HTML
Essentials

Second Edition

Paradigm PUBLISHING

D1318414

Callihan

Editorial Director: Sonja Brown
Senior Developmental Editor: Christine Hurney
Production Editor: Bob Dreas
Cover and Text Designer: Jaana Bykonich

Desktop Production: Jack Ross; John Valo at Desktop Solutions
Proofreader: Julie McNamee
Indexer: Teresa Casey

Care has been taken to verify the accuracy of information presented in this book. However, the authors, editors, and publisher cannot accept responsibility for Web, e-mail, newsgroup, or chat room subject matter or content, or for consequences from application of the information in this book, and make no warranty, expressed or implied, with respect to its content.

Trademarks: Some of the product names and company names included in this book have been used for identification purposes only and may be trademarks or registered trade names of their respective manufacturers and sellers. The authors, editors, and publisher disclaim any affiliation, association, or connection with, or sponsorship or endorsement by, such owners.

We have made every effort to trace the ownership of all copyrighted material and to secure permission from copyright holders. In the event of any question arising as to the use of any material, we will be pleased to make the necessary corrections in future printings. Thanks are due to the aforementioned authors, publishers, and agents for permission to use the materials indicated.

ISBN 978-0-76383-642-9

© 2010 by Paradigm Publishing, Inc.
875 Montreal Way
St. Paul, MN 55102
E-mail: educate@emcp.com
Web site: www.emcp.com

All rights reserved. No part of this publication may be adapted, reproduced, stored in a retrieval system, or transmitted in any form or by any means, electronic, mechanical, photocopying, recording, or otherwise, without prior written permission from the publisher.

Printed in the United States of America

18 17 16 15 14 13 12 11 10 09   1 2 3 4 5 6 7 8 9 10

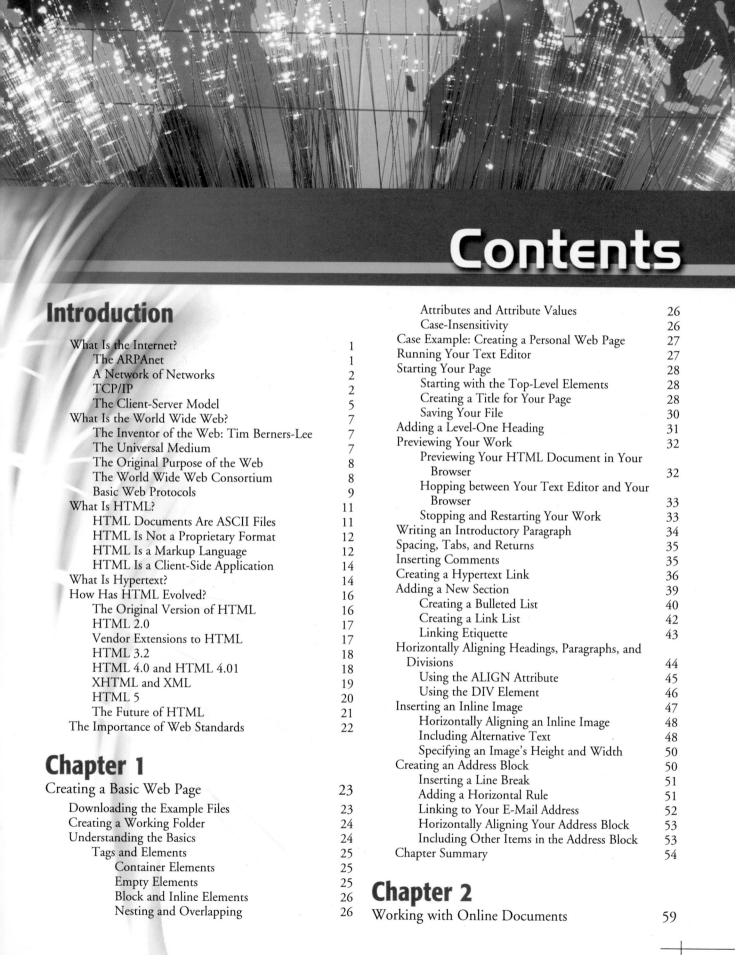

Contents

Chapter 7

Appendix A

Appendix B

Appendix C

Appendix D

Appendix E

Appendix F

Appendix G

Glossary

Index

Preface

In a short period of time, the Web has become a ubiquitous presence in the lives of many people, be they workers, students, business people, or even children. Today, many rely on the Web for research, communication, social networking, job searches, entertainment, and more.

HTML IS FOR EVERYONE

From the beginning, the Web was conceived as a two-way medium. Anyone who surfs the Web can also create and publish documents that others can surf. These Web sites are created using HTML, or *Hypertext Markup Language*. Many think HTML must be overly technical or too difficult for the average person to learn and master. From the beginning, however, HTML was conceived as a tool that anyone could use without a great deal of previous technical experience or know-how.

Graduated Learning Process

The chapters in this book organize the material covered and skills taught into logically consistent steps that move from basic to intermediate and then to advanced topics. In each chapter, the student develops new skills, which can then be applied to addressing more challenging examples in the next chapter, and so forth, with each chapter representing a higher step upon which the student can stand toward mastery of the subject. Chapter work might take one to two class periods to complete, with review exercises, quizzes, online research, and independent projects requiring additional time. Examples, exercises, and projects can be done in class, in a computer lab, or at home. Students can break off at any time, save their work, and then later pick up where they left off, in the same or another place.

Special Features

This book is designed to make learning Web development with HTML both easy and productive by including these special features:

- **Downloadable Example Files.** These files are used to complete each chapter's examples and exercises and can be downloaded by the instructor or by students from this book's Internet Resource Center at **www.emcp.net/html2e**. Example files are available in two formats: Windows and Macintosh OS X/Linux/UNIX. Additional student resources and instructional support are also available at this book's Internet Resource Center.

- **Differentiation of Action and Content Material.** This book makes it easy for students to differentiate between material included for understanding and material that should be acted upon. The in-context code examples enable the student to see and complete the tasks quickly and easily.
- **Notes, Tips, and Margin Hints.** These features highlight additional information the student might find useful or helpful in comprehending information or completing examples.
- **Trouble Spots.** Trouble Spots highlight points at which problems might occur and provide relevant advice and solutions.
- **Real-World Case Examples and Scenarios.** Examples and scenarios are used in each chapter to demonstrate topics, features, and methods.
- **Online Research and Extended Learning.** These opportunities are frequently referenced at relevant points within each chapter. Students can visit the Web addresses to find out more about chapter topics.
- **Chapter Summaries.** This feature summarizes the topics that should be comprehended and the skills that should be gained in each chapter.
- **Code Reviews.** This section reviews all elements, attributes, or other codes introduced in a chapter.
- **Online Quizzes.** These quizzes are available online at this book's Internet Resource Center to check comprehension and retention of key topics and information. Students receive immediate feedback, highlighting areas in which further study or review might be helpful.
- **Review Exercises.** These exercises can be done by students who finish the chapter work early. Review exercises also can be completed during lab time or at home.
- **Web-Based Learning Activities.** Students can access online resources for each chapter to further explore and research relevant topics, issues, and techniques. Results from online research can be used to create reviews, reports, or presentations.
- **Projects.** Projects present real-world Web publishing jobs that students can work on independently or the instructor can assign to provide additional practical experience in applying the skills and knowledge gained in each chapter.
- **Key Term Glossaries.** A glossary of all key terms used in the book is included at the end of the book. Individual chapter glossaries are available at the book's Internet Resource Center.

WHAT IS NEW IN THIS EDITION

The *essentials* of HTML remain largely the same from when this book's original edition was published—HTML 4.01, the current standard, has remained unchanged since 1999. Time never stands still, however. Developments since the original edition was published in 2004 impact how Web authors and designers approach and implement different features and aspects of the HTML standard and have influenced the coverage, examples, and recommendations included in this edition:

- **HTML 5 "draft" specification.** A new HTML specification, HTML 5, was announced in January 2008. While it is still a draft and will not be finalized for many years, current browsers are already supporting some HTML 5 features. While this book primarily teaches HTML 4.01, which is still the standard for HTML, changes have been incorporated into its coverage, examples, and recommendations to emphasize forward-compatibility with HTML 5. The best way to prepare for HTML 5 is to write and design HTML 4.01-compliant Web pages and sites.
- **Much improved support for standards in browsers.** Current browsers, such as Internet Explorer 8 for Windows, Firefox 3, and Apple Safari 4, feature fuller and more consistent support for the HTML and Cascading Style Sheets (CSS) standards, while browsers with flawed implementations of those standards have largely passed from usage. As a result, this edition is less concerned with backward-compatibility and cross-browser workarounds and more concerned with forward-compatibility and standards-compliance.
- **Wider range of display resolutions.** At the time of the original edition, most users were using displays of 800 x 600 pixels or smaller. Now over 85 percent are using displays of 1024 × 768 pixels or larger, and many have display resolutions that far exceed that. Accessing the Web using alternative devices with smaller screens and resolutions, such as cellular phones and PDAs, has increased significantly. Information on how these factors might impact design decisions has been incorporated into this edition where relevant.
- **Less conflict between accessibility and design.** Better browser support for standards means that Web authors are better able to support accessibility for users with visual disabilities, while making fewer design tradeoffs and compromises. The FONT element and using tables or frames for page layout, considered to be detrimental to accessibility, are still covered, but in somewhat truncated form, if only because students might need to revise legacy pages that contain them. Wherever relevant, this edition presents or references CSS-based alternatives to such elements and methods.
- **Expanded coverage.** Coverage of related features and technologies has been expanded, including Cascading Style Sheets (CSS), JavaScript, XHTML, XML, Image Maps, Server-Side Includes (SSI), password protection, (PHP, online databases, secure forms and servers, and wireless Web protocols. Four new appendixes have been added: Appendix B: *HTML/XHTML Conversion Chart*, Appendix C: *Cascading Style Sheets Sampler*, Appendix F: *Working with JavaScript*, and Appendix G, *Miscellaneous Technologies and Features*.
- **Key term definitions.** Key terms for each chapter are highlighted in bold. A glossary of all key terms in the book and their definitions is presented at the back of the new edition. Individual key term glossaries for each of the chapters are available at this book's Internet Resource Center at **www.emcp.net/html2e**.

WHAT THIS BOOK COVERS

This book covers all the essential features and capabilities of HTML:
- The Introduction includes background information and perspectives on the evolution of the Internet, the Web, and HTML.

- Chapter 1, *Creating a Basic Web Page*, covers using the example files, using a text editor and a browser, and creating a Web page using common features such as headings, paragraph text, bulleted lists, hypertext links, and inline images.
- Chapter 2, *Working with Online Documents*, covers using bold and italic inline highlighting, superscripts and subscripts, numerical lists, non-keyboard characters, monospaced and preformatted text, and other key features commonly used in creating online documents.
- Chapter 3, *Working with Fonts, Colors, and Backgrounds*, covers using HTML elements and attributes to control the size, color, and face of fonts; the color of text, links, and backgrounds; and background images. Why elements and attributes controlling appearance are "deprecated" in HTML 4 is discussed, with alternatives provided using Cascading Style Sheets (CSS).
- Chapter 4, *Working with Images and Other Media*, covers working with inline images in more depth, including floating images; designing online galleries using thumbnail images and image links; using graphic rules, banners, and buttons; learning about creating your own Web images; and using relative URLs to display images saved in other folders. Adding GIF animations, embedding audio and video files, and creating image maps are also covered. Copyright issues involved in using images, audio, and video in Web pages are also discussed.
- Chapter 5, *Working with Tables*, covers displaying and formatting tabular data arranged in rows and columns in Web pages, including importing and formatting an Excel worksheet, structuring and aligning HTML tables, controlling table appearance using HTML codes and styles, creating indented icon link lists, and formatting an online resume.
- Chapter 6, *Working with Forms*, covers using common form elements to elicit user feedback, including text boxes, radio buttons, check boxes, list menus, text area boxes, and submit and reset buttons, and also improving the appearance of forms using colors and backgrounds, preformatted text, and tables. Coverage is also included on creating mailto and CGI forms, submitting and receiving form responses, and configuring and setting access permissions for the most commonly used form–processing CGI script.
- Chapter 7, *Designing Multi-Column Web Sites*, covers creating multi-column layouts using three methods: frames, tables and styles, and styles alone. The pros and cons of these methods are discussed, as they apply to issues of compatibility, usability, and accessibility. Two methods are presented for designing multi-column Web sites using styles: fixed and fluid. Also covered is using an external or global style sheet to control the appearance of multiple pages.
- Appendix A, *HTML Quick Reference*, provides descriptions, attributes, and examples for HTML 4 and HTML 5 elements. It also includes a brief introduction to using the W3C HTML Validator.
- Appendix B, *HTML-to-XHTML Conversion Chart*, shows all syntactical differences between HTML 4.01 and XHTML 1.0 documents. Using this chart, any HTML 4.01 file can easily be converted to an XHTML 1.0 file.
- Appendix C, *Cascading Style Sheets Sampler*, provides descriptions and examples for the most commonly used and widely supported CSS 1 and CSS 2 properties.
- Appendix D, *Special Characters Chart*, covers all ISO-8859-1 extended characters and an extensive selection of UTF-8 Unicode characters, including their numbered and named entity codes for inserting them into HTML documents.

- Appendix E, *Web-Safe Colors Chart*, shows 216 colors and their hexadecimal RGB values that will be displayed without dithering on any system capable of displaying 256 or more colors.
- Appendix F, *Working with JavaScript*, provides a basic introduction to using JavaScript in Web pages, including using functions, loops, variables, and arrays. Examples of some of the more commonly used types of scripts are included.
- Appendix G, *Miscellaneous Technologies and Features*, provides rundowns, and some examples, of various technologies and features not covered earlier in the book, including using an FTP program to files to a Web server, Server-Side Includes (SSI), password protection, cookies, ASP and PHP, online databases, secure forms and servers, XML, DHTML, Adobe Flash, and XHTML Basic and XHTML Mobile Profile (for coding pages to be accessed through small-format wireless or mobile devices).

STANDARDS-BASED INSTRUCTION

All instruction in this book is based on the official specifications and standards for HTML and CSS, as established by the World Wide Web Consortium (W3C), the organization in charge of setting standards for the World Wide Web. Except where clearly noted in the book, all of the HTML examples presented conform to the W3C's HTML 4.01 specification, which is the official HTML standard at the time of this edition's publication.

Additional information is also provided, where relevant and helpful, on the potential or likely impacts of the HTML 5 "draft" specification on current Web design practices. It is important to note that, while browsers are already supporting parts of HTML 5, it is not expected to become a finalized standard for many years to come. The first step toward adopting HTML 5 is simply conformance to HTML 4, which is largely incorporated into HTML 5.

It is important that students learn not merely what happens to work at the moment in current Web browsers, but what will continue to work in future Web browsers as well. There is no guarantee that non-standard methods and techniques will continue to be supported in the future.

SOFTWARE REQUIREMENTS

Although most of the figures in this book use screen captures taken on a Windows system, the execution of the examples, projects, and other assignments does not require system-specific software or facilities. The example files used in this book are available for download in two formats, one for Windows computers and the other for Macintosh OS X, Linux, and UNIX computers, from this book's Internet Resource Center at **www.emcp.net/html2e**.

The only software required to complete this book's examples, assignments, and projects is a simple text editor and a current graphical Web browser:

- **A text editor.** You do not need anything fancy to create HTML files, which are just straight text files. Most operating systems include text editors you can use, such as Windows Notepad or TextEdit on OS X for the Macintosh. More full-featured text editors can be downloaded and installed from the Web.

- **A current graphical Web browser.** To preview and debug all the examples, assignments, and projects, you should use a current graphical Web browser. It is recommended that students use any of these or higher browser versions to create or preview this book's case examples: Internet Explorer 8 (for Windows), Mozilla Firefox 3 (for Windows, Macintosh OS X, and Linux), or Apple Safari 4 (for Macintosh OS X or Windows).

- **A connection to the Internet.** You can create Web pages without being connected to the Internet and the Web, but if you want to download the example files, additional software tools, or Web art images, or want to publish projects you create to the Web, you will need an Internet connection. An Internet Resource Center has also been created for this book that provides downloadable example files and many additional resources that complement and extend the material in this book.

No other software tools are required to create and preview this book's examples and assignments. Students, however, may choose to use optional software tools for creating individual projects, such as image editors, GIF animators, image map editors, image splicers, interactive animation programs, and so on. Examples and projects, however, should be created using a text editor and not in a Web publishing program (such as Adobe Dreamweaver, for instance), since only in that way can mastery of HTML be demonstrated.

Students also will need to use an FTP program if they want to publish Web pages or projects they create on the Web. Additional software tools that students can choose to employ will be discussed in more depth in the relevant chapters.

ABOUT THE AUTHOR

Steve Callihan has authored numerous books on Web design, HTML, Web animation, and Cascading Style Sheets; published articles on Web publishing in major computer magazines; and worked extensively in the technical writing, desktop publishing, and Web design fields. He has an extensive background designing training materials, producing hardware and software user documentation, and designing, optimizing, and promoting Web sites. He has more than 20 years' experience as a team member, team leader, department supervisor, independent contractor, and sole proprietor working in a wide variety of computer document processing and production capacities.

Introduction

Before you start working with HTML, you should understand what HTML is and where it came from. HTML is a key aspect of the World Wide Web, which is an evolution of the Internet.

WHAT IS THE INTERNET?

How the Internet came to be is an interesting story. The Internet actually is rooted in the Cold War. The researchers who established the network that was to eventually become the Internet were motivated by a desire to establish a communication system that could survive an atomic attack.

Following the launch of the Sputnik satellite by the Soviet Union in 1957, the U.S. Defense Department established the Advanced Research Projects Agency (ARPA) to develop the first U.S. satellite, which was launched 18 months later. Later, ARPA undertook a new challenge, establishing a communication system to command and control the U.S.'s ICBM missile system and strategic bomber fleet. In 1963, the Rand Corporation was asked by ARPA to conceptualize the design principles behind such a system, a primary requirement being the ability to survive and remain functioning after a nuclear attack.

The ARPAnet

The Rand Corporation responded that the system would need to have "no central authority" and would need to be designed from the beginning to "operate while in tatters." These two characteristics define the essence of what later was to become first the **ARPAnet** and then later the Internet: a communication system, or network, that has no central authority (that could be knocked out in nuclear strike) and operates in a condition of assumed unreliability (cities destroyed by nuclear blasts, telephone lines down). The irony, of course, is that what was to eventually become the anarchic Internet we know today, which even nation states have great difficulty controlling, had its roots in a severe case of Cold War paranoia.

The ARPAnet was commissioned by the Department of Defense in 1969, initially linking research centers at four universities involved in defense research (UCLA, Stanford, University of California at Santa Barbara, and the University of Utah). Within the next

On a network, a *node* is a point of access that is connected to other points of access (or nodes). For instance, if your computer is connected to a network, it is a node in the network.

two years, the ARPAnet grew to 15 nodes (including MIT, Harvard, NASA/Ames, and others). By 1973, the ARPAnet had expanded to England and Norway.

A number of key technologies that are associated with the Internet were also developed in the early days of the ARPAnet. Telnet was introduced in 1972, standardizing the capability to dial in and log on to a computer on the network. FTP (File Transfer Protocol) was introduced in 1973, standardizing how files were transferred between computers on the network. The first network-wide e-mail system was established in 1977. Newsgroups (USENET) were introduced in 1979.

A Network of Networks

The problem initially faced by the founders of the Internet was that many different network topologies were in use. What would work to communicate with one network might not work with another network. The system needed a shared set of **protocols**, or agreed upon rules, by which these different networks could all communicate with each other.

It doesn't matter what kind of system or device is connected to the Internet—it only matters that systems or devices connected to the Internet speak the same language when sending and receiving data over the Internet. That language, in the form of a set of common protocols, is **TCP/IP** (Transmission Control Protocol/Internet Protocol), which was introduced in 1982. Thus was born a "network of networks," or an **internet**.

TCP/IP

In 1982, the ARPAnet adopted TCP/IP as the standard set of rules for sending and receiving data across the network. Today, TCP/IP remains the key suite of protocols that enables the exchange of data over the Internet. TCP/IP actually comprises two different protocols:

- **TCP (Transmission Control Protocol).** Breaks the message down into smaller pieces, or **packets**, which makes the transmission of larger files or messages across the network more efficient. Each packet is individually labeled, identifying its origin, destination, and position within the file. When the packets arrive at their destination, TCP checks the packets for errors, verifies that all the packets that belong to the file have arrived, and then reassembles them in the proper order to reconstitute the full file. If errors are found or a packet fails to arrive, a request is sent to the sender to resend the file.

- **IP (Internet Protocol).** At each node along the way, a device called a **router** reads a packet's address and then, if the current node is not its destination, forwards it on toward its destination.

Any system—whether a network gateway, a mainframe computer, a **Web server** delivering content over the Web, or your own personal computer you use to connect to the Internet—uses TCP/IP to connect to and share information over the Internet (see Figure I.1).

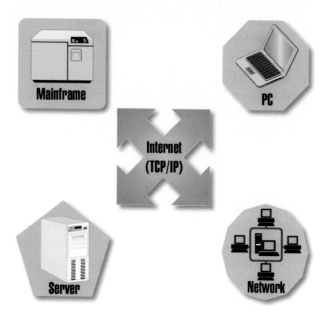

FIGURE I.1 • The Internet uses a common language (TCP/IP) that connects systems and devices to share (send and receive) data between them.

TCP has been compared with packing up the contents of your house and moving it across the country. The movers come in and pack everything up into boxes (or "packets"), which are then shipped across country. When they finally arrive at their destination, simply checking the shipment's manifest shows whether all the packets have arrived, or whether any have been lost along the way. The movers then unpack the packets, which then become the contents and furniture of your new house. This way of transferring data over a network is also called **packet switching**. For an illustration of how this works, see Figure I.2.

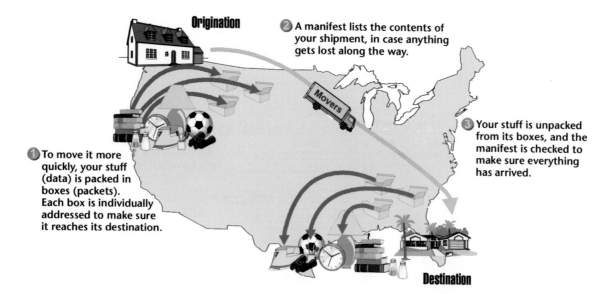

FIGURE I.2 • Breaking data into smaller packets can speed its transmission to its destination.

IP has been compared with sending a letter across the country. You place the letter in an envelope, and as long as the address on the envelope is correct, barring mishaps, the letter should eventually be delivered safely to its address. A mail sorter doesn't have to know anything about the contents of the letter; a mere look at the ZIP code for the letter is sufficient to send the letter off in the right direction.

Over the Internet, the packets that compose a message might take different routes to get to the same destination. In other words, based upon changing traffic conditions, one packet might go from New York to Seattle by first going via St. Louis, San Francisco, and Portland, before finally arriving, safe and sound, in Seattle. Another packet, on the other hand, due to sudden congestion on the route to St. Louis, might go from New York to Seattle by following an entirely different route, traveling via Chicago, St. Paul, Missoula, and Spokane, before arriving in Seattle (see Figure I.3). On the Internet, if any packets that are part of a message fail to arrive (are lost along the way), the receiver of the message simply requests that the sender resend the message. After all the packets have arrived, they are reassembled into the full message, which is then read or executed.

The advantage of packet switching is that it makes it easier for multiple message streams to share the same network space. If only whole files, for instance, could be sent over the Internet, one large file could block other smaller files from getting through. Breaking messages and files—transmissions—into smaller packets is more efficient and much less prone to bottlenecks.

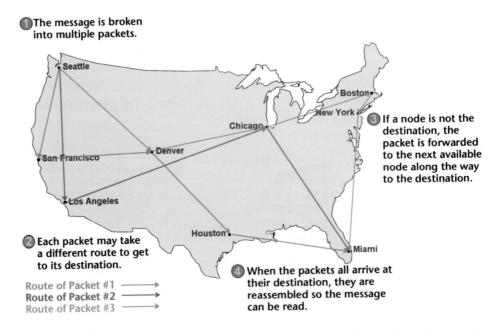

① The message is broken into multiple packets.

② Each packet may take a different route to get to its destination.

Route of Packet #1 ⟶
Route of Packet #2 ⟶
Route of Packet #3 ⟶

③ If a node is not the destination, the packet is forwarded to the next available node along the way to the destination.

④ When the packets all arrive at their destination, they are reassembled so the message can be read.

FIGURE I.3 • When a file or message is broken down into packets, each packet can take a different route to get to its destination.

NOTE

For TCP/IP, TCP (Transmission Control Protocol) defines the "packet," and IP (Internet Protocol) does the "switching" that routes the packets to their destination. You can think of TCP as boxcars in a train and IP as a train switch that moves the train from one track to another, except that in the case of TCP/IP, the individual boxcars could be switched onto different tracks.

One of the main points to remember about TCP/IP is that the essence of what makes up the Internet is not the wire, or the means of transmission, but the protocols that determine how information is sent, forwarded, and received over the wire. The Internet, in other words, is not the wires and connections (the hardware) that makes up the physical network, but rather the intelligence (or software) that directs and orders the traffic, or transmission stream, over the Internet. That directing and ordering intelligence is TCP/IP.

Thus, many and varied systems can be connected to the Internet. The only thing that matters is that they all use the same set of protocols—TCP/IP—to communicate with each other. When you connect to the Internet, you are connected in exactly the same fashion as a whole network of computers might be connected at your local university, through TCP/IP.

The standardization upon TCP/IP as the common means for exchanging information across the network allowed the ARPAnet to grow and expand to eventually become the Internet we know today. In 1986, the National Science Foundation (NSF) formed the **NSFNet**, which initially linked five supercomputing centers to form the first high-speed backbone, running at what was then a blazing speed of 56 KBps. Unlike the ARPAnet, which linked together academic centers that were involved in defense research, the NSFNet opened up the network to the rest of the academic community, allowing anyone connected through a university to exchange information and ideas with anyone else who was also connected. Soon afterwards, the speed of the NSFNet backbone increased to 1.544 Mbps (called a "T1" connection). In 1990, the ARPAnet ended and was absorbed into the NSFNet. In the same year, the first commercial provider of dial-up access to the Internet, the World (world.std.com), came online, with many other ISPs (Internet Service Providers) coming along shortly after. The NSFNet finally became the full Internet, to which anyone could connect, that we know today.

In 1991, the **Internet Society** was founded in response to the growing internationalization of the Internet and the need to consolidate responsibility for establishing Internet infrastructure standards.

NOTE — Look at the Internet Society's site at **www.isoc.org/internet/history/** for additional resources and information about the history and development of the Internet.

The Client-Server Model

TCP/IP enables the exchange of information and data over the Internet, but it does not, by itself, enable the distribution of services or the sharing of resources. Over a network, whether your local-area network (or LAN) or the Internet, this is done by means of a process by which computers make and respond to requests over the network, a process that is often referred to as the **client-server model**. A **client** is a computer that requests a service from another computer (a server). A **server** is a computer that responds to requests for services from another computer (a client).

A computer can be both a client and a server. A server is simply a computer operating on the Internet running software that enables it to function as a server. Besides Web servers, for instance, Gopher, FTP, e-mail, news, and other servers also function on the Internet and the Web. The same computer might function as a Web, FTP, and e-mail server, simply by running software that enables these functions. A server also can request a service from another server, in which case it is functioning as a client.

Most personal computers connected to the Internet are not running as servers but only as clients. Not that long ago, such computers were normally connected at a transmission speed of 56 KB or slower, which was just too slow to successfully function as a server. These days, many more users have some form of broadband connection. Most ISPs (Internet Service Providers), however, randomly assign an available IP address. An **IP address** is a series of numbers that uniquely identifies any computer (server or client) that is connected to the Internet. To be continually available as a server on the Internet, a computer needs to have the same permanent (or "static") IP address and not a different IP address each time it is connected. You can think of an IP address as a street address: if you were to continually change your street address, nobody would be able to find you. They would be showing up looking for you where you were last but not where you are.

You can think of the client-server model functioning much like a pizza delivery service. You, the client, feeling the irresistible urge for a three-cheese pizza with mushrooms and anchovies, call up the pizza delivery service, the server, and make your request: a 16-inch pizza with three cheeses (mozzarella, parmesan, and romano), mushrooms, and anchovies. As part of your request, you also tell the pizza order person what your address is, so the pizza delivery person can deliver it to your front door. The person taking your order confirms that they can supply the request. After the pizza is cooked according to your specification, it is loaded into a truck and rushed to your door, so you can eat it while it is still hot and steaming. Transactions occurring over the Internet happen in much the same manner, with a client requesting a service from a server, and then the server delivering the requested service to the client (see Figure I.4).

A client is simply software running on a computer. You should already be familiar with one client: your **Web browser**. Another term for a Web browser is a **user agent** (which might encompass non-visual browsing agents as well, for instance). Web browsers aren't the only kind of clients that operate across the Internet. Other clients include Gopher, WAIS, Archie, and FTP clients, for instance. In each case, these all work relatively the same: a Gopher client makes a request of a Gopher server, or an FTP client

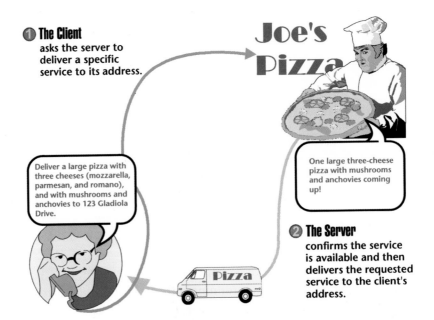

① The Client asks the server to deliver a specific service to its address.

Deliver a large pizza with three cheeses (mozzarella, parmesan, and romano), and with mushrooms and anchovies to 123 Gladiola Drive.

One large three-cheese pizza with mushrooms and anchovies coming up!

② The Server confirms the service is available and then delivers the requested service to the client's address.

FIGURE I.4 • The client-server model is similar to a pizza delivery system, in which a customer places an order for a pizza, specifying size and toppings, to be delivered to her door.

makes a request of an FTP server, which then responds by delivering the service that is being requested by the client. A Web browser, on the other hand, can function as several different clients in one—functioning as a Gopher, FTP, or WAIS client, for instance. All it needs to know is the IP address on the Internet of the particular server to which it wants to make a request.

WHAT IS THE WORLD WIDE WEB?

If the Internet is said to have begun with the formation of the ARPAnet around 1970, then it predates the **World Wide Web** ("the Web") by over 20 years. If the start of the Internet is dated, however, from the formation of the NSFNet, which came about in 1986, then it predates the World Wide Web by a mere 4 or 5 years. In fact, without the formation of the NSFNet, or something like it, the Web could not have developed in the first place. NSFNet opened up the Internet to allow the participation of anyone connected through participating universities and research centers, which allowed the Web—the brainchild of an academic and scientist who was also connected to the Internet—to come to fruition.

The Inventor of the Web: Tim Berners-Lee

In 1989, a British scientist working at CERN (*Conseil European pour la Recherche Nucleaire* or European Organization for Nuclear Research) in Bern, Switzerland, made a radical proposal to facilitate the sharing and exchange of information and ideas between academics across the Internet. That scientist was Tim Berners-Lee, and his radical proposal was for something he called "the World Wide Web." In his original proposal for the World Wide Web, Berners-Lee described it as "a wide area hypermedia information retrieval initiative aiming to give universal access to a large universe of documents." More recently, he provided an updated description and definition for the Web: "the universal space of all network-accessible information." He also has used the term "universal space" in online presentations to describe the nature and character of the Web.

NOTE You can find CERN's home page at **www.cern.ch/**. To learn about CERN's role in the invention and early evolution of the Web, click the About us link.

The Universal Medium

Another way of looking at the Web is as a universal medium. The Web, in other words, encompasses all media—print, radio, television, and so on—within a single universal medium. This is actually already implicit in Berners-Lee's description of the Web as a *"hypermedia* information retrieval initiative.

The original focus of the Web was on the sharing and exchanging of textual information. Web documents are referred to as "pages" for that reason. The term **Web page**, however, is a bit of a misnomer, in that a document on the Web can be of virtually any length. It would be more accurate to refer to a Web document as a *Web scroll*, but somehow that just does not have the right ring.

The Original Purpose of the Web

As it was originally conceived, the Web was designed to facilitate the exchange of ideas and the sharing of information between individuals or groups, with little distinction between those who create and those who consume what was being exchanged and shared. From the beginning, it was intended that the Web would be a medium (or "information retrieval initiative") that would allow anyone to communicate with anyone. The initial participants on the Web were mostly academics and scientists, only because the Internet at the time of the introduction of the Web was still largely an academic affair. The first ISP, the World (world.std.com), made access to the Internet available outside of connected universities and other research facilities in 1990, a year after the Berners-Lee's initial proposal for the formation of the Web. From the beginning, however, Berners-Lee's vision for the Web was one in which no group, community, or individuals held privileges over any other, with all having equal rights to not only consume but also to originate and create the content that composes the Web.

Thus, although the Web has evolved into much more than its initial vision—becoming both an entertainment medium and a platform for the distribution of commercial applications, programs, and services—the original vision of the Web as a "universal space" within which everyone could, and should, be able to communicate and interact with everyone else, remains at the heart of what the Web is and will continue to be.

In other words, on the Web, large-scale economic or political concerns, such as General Motors, Universal Studios, or the federal government, for instance, really have no greater privilege to conceptualize, produce, and distribute (or share) information, ideas, or even software products, across the Web than the plain ordinary individual. On the Web, all addresses are coequal; in other words, Joseph Schmoe's Web address of www.joseph-schmoe.com/, to cite an entirely fictional example, is just as easily reachable as Yahoo!'s Web address of www.yahoo.com/. Joe, of course, being just an ordinary guy, does not have the advertising budget of a Yahoo!, nor would the traffic limitations of his Web hosting account stand up to even a small fraction of the traffic Yahoo! attracts, but anyone knowing his address should be able to reach his site just as quickly and easily as they can reach Yahoo! From that perspective, Yahoo!'s multi-billion dollar presence and Joseph Schmoe's presence on the Web (very much a shoestring affair) are equal. The same holds for a grandmother in Ireland, a schoolboy in France, or even a homeless person in Seattle—anyone with access to the Internet and the Web can be a creator and producer, not just a consumer, of content on the Web.

The World Wide Web Consortium

Although the World Wide Web was born at CERN in Switzerland, the fostering of a worldwide communication network was neither CERN's primary mission nor its mandate. In 1994, under the auspices of INRIA (the National Institute for Research in Computer Science and Controls, located in France), the **World Wide Web Consortium** (W3C) was formed in collaboration with the Laboratory of Computer Science at MIT (Massachusetts Institute of Technology) in the United States, where Berners-Lee took up a research position.

NOTE You can find the W3C's home page at **www.w3.org/** (see Figure I.5). To find out about the W3C's work on the different HTML standards, just click the HTML link in the left sidebar.

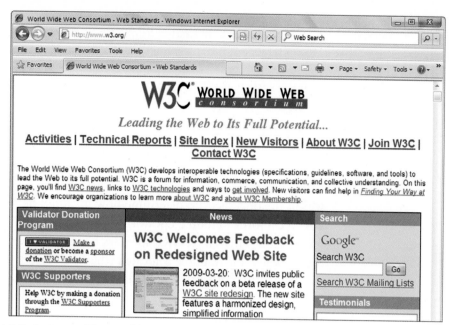

FIGURE 1.5 • The World Wide Web Consortium is in charge of establishing consensus on Web standards, including HTML.

The W3C's stated mission is "leading the Web to its full potential." The W3C is responsible for fostering and developing the specifications, guidelines, protocols, software, and tools that provide the standard foundation upon which the Web can stand and grow. Without the W3C, we might otherwise have ended up with a bevy of less-than-worldwide "webs," each based on separate proprietary protocols and accessed through different interfaces. As a standards-setting organization, the W3C is responsible for creating consensus among the various member organizations and vendors in the W3C, forging a path forward that all agree they can follow. The W3C, in other words, is not a governing organization charged with enforcing dictates from some kind of elite council of technological elders but rather simply establishes the forums and working groups within which organizations and vendors with a stake in the future development of the Web can come together and work out common agreements and commitments. The W3C is a bottom-up, "grass roots" organization that is run by and functions on the basis of consensus among its members, in other words, and not a top-down organization charged with enforcing rules and regulations. In fact, the W3C does not even refer to its specifications as "standards" but merely as "recommendations."

Basic Web Protocols

As is the case with the Internet, the Web is really nothing more than a set of agreed upon protocols and specifications. The essential protocols and specifications that comprise the Web are:

- **HTTP** (Hypertext Transfer Protocol) formalizes the interchange (requests and responses) that occurs between Web-based clients (Web browsers, for instance) and Web-based servers (**Web servers**). All Web addresses, for instance, begin with "http://".

NOTE — In this book, the "http://" is omitted from Web addresses referenced to lessen the chance that a Web address will take up more than the available space on a line. All current browsers allow you to omit "http://" when typing a Web address in their Address or Location bars. Non-HTTP URLs (such as FTP or Gopher URLs, for instance) still need to be typed in full.

- **HTML** (Hypertext Markup Language) establishes the common language that allows for the universal exchange of information over the Web. HTML defines elements and attributes that facilitate the presentation of structured information and data. User agents (Web browsers, for instance) then interpret the HTML coding within the document to determine how it should be presented.
- **URL** (Uniform Resource Locator) which defines the "Web address" of any resource on the Web. A URL specifies how a resource is to be accessed (the protocol), where the resource is located (the host server), and what the resource is (its path and name). A URL is also called a **URI** (Uniform Resource Identifier) by the W3C.
- **CGI** (Common Gateway Interface) allows Web server software running HTTP can interface with the host computer on which it is running. CGI allows server-side programs and scripts to be executed across the network. An example of this might be a CGI script written in Perl (a programming language common to UNIX servers) that processes requests sent from HTML forms embedded in Web documents.

An HTTP request, for instance, might use the following commands to ask a server to

- GET a particular document or file, providing the name and location of the file on that server.
- SEARCH for keywords within a particular document or subset of documents.
- Request only return documents created SINCE or BEFORE a particular date and/or time.
- Return a document's HEAD (header information), which allows a Web browser, for instance, to compare the creation date of a cached copy of a document residing on the browser's local machine against the non-cached remote copy of the document residing on the server. That way, if the remote copy hasn't been updated since the local copy was cached, the browser can just open and display the local copy, rather than having to download the entire remote copy.
- Identify the USER, the user's HOST, and the client software that is making the request so that requests can be logged and tracked.

After receiving a request, an HTTP server informs the client of the *status* of the requested resource or service. A server can signal back to a client the status of requests for resources or services in a variety of ways. For instance, a Web server might

- Respond that the request is successful (the document is present and available for delivery).
- Forward the client to a new address, if the resource has been moved.
- Inform the client that the document cannot be found (does not refer to a valid document path and name on the server).
- Inform the client that access to the document is not authorized, forwarding the client to a form for inputting a user name and password, for instance, or simply telling the client that access has been refused.
- Inform the client that the resource is not available due to a server error.

- Inform the client that the resource is temporarily unavailable and that the client might check back later.
- Tell the client that a keyword search of documents came up with no results.
- Tell the client the format on the server to which the requested document corresponds.

After the server signals back to the client, the client can then request that the server deliver the resource if it is available. The client also can go to a forwarded address and start the whole transaction over again, or simply relay the information to the user that the resource is not available for one reason or another and wait for the user to provide a different address to go to. The client also can decide to display a locally cached copy of the resource, if it is available.

HTTP is just one of several protocols used to exchange documents and information over the Internet. Other protocols that share the Internet with HTTP include FTP, Gopher, Archie, Telnet, and WAIS. All of these other protocols require server software that can respond to requests and deliver the requested resource, as well as client software that can communicate and interact with the specific server software.

 **Visit the Internet Resource Center.** You can find additional online resources that discuss the history of the Internet and the Web in the Introduction section of this book's Internet Resource Center at **www.emcp.net/html2e**.

WHAT IS HTML?

The acronym HTML stands for Hypertext Markup Language. HTML was a key part of the original proposal for the Web. Without HTML, the Web would be much different than it is now. HTML was originally conceived as a subset of **SGML** (Standard Generalized Markup Language). SGML is the standard markup language used to prepare computer-generated documents for publishing on a printing press. HTML has a similar function, except it is used to prepare computer-generated documents for publishing on the Web.

HTML Documents Are ASCII Files

HTML documents are straight ASCII text documents. **ASCII** (American Standard Code for Information Interchange) defines a standard set of characters and control codes that are automatically recognized by almost all computer systems. The only exceptions are IBM's mainframe computer systems that use EBCDIC (Extended Binary Coded Decimal Information Code), a standard that predated ASCII. Because the standard ASCII codes are represented by 7-bit binary numbers (0000000 to 1111111), there are 128 standard ASCII codes. These include the alphabetic characters (a to z and A to Z), numbers (0 to 9), punctuation (period, comma, colon, semicolon, and so on), the space character, and various other commonly used characters (@, #, $, and so on). Also included are a number of control characters that command actions (tab, carriage return, line feed, backspace, delete, and so on).

NOTE ——— ASCII is also referred to as US-ASCII because it includes the "$" symbol for U.S. currency. It doesn't include any of the accented characters used by many European languages. Many international variants of ASCII have been developed; in UK-ASCII (BS 4730), for instance, the number symbol (#) is replaced by the British pound symbol (£).

ASCII text files can be read and written by a simple **text editor**, such as Notepad on the Windows platform, SimpleText on the classic Macintosh platform, TextEdit on the Mac OS X platform, and vi (pronounced "vee eye") on the UNIX (or Linux) platform.

You do not need to know the ASCII codes, however, to create HTML files. In Chapter 1, *Creating a Basic Web Page*, you use a simple text editor to create an HTML file. A text editor has one purpose, to read and write ASCII text files. An ASCII text file is also sometimes referred to as a "plain" text file because it does not include any additional formatting codes (such as for bold, italics, indents, and so on) that a word processor might include in a word processing document. Text editors are also commonly used to read and write program code, which also does not require any formatting or extra characters.

HTML Is Not a Proprietary Format

HTML is not a proprietary document format, such as is the case with documents created by word processing programs, for instance. When you create a document in a word processing program, such as Microsoft Word or Corel WordPerfect, you can include all sorts of additional formatting and other characteristics that are invisibly coded beneath the surface. You might decide to bold a phrase, set a heading in a different font face or size, apply a color to a paragraph, set margins, create footnotes, add page numbers, and so on. You are limited only by the capabilities of the program you are using.

There is a penalty, however, for being able to format word processing documents in various and fancy ways—a word processing document will be much larger than an equivalent ASCII text file containing the same textual characters. On your local computer system, the difference in file sizes between the two formats is not very important because the speed of processing files locally renders the difference in file sizes as having a negligible effect on how fast a file is displayed or updated. For that reason, you undoubtedly use a word processor to create any documents for local use (or for sharing across your local network or via "sneakernet").

HTML documents, however, need to be transmitted across the Internet and the Web, which means they need to be no larger than is absolutely necessary. Using only ASCII codes to compose HTML documents achieves that. The choice of using ASCII for HTML files, in other words, is an important aspect of ensuring that HTML files can easily and quickly be transmitted and exchanged over the Internet and the Web. If a proprietary format had been used for HTML instead, the Internet traffic jams would have been much worse much earlier, and special software would have been required to interpret and read HTML documents.

HTML Is a Markup Language

Many people think HTML is a programming language because it is represented by an acronym. However, HTML is actually a **markup language**. The term *markup* originates from the world of printing and publishing. A formatter or designer would actually "mark up" the copy or layout, indicating how different elements should be printed. For instance, markup might be added to indicate that a heading at the top of the document should be printed in a bold 24-point Helvetica font. Other markup on the document might indicate color, margins, indents, leading, kerning, and so on. Back before mechanical or electronic typesetters, a person would then physically set the type for the document in the specified typefaces and sizes. Later, mechanical and electronic typesetting machines were invented that automated this process. Markup in an HTML file works in a somewhat similar fashion, with a Web browser functioning as a kind of typesetter.

With HTML, you mark up your textual copy to specify the structural elements that compose your document, such as headings, paragraphs, bulleted lists, bolding, italics, superscripts, and so on. A Web browser then interprets (or "parses") your markup code to appropriately display your document according to your instructions.

A primary difference between markup for printing and for the Web is that when designing a flyer, for instance, you already know the size of the media on which the flyer will be printed, whereas a Web page may be displayed on monitors of widely different sizes, at different resolutions, and using different default font-pitches. The actual dimensions of a Web page, in other words, are unknown and variable and might even have no dimensions at all, if presented through a Braille or speech browser, for instance. Because of this, the original philosophy of HTML has been to indicate what an element is, with the identity of the element indicating its function and structural import, rather than to try to describe what an element should look like.

HTML is based on SGML. SGML is generally used to mark up electronic documents for processing, whether for printing on a printer or for displaying on a computer monitor. A desktop publisher, for instance, might use SGML conventions to identify (or tag) the different elements that compose an electronic document (whether a newsletter, a brochure, a calendar, a catalog, and so on). A separate program (a desktop publishing application such as PageMaker, Quark Express, or InDesign) then applies the formatting characteristics specified for the indicated elements.

HTML shares many common characteristics and features with SGML. Both are used to specify the hierarchical structure of a document in the form of elements and their attributes. An HTML standard is defined by means of a **DTD** (Document Type Definition), which originates from SGML. A DTD defines the elements, attributes, and other conventions that pertain to the processing of a specific type of document—an HTML file versus some other kind of file, such as some kind of DTP (Desktop Publishing) file that is intended for printing on a printing press, for instance. HTML is much simpler than SGML, however, because it is intended for a specific purpose (specifying the structure of electronic documents for presentation over the Web), whereas SGML is intended to take into account any and all purposes that an electronic document might be used for.

Two other markup languages are also in use: **XHTML** (Extensible Hypertext Markup Language) and **XML** (Extensible Markup Language). XHTML is a version of HTML that has been brought into conformance with XML. XML is intended to facilitate the presentation of structured data (database records, spreadsheets, catalogs, address books, financial transactions, bibliographies, or any data that can be given a structure). XML also makes possible the formulation of more specific markup languages, or modules, to be used for presenting documents and data over the Web—XHTML is, in fact, an XML module. Any individual or organization can formulate an XML-based markup language simply by publishing its DTD on the Web, as long as it is otherwise in conformance with XML. Other XML-based markup languages that have been or are being developed include MathML (Mathematical Markup Language), SMIL (Synchronized Multimedia Integration Language), RDF (Resource Description Framework), SVG (Scalable Vector Graphics), and XForms (Next-Generation Web Forms).

HTML Is a Client-Side Application

In its original conception at least, HTML markup was not intended to specify individual formatting characteristics. Rather, it was intended to specify only the structural aspects of a document, leaving the question of how the different elements in the document should be displayed entirely up to the Web browser (or other user agent used to interpret the HTML code). Thus, the idea was to specify only that an element was a level-one heading, for instance—a browser might then decide to display the heading in whatever typeface and font size it determined to be appropriate.

NOTE As HTML became more a visual media and less a textual media, how elements appeared on the screen came to matter much more. Recent browsers display elements and attributes with a high degree of uniformity. This uniformity is not due to any dictates from the W3C. Rather, it is the result of market forces. Other browsers are emulating how the market leaders— whether Mosaic, Netscape Navigator, or Internet Explorer—display elements and attributes.

Leaving how elements and attributes are to be displayed up to the browser enables HTML files to remain relatively small because information does not need to be included in the file to specify how a level-one heading is to be formatted. Rather, an element is simply marked up as being a level-one heading, and the browser determines on its own how to display it.

This means that decisions about how a document is to be displayed do not have to be made until the document has been downloaded to the client (the Web browser). In other words, the load of determining formatting characteristics is assigned to the client (the local Web browser), while the server (the Web server) is only responsible for conveying the structural components of the documents to the client. This is referred to as a **client-side application** or process, in that instructions are downloaded and delivered to a client (your local Web browser, for instance) before they are executed. With a **server-side application** or process, on the other hand, a script or program located on the server might be executed (via CGI), with the results then downloaded and delivered to the client.

WHAT IS HYPERTEXT?

Besides being a markup language, HTML is a language that facilitates the dynamic and nonlinear interlinking of documents by means of **hypertext**. The prefix, *hyper-*, is from the Greek and is generally translated as meaning "over" or "above." The term *hypertext*, thus, indicates an additional set of nonlinear and nonsequential relations or linkages that can be defined within and between textual documents, over and above the normal flow that a straight linear or sequential reading of a document's text would encompass. This is actually not an entirely new or radical idea. Regular books, for instance, include something similar to hypertext links—they are called cross-references, footnotes, and endnotes. With a book's cross-reference, however, you have to thumb through to the page that is being referenced to find the object of the cross-reference. With a footnote, you might have to put on your hat, coat, and shoes, head on down to the library, search through the catalog or shelves to retrieve the actual book, and then turn to the chapter and page being referenced.

With a **hypertext link**, however, you can immediately jump to the object of the link. That object might be another HTML document, a map or chart, a figure illustration, a section in another document, and so on. The object can be in the same file, in the same folder, in the same Web site, on the same server, or located anywhere else in the Web or on the Internet. A hypertext link, for instance, can jump to a location two-thirds down from the top of another HTML file that is located halfway around the World. Besides HTML files and locations within HTML files, other objects also can be linked, including images, audio files, animations, videos, and more. In fact, anything that has an address on the Internet can be linked to, including many Internet services that predate the Web but still continue to exist on the Internet along with the Web, including Gopher files, FTP directories, WAIS files, Archie databases, Veronica searches, and so on.

In July 1945, Vannevar Bush, who had been the head of the Office of Scientific Research and Development during World War II, wrote an article, "As We May Think," that was published in *Atlantic Monthly*. In the article, he made the earliest proposal for what might be interpreted as a hypertext system. He proposed a system called a **memex**, which he described as working along similar lines to the human brain, being characterized by the association of an "intricate web of trails."

NOTE ———— You can read Vannevar Bush's article, "As We May Think," online at the *Atlantic Monthly* site at **www.theatlantic.com/doc/194507/bush**.

Twenty years later, in 1965, Ted Nelson, a graduate student at Harvard, inspired by reading Vannevar Bush's article, coined the term *hypertext* and worked out the basic characteristics of what a hypertext system might be. Nelson described hypertext as being "nonsequential writing" in *Literary Machines*, a book that he self-published in 1974. He worked for many years on elaborating a full-fledged hypertext system that he called Zanadu, but which was never completed. Nelson also coined the term **hypermedia** to describe the nonsequential linking of different media, as well as another wonderfully apt term, the **docuverse**, which encompasses the universe of hypertext-linked documents.

Prior to the invention of the Web, a number of hypertext systems were implemented. The earliest was Xerox's NoteCards system created in 1985. The Owl Guide hypertext system was released in 1986, and Apple released the HyperCard system, created by Bill Atkinson, in 1987. Asymmetrix Toolbox, a clone of the HyperCard system, was later developed for Windows.

In 1989, Berners-Lee was directly influenced by Nelson's ideas when he formulated his concepts for the creation and formation of what soon became the World Wide Web. It is no accident that the term *hypermedia* is prominently featured in Berners-Lee's initial description of the Web as a "wide-area hypermedia information retrieval initiative." Nelson's term, docuverse, is also a very close analog for Berners-Lee's description of the Web as "the universal space of all network-accessible information." Figure I.6 provides a graphic illustration of how hypertext and hypermedia interact within the universal space, or docuverse, that they inscribe.

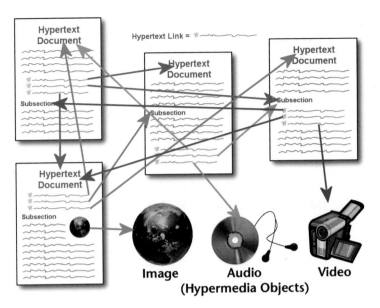

Image (Hypermedia Objects) Audio Video

FIGURE 1.6 • A hypertext link can jump to another document, a subsection within a document, a hypermedia object (image, audio, video, animation, and so on), or any other object or resource that has an address on the Internet.

Visit the Internet Resource Center. For links to resources on the Web that discuss the history of hypertext, see the Introduction section of this book's Internet Resource Center at **www.emcp.net/html2e.**

HOW HAS HTML EVOLVED?

Although Berners-Lee defined the original principles and specifications for HTML, HTML has undergone change. Many other individuals, organizations, companies, and factors have had a hand in determining what HTML was eventually to become.

The Original Version of HTML

HTML has evolved over time. Berners-Lee introduced the original version of HTML in 1989 along with the proposal for the formation of the World Wide Web. The original version of HTML provided for the following features:

- A document title.
- Heading elements used to structure an HTML document hierarchically.
- Standalone paragraph elements, but used as separators, not as containers, as in later versions of HTML. (There was no provision for adding line breaks, however.)
- Hypertext anchors (the A element) for creating hypertext links to documents or locations within documents.
- Bulleted and glossary lists, but not numbered lists.
- Non-keyboard character entities (such as for the copyright and registered symbols).
- An address block designator (the ADDRESS element).

NOTE To find out more about the original version of HTML at the W3C site at **www.w3.org/ History/19921103-hypertext/hypertext/WWW/MarkUp/MarkUp.html**. Reading the earlier versions of HTML can be a great way to find out more about why HTML is what it is and how it has evolved and changed in response to the evolution and growth of the Internet and the Web.

HTML 2.0

The original version of HTML, although functional, was simple and missing many of the key features taken for granted by today's Web authors. A number of proposals were made for extending the original version of HTML, which as a group were generally referred to as "HTML+," but which were never formalized into a final recommendation (or standard).

The first official new version of HTML, following the original version, was HTML 2.0, which was formalized as an official recommendation in 1995. HTML 2.0 added the following features:

- HTML, HEAD, and BODY elements, to provide a more explicit structure to an HTML document (specifying separate "header" and "body" sections within an HTML document).
- The paragraph element goes from being a standalone "separator" to being a container element but with an implied ending.
- Display of inline images.
- Bold, italic, and monospace highlighting.
- Horizontal rules and line breaks.
- Numbered lists.
- Various other elements still in common use in HTML, including block quotes, preformatted text, metadata, HTML comment codes, and input forms.

NOTE To find out more about HTML 2.0, you can read its specification at the W3C site at **www.w3.org/MarkUp/html-spec/**.

Vendor Extensions to HTML

Early on, browser vendors began adding their own extensions to HTML in response to the clear desire of authors and surfers for more richly formatted documents. For instance, the capability to display inline images in an HTML document was originally an extension to HTML created by the makers of the first widely distributed graphical Web browser, **Mosaic**. Many of these extensions to HTML are commonly referred to as **Netscape extensions** because the makers of the Netscape Navigator browser, the first widely distributed commercial Web browser, introduced them. Some of these extensions allowed authors of HTML documents to specify changes in font colors and sizes, as well as background colors and images, for instance. Later, Microsoft, when its Internet Explorer browser began to overtake the Netscape browser in popularity, introduced some of its own extensions to HTML, which are commonly referred to as **Microsoft extensions**. Examples of Microsoft extensions include changing the typeface being used to display an element (using the FONT element's FACE attribute) and creating text that scrolls horizontally across the screen (the MARQUEE element).

Many of the extensions originally introduced as extensions to HTML have since been incorporated into the official specifications (or "standards") for HTML. Some extensions to HTML, however, remain as unofficial and proprietary extensions of HTML, including Netscape's BLINK element and Microsoft's MARQUEE element.

HTML 3.2

After failing to come to consensus on a more comprehensive reformulation of HTML (the proposed HTML 3 specification), the W3C ended up approving a somewhat less ambitious proposal in January of 1997, which it termed HTML 3.2. This new HTML standard brought into the fold a number of extensions to HTML that had been introduced by Netscape, as well as several features that had originally been proposed as part of HTML 3.0:

- Variable font sizes and colors, text and link colors, and background colors and images
- Flowing text around images and image borders
- Tables for displaying data in rows and columns
- Horizontal alignment of document divisions (new), headings, paragraphs, and rules
- Superscripts and subscripts, strikethrough, and underlining
- Client-side image maps
- Scripts and styles (the latter, however, not implemented until HTML 4)

NOTE   To find out more about HTML 3.2, you can read its specification at the W3C site at **www.w3.org/TR/REC-html32**.

HTML 4.0 and HTML 4.01

Less than a year later, in December of 1997, the W3C recommended a new specification, HTML 4.0. HTML 4.0 included the following new features:

- Frames and inline frames
- Fully implemented style sheets
- Font typeface changes
- New form and table elements
- New text highlighting elements, including insertions and deletions, quotations, abbreviations, acronyms, and text spans
- Java applets and multimedia objects (not just inline images but other hypermedia objects, such as videos, animations, audio consoles, and so on)
- Triggering of scripts in response to mouse and user actions

The W3C came out with the HTML 4.01 recommendation in 1999, which was largely a fine-tuning of the HTML 4.0 specification. The W3C announced that HTML 4.01 was the final version of HTML, with future development focused in other related technologies (style sheets, scripting technologies, the document object model, as well as XHTML and XML). In 2008, however, the W3C announced a draft specification for HTML 5, which will likely not be finalized for several years. This book focuses on teaching the HTML 4.01 standard, while ensuring forward-compatibility with the future HTML 5.0 standard. See "HTML 5" later in this section for more information on HTML 5.

NOTE To find out more about HTML 4.01, you can read its specification at the W3C site at **www.w3.org/TR/html401/**.

XHTML and XML

The W3C recommended the XML (Exstensible Markup Language) 1.0 specification in February of 1998 and the XHTML (Extensible Hypertext Markup Language)1.0 specification in January of 2000. The W3C describes XML as "a universal format for structured documents and data on the Web." Unlike HTML, XML does not possess a specific set of named elements and attributes but allows authors to freely invent the elements and attributes that describe the structure of a document or data set. Elements and attributes can be created to take advantage of specific applications, or applications can be created to take advantage of specific element and attribute sets. XML, by itself, provides no formatting or display characteristics, but relies on style sheets to determine the presentation or appearance of an XML document. For an example of using XML to structure and format a bibliography of the Harry Potter series of books, see Appendix G, *Miscellaneous Technologies and Features*.

XHTML 1.0 XHTML 1.0 is an attempt to reformulate HTML as a conforming XML application. While adopting its syntactical rules from XML, it lacks the freedom to liberally create new elements and attributes that is present in XML. Although included as a **namespace** under the XML umbrella standard, XHTML 1.0 is identical to HTML 4.01 in structure and function, sharing the same elements and attributes.

Appendix B, *HTML-to-XHTML Conversion Chart*, presents all of the differences between HTML 4.01 and XHTML 1.0 in a handy side-by-side format. Using this chart, any HTML 4.01 file can easily be converted to an XHTML 1.0 file.

XHTML 1.1 The Modularization of XHTML specification reached recommendation status in 2001, providing a framework within which XHTML could be extended to address emerging platforms, including small-format wireless and mobile devices, Web-enabled televisions, and other technologies. The first three XHTML-family modules were XHTML 1.1, XHTML Basic, and XHTML Print.

XHTML 1.1 is similar to XHTML 1.0 Strict, with deprecated elements and attributes included in 1.0 not allowed in 1.1. Also not allowed in HTML 1.1 is the lang attribute (in favor of xml:lang) and the name attribute for the A and MAP elements (in favor of the id attribute).

XHTML Basic 1.0, XHTML Mobile Profile, and XHTML Basic 1.1 are subsets of XHTML 1.1 that allow producing documents and applications that address the rapidly increasing numbers of users who access the Web through cellular phones and PDAs.

XHTML is just one of a family of new XML-based applications. Other XML-based applications include MathML (Mathematical Markup Language), SMIL (Synchronized Multimedia Integration Language), and RDF (Resource Description Framework).

XHTML 2.0 XHTML 2.0 was introduced as a working draft in 2006. Like XHTML 1.1, it does not allow deprecated elements or attributes. Some features of XHTML 2.0 include XForms, XFrames, XML Events, a new NL element (for navigation lists), the ability for any element to be a link, and a new H element (for document headings). The I, B, and TT elements are removed, as is the ALT attribute for the IMG element (alternate text is provided by the content of the IMG element, which is a container element in XHTML 2.0).

XHTML documents can be delivered as either HTML or XHTML+XML documents. If the first, a browser's HTML parsing engine is used to render the document; if the second, a browser's XML parsing engine is supposed to be used. However, Microsoft has never supported parsing XHTML+XML documents as XML in its Internet Explorer browser, which parses them as HTML documents (rendered using its HTML parser), and has stated it has no plans to do so in the future. This has caused many Web designers to question the value of migrating from HTML to XHTML.

An additional factor that has slowed the acceptance of XHTML has been more draconian error checking when a document is parsed as an XHTML+XML document, compared to when it is parsed as an HTML document. A single coding error in an XHTML+XML document will cause it to fail to display, displaying an error instead, while HTML parsers use error-correction routines to attempt to correct coding errors on the fly.

HTML 5

In 2004, three browser vendors—Mozilla, Opera Software, and Apple—formed the Web Hypertext Application Technology Working Group (WHATWG) to further the development of HTML and APIs (Application Programming Interfaces) to ease the authoring of Web applications. In September 2005, WHATWG announced an early working draft of Web Applications 1.0, described as "a new version of HTML4 and XHTML1."

In October 2006, in response to the "breakaway WHATWG," Tim Berners-Lee of the W3C wrote in his blog: "The attempt to get the world to switch to XML, including quotes around attribute values and slashes in empty tags and namespaces all at once didn't work." Instead of a revolution, it was "necessary to evolve HTML incrementally."

A year later, the W3C re-chartered its HTML Working Group to further the development of the next version of HTML. Mozilla, Opera, and Apple allowed the publication of the Web Applications 1.0 specification under W3C copyright, which then became the starting point for HTML 5. The WHATWG continues to collaborate on the development of HTML 5 but in a more open and less formal fashion than the HTML Working Group—anyone can join and participate in the WHATWG, while the HTML Working Group is restricted to "invited experts." Mozilla, Opera, and Apple belong to both working groups, while the HTML Working Group also includes Microsoft and Google (maker of the Chrome browser).

A "draft" specification for HTML 5 was announced in January 2008. Some of its promised features include

- New elements to facilitate the semantic structuring of HTML documents, including the HEADER, FOOTER, ASIDE, SECTION, and FIGURE elements. The ASIDE element in conjunction with CSS positioning could be used to format a sidebar, for instance.
- The CANVAS element, for displaying direct-mode graphics. Already implemented in the Opera 9 browser.
- Multimedia elements—AUDIO, VIDEO, EMBED, SOURCE, and SVG. The EMBED element, originally a Netscape extension, never made it into HTML 3.2 or HTML 4 but is in HTML 5.
- Other new elements—COMMAND, DIALOG, DETAILS, DATAGRID, DATALIST, EVENTSOURCE, MARK, METER, OUTPUT, PROGRESS, RUBY (with RP and RT), and TIME.

- Web application APIs to speed the development of online applications. Local and session storage.
- Context menus, editable content, cross-document messaging, drag and drop interface, and other features.
- Obsolete elements: ACRONYM, APPLET, BASEFONT, BIG, CENTER, DIR, FRAME, FRAMESET, NOFRAMES, S, STRIKE, TT, and U. FONT is only allowed when inserted by a WYSIWYG editor.

Some HTML 5 features are already being implemented in current browsers (the CANVAS element in the Opera 9 browser, for instance). HTML 5 is projected to become a "candidate recommendation" by September 2012, but when it will become a final recommendation is unclear.

Many of the new elements, such as the HEADER, FOOTER, and ARTICLE elements, are "sectioning" elements that operate in the same way as the DIV element, relying entirely on styles to specify display characteristics but with more semantically specific names. Wide adoption will depend on non-supporting browsers passing out of usage—something that is accelerated by increased use of "automatic updates" due to security concerns.

The W3C's strategy for implementing HTML 5 includes

- A new simplified DocType statement: `<!doctype html>`
- One version of HTML (no more strict, transitional, and frameset "flavors")
- Default to standards mode (no more "quirks" or "almost standards" modes triggered by DocType statements)
- Browsers responsible for error-handling and backward-compatibility
- Authors responsible for forward-compatibility and standards-compliance

The HTML 5 specification encompasses both HTML 5 and XHTML 5, both of which share the same DocType statement (`<!doctype html>`). The combined specification is sometimes referred to as X/HTML 5.

NOTE — To find out more about HTML 5, you can read its specification at the W3C site at **www.w3.org/TR/html5/**.

The Future of HTML

Prior to the announcement of the working draft of the HTML 5 specification, it was assumed that the path of evolution for HTML led from HTML 4.01 to XHTML 1.0, and then from XHTML 1.0 through XHTML 1.1 to XHTML 2.0 and beyond. The W3C even went so far as to declare that HTML 4.01 would be the last version of regular HTML.

However, the adoption of XHTML in place of HTML 4.01 was frustrated by the failure of large numbers of Web designers and content developers to migrate from what they were familiar with (HTML 4.01 and CSS 2.1) to what they were not (XHTML and XSLT or CSS), as well as by the failure of Microsoft to support parsing XHTML documents as XHTML+XML in its Internet Explorer browser.

Currently, there are two separate paths forward for HTML: XHTML 2.0 and HTML 5. Both are represented by separate working groups at the W3C, but there have been calls for merging them so the future development of the two standards can be coordinated. In general, it is expected that XHTML 2.0 will attract developers who need the special features offered by that markup language, whereas most other Web designers and authors are more likely to opt for using HTML 5.

NOTE — **Visit the Internet Resource Center.** For links to resources on the Web that discuss the history of the Internet, The Web, and HTML, see the Introduction section of this book's Internet Resource Center at **www.emcp.net/html2e**.

THE IMPORTANCE OF WEB STANDARDS

Even though the W3C does not term its recommended specifications as being "standards," the intent is clearly to arrive at a degree of agreement and consensus that can result in the establishment of a standard. For instance, browser vendors are members of the W3C and vote, along with other members, on whether proposed specifications should be formally recommended by the W3C. Although the W3C has no power to force anyone to follow a recommendation, those who are expected to follow the recommendation, such as browser vendors, for instance, have been directly involved in formulating the recommendation and voted for its approval. The likelihood of their implementing the recommendation is therefore considerably enhanced. Only a broad-based implementation of a recommendation will cause it to become a "standard."

This brings up an important consideration for anyone who wants to produce HTML documents for wide distribution over the Web. Only by sticking to the agreed upon recommendations for HTML (the HTML "standards") can you be relatively assured that your documents will be reliably displayed not only in all current Web browsers but in future Web browsers as well. Browser vendors are committed to supporting standard features in future browsers but can drop non-standard ("proprietary") features at their whim. By sticking to using only standard elements and attributes in your HTML documents, you help to ensure that your documents will remain *forward-compatible* with future browsers and user agents.

KEY TERMS

For a review of the key terms bolded in this introduction, visit the Introduction section of this book's Internet Resource Center at **wwww.emcp.net/html2e**. A complete glossary appears at the end of the book.

WEB-BASED LEARNING ACTIVITIES

The following Web-based learning activities can help you to further extend your learning and shore up your understanding of specific topic-areas:

- Visit this Introduction's section at the Internet Resource Center for this book at **www.emcp.net/html2e** to find online resources that you can use to further investigate and explore the topics and subjects covered.
- Further research a specific topic introduced in this Introduction using Google (**www.google.com/**), Yahoo! (**www.yahoo.com/**), Wikipedia (**www.wikipedia.org/**), Open Directory Project (**www.dmoz.org/**), or other online sources. Some topics covered include:
  - The beginnings and evolution of the Internet.
  - The invention of hypertext by Ted Nelson.
  - The invention of the World Wide Web and HTML by Tim Berners-Lee at CERN.
  - The development of the W3C at MIT.

CHAPTER 1

Creating a Basic Web Page

PERFORMANCE OBJECTIVES

- Use your text editor and a graphical Web browser to create and preview your HTML files.
- Create your page's top-level elements.
- Use heading and paragraph elements to structure and create the base content for your page.
- Create hypertext links, lists, and link lists.
- Align elements horizontally on the page.
- Insert inline images in your page.
- Create an address block for your page.

Learning how to use HTML to create a Web page is similar to learning how to ride a bicycle. No amount of theorizing or reading about it is going to teach you how to ride, in other words. You just have to get on and ride, although some training wheels, and someone to grab the handlebars if you start to teeter after the training wheels come off, can definitely be helpful.

In this chapter, you learn how to use this book's example files, review basic HTML pointers, and create a basic Web page. You will not be doing anything particularly fancy, but you will use everything you learn in this chapter in virtually every Web page you create in the future.

DOWNLOADING THE EXAMPLE FILES

In this book's chapters, you use the author-prepared **example files** to complete the included **case examples**, review exercises, and end-of-chapter projects. Your instructor might provide these to you or ask you to download them from the Web.

Visit the Internet Resource Center. To download the example files, go to the Download the Example Files section of this book's Internet Resource Center at **www.emcp.net/html2e**. Downloading instructions are provided, if you need them.

The example files are available for download as **ZIP archive files** (*.zip). Two versions are available, one for use with Microsoft Windows and the other for use with either Macintosh OS X or Linux/UNIX. ZIP archive files use compression algorithms to reduce the size of files so they can be more quickly downloaded over the Internet. Both Windows (XP and Vista) and Macintosh OS X (10.3 and later) have built in support for ZIP format files.

Visit the Internet Resource Center. You can find listings of third-party file compression programs that extract ZIP archive files that you can download and install in the Chapter 1 section of this book's Internet Resource Center at **www.emcp.net/html2e.**

CREATING A WORKING FOLDER

When the contents of the ZIP file containing the example files for this book are extracted, an **HTML_Examples** folder will be created within the current drive or folder. This is the **working folder** you will be using to save any files you create while doing this book's case examples, review exercises, or projects.

You can rename your working folder or move it to another location, as long as you remember what you named it and where you put it. For instance, if your last name is Smith, you might rename it as Smith_HTML_Examples and move it to your Desktop, where it will be easily accessible, or to your My Documents folder, if using Windows. If you are on a network, you might move it to your network folder.

If you plan on working on more than one computer, you can move your working folder to a flash memory drive ("memory stick") or other portable device or media (portable USB hard drive, DVD-RW disc, CD-RW disc, and so on), so you can work easily transfer examples, exercises, and projects you are working on between computers.

In your working folder (HTML_Examples, if you have not renamed it), you will now find separate folders (**chap01**, **chap02**, and so on) that contain the example files for each chapter. When working on a chapter's examples and exercises, you need to save the files you create in that chapter's folder within your working folder.

If you need more help in downloading or using the example files, ask your instructor for assistance. For detailed instructions for downloading and extracting the example files, see this book's Internet Resource Center at **www.emcp.net/html2e.**

When working with the example files and saving files you create, you will need to perform basic computer operations, such as copying, moving, renaming, deleting, saving, or opening folders or files. You should already be familiar with these kinds of basic operations. If you are confused about how to complete a particular folder or file operation on the system you are using, consult your system's help system or ask your instructor for assistance.

UNDERSTANDING THE BASICS

Before you actually start creating an HTML file, it might be helpful to review some basic pointers about how an HTML file is organized and composed.

Tags and Elements

The **element** is the basic building block of an HTML document. Anything included within an HTML document is either an element or is contained within an element. HTML uses codes called **tags** to delimit elements within an HTML document. In HTML, you can set two different element types: a container element and an empty element.

CONTAINER ELEMENTS A **container element** brackets text (or other elements) between two tags, a **start tag** and an **end tag**, with the end tag distinguished from the start tag by a leading forward slash, like this:

```
<tagname>element content</tagname>
```

For instance, the following is an example of setting a level-one heading element (a container element with h1 as the start and end tag names):

```
<h1>This Is a Level-One Heading</h1>
```

In this case, the start of the container is *tagged* with an **<h1>** start tag, while its end is tagged with an **</h1>** end tag. Both start and end tags are enclosed inside of left and right angle-brackets (< and >), while in the end tag, the element name is preceded by a forward slash (/).

HTML elements are often loosely referred to as tags. It is important to stress, however, that an element comprises both the tags that are used to mark the start and end of the element *and* anything that is enclosed within those two tags. The **element content** is the content between the start tag and end tag (see Figure 1.1).

HTML element

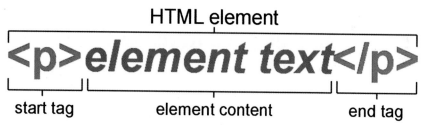

start tag   element content   end tag

FIGURE 1.1 • An element is not only the tags (codes) used to delimit it, but everything in between as well.

EMPTY ELEMENTS An **empty element** uses a single tag, without an end tag, and does not contain text or other elements. An empty element is also called a *standalone element* because it stands on its own and does not bracket anything. (In HTML 5, an empty element is called a *void element*.)

In the following example, the HR (Horizontal Rule) element, which is an empty element, indicates where a browser should draw a horizontal rule across the page:

```
<h1>This Is a Level-One Heading</h1>
<hr>
```

HTML does not have many empty elements; most elements are container elements. Besides the HR element, some other empty elements that are frequently used include the IMG (Image) and BR (Line Break) elements.

You will also run into some instances where a container element will look like an empty element, with just a start tag but no end tag. Rather, the element actually has an implied end tag, where the end of the element is implied by the start of a following element. For example, the LI (List Item) element, used with the OL (Ordered List) and UL (Unordered List) elements, is a container element for which the end tag can be omitted. (You will be alerted to this when such an element is first utilized in the examples.)

BLOCK AND INLINE ELEMENTS An HTML element that is contained in the body of an HTML document (in the BODY element) also can function as a block element or an inline element. **Block elements** are presented as separate blocks, starting on a new line with vertical spacing inserted above and below the element. **Inline elements** are presented "in a line" in the position where they are inserted, without starting a new line (and without any additional vertical spacing inserted above or below the element).

NESTING AND OVERLAPPING **Nesting** means including an element within another element. Because HTML documents are hierarchical in structure, elements must always be nested inside of or bracket other elements, but should never overlap. For instance, the following two examples apply both italics and bolding to text within an HTML document:

```
<b><i>bolded and italicized</i></b>
<i><b>italicized and bolded</b></i>
```

Both of these are correct—all that matters is that one be nested inside the other.
    On the other hand, here is an example of how you should not do it:

```
<b><i>bolded and italicized</b></i>
```

In this case, the B (Bold) element overlaps the I (Italic) element, which might confuse a browser about what should be nested inside of what.

Attributes and Attribute Values

In HTML elements, attributes can be used to further specify the presentation or function of an element. An **attribute** has two parts: the **attribute name** and an **attribute value**. An attribute included in an HTML element in the following manner:

```
<tagname attribute="value">
```

The following example shows a series of attributes being applied to the IMG (Image) element:

```
<img src="myimage.jpg" height="200" width="150">
```

In HTML 4, you are free not to quote an attribute value as long as it contains only letters (a–z and A–Z), digits (0–9), hyphens, periods, underscores, and colons. The W3C recommends, however, that all attribute values in HTML files be quoted. Quoting of attribute values is required in XHTML.

Case-Insensitivity

In HTML, both element and attribute names are case-insensitive. Both of the following lines of code are perfectly valid, for instance:

```
<img src="myimage.jpg" height="200" width="150">
<IMG SRC="myimage.jpg" HEIGHT="200" WIDTH="150">
```

In this book, element and attribute names included in code examples are all presented in lowercase. Part of the reason for this is that XHTML, unlike HTML, is case-sensitive; XHTML requires that all element and attribute names be lowercased. Following the same rule in your HTML documents will make your task much easier if you ever decide you need to convert any of them to XHTML.

NOTE — In this book, HTML code or other code that you need to key is printed in a magenta color. Code printed in a black color is presented for example purposes or for context and need not be keyed. You will be prompted later in this chapter when you need to run your text editor and start keying in any HTML codes.

CASE EXAMPLE: CREATING A PERSONAL WEB PAGE

To gain experience creating a basic Web page, you will create one of the more common pages found on the Web: a **personal Web page**. A personal Web page might include information about a person's life, family, and other interests, for instance. It might provide further details about a person's educational, professional, or career background and involvements. It might also focus on particular interests or hobbies that the person creating the page might have. In other words, a personal Web page can include just about anything under the sun that is related to the person creating the page.

"Johnny Watson is a college student who wants to create his own personal Web page. He does not yet know a lot about HTML, so he wants to keep things simple. He has two primary interests—sports and gardening—that he wants to feature in his page, although he wants to include other information, too. Soon to be graduating, he wants to include links to his biography and his resume. He also wants to share links to his favorite sports and gardening Web sites, and to Web pages created by his friends."

RUNNING YOUR TEXT EDITOR

You will be using a text editor to create, edit, and save your HTML documents. Web authors use a text editor to save an HTML document as an **ASCII text file**, which includes only codes included in the American Standard Code for Information Interchange encoding scheme. It includes only the basic characters included on the typical keyboard and is sometimes referred to as a plain text file, for that reason. A text editor does not add bolding or italic highlighting, set margins, change font sizes, or add any of the other kinds of formatting a word processor can do, for instance.

If using Windows, you can use Notepad, as your text editor. Notepad is included with XP or Vista. If using the Macintosh, you can use TextEdit, which is included with OS X. Older versions of the Macintosh OS include SimpleText.

action

Windows. In Windows XP and Vista, without the Classic Desktop theme selected, to run Notepad, click the Start button, and select All Programs, Programs, Accessories, and Notepad. If the Classic Desktop theme is selected, select Programs, Accessories, and Notepad.

To enable word wrap in Windows XP and Vista, select Format and Word Wrap (if it is not already checked). In earlier versions of Windows, select Edit and Word Wrap. When Word Wrap is turned on, a check mark is displayed next to the Word Wrap option.

tip

For a shortcut for running Notepad, click the Start button, then in Windows Vista, click in the Start Search bar, key **notepad**, and press Enter; in Windows XP, select Run, key **notepad**, and press Enter.

To edit and save HTML files, run TextEdit from the Dock or the Applications folder. TextEdit defaults to saving files in **rich text format** (RTF). To set TextEdit to default to opening new files as plain (or ASCII) text files, select TextEdit, Preferences, click the New Document tab, and select Plain Text (under Format). To enable word wrap, check the Wrap to Page check box (under Format).

Macintosh. To enable saving plain text files, but with a ".html" instead of a ".txt" extension, select TextEdit, Preferences, click the Open and Save tab, uncheck the Add ".txt" extension to plain text files check box (under When Saving a File), and check the Ignore rich text commands in HTML files check box (under When Opening a File).

Included text editors for Linux vary, depending on the environment being used. For instance, gedit text is included with the GNOME environment and kate with the KDE environment. See your system documentation or help system to find out how to run any text editor that is included with your system's software. You also can download text editors for many platforms, including Linux, OS/2, BeOS, and QNX, from Tucows at **www.tucows.com/**.

STARTING YOUR PAGE

For this example, you will be creating an HTML file from scratch. You do not need to open an example file to get started. Just key the indicated example codes directly into your text editor's window. Any text that you need to key is displayed within a code example in a magenta font.

Let any long lines wrap—you do not need to insert a hard return at the end of every line in the example codes. Additional leading is inserted between code blocks to indicate where you need to insert a hard return.

Starting with the Top-Level Elements

The HTML, HEAD, and BODY elements are the **top-level elements** and specify the top-level hierarchy of a Web page. The HTML element identifies that the document is an HTML document, while the HEAD and BODY elements are nested inside the HTML element.

Key the following codes into your text editor's window to create the top-level elements for your page:

```
<html>
<head>
</head>
<body>
</body>
</html>
```

In the HEAD element, elements are inserted that define characteristics of the document, such as a title, a style sheet, meta data elements that describe the document, and so on.

In the BODY element, elements are inserted that will be displayed in a browser's viewport, such as headings, paragraphs, lists, and so on. Because you have not yet included anything in the BODY element, opening your document in a browser at this point would just display a blank browser window. The action text will prompt you later when you should run your browser to check out the visual results of your work.

Creating a Title for Your Page

The TITLE element is a required element that is nested inside the HEAD element. Every HTML document should have a TITLE element.

Add the following TITLE element to your HTML document:

```
<html>
<head>
<title>Johnny Watson's Home Page</title>
</head>
<body>
</body>
</html>
```

The content of the TITLE element is generally displayed in a browser's title bar. Including additional text in your title that summarizes the content of your page may improve the chances of your page being displayed, or cause it to be displayed earlier, in a search engine's list of search results. There is effectively no limit on the amount of text you can include in your title, but search engines vary on how much of an extended title content they will display or index. The Google search engine (**www.google.com/**), for instance, only displays up to 60 characters in a page's title.

Add additional text to your title that more specifically indicates the actual content of your page to make your title more informative and more likely to be found in a search engine's list of search responses. Because Johnny Watson's two favorite interests are sports and gardening, add additional text to the title to indicate that:

```
<html>
<head>
<title>Johnny Watson's Home Page: Sports and Gardening</title>
</head>
<body>
</body>
</html>
```

A number of other elements can be included in the HEAD element. These include the META, BASE, LINK, STYLE, and SCRIPT elements. Because you are creating a basic Web page in this chapter, these other elements are not discussed at this point. You will learn about using the META element in Chapter 2, *Working with Online Documents*. For more information on the other HEAD elements, see Appendix A, *HTML Quick Reference*.

Saving Your File

Earlier in this chapter, you were prompted to download a ZIP file containing the example files that are used in creating this book's case examples—when you extracted its contents, an **HTML_Examples** folder was created in the current folder or drive. This folder is the folder where you need to save any files you create while doing this book's case examples. Since you are free to rename or move this folder, in this book it will simply be referred to as your "working folder." It is up to you to remember what you have named it and where it is located.

If you have not yet downloaded the example files or created your working folder, return to "Downloading the Example Files" earlier in this chapter and follow the instructions that are given there.

Turning on Display of File Extensions in Windows

By default, Windows hides file extensions, using file icons to indicate file types. The file extensions are still there, however, but are just hidden. On the Web, files are identified by their file extensions, so it is important that they be visible to you. To make working with files easier in Windows, you should turn on the display of file extensions. To turn on the display of file extensions:

1. In Vista, click Start, select Control Panel from the side menu, select Appearance and Personalization, and then Folder Options; in Windows XP, double-click My Computer on your Desktop and then select Tools and Folder Options.
2. In Vista or XP, click the View tab, and uncheck the Hide extensions [or file extensions] for known file types check box.

Turning on the display of file extensions also can help reduce your vulnerability to e-mail viruses. Many e-mail viruses use a visible and a hidden file extension to fool you into thinking that a file is a type of file that is safe to open.

Windows. Save your HTML document as **watson.html** in your working folder:
1. In Notepad, select File and Save.
2. Click on the Browse Folders button (in Windows Vista) or the Save in box (in Windows XP) and navigate to your working folder. Open the chap01 folder.
3. Click on the Save as type box, and select All Files.
4. In the File name box, key **watson.html** as the file name, and click Save.

Macintosh. Save your HTML document as **watson.html** in the chap01 folder in your working folder:
1. In TextEdit, select File and Save As.
2. If not already selected, select Western (Mac OS Roman) in the Plain Text Encoding box.
3. Use the Where box to navigate to your working folder, and then choose the chap01 folder.
4. In the Save As box, key **watson.html**. Click Save.
5. If prompted that the standard extension is ".txt", click the Use .html button.

When saving an HTML file, do *not* include any spaces in the file name. Although this is allowed in both Windows and the Macintosh (Classic or OS X), it is not allowed on a UNIX server (and most Web servers run UNIX). More recent UNIX Web servers will substitute the space character's escape code (**%20**) for spaces in folder and file names, but any link to the file would also have to reduplicate the escape character in place of the space, or the link will not work. Other UNIX Web servers might simply generate a "file not found" or other error when encountering spaces in folder or file names. Substitute underscores (_) for spaces, if necessary.

Also, always add an **.html** (or **.htm**) file extension to any HTML file that you save. Internet Explorer 8 and Mozilla Firefox 3 will display an HTML file without the file extension as an HTML file, but other browsers might treat it as a straight text file and simply display the raw HTML codes.

All HTML files start out the same way. Saving a template file can save you some keystrokes when creating an HTML file from scratch. In Windows Notepad, for instance:
1. Save watson.html (select File and Save).
2. Delete the content of the TITLE element.
3. Resave the file (select File and Save As) as start.html in your working folder so you can use it later to start a new HTML file with the opening codes already keyed in.
4. Reopen watson.html (select File and Open) from the chap01 folder to continue working with the current case example.

ADDING A LEVEL-ONE HEADING

HTML includes six **heading-level elements** (H1, H2, H3, and so on) that can be used to create headings. Generally, only one H1 heading is included, at the top of the BODY element, functioning as a heading, or title, for the whole document. The other heading elements are then used to indicate sections and subsections within a document.

Unlike the content of the TITLE element, which is only displayed on a browser's title bar, the content of the H1 element is displayed within the browser window and serves as the displayable title for the document.

Edit the H1 element as shown here to include keywords in the level-one heading:

```
<html>
<head>
<title>Johnny Watson's Home Page: Sports and Gardening</title>
</head>
<body>
<h1>Sports, Gardening, and Other Interests</h1>
</body>
</html>
```

PREVIEWING YOUR WORK

To preview your work while creating the document examples that are presented in each chapter, you need to have your HTML document open in both your text editor and your browser. You should frequently switch between your text editor and your browser, saving your work in your text editor and then refreshing the display of your document in your browser.

Previewing Your HTML Document in Your Browser

Now that you have added something to your HTML document that will be displayed within a browser's window, you should preview your results in your browser.

action

Save your document and then open it in your browser, so you can see your results for yourself:

HINT

If Internet Explorer 8's Menu Bar is not visible, just tap the Alt key to make it temporarily visible.

1. Resave **watson.html**. In Windows Notepad, select File and Save, or press Ctrl+S to resave your document (some earlier versions of Notepad do not recognize Ctrl+S, however). In TextEdit Macintosh OS X, you can press Command+S to resave your document.

tip

To toggle display of the menu bar on or off by default in Internet Explorer 8, select View, Toolbars, and Menu Bar. You can also right-click in the toolbar area and select Menu Bar.

2. Run your browser and open **watson.html**. In Internet Explorer 8 for Windows, for instance, select File, Open, and click the Browse button; in Mozilla Firefox 3 for Windows, select File and Open Page. Navigate to and open your working folder, open the **chap01** folder, double-click **watson.html,** and click OK to open it. Figure 1.2 shows watson.html opened in a Web browser.

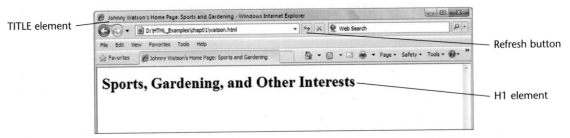

FIGURE 1.2 • The HTML document, watson.html, is opened in a Web browser.

tip

Alternatively, you can open a local HTML file in your browser by dragging it from its folder and dropping it in your browser's window. You will need to arrange your HTML file's open folder and your browser's window so you can drag your file from one and drop it in to the other. Whether this is easier than just using the File menu, however, is debatable.

HINT

You also can press the keyboard shortcut Ctrl+R in Windows or Command+R on the Macintosh to refresh your page in your browser.

As you add more example code to your HTML document, do not just rely on the figures to show you what your results should look like. Instead, use the figures as prompts to save your HTML document in your text editor, and switch over to your browser. Just click the **Refresh button** (in Internet Explorer), or the **Reload button** (in Mozilla Firefox), to refresh the display of your page.

Hopping between Your Text Editor and Your Browser

Both Windows and the Macintosh OS X support similar shortcut key combinations that you can use to quickly hop back and forth between your text editor and your browser.

action

Practice hopping back and forth between your text editor and your browser:

Windows. Hold down the **Alt key** and tap the **Tab key** to cycle through the icons for any open applications. Release the **Alt key** when the icon for the application you want to hop to is highlighted to bring its window to the foreground. You also can just press **Alt+Tab** once to jump to the previously opened application window.

Macintosh OS X. Hold down the **Command key** and tap the **Tab key** to cycle through any open application windows. Release the **Command key** when the application window you want to hop to is in the foreground.

You can also click the Window you want to bring to the foreground, if your text editor and your browser's windows overlap each other in the display, or click its icon in the Taskbar (in Windows) or in the Dock (in Macintosh OS X).

Stopping and Restarting Your Work

Depending on your learning style and computer experience, the amount of time required to complete this chapter's examples and exercises varies. It is not how fast you learn HTML that matters but how well you learn it, so do not feel that you have to rush to complete a chapter. You can stop at any point within a chapter, save your work, and then pick up where you left off at another time or location.

action

Follow these steps to resume work on a chapter's examples and exercises at home or in a computer lab, for instance:

1. In your text editor, save your HTML file in the chapter folder in which you are working.
2. Copy the chapter folder you are working in (the chap01 folder for Chapter 1) to a portable memory device or media (a memory stick, DVD-RW disc, or CD-RW disc, for instance). Be sure to copy the chapter folder and not just the file you are working on.

3. Take the portable memory device or media to any other location where you want to resume working on a chapter's examples or exercises. In the new location, just run your text editor, select File, then Open, and reopen the HTML file you are working on.

Windows. When opening a file in Notepad, the Open dialog box defaults to displaying only text files (with a .txt extension). To see HTML files (with an .html extension), you need to first select All Files (*.*) in the Files of type box.

WRITING AN INTRODUCTORY PARAGRAPH

The P (Paragraph) element is used to tag regular text paragraphs in an HTML document. An HTML document should contain no untagged text.

Using an introductory paragraph in an HTML document allows you to include additional **keywords** that search engines and Web directories can index, improving the chances of visitors finding your page.

Add the following introductory paragraph to your HTML document (see Figure 1.3):

```
<body>
<h1>Sports, Gardening, and Other Interests</h1>
<p>Welcome to my home page! My name is Johnny Watson and I'm a
big nut about two things: sports and gardening! You may think
that is an odd combination, but they really have more things in
common than you might suppose. First they are both largely
outside activities: I enjoy participating in, rather than just
watching, sports, for one thing. When the weather is bad, there
can be an indoor component to both activities. I enjoy following
some of my favorite teams on TV, while watering my indoor plants
at the same time!</p>
</body>
</html>
```

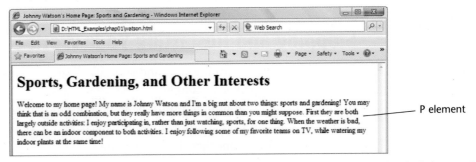

FIGURE 1.3 • An introductory paragraph can both describe your page and include keywords that search engines and Web directories can use to index your page.

Beginning HTML authors often think they can just insert multiple empty P elements to add vertical spacing within a Web page. That will not work. Browsers completely ignore multiple empty P elements in an HTML document. In Chapter 2, you will learn how to use the PRE element, which is the only element in which nested spaces, tabs, and returns are displayed and can be used to insert vertical spacing within an HTML document (by nesting two or more returns).

SPACING, TABS, AND RETURNS

Web browsers ignore any spacing, tabs, and hard returns you insert into an HTML document. You can use these to make your document's raw codes easier to read and interpret visually.

Test what happens when you insert hard returns or spaces into an HTML document:

1. Insert hard returns where ¶ characters are shown, and insert spaces where · characters are shown:

```
<html>
<head>
¶
···<title>Johnny Watson's Home Page: Sports and Gardening</title>
¶
</head>
<body>
¶
···<h1>Sports, Gardening, and Other Interests</h1>
¶
···<p>Welcome to my home page! My name is Johnny Watson and I'm a
big nut about two things: sports and gardening! You may think
that is an odd combination, but they really have more things in
common than you might suppose. First they are both largely
outside activities: I enjoy participating in, rather than just
watching, sports, for one thing. When the weather is bad, there
can be an indoor component to both activities. I enjoy following
some of my favorite teams on TV, while watering my indoor plants
at the same time!</p>
¶
</body>
</html>
```

You also can use tabs, instead of three spaces, to indent the first line of nested elements within your text editor.

2. Save watson.html (select File and Save in Notepad), switch to your browser, and refresh its display by clicking the Refresh button (or pressing Ctrl+R).

You should not see any change in your page, which should still look like Figure 1.3. That is because spaces, tabs, and hard returns, while visible in your text editor, should have no effect when displayed in a Web browser.

3. Delete the hard returns and spaces you just entered. Resave your file.

INSERTING COMMENTS

You can annotate your HTML document by inserting **comments**, which can be helpful if you or someone else has to revise your document at a later date, for instance. Later you might not remember why you did something a certain way, but a comment can remind you.

In HTML, bracket anything you want to include as a comment within <!-- and --> codes. Any text or codes included within these two codes can be read within your text editor but will not be displayed in a browser.

action

Test using comments in your document:

1. Add the following comments to your document:

```
<body>
<!--Top-level heading for document-->
<h1>Sports, Gardening, and Other Interests</h1>
<!--Introductory paragraph-->
<p>Welcome to my home page! My name is Johnny Watson and I'm a
big nut about two things: sports and gardening! You may think
that is an odd combination, but they really have more things in
common than you might suppose. First they are both largely
outside activities: I enjoy participating in, rather than just
watching, sports, for one thing. When the weather is bad, there
can be an indoor component to both activities. I enjoy following
some of my favorite teams on TV, while watering my indoor plants
at the same time!</p>
```

2. Select File, then Save to save your document, switch over to your Web browser, and refresh the display of your page by clicking the Refresh (or Reload) button.

After refreshing the display of your page, you should not see any change in your page, which should still look like Figure 1.3, because HTML comment codes and any text or other elements contained within them, although visible in your text editor, have no effect when displayed in a Web browser.

In this case, you are using HTML comments to identify and annotate the different sections of your page's code, with simple text statements as their content. You can also nest HTML elements inside of HTML comments, which can be helpful in revising or debugging your code. For instance, you might want to change the content of the heading-one element, while keeping the former version so you can return to it later:

```
<!--
<h1>Sports, Gardening, and Other Interests</h1>
-->
<h1>My Sports and Gardening Page</h1>
```

TROUBLE spot Although you can nest both text and HTML elements inside HTML comment codes, you cannot nest an HTML comment inside another HTML comment.

You also should make sure that any HTML comment codes you add to your document are properly nested and not overlapping any elements. If commenting out an element's start tag, make sure that its corresponding end tag, if it has one, is also commented out.

CREATING A HYPERTEXT LINK

In HTML, the A (Anchor) element is used to add a **hypertext link** to a Web page. Hypertext links can be added anywhere you can add text within an HTML document.

" Johnny Watson wants to link the word "sports" in the first sentence of his introductory paragraph to his favorite sports-related Web site. "

Add the following codes to link the word "sports" to ESPN.com:

```
Welcome to my home page! My name is Johnny Watson and I'm a big
nut about two things: <a href="http://www.espn.com/">sports</a>
and gardening!
```

Johnny Watson also wants to link the word "gardening" in his introductory paragraph's first sentence to his favorite gardening site.

To get some practice creating a hypertext link on your own, follow the previous example of linking the word "sports" to the ESPN Web site, but this time link the word "gardening" in the same sentence to the BBC's Lifestyle/Gardening site, using **http://www.bbc.co.uk/gardening/** as the value of the HREF attribute.

You should have now inserted two inline hypertext links, linking the words "sports" and "gardening" to actual sites that exist on the Web (see Figure 1.4).

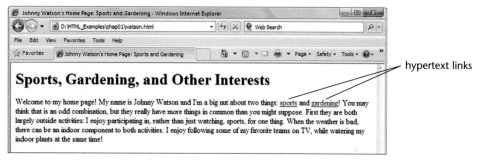

FIGURE 1.4 • Any word or phrase within an HTML document can be turned into a hypertext link.

You can test any links to pages on the Web that you create on your local machine, without having to publish your page to the Web, as long as you are connected to the Internet. If you are working on a computer without an Internet connection, skip the following Action section.

Test the "sports" and "gardening" links you just created:
1. Save your document in your text editor, switch to your browser, and refresh the display of your page.
2. Click the "sports" and "gardening" links to test them. Your browser should jump to the ESPN site and the BBC gardening site, respectively. Click your browser's Back button to return to your example page.

A common error when creating hypertext links is to leave off the second quotation mark that encloses the A element's HREF value. This omission causes most browsers to simply ignore anything that follows because it is considered to still be part of the HREF value, until a following A element start tag is encountered. This can result in a single word, a whole paragraph, or even the rest of a page not being displayed. Figure 1.5 shows what this looks like in a browser.

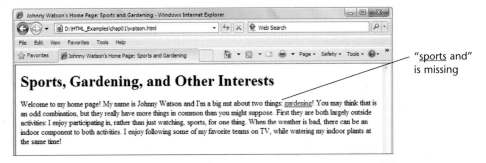

"sports and"
is missing

FIGURE 1.5 • Leaving off a following quote in a hypertext link can cause following text to disappear.

Other common errors when creating hypertext links include leaving off the closing > character of the A element's start tag and leaving out the / character in the A element's end tag. Browsers may react to either of these errors by considering all following text to be part of the same hypertext link (and underlining it), until another A element is encountered.

These link examples illustrate that you can turn any word (or phrase) within an HTML document into a hypertext link. Additionally, if Johnny Watson also had created a biography page for himself, he could have linked his name to that page.

The A element must include either an HREF (Hypertext Reference) attribute or a NAME attribute. To create a hypertext link, you use the HREF attribute. The NAME attribute is used for targeting a location within an HTML document that can be jumped to via a hypertext link—you will learn about doing that in Chapter 2.

The HREF attribute references the Web address, or **URL** (Uniform Resource Locator), of an object or resource on the Web. For an explanation of the different components that make up a URL, see the "What Is a URL?" sidebar later in this chapter.

In this chapter's code examples, two types of URLs are used: an **absolute URL** that points to a location on the Web and a **relative URL** that states the position of a linked object *relative to* the location of the linking file. An example of an absolute URL is `http://www.google.com/`. When you use just a file name to link to a file, for instance, you are actually using a relative URL, in that you are telling a browser that the linked file is located in the same folder as the linking file. You also can use relative URLs to link to files located in other folders within your own site. This allows the same file to be linked to from multiple files within your site. It is common, for instance, to save images in their own folder and then use relative URLs to link to them. For a full explanation of how to use relative URLs in your Web pages, see "Using Relative URLs" in Chapter 4, *Working with Images and Other Media*.

Links are generally displayed in a browser as colored blue and underlined (as shown previously in Figure 1.5), while links to sites you have already visited are generally colored purple.

For a graphical illustration of the different parts that compose a hypertext link, see Figure 1.6.

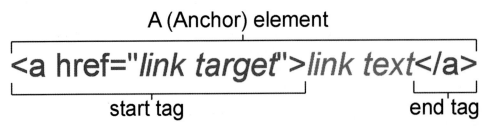

A (Anchor) element

`<a href="link target">link text</a>`

start tag   end tag

FIGURE 1.6 • A hypertext link is composed of several parts.

ADDING A NEW SECTION

As was stressed earlier, an HTML document is structured hierarchically. Heading-level elements are generally used to indicate the hierarchical structure of a document, with an H1 element marking the document heading, H2 elements marking major section headings, and H3 elements marking subsection headings within major sections. If an additional heading level is required, an H4 element can mark subsection headings within other subsections. Six heading-level elements are available, from the largest (H1) to the smallest (H6). Of these, only the four largest are normally used because the two smallest (H5 and H6) are displayed in font sizes that are smaller than the default paragraph text font.

To see this for yourself, look at the HTML document included with this chapter's example files, which shows all six heading-level elements in relation to the default paragraph text. Just open **headings.html** in your browser from the chap01 folder (see Figure 1.7).

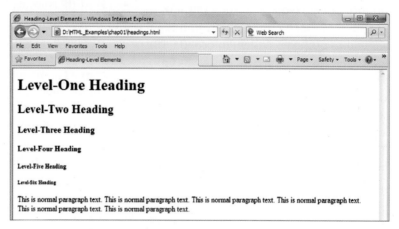

F I G U R E   1 . 7   •   Six different heading-level elements are available, but only four are as large as or larger than normal paragraph text.

> Johnny Watson wants to add a list of links to his page linking to both local Web pages, such as his biography and resume, and to other Web pages that are located at other sites on the Web. He also wants to include his link list inside its own section, with an H2 element heading the section and a following text paragraph introducing the list of links.

Add a level-two heading and a following paragraph element (see Figure 1.8):

```
<p>Welcome to my home page! My name is Johnny Watson and I'm a big
nut about two things: <a href="http://www.espn.com/">sports</a>
and <a href="http://www.bbc.co.uk/gardening/">gardening</a>! You
may think that is an odd combination, but they really have more
things in common than you might suppose. First they are both
largely outside activities: I enjoy participating in, rather than
just watching, sports, for one thing. When the weather is bad,
there can be an indoor component to both activities. I enjoy
following some of my favorite teams on TV, while watering my
indoor plants at the same time!</p>
<h2>Biography, Interests, and Friends</h2>
<p>In the following list, I've included links to biographical and
career info, resources focused on topics that I'm especially
interested in, and pages that have been created by friends of
mine:</p>
```

What Is a URL?

The Web forms a space (a "universal space," as Tim Berners-Lee puts it) through which users ("surfers") can navigate to find information, objects, or other resources. To locate something, however, that something must have a discreet and unique location and identity. On the Web, a *Uniform Resource Locator* (URL) identifies the location and identity of any object. An object's URL is also commonly referred to as a *Web address*. A URL can be divided into the following functional parts:

- **Scheme.** A URL's scheme identifies the service (and protocol) being requested. For a URL linking to an object located on a Web server, `http:` specifies that HyperText Transfer Protocol (HTTP) be used to transfer the requested object. `https:` specifies that HyperText Transfer Protocol Secure is used (this protocol is used to access objects on a secure server). Any other valid URL scheme can be used (`ftp:`, `gopher:`, `telnet:`, and so on). A double forward-slash (//) following the scheme indicates it is a hierarchically structured service (organized in folders and subfolders). For instance, Web servers and FTP servers organize the documents and objects they contain in folders (and subfolders) and thus require the double forward-slash following their URL's scheme: `http://www.yahoo.com/` or `ftp://ftp.netscape.com/`, for instance. On the other hand, USENET news servers and e-mail addresses are not hierarchically organized and thus should not have the double-slash following the scheme (`news:comp.infosystems.www.authoring.html` or `mailto:peterpiper@picklepicker.com`, for instance).

- **Host (IP Number or Alias/Domain Name).** Every device connected to the Internet has an **IP address**, which is a set of numbers that uniquely identifies it on the Internet (221.196.64.21, for instance). In place of an **IP number**, a **host name**, which is the combination of an **alias** and a **domain name**, also can be used, which is how most people connect to servers on the Web. An alias is a prefix to a domain name that stands for (is an alias for) a resource located within that domain. It precedes, rather

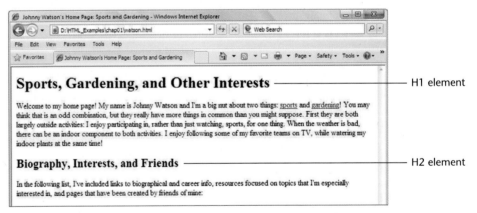

FIGURE 1.8 • An H2 (Level-Two Heading) element is added to the page, along with a following text paragraph.

Creating a Bulleted List

A **bulleted list** is created using the UL (Unordered List) element, displaying bullet characters preceding the list items. To create a bulleted list, you use two HTML elements: a UL element brackets the list as a whole, indicating that it is a bulleted (or unordered) list, while LI (List Item) elements indicate the individual items that are included in the list.

than follows, the domain name because it is not a hierarchically located object under that domain, but rather is an alias for such an object. The most commonly used URL alias on the Web is www (as in `http://www.altavista.com/`). Not all Web addresses use a www alias. For instance, `http://maps.yahoo.com/` uses an alias, maps, to point to the location of the Yahoo! Maps home page within the yahoo.com domain. A domain name, such as yahoo.com, on the other hand, is a unique name that identifies a resource on the Internet and the Web.

- **Port Number (Optional).** A port number is included in a URL only if a server is using a port number other than the default: `http://www.somehost.org:81/`, for instance. The default port number for a Web server is 80, whereas the default port number for an FTP server is 21; generally, you should only have to include a port number in your own URLs if your hosting server requires it (a rarity).
- **Resource Path.** If the linked object is not located in the host's root folder, the **resource path** speci-

fies the folder path to the object's location. For instance, `http://www.somehost.org/users/jwatson/` specifies that the URL's object is located in the **jwatson** folder, which is located in the **users** folder, which is itself located in the root folder of www.somehost.org.

- **Object.** The **object of a URL** is the actual file that is being linked to. For instance, `http://www.somehost.org/users/jwatson/watson.html` specifies that the object of the URL is a file named watson.html. Note, however, that a Web server administrator can specify a default file name, usually index.html, which is implied if an object file name is not included in a URL. This file is often called an **index page**. Thus, `http://www.somehost.org/users/jwatson/` and `http://www.somehost.org/users/jwatson/index.html` may represent the same URL. Other default file names also can be used (index.htm, default.html, welcome.html, or main.html, for instance), but index.html is by far the most commonly used.

Use the UL and LI elements to create a bulleted list, following the introductory paragraph you added previously (see Figure 1.9):

```
<h2>Biography, Interests, and Friends</h2>
<p>In the following list, I've included links to biographical and
career info, resources focused on topics that I'm especially
interested in, and pages that have been created by friends of
mine:</p>
<ul>
<li>My biography
<li>My resume
<li>Get the latest sports scores
<li>Get indoor gardening tips and advice
<li>My friend Joe's site
<li>My friend Jane's site
</ul>
```

Biography, Interests, and Friends

In the following list, I've included links to biographical and career info, resources focused on topics that I'm especially interested in, and pages that have been created by friends of mine:

- My biography
- My resume
- Get the latest sports scores
- Get indoor gardening tips and advice
- My friend Joe's site
- My friend Jane's site

— unordered list

FIGURE 1.9 • A series of bulleted list items are added to the page.

That is all you have to do to create a bulleted (or unordered) list. Lists are simple to create and add to your Web pages, so do not hesitate to use them.

Notice that the LI element, used to create a list item, has no end tag. The LI element is not an empty element, but in HTML 4 its end tag is implied, either by the start of a following LI element or by the end of the list. In XHTML, however, element end tags are required and cannot be implied, with the first list item in the previous example having to be inserted like this: `<li>My Biography</li>`.

You can nest bulleted lists inside of each other. Browsers automatically alter the bullet character for different levels of bulleted lists. Following is a code example of nesting one bulleted list inside of another:

```
<ul>
<li>First list item
<li>Second list item
   <ul>
   <li>First nested list item
   <li>Second nested list item
   </ul>
<li>Third list item
</ul>
```

Other types of lists can be created using HTML. **Numbered lists** are created using the OL (Ordered List) element and are covered in Chapter 2, *Working with Online Documents*. Definition lists are created using the DL (Definition List) element, in combination with the DT (Definition Term) and DD (Definition Data) elements, and can be useful for creating online glossaries. The DIR and MENU elements, which most browsers display identically to the UL element, are seldom used and should probably be avoided. You can find out more about the DL, DIR, and MENU elements in Appendix A, *HTML Quick Reference*.

Including the P element end tag (`</p>`) is also optional in HTML 4 and 5. In many instances, however, this omission can cause problems or produce differing results in different browsers—for that reason, you should always add the end tag at the end of your paragraph elements.

Creating a Link List

After you have created a bulleted list, you only need to add the links to create a **link list** (or list of hypertext links).

Create a link list, and test it in your browser:

1. Create a link list by nesting the list item text within hypertext links (see Figure 1.10):

```
<ul>
<li><a href="mybio.html">My biography</a>
<li><a href="myresume.html">My resume</a>
<li><a href="http://www.usatoday.com/sports/scores.htm">Get the
latest sports scores</a>
<li><a href="http://www.about-house-plants.com/">Get indoor
gardening tips and advice</a>
<li><a href="http://blank.emcp.com/jshmoe/">My
friend Joe's site</a>
```

```
<li><a href="http://wherever.emcp.com/jdoe/homepage.html">My
friend Jane's site</a>
</ul>
```

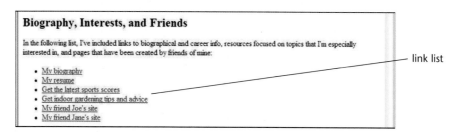

FIGURE 1.10 • A link list is just a list with links.

2. Save your file, switch over to your browser, and refresh the display of your page.
3. Test the biography and resume links. Dummy example pages are included with the example files that should display in your browser when you click on the links. Click the Back button to return to your example page.
4. The next two links are to actual sites on the Web; test them if you are connected. The last two links, however, to Joe's and Jane's sites, are fictional links that should not connect to anything—test either one to find out what happens when the object of a link does not exist.

In Windows and on the Macintosh, file and folder names are case-insensitive. However, on a UNIX computer, file and folder names are case-sensitive. For example, on a UNIX computer, the file names MyPage.html and mypage.html actually represent two different file names.

This UNIX naming convention matters because most Internet Web servers are UNIX servers. If you find that links that worked on your local Windows or Macintosh machine suddenly stop working after you transfer your Web page files to a Web server, the problem might be due to the case-sensitivity of file and folder names on a UNIX server. To avoid the problem, make sure that file and folder names included in your URLs match the actual file and folder names *exactly*.

The same holds true for absolute URLs that link to sites located on the Web. Although domain names are not case-sensitive, any folder or file names may be—so whenever you include an absolute URL in your page, make sure that you include it exactly as it is given (including any uppercase characters).

Linking Etiquette

At one time it was considered proper *netiquette* to request permission before linking to someone else's page. That was because unwanted traffic could easily push a page or site beyond its traffic allowance, when such allowances were much smaller than they are now. If running a major site, you should still request permission to link to a smaller site for that very reason. In general, especially when linking to a site's front page, you should not feel constrained to ask permission to link. These days most people want all the links they can get. However, if someone requests that you not link to their page, especially if it is a personal or family page, it is only good manners to comply.

Even linking to a page within someone else's site should not be a problem, as long as you properly identify both the site and page you are linking to. It is the responsibility of the Web author to code a site's pages so that the home or front page can easily be reached from any page within the site. The basic nature of hypertext and the Web, as enunciated in the visions of Ted Nelson and Tim Berners-Lee, is that any page can be linked to from any other page. Without links, there would be no Web, after all.

If using frames, however, you should not link to another's page so that it is displayed within a frame within your site without first getting permission. Always include `target="_blank"` or `target="_top"` in your link's A element when linking within a framed page to an external site or page, so the page will be displayed outside of your frame.

When linking to content that is within a frame in someone else's site, you should try to link to the pages that contains the frame, rather than simply the page within the frame. Where this is not possible, you might include a link to the site's front page, along with a link to their framed page. You will learn about using frames in Chapter 7, *Designing Multi-Column Web Sites*.

It is, however, unethical to link to someone else's images or other media files without permission, whether using the A, IMG, EMBED, or OBJECT elements, because doing so can significantly increase their traffic, which they have to pay for. Such linking on the Web is usually considered to be a form of theft (stealing someone else's bandwidth and intellectual property). Instead, you should always link to the site or page where the image or other media file is located, rather than directly to the file. If the image or media file is the only content of a page, you should link to a page that links to that page, has content that identifies the site, and provides a link to its front page.

HORIZONTALLY ALIGNING HEADINGS, PARAGRAPHS, AND DIVISIONS

So far, all of the elements you have added to your example page are left-aligned (horizontally aligned with the left margin). That is because left-alignment is the default horizontal alignment for block elements, except for the CENTER element.

Gathering URLs

If you later want to create your own list of hypertext links, you will need to gather the URLs and other link information you want to use. You can gather URLs for use in your Web pages in several ways:

- **While Surfing.** Open the page you want to create a link to in your browser, click and drag to highlight the contents of the Address (or Location) box, and press Ctrl+C (Windows) or Command+C (Macintosh). Press Ctrl+V (Windows) or Command+V (Macintosh) to paste the URL into your text editor. Copy and paste the level-one heading content to use it as your **link text**.
- **Copying a Link.** Just right-click on the link (in Macintosh OS X, hold down the Control key and click) and select to copy the link. The actual menu option varies from browser to browser:

Copy Shortcut, Copy Target, Copy Link Address, Copy Link Location, and so on.

- **From Internet Explorer Favorites.** Open your Favorites in the Explorer bar (select View, Explorer Bar, and Favorites). Locate a favorite you want to use, right-click on it (in Macintosh OS X, hold down the Control key and click), and select Properties. Copy the contents of the URL box, and paste it into your text editor. For the link text, you can type in the name of the Favorite (or any other text you want to use).
- **From Mozilla Firefox Bookmarks.** In Firefox 3, select Bookmarks and Organize Bookmarks. Find the Web page you want to link to, click on it, copy the contents of the Location box, and paste it into your text editor; copy the contents of the Name box and paste it to use it as the link text.

N O T E ———— The CENTER element was originally a Netscape extension to HTML that was included in HTML 3.2 and 4. Because it has been superceded by the DIV element `<div align="center">`, is deprecated in HTML 4, and is obsolete in HTML 5, its use should be avoided.

Using the ALIGN Attribute

You can use the ALIGN attribute to center, right-align, left-align, or justify text contained in a number of block elements, including heading level and paragraph elements.

Right-align the level-one heading, justify the text paragraphs, and center the level-two heading (see Figure 1.11):

```
<h1 align="right">Sports, Gardening, and Other Interests</h1>
<!--Introductory paragraph-->
<p align="justify">Welcome to my home page! My name is Johnny
Watson and I'm a big nut about two things: <a href="http://www.
espn.com/">sports</a> and <a href="http://www.bbc.co.uk/
gardening/">gardening</a>! You may think that is an odd
combination, but they really have more things in common than you
might suppose. First they are both largely outside activities: I
enjoy participating in, rather than just watching, sports, for
one thing. When the weather is bad, there can be an indoor
component to both activities. I enjoy following some of my
favorite teams on TV, while watering my indoor plants at the same
time!</p>
<h2 align="center">Biography, Interests, and Friends</h2>
<p align="justify">In the following list, I've included links to
biographical and career info, resources focused on topics that
I'm especially interested in, and pages that have been created by
friends of mine:</p>
```

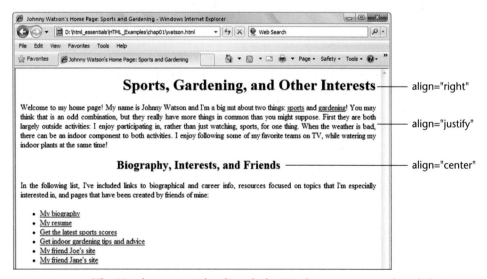

F I G U R E 1 . 1 1 • The H1 element is right-aligned, the H2 element is centered, and the P elements are justified.

NOTE
The ALIGN attribute is deprecated in HTML 4 and obsolete in HTML 5. **Deprecated elements** and attributes have been outdated by newer constructs. While Web authors are discouraged from using them, and encouraged to use Cascading Style Sheets (CSS) to achieve the same or similar results to improve usability and accessibility on the Web, their use is not forbidden. **Obsolete elements** and attributes should not be used, however. You will learn more about deprecation in Chapter 3, *Working with Fonts, Colors, and Backgrounds*. CSS-based alternatives to using the ALIGN attribute are presented in Chapter 7, *Designing Multi-Column Web Sites*.

Using the DIV Element

You cannot use the ALIGN attribute to horizontally align the UL (or OL) element. You can, however, horizontally align a list by nesting it inside a centered or right-aligned DIV (Division) element. The DIV element is a block element that is used to delineate a division within a document. Any element that can be nested in the BODY element can also be nested in a DIV element.

Center the link list by nesting it inside a center-aligned division (see Figure 1.12):

```
<div align="center">
<ul>
<li><a href="mybio.html">My biography</a>
<li><a href="myresume.html">My resume</a>
<li><a href="http://www.usatoday.com/sports/scores.htm">Get the
latest sports scores</a>
<li><a href="http://www.about-house-plants.com/">Get indoor
gardening tips and advice</a>
<li><a href="http://blank.emcp.com/jshmoe/">My friend Joe's
site</a>
<li><a href="http://wherever.emcp.com/jdoe/homepage.html">My
friend Jane's site</a>
</ul>
</div>
```

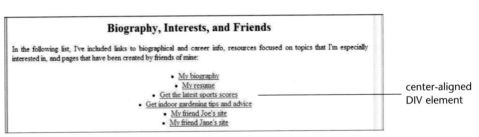

center-aligned
DIV element

FIGURE 1.12 • The bulleted list is nested inside a centered DIV element.

Apple's Safari browser renders the centered bulleted list differently from other browsers, centering the list item text but leaving the bullets aligned flush with the left margin. The only way to cause the centered bulleted list to display the same in Safari as in other browsers is to apply an inline style to the UL element:

```
<ul style="list-style-position: inside; padding-right: 1em">
```

Using styles will be discussed in Chapter 3, *Working with Fonts, Colors, and Backgrounds*, and Chapter 7, *Designing Multi-Column Web Sites*.

NOTE
By itself, a DIV element has no formatting. Using HTML alone, you can only change the horizontal alignment of text or other elements nested in a DIV element (setting them to be left-, right-, or center-aligned). To apply additional formatting directly to a DIV element, you need to use styles. You will work with some basic examples of using styles in Chapter 3, *Working with Fonts, Colors, and Backgrounds*, and with more advanced examples in Chapter 7, *Designing Multi-Column Web Sites*.

INSERTING AN INLINE IMAGE

The IMG (Image) element is used to insert an **inline image** in an HTML document. The IMG element is an inline element and not a block element. When you insert an inline image, it is displayed in the position—in the middle of a line of text, for instance—where it is inserted. The IMG element is also an empty (or standalone) element.

An example banner image, banner.gif, is included with the example files for this chapter. A banner image is an image that is displayed along the top of a Web page and thus is normally wider than it is high. A logo image is similar to a banner image and is also displayed at the top of a Web page, but is usually of relatively equal height and width.

NOTE
Image formats other than GIF (Compuserve Graphics Interchange Format) can be used to insert inline images, including JPEG (Joint Photographic Experts Group) and PNG (Portable Network Graphics) graphic formats. GIF, JPEG, and PNG images are compressed; non-compressed image formats, such as TIF or BMP, should not be inserted as inline images. Differences between image formats and how to decide which image format is best to use in a given situation are discussed in Chapter 4, *Working with Images and Other Media*.

action

Remove the H1 element's right-alignment, and then use the IMG element to insert a banner image as an inline image at the top of the page (see Figure 1.13):

```
<p><img src="banner.gif"></p>
<h1 align="right">Sports, Gardening, and Other Interests</h1>
```

FIGURE 1.13 • A banner image can add visual appeal to a Web page.

In the IMG element, the SRC (Source) attribute specifies the URL of the image file that is to be inserted into the HTML document. This attribute works just like the HREF attribute in the A element. To specify an image file that is located in the same folder as the HTML file in which it is to be inserted, you just need to specify the image's file name.

Notice in the code example that the IMG element is nested inside a P element. That is because the IMG element is an inline element and should not be nested directly inside the BODY element. An inline element should always be nested inside a block element.

NOTE

Alternatively, you can nest the banner image at the start of the level-one heading, with a line break providing vertical separation between the image and the following heading text:

```
<h1><img src="banner.gif"><br>Sports, Gardening, and Other
Interests</h1>
```

Nesting in this way adds less vertical spacing between the inline image and the following heading text than nesting the inline image in a separate P element. Use of the BR (Break) element to add a line break is discussed later in this chapter, in the "Creating an Address Block" section.

Horizontally Aligning an Inline Image

Because the IMG element is an inline element, you cannot directly align it horizontally relative to the page. Instead, you must nest it inside a block element that is horizontally aligned.

action

Center the inline image by nesting it inside the centered paragraph element (see Figure 1.14):

```
<p align="center"><img src="banner.gif"></p>
<h1 align="center">Sports, Gardening, and Other Interests</h1>
```

FIGURE 1.14 • Nesting it in a centered paragraph centers the inline image.

Including Alternative Text

Not everyone uses a graphical Web browser to access Web pages. Some surfers still use text browsers, such as Lynx, which cannot display images. Individuals with visual impairments may use a Braille browser or a screen reader to access Web pages. Some surfers also surf the Web with the display of graphics turned off in their browsers because they can find and access information on the Web faster by just downloading text and not the accompanying images.

Inclusion of **alternative text** for images is required for Web pages created for government organizations and agencies, which must comply with the Americans with Disabilities Act (ADA). Schools, libraries, businesses, or other entities that accommodate the public may have their own policies that mandate the inclusion of alternative text in Web pages, as well as other requirements to ensure accessibility.

If you include only an SRC attribute in an IMG element, some users may have a hard time identifying what the significance of your image is or even that it is an image. Figure 1.15 shows watson.html as it is displayed in Lynx, a text-only browser.

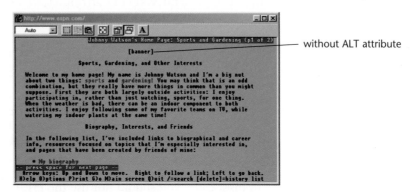

— without ALT attribute

FIGURE 1.15 • When viewing a Web page in Lynx, a text-only browser, a user might have difficulty identifying that an image is an image or its function or content.

To make it easier for anyone using these alternative means to access a Web page, you should include an ALT (Alternative Text) attribute in your IMG elements to further identify your image.

Use the ALT attribute to add alternative text to the IMG element's start tag, indicating the function and content of the image:

```
<p align="center"><img src="banner.gif" alt="Banner Image: Sports
& Gardening"></p>
<h1 align="center">Sports, Gardening, and Other Interests</h1>
```

As shown in Figure 1.16, the inline image is now more helpfully identified in Lynx.

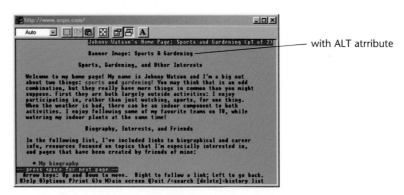

— with ALT atrribute

FIGURE 1.16 • Alternative text helps users of text-only or non-visual browsers to identify the function and content of images used in your Web pages.

For additional information and resources on Web design accessibility issues, see the Blindness Resource Center's "Access to the Internet and Web" site at **www.nyise.org/access.htm**. Accessibility is an important issue in Web design, so look for additional comments, notes, and tips in the remainder of this book that highlight measures you can take to make your own Web designs accessible to everyone.

Specifying an Image's Height and Width

Whenever you include an inline image in your page, you should specify its dimensions. That way, browsers can allocate display space for your image before it has been completely downloaded, which can allow the remainder of the page to be displayed quicker. The HEIGHT and WIDTH attributes are used in the IMG element to set the dimensions, in pixels, of an inline image.

Add HEIGHT and WIDTH attributes to the IMG element that specify the actual dimensions of the image:

```
<p align="center"><img src="banner.gif" alt="Banner Image: Sports
& Gardening" height="75" width="300"></p>
<h1 align="center">Sports, Gardening, and Other Interests</h1>
```

In most cases, you should not use the HEIGHT and WIDTH attributes to change the dimensions of an inline image, but you should use these attributes to specify the actual dimensions of the image. Instead of resizing an image in the browser, you should open it in your image editor and resize it there. Reducing the size of an image in a browser is a waste of **bandwidth** because the full-size image still must be downloaded over the Internet. Increasing the size of an image in a browser might magnify any image flaws or deficiencies.

CREATING AN ADDRESS BLOCK

In HTML, the ADDRESS element is used to create an **address block** within your page. The address block can identify the author or owner of a page, include contact information, and provide a means for visitors to provide feedback. Most often, the address block is inserted at the bottom of the page.

Use the ADDRESS element to add an address block to the example document that contains the author's name and e-mail address:

```
<address>
Johnny Watson<br>
E-mail: jwatson@whatnot.emcp.com
</address>
</body>
</html>
```

Spam is unsolicited and unwanted e-mail messages. Spammers use spiders (or robots) to crawl the Web looking for e-mail addresses listed in Web pages. Including your e-mail address in your Web page might expose you to more spam than you are already receiving.

One option is to sign up for a free *Web-mail* (Web-based e-mail) address and include it in your Web pages to provide visitors a way to contact you or give you feedback. A Web-mail account is accessed through a Web site's address using your browser, rather than through a mail server using a mail program (such as Outlook Express, for instance) that you may have installed on your computer. If your Web-mail address starts to get spammed too much, just dump it, and sign up for another Web-mail address and use it instead, editing your pages to include the new address. Most Web-mail accounts limit the amount of space available to store messages, so you should delete messages after you have read them, or move them to your own hard drive. You can then let only close friends and relatives know your permanent e-mail address, which should help limit the amount of spam sent to that address.

For a comprehensive listing of free Web-mail providers, just go to Yahoo! and do a search on **free e-mail**.

Alternatively, there are free services on the Web that will encrypt your e-mail address (and the link code containing it) so that spambots will not be able to read it, such as Hivelogic Enkoder at **www.danbenjamin.com/enkoder/**.

Most browsers display text nested in an ADDRESS block in an italic font. Nothing in the HTML specifications, however, dictates that text in an ADDRESS element should be italicized. Some earlier browsers do not italicize address block text, and nothing compels future browsers to do so, either.

Nest the text in the address block inside an I (Italic) element to insure that every browser italicizes it:

```
<address><i>
Johnny Watson<br>
E-mail: jwatson@whatnot.emcp.com
</i></address>
```

Inserting a Line Break

You might notice in the previous example that a BR (Break) element is used. This is an empty element that is used to insert a line break. A line break, unlike a paragraph break (**</p><p>**), does not insert extra vertical spacing. It can be used to demarcate the ends of lines in the stanzas of a poem, for instance.

Block elements cannot be nested inside the ADDRESS element. Only inline elements can be included. If you want to include vertical white space between lines in your address block, you should use double BR elements (**

**. Generally, however, you should avoid using multiple BR elements just to space text down on a page.

An alternative is to use the PRE (Preformatted Text) element, which displays contained hard returns. The HTML 4 and HTML 5 specifications, however, discourage the counter-semantic use of elements as being deleterious to accessibility. The PRE element is covered in Chapter 2, *Working with Online Documents*.

A better solution is to use styles, which separate presentation from content. See Chapter 7, *Designing Multi-Column Web Sites*, for coverage of using styles to increase (or decrease) margin space above or below an element.

Adding a Horizontal Rule

To help demarcate your address block from the remainder of your document's body, you can use the HR (Horizontal Rule) element as a separator. The HR element is an empty element that draws a horizontal line between the margins of the page.

Insert an HR element to separate the address block from the rest of the page (see Figure 1.17):

```
<hr>
<address><i>
Johnny Watson<br>
```

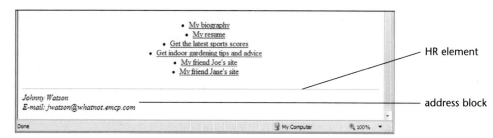

FIGURE 1.17 • An address block is used to identify, and provide a means to contact, the author or owner of a Web page.

Linking to Your E-Mail Address

You can use a special form of URL to link to your e-mail address. This type of URL is commonly referred to as a **mailto address**. A link to a mailto address is created the same way you create a link to a regular Web address, except that mailto: is used as the URL scheme, instead of http://, and an e-mail address is used instead of a domain name address.

Add the following codes to turn Johnny Watson's e-mail address into a mailto link (see Figure 1.18):

```
Johnny Watson<br>
E-mail: <a href="mailto:jwatson@whatnot.emcp.com">jwatson@
whatnot.emcp.com</a>
```

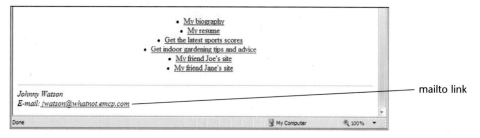

FIGURE 1.18 • You can use a mailto address to link to your e-mail address.

A mailto link provides a convenient and easy way for visitors to your page to give you feedback by sending you an e-mail message. Not everyone can use a mailto link, however. Users need to have a mail program, such as Outlook Express or Thunderbird, installed and configured to send mail and specified as their default mail program to be able to use a mailto link. Many users use Web-mail services for sending e-mail, which will not work with a mailto link.

Because not everyone can use a mailto link, it is important to always include your e-mail address *both* as the mailto URL and as the link text, for instance:

```
<a href="mailto:your@address.com">your@address.com</a>
```

That way, if some users cannot use your mailto link, they can still click and drag to copy your e-mail address and then paste it into their e-mail program's mail composition window.

NOTE Before publishing a mailto link containing your e-mail address to the Web, be sure to read the Trouble Spot on unwanted e-mail spam and how to prevent it that is presented earlier in this chapter.

Horizontally Aligning Your Address Block

The content of the ADDRESS element is left-aligned by default. However, as is the case with the UL element, the ALIGN attribute cannot be used to horizontally align the content of the ADDRESS element. To horizontally align the content of your ADDRESS element, you need to nest it inside a horizontally aligned DIV element.

action Center the content of the ADDRESS element by nesting it in a center-aligned DIV element (see Figure 1.19):

```
<hr>
<div align="center">
<address><i>
Johnny Watson<br>
E-mail: <a href="mailto:jwatson@whatnot.emcp.com">jwatson@
whatnot.emcp.com</a>
</i></address>
</div>
```

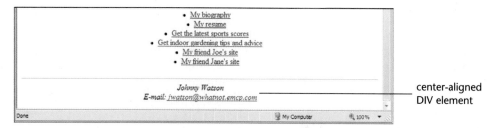

center-aligned DIV element

FIGURE 1.19 • For a different look, you can center your address block.

Including Other Items in the Address Block

You can include other things in your address block. If you are representing a business, you could include your toll-free number, fax number, and so on. You can include a link to your home page, for instance—this can be a good thing to do, even if the current page is your home page because it lets others know that it is your home page. Some authors like to include the date when the page was created or last updated, as well.

Another option is simply to include a link in your address block to a contact page. This can be helpful if you have multiple e-mail contacts, phone numbers, and so on, especially if you need to update them frequently. If you use a link to a contact page, you will only need to update that page if you need to make a change, rather than updating your address block on every page.

CHAPTER SUMMARY

In this chapter, you set up your working folder, learned how to extract and use the example files, reviewed basic HTML pointers, and created a basic Web page. You also gained experience using a text editor and your Web browser to dynamically review changes to an HTML document. You should now be familiar with many of the most commonly used HTML elements, including the top-level elements of an HTML document and the elements used to create headings, paragraphs, unordered (bulleted) lists, hypertext links, inline images, horizontal rules, line breaks, and address elements.

Code Review

`<html>...</html>`	HTML element. Contains all other elements within an HTML document.
`<head>...</head>`	HEAD element. Contains any elements used to provide "header information" about a document that is not displayed in a browser window.
`<body>...</body>`	BODY element. Contains any elements that compose the "body" of an HTML document and that are directly displayed within a browser window.
`<title>...</title>`	TITLE element. A required element within the HEAD element that specifies the title of the document. The title is not displayed within a browser window, but is displayed on a browser's title bar.
`<h1>...</h1>`	H1 (Level-One Heading) element. A top-level heading, or document title, that is displayed in a browser's window.
`<h2>...</h2>`	H2 (Level-Two Heading) element (Level-Two Heading). Marks the beginning of a major section within an HTML document. The H3 and H4 elements can be used to mark further subsection levels.
`<p>...<p>`	P (Paragraph) element. Contains paragraph text that is included in an HTML file. There should be no untagged text within an HTML document.
`<!--...-->`	HTML comments. Anything nested inside HTML comments will not be displayed in a browser.
`<a>...</a>`	A (Anchor) element. When used in conjunction with the HREF attribute, specifies that included text or elements is to operate as a hypertext anchor (or link).
`<a href="url"...`	HREF (Hypertext Reference) attribute. Within an A element, specifies the URL of a linked object.
`<ul>...</ul>`	UL (Unordered List) element. A bulleted list (or unordered list).
`<li> or <li>...</li>`	LI (List Element) element. A list item that is included within a list. End tag is optional.
`align="value"`	ALIGN attribute. Used in the H1, H2, P, DIV, and ADDRESS elements, among others, to horizontally align their content on the page.
`<div>...</div>`	DIV (Division) element. Defines a document division, which can contain any other "body" elements.
`<img>`	IMG (Image) element. An inline image in an HTML document.
`<img src="url"...`	SRC (Source) attribute. Specifies the URL of an inline image.

`<img alt="text">`	ALT (Alternate Text) attribute. Provides alternate text that can be displayed in place of an image.
`height="n"`	HEIGHT attribute. Specifies the actual vertical dimension of an image in pixels.
`width="n"`	WIDTH attribute. Specifies the actual horizontal dimension of an image in pixels.
`<address>...</address>`	ADDRESS element. Specifies an address block within an HTML document, in which the author or owner is identified and a means for feedback is provided.
`<hr>`	HR (Horizontal Rule) element. Creates a horizontal rule that can be used as a separator in an HTML document.
` `	BR (Break) element. Inserts a line break inside another element.

KEY TERMS

For a review of the key terms bolded in this chapter, visit the Chapter 1 section of this book's Internet Resource Center at **wwww.emcp.net/html2e**. A complete glossary appears at the end of the book.

ONLINE QUIZ

An online self-check quiz that you can use to test your knowledge of the topics covered in this chapter can be found in the Chapter 1 section of this book's Internet Resource Center at **www.emcp.net/html2e**.

REVIEW EXERCISES

This section provides hands-on review exercises to reinforce your understanding of the information and material included within this chapter. To do these exercises, save **watson.html** as **watson_review.html** in the **chap01 folder** and then use that new document to review using the elements, attributes, and other features that were covered in this chapter:

1. Combine H2 or H3 elements with paragraph elements to add additional sections or subsections to your HTML document. Type dummy text for the paragraphs, if you wish—the main thing is to experiment with how heading and paragraph elements work, without worrying about the actual content.
2. Practice using the HTML comment codes (<!-- and -->). Do not worry at this point whether the comments you add help to annotate your code or not—the idea is to just get practice inserting comments, so feel free to use dummy text to create the comments.
3. Experiment using the ALIGN attribute to center, right-align, or justify headings, paragraphs, and divisions (DIV elements). Experiment using a center-aligned DIV element to center nested text and elements.
4. Practice creating additional in-context hypertext links. Look for additional words or phrases that can be turned into hypertext links. For instance, turn the word "weather" into a link to the Weather Channel (**www.weather.com/**). Look for or add other

words or phrases that you can turn into in-context hypertext links to related sites you have discovered on the Web.

5. In the link list, add additional link items that link to sites on the Web. For instance, do research on the Web to find the URLs for any of the following: a major newspaper (Washington Post, Los Angeles Times, Chicago Tribune, and so on), a TV or cable news outlet (ABC News, PBS News, BBC News, and so on), a friend's Web site, or any other links you want to try creating.

WEB-BASED LEARNING ACTIVITIES

The following Web-based learning activities can help you to further extend your learning and shore up your understanding of specific topic-areas:

- Visit the Chapter 1 section of this book's Internet Resource Center at **www.emcp. net/html2e** to find online resources that you can use to further investigate and explore the topics and subjects covered in this chapter. You can also find all Web sites cited in this chapter's notes listed there.
- Further research a specific topic introduced in this chapter using Google (**www. google.com/**), Yahoo! (**www.yahoo.com/**), Wikipedia (**www.wikipedia.org/**), Open Directory Project (**www.dmoz.org/**), or other online sources. Some topics covered in this chapter that you can further research include:
  - The basics of HTML
  - Text editors available for your platform
  - The different kinds of URLs that can be created
  - What *netiquette* is and why it is important
  - What *alternative text* is and why it is important to help ensure *accessibility*
  - How mailto links can expose your e-mail address to spam and ways in which that can be effectively addressed
- Use the results of your online research into a particular topic to:
  - Write a review to be read in front of your classmates
  - Write a report that can be read by your classmates
  - Design a diagram, chart, or other graphic that illustrates a key topic or concept
  - Create a presentation using PowerPoint (or other software) that can be shared with your classmates
  - Give a stand-up presentation to your classmates
  - Team up with one or more classmates to give a group presentation to your classmates

PROJECTS

These projects can be done in class, in a computer lab, or at home. In your project, demonstrate the correct use of the following HTML features covered in this chapter:

- HTML, HEAD, and BODY elements.
- TITLE element (include a descriptive title).
- H1 and H2 elements.
- P elements, bracketing any text paragraphs.
- UL and LI elements to add a bulleted list.
- At least one HTML comment.
- A element and HREF attribute (include at least three hypertext links, correctly

using URLs and link text to link to and identify sites located on the Web).
- ALIGN attribute to center or right-align the H1 or H2 element.
- IMG element and SRC, ALT, HEIGHT, and WIDTH attributes. Include at least one .GIF, .JPG, or .PNG graphic.
- ADDRESS element and a mailto e-mail link.
- HR and BR elements.

Use the skills learned in this chapter to create any of the following projects:

Project 1. Create your own personal Web page.

Plan, write, and create your own personal Web page:

1. Plan and write the content of your personal page, including content to be used for a title, level-one heading, and introductory paragraph.
2. Gather any URLs, site names, and accompanying descriptive text you want to use in creating hypertext links, to be used either in-context or in a link list. Remember that any word or phrase in an HTML document can be a link, so look for opportunities to create interesting links to other sites or resources on the Web.
3. At the bottom of your text document, type the text you want to use as your address block. At minimum, type your name and an e-mail address. *Note: See the caution earlier, however, about the danger of exposing your e-mail address to spammers.* Use a dummy e-mail address here, if you like, or you can sign up for a free Web-mail address that you can use.
4. Optionally, gather any JPEG or GIF images you want to include as inline images. Scan a snapshot of yourself, for instance, in the image-editing software that came with your scanner, and resize the image (keep it under 500 pixels wide, and 250 pixels wide is not too small for a personal snapshot). (You do not need to include any images, and you also do not need to include more than one, so you should not go overboard adding images at this stage.)
5. Tag your file with HTML tags to define the HTML elements of your page. Create your top-level elements (HTML, HEAD, TITLE, and BODY). Tag the level-one heading and any paragraphs. Tag any sublevel headings, bulleted lists, hypertext links, and your address block (inserting line breaks where needed). Insert any GIF or JPEG image you want to include as an inline image (adding HEIGHT and WIDTH attributes and alternative text).

Project 2. Create a topical Web page.

Plan, write, and create a basic Web page based on a topic you are interested in or know something about. Follow the directions given previously for creating a personal Web page, but substitute text and links (and any images you want to use) focused on the topic you want to present (instead of on yourself).

Project 3. Create a Web page for a club or organization.

Do you belong to or participate in a club or organization that does not yet have its own Web page? Create a Web page that includes a description of the club or organization, a list of its activities, and an e-mail link that visitors can use to find out about joining or contributing. Include a link list to other related clubs, organizations, and sites.

CHAPTER 2

Working with Online Documents

PERFORMANCE OBJECTIVES

- Add a DocType declaration to identify the HTML version and compatibility level of your document.
- Use the META element to add a document description, a list of keywords, and other metadata.
- Add emphasis such as bolding and italics to text.
- Format quotations and citations.
- Create superscripted footnote and endnote links.
- Insert copyright, register, and trademark symbols.
- Create a document menu.
- Use monospaced highlighting.
- Work with numerical lists.
- Use preformatted text.

In Chapter 1, *Creating a Basic Web Page*, you learned how to create a simple personal Web page. In this chapter, you will learn more about how you can use HTML to format online documents, including creating an online academic paper, a frequently asked questions (FAQ) page, and online technical documentation.

USING THE EXAMPLE FILES

You will find the example files for this chapter located in the **chap02** folder within your working folder. You should save any HTML files you create in this chapter in that folder. If you have yet to create a working folder, return to "Downloading the Example Files" in Chapter 1 for instructions on how to do that.

CASE EXAMPLE: FORMATTING AN ONLINE ACADEMIC PAPER

Increasingly, both students and instructors are choosing to publish academic papers and essays online, rather than just in paper form. Publishing a paper online can be a great way to get feedback and to stimulate discussion on a topic or position. In this exercise, you will add formatting to an example academic paper that is included with this book's example files.

> Crystal Porter is a junior in college majoring in sociology. She is writing a paper titled "Commerce and Civilization" for her "Origins of Civilization" class. In this paper, she is arguing for commerce as a root cause, rather than simply a consequence, of the transition from simpler and more primitive "folk societies" to more complex urbanized civilizations.
>
> Crystal wants to format her online document so that it looks and works like a regular academic paper that she would print out on a printer. However, she also wants to take advantage of some of the additional facilities afforded by HTML, such as using hypertext links to connect footnote numbers with their respective footnote text.
>
> Although the paper is still in draft form and incomplete, Crystal wants to put it online to start getting feedback from her professor and fellow students while she is still writing the paper.

Opening an HTML File in Your Text Editor

In this case example, you will be working with an example file, acad_paper_ex.html, which has been created for you. You will find this file in the **chap02** folder located inside your working folder.

Open **acad_paper_ex.html** in your text editor:
1. Run your text editor (Notepad in Windows or TextEdit in Macintosh OS X, for instance).
2. Open the **chap02** folder in your working folder. For instance, in Notepad in Windows or TextEdit in Macintosh OS X, select File, Open, and navigate to and open your working folder (named HTML_Examples, or whatever you renamed it).

    Your working folder was extracted to the current folder when you downloaded and extracted the example files in Chapter 1. If you cannot remember where you extracted it to, you can use Search in Windows or the Finder in Macintosh OS X to find it. If you still cannot find it, ask your instructor for help.
3. If you are using Windows, click on the Files of type box, and select All Files; otherwise, you will not be able to see files with other than a .txt extension.
4. Double-click **acad_paper_ex.html** in the chap02 folder to open it in your text editor.

Windows. If you are using Windows, the display of file extensions for known file types is turned off by default. If you have not turned on the display of these file extensions, you will not be able to see the file extensions for most file types when lists of files are displayed on your system. For instance, when opening "acad_paper_ex.html," you will only see "acad_paper_ex" displayed as the file name, with only the file icon helping to identify the file type. See "Turning on Display of File Extensions in Windows" in Chapter 1 if you cannot see file extensions in Windows.

Saving and Previewing Your HTML File

To avoid overwriting the example file, you can resave it under another name. That way, you can use it as a reference point, or backtrack to the beginning and start over fresh, if you need to.

1. Select File, Save As, and resave the example file as **acad_paper.html** in the chap02 folder in your working folder.
2. Run your browser (or switch over to it if it is already open), and open **acad_paper.html** from the chap02 folder in your working folder. (If you are unclear about how to open a local HTML file in your browser, see "Previewing Your HTML Document in Your Browser" in Chapter 1.)

When working through this chapter's examples, be sure to frequently save your HTML file, switch over to your browser, refresh the display of your Web page, and then preview any changes you have made to the example code you have created. Use the screen captures in this chapter's figures as prompts to switch over to your browser to check out the results of your work for yourself, rather than simply depending upon the figures to show you how the results of your code should look. If the results you see in your browser are significantly different than what you see in the figures, check your code against the code shown in the preceding code example to see if you have made any errors, such as failing to add a "/" character to an end tag, for instance.

If you are using a browser other than Internet Explorer 8 to preview your work, what you see in your browser might not always exactly match what you see in the figures.

DECLARING THE DOCUMENT TYPE

According to the HTML 4.01 and XHTML 1.0 specifications, a valid HTML document should declare the version of HTML that is used in the document. This is done by inserting a special code, a **DocType declaration** (or document type declaration), at the top of the document, above the HTML element. The DocType declaration specifies the HTML version used in a document and the conformance level being enforced.

A number of elements and attributes were introduced as extensions to HTML by browser vendors with little concern for usability or accessibility. These were included in HTML 4, but their use was **deprecated**, or discouraged, and the use of newer constructs such as Cascading Style Sheets (CSS), which were formulated with usability and accessibility in mind, was encouraged instead.

Understanding Conformance Levels

The HTML 4 specification anticipated that as older browsers passed out of use and new browsers supporting the new HTML 4 features came into use, the need to use deprecated features would diminish and eventually disappear over time. To allow for that transition, the W3C defined three different **conformance levels** for HTML 4 and XHTML 1.0:

- **Strict conformance.** Disallows any deprecated or frameset elements or attributes. Is intended for use with pages to be displayed in browsers that fully implement the HTML 4.01 or XHTML 1.0 standards.
- **Transitional conformance.** Also called "loose" conformance. Allows deprecated elements or attributes. Is intended for use until browsers fully support newer constructs such as Cascading Style Sheets (CSS) and newer elements and attributes introduced as part of HTML 4.01 and XHTML 1.0.

- **Frameset conformance.** Allows both deprecated and frameset elements or attributes. Is intended for use in pages that use the FRAMESET element, the FRAME element, and other related elements or attributes to create framed Web sites.

Web authors are discouraged from using deprecated elements and attributes and are encouraged to use alternatives, such as style sheets, that further rather than harm accessibility and usability.

Deprecated elements and attributes are valid, however, as long as documents that include them are declared as conforming to the transitional conformance level of HTML 4.01 or XHTML 1.0. Web authors were warned that deprecated elements and attributes could be declared as **obsolete** in future versions of HTML—and, indeed, most deprecated features have been declared obsolete in the HTML 5 draft specification.

You will learn more about deprecated elements and attributes, and about using styles instead to achieve similar or superior results, in Chapter 3 and Chapter 7.

The frameset elements (FRAMESET, FRAME, and NOFRAMES), which were originally introduced as extensions to the Netscape browser, although not specifically deprecated in HTML 4.01 or XHTML 1.0, were not included in the strict conformance level for either and should be regarded as also being deprecated. The frameset elements have also been declared obsolete in HTML 5.

Following are three examples of DocType declarations that can be included in an HTML document to specify conformance to the strict, transitional, or frameset definitions for HTML 4.01:

```
<!DOCTYPE HTML PUBLIC "-//W3C//DTD HTML 4.01//EN"
 "http://www.w3.org/TR/html4/strict.dtd">

<!DOCTYPE HTML PUBLIC "-//W3C//DTD HTML 4.01 Transitional//EN"
 "http://www.w3.org/TR/html4/loose.dtd">

<!DOCTYPE HTML PUBLIC "-//W3C//DTD HTML 4.01 Frameset//EN"
 "http://www.w3.org/TR/html4/frameset.dtd">
```

You should declare your document as conforming to the strict definition for HTML 4.01 only if it contains no deprecated or frameset elements or attributes. Otherwise, you should declare it as conforming to either the transitional or frameset definition.

Understanding DocType Switching

Recent browsers use the DocType declaration to do what has commonly been referred to as **DocType switching**.

Depending on the type of DocType declaration included in your document, a browser that does DocType switching can switch between various display modes. This was initially limited to two modes: standards mode and quirks mode.

In **standards mode**, a browser's most up-to-date implementation of the HTML and CSS standards is adhered to, even if that will cause problems when displaying a page that was coded to take advantage of the non-standard quirks of an earlier browser version.

In **quirks mode**, earlier non-standard quirks are reduplicated, even if that will cause problems when displaying a page that was coded to be standards-compliant.

A third mode, **almost standards mode**, was later introduced to account for behavior in browsers that correctly implement almost all of the HTML 4.01 and CSS 2 standards. This mode arose because of differences between the standards modes in Internet

Explorer and the Mozilla browsers in how images nested directly inside table cells were treated. However, unless you are doing page layouts using sliced images in tables, the two modes are the same.

If you use any of the previously listed DocType declarations in your document, browsers that do DocType switching will switch to using standards mode or almost standards mode. If you omit a DocType declaration, such browsers will default to using quirks mode. DocType declarations other than those previously listed might also trigger quirks mode.

Generally, you should stick to using one of the DocType statements listed previously, to ensure that your document is displayed, as much as possible, in accordance with the latest standards. Intentionally triggering quirks mode should be avoided.

Use of the new HTML 5 DocType statement will cause current browsers, including Internet Explorer 8, to default to standards mode but could cause earlier browsers that do not recognize that DocType statement to revert to quirks mode.

In most cases, when you are just using straight HTML, there should be little if any differences in browsers running in standards, almost standards, or quirks modes. It can make a difference, however, if you are using styles, scripts, or dynamic HTML features in your document.

 **Visit the Internet Resource Center.** To find resources on the Web that discuss DocType declarations and DocType switching, see the Chapter 2 section of this book's Internet Resource Center at **www.emcp.com/html2e.**

Internet Explorer 8 Standards Mode

Internet Explorer 8 defaults to what Microsoft calls Internet Explorer 8 Standards mode, which strictly enforces the current HTML 4.01 and CSS 2.1 standards. A second standards mode, Internet Explorer 7 Standards mode, which applies those standards less strictly, is invoked by inserting a special META-equiv statement in a page's HEAD section, causing pages to display as they would appear in Internet Explorer 7:

```
<head>
<meta http-equiv="X-UA-Compatible" content="IE=7">
<title>Commerce and Civilization by Crystal Porter</title>
```

These two modes correspond to standards mode and almost standards mode in Internet Explorer 8. In almost standards mode, the page is displayed as it would appear in Internet Explorer 7. Quirks mode in Internet Explorer 8, which can be triggered by a foreshortened DocType statement, causes pages to display as they would appear in Internet Explorer 6.

HTML 5 DocType

The "draft" specification of HTML 5 replaces the three HTML 4.01 DocType declarations with a single and much simpler declaration:

```
<!DOCTYPE html>
```

The declaration is case-insensitive, so **<!DocType html>** is the same as **<!doctype html>**. Most current browsers recognize the HTML 5 DocType declaration, even if they do not yet support many elements that are new to HTML 5.

Web authors can begin experimenting with the new DocType now, which should force standards mode in all current browsers. Some recent browsers that do not recognize the new DocType, but do DocType switching, could invoke quirks mode, breaking pages that display properly, in standards or almost standards mode, when using one of the HTML 4.01 DocTypes.

Adding a DocType Declaration

The DocType declaration is inserted at the top of an HTML document, above the HTML element.

Insert a DocType declaration declaring that your HTML document is compatible with the transitional definition for HTML 4.01:

```
<!DOCTYPE HTML PUBLIC "-//W3C//DTD HTML 4.01 Transitional//EN"
  "http://www.w3.org/TR/html4/loose.dtd">
<html>
<head>
```

USING META ELEMENTS

The META (Meta Data) element is an empty element that allows authors to include metadata in their HTML documents. **Metadata** is information that is about, or describes, a document, rather than content that is displayed in a document. It is further described by the W3C as "machine understandable information," which highlights that this data is less likely to be consumed by human surfers as by parsing engines, validation checkers, indexing robots, and other computer-based processes and programs. META elements are inserted in a document's HEAD element.

Specifying the Document's Character Set

As the Web becomes more and more of a global phenomenon, pages are being published in many languages, many of which (such as Chinese and Japanese) do not use the Latin-based alphabet used by Western European languages. Because of this, the specific character set being used in a document is a much more important issue than it once was (when virtually all Web pages were published in English). If you try to display a page originating from China or Japan, and square blank boxes appear where text characters would normally be, it could be because the character set being assumed by your browser does not match the character set being used by the page you are trying to access.

Also, you are required to specify your document's character set when validating an HTML document using the W3C's HTML Validator. The W3C recommends that Web authors specifically declare their document's character set.

You declare your document's character set by inserting it as metadata in your document's HEAD element. This should be inserted ahead of any other element within the HEAD element.

Insert the following META element at the start of your document's HEAD element to declare that your document is using the UTF-8 character set:

```
<head>
<meta http-equiv="Content-Type" content="text/html;
charset=utf-8">
<title>Commerce and Civilization by Crystal Porter</title>
```

Alternatively, you can declare ISO-8859-1, which contains characters specific to western European languages, as the character set. UTF-8 is a superset of ISO-8859-1, so the difference between the two is that UTF-8 also allows the inclusion of Unicode characters, greatly expanding the number and kinds of characters that can be displayed in Web pages.

The various ins and outs of using different character sets can get complex. See Appendix D, *Special Characters Chart*, to find all of the displayable characters included in the ISO 8859-1 character set, as well as examples of Unicode characters you can include in your HTML documents.

Visit the Internet Resource Center. You can find additional online resources that discuss using ISO 8859-1, Unicode, and other character sets in the Chapter 2 section of this book's Internet Resource Center at **www.emcp.com/html2e**.

Including a Description and Keyword List

Probably the two most common uses of the META element are to include a description of your page and a list of keywords that are related to the content of your page. Many search engines use these META elements when listing or indexing your site. These kinds of META elements are included in an HTML document using the following general format:

```
<meta name="metadata name" content="metadata content">
```

Add a META element below your document's TITLE element that provides a description of the document's content:

```
<title>Commerce and Civilization by Crystal Porter</title>
<meta name="description" content="Discussion of the impact of
commerce on the development of civilization, contrasting folk and
urban societies, and debating the role of trade and commerce in
the transition between the two.">
</head>
```

Some search engines and Web directories display your META element description, instead of the initial text of your document, in a list of search responses. This can be useful, for instance, if the initial text of your document does not provide a good description or is short on information about your document. A good META element description makes it more likely that someone interested in a document such as yours will actually click on its link in a search engine list, rather than pass on to the next link.

Add a META element below the one you just added that provides a list of keywords a search engine might use in indexing your document:

```
<title>Commerce and Civilization by Crystal Porter</title>
<meta name="description" content="Discussion of the impact of
commerce on the development of civilization, contrasting folk and
urban societies, and debating the role of trade and commerce in
the transition between the two.">
<meta name="keywords" content="civilization, society, societies,
culture, higher societies, folk society, folk societies, sociology,
primitive, tribal, urban, egypt, sumeria, trade, commerce, import,
export, market, generalist, specialist">
</head>
```

Search engines and directories that support use of the META element can use your keyword list to help index your document. This can increase the likelihood that someone doing a search on a keyword you have listed will be able to find your document.

Visit the Internet Resource Center. To find online resources that further discuss these and other uses of the META element, go to the Chapter 2 section of this book's Internet Resource Center at **www.emcp.com/html2e.**

ADDING INLINE HIGHLIGHTING

Bold and italic often are used to add highlighting and emphasis to text within a document. HTML includes a number of inline elements that can be used to add bolding or italics to an HTML document.

Using the I and B Elements

The I (Italic) and B (Bold) elements are used to add italic or bold highlighting to enclosed text. They are sometimes referred to as **literal elements** because they literally specify a display characteristic, italics or bolding.

Use the I and B elements to apply italics and bolding to the example text:

1. Use the I element to italicize the included text (see Figure 2.1):

```
<p>Civilizations have often been referred to as <i>advanced
societies</i>, in contrast to less developed societies.
```

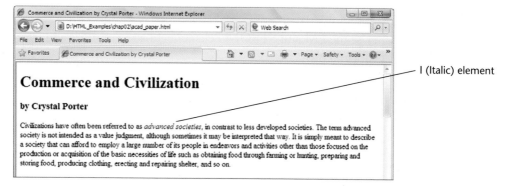

FIGURE 2.1 • A Web browser displays text tagged with the I (Italic) element in an italic font.

2. Use the B element to create bolded lead-in headings for the first two items in the bulleted list (see Figure 2.2):

```
<ul>
<li><b>Geographical expansion.</b> A civilization occupies a
relatively wide expanse of territory.
<li><b>Population growth and concentration.</b> A civilization
requires sufficient population and sufficient population density
to be able to employ large numbers of individuals in activities
with no direct economic return. These individuals include those
involved in government, ceremonial activities, art, philosophy,
and scientific inquiry.
```

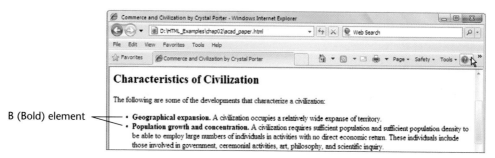

FIGURE 2.2 • A Web browser displays text tagged with the B (Bold) element in a bold font.

Using the EM and the STRONG Elements

The EM (Emphasis) and STRONG (Strong Emphasis) elements are used to emphasize or strongly emphasize enclosed text. They are inline elements and are sometimes referred to as **logical elements** because they specify a logical display characteristic, emphasis or strong emphasis, rather than a literal one (italics or bolding). In a graphical Web browser, an EM element is displayed in an italic font, while a STRONG element is displayed in a bold font.

It is customary in publications to use italics to emphasize book, journal, or magazine titles, rather than set them in quotes. In HTML, you can use either the I or the EM element to italicize (or emphasize) these kinds of text strings.

Use the EM and STRONG elements to add emphasis and strong emphasis to the example document:

1. Use the EM element to emphasize the journal and book titles included in the following example (see Figure 2.3):

```
<h2>Distinguishing Between Folk and Urban Societies</h2>
<p>In an article published in the <em>American Journal of
Sociology</em>, Robert Redfield described the more primitive and
pre-urbanized state of society as forming "folk societies."(1)
John A. Wilson, in <em>The Culture of Ancient Egypt</em>,
summarizes Redfield's conclusions in the following manner:</p>
```

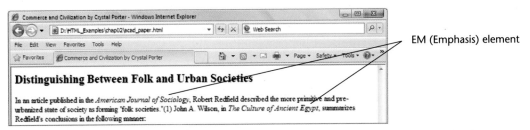

EM (Emphasis) element

FIGURE 2.3 • A Web browser displays text tagged with the EM element in an italic font.

2. Use the STRONG element to add stronger emphasis. Scroll down to the bottom part of the document, and insert the following codes where indicated to strongly emphasize the included text (see Figure 2.4):

```
<hr>
<p><strong>Notes</strong></p>
<p>
1. Robert Redfield, "The Folk Society," American Journal of
Sociology, LII (1947), pp. 293-308.<br>
```

STRONG (Strong Emphasis) element

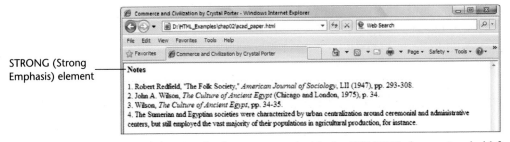

FIGURE 2.4 • A Web browser displays text tagged with the STRONG element in a bold font.

Whether you use logical or literal highlighting elements to apply italics to your Web pages is up to you; all graphical browsers, at least, treat the I and EM elements and the B and STRONG elements as interchangeable. The I and B elements are more economical and easier to type. The logical character of the EM and STRONG elements, however, still holds when the presentation media is not a visual media. In a speech browser, for instance, emphasized text might be preceded and followed by a pause and expressed through a somewhat louder voice, while strongly emphasized text might be expressed through both a louder and deeper voice.

Creating Bold Italic Highlighting

You can create text that is both italicized and bolded by nesting an I and a B element. It does not matter which is nested inside of which; just do not overlap them. You can also nest an EM and a STRONG element to get the same bold italic text. You can even nest an I and a STRONG element, or an EM and a B element, to get bold italic text.

action

Nest the STRONG element you defined in the preceding code example inside of an EM element (see Figure 2.5):

```
<p><em><strong>Notes</strong></em></p>
<p>
1. Robert Redfield, "The Folk Society," American Journal of
Sociology, LII (1947), pp. 293-308.<br>
```

EM and STRONG
elements

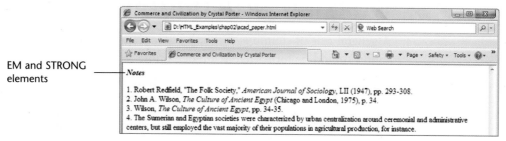

FIGURE 2.5 • A Web browser displays text tagged with both the EM and STRONG elements in a bold italic font.

tip

Alternatively, you can use the CITE element to highlight citations: `<cite>American Journal of Sociology</cite>`. Because this is more semantically specific, it is thought by some to enhance accessibility, compared to the more general I or EM elements. All current graphical browsers display I, EM, and CITE elements identically, in an italicized font.

practice

So far you have only marked up some of the instances in the example file where the I (Italics), B (Bold), EM (Emphasis), and STRONG (Strong Emphasis) elements could be used to further mark up the document for display on the Web. To gain more practice, look for other places in the document where you can use these elements, as well as the CITE element. For instance:

- The I element was used to italicize a phrase that benefited from being so highlighted in the text. Look for other instances within the document's text paragraphs where you might use the I element.
- The B element was used to bold the lead-in phrases of the first two bulleted list items. Use the B element to bold the remaining lead-in phrases in the bulleted list.
- The EM element was used to emphasize (and thus italicize) the titles of a journal and a book. Look for other journal or book titles in the footnote items at the bottom of the document, and use the EM element to emphasize those titles as well.
- The CITE element can also be used to highlight book titles, publications, works of art, and so on. Look for such instances in the text and use the CITE element to highlight them instead of using the I or EM element.

N O T E

Additionally, the U (Underline) element can be used to underline text. Underlining, however, is generally discouraged in Web pages because it is too easily confused with a hypertext link, which is also usually displayed in an underlined font. Underlining in a computer document is also somewhat of an anachronism, dating back to when early computer displays and printers lacked the capability to produce an italic font.

The U element was introduced in HTML 4 and might not be supported by some earlier browsers. It is also obsolete in HTML 5. Thus, it is best avoided, for reasons of both backward and forward compatibility.

If you wish to use underlining for decorative purposes, rather than for emphasis, you should use styles. For instance, the following sets underlining for an H2 heading element:

```
<h2 style="text-decoration: underline">
```

WORKING WITH QUOTATIONS

A general rule of thumb is that any quote that is four lines or longer in a printed publication should be formatted as a block quote (as a separate text block indented from the margins). The same idea applies to Web pages for quotations likely to extend more than a few. In HTML, the BLOCKQUOTE element tags a block of text as a block quote.

"Crystal's paper includes two extended quotations."

Nest the indicated paragraph inside of a BLOCKQUOTE element to format it as a block quote, and delete the quotation marks, because block quotes do not need to be quoted (see Figure 2.6):

```
<h2>Distinguishing Between Folk and Urban Societies</h2>
<p>In an article published in the <em>American Journal of
Sociology</em>, Robert Redfield described the more primitive and
pre-urbanized state of society as forming "folk societies."(1)
John A. Wilson, in <em>The Culture of Ancient Egypt</em>,
summarizes Redfield's conclusions in the following manner:</p>

<blockquote><p>"This ideal folk society is homogenous, small, and
has a strong sense of community. It is nonliterate, and its
economy is one of self-sufficiency rather than of buying and
selling. In general, the ties of family provide the community.
The society is deeply rooted in religious belief and custom, and
relations are personal, so that the secular and impersonal have
not yet come into being. The behavior of such a society is
strongly traditional, so that there is no encouragement to
speculation or to experimentation, since sanctified tradition has
provided all the answers. Such a folk society could exist as a
pure culture only if the conditions of its maintenance and
security from disturbance were assured."(2)</p></blockquote>
```

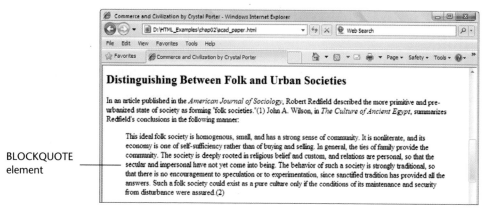

BLOCKQUOTE element

FIGURE 2.6 • An extended quotation should be formatted as a block quote.

Nesting Paragraphs in Block Quotes

In the example, you nested a P element, rather than raw text, within a BLOCKQUOTE element. This is not required by the transitional and frameset versions of HTML 4.01 or XHTML 1.0, which allow both block and inline elements to be nested directly inside of a BLOCKQUOTE element. The strict version of HTML 4.01, however, allows only block elements to be nested directly inside of a BLOCKQUOTE element.

Nesting P elements (or other block elements) instead of raw text inside of a BLOCKQUOTE element is a good idea, nonetheless. Nesting P elements, for one thing, lets you include more than one paragraph of text in a block quote. An additional consideration comes into play when using styles, in which case, a P element and raw text nested inside of a BLOCKQUOTE element might differ in their display characteristics if the styles for the P and BLOCKQUOTE elements are not identically defined.

NOTE Using the BLOCKQUOTE element purely as a formatting device should be avoided. The **counter-semantic use** of elements, such as using the BLOCKQUOTE element to indent the body or sections of a Web page from the margins, can be confusing to individuals with visual disabilities using non-visual user agents, such as Braille browsers or screen readers. Examples of using styles to indent text from the margins can be found in Chapter 7.

practice Just a little further down in the document, another paragraph is enclosed within quotation marks. Delete the quotation marks, and then use the BLOCKQUOTE element to turn that paragraph into a block quote also.

Using the Q (Quote) Element

The Q (Quote) element is an inline element that was introduced in HTML 4 and can be used to set quote marks around a quotation from another source. The advantage of using the Q element is that it is language independent and can set whatever quote marks are appropriate for the language being used—in a document using the UTF-8 character set, quoted text is displayed using "curly" double quotation marks by default, whereas nested quoted text is displayed using "curly" single quotation marks.

The LANG attribute can be used to specify the language of the quote. For instance, if `lang="fr"` is used, then French quotation marks will be displayed (« and » for double quotes and ‹ and › for single quotes).

The following shows some example code using the Q element:

```
<p>Without an <q lang="en" cite="http://www.somesource.emcp.com/">
interdependence of commercial transactions,</q> it is difficult to
see how radical change might occur in a pre-urban folk society.
```

The disadvantage of using the Q element is that only the most recent browsers support it, and it **degrades ungracefully** in browsers that do not support it (with no quotes being displayed). For those reasons, the Q element is best avoided, at least until all recent browsers support it.

NOTE — An element or attribute is not determined to degrade ungracefully merely because it produces an unexpected or unpleasant visual effect in a browser but only if it also makes accessing or understanding the content of the element or document more difficult or impossible.

MARKING REVISIONS

HTML includes a number of elements that can be used to mark up insertions or deletions within an HTML document.

Using the DEL and INS Elements

The DEL (Delete) and INS (Insert) elements let you mark deletions and insertions within an HTML document. Browsers that support these inline elements display deletions as strikethrough text and insertions as underlined text.

 Cynthia wants to display deletions and insertions as she revises her online paper.

 Use the INS and DEL elements to mark insertions and deletions in the following example text (see Figure 2.7):

```
<p><ins>As described</ins><del>Admittedly</del>, these
characteristics of folk societies and urban societies <ins>place
</ins><del>situate</del> them as extremes at either end of a<ins>n
overall</ins> continuum<ins> that is defined by society in all of
its forms</ins>. However, in reality, societies tend to contain
characteristics of both of these societ<ins>al</ins><del>y</del>
types. For example, most societies have both generalists and
specialists, but in a community considered to be a folk society,
generalists predominate. In a community considered to be an urban
society, specialists predominate at least in rank, if not
necessarily always in numbers.(4)</p>

<h2>Commerce as a <ins>Cause of</ins><del>Means Toward</del>
Urbanization</h2>
```

INS (Insert)
elements

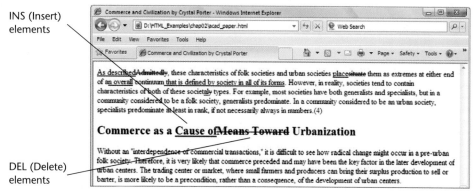

DEL (Delete)
elements

FIGURE 2.7 • In a browser that supports the DEL and INS elements, deletions are displayed as strikethrough text, while insertions are displayed as underlined text.

One of the main drawbacks of using the DEL and INS elements is lack of support in earlier browsers. These elements do not degrade gracefully in non-supporting browsers, with both deletions and insertions indistinguishably displayed as normal text in those browsers. Only a very small percentage of users, however, are still using browsers that do not support these elements.

Striking Out Text

HTML provides two additional inline elements that can create strikeout text: the STRIKE and S elements. The STRIKE element had a long history as a Netscape extension before it was included in HTML 3.2. The more concise S element was proposed for the failed HTML 3.0 proposal but was not included in standard HTML until HTML 4.0. Both of these elements are deprecated in HTML 4.01 and obsolete in HTML 5, in favor of using the DEL element or styles to achieve similar or better results.

CREATING FOOTNOTES AND ENDNOTES

Footnotes or endnotes are often needed in academic papers. In this section, you learn how to incorporate both footnotes and endnotes in an online document, including how to superscript note numbers and create hypertext footnote and endnote links.

Superscripting Note Numbers

Note numbers are superscripted in documents. In HTML, the SUP (Superscript) element is used to superscript text. Example note numbers are already included in the example document.

Find the first note number, and use the SUP element to superscript it, as shown here (see Figure 2.8):

```
<h2>Distinguishing Between Folk and Urban Societies</h2>
<p>In an article published in the <em>American Journal of
Sociology</em>, Robert Redfield described the more primitive and
pre-urbanized state of society as forming "folk
```

```
societies."<sup>(1)</sup> John A. Wilson, in <em>The Culture of
Ancient Egypt</em>, summarizes Redfield's conclusions in the
following manner:</p>
```

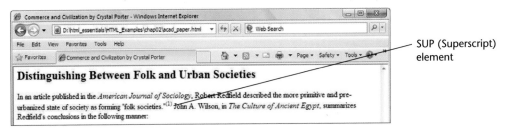

FIGURE 2.8 • The SUP element is used to superscript included text.

Notice in the example that the superscripted note number is enclosed within parentheses. The primary reason for doing this is to avoid ungraceful degradation in non-supporting browsers or in browsers, such as text browsers, that cannot display superscripted text. In those browsers, an unsuperscripted note number would be displayed immediately following the preceding text, displaying **text1**, instead of **text[1]**, for instance.

practice

Three additional footnote numbers (within parentheses) are included in the example document. Find each additional footnote number, and use the SUP element to superscript the number and the surrounding parentheses.

tip

Although not included in the current example, just as you can use the SUP element to superscript nested text, you also can use the SUB (Subscript) element to subscript nested text. For instance, to format the chemical formula of water, you might do this:

```
H<sub>(2)</sub>0
```

This should then display in a browser as $H_{(2)}0$, for instance.

Creating Hypertext Footnote Links

Besides simply formatting superscripted note numbers, you can turn them into hypertext links that will jump from the note number to a footnote located at the bottom of the page.

When creating a hypertext link that jumps to a location within a document, you need to create two separate anchor elements (A elements): a **destination anchor** that marks a location in the document that you want to jump to and a **jump link** that links to the destination anchor.

CREATING A DESTINATION ANCHOR A destination anchor marks an object within a document to which a hypertext link can jump. A destination anchor is created using the A element but with a NAME attribute instead of an HREF attribute. A destination anchor is created in the following general format:

```
<a name="anchorname">anchor object</a>
```

Each destination anchor you create within your document must have a unique name. If you create two destination anchors with the same name, a browser will not be able to decide which one it should jump to and, therefore, will not jump anywhere. The anchor object can be text, even a single letter, or an element (an IMG element or OBJECT element, for instance).

You can find several example footnotes at the bottom of the example document.

action

Add a destination anchor to mark the location of the first footnote:

```
<hr>
<p><em><strong>Notes</strong></em></p>
<p>
<a name="note1">1</a>. Robert Redfield, "The Folk Society,"
<em>American Journal of Sociology</em>, LII (1947), pp. 293-
308.<br>
```

The HTML 4.01 specification also allows the use of an empty destination anchor (`<a name="note1"></a>`, for instance) to mark a location rather than bracket an object but warns that some user agents may not be able to find it. The HTML 5 draft specification, however, does not allow empty destination anchors but requires that they have text or at least one element as their content. It also disallows using "inter-element white space" (a space or non-breaking space entity code, for instance) as the sole content of the element. Thus, for both backward- and forward-compatibility reasons, empty destination anchors should probably be avoided.

The ID attribute can also be used to set a destination anchor (`<a id="note1">1 </a>`, for instance) but might not be supported by some older browsers. To satisfy both newer and older browsers, you can include both in an A element (`<a name="note1" id="note1">1</a>`, for instance). When including both a NAME and an ID attribute in an element, their values must be identical.

While the NAME attribute can only designate an A element as a destination anchor, the ID attribute can designate any element as a **destination element** to which links can jump to within a document. This considerably broadens what can be linked to in an HTML document, allowing third parties, for instance, to link to any element to which an ID attribute has been assigned within any document anywhere. While this should work in all current browsers, some older browsers might not recognize it.

NOTE

The NAME attribute is included in XHTML 1.0 for transitional purposes but is deprecated in favor of using the ID attribute instead. Thus, using the NAME attribute in a "strict" XHTML 1.0 document is not valid, even though it is valid in a "strict" HTML 4.01 document (and in an HTML 5 document). For other differences between HTML 4.01 and XHTML 1.0, see Appendix B, *HTML to XHTML Conversion Chart*.

CREATING A JUMP LINK Now that you have created a destination anchor, you can create a hypertext link that will jump to the location you have marked. A jump link that jumps to another location in a document is created in the following general format:

```
<a href="#anchorname">link text</a>
```

Within the HREF attribute value, the text string following the # character is the name of an anchor (or the value of an A element's NAME attribute). The # character and the following text string together are referred to as a **fragment identifier**.

Create a jump link that jumps from a note number in the text to a footnote at the bottom of the document:

1. Return to the first note number that you previously superscripted, and apply the following codes to turn it into a jump link (see Figure 2.9):

```
<h2>Distinguishing Between Folk and Urban Societies</h2>
<p>In an article published in the <em>American Journal of
Sociology</em>, Robert Redfield described the more primitive and
pre-urbanized state of society as forming "folk
societies."<sup><a href="#note1">(1)</a></sup> John A. Wilson, in
<em>The Culture of Ancient Egypt</em>, summarizes Redfield's
conclusions in the following manner:</p>
```

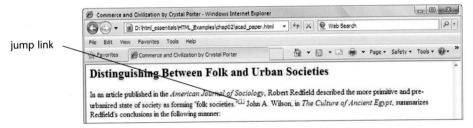

FIGURE 2.9 • The superscripted note number has been turned into a jump link that, when clicked on, will jump to the specified destination anchor.

2. Save your document, switch over to your browser, refresh the display of your page, and then click on the **(1)** note link. Your browser should jump to the first footnote at the bottom of the page (see Figure 2.10).

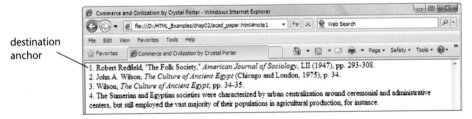

FIGURE 2.10 • A note at the bottom of a page can be linked with its corresponding note number in the body of the document.

tip

At the bottom of the BODY element, a PRE (Preformatted Text) element has been inserted that contains 30 hard returns. The reason for doing this is to add vertical spacing at the bottom of the document, so that when a hypertext footnote link jumps to one of the footnotes at the bottom of the page, the footnote will be displayed at the top of the browser window, rather than partway down in the window. The PRE element can be used for this because it is the only element that does not ignore nested hard returns. Alternatively, a style could be used to add additional margin space at the bottom of the page.

CREATING A RETURN LINK Visitors can just click the browser's Back button to return to the location they were at before clicking a hypertext link. It is not a bad idea, however, to provide a more explicit means by which visitors can return to their previous position within the document. You can do this by creating a **return link** that jumps the other way, from the end of a footnote back up to its corresponding note number in the document's text.

An anchor element can include both an HREF and a NAME attribute (or an HREF and an ID attribute), so you do not have to create a separate destination anchor next to the jump link you created previously. It is permissible to include both an HREF and a NAME attribute in an A element's start tag to create an anchor element that can serve as both a jump link and a destination anchor. For elements other than the A element, however, you should avoid including both a NAME attribute and an ID attribute with the same value.

Create a hypertext link that jumps back up from the footnote to its corresponding note number in the text:

1. Edit the hypertext note link you previously created, giving it a unique name using the NAME attribute:

```
<p>In an article published in the <em>American Journal of
Sociology</em>, Robert Redfield described the more primitive and
pre-urbanized state of society as forming "folk
societies."<sup><a href="#note1" name="return1">(1)</a></sup>
John A. Wilson, in <em>The Culture of Ancient Egypt</em>,
summarizes Redfield's conclusions in the following manner:</p>
```

2. Scroll back down to the list of footnotes at the bottom of the document body. At the end of the first footnote, create a jump link that will jump back to the note number link that you just named (see Figure 2.11):

```
<p><em><strong>Notes</strong></em></p>
<p>
<a name="note1">1</a>. Robert Redfield, "The Folk Society,"
<em>American Journal of Sociology</em>, LII (1947), pp. 293-308.
<a href="#return1">[Return]</a><br>
```

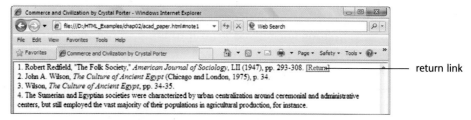

FIGURE 2.11 • Including a return link following a footnote provides visitors with an explicit means to return to their previous location in the document.

3. In your browser, click on the **[Return]** link at the end of the first footnote. Your browser should jump back to the first note number (see Figure 2.12).

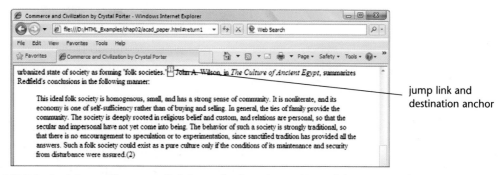

FIGURE 2.12 • The return link jumps back to the position of the note number.

The easiest way to keep jump links and destination anchors straight in your mind is to remember these simple differences between the two:

- A jump link always includes an HREF attribute with a fragment identifier (beginning with a # character) that identifies the name and/or ID of the destination anchor it jumps to (for example: **href="#Part1"**).
- A destination anchor includes a NAME attribute and/or ID attribute (*not* beginning with a # character) that names or identifies it, so it can be targeted by a jump link (for example: **name="Part1"**, **id="Part1"**, or both together).

TROUBLE *spot* Fragment identifiers and anchor names are case-sensitive. Whatever you specify as the name of a destination anchor must be duplicated exactly, including any uppercase characters, in the fragment identifier used to jump to it. In other words, if you specify **name="note1"** as the name of a destination anchor, then **href="#note1"** must be used in the corresponding jump link, and not **href="#Note1"** or **href="#NOTE1"**.

practice So far, you have created one hypertext note link (a jump link) that jumps from the first note number in the document to the first footnote listed at the bottom of the page (marked by a destination anchor). Using that experience as a guide, do the same for the three remaining note numbers and footnotes:

1. Create the destination anchors that mark the location of the remaining three footnotes at the foot of the page. Using the A element's NAME attribute, give each one a unique name (**note2**, **note3**, and **note4**).
2. Find each of the remaining note numbers in the document (they are the same note numbers, surrounded by parentheses, that you superscripted earlier). Turn each note number (and surrounding parentheses) into a jump link by nesting it inside of an A element with an HREF attribute targeting the name of the destination anchor you want it to jump to (**#note2**, **#note3**, and **#note4**).
3. In your browser, test each of the links you have created.

You also previously created a return link at the end of the first footnote that jumps back up to the corresponding note number in the document's text. Using that experience as a guide, create return links at the end of the other three footnotes:

1. Find the three remaining note numbers. In the jump links you created for them, use the NAME attribute to give each one a unique name (**return2**, **return3**, and **return4**). These anchor elements now serve as both jump links and destination anchors.
2. Use the A element's HREF attribute to create return links at the end of the remaining footnotes at the foot of the page that jump back up to the corresponding note numbers. For the HREF attribute value, use fragment identifiers that target the names of the destination anchors you want to return to (**#return2**, **#return3**, and **#return4**).
3. In your browser, test each of the return links you have created.

CREATING A FOOTNOTE SEPARATOR LINE In the example text, an HR (Horizontal Rule) element is inserted above the footnotes to create a separator line between them and the rest of the document's text. An HR element, however, draws a line all the way across the page, while in printed documents with footnotes, a footnote separator line is usually drawn only part of the way across the page. Horizontal rules are also center-aligned when their width is set to less than 100 percent.

 Create a left-aligned footnote separator line with a size of 1 pixel and a width of 150 pixels:

1. Reduce the width of the horizontal rule to 150 pixels, and set a size of 1 pixel, as shown in the following example:

```
<hr width="150" size="1">
<p><em><strong>Notes</strong></em></p>
<p>
<a id="note1"></a>1. Robert Redfield, "The Folk Society,"
<em>American Journal of Sociology</em>, LII (1947), pp. 293-308.
<a href="#return1">[Return]</a><br>
```

2. Left-align the horizontal rule (see Figure 2.13):

```
<hr width="150" size="1" align="left">
<p><em><strong>Notes</strong></em></p>
```

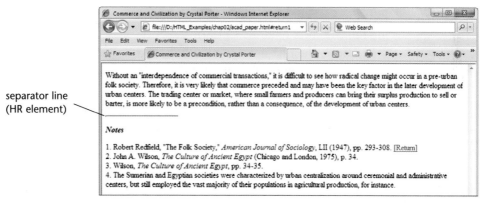

FIGURE 2.13 • The horizontal rule is left-aligned.

tip You also can set the width of a horizontal rule using a percentage value. For instance, **width="25%"** would set the width of the horizontal rule to 25 percent of the width of the browser viewport.

Creating Endnote Links

In a published article or book, the only difference between footnotes and endnotes is that footnotes are listed at the bottom of a page, and endnotes are listed at the end of an article, chapter, or book. A Web page, of course, is a single page of indeterminate length, so the foot and the end of the document are really the same. When working in HTML, endnotes are generally grouped in a separate document, whereas footnotes are displayed at the foot of the current document.

You might want to consider using endnotes, rather than footnotes, if you have many notes in your document or they include an extensive amount of text. If you only have a handful of relatively brief notes, then you might want to consider using footnotes.

You link to an endnote in the same way that you link to any location in another document. You create such a link in the following fashion:

```
<a href="url#anchorname">link text</a>
```

In the example, *url* stands for the object file that is targeted by the link, which can be just a file name (if the name of the file you are linking to is located in the same folder), an absolute Web address (**http://www.*yourhost*.com/*yourfolder*/*yourpage*.html**), or a relative Web address that points to a file located in your own site (***yoursubfolder*/ *yourpage*.html**). Using relative URLs is covered in more detail in Chapter 4.

When working with Web pages, endnotes are generally grouped in their own separate document. You might want to do this, for instance, if you have a lot of notes that need to be listed, and for the sake of brevity or design, you do not want to display them at the foot of your page. You might also want to group notes from a collection of documents (or chapters) in a single file, which can then be referenced from those documents (these notes would function like endnotes at the end of a book, for instance).

This example uses an endnotes_ex.html example file that is included with the other example files for this chapter (in the chap02 folder). In creating the following example, you will be instructed to open endnotes_ex.html in your text editor and resave it as endnotes.html in the chap02 folder in your working folder or disk.

action

Edit the jump links for the note numbers so they point to the name of the file containing the endnotes (endnotes.html):

1. Locate the first note number link, and, in the HREF attribute, insert the name of the file that will contain the endnotes (endnotes.html) in front of the fragment identifier (#note1):

```
<h2>Distinguishing Between Folk and Urban Societies</h2>
<p>In an article published in the <em>American Journal of Sociology
</em>, Robert Redfield described the more primitive and pre-
urbanized state of society as forming "folk societies."<sup><a
href="endnotes.html#note1" name="return1">(1)</a></sup> John A.
Wilson, in <em>The Culture of Ancient Egypt</em>, summarizes
Redfield's conclusions in the following manner:</p>
```

2. Do the same with the three other note number links you have created, so they each point to endnotes.html. Resave your file.
3. Run a second copy of your text editor, and open **endnotes_ex.html** from the chap02 folder in your working folder. (If using a text editor that lets you open multiple windows, just open endnotes_ex.html in a separate window.)
4. Resave **endnotes_ex.html** in the chap02 folder as **endnotes.html**, so you will not overwrite the original example file.

NOTE

In viewing the example file in your text editor, you will notice that the endnotes in endnotes.html are identical to the footnotes in your other document, including the destination anchors and return links you added to your footnotes. This demonstrates that you can link to a location within any document anywhere, even halfway around the world, as long as a destination anchor marks it.

5. Edit the return links, so they target your academic paper's file name (if you resaved your document under a different file name, substitute that file name in the following code). Resave your file.

```
<p>
<a id="note1">1</a>. Robert Redfield, "The Folk Society,"
American Journal of Sociology, LII (1947), pp. 293-308. <a
href="acad_paper.html#return1">[Return]</a><br>
```

```
<a id="note2">2</a>. John A. Wilson, The Culture of Ancient Egypt
(Chicago and London, 1975), p. 34. <a href="acad_paper.
html#return2">[Return]</a><br>
<a id="note3">3</a>. Wilson, The Culture of Ancient Egypt, pp.
34-35. <a href="acad_paper.html#return3">[Return]</a><br>
<a id="note4">4</a>. The Sumerian and Egyptian societies were
characterized by urban centralization around ceremonial and
administrative centers, but still employed the vast majority of
their populations in agricultural production, for instance. <a
href="acad_paper.html#return4">[Return]</a>
</p>
```

6. Switch to your browser, and refresh the display of your page (it should still be displaying your academic paper). Find the first note number link, and click on it. Your browser should open endnotes.html and jump down to the position of the first endnote (see Figure 2.14).

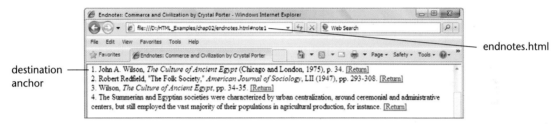

destination anchor

endnotes.html

FIGURE 2.14 • Note links can be created that jump to a list of endnotes grouped in a separate file.

7. Click the **[Return]** link at the end of the first endnote. Your browser should reopen your academic paper's file and return to the note number link that you just jumped from. You also can click the Back button to do the same thing.

8. Test the remaining note number links. They should each jump to endnotes.html, displaying the corresponding endnote at the top of the browser window.

NOTE — The endnotes.html example file also includes a PRE element containing multiple hard returns at the bottom of the page to help ensure that the endnotes are displayed at the top of the browser window when they are jumped to. The actual number of returns needed to cause this can vary depending upon the length of the page and the width and height of the browser's viewport.

INSERTING ENTITY CODES

An **entity code** allows you to insert **special characters** that are not available on the keyboard. There are two types of entity codes—numeric and named.

A **numeric entity code** identifies a character by its numerical position in the ISO 8859-1 character set and is inserted in this general format:

```
&#entitynumber;
```

The HTML specifications list many entity names that can be used to reference many special characters. A **named entity code** is inserted in this general format:

```
&entityname;
```

Inserting a Copyright Symbol

If you publish original material on the Web, you might want others to understand that your material is copyrighted and not part of the public domain. Including a copyright notice will not necessarily stop someone else from copying and reusing your material, but it will at least put them on notice that it is illegal for them to do so.

The copyright symbol is not included on your keyboard, so you have to use its named or numeric entity code to insert it into your page.

The copyright symbol's named entity code is **©**, whereas its numeric entity code is **©**.

Use the named entity code for the copyright symbol to add a copyright notice at the bottom of your example document (see Figure 2.15):

```
<hr>
<address>
Crystal Porter<br>
E-Mail: <a href="mailto:cporter@pinebough.emcp.net">cporter@
pinebough.emcp.net</a><br>
</address>
<p>&copy; Copyright 2009 by Crystal Porter. All rights
reserved.</p>
```

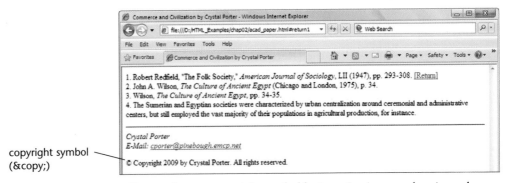

copyright symbol
(©)

FIGURE 2.15 • You can insert a copyright symbol by inserting its named entity code.

Including a copyright notice on your page is not required to protect your copyright; under current copyright law, anything you create is automatically copyrighted. You are also not required to register your copyright. Including a copyright notice on your work, however, puts others on notice that your work is copyrighted and strengthens your case against someone who infringes on your copyright. Registering your copyright makes you eligible to receive statutory damages of as much as $100,000.

Visit the Internet Resource Center. To find online resources that discuss copyrights and fair use rights and laws for material published to the Web, go to the Chapter 2 section of this book's Internet Resource Center at **www.emcp.com/html2e.**

Inserting Other Entity Codes

Although many named entity codes are allowed by the HTML specifications, some earlier browsers might not recognize all of them. This is a case of ungraceful degradation because in a non-supporting browser, the raw code is displayed instead of the character. Figure 2.16 shows what the named entity for the trademark symbol looks like, when displayed in a browser that does not support its named entity code (™).

> ### Gombo™ Galvinator
>
> Price: $50
>
> This is just some dummy text. This is just some dummy text. This is just some dummy text. This is just some dummy text. This is just some dummy text. This is just some dummy text. This is just some dummy text. This is just some dummy text. This is just some dummy text. This is just some dummy text. This is just some dummy text. This is just some dummy text. This is just some dummy text. This is just some dummy text. This is just some dummy text. This is just some dummy text. This is just some dummy text. This is just some dummy text.

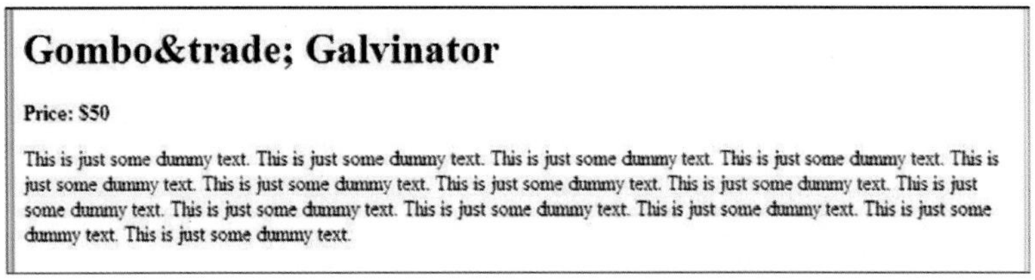

FIGURE 2.16 • If a browser does not recognize a named entity code, it displays the raw code.

Later in this chapter, including trademark and registered symbols is covered in the "Inserting the Registered and Trademark Symbols" section.

Because named entity codes do not degrade gracefully in non-supporting browsers, it is better to use named entity codes to insert only the characters shown in Table 2.1, which are supported by all recent browsers, and use numeric entity codes to insert all other characters.

TABLE 2.1 • Named Entity Codes Supported by All Recent Browsers

Decription	Named Entity Code	Character/Symbol
Copyright	&copy;	©
Registered	&reg;	®
Left Angle	&lt;	<
Right Angle	&gt;	>
Ampersand	&amp;	&
Double-quote	&quot;	""
Most accented characters	À, Õ, and ä for instance	À, Ô, and ä, for instance

In HTML 4.01 documents, you do not generally have to substitute entity codes for left angle (<), right angle (>), ampersand (&), or double-quote ("") characters that are included in regular text, unless you want to display them "as is" in a Web page. For instance, to display `<img src="myimage.jpg">` as it appears, rather than as it is parsed by a browser, you would include the following in an HTML document:

```
&lt;img src=&quot;myimage.jpg&quot;&gt;
```

Standalone ampersands included in attribute values and URLs, however, should be inserted using the entity code, &.

In XHTML 1.0 documents, however, standalone ampersands or left angle characters must be inserted using their entity codes, regardless of where they appear in the document.

Some browsers for Macintosh OS 9 and earlier ("Classic Macintosh") were unable to display some special characters included in the ISO 8859-1 character set because those characters were missing from those systems' native character set (Mac Roman). That is no longer a problem with Macintosh OS X, however, which uses UTF-8 (Unicode) as its native character set; UTF-8 is a superset of ISO 8859-1.

TROUBLE *spot* Do not use keyboard shortcuts, Window's Character Map, or the Macintosh OS X's Character Palette or Keyboard Viewer to insert non-keyboard characters into an HTML document. Different systems might have different characters included at different locations in their native character sets, meaning that what displays as one character on one system might be displayed as an entirely different character on another system. Always use HTML entity codes to insert non-keyboard characters into HTML documents.

NOTE See Appendix D, *Special Characters Chart*, for a listing of all ISO 8859-1 special characters, as well as a selection of Unicode characters, that can be inserted into HTML documents.

CASE EXAMPLE: CREATING A FREQUENTLY ASKED QUESTIONS PAGE

A frequently asked questions (or FAQ) page is one of the most common types of pages that can be found on the Web. You can find FAQ pages on just about every topic or subject. Most FAQ pages are organized as a series of questions and answers, with a menu at the top of the page to make it easier to find the answer to a particular question.

"Eddie Lopez is a support technician at CD Bunson Burners, Inc., which manufactures multi-drive CD-R recording systems. He has been tasked with creating a frequently asked questions (FAQ) page that compiles answers to questions that are frequently asked by customers. While compiling the questions and answers, Eddie noticed that a menu system at the top of the page would make it easier for users to find the particular question for which they are seeking an answer."

This example uses the cdr-faq_ex.html example file that is included with the other example files for this chapter (in the chap02 folder).

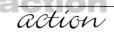

action To start using the example file for this case example:
1. In your text editor, open **cdr-faq_ex.html** from the chap02 folder within your working folder or disk.
2. Resave your document as **cdr-faq.html** in the chap02 folder.
3. In your browser, open **cdr-faq.html** from the chap02 folder.

TROUBLE *spot* If you need more help opening and resaving an HTML file in your text editor, see "Opening an HTML File in Your Text Editor" earlier in this chapter. If you need more help opening an HTML file in your Web browser, see "Saving and Previewing Your HTML File" earlier in this chapter.

Many of the HTML codes have already been added to this example document. You will be adding codes to the example document to help demonstrate a variety of different features, including creating a menu (or table of contents), making text bigger or smaller, creating multi-level numbered lists, inserting registered and trademark symbols, and using monospaced text to format input, output, and program code.

CREATING A DOCUMENT MENU

A **document menu** is any arrangement of links at or near the top of a document that visitors can use to more easily access subsections, which they might otherwise have to scroll down to find, such as in a longer, multi-part document. A document menu can be presented as a bulleted link list (using the UL and LI elements), as a horizontal series of links separated by spaces or other characters, or as a sidebar menu in a page using a multi-column layout.

Creating the Menu Links

A bulleted list is already included at the top of the example document. You just have to add the links to turn it into a menu. The menu links you will be creating work the same as the note links you created in the previous case example, except that they link to document sections, instead of to footnotes at the bottom of the page.

Add the following codes to turn the text in the list items into hypertext links (or jump links) that will jump to locations in your document (see Figure 2.17):

```
<h3>CD Bunson Burners, Inc.</h3>
<h1>CD-R Frequently Asked Questions</h1>

<ul>
<li><a href="#quest1">What is CD-R?</a>
<li><a href="#quest2">What is the difference between CD-R and
CD-ROM?</a>
<li><a href="#quest3">How long is a CD-R disc?</a>
<li><a href="#quest4">How do I back up an audio CD?</a>
<li><a href="#quest5">Can I batch process recording jobs?</a>
</ul>
```

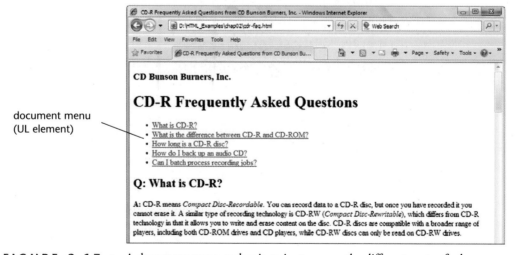

document menu
(UL element)

FIGURE 2.17 • A document menu makes it easier to access the different parts of a longer document.

Inserting the Destination Anchors

Before your menu links will work, destination anchors need to be inserted to mark the locations to which the menu links are going to jump.

The questions in the document are formatted as level-two headings (H2 elements). For the menu links to be able to jump to them, they need to be marked with named destination anchors.

Insert the destination anchor that marks the first question-and-answer section, and then test the link that jumps to it to make sure it works:

1. Scroll down to the first H2 element, and insert a destination anchor that will be jumped to from the first menu link:

```
<h2><a name="quest1">Q:</a> What is CD-R?</h2>
<p><b>A:</b> CD-R means <i>Compact Disc-Recordable</i>. You can
record data to a CD-R disc, but once you have recorded it, you
cannot erase it.
```

2. Save your file in your text editor, switch over to your browser, and refresh the display of your page. Click on the first menu link to test it. Your browser should jump down to the position of the destination anchor you inserted, displaying the first question and answer at the top of the browser window (see Figure 2.18).

destination anchor
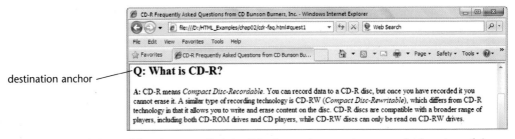

FIGURE 2.18 • After the menu link is clicked on, a browser jumps to the location of the corresponding named destination anchor.

3. Create the other destination anchors. Using the first destination anchor you created as a guide, insert destination anchors that mark the locations of the other question-and-answer sections. Name these destination anchors so they match the anchor names that are used in the menu links (**quest2**, **quest3**, **quest4**, and **quest5**).

4. Save your file, switch over to your browser, refresh your page, and then test the other links in your menu. For instance, click on the third menu link ("How long is a CD-R disc?"); your browser should jump down to the third question-and-answer section (see Figure 2.19).

destination anchor
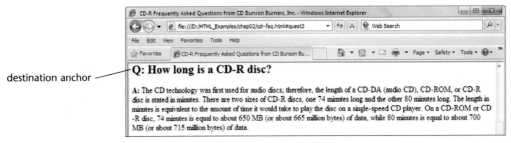

FIGURE 2.19 • After the third menu link is clicked, the browser jumps to the third question-and-answer section.

NOTE

You cannot always rely on the content of a destination anchor being displayed at the top of a browser's viewport after jumping to it from a jump link. If the page content following the destination anchor is not sufficient to fill the browser's viewport, the destination anchor will be displayed part way down in the viewport rather than at the top. In most cases, such as with the current document, this is fine. In other cases, however, such as with the previous case example, it might be more important that jump links jump all the way to their corresponding foot notes. To ensure that happens, a PRE element containing 30 hard returns was inserted at the bottom of the BODY element.

Creating Return Links

When you create a menu that jumps to different sections within an HTML document, you can also add links at the end of each section that will return a visitor to the menu. These links are similar to the return links you added at the end of the footnotes in the previous case example, except they all return to the same destination anchor.

1. Add a **name="menu"** attribute to the A start tag in the menu, so it will also function as a destination anchor that your return links can jump back to:

```
<ul>
<li><a href="#quest1" name="menu">What is CD-R?</a>
<li><a href="#quest2">What is the difference between CD-R and
CD-ROM?</a>
```

2. Create the return link following the first question-and-answer section (see Figure 2.20):

```
<h2><a name="quest1">Q:</a> What is CD-R?</h2>
<p><b>A:</b> CD-R means <i>Compact Disc-Recordable</i>. You can
record data to a CD-R disc, but once you have recorded it you
cannot erase it. A similar type of recording technology is CD-RW
(<i>Compact Disc-Rewritable</i>), which differs from CD-R
technology in that it allows you to write and erase content on
the disc. CD-R discs are compatible with a broader range of
players, including both CD-ROM drives and CD players, while CD-RW
discs can only be read on CD-RW drives.</p>
<p>Return to the <a href="#menu">Menu</a>.</p>
```

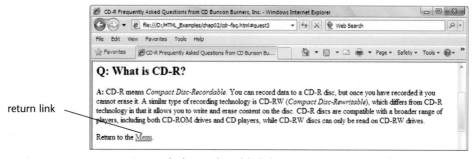

return link

FIGURE 2.20 • Return links can be added that jump back to a document menu.

3. In your browser, click the return link you just added. Your browser should jump back up and display the document menu you created (see Figure 2.21).

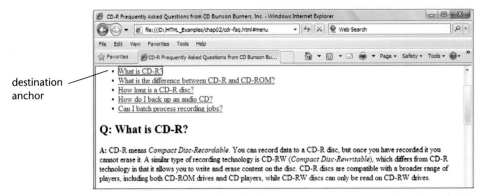

destination anchor

FIGURE 2.21 • After a return link is clicked on, a visitor is returned to the top of the document menu.

4. Copy the return link you just created and paste it in following the other question-and-answer sections to create the other return links. All of your return links are identical because they all jump back to the same destination anchor.
5. Test your return links in your browser. They should all return you back to the document menu.

MAKING BIGGER AND SMALLER TEXT

The BIG and SMALL elements can be used to increase or decrease the size of nested text. You can also increase and decrease the size of text using the FONT element. You should be aware, however, that while the FONT element is deprecated in HTML 4.01, the BIG and SMALL elements are not. Use of the FONT element to control font sizes and the issue of deprecation are covered in more detail in Chapter 3.

Making Text Bigger

In the example file, increasing the size of the "Q:" and "A:" text strings that precede each question and answer can help the reader identify them.

Use the BIG element to increase the size of the "Q:" and "A:" text strings for the first question and answer (see Figure 2.22):

```
<h2><a name="quest1"><big>Q:</big></a> What is CD-R?</h2>
<p><b><big>A:</big></b> CD-R means <i>Compact Disc-Recordable</i>.
```

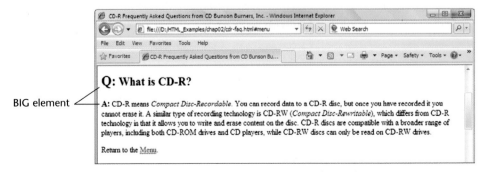

BIG element

FIGURE 2.22 • The BIG element increases the size of nested text.

You also can nest multiple BIG elements to further increase the size of nested text.

Nest the "A:" text string within another BIG element to further increase its size (see Figure 2.23):

```
<h2><a id="quest1"><big>Q:</big></a> What is CD-R?</h2>
<p><b><big><big>A:</big></big></b> CD-R means <i>Compact Disc-
Recordable</i>.
```

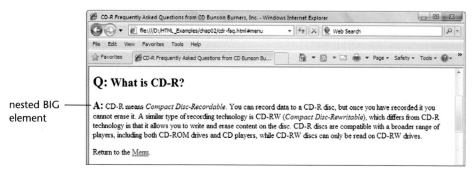

nested BIG element

FIGURE 2.23 • Two BIG elements increase the size of nested text even more.

You can nest up to four BIG elements to increase the text size (more than four nested BIG elements will not further increase the text size). That is because HTML only provides for seven font sizes, only four of which are larger than the default paragraph font size. Text in heading-level elements can be increased even fewer times—the size of text can be increased once in an H1 element, twice in an H2 element, three times in an H3 element, and so on. You will learn more about setting font sizes in Chapter 3.

Use the BIG element to increase the "Q:" and "A:" text strings for the other four question-and-answer sections. Be sure you nest the two BIG elements used to increase the size of the "A:" text strings inside of the B element's start and end tags, rather than overlap them.

Making Text Smaller

In some situations, you might want to make text smaller. For example, you might not want certain text to be as noticeable as the other text on your page, while still being legible.

Use the SMALL element to decrease the size of the copyright statement at the bottom of the page (see Figure 2.24):

```
<p><small>&copy; Copyright 2009 by CD Bunson Burners, Inc. All
rights reserved.</small></p>
</body>
```

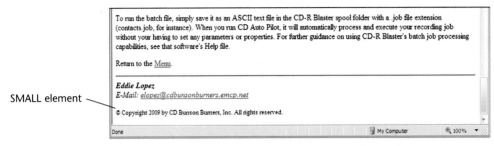

To run the batch file, simply save it as an ASCII text file in the CD-R Blaster spool folder with a .job file extension (contacts.job, for instance). When you run CD Auto Pilot, it will automatically process and execute your recording job without your having to set any parameters or properties. For further guidance on using CD-R Blaster's batch job processing capabilities, see that software's Help file.

Return to the Menu.

Eddie Lopez
E-Mail: elopez@cdbunsonburners.emcp.net

© Copyright 2009 by CD Bunson Burners, Inc. All rights reserved.

Done   My Computer   100%

SMALL element

FIGURE 2.24 • The SMALL element decreases the size of nested text.

Generally, it is not a good idea to nest SMALL elements to decrease the size of text even further because doing so might render the nested text unreadable on some systems.

BIG and SMALL in HTML 5

The BIG element, although not deprecated in HTML 4, is obsolete in HTML 5, in line with the general approach that HTML should handle structure and meaning, while CSS should handle presentation, to optimize accessibility. The SMALL element is redefined in HTML 5 as semantically referring to "small print," as in contracts or disclaimers.

See Chapter 3, *Working with Fonts, Colors, and Backgrounds*, for coverage of using both the FONT element's SIZE attribute and the CSS font-size property to increase or decrease the size of fonts.

USING NUMBERED LISTS

The FAQ includes one answer that provides instructional steps formatted as a numbered list. Technical documents often include numbered instructional steps. In HTML, the OL (Ordered List) element is used to create a numbered list.

In the example document, one question-and-answer section contains instructions formatted as separate paragraphs instead of numbered steps. The paragraphs are marked by single **<p>** start tags, without corresponding end tags, which is legal in HTML, because including end tags for paragraph elements, although generally advisable, is not required. You will be deleting the **<p>** start tags anyway, so leaving off the end tags just means you do not have to delete them as well. You create a numbered list in exactly the same way you created a bulleted list in the previous chapter, except you use an OL element, rather than a UL element.

Delete the **<p>** start tags, and use the OL and LI elements to create a numbered list (see Figure 2.25):

```
<h3>Create an Image File:</h3>
<ol>
<li><p>Click the Start button and select Programs, Adaptec Easy
CD Creator 4, and Create CD.
<li><p>Click the Audio CD button.
<li><p>Insert the audio CD you want to copy in your CD-ROM or
CD-R drive. Click on the first track to highlight it. Hold down
the Shift key and click on the last track to highlight all of the
tracks. Click the Add button on the Toolbar.
<li><p>Select File, then Create CD Image. Change to the folder
```

```
where you save your image files (or you can create a folder for
this) and then save your image file, ending the file name with a
.cif file extension. For instance, type myimage.cif as the name
of your image file.
<li><p>The message "CD created successfully" will be displayed
when the image file has been successfully created. Click the OK
button.
</ol>
```

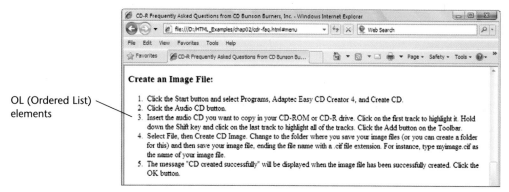

OL (Ordered List) elements

FIGURE 2.25 • The OL element is used in combination with the LI element to format a numbered list.

Although no `</li>` end tags are included in the preceeding example, that does not mean that LI is an empty element. Rather, it is a container element for which adding the end tag is optional. The end tag is implied by the start of the following list item or the end of the containing list element. The LI end tag, however, is required in XHTML (which does not allow implied end tags).

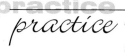

The next two H3 elements ("Select Recording Options" and "Select Advanced Options") are also followed by paragraphs that can be turned into numbered lists. To gain more practice creating numbered lists, use the OL and LI elements to turn paragraphs following those headings into numbered list items as well.

Creating Multi-Level Numbered Lists

If you nest bulleted lists inside each other, a browser automatically changes the bullet type for each nested list level. Nesting numbered lists inside each other does not work in the same way; each nested list level still has the same number type (Arabic numerals).

The TYPE attribute is used in the UL or OL elements to change the bullet or number type, respectively. The OL element's TYPE attribute takes the following values: **I** (uppercase Roman), **i** (lowercase Roman), **A** (uppercase alphabetic), **a** (lowercase alphabetic), and **1** (Arabic numerals).

Change the H3 elements into list items in an ordered list, and then set an uppercase alphabetic number type for the list:

1. Nest all of the H3 elements (and following numbered steps) inside an OL element, and then change the H3 elements into LI elements:

```
<ol>
<li><h3>Create an Image File:</h3>
```

```
<ol>
<li>Click on the Start button and select Programs, Adaptec Easy
CD Creator 4, and Create CD.

[...]

<li><h3>Select Recording Options:</h3>
<ol>
<li>Insert a blank (unrecorded) CD-R disc in your CD-R drive.

[...]

<li><h3>Select Advanced Options:</h3>
<ol>
<li>If the Advanced options are not displayed, click the Advanced
button.

[...]

<li>The message "CD created successfully" will be displayed when
the image file has been successfully recorded to the CD-R disc.
Click the OK button.
</ol>
</ol>
```

2. Use the TYPE attribute in the first OL element to specify that it should be numbered using uppercase alphabetic characters (see Figure 2.26):

```
<ol type="A">
<li>Create an Image File:
<ol>
<li>Click on the Start button and select Programs, Adaptec Easy
CD Creator 4, and Create CD.
```

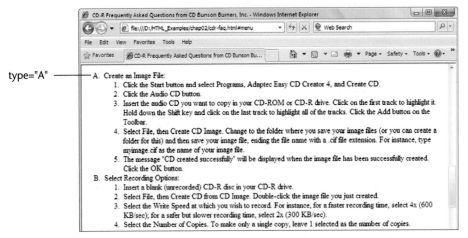

FIGURE 2.26 • You can nest numbered lists inside each other that use different numbering schemes.

The TYPE attribute can also be used with the UL (Unordered List) element to change the bullet character used for bulleted list items. Values that can be used include **disc** (the default), **circle**, or **square**.

The TYPE attribute can be applied to the OL or UL elements to change the number or bullet type for a whole list or to an LI element to change a specific list item.

Adding Vertical Spacing between List Items

By default, browsers do not add extra vertical spacing above or below list items (in the OL or UL elements). When creating instructional steps, however, it is nice to include a little more air in the list. One way to do that is to insert two BR (Line Break) elements at the end of the list items.

action

action

HINT

To insert the same text in multiple locations, just highlight it with the mouse, copy it, and then paste it in wherever you want to insert it. In Windows, press Ctrl+C to copy and Ctrl+V to paste; on the Macintosh, press Command+C to copy and Command+V to paste.

Add two BR elements at the end of all the LI elements in your nested OL elements:

1. Insert two BR elements at the end of the following LI elements (at the end of the first list item in the top-level list and the first nested list, respectively):

```
<ol type="A">
<li>Create an Image File:<br><br>
<ol>
<li>Click on the Start button and select Programs, Adaptec Easy
CD Creator 4, and Create CD.<br><br>
```

2. Insert double BR elements at the end of all the other LI elements in the numbered lists (see Figure 2.27).

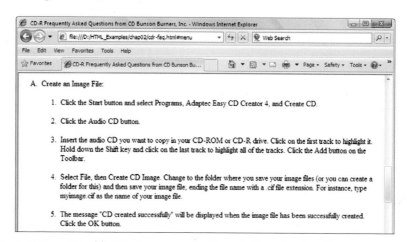

FIGURE 2.27 • Double BR elements can add vertical spacing in a list.

Although using multiple BR elements to force white space is generally discouraged, nothing in the HTML 4 or 5 specifications forbids using double BR elements. In fact, in the original definition of HTML, the P element was an empty element that simply represented two line breaks (or carriage returns).

Earlier HTML standards seemed to imply that multiple BR elements should be collapsed to a single BR element, but the browser vendors ignored that injunction. The current specifications for HTML and XHTML do not define any specific behavior for multiple BR elements. (Even if there is a browser somewhere that collapses double BR elements, it would be a case of graceful, rather than ungraceful, degradation.)

Inserting multiple BR elements, however, also cannot be considered to be non-standard, at least according to the latest HTML specifications, as long as they are nested inside of a block element. Adding two BR elements at the end of an LI element should not be harmful to accessibility, although the same cannot be said for using them in place of a P element.

An alternative to using double BR elements is to use styles to increase the LI element's bottom margin. See Chapters 3 and 7 for coverage of using styles in your documents.

INSERTING THE REGISTERED AND TRADEMARK SYMBOLS

Earlier, in the academic paper example, you learned how to insert the entity code for the copyright symbol. The named entity code for the registered symbol was also mentioned, although no example was given. Another common symbol that you may want to include in an HTML document is the trademark symbol.

The named entity code for the registered symbol (**®**) is supported by both current and earlier browsers. The named entity code for the trademark symbol (**™**), however, while supported in current browsers, might not be supported in some earlier browsers and should be avoided.

Complicating matters somewhat, in the ISO 8859-1 character set, the trademark symbol is listed outside of the range of displayable characters, among the "unused characters," which means that it is not a legal character that should be included in an HTML document, even when inserted using its numeric entity code (**™**). In practice, however, the trademark symbol's numeric entity code works in Windows, Macintosh, and UNIX browsers, but because it is not a legal character, there is no guarantee that it will display on every possible system.

The only standard way to insert a trademark symbol that should display in most current browsers is to insert it as a Unicode character (**™**). As its name implies, Unicode is a universal character set that aims ultimately to include all characters that are used in every language. As it stands, Unicode includes many thousands more characters than the ISO 8859-1 character set.

> Eddie Lopez's boss told him to insert trademark or registered symbols wherever required.

action

Insert the registered and trademark symbols as shown in the following example (see Figure 2.28):

```
<h2><a
name="quest4"><big>Q:</big> How do I back up an audio CD?</h2>
<p><b><big><big>A:</big></big></b> To make a copy of an audio CD
(CD-DA), so that you can play the copy in your CD player, you
need to record the disc in a single session and close the disc
when you are finished recording. If you record the disc using
multiple recording sessions or do not close the disc, you will
only be able to play the disc in a CD player or CD-ROM drive that
is <i>multisession capable</i>.</p>
<p>To make a copy of an audio CD using Adaptec&reg; Easy CD
Creator&#8482; 4:</p>
```

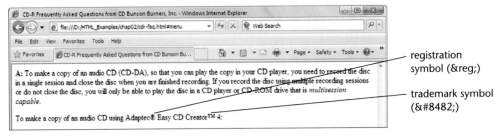

FIGURE 2.28 • The registered and trademark symbols are two of the more common special characters that can be displayed on a Web page.

The main problem with using the Unicode trademark symbol, however, is that it might not display in all browsers. Earlier browsers that do not recognize Unicode (UTF-8) also will not display it.

If it is important to include a trademark symbol that can be displayed by all browsers (your lawyers, for instance, might insist that it be used wherever required within any corporate documents), even in non-graphical browsers, you can include a trademark symbol in a Web page by parenthesizing and superscripting the "tm" letter pair: `<sup>(tm)</sup>`. This is the same somewhat ungraceful workaround, or *kludge*, that you used before to get around the problem of superscripted note numbers in browsers that do not support superscripting.

For more information about the ISO 8859-1 and Unicode character sets, see Appendix D, *Special Characters Chart*.

USING MONOSPACED TEXT

HTML provides a number of elements that cause text to be displayed in a **monospaced font**, including the CODE, KBD, SAMP, and TT elements. In a monospaced font, also called a fixed-pitch font, all characters, including letters, numbers, punctuation marks, and even spaces, are the same width, taking up exactly the same amount of horizontal space. The default monospaced font varies from system to system: Courier New (Windows XP), Courier (Macintosh OS 9), Lucida Console (Windows Vista), or Monaco (Macintosh OS X). By contrast, text in other non-monospaced elements is displayed in a proportional font, such as Times New Roman or Times Roman, for instance, in which each character may have a different (or "proportional") width.

Monospaced text is most common in technical documents, where it is generally used to represent different kinds of computer-generated output or input and to distinguish it from other surrounding text that is purely informational (rather than representational).

In HTML, the TT (Teletype) element is a generic element for producing monospaced text. The name of the element comes from a device, the teletype, which was used for both input and output on mainframes and minicomputers before the introduction of computer monitors using cathode ray tubes. The teletype was both a typewriter and a printer, which is why the TT element is a generic monospaced element that can be used to highlight both input and output text. Timothy Berners-Lee, and many others who helped pioneer the formation of the Web, worked with teletypes both as computer science students and later on the job, which is undoubtedly how the teletype element got its name in the first place. Bill Gates and Paul Allen, the founders of Microsoft, first learned how to program on a teletype at Lakeside Prep School in Seattle. (To read more about Bill Gates' early computer learning experiences, see "William H. Gates III: Before Microsoft" by John Mirick at **ei.cs.vt.edu/~history/Gates.Mirick.html**.) Perhaps to accommodate younger users who have never heard of nor seen a teletype, the TT element is sometimes referred to as the "typewriter text" element.

NOTE Although the TT element is not deprecated in HTML 4, it is obsolete in HTML 5, probably because its semantic meaning is considered to be anachronistic. The TT element remains perfectly valid, however, as long as you declare your document as conforming to HTML 4.01 or XHTML 1.0. If you want to code your HTML with forward-compatibility with HTML 5 in mind, however, you might use the SAMP element to represent computer output and the KBD element to represent computer input, while the CODE element could be used for actual program code.

action

Use the SAMP and KBD elements to highlight computer output and input:

1. Use the SAMP element, combined with the BIG element, to highlight screen labels and other output in the following example code; delete the quotation marks around "CD created successfully":

```
<li>Select <samp><big>File</big></samp>, then <samp><big>Create
CD Image</big></samp>. Change to the folder where you save your
image files (or you can create a folder for this) and then save
your image file, ending the file name with a .cif file extension.
For instance, type myimage.cif as the name of your image
file.<br><br>
<li>The message <samp><big>"CD created successfully"</big></samp>
will be displayed when the image file has been successfully
created. Click the <samp><big>OK</big></samp> button.<br><br>
</ol>

<li>Select Recording Options:<br><br>
```

2. Use the KBD element, combined with the B and BIG elements, to highlight computer input (see Figure 2.29):

```
<li>Select <samp><big>File</big></samp>, then <samp><big>Create
CD Image</big></samp>. Change to the folder where you save your
image files (or you can create a folder for this) and then save
your image file, ending the file name with a .cif file extension.
For instance, type <kbd><b><big>myimage.cif</big></b></kbd> as
the name of your image file.<br><br>
```

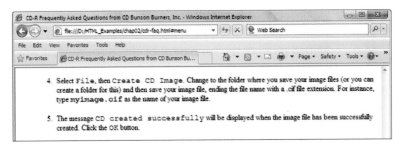

FIGURE 2.29 • Nesting a B element distinguishes the KBD element from the SAMP element.

NOTE The BIG element was used with the SAMP and KBD elements because monospaced text looks shorter than surrounding non-monospaced text, even though they are the same size.

You also might want to display strings or blocks of computer code as monospaced text. The CODE element is an inline element, the purpose of which is to display strings of computer code. By inserting BR elements at the end of lines, the CODE element also can be used to display short blocks of computer code.

action

Format the example document's listing of a computer batch file in a monospaced font using the CODE element (the BR elements have already been inserted for you), as shown here (see Figure 2.30):

```
<p><code>[CD-R Blaster Job]<br>
Job Name = Contact Database<br>
Image File = F:\contacts.cif<br>
Label File = F:\Label templates\contacts.lbl<br>
Merge File = F:\contacts.mrg<br>
Type = Disk-At-Once<br>
Session = Single<br>
Disk = Close<br>
Number of Discs = 20<br>
Verify Type = None<br>
CRC32 = FFFFFFFF<br>
Serialize = No<br>
Serial Number Field = 1<br>
Serial Number Start = 123<br>
Serial Number Step = 1</code></p>
```

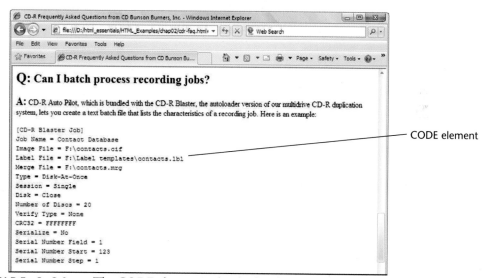

CODE element

FIGURE 2.30 • The CODE element is also displayed in a monospaced font.

USING PREFORMATTED TEXT

Preformatted text is text that you want to display "as is," preserving any hard returns, spaces, or tabs that have been used to visually organize the text or code. In HTML, the PRE (Preformatted Text) element is the only element that does not ignore hard returns, spaces, or tabs.

Nest the code text inside a PRE element, and space out the text following the "=" character to form a second column:

1. Nest the code text inside a PRE element, and delete the tags for the P, BR, and CODE elements:

```
<pre>
<p><code>[CD-R Blaster Job]<br>
Job Name = Contact Database<br>
Image File = F:\contacts.cif<br>
Label File = F:\Label templates\contacts.lbl<br>
Merge File = F:\contacts.mrg<br>
Type = Disk-At-Once<br>
Session = Single<br>
Disk = Close<br>
Number of Discs = 20<br>
Verify Type = None<br>
CRC32 = FFFFFFFF<br>
Serialize = No<br>
Serial Number Field = 1<br>
Serial Number Start = 123<br>
Serial Number Step = 1</code></p>
</pre>
```

2. Insert spaces (shown by dot characters) following the "=" characters so that a second, left-aligned column is formed (see Figure 2.31):

```
<pre>
[CD-R Blaster Job]
Job Name = ··············Contact Database
Image File = ··········F:\contacts.cif
Label File = ··········F:\Label templates\contacts.lbl
Merge File = ··········F:\contacts.mrg
Type = ················Disk-At-Once
Session = ·············Single
Disk = ················Close
Number of Discs = ······20
Verify Type = ··········None
CRC32 = ················FFFFFFFF
Serialize = ············No
Serial Number Field = ···1
Serial Number Start = ···123
Serial Number Step = ····1
</pre>
```

TROUBLE *spot*

To complete this step, the example code needs to be displayed in your text editor using a monospaced font. Most text editors default to using a monospaced font but if you have switched to using a proportional font, the second column will not line up vertically. To switch back to using the default monospaced font in Notepad, select Format, Font, and Lucida Console; in TextEdit, select Format, Font, Show Fonts, and Monaco.

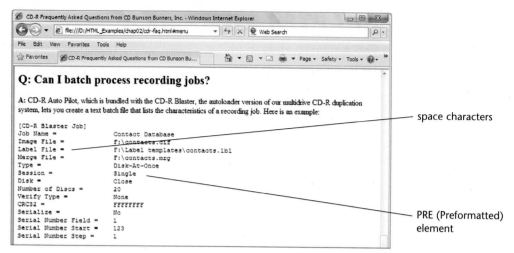

space characters

PRE (Preformatted) element

FIGURE 2.31 • The PRE element displays a block of text in a monospaced font, while preserving any included spaces, tabs, or hard returns.

CHAPTER SUMMARY

You should now be familiar with many of the HTML features and elements that are commonly used in creating and formatting online documents, including adding DocType declarations, META elements, inline highlighting (italics, bolding, underlining, monospacing, and so on), commonly used special characters (copyright, registered, and trademark), superscripted notes, hypertext note links, big and small text, and document menus.

Code Review

`<!DOCTYPE...>`	DocType declaration. Declares the version of HTML (or XHTML) to which the document conforms.
`<meta...>`	META (Meta Data) element. Empty element used to include metadata in an HTML document's HEAD element.
`<i>...</i>`	I (Italics) element. A literal element that highlights text as italic.
`<b>...</b>`	B (Bold) element. A literal inline element that highlights text as bold.
`<em>...</em>`	EM (Emphasis) element. A logical element that marks text as emphasized (displayed as italic in graphical browsers).
`<strong>...</strong>`	STRONG (Strong Emphasis) element. A logical element that marks text as strongly emphasized (displayed as bold in graphical browsers).
`<u>...</u>`	U (Underline) element. Inline element that applies underlining to a text string. Considered to be anachronistic and harmful to usability. Deprecated in HTML 4; obsolete in HTML 5.
`<blockquote>...</blockquote>`	BLOCKQUOTE element. Specifies that a text block is to be formatted as a block quote, indented in from the margins. Should not be used, counter-semantically, as a layout device.
`<q>...</q>`	Q (Quote) element. Specifies text to be quoted, with quotation marks for the language being used inserted before and after the quotation.
`<q lang="langcode"...`	LANG (Language) attribute. In the Q element, causes language specific quote marks to be displayed: **en** (English), **fr** (French), **de** (German), **es** (Spanish), **it** (Italian), and so on.
`<q cite="url"...`	CITE attribute. In the Q (Quote) elements, cites a URL where the source of the quote can be found.
`<del>...</del>`	DEL (Delete) element. Specifies that nested text is a deletion. Displayed in graphical browsers as strikeout text.
`<ins>...</ins>`	INS (Insert) element. Specifies that nested text is an insertion.
`<strike>...</strike>`	STRIKE element. Specifies strikeout text. Deprecated in HTML 4; obsolete in HTML 5.
`<s>...</s>`	S (Strikeout) element. A more concise, but less universally supported element that specifies strikeout text. Deprecated in HTML 4; obsolete in HTML 5.
`<sup>...</sup>`	SUP (Superscript) element. Superscripts a nested character or characters.
`<sub>...</sub>`	SUB (Subscript) element. Subscripts a nested character or characters.
`<ul>...</ul>`	UL (Unordered List) element. Creates an unordered (or bulleted) list.

`<a name="anchorname">...</a>`	A destination anchor that can be jumped to from a hypertext link (or jump link).
`<a id="identity">...</a>`	ID element. A destination anchor (or element) that can be jumped to from a jump link.`<a href="#anchorname">...</a>` A jump link that uses a fragment identifier (#*anchorname*) to jump to a destination anchor.
`<a href="#identity">...</a>`	A jump link that uses a fragment identifier (#*identity*) to jump to a destination anchor or element.
`<hr width="n"...`	WIDTH attribute. Sets the HR (Horizontal Rule) element to a width in pixels. A percentage value can also be set (**width="25%"**, for instance).
`<hr align="alignment"...`	ALIGN attribute. In the HR element, sets horizontal alignment. Values are: **left**, **center**, and **right**.
`<hr size="n"...`	SIZE attribute. In the HR element, sets the height (size) of the rule in pixels.
`&amp;`	Named entity code for the ampersand (&) symbol.
`&copy;`	Named entity code for the copyright symbol.
`&reg;`	Named entity codes for the registered symbol.
`&#8482;`	Unicode numeric entity code for the trademark symbol.
`<big>...</big>`	The BIG element. Increases the size of a text string by one step. Obsolete in HTML 5.
`<small>...</small>`	The SMALL element. Decreases the size of a text string by one step. Redefined in HTML 5 as marking text as "small print."
`<ol>...</ol>`	OL (Ordered List) element. Creates an ordered (or numbered) list.
`<li> or <li>...</li>`	LI (List Item) element. Creates a list item in an unordered or ordered list. Can have an implied or real end tag.
`<ol type="numbertype">...`	Specifies the type of number (**I**, **i**, **A**, **a**, or **1**) to be used in an ordered list.
`<ul type="bullettype">...`	Specifies the type of bullet (**disc**, **circle**, or **square**) to be used in an unordered list.
`<tt>...</tt>`	TT (Teletype or Typewriter Text) element. A general-purpose element for marking up computer input or output to be displayed in a monospaced font. Obsolete in HTML 5 due to being anachronistic and semantically unspecific.
`<kbd>...</kbd>`	KBD (Keyboard) element. Indicates keyboard input (normally displayed in a monospaced font).
`<samp>...</samp>`	SAMP (Sample) element. The Sample element. Indicates sample text or output (normally displayed in a monospaced font).
`<code>...</code>`	CODE element. Indicates program or script code (normally displayed in a monospaced font).
`<pre>...</pre>`	PRE (Preformatted Text) element. Displays a text block with all spaces, tabs, and hard returns displayed rather than ignored (normally displayed in a monospaced font).

KEY TERMS

For a review of the key terms bolded in this chapter, visit the Chapter 2 section of this book's Internet Resource Center at **www.emcp.net/html2e**. A complete glossary appears at the end of the book.

ONLINE QUIZ

An online self-check quiz that you can use to test your knowledge of topics covered in this chapter can be found in the Chapter 2 section of this book's Internet Resource Center at **www.emcp.net/html2e**.

REVIEW EXERCISES

This section provides some hands-on review exercises to reinforce the information and material included within this chapter. To do these exercises, save **acad_paper.html** and **cdr-faq.html** as **acad-paper_review.html** and **cdr-faq_review.html** in the **chap02 folder,** and then use those new documents to review using the elements, attributes, and other features that were covered in this chapter:

1. In either review document (or both), delete the META element description and keyword list in the HEAD element, and create a new description and keyword list based on the actual topic and content of the document. Do not use the description and keyword list provided in the chapter, but write your own from scratch.

2. In both review documents, look for additional instances in both case example documents where you can apply any of the inline highlighting elements (I, B, EM, STRONG, CITE, TT, KBD, SAMP, and CODE).

3. For either review document, find a poem that you like, and format it using the BLOCKQUOTE element. Do not worry about context or realism; this is merely to get some practice formatting poetry as a block quote. Write an introductory paragraph that cites the poem and its author, and then insert the poem as a block quote. For a single-stanza poem, nest the entire poem within a paragraph element; for a multi-stanza poem, nest the stanzas inside paragraph elements. Insert line breaks at the end of the individual verse lines.

4. In acad_paper_review.html, add a fifth superscripted note number (following the other four note numbers) anywhere in the text. Do not worry about it being related to the text where you insert it; this is just for practice. Create a mock fifth footnote at the bottom of the page (using the other footnotes as examples). Create a unique destination anchor that brackets the new note number. Turn the superscripted note number into a jump link that jumps to the destination anchor you just created. Finally, create a return link that jumps back from the end of the footnote to the corresponding note number in the document text.

5. In cdr_faq_review.html, create a mock question-and-answer section. Do not worry about it relating to CD-R; any question and answer will do. Format it exactly like the other question-and-answer sections. Finally, add a new option to the document menu (using the question as the link text) that jumps to your new question-and-answer section. Add a return link below the question-and-answer section that jumps back up to the document menu.

6. In cdr_faq_review.html, add a mock nested number list following any of the

answer sections. Do not worry about the content; use dummy text if you wish. Just make sure that you create a numbered list that has at least three levels of nested lists (including a list nested in a list that is nested in a list, in other words). Use the OL element's TYPE attribute to assign a different number-type (or letter-type) to each level of nested list. Use any of these values: **I** (uppercase Roman), **i** (lowercase Roman), **A** (uppercase alphabetic), **a** (lowercase alphabetic), **1** (Arabic numerals).

7. In either review document, experiment further with using the BIG and SMALL elements. Do not worry about context or content. The point is to see what the BIG and SMALL element will do when applied in different circumstances. Try nesting up to four BIG elements to get even bigger text. Try nesting multiple instances of SMALL elements, just to see in your browser why you should not nest SMALL elements.

8. In either review document, experiment with using the HR element's WIDTH, SIZE, and ALIGN attributes. Try different combinations, and then check them out in your browser.

9. In the CD-R FAQ document, experiment further with inserting non-keyboard characters. Look for any additional instances in the document where you think a copyright, registered, or trademark symbol might be appropriate, or write additional example text of your own. Use named entity codes referenced in the chapter to insert the copyright and registered symbols. Use the Unicode numeric entity code referenced in the chapter to insert the trademark symbol. Alternatively, insert a trademark symbol that can be viewed in all browsers, by using the somewhat inelegant solution, or *kludge*, mentioned in the chapter to insert a trademark symbol by superscripting a parenthesized "tm" text string.

   Look at the "Special Characters (ISO 8859-1)" section in Appendix D, choose six characters listed there, and insert them into your review document using their numeric entity codes for the first three and their named entity codes for the second three.

   Look at the "Unicode Characters" section in Appendix D, choose six characters there, and insert them into your review document, using their numeric entity codes for the first three and their named entity codes for the second three. Note if your browser fails to display any of the Unicode characters you have chosen, which means that you do not have a Unicode-compatible font on your system that contains that character.

10. In either review document, experiment with creating a nested bulleted list. Using dummy text, if you wish, create a nested bulleted list with at least three nested levels. A browser automatically displays different bullet characters for different nested bullet list levels, in this sequence, corresponding to the TYPE attributes that assign bullet-types: disc, circle, and square. Using these TYPE attribute values, assign bullet types to each nested bullet level that is different from the default sequence.

WEB-BASED LEARNING ACTIVITIES

The following Web-based learning activities can help you to further extend your learning and shore up your understanding of specific topic-areas:

- Visit the Chapter 2 section of this book's Internet Resource Center at **www.emcp. net/html2e** to find online resources that you can use to further investigate and explore the topics and subjects covered in this chapter. You can also find all Web sites cited in this chapter's notes listed there.

- Further research a specific topic introduced in this chapter using Google (**www.google.com/**), Yahoo! (**www.yahoo.com/**), Wikipedia (**www.wikipedia.org/**), Open Directory Project (**www.dmoz.org/**), or other online sources. Some topics covered in this chapter that you can further research include:
  - Conformance levels: strict, transitional, and frameset
  - DocType switching and quirks, almost standards, and standards modes
  - Using META elements to add metadata to Web pages
  - Why some elements and attributes are deprecated
  - Character sets: ASCII, ISO 8859-1, and Unicode
  - How copyright and fair use law applies to Web pages
  - Style guides for citing online sources
- Use the results of your online research into a particular topic to:
  - Write a review to be read in front of your classmates
  - Write a report that can be read by your classmates
  - Design a diagram, chart, or other graphic that illustrates a key topic or concept
  - Create a presentation using PowerPoint (or other software) that can be shared with your classmates
  - Give a stand-up presentation to your classmates
  - Team up with one or more classmates to give a group presentation to your classmates

PROJECTS

These projects can be done in class, in a computer lab, or at home. Use the skills you have developed in this and the previous chapter to create any of the following projects. In your project, demonstrate the correct use of the following HTML features covered in this chapter:

- DocType declaration, declaring conformation to the transitional definition of HTML 4.01.
- META element, declaring the document's character set as UTF-8.
- META element, specifying a project description.
- META element, specifying a list of keywords and/or keyphrases associated with the project.
- I and B elements or EM and STRONG elements. Alternately, use the CITE element in place of the I element.
- One or a combination of the following: 1) One or more links that jump to named anchor links within the page, 2) one or more superscripted footnote links that jump to a footnote at the bottom of the page, or 3) a numbered list or outline.
- A copyright statement using the named or numeric entity code for the copyright symbol.
- Other required or common elements (HTML, HEAD, TITLE, BODY, H1, H2, P, UL, ADDRESS, etc.)

Project 1. Format a paper or essay you have authored as an online document.

Take the lessons learned in this chapter and apply them to formatting a paper or essay that you have written so it can be displayed as an online document. Some guidelines for completing this assignment follow:

1. In your word processor, save your paper or essay under another name as a text file in this chapter's folder (chap02). For instance, you might save it as mypaper.html.

(Note: Do not save your paper or essay as an HTML file in your word processor—that is likely to generate a bunch of unnecessary and redundant HTML codes, sometimes referred to as spaghetti code.*)*

2. Using the example online paper you created in this chapter, in your text editor, tag the text file you saved with the appropriate HTML elements, including the top-level HTML elements, a title element, heading elements, paragraph elements, bulleted or numbered list elements, block quote elements, and so on. No untagged text should be nested directly inside your BODY element. Optionally, also add a DocType declaration and META elements specifying your document's character set, a description of your page, and a list of keywords.

3. Scan your document's text for any special characters or symbols that have been carried over from your word processing document. Replace them with appropriate entity codes (see Appendix B), or type a substitute (replacing an e character with a grave accent, for instance, with a simple *e* character).

4. Look for instances in your original word processing document where you included italicized, bolded, or underlined text. Tag the same text in your text file using the I and B elements (or the EM and STRONG elements). Decide whether you want to carry over any underlined text—a better solution may be to simply format underlined text as italicized text.

5. Look for instances where you have included footnotes in your document. Use the SUP element to superscript footnote numbers and create hypertext links that jump to any footnotes listed at the bottom of your page.

6. Use the ADDRESS element to create an address block at the bottom of your page's BODY element. At minimum, type your name and an e-mail address. Sign up for a free Web-mail address that you can use here, if you do not want to expose your regular e-mail address to spammers.

Project 2. Create a Frequently Asked Questions page.

Using the FAQ page you worked with in this chapter as an example, create an FAQ page on a topic or subject about which you have some expertise. Create a list of questions and then write answers to them. Create a menu at the top of the page (listing only the questions) that uses hypertext links to jump to the corresponding question-and-answer sections. Insert return links following each question-and-answer section that jump back to the menu. Add an address block to the bottom of your page.

Project 3. Write instruction steps for a computer or application procedure you are familiar with.

Create a Web page that features instruction steps that will give you an opportunity to use the TT, KBD, SAMP, CODE, and PRE elements in appropriate circumstances, as well as the I and B (or EM and STRONG) elements.

Project 4. Create a poetry page.

If you write poetry, create a Web page to show off your poems. Insert the poems inside block quote elements to indent them from the margin. Nest stanzas inside paragraph elements and insert BR elements to break the verse lines. Use any other elements or attributes you have learned to use.

CHAPTER 3
Working with Fonts, Colors, and Backgrounds

PERFORMANCE OBJECTIVES

- Change the size of fonts for elements and text.
- Change the face of fonts for elements and text.
- Change the color of fonts, text, and links.
- Use background colors and images in Web pages.
- Set font characteristics and element backgrounds using styles.

In the first two chapters, you learned how to use basic and common features of HTML to create typical Web pages. In this chapter, you learn how to change the appearance of your Web pages by changing font sizes and faces, applying color changes to fonts and links, and using background colors and images.

USING THE EXAMPLE FILES

You will find the example files for this chapter located in the **chap03** folder within your working folder. You should save any HTML files you create in this chapter in that folder. If you have yet to create a working folder, return to "Using the Example Files" in Chapter 1 for instructions on how to do that.

CASE EXAMPLE: UPDATING THE APPEARANCE OF A PERSONAL WEB PAGE

In this example, you revise the personal Web page you created in Chapter 1, *Creating a Basic Web Page*, by using fonts, colors, and backgrounds to make it more attractive and visually appealing.

"Johnny Watson made some changes to his personal Web page, adding a DocType statement, a META element declaring the character set his page uses, and two other META elements that provide a description and keyword list that search engines and directories can use to index or list his page. He also made a few other minor changes to the text in his page but not to the HTML codes. His friends like the content and links he included in his page but have commented that it might look better if he varied the size and face of his fonts and incorporated colors and backgrounds into his page's design. When Johnny Watson first created his personal Web page, he was still learning HTML and had not learned yet how to make font or color changes. He has since learned more about using these features and wants to apply them to update the appearance of his personal Web page. "

To get started working with this example:

1. Run your text editor, and open **watson2_ex.html** from the chap03 folder in your working folder or working disk.
2. Save watson2_ex.html as **watson2.html** in the chap03 folder.
3. Run your browser, and open **watson2.html** from the chap03 folder.

If you need more guidance on opening and saving an HTML file in your text editor and opening and previewing it in your Web browser, see "Opening an HTML File in Your Text Editor" and "Saving and Previewing Your HTML File" in Chapter 2, *Working with Online Documents*.

CHANGING FONT SIZES

In HTML, the FONT element can be used to change the appearance of nested text, including the size, color, and face of the **font** in which text is displayed. In this section, you will focus on the first of these features, changing the size of the font used to display nested text. In the FONT element, the SIZE attribute is used to change the size of nested text.

Using Absolute Font Sizes

The FONT element's SIZE attribute enables you to specify seven different absolute font sizes by using an integer value from 1 to 7. An **absolute font size** will not change, even if the default base font size is changed. For instance, the following sets an absolute font size of 5 for the nested text:

```
<font size="5">nested text</font>
```

Figure 3.1 shows the seven font sizes in relation to the default sizes of a level-one heading and paragraph text.

The HTML file shown in Figure 3.1 is available with the example files for this chapter. To look for yourself, open **fontsizes.html** in your browser from the **chap03** folder. After viewing it, click the Back button to return to watson2.html in your browser. If the file was opened in a new window (the Back button is not available), just close the window, which should bring watson2.html back to the foreground.

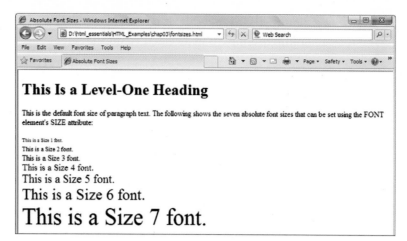

FIGURE 3.1 • Seven absolute font sizes can be set in HTML.

As shown in Figure 3.1, two of the font sizes (sizes 1 and 2) are smaller than the default size of paragraph text, one (size 3) is the same size, and four (sizes 4 through 7) are larger.

"Johnny Watson discovered that by using the FONT element, he can set a font size that is one size larger than the default font size of a level-one heading. He decided to take advantage of this to increase the size of the initial letters in each word of his level-one heading."

action

Use the FONT element's SIZE attribute to increase the initial letters in the level-one heading to size 7 (see Figure 3.2):

```
<h1><font size="7">S</font>ports, <font size="7">G</font>
ardening, and <font size="7">O</font>ther <font size="7">I
</font>nterests</h1>
```

size 7 fonts

FIGURE 3.2 • The initial letters of the level-one heading are set to a size 7 font.

> Johnny liked the result of increasing the size of the initial letters in his level-one heading so much, he decided to do the same with his level-two heading.

action

Use the FONT element's SIZE attribute to increase the initial letters in the level-two heading to size 6 (see Figure 3.3):

```
<h2 align="center"><font size="6">B</font>iography,
<font size="6">I</font>nterests, and <font size="6">F
</font>riends</h2>
```

FIGURE 3.3 • The initial letters of the level-two heading are set to a size 6 font.

Using Relative Font Sizes

Alternatively, you can set font sizes relative to the default base font size. **Relative font sizes** are adjusted, up or down, if the default base font size is increased or decreased. A relative font size is indicated by a "+" or "-" character in front of the SIZE attribute integer value. For instance, the following increases the font size of text one size above the base font size:

```
<font size="+1">nested text</font>
```

> Johnny wants to increase the font size of the two in-context hypertext links that are in his introductory paragraph. He has decided to try using relative font size changes to do this.

action

Set relative font sizes that will increase the size of text nested inside of the two hypertext links in the introductory paragraph (see Figure 3.4):

```
<p>Welcome to my home page! My name is Johnny Watson and I'm a
big nut about two things: <a href="http://www.espn.com/">
<font size="+1">sports</font></a> and
<a href="http://www.bbc.co.uk/gardening/"><font size="+1">
gardening</font></a>!
```

size="+1"

FIGURE 3.4 • A relative font size increases the size of text relative to the default base font size.

In the previous chapter, you used the BIG and SMALL elements to increase and decrease the size of nested text. At first glance, a BIG element and a FONT element with a `size="+1"` attribute seem to do the same thing, but that is not true.

A BIG element increases the font size of nested text relative to the font size of the current element. A FONT element with a `size="+1"` attribute increases the size of nested text one size relative to the size of the base font, which is the default font size of the BODY element. The BODY element font size is inherited by text-level elements such as paragraphs, list elements, and block quotes.

action

Add a relative font size change to the HTML file, and review its effect in your browser:

1. Add an H2 element that brackets both a BIG element and a FONT element with `size="+1"`:

```
<h1><font size="7">S</font>ports, <font size="7">G</font>
ardening</font>, and <font size="7">O</font>ther <font size="7">
I</font>nterests</h1>
<h2>by <big>Johnny</big> <font size="+1">Watson</font></h2>
</div>
```

BIG element

size="+1"

FIGURE 3.5 • A relative font size increases the size of text relative to the base font size.

2. Review the result in Figure 3.5 and in your browser. Notice that, relative to the H2 element ("by"), the BIG element ("Johnny") is displayed in a larger font, but the

FONT element with a +1 relative font size ("Watson") is actually smaller than the H2 element in which it is nested. The difference is because a BIG element resizes text relative to the font size of the element in which it is nested (the H2 element, in this case), whereas a relative font size resizes text relative to the font size of the base font.

3. When you are finished reviewing the example in your browser, delete the text and codes you just added.

CHANGING THE FONT FACE

The FONT element's FACE attribute lets you specify a **font face** (or typeface) or a comma-delimited list of font faces to be used in displaying nested text.

Understanding Font Availability

You might see some neat font on the Web and think you would like to use that font in your Web page. You download and install it, reference it in your Web page, and it works! You publish your page to the Web, and then ask all your friends to check out your page, adding as your final words, "Be sure to check out the snazzy font I'm using!" One by one, however, your friends report that all they can see is the same font that is displayed on almost every Web page (Times New Roman or Times).

The problem is that your friends, unlike yourself, have not downloaded and installed the font you are using, and thus do not have it available on their systems. For a font to be displayed in a Web page using the FONT element's FACE attribute, it must be available on a user's system. Just because a particular font is available on your system does not mean that others will have the same font available on their systems, and no one font is guaranteed to be available on all systems. When specifying fonts for display in your Web page, you need to stick with specifying the most commonly available fonts, avoiding less commonly available fonts you may have installed on your system or can download from the Web. See "Specifying a Font List" a little later in this chapter for a rundown of the more commonly available fonts.

Specifying a Single Font Face

To specify that a particular font face, if available, should be used to display an element, you specify the name of the font as the value for the FACE attribute.

Johnny Watson wants to change the look of his heading-level elements from using the default serif font that browsers normally use for heading-level elements to a sans serif font. He wants to add more visual variety to his page and believes that a sans serif font will give his headings a cleaner and more contemporary look because it lacks the strokes, or serifs, that accentuate the letterforms of serif fonts. He has decided to use the Arial font because it is one of the more common sans serif fonts. He understands that it might not be available on every system. He is willing to have a different font displayed on some systems than the font he has specified. The font switch would be a case of graceful degradation that should not pose accessibility problems.

He has also removed the font size changes he added earlier to his level-one and level-two headings to get a cleaner, less busy look. 99

Use the FONT element to specify that the level-one and level-two heading elements should be displayed in an Arial font, if available:

1. Delete the font size changes that you added earlier, and set a single FONT element that sets an Arial font for the H1 element.

```
<h1><font face="Arial">Sports, Gardening, and Other Interests
</font></h1>
```

2. Do the same for the H2 element (see Figure 3.6):

```
<h2 align="center"><font face="Arial">Biography, Interests, and
Friends</font></h2>
```

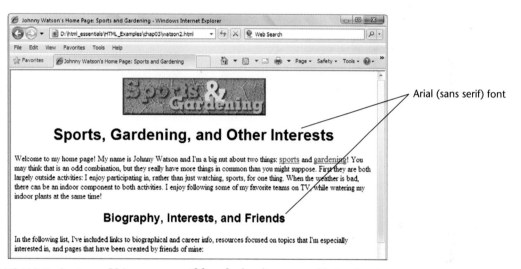

Arial (sans serif) font

FIGURE 3.6 • Using a sans serif font for headings can add visual variety to a page.

The FONT element is an inline element and, thus, should always be nested inside of a block element and should not have block elements nested inside of it. For instance, you should *not* apply a font face change to the H2 element like this:

```
<font face="Arial"><h2>Biography, Interests, and Friends</h2>
</font>
```

Specifying a Font List

The problem with only specifying a single font face is that there are many systems that may not have that font installed. The Arial font should be present on almost every Windows system, but many Macintosh and Linux users might not have that font. To get around that problem, HTML enables you to specify a comma-delimited list of fonts, or **font list**. The second listed font can be displayed if the first font is not available, the third listed font if the second font is not available, and so on.

66 Johnny Watson wants to specify a list of fonts, rather than just a single font, to increase the chances that one of the listed fonts will be available on a user's system. 99

 Specify a list of fonts to be used to display the level-one and level-two headings:

1. Specify a list of fonts for the H1 element:

```
<h1><font face="Arial, Geneva, Helvetica">Sports, Gardening and
Other Interests</font></h1>
```

2. Make the same change for the H2 element.

Arial, Times New Roman, and Courier New are **TrueType fonts**, which were originally introduced in Windows as replacements for Adobe's **PostScript fonts**: Helvetica, Times, and Courier. Later, Apple introduced their own set of TrueType replacements: Geneva, New York, and Monaco.

NOTE — The Geneva and Monaco fonts are built into Macintosh OS X, but Times New Roman has replaced New York as the default "text" font on that system.

Some earlier browsers treat font-face names as case-sensitive. When specifying font-face names, you should type them using any initial uppercase characters that are included in the font-face name. For instance, you should type **Arial** and not **arial** as the FACE attribute value.

If PostScript fonts are not available on a system, current browsers will substitute TrueType equivalents for Times and Helvetica in a font list. You cannot rely on that, however, for other PostScript fonts or in many earlier browsers. For instance, both Internet Explorer 8 and Mozilla Firefox 3 substitute a lower-quality bitmap font for Courier, if PostScript fonts are not available. Besides Times, Helvetica, and Courier, other commonly available PostScript fonts include Palatino, New Century Schoolbook, Bookman, Avant Garde, and Zapf Chancery.

If you are targeting a general audience, you should list a broadly available Windows font first, even if creating your page on a Macintosh, since the vast majority of users on the Web are using Windows, while listing a broadly available Macintosh font second. On the other hand, if you are primarily targeting Macintosh users, you might lead with a broadly available Macintosh font followed by one that is broadly available on Windows. A PostScript font should only be listed as a final fallback option for those few systems that might only have PostScript fonts available.

Table 3.1 shows the names of some of the most commonly available fonts for Windows, Macintosh OS X, or UNIX/Linux systems.

TABLE 3.1 • Fonts Commonly Available on Different Systems

System	Most Available Fonts
Windows	**Serif:** Palatino Linotype, Georgia, Sylfaen, Times New Roman **Sans Serif:** Microsoft Sans Serif, Verdana, Arial, Tahoma, Franklin Gothic Medium, Trebuchet MS, Lucida Sans Unicode **Monospace:** Courier New, Lucida Console **Display:** Arial Black, Comic Sans MS, Impact **Narrow:** Arial Narrow
Macintosh	**Serif:** Georgia, Times New Roman, Times **Sans Serif:** Arial, Helvetica, Verdana, Lucida Grande, Lucida Grande, Geneva, Helvetica Neue, Trebuchet MS, Futura, Gil Sans **Monospace:** Monaco, Courier, Courier New, Andale Mon **Display:** Arial Black, Comic Sans MS, Impact **Narrow:** Arial Narrow

TABLE 3.1 • Fonts Commonly Available on Different Systems—Continued

System	Most Available Fonts
UNIX/Linux	**Serif:** Century Schoolbook L, URW Bookman L, URW Pallido L, Bitstream Charter **Sans Serif:** URW Gothic L, Nimbus Sans L, DejaVu Sans **Monospace:** DejaVu Sans Mono, Nimbus Mono L, Bitstream Vera Sans Mono **Display:** Arial Black, Impact, Comic Sans MS

Note: PostScript fonts are *italicized*. Fonts are listed in order of their availability and were available on at least 88 percent of the systems for which they are listed, with the exception of the Display fonts for Linux, which were available on 58 to 54 percent of Linux systems. For an ongoing survey of the availability of fonts on Windows, Macintosh, and Linux systems, see the CSS font sampler and survey at **www.codestyle.org/css/font-family/**.

You cannot rely on any one font being available on all systems. Any font face you specify using the FONT element's FACE attribute is a suggestion only that may or may not be displayed on someone else's system.

You should also realize when using uncommon fonts that different fonts can have the same name. Thus, the Carumba font installed on your system might be an entirely different font than the Carumba font installed on someone else's system. This is another good reason to stick to using only commonly available fonts in your Web pages.

TROUBLE *spot*

Different fonts of the same size can have a different x-height. The **x-height** is the height of the lowercase letters in a font (generally the height of the lowercase "x"). A font with a larger x-height will take up more horizontal space on a line than another font of the same size but with a smaller x-height. This is because its lowercase characters are not only taller but also wider than those in a font with a lower x-height. The same applies to fonts displayed in different weights (lighter or bolder).

Figures 3.7 and 3.8 show a series of sans serif and **serif fonts** commonly available on Windows systems. They each show a series of different fonts, one sans serif and the other serif, set at 28 pixels, arranged according to how much horizontal space they take up. To see these files for yourself, open **fontfaces-sans.html** and **fontfaces-serif.html** in your browser from the chap03 folder. Only fonts available on your system, however, will display in your browser. For instance, Corbel, Candara, Calibri, Cambria, and Constantia are fonts included with Windows Vista, but the default text font might be displayed instead on systems on which those fonts are not available.

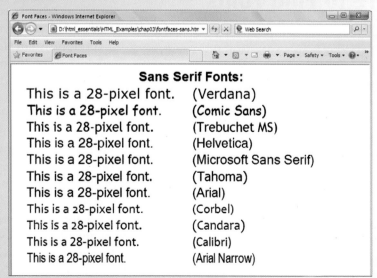

FIGURE 3.7 • Fonts the same size can have different x-heights or weights, which can affect the amount of horizontal space the fonts use.

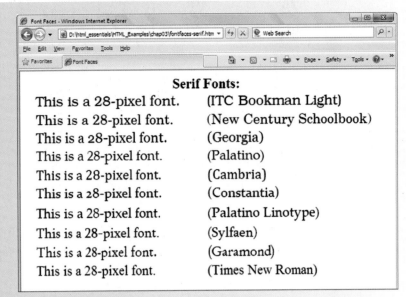

FIGURE 3.8 • Fonts of the same size can have different x-heights or weights, which can affect the amount of horizontal space the fonts use.

Notice that the amount of horizontal space occupied by these fonts can vary significantly, even though they are the same size (28 pixels high) and contain the same text. When specifying a list of fonts, be aware that while your preferred font (Arial, for instance) may not cause an H1 heading to wrap, another font in your font list with a larger x-height (Verdana, for instance) may cause the heading to wrap to a second line.

Specifying a Generic Font-Family Name

Generic font-family names (serif, sans-serif, monospace, cursive, and fantasy) are defined as part of the CSS specifications, but can also be used with the FONT element's FACE attribute. However, because generic font-family names used with the FACE attri-

Where to Find Fonts

Starting in 1996, Microsoft provided a selection of free TrueType core fonts for the Web that Windows, Macintosh, and UNIX/Linux users can download and install if they are not already available on their systems: Andale Mono, Arial, Arial Black, Comic Sans MS, Courier New, Georgia, Impact, Times New Roman, Trebuchet MS, Verdana, and Webdings (Windows only). Many Microsoft applications also install these fonts. As a result, these fonts are widely available on the Web and should be available on most Windows systems.

Although Microsoft ceased making these fonts available for download from their site in 2002, third parties were allowed to continue making them available. Windows and Macintosh users can download

any of these fonts not currently on their systems at:
web.nickshanks.com/typography/corefonts
Linux users can download these fonts at:
corefonts.sourceforge.net/

Additionally, Microsoft included a selection of fonts with Windows Vista that are optimized for display on the Web: Calibri, Cambria, Candara, Consolas, Constantia, and Corbel. Non-Vista Windows users can get these fonts by downloading and installing the free PowerPoint Viewer 2007 from the Microsoft Download Center (search for "PowerPoint Viewer 2007"):
www.microsoft.com/downloads/

For additional links to font resources on the Web, see the Chapter 3 section of this book's Internet Resource Center at **www.emcp.net/html2e**.

bute might not be supported by earlier browsers and are not part of the HTML 4.01 specification, you should include a generic font-family name only at the end of a font list as a stop-gap in case none of your listed fonts are available on a user's system.

> Johnny Watson discovered that most current browsers also support using a generic font-family name in a list of font names for the FACE attribute. He has decided to include the sans serif generic font-family name in his font list to increase the chances that a browser will display a sans serif, rather than a serif, font.

Include a generic font-family name at the end of the document's font lists to increase the chances of a sans serif font being displayed on a user's system:

1. Add a generic font-family name, sans serif, to the end of the font list for the H1 element:

```
<h1><font face="Arial, Geneva, Helvetica, sans-serif">Sports,
Gardening, and Other Interests</font></h1>
```

2. Make the same change for the H2 element.

Of the generic font-family names, only the **serif**, **sans serif**, and **monospace** names are consistently supported by browsers. Browsers that support using these names generally display a Times New Roman or Times font when a serif generic font-family name is specified, Arial or Helvetica when a sans serif generic font-family name is specified, and Courier New or Courier when a monospace generic font-family name is specified. The other generic font-family names are inconsistently supported by browsers and should be avoided.

Using Sans Serif and Serif Fonts

Most browsers use a serif font for displaying text, generally some variant of Times or Times New Roman. The Times font is so named because it was first used to print columnar text in the London *Times* newspaper. A **serif font**, such as used in this book's paragraph text, has strokes (serifs) that accentuate the ends of the letterforms, whereas a **sans serif font**, such as is used in this book's headings, lacks any accentuating strokes. Serifs make larger amounts of a smaller-sized font, such as paragraph text, for instance, easier to read and scan because the serifs guide your eyes along as you read. For that reason, books and newspapers generally use a serif font for body text that needs to be read for content, and a sans serif font only in headings and display type.

Designers, on the other hand, often use sans serif fonts in advertising copy, especially where the text also serves as a design element, but also to create a contrast with serif fonts used in a magazine's text columns. Some magazines have gone to printing body text in a sans serif font, to give their pages a look they consider more modern and stylish; when that is done, however, the space between the text lines, called the leading, is usually also increased to help make the sans serif body text easier to read.

Web page designers also sometimes opt for using sans serif fonts for body text (paragraph text), for much the same reasons print designers do, because it gives their pages more of a "designed" (and less "bookish") look. This is fine in a shorter page, such as Johnny Watson's personal page, which contains less than two screens worth of text.

However, if you are presenting larger amounts of text that need to be read for comprehension, a serif font is probably the better choice. Crystal Porter, for instance, would not want to present her online academic paper in a sans serif font, not simply because a serif font is what is expected but also because a sans serif font would make her text more difficult to read and comprehend.

Compare reading the text of the *Declaration of Independence* in a serif and a sans serif font:
1. Open **textcompare.html** in your browser from the chap03 folder (see Figure 3.9).

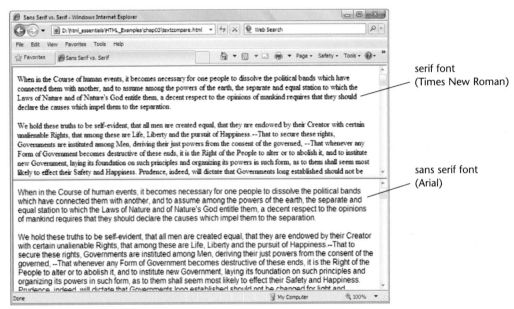

serif font (Times New Roman)

sans serif font (Arial)

FIGURE 3.9 • According to one school of thought, text displayed in a serif font is easier to read and comprehend than text displayed in a sans serif font.

2. The two versions are displayed in separate frames. Read the text in each frame. You can grab the divider line between the two frames with the mouse pointer and pull it up or down to display more text in either frame.
3. Understanding that you are making an entirely subjective and unscientific judgment, make note of which of the two fonts you feel is the most readable.

Visit the Internet Resource Center. To find online resources that discuss fonts, typography, and readability, go to the Chapter 3 section of this book's Internet Resource Center at www.emcp.net/html2e.

WORKING WITH COLORS

The FONT element's COLOR attribute is used to specify a **foreground color** to be displayed for nested text. A font color can be assigned by using either a **color name** or a **hexadecimal RGB code**.

Using Color Names

These are the 16 standard color names that can be used as values for the FONT element's COLOR attribute: white, black, gray, silver, white, maroon, red, fuchsia, green, lime, olive, yellow, navy, blue, teal, and aqua. These color names are derived from the 16 colors available on a 16-color VGA display.

" Johnny Watson's friends told him that, other than his banner graphic, his page is a drab affair that could stand to be touched up with a little color. Johnny learned that he can use the FONT element's COLOR attribute to specify any of 16 standard color names. "

Use the FONT element's COLOR attribute to assign foreground colors to the text nested inside the H1 and H2 elements:

1. Specify that text nested inside the H1 element should be displayed in a blue color:

```
<h1><font color="blue" face="Arial, Geneva, Helvetica,
sans-serif">Sports, Gardening, and Other Interests</font></h1>
```

2. Specify that text nested inside the H2 element should be displayed in a red color (see Figure 3.10):

```
<h2 align="center"><font color="red" face="Arial, Geneva,
Helvetica, sans-serif">Biography, Interests, and Friends</font>
</h2>
```

FIGURE 3.10 • A Web page need not be a purely black-and-white affair.

As shown in Figure 3.10, the text nested inside the H1 element is now displayed in a blue color, and the text nested inside the H2 element is now displayed in a red color. An example file, colornames.html, is included in the chap03 folder with the other example files for this chapter. You can open and view **colornames.html** in your browser, as shown in Figure 3.11.

FIGURE 3.11 • There are 16 standard color names that can be used to specify colors in Web pages.

NOTE

The CSS 2.1 specification added orange to the list of standard color names. To create a valid HTML 4.01 or XHTML 1.0 document, however, the orange color name should only be applied using CSS styles and not using the FONT element's COLOR attribute. See the next section, "Using Hexadecimal RGB Codes," for ways to set many more colors than the standard color names provide, including orange.

Most current browsers actually support many more than the standard 16 color names specified in the HTML 4 specifications. There are 140 color names that date back to the beginnings of the Web—they were part of the X-Windows system under UNIX. Many current browsers still recognize these same color names. Because none of these color names are included in the HTML 4.01 or XHTML 1.0 specifications, you should avoid using them in Web pages.

You do not need to use non-standard color names, however, to make use of a much wider selection of colors in your Web pages. Any of the non-standard color names can also be specified using a hexadecimal RGB code, which all browsers that recognize colors support.

Using Hexadecimal RGB Codes

The 16 color names are admittedly somewhat limiting. To display a color different from those specified by the standard color names, you can use a hexadecimal RGB code. A hexadecimal RGB code states the RGB (red-green-blue) values for a color in hexadecimal numbers, in the following format:

```
color="#rrggbb"
```

The hash character (#) indicates that the following six characters correspond to three hexadecimal color values (*rr*, *gg*, and *bb*) that together represent a specific RGB color value.

The U.K. keyboard for the Macintosh does not have the "#" (hash) character at the Shift+3 position but has the "£" (British pound) symbol instead. To insert the "#" character using a U.K. keyboard, just press Option+3 (or Alt+3).

The **hexadecimal numbering system** uses a 16-number base (0, 1, 2, 3, 4, 5, 6, 7, 8, 9, A, B, C, D, E, and F), as opposed to the 10-number base that forms the decimal numbering system. Programmers tend to prefer using hexadecimal numbers because up to 256 numerical values can be stated using only 2 characters, whereas using a decimal

Hex = Dec	Hex = Dec	Hex = Dec	Hex = Dec
0 = 0	4 = 4	8 = 8	C = 12
1 = 1	5 = 5	9 = 9	D = 13
2 = 2	6 = 6	A = 10	E = 14
3 = 3	7 = 7	B = 11	F = 15

numbering system 3 digits are required. Table 3.2 shows the 16 hexadecimal numbers and their decimal equivalents.

To derive the decimal value of a hexadecimal number, just apply the following formula:

$$(h^1 \times 16) + h^2 = d$$

The variable h^1 corresponds to the decimal value of the first hexadecimal digit, h^2 corresponds to the decimal value of the second hexadecimal digit (as shown previously in Table 3.2), and d equals the number's decimal value. In other words, the decimal value of AD (where the hexadecimal numbers A and D are equal to decimal values of 10 and 13, respectively) can be calculated in this fashion:

$$(10 \times 16) + 13 = 173$$

By using hexadecimal RGB codes, you can set 256 different values for each RGB color component, meaning that a total of 16,777,216 (16.7 million) separate colors (256 × 256 × 256) can be set using hexadecimal RGB codes.

A number of sites on the Web list the hexadecimal codes for the non-standard color names supported by most current browsers. Although you should not use these color names, you can use them to identify a particular color that you like, and then use its listed hexadecimal code to apply it to your Web page. Thus, instead of using the non-standard DarkGoldenRod color name to specify a gold-like color, just use its hexadecimal equivalent (#b8860b). There are many sites on the Web that provide color charts that show the non-standard color names along with their corresponding hexadecimal RGB codes.

Visit the Internet Resource Center. To find a selection of color charts, color pickers, and other color resources, including sites that list the hexadecimal color codes for all 140 non-standard color names, go to the Chapter 3 section of this book's Internet Resource Center at **www.emcp.net/html2e.**

Use hexadecimal RGB codes to change the colors of the level-one and level-two heading elements:

1. Use the hexadecimal RGB code, **#b8860b**, to change the color of the level-one heading to a color corresponding to the non-standard "DarkGoldenRod" color:

```
<h1><font color="#b8860b" face="Arial, Geneva, Helvetica,
sans-serif">Sports, Gardening, and Other Interests</font></h1>
```

2. Use the hexadecimal RGB code, **#2e8b57**, to change the color of the level-two heading to a color corresponding to the non-standard "SeaGreen" color (see Figure 3.12):

```
<h2 align="center"><font color="#2e8b57" face="Arial, Geneva,
Helvetica, sans-serif">Biography, Interests, and Friends</font>
</h2>
```

color="#b8860b"
("DarkGoldenRod")

color="#238b57"
("SeaGreen")

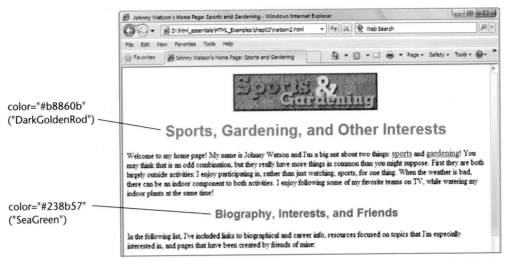

FIGURE 3.12 • Use hexadecimal color codes to set colors other than those specified by the 16 standard color names.

A common mistake when setting colors using hexadecimal RGB codes is to omit the # character at the start of the code. Internet Explorer and Safari will let you get away with doing this if setting the color using the FONT element but not if using a style. Firefox, however, will not apply the color, whether using the FONT element or a style, if the # character is missing.

While the orange color name is available for use when setting colors using styles, as of CSS 2.1, it is not included in the 16 standard color names that are defined for use with the FONT element's COLOR attribute. You can, however, specify the same color as the orange color name using hexadecimal color codes: **<font color="#ffa500">**.

Using Web-Safe Colors

Web-safe colors are colors that will be displayed without dithered on systems only capable of displaying 256 colors. Although most users currently surfing the Web can display colors from a palette of at least 16.7 million colors (also known as a True Color palette), a small number of users are still using graphic cards or monitors that limit them to 256 or fewer colors. **Dithering** is the adjustment of the colors in adjacent pixels so that they appear to the eye to be a single color. When successful, dithering realistically reproduces a color that is not otherwise available; when unsuccessful, it produces a noticeably splotchy or speckled color that may only remotely resemble the desired color.

The **Web-safe palette** was originally developed by Netscape and is sometimes called the "Netscape palette" because of that. It contains 216 colors that are guaranteed to be displayable on virtually all computer systems without having to be dithered. The Web-safe palette is composed entirely of colors with hexadecimal RGB codes that include only these hexadecimal numbers: 00, 33, 66, 99, CC, and FF. For instance, the hexadecimal RGB code of #996600 produces a color that is somewhat darker than the "DarkGoldenRod" color used previously but which still produces a recognizably "gold" color.

Use the #996600 hexadecimal code to apply a Web-safe "gold" color to the H1 element (see Figure 3.13):

```
<h1><font color="#996600" face="Arial, Geneva, Helvetica,
sans-serif">Sports, Gardening and Other Interests</font></h1>
```

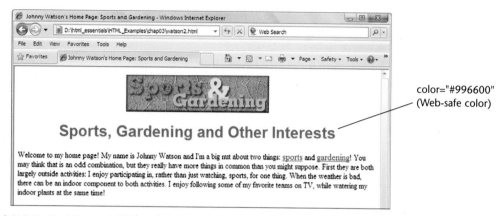

color="#996600"
(Web-safe color)

FIGURE 3.13 • A Web-safe RGB color, including only the 00, 33, 66, 99, CC, or FF hexadecimal numerical values, will not be dithered on a 256-color system.

Appendix E, *Web-Safe Colors Chart*, shows all the Web-safe colors along with the hexadecimal RGB codes you need to use to apply them to your Web pages. Using the chart, choose a Web-safe color and apply it to your document's H2 element. Be sure to check out the result in your browser. If you do not like how your first choice looks, try another one. Experiment with setting different Web-safe colors for your H1 element as well. Repeat until you are satisfied with your choices of Web-safe colors for the H2 and H1 elements.

You can also find an HTML file, **colorchart.html**, included with the example files in the chap03 folder. Open this file in your browser to see all of the Web-safe colors along with their corresponding hexadecimal RGB codes.

Setting Text, Link, and Background Colors

The BODY element's TEXT, LINK, VLINK, ALINK, and BGCOLOR attributes enable you to set colors for your page's text, unvisited links, visited links, activated links, and background. Unvisited and visited links connect to sites you have not visited and sites you have already visited. An activated link's color is displayed when the mouse button is held down on a link. Usually, unvisited links are colored blue, and visited links are colored purple, for instance.

NOTE

If you click a link to access another page and then click the Back button to return to the first page, the link will be displayed as an active link in Internet Explorer, until you click or hold the mouse down on something else. In other browsers, however, the link will be displayed as a visited link after returning to the page.

Test applying the TEXT, LINK, VLINK, ALINK, and BGCOLOR attributes to the BODY element:

1. Use a combination of color names and hexadecimal RGB codes to set colors for text, links, and the page background:

```
<body text="navy" link="#ff6600" vlink="#996699" alink="blue"
bgcolor="#ffffcc">
```

2. Save your file in your text editor, and refresh its display in your browser.

3. Click the **My biography** link, which will open a dummy page (mybio.html). Click the **Back** button to return to watson2.html.

4. Hold the mouse button down on the **My resume** link. You should now see the page's text, unvisited links, visited link (My biography), activated link (My resume), and background displayed in the colors you set in step 1 (see Figure 3.14).

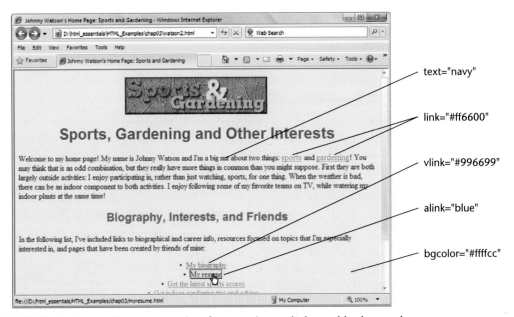

FIGURE 3.14 • You can set colors for a page's text, links, and background.

Figure 3.14 shows the result of the action as it would occur if a visitor had not previously visited any of the linked pages. Since you have worked with this same example in Chapter 1, some of the other links might also be displayed in your browser as visited links. This shows that while you can specify a color for visited links, you cannot specify which links have been visited since that is controlled by each visitor's browsing history.

If you wish to see the same result in your browser as what is shown in Figure 3.14, you have the option of deleting your browsing history, which will revert all links back to being unvisited, and then repeat the previous action steps. In Internet Explorer 7 and 8, select Tools and Delete Browsing History. In Safari 3, select History and Clear History. Doing the same in Firefox 3 is a little more complicated: select Tools and Options, click the Privacy tab and the Settings Button (under Private Data), uncheck all but the Browsing History check box, click OK, and then click the Clear Now button.

Whenever you set a foreground color for your page's text, you should also set a **background color** as well, if only a white color. That is because many browsers let users also set foreground and background colors in their browser preferences. If you only set the foreground color, your foreground color could clash or lack contrast with a user's background color. You could even end up with navy blue text displayed against a navy blue background.

You also should be mindful when setting foreground and background colors that some people have **color-vision deficiencies** that make it difficult to distinguish between certain color combinations. About ten percent of males have some form of color-vision deficiency. Some people see red text as yellow text, for instance, whereas others may have trouble distinguishing between red and green. Others may see blue text as yellow text.

Make sure that you have sufficient tonal contrast between foreground and background colors in your pages to assist people with color-vision deficiencies. Do not rely simply on a color contrast, especially between red and green or blue and yellow, to distinguish foreground and background colors.

Visit the Internet Resource Center. To find resources on the Web that discuss color-vision deficiency and Web design, go to the Chapter 3 section of this book's Internet Resource Center at **www.emcp.net/html2e**.

USING A BACKGROUND IMAGE

The BODY element's BACKGROUND attribute lets you assign a **background image** to your page. Using a background image can add to the visual appeal of your page; however, it also can make your page more difficult to access and read, if the image is busy or high contrast, or if its colors clash or do not provide sufficient contrast with your page's foreground and link colors. An example background image, **back_light.jpg**, is included with this chapter's example files.

Displaying a Background Image

The BODY element's BACKGROUND attribute is used to display a background image in a Web page. Its value is a URL or file name of an image, which can be any of the same kinds of image formats that are normally used for displaying inline images, including JPEG (.jpg), GIF (.gif), and PNG (.png) images. A background image is normally a smaller image, often less than 100 pixels wide or high, which when tiled, or repeated, will seamlessly fill a browser's background.

Use the BODY element's BACKGROUND attribute to assign a background image to your page (see Figure 3.15):

```
<body text="navy" link="#ff6600" vlink="#996699" alink="blue"
bgcolor="#ffffcc" background="back_light.jpg">
```

background=
"back_light.jpg"

FIGURE 3.15 • A carefully chosen background image can further enhance the appearance of a Web page.

Notice that both a background color and a background image are specified for the BODY element. That is because some users surf the Web with the display of graphics turned off to speed up access to Web pages over a slow connection. By specifying a background color that is close in color to your background image, you can insure that such users will still see your intended foreground-background color combination. This is especially important when displaying light text against a dark background image, which could end up displaying light text against a white background if the background image is not displayed.

 **Visit the Internet Resource Center.** To find online resources that provide background images you can download and use in your Web pages, go to the Chapter 3 section of this book's Internet Resource Center at **www.emcp.net/html2e.**

Creating Your Own Background Images

You can create your own seamless background image from scratch. In your image editor, select or crop an image that you want to use. For instance, you might want to select and crop a section of cloudy sky from a photograph. To turn the cropped image into a seamless background:

1. Select or create an image (Image A) that you want to use, and size it to 50 × 50 pixels. Open a second (blank) image (Image B) that is sized at 100 × 100 pixels. Copy and paste Image A into the upper-left corner of Image B.
2. Flip Image A horizontally, so that what was on the left is now on the right, and vice versa. Copy and paste this image into the upper-right corner of Image B.

3. Using the mirrored image you created in step 2, flip Image A vertically, so that what was the top is now the bottom, and vice versa. Copy and paste this image into the lower-right corner of Image B.

4. Using the mirrored image you created in step 3, flip Image A horizontally, so that what was on the left is now on the right, and vice versa. Copy and paste this image into the lower-left corner of Image B (see Figure 3.16.)

5. Optionally, resize Image B to a smaller size (75 × 75 pixels, for instance), and then save it as a JPEG image (as myback.jpg, for instance).

The result is that myback.jpg matches up on all four sides, creating a seamless background tile (see Figure 3.17).

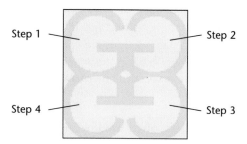

FIGURE 3.16 • A seamless background image can be created by mirroring it horizontally and vertically.

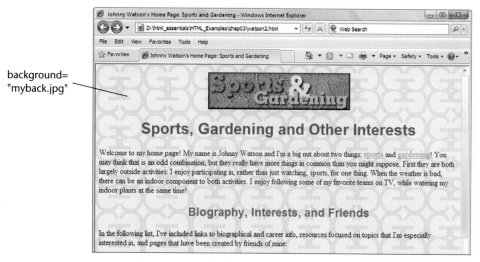

background= "myback.jpg"

FIGURE 3.17 • The seamless background image shown in Figure 3.16 is shown here displayed in a Web page.

CONTROLLING FONTS, COLORS, AND BACKGROUNDS USING STYLES

The FONT and BASEFONT elements, as well as the BODY element's TEXT, LINK, VLINK, ALINK, BGCOLOR, and BACKGROUND attributes, have been **deprecated** in HTML 4.01 and XHTML 1.0 in favor of using Cascading Style Sheets (CSS) to achieve similar or better results. The primary reason for this is to provide for improved accessibility by separating appearance and presentation from structure and content. Deprecated elements and attributes are entirely legal, as long as you declare your document to conform to the transitional or frameset definition of HTML 4.01 or XHTML 1.0. See the sidebar,

"Why Use Styles Instead of Deprecated Elements and Attributes?," for a rundown of the reasons you should use styles instead of deprecated HTML features.

NOTE

If working under a federal government contract or for a federal agency, ensuring accessibility is mandatory under Section 508 of the Rehabilitation Act. The same can also be true if working under a state governmental contract or for a state agency or non-profit organization that receives federal funds.

Many government agencies, educational institutions, non-profit organizations, and companies now require the use of styles in place of deprecated elements and attributes, in order to help ensure that documents they publish on the Web are accessible to all. Many of these agencies, institutions, organizations, and companies have subscribed to the W3C's Web Accessibility Initiative (WAI), which promotes the use of CSS in place of deprecated elements and attributes and provides guidelines that Web designers can follow in ensuring that their Web page designs are compliant, not only with the letter, but also the spirit of the Rehabilitation Act and the Americans with Disabilities Act (ADA). You can find out more about the WAI at **www.w3.org/WAI/**.

Screen readers, often used by individuals with visual impairments to access the content of Web pages, can easily ignore any CSS styling added to a page while conveying the page's structure and content as indicated by its HTML coding. Separating appearance from content is a much more difficult task, however, if HTML elements and attributes are also being used to determine a page's visual presentation and appearance.

In the past, many Web designers chose to continue to use deprecated elements and attributes, rather than implement styles, because of the **backward-compatibility** issues that the use of styles posed. Early browsers (such as Internet Explorer 2 or Netscape 3) did not support CSS and completely ignored any CSS styles included in a page. Later browsers (such as Internet Explorer 3 and Netscape 4) supported CSS, but did it badly.

The purpose of this section is not to teach you everything you need to know about using styles but to provide you with examples of and some hands-on experience with using styles in place of deprecated elements and attributes to control fonts, colors, and backgrounds.

In this section, you will learn how to use CSS-based alternatives that are easy to implement and supported by all recent browsers, including using:

- Inline styles to replace the FONT element and its SIZE, COLOR, and FACE attributes.
- A simple style sheet to replace the BODY element's TEXT, LINK, VLINK, ALINK, BGCOLOR, and BACKGROUND attributes.

Johnny Watson has decided he wants to revise his personal page so that it is more accessible and less likely to cause problems for visitors with visual disabilities. He is going to apply **inline styles** using the STYLE attribute, instead of using the FONT element, and a simple **style sheet** using the STYLE element, instead of using the BODY element's TEXT, LINK, VLINK, ALINK, BGCOLOR, and BACKGROUND attributes.

Save your current file so you can reference it later, and then resave it under another file name for doing this section's examples:

1. In your text editor, first save **watson2.html** (File, Save) to keep any changes you have made to that file.
2. Resave watson2.html as **watson3.html** in the chap03 folder.
3. Open **watson3.html** in your browser from the chap03 folder.

Later, you can refer to your finished version of watson2.html to refresh your understanding of using the FONT element to set font changes, and you can refer to your finished version of watson3.html to refresh your understanding of using styles to set font changes.

Why Use Styles Instead of Deprecated Elements and Attributes?

Many deprecated features, such as the FONT element and its SIZE, COLOR, and FACE attributes and the BODY element's TEXT, LINK, VLINK, ALINK, BGCOLOR, and BACKGROUND attributes were originally introduced as unofficial extensions to HTML in Netscape's Navigator and Microsoft's Internet Explorer browsers. These features were offered in response to commercial pressures for a visually richer Web. However, they were implemented with little consideration of their impact on users with visual impairments and disabilities.

In the interest of promoting a transition to a more accessible Web, the W3C included these previously unofficial extensions in the HTML 3.2 and HTML 4 specifications but declared them as being deprecated. The W3C states that a deprecated element or attribute is one that has been "outdated by newer constructs" and that, in general, "authors should use style sheets to achieve stylistic and formatting effects rather than HTML presentational attributes."

To deprecate means to disapprove or disparage, but it does not mean to forbid. Deprecated features are not *obsolete* (and thus are not forbidden). Deprecated features are valid as long as you declare your document as conforming to the "transitional" or "frameset" definition of HTML 4.01 (or XHTML 1.0).

However, with the introduction of Internet Explorer 8, all current browsers now support CSS 2. There are also relatively simple workarounds available that enable creating advanced style sheets that are compatible with almost all recent browsers, including Internet Explorer 5 (see Appendix C, *Cascading Style Sheets Sampler*, for examples of several of them). Earlier browsers with poor or no support for CSS have almost completely passed from usage. Thus, in almost all cases, concerns about backward-compatibility or cross-browser support no longer stand as legitimate reasons to continue using deprecated elements and attributes instead of styles.

Government agencies, educational institutions, non-profit organizations, or larger companies may also decide on their own to require the use of styles in place of deprecated elements and attributes in order to help ensure that documents they publish on the Web are accessible to all and are compliant, not only with the letter, but also with the spirit of the Americans with Disabilities Act (ADA). Anyone contemplating working in the Web design field needs to be conversant with using Cascading Style Sheets to produce Web pages that are accessible to all.

Using styles, in most cases, is not inherently more difficult than using presentational HTML elements and attributes. In many cases, styles can make designing and maintaining Web pages easier and less labor-intensive. Styles also allow much fuller control over the appearance of Web pages than is possible using HTML alone, while helping to ensure that everyone, including individuals with visual disabilities and impairments, can access content you publish to the Web.

Most elements and attributes that were deprecated in HTML 4 are obsolete in HTML 5. The best way to assure **forward-compatibility** with HTML 5 is simply to write valid HTML 4.01 or XHTML 1.0 code that does not rely on deprecated elements and attributes.

Using Inline Styles to Replace the FONT Element

Some of the accessibility and usability disadvantages of the FONT element include:

- Setting font sizes using the SIZE attribute can prevent users with visual impairments, such as being severely near-sighted, from setting their own font-size preferences.
- Setting font colors using the COLOR attribute, along with setting background colors or images using the BODY element's BGCOLOR or BACKGROUND attributes, can prevent colorblind users from setting their own color and background preferences. Ten percent of males are colorblind and unable to distinguish red and green or blue and yellow unless they are tonally contrasted.
- Using the FACE attribute to specify a font face can have unpredictable results on systems on which that font is not installed. For instance, if Verdana, which has a larger x-height (or larger lowercase letters relative to its uppercase letters), is not on a system, a font with a much lower x-height might be substituted, impacting the readability of the text.
- The FACE attribute can also cause problems when used to create multi-lingual documents, by specifying an "international" font face to display quotes in another language, in that those quotes will likely be turned into gibberish on systems without that font. For alternatives, see Appendix D, *Special Characters*, and the W3C's "International Quick Tips for the Web" at **www.w3.org/International/quicktips/**.

In this section, you will learn how to use the STYLE attribute in combination with the SPAN element to create an inline style to control the appearance of HTML elements. In the next section, you will learn how to create a simple style sheet to control a page's text, link, and background characteristics.

The advantage of using inline styles is they are easier and simpler to implement than style sheets. The disadvantage is that inline styles can be applied to only one element at a time, whereas a style sheet gives you a lot more flexibility, allowing you to set the display characteristics of every instance of an element.

SETTING FONT SIZES   The font-size property in CSS allows you to set font sizes using a number of different measurements, but the most commonly used are *ems* and *pixels*.

An **em** is a traditional printer's measurement that originally signified the width of the letter M in a particular typeface. In CSS, it is a relative measurement that sets an element's font size relative to its parent (or bracketing) element's font size. For instance, assuming that the font size of body text is 16 pixels (the default in most browsers), a font size of 1.5 ems set on a P element nested directly inside the BODY element would be 24 pixels (1.5 × 16). To set the font size of a specific P element to 1.2 ems, you could do the following:

```
<p style="font-size: 1.2em;">nested text</p>
```

A **pixel** (short for "picture element") represents the smallest piece of information in a digital image. In CSS, font sizes set in pixels are inversely relative to the screen resolution—the higher the screen resolution, the smaller a font set in pixels will appear relative to the screen size.

For instance, to set the font size of a specific P element to 20 pixels, you could do the following:

```
<p style="font-size: 20px;">nested text</p>
```

The SPAN element is an inline element that has no default formatting and can be used in conjunction with styles to replace all usages of the FONT element.

Replace the FONT elements that are nested inside the "sports" and "gardening" anchor elements with SPAN elements that use the STYLE attribute to set the font size to 1.2 ems:

1. Delete the FONT elements that were set previously in the introductory paragraph.
2. Add SPAN elements that set nested text to a font size of **1.2em** (see Figure 3.18):

```
<p>Welcome to my home page! My name is Johnny Watson and I'm a
big nut about two things: <a href="http://www.espn.com/">
<span style="font-size: 1.2em">sports</span></a> and
<a href="http://www.bbc.co.uk/gardening/">
<span style="font-size: 1.2em">gardening</span></a>!
```

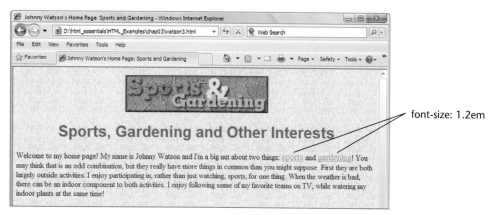

font-size: 1.2em

FIGURE 3.18 • The size of the "sports" and "gardening" links are set to 1.2 ems (1.2 times the size of the surrounding text).

Alternatively, you can use styles to set font sizes using a percentage (%) value. A **font-size: 100%** value and a **font-size: 1em** are generally equivalent.

The one case where percentages and ems are not equivalent is if a user has increased or decreased the text size in the browser. If the text size has been increased, for instance, a **1em** font size, when applied to the BODY element, results in a much larger body text size than a **100%** font size.

Users can increase or decrease the size of text in Internet Explorer 7 by selecting View and Text Size; in Mozilla Firefox 3 by selecting View and Zoom; and in Safari 4 by selecting View and Zoom Out or Zoom In.

Thus, ems should not be used to set a font size for the BODY element but only percentages. Better yet is to not set a font size for the BODY element at all (while setting font sizes for elements nested inside the BODY element using ems or percentages).

The ex (x-height) relative measurement is potentially useful, setting sizes relative to the height of lowercase text (or the height of an "x"). However, the ex relative mesurement should be avoided because of inconsistent implementation in browsers. Some browsers will simply compute an ex as equal to half an em.

The pt (point), pc (pica), cm (centimeter), in (inch), and mm (millimeter) absolute measurements should not be used in documents to be displayed on the Web, because Web pages (and browser viewports) are of uncertain dimensions and resolutions. In

CSS, there are 72 points to an inch, and 12 points to a pica (6 picas to an inch), but that only has relevance if you know the dimensions of the medium (such as an 8.5 × 11-inch piece of paper).

EMS OR PIXELS? The choice between using ems or pixels in Web pages has generated reams of debate on the Web. Ems are good for creating page designs that scale relative to user font size preferences. These kinds of designs are sometimes referred to as **fluid designs**. Pixels are good for designing layouts where element sizes need to be nailed down relative to each other. Designs with these layout requirements are sometimes referred to as **pixel-perfect designs**. There are drawbacks to using both ems and pixels:

- Some earlier browsers with poor support for styles incorrectly implemented the em measurement—Internet Explorer 3, for instance, treated one em as equivalent to one pixel. Fortunately, very few users still use that browser.
- Text set in pixels cannot be resized by users in Internet Explorer 7 or earlier, which makes it more difficult for users with visual impairments to set their own font size preferences. Internet Explorer 8, however, does let users resize text set in pixels.

The number of users using browsers that do not handle ems properly, however, is now extremely low. All recent graphical browsers handle ems just fine. If all you want to do is increase or decrease the size of a font relative to the current font size, there is no longer any reason to not use ems (**font-size:1.2em** to increase it, or **font-size:.8em** to decrease it, for instance).

Current browsers allow users to increase or decrease the size at which text is displayed, making it much easier for users to adjust the size of text in their browsers if it should be too small for them, helping to alleviate some of the accessibility issues involved with setting font sizes using pixels. For instance, in Internet Explorer 8, select View and Text Size to select from five text sizes, from Largest to Smallest, with Medium being the default (see Figure 3.19). If you select Larger from the Text Size menu, the text size is increased by one step (see Figure 3.20). Selecting View and Zoom in Internet Explorer 8 lets you zoom the whole page (both text and graphics).

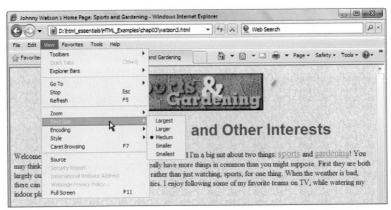

FIGURE 3.19 • In Internet Explorer 8, users can adjust the size of the default text font.

Larger text

FIGURE 3.20 • The text size has been increased from Medium to Larger in Internet Explorer 8.

You can increase the text size in Mozilla Firefox 3 by selecting View, Zoom, and Zoom In. Depending on whether the Zoom Text Only option is selected or not, either just the text or the whole page will be zoomed.

TROUBLE *spot*

Points and pixels were traditionally equivalent by default on Macintosh systems. That only holds true, however, if the default **dot pitch** is set to 72 dpi (dots per inch), with a point equaling 1/72 of an inch. Points and pixels are not equivalent on a Windows system, however, because the default dot pitch for fonts is 96 dpi in Windows. The result is that text set in an 8-point font, for instance, which is legible in a Windows browser displaying text at 96 dpi, will be illegible in a Macintosh browser displaying text at 72 dpi.

This is less a factor in Macintosh OS X, which, starting with the Tiger release, allows applications to apply scaling factors that are multiples of the base resolution of 72 dpi, which current browsers use to cause font sizes to appear the same as in Windows browsers. Internet Explorer 4 and 5 for the Macintosh also automatically adjusted font resolution to match what is seen in Windows.

Because points are only equivalent to pixels at 72 dpi, they should *never* be used to specify font sizes or other dimensions in Web pages. If you want to specify a font size that is relative to the display resolution (actual or factored), you should use pixels, not points.

SETTING FONT FACES When specifying font families using styles, you use the same font names you used when specifying font-face names using the FONT element's FACE attribute.

action

Set a style that specifies a list of font families to be used in displaying the H1 and H2 elements:

1. Delete the FONT elements that were previously nested in the H1 and H2 elements.
2. Insert a STYLE attribute in the H1 start tag to specify a list of font-family names (see Figure 3.21):

```
<h1 style="font-family: 'Comic Sans MS', Arial, Geneva, Helvetica,
sans-serif">Sports, Gardening, and Other Interests</h1>
```

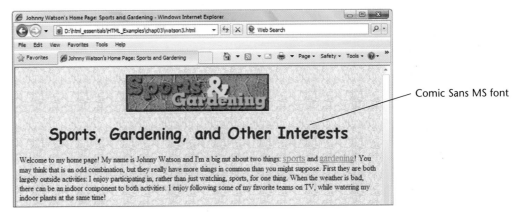

— Comic Sans MS font

FIGURE 3.21 • An inline style causes the H1 element to be displayed in a Comic Sans MS font on systems that have that font available.

As with using the FONT element's FACE element, if Comic Sans MS is not available on a system, the next font in the list that is available will be displayed. If none of the listed fonts are available, the system's default sans serif font will be displayed.

NOTE

Note that in the previous code example, the font name, Comic Sans MS, is enclosed within single quote marks. Single quote marks are required whenever specifying a font name that contains spaces.

SETTING FONT COLORS The color property in CSS allows you to set a foreground color for the BODY element, as well as for any block or inline element, using the same 16 standard color names and hexadecimal RGB codes that you used previously to specify colors for the FONT element's COLOR attribute. Additionally, CSS' background property lets you set a background color.

action

Use the STYLE attribute to set foreground colors for the H1 and H2 elements, along with a transparent background color for both:

1. Edit the H1 element's STYLE attribute, setting an orange foreground color and a transparent background:

```
<h1 style="color: #ff6600; background: transparent; font-family:
'Comic Sans MS', Arial, Geneva, Helvetica, sans-serif">Sports,
Gardening, and Other Interests</h1>
```

2. Edit the H2 element's STYLE attribute, setting a green foreground color and a transparent background (see Figure 3.22):

```
<h2 style="color: #339900; background: transparent; font-family:
Arial, Geneva, Helvetica, sans-serif" align="center">Biography,
Interests, and Friends</h2>
```

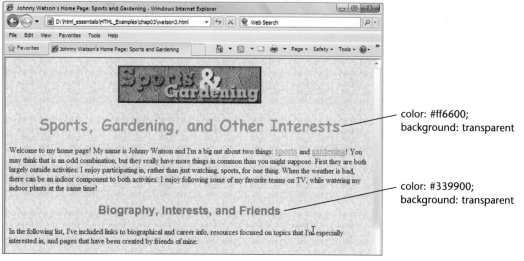

color: #ff6600;
background: transparent

color: #339900;
background: transparent

FIGURE 3.22 • Different colors are set for the H1 and H2 elements using styles.

tip

Notice that a transparent background is also specified for the H1 and H2 elements. Whenever you specify a foreground color using styles, you should also specify a background color, if only as transparent. The reason for this is that a user might be using a user-defined style sheet that assigns foreground and background colors to the H1 and H2 elements—if you only set a foreground color, it could end up being displayed against a user's background color. You could end up with yellow text against a yellow background, for instance, or red text against a green background that someone who has red-green color-vision deficiency might have difficulty reading.

Setting Text, Link, and Background Colors Using the STYLE Element

The BODY element's TEXT, LINK, VLINK, ALINK, and BGCOLOR attributes also are deprecated in HTML 4.01 in favor of using styles to achieve similar or better results. You can control the display characteristics of your page's text, link, and background colors using a simple style sheet.

Use the STYLE element to add a simple style sheet to the HEAD element to control text, link, and background colors:

1. Delete the TEXT, LINK, VLINK, ALINK, BGCOLOR, and BACKGROUND attributes you previously set in the BODY element:

```
<body text="navy" link="#ff6600" vlink="#996699" alink="blue"
bgcolor="#ffffcc" background="back_light.jpg">
```

2. Add a STYLE element to your document's HEAD element:

```
<meta name="keywords" content="sports, gardening, espn, bbc,
football, baseball, indoor gardening, house plants, container
gardening, plant diseases">
<style type="text/css">
</style>
</head>
```

3. Set a style for the BODY element that sets a dark green text color and a light yellow background color (uses spaces or a tab to create the code indents):

```
<style type="text/css">
body {
    color: #333300;
    background: #ffffcc;
    }
</style>
</head>
```

4. Set styles that specify colors for unvisited (**a:link**), visited (**a:visited**), and active (**a:active**) links:

```
<style type="text/css">
body {
    color: #333300;
    background: #ffffcc;
    }
a:link {
    color: #cc0000;
    background: transparent;
    }
a:visited {
    color: #9900cc;
    background: transparent;
    }
a:active {
    color: blue;
    background: transparent;
    }
</style>
</head>
```

5. CSS also lets you set an **a:hover** style to control the appearance of a link when the mouse hovers over it (see Figure 3.23):

```
a:active {
    color: blue;
    background: transparent;
    }
a:hover {
    color: #ffcc00;
    background: green;
    }
</style>
```

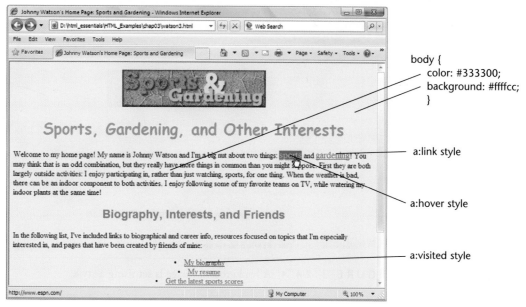

body {
    color: #333300;
    background: #ffffcc;
}

a:link style

a:hover style

a:visited style

FIGURE 3.23 • Styles can control text, link, and background colors.

A common error when typing styles is to type a colon where a semicolon is called for, or vice versa. Another common error is to type a regular opening or closing parenthesis, rather than an opening or closing squiggly bracket ("{" or "}"), before or after a style rule's properties. Also, if your style is not nested inside of a properly formed STYLE element (starting with `<style type="text/css">` and ending with `</style>`), it will not be displayed. If you find that a style is not working, check to make sure you have not made any of these errors.

When setting link properties using styles, you should always list a:hover and a:active after a:link and a:visited. If you do not, the hover and active link states will not be displayed. If you list a:hover after a:active, for instance, the activated state will not be visible when the mouse pointer is held down on the link.

Setting a Background Image Using a Style

The final touch you need to add now is a background image.

Add a background image to your style sheet that will display behind the BODY element (see Figure 3.24):

```
<style type="text/css">
body {
    color: #333300;
    background: #ffcc99 url(tanparch.gif);
    }
```

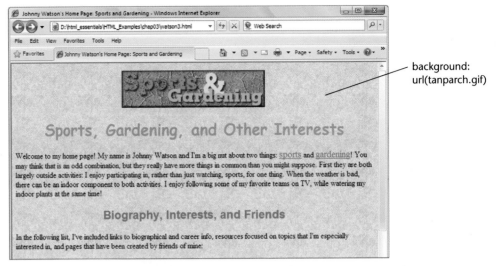

background:
url(tanparch.gif)

FIGURE 3.24 • A background image is set using a style.

When specifying a background image URL in a style, be sure to surround it with regular parentheses—(and)—and not squiggly brackets—{ and }. As with setting a background image using a BODY element attribute, when setting a background image using a style, you should always specify a background color that is similar to your background image's coloration because some users surf the Web with the display of graphics turned off.

Table 3.3 shows the equivalent codes for setting font colors and backgrounds using BODY attributes and a style sheet.

TABLE 3.3 • BODY Attribute and Style Sheet Equivalencies

Effect	BODY Attributes	Style Sheet
Text Color	text="navy"	body { color: navy }
Link Color	link="#ff6600"	a:link { color: #ff6600 }
Visited Link Color	vlink="#996699"	a:visited { color: #996699 }
Active Link Color	alink="blue"	a:active { color: blue }
Hover Link Color	(none)	a:hover { color: blue }
Background Color	bgcolor="#ffffcc"	body { background: #ffffcc }
Background Image	bgcolor="#ffffcc"	body { background: url (back_light.jpg) }

SPECIFYING A DARK BACKGROUND IMAGE To make a more dramatic statement, you can use a dark background image. To do this, you must adjust your page's foreground colors so they provide proper contrast, as well as the background color you have specified. A dark background image, back_dark.jpg, is included with the other example files in the chap03 folder.

Save your current file so you can reference it later, and then resave it under another file name for doing this section's examples:

1. In your text editor, first save **watson3.html** (File, Save) to keep any changes you have made to that file.
2. Resave watson3.html as **watson4.html** in the chap03 folder.
3. Open **watson4.html** in your browser from the chap03 folder.
4. Set a dark background image, and reset your page's text, link, and background colors to match (see Figure 3.25):

```
<style type="text/css">
body {
      color: #ffffcc;
      background: navy url(back_dark.jpg);
      }
a:link {
      color: #33ffcc;
      background: transparent;
      }
a:visited {
      color: #00cccc;
      background: transparent;
      }
a:active {
      color: aqua;
      background: transparent;
      }
a:hover {
      color: yellow;
      background: maroon;
      }
</style>
</head>
```

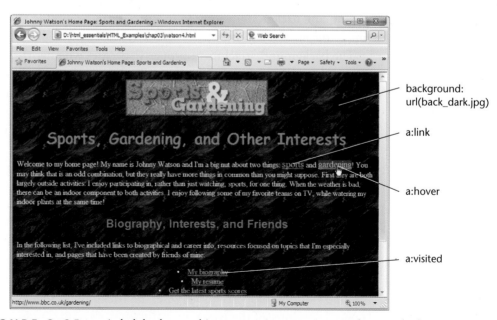

FIGURE 3.25 • A dark background image can give a page a more dramatic look.

TROUBLE *spot*

When printing a Web page, many browsers do not print background colors or images, which in some browsers, such as Internet Explorer, can result in light-colored text being printed against a white background. If displaying white text against a white background, the result can be no visible text. One way to deal with this problem is to create and link to a "printer-ready" version of your page that substitutes dark text against a white background. Another and easier way is to include a second style sheet in your document's HEAD element but with a **media="print"** attribute set:

```
<style type="text/css" media="print">
body {
    color: black;
    background: white;
    }
</style>
</head>
```

With watson4.html, this will cause the body text, and any other nested text for which a foreground or background color has not been set, to print in a black color against a white background in browsers that recognize a print media style sheet. If white or light foreground colors were set for other elements in the page, you would need to include those in your print media style sheet. For instance:

```
<style type="text/css" media="print">
body, p, li, a:link, a:visited, address {
    color: black;
    background: white;
    }
</style>
</head>
```

USING OTHER BACKGROUND PROPERTIES   There are a number of other background properties you can set using styles. The background-attachment, background-repeat, and background-position properties can be used to vary how a background image displays in a browser.

The background-attachment property specifies whether the background image is fixed relative to the browser window or scrolls along with the page. The default value is **scroll**, which causes the background to scroll along with the page. A **fixed** value, on the other hand, causes the background image to remain fixed relative to the browser window (so the document text scrolls within the browser window, but the background image remains fixed).

The background-repeat property specifies whether the background image is to be repeated (or tiled) and whether it should be repeated vertically or horizontally. The default value is **repeat**, which caused a background image to be tiled both vertically and horizontally within the browser background. The **repeat-y** value causes the background image to be repeated vertically only, whereas a **repeat-x** value causes it to be repeated horizontally only. The **no-repeat** value causes the background image to be displayed only once (not tiled). The no-repeat value is usually used in conjunction with the background-position property (otherwise, the background image is displayed, untiled, in the upper-left corner of the page).

The background-position property specifies the position of a non-tiled background image. A percentage value or a length value (using pixels or ems) can be used to space the background image in from the top-left corner of a page or element. If only one value is given, it is assumed that only the horizontal position of the background image is being set. If two values are given, the first is used to set the horizontal position and the second to set the vertical position. The keywords **left**, **center**, and **right** can also be used to set the horizontal position of the background image, while the keywords **top**, **middle**, and **bottom** can be used to set the background image's vertical position. The keyword values cannot be combined with the percentage or length values. Here are some possible styles that could be set using these properties:

```
body {
background-image: url("backimg.jpg");
background-attachment: fixed;
background-repeat: no-repeat;
background-position: 50% 50%
}
```

or

```
body {
background-image: url("backimg.jpg");
background-repeat: repeat-y;
background-position: center
}
```

or

```
body {
background-image: url("backimg.jpg");
background-repeat: no-repeat;
background-position: 50% 100px
}
```

You can also use the background property to set all background properties at once. For instance:

```
body {
        color: #ffffcc;
        background: navy url("watermark.gif") no-repeat fixed 50% 50%;
        }
```

When vertically positioning a non-tiled background image using a percentage value or a keyword value (middle or bottom), some earlier browsers position the background image relative to the browser window, whereas others position it relative to the length of the document. To insure that your watermark background image will always be displayed the same distance from the top of the page in all browsers that support this feature, set a specific length amount from the top of the page.

CHAPTER SUMMARY

You should now be familiar with using both HTML and CSS to control fonts, colors, and backgrounds in Web pages you create. You should know how to set absolute and relative font sizes, specify font-face names and font lists, apply colors using the 16 standard color names and hexadecimal RGB codes, use Web-safe colors in your pages, set foreground and background colors, and use background images. You should also be familiar with CSS-based alternatives to using the SIZE, FACE, and COLOR attributes in the FONT element and the TEXT, LINK, VLINK, ALINK, BGCOLOR, and BACKGROUND attributes in the BODY element, which are deprecated in HTML 4. In addition, you should be aware of accessibility concerns that can arise when setting fonts, colors, and backgrounds in Web pages.

Code Review

`<font>...<font>`	FONT element. Specifies the font size, color, or face for an element. Deprecated in HTML 4.
`<font size="size"`	SIZE attribute. In the FONT element, specifies the font size for the element. You can set seven absolute font sizes (1 to 7), or relative font sizes (+1 or -1, for instance).
`<font face="font"`	FACE attribute. In the FONT element, specifies the font face for the element, in the form of a font-face name.
`<font face="fontlist"`	Specifies a comma-delimited list of fonts that might be available on a users system.
`<font color="color"`	COLOR attribute. In the FONT element, specifies the foreground color of nested text. Colors can be specified using any of the 16 standard color names or hexadecimal RGB codes.
`<body text="color"`	TEXT attribute. In the BODY element, sets the color of body text.
`<body link="color"`	LINK attribute. In the BODY element, sets the color of unvisited links.
`<body vlink="color"`	VLINK attribute. In the BODY element, sets the color of visited links.
`<body alink="color"`	ALINK attribute. In the BODY element, sets the color of activated links.
`<body bgcolor="color"`	BGCOLOR attribute. In the BODY element, sets a background color for a page.
`<body background="url"`	BACKGROUND attribute. In the BODY element, states the URL of a background image for a page.
`<style type="text/css">`	STYLE element. Element in the document head that specifies nested text in a style sheet; `type="text/css"` specifies it is a CSS style sheet.
`style="stylelist"`	STYLE attribute. Inserts an inline style within an element's start tag, in the form of one or more style declarations, separated by semi-colons. For instance: `style="color: red; background: yellow;"`
`font-size: size;`	font-size property. In a CSS style sheet, sets the font size of an element, most often in pixels (15px), ems (1.2em), or percentages (150%).

`<span>`	SPAN element. A generic inline element that has no formatting characteristics of its own but which can be used to create custom inline elements by using styles.
`font-family:` *`font`*`;`	font-family property. Specifies a specific or generic font-family name or a font-family list.
`color:` *`color`*`;`	color property. Specifies the foreground color of an element using a color name or hexadecimal RGB code.
`background:` *`color`*`;`	background property. Specifies a background color for an element.
`background:` `url("`*`image`*`")`	Specifies a background image for an element. For instance: `background: blue url("sky.jpg");`
`a:link {`*`properties`*`}`	A CSS selector that specifies the properties of an unvisited link.
`a:visited` `{`*`properties`*`}`	A CSS selector that specifies the properties of a visited link.
`a:hover {`*`properties`*`}`	A CSS selector that specifies the properties of a link when the mouse pointer is hovering over it.
`a:active` `{`*`properties`*`}`	A CSS selector that specifies the properties of an activated link.
`background-image:` `url("`*`image`*`");`	Style property that specifies a background image for the BODY or other elements.
`background-attach:` *`value`*`;`	Style property that specifies whether a background image is **fixed** or **scrolled** (the default).
`background-repeat:` *`value(s)`*`;`	Style property that specifies whether a background image is repeated (tiled) or not; **repeat** is the default, **none** turns tiling off, while **repeat-y** and **repeat-x** tile the background image along the y-axis and x-axis, respectively.
`background-position:` *`value(s)`*`;`	Style property that controls how a background image is positioned on the screen. For instance: `background-position: top center;`

KEY TERMS

For a review of the key terms bolded in this chapter, visit the Chapter 3 section of this book's Internet Resource Center at **www.emcp.net/html2e**. A complete glossary appears at the end of the book.

ONLINE QUIZ

An online self-check quiz that you can use to test your knowledge of the topics covered in this chapter can be found in the Chapter 3 section of this book's the Internet Resource Center at **www.emcp.net/html2e**.

REVIEW EXERCISES

This section provides some hands-on review exercises to reinforce the information and material included within this chapter. Review using the elements, attributes, styles, and other features that were covered in this chapter, checking your results in your browser and troubleshooting any errors:

1. Open **watson2_ex.html** from the **chap03** folder and resave it as **watson2-review.html** in that same folder. Further experiment with using the FONT element to set font sizes, faces, and colors, using codes that were not previously exampled in this chapter:

   A. Review using the SIZE attribute to specify font sizes. Specify all seven absolute font sizes and at least four relative font sizes, using both positive and negative values. Nest two inside a P element and two inside the H1 or H2 elements.

   B. Review using the FACE attribute to set font faces. Using Table 3.1 as a reference, specify at least five fonts that are listed as widely available for your system. Be sure to properly quote any font names that include spaces. If you are not sure which fonts are available on your system, you should be able to access a list of available fonts in your word processing program.

   C. Review using the FACE attribute to specify lists of font faces. Using Table 3.1 as a reference, specify at least three different font lists, using non serif, serif, and monospaced fonts, respectively. In each list, include fonts that are widely available on Windows, Macintosh, and Linux systems, as well as the appropriate generic font name.

   D. Review using the COLOR attribute to set font colors. Using Figure 3.11 as a reference, use two of the 16 standard color names, not including black or white, to set colors for the H1 and H2 elements. Using Appendix D, *Web-Safe Color Chart*, as a reference, use two hexadecimal RGB codes to set colors for the two in-context links included in the introductory paragraph.

2. Continuing to work in **watson2-review.html**, further experiment with using the BODY element's TEXT, LINK, VLINK, ALINK, BGCOLOR, and BACKGROUND attributes to set text and link colors and background colors and images, using codes that were not previously exampled in this chapter:

   A. Review using the TEXT, LINK, VLINK, and ALINK attributes to set a foreground colors for text and links, using both standard color names and hexadecimal RGB codes. Select colors that provide good contrast with a white background.

   B. Review using the BGCOLOR attribute to set a lighter background color using either a standard color name or a hexadecimal RGB code that provides good contrast with the text and link colors you previously set.

   C. Review using the BACKGROUND attribute to set a lighter background image that provides good contrast with the text and link colors you previously set. Use the file manager or any other image-viewing software on your system to find and copy a background image you want to use from the **art** folder to the **chap02** folder in your working folder. You can also download a background image you want to use from the Web, saving it in the **chap02** folder.

   D. In conjunction with the background image you just specified, change any of the other foreground colors you have chosen to create what you think is a pleasing or effective color scheme. Do not be satisfied with your first result, but try several different schemes, before deciding on your favorite.

3. Save **watson2-review.html** as **watson2b-review** in the **chap03** folder, and use that file to further experiment with creating a page with a dark background using the BODY element's BGCOLOR and BACKGROUND attributes:

A.	Delete the BACKGROUND attribute you previously set and then review using the BGCOLOR attribute to set a darker background color, using any of the hexadecimal RGB codes shown in Appendix D. Change any of the colors you previously set for the TEXT, LINK, VLINK, and ALINK attributes so they provide good tonal contrast with your new background color. Do the same with any other colors you previously set using the FONT element's COLOR attribute.

B.	Review using the BACKGROUND attribute to set a darker background image for the page. Find and copy a darker background image you want to use from the **art** folder to the **chap03** folder in your working folder, or download one from the Web and save it in the **chap02** folder. If necessary, adjust any of the foreground colors you set previously so that they provide good tonal contrast with the background image you are using.

NOTE The art folder is located inside your working folder, along with the chapter folders. It contains extra images that you can use when completing this book's review exercises and projects.

C.	In conjunction with the darker background image you specified, change any of the other foreground colors you have chosen to create what you think is a pleasing or effective color scheme. Do not be satisfied with your first result, but try several different schemes, before deciding on your favorite.

4.	Open **watson2_ex.html** from the **chap03** folder and resave it as **watson3-review.html** in that same folder. Further experiment with using inline styles to set font sizes, faces, and colors, using codes that were not previously exampled in this chapter:

A.	Review using the STYLE attribute and the font-size property to replace using the FONT element to specify font sizes. Apply inline styles to SPAN elements to set at least four font sizes, with two using ems and two using pixels, for nested text.

B.	Review using the STYLE attribute and the font-family property to replace using the FONT element to specify font faces. Apply inline styles to the H1 and H2 elements to specify a sans serif font family.

C.	Review using the STYLE attribute and the font-family property to replace using the FONT element to specify font lists. Edit the inline styles you just set for the H1 and H2 elements and specify a list of sans serif fonts in place of the single font name you set previously. In the font list, include fonts for Windows, Macintosh, and Linux, as well as the appropriate generic font name.

D.	Review using the STYLE attribute and the color property to replace using the FONT element to specify colors. Set colors for the H1 and H2 elements and for the two in-context links included in the introductory paragraph, using both standard color names and hexadecimal RGB codes.

5.	Continuing to work in **watson3-review.html**, further experiment with using the STYLE element to replace using the BODY element's TEXT, LINK, VLINK, ALINK, BGCOLOR, and BACKGROUND attributes for specifying text and link colors and background colors and images:

A.	Review adding a style sheet to the document's HEAD element using the STYLE element and its TYPE attribute.

B. Review adding a style to the style sheet that applies the color and background properties to the BODY element. Set the background to be transparent.

C. Review adding a style that applies the color and background properties to links, visited links, and active links. Set the backgrounds to be transparent.

D. Review editing the style for the BODY element, replacing the transparent value with both a lighter background color and a lighter background image.

E. In conjunction with the lighter background image you just set, change any of the other foreground colors you have set to create what you think is a pleasing or effective color scheme. Do not be satisfied with your first result, but try several different schemes, before deciding on your favorite.

6. Save **watson3-review.html** as **watson3b-review** in the **chap03** folder, and use that file to further experiment with using styles to create a page using a darker background color and darker background image:

A. Revise the style sheet, specifying a darker background color and a darker background image for the BODY element.

B. In conjunction with the darker background image you just set, change any of the other foreground colors you have set to create what you think is a pleasing or effective color scheme. Do not be satisfied with your first result, but try several different schemes, before deciding on your favorite.

7. Get critiques from at least three other classmates of the color scheme of which you are most proud, chosen from watson2-review.html, watson2b-review.html, watson3-review.html, or watson3b-review.html. Seriously consider the critiques and make any changes to your color scheme you think are merited.

WEB-BASED LEARNING ACTIVITIES

The following Web-based learning activities can help you to further extend your learning and shore up your understanding of specific topic-areas:

- Visit the Chapter 3 section of this book's Internet Resource Center at **www.emcp.net/html2e** to find online resources that you can use to further investigate and explore the topics and subjects covered in this chapter. You can also find all Web sites cited in this chapter's notes listed there.

- Further research a specific topic introduced in this chapter using Google (**www.google.com/**), Yahoo! (**www.yahoo.com/**), Wikipedia (**www.wikipedia.org/**), Open Directory Project (**www.dmoz.org/**), or other online sources. Some topics covered in this chapter that you can further research include:
  - Typography on the Web.
  - Usability and readability issues with fonts and text on the Web.
  - TrueType vs. PostScript fonts.
  - Accessibility issues with using colors on the Web.
  - How color theory applies to Web design.
  - Reasons why certain elements and attributes are deprecated.
  - The use of ems or pixels in creating Web designs.

- Use the results of your online research into a particular topic to:
  - Write a review to be read in front of your classmates.
  - Write a report that can be read by your classmates.
  - Design a diagram, chart, or other graphic that illustrates a key topic or concept.
  - Create a presentation using PowerPoint (or other software) that can be shared with your classmates.

- Give a stand-up presentation to your classmates.
- Team up with one or more classmates to give a group presentation to your classmates.

PROJECTS

These projects can be done in class, in a computer lab, or at home. Use the skills you have developed in this and the previous chapters to create any of the following projects. In your project, demonstrate the correct use of the following HTML features covered in this chapter:

- The FONT element's SIZE attribute OR CSS' **font-size** property to make font size changes for elements and text.
- The FONT element's FACE attribute OR CSS' **font-family** property to make font face changes for elements and text.
- The FONT element's COLOR attribute OR CSS' **color** property to make font color changes for elements and text.
- The BODY element's TEXT, LINK, and VLINK attributes OR CSS' **color** property OR CSS' **a:link**, **a:visited**, and **a:active** to set text and link colors for the document.
- The BODY element's BGCOLOR attribute OR CSS' **background** property to set a background color for the document.
- The BODY element's BACKGROUND attribute OR CSS' **background** property to set a background image for the document (optional).

You can find additional background and other images you can use in your project in the **art** folder included with this book's example files. Also, see the Chapter 3 section of this book's Internet Resource Center at **www.emcp.net/html2e** for links to online resources where you can find additional background and other images that you can download and use in your project.

Project 1. Update the appearance of a personal Web page using fonts, colors, and backgrounds.

If you created your own personal Web page as a project at the end of Chapter 1, apply the lessons learned in this chapter to update the appearance of your personal page, using the FONT element's SIZE, FACE, and COLOR attributes and the BODY element's TEXT, LINK, VLINK, ALINK, BGCOLOR, and BACKGROUND attributes. Experiment with using different color schemes and background images, until you find the combination you like best.

Project 2. Update the appearance of a personal Web page using styles.

If you created your own personal Web page as a project at the end of Chapter 1, apply the lessons learned in this chapter to update the appearance of your personal page, using only styles (without using the FONT element's SIZE, FACE, and COLOR attributes or the BODY element's TEXT, LINK, VLINK, ALINK, BGCOLOR, and BACKGROUND attributes). Experiment with using different color schemes and background images, until you find the combination you like best. Pay special attention to making your page accessible to visitors with visual handicaps, by using em measurements for font sizes and avoiding color combinations that can cause difficulties for users with different forms of color-vision deficiency, for instance.

Project 3. Update the appearance of a topical Web page using fonts, colors, and backgrounds.

If you created a topical page as a project at the end of Chapter 1, apply the lessons learned in this chapter to update the appearance of your personal page using the FONT element's SIZE, FACE, and COLOR attributes and the BODY element's TEXT, LINK, VLINK, ALINK, BGCOLOR, and BACKGROUND attributes. See the guidelines for Project 1 for more details.

Project 4. Update the appearance of a topical Web page using styles.

If you created a topical page as a project at the end of Chapter 1, apply the lessons learned in this chapter to update the appearance of your topical page using only styles. See the guidelines for Project 2 for more details.

Project 5. Update the appearance of a page you created for a club or organization.

If you created a page for a club or organization at the end of Chapter 1, apply the lessons learned in this chapter to update the appearance of that page using either HTML elements and attributes or styles to control fonts, colors, and backgrounds. See the guidelines for Projects 1 and 2 for more details.

Project 6. Create a new Web page from scratch that uses fonts, colors, and backgrounds.

Create any kind of new page from scratch: a personal page, a topical page, a page for a club or organization, or a page created for any other purpose. If you are not sure what kind of page you want to create, look on the Web for examples that you can try to emulate. Apply the lessons learned in this chapter or previous chapters to create an effective and visually attractive page featuring font size, face, and color changes, combined with a background color or background image. Try to combine features learned in this chapter with features learned in earlier chapters. For instance, you might combine a document menu that jumps to subsections within a document, as was demonstrated in Chapter 2, with hover links (using a:hover), as was demonstrated in this chapter.

CHAPTER 4
Working with Images and Other Media

PERFORMANCE OBJECTIVES

- Flow text and other elements around a floating image.
- Create a thumbnail image gallery.
- Use graphic rules, banners, and buttons.
- Create GIF and JPEG Web graphics.
- Understand color palettes.
- Use transparent GIF images.
- Use GIF animations.
- Embed sound and video.
- Use relative URLs.
- Create a graphical front end using an image map.

In Chapter 1, *Creating a Basic Web Page*, you learned how to include an inline image in an HTML document using the IMG element. In this chapter, you will learn much more about working with and using images and other media in HTML documents.

The original version of HTML had no means for including images. As has often happened in HTML, the market perceived a deficit, and supplied it. The IMG element was actually the first unofficial extension to HTML, supported by the first widely available graphical browser, the Mosaic browser.

The old adage that a picture is worth a thousand words is proven true by how the deft usage of carefully chosen images augments and supplements the textual content of a page. In fact, an image or group of images can even stand by itself as the main content of a page.

USING THE EXAMPLE FILES

If you created a working folder for storing files you create, you will find the example files for this chapter located in the **chap04** folder within your working folder. Save any HTML files you create in this chapter in that folder.

CASE EXAMPLE: CREATING A REPORT WITH FLOATING IMAGES

In this example, you will create a report on the history of NASA's Project Mercury space program to place a manned space vehicle into orbit around the earth. To supplement the textual content of the report, you will include actual NASA photographs at key points, which are included with the example files for this chapter.

> Shirley Johnson is a science major who is particularly interested in astronomy and space exploration. For a class, she is writing a report on the history of the Project Mercury space program, which placed the first American, John Glenn, into orbit around the earth.
>
> Shirley has already done quite a bit of work developing her page. She has written the report text, set up a document menu that jumps to sections within the report, created note links that jump to footnotes at the bottom of the page, and set up the colors, fonts, and backgrounds she wants to use. For the background, she created her own seamless background image, taken from one of NASA's photographs of a star cluster in outer space.

To get started working with this example:

1. Run your text editor, and open **mercury_ex.html** from the chap04 folder in your working folder.
2. Save mercury_ex.html as **mercury.html** in the chap04 folder.
3. Run your browser, and open **mercury.html** from the chap04 folder (see Figure 4.1).

FIGURE 4.1 • The color scheme, background image, document menu, and hypertext note links have already been created for mercury.html.

This chapter uses a number of image files that are included with this chapter's example files in the chap04 folder. Any HTML files you create in this chapter must be saved in the same folder in which the example graphic files for this chapter are located; otherwise, the example graphics will not display when you preview the HTML files in your browser.

FLOATING IMAGES

You added an **inline image** to an HTML document in Chapter 1 but nested it by itself inside an otherwise empty P element, which added space above and below the image, separating it from other elements. You had to do that because an IMG element is an **inline element** that is displayed in a line at the point at which it is inserted and, as such, does not insert line breaks or vertical spacing above or below an image.

> Shirley decided to illustrate her report by using actual NASA photographs that are available online. She researched NASA's copyright and reproduction guidelines and discovered that most of NASA's photographs are not copyrighted, so she is free to use them for non-commercial or educational purposes.

action

Insert an inline image at the start of a paragraph containing text (see Figure 4.2):

```
<h2><a name="sect1"></a>1915 to 1957</h2>
<p>In 1915, the U.S. Congress formed the National Advisory
Committee for Aeronautics to "supervise and direct the scientific
study of the problems of flight, with a view to their practical
solutions."<sup><a href="#note1" name="return1">(1)</a></sup>
That organization evolved four decades later into the National
Aeronautics and Space Administration (NASA).</p>
<p><img src="atlas_mercury.jpg" alt="Atlas rocket with Mercury
spacecraft" width="175" height="238">The Atlas rocket launch
vehicle, which lifted John Glenn into orbit, began being used
following World War II. Its initial test occurred in 1948.<sup>
<a href="#note2" name="return2">(2)</a></sup> The first launch
was not attempted until June 11, 1957, however, just four months
prior to the launching of the Sputnik I. Unfortunately, the first
Atlas launch ended with the missile exploding at 10,000 feet. A
second Atlas test launch also ended in failure on September 25,
1957. It was not until January 10, 1958, that the Atlas rocket
was successfully launched.</p>
```

HINT

Setting WIDTH and HEIGHT attributes for inline images can speed up display of the rest of the page, because the browser can allocate space for images before they have finished downloading.

inline image (non-floating)

FIGURE 4.2 • An inline image is displayed at the position where it is inserted within a line.

Flowing Text around a Left-Aligned Image

The IMG element's ALIGN attribute has two different functions. It can be used to vertically align an image relative to the line of text it is inserted on (you will learn how to do that later in this chapter). ALIGN also can be used to **float** an image to the left or right margin and cause following text or elements to flow around the image.

Set the inline image you just added so that it floats to the left margin, with following text and elements flowing around the right side of the image (see Figure 4.3):

```
<p><img src="atlas_mercury.jpg" align="left" alt="Atlas rocket
with Mercury spacecraft" width="175" height="238">The Atlas
rocket launch vehicle, which lifted John Glenn into orbit, began
being used following World War II.
```

left floating image
(align="left")

FIGURE 4.3 • A left-aligned image floats to the left margin, with following text and elements flowing around the right side of the image.

Setting Horizontal Spacing

The only problem with the floating image is that no **horizontal spacing** separates it from the flowing text. The IMG element's HSPACE attribute lets you set horizontal spacing that will be added on each side of the image.

Add 10 pixels of horizontal spacing to the inline image (see Figure 4.4):

```
<p><img src="atlas_mercury.jpg" align="left" hspace="10"
alt="Atlas rocket with Mercury spacecraft" width="175"
height="238">The Atlas rocket launch vehicle, which lifted John
Glenn into orbit, began being used following World War II.
```

horizontal spacing (hspace="10")

FIGURE 4.4 • Ten pixels of horizontal spacing are added to both sides of the image.

Use the VSPACE attribute, which works the same as the HSPACE attribute, to add **vertical spacing** above and below an inline image.

As shown in Figure 4.4, any horizontal spacing you add to the image is added to both sides of the image.

Flowing Text around a Right-Aligned Image

You also can float an image to the right margin, with following text and elements flowing around the left side of the image.

action

Insert a right-aligned inline image with 10 pixels of horizontal spacing set (see Figure 4.5):

```
<h2><a name="sect2"></a>1958 to 1960</h2>
<p>In June, 1958, the initial specifications were established for
what was to become the Project Mercury manned spacecraft. On
November 5, the Space Task Group was formed to implement a manned
satellite program; on November 26, the manned satellite program
was officially designated as Project Mercury.</p>
<p><img src="astronauts.jpg" align="right" hspace="10" alt="The
seven original Mercury astronauts" width="200"
height="197">Project Mercury was approved on October 7, 1958,
which led to the first orbital flight by an American astronaut,
John Glenn, in the "Friendship 7" spacecraft, about three years
and four months later, on February 20, 1962.</p>0
```

right floating image (align="right")

FIGURE 4.5 • A right-aligned image with 10 pixels of horizontal spacing is added to the page.

Notice that an ALT attribute is included in both IMG elements you have added so far, specifying **alternative text** that describes the images. Adding an ALT attribute to an inline image informs users of non-visual browsers, such as a Braille browser, of the content or purpose of the image. Some, but not all, browsers display the content of the ALT attribute when the mouse hovers over the image.

Flowing Text between Two Images

You also can flow text between a left-aligned and a right-aligned image.

Add both a left-aligned and a right-aligned image at the same location within the page (see Figure 4.6):

```
<h2><a name="sect3"></a>1961</h2>
<p><img src="chimp_ham.jpg" align="left" hspace="10" alt="Ham,
the first chimpanzee to go into outer space" width="175"
height="211"><img src="glenn_grissom_shepard.jpg" align="right"
hspace="10" alt="John Glenn, Virgil Grissom, and Alan Shepard in
front of the Redstone rocket" width="191" height="211">On January
31, 1961, a Redstone rocket launched a Mercury space vehicle from
Cape Canaveral with Ham, a 37-pound chimpanzee, as its passenger
in a suborbital flight. Ham survived the flight in good shape,
but when he was shown the space vehicle again later, made clear
he wanted no part of it. On February 1, John Glenn, Virgil
Grissom, and Alan Shepard were selected to train for the first
manned space flight.</p>
```

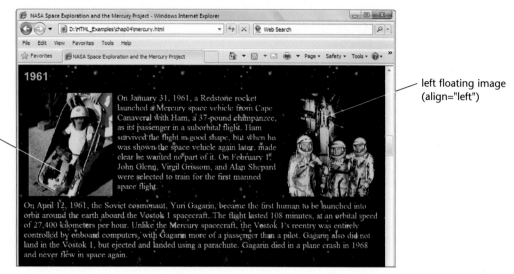

right floating image
(align="right")

left floating image
(align="left")

FIGURE 4.6 • Text flows between a left-aligned and a right-aligned image.

Overlapping Floating Images

You also can overlap floating images, so that text first flows just around the right side of the first image, then between both images, and finally just around the left side of the second image.

Move the second image down, so the two floating images overlap (see Figure 4.7):

```
<h2><a name="sect3"></a>1961</h2>
<p><img src="chimp_ham.jpg" align="left" hspace="10" alt="Ham,
the first chimpanzee to go into outer space" width="175"
height="211"><img src="glenn_grissom_shepard.jpg" align="right"
hspace="10" alt="John Glenn, Virgil Grissom, and Alan Shepard in
front of the Redstone rocket" width="191" height="211">On January
31, 1961, a Redstone rocket launched a Mercury space vehicle from
Cape Canaveral with Ham, a 37-pound chimpanzee, as its passenger
in a suborbital flight. Ham survived the flight in good shape,
but when he was shown the space vehicle again later, made clear
he wanted no part of it. <img src="glenn_grissom_shepard.jpg"
align="right" hspace="10" alt="John Glenn, Virgil Grissom, and
Alan Shepard in front of the Redstone rocket" width="191"
height="211">On February 1, John Glenn, Virgil Grissom, and Alan
Shepard were selected to train for the first manned space
flight.</p>
```

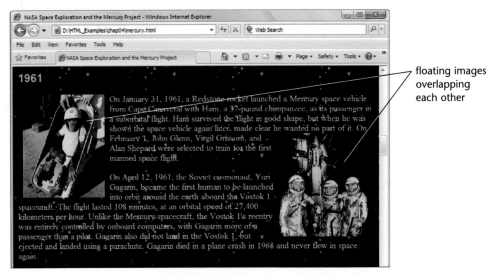

floating images overlapping each other

FIGURE 4.7 • You can overlap a left-aligned and a right-aligned image.

Practicing Using Floating Images

You should now have a good understanding of flowing text around left-aligned and right-aligned images, flowing text between floating images, and overlapping floating images. A number of additional example graphics are included with this chapter's example files that you can use to get more practice using floating images.

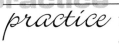

Using the previous examples of inserting left-aligned and right-aligned images as a guide, insert additional floating images at appropriate points within the document. Be sure to specify the actual height and width of the images, add horizontal spacing, and include alternative text that describes the image. The following are some images included with the example images for this chapter that you can use:

- **alan_shepard.jpg** Close-up view of astronaut Alan Shepard in his pressure suit for the first manned Mercury suborbital flight (MR-3). Width: 175; height: 201.
- **mercurylaunch.jpg** Launch of the Mercury-Atlas 6 mission that put John Glenn into orbit around the earth. Width: 200; height: 214.
- **glenn_orbit.jpg** View of earth taken by astronaut John Glenn during his space flight. Width: 200; height: 153.
- **john_glenn.jpg** Astronaut John Glenn poses in Mercury space suit. Width: 175; height: 199.
- **schirra_splash_down.jpg** Navy frogman secures tow line to Sigma 7 flotation collar. Width: 200; height: 184.
- **white_eva.jpg** Astronaut Edward White during first EVA performed during Gemini 4 space flight. Width: 200; height: 171.
- **flagonmoon.jpg** Astronaut Edwin Aldrin poses for photograph beside deployed U.S. flag (Apollo 11 landing on moon). Width: 200; height: 171.
- **earth_apollo17.jpg** View of the Earth seen by the Apollo 17 crew traveling toward the moon. Width: 200; height: 192.

VIEWING IMAGES

For a shortcut for running Windows Explorer, click the Start button, then in Windows XP, select Run, type **explorer**, and press Enter; in Windows Vista, click in the Start Search bar, type **explorer**, and press Enter.

Both Windows and Macintosh OS X have built-in support for viewing images. To view **thumbnails** (or icons) of images stored in a folder, in Windows Explorer, select Tools, View, and Thumbnails; in the Macintosh's Finder, select View, then click as Icons.

You also can open an image in a Web browser if it is a GIF, JPEG, or PNG image. Just open it as you would open a local HTML file, except that in Internet Explorer, you will need to select All Files as the file type. (Firefox and Safari default to displaying all files.)

There are many shareware and freeware image-viewing utilities available on the Web that let you view galleries of smaller-sized thumbnail (or icon) images. You can also use an image editor as an image viewer.

Visit the Internet Resource Center. To find online resources that provide freeware and shareware image viewers for Windows, Macintosh OS X, and Linux that you can download and use, visit the Chapter 4 section of this book's Internet Resource Center at **www.emcp.net/html2e** or the Tucows site at **www.tucows.com/**.

CASE EXAMPLE: CREATING AN ONLINE PICTURE GALLERY

A common way to present images on the Web is in an online picture gallery. Web authors might choose to display many different kinds of images in an online picture gallery, including personal snapshots, vacation photos, photographic artworks, paintings, drawings, sculptures, and so on.

Images can be presented as a gallery in many ways as well. One common way is to use left-aligned and right-aligned images in conjunction with caption text that describes the images. Additionally, online picture galleries usually use smaller-sized thumbnail images that link to fuller-sized images that can be viewed in a separate window. This method maximizes the number of images that can be shown on a gallery page, while keeping the size of the page as small as possible.

"In addition to creating her online report on the Mercury spaceflight program, Shirley Johnson decided to create an online picture gallery of NASA space exploration images. Shirley already has a good start on her online gallery. She created her color scheme, set a background image, inserted images she wants to use, and wrote headings and captions for the gallery images."

To get started working with this example:

1. In your text editor, open **spacegallery_ex.html** from the **chap04** folder in your working folder.
2. Resave it as **spacegallery.html** in the same folder.
3. In your browser, open **spacegallery.html** from the **chap04** folder (see Figure 4.8).

FIGURE 4.8 • The color scheme, background image, images, headings, and captions are already set.

CREATING A FLOWING LEFT-RIGHT GALLERY LAYOUT

To create this example, you alternate left-aligned and right-aligned floating images, with headings and captions flowing around the images. You also set up the floating images to function as hypertext links to larger-sized versions of the images.

Floating the Gallery Images

Starting out, the gallery images are just inserted as regular inline images. You can float an image to either the left or right margin, but you need to be careful that following floating images do not also flow around the image. The BR (Break) element's CLEAR attribute lets you stop following text or elements from flowing around a floating image.

Float the first image, and use the BR element's CLEAR attribute to stop following elements from flowing around the image (see Figure 4.9):

```
<hr>
<h2><img align="left" hspace="10" src="spacecapsules_th.jpg"
width="200" height="166" alt="Mercury, Gemini, and Apollo
spacecraft."> Mercury, Gemini, and Apollo Spacecraft</h2>
<p>The Mercury spacecraft carried one pilot, the Gemini
spacecraft carried two crew members, and the Apollo spacecraft
carried three crew members.<br clear="all"></p>

<hr>
<h2><img align="right" hspace="10" src="flagonmoon2_th.jpg"
width="200" height="169" alt="Astronaut Edwin Aldrin posing next
to U.S. flag on the moon.">U.S. Flag and Edwin "Buzz" Aldrin on
the Moon</h2>
<p>The Lunar Module "Eagle" is on the left. You can see the
footprints of the astronauts on the surface of the moon. The
picture was taken by Neil Armstrong on July 20, 1969.
<br clear="all"></p>
```

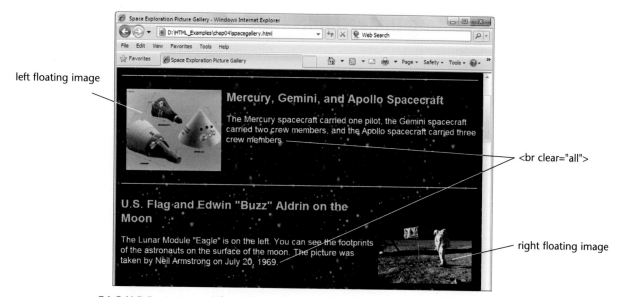

left floating image

<br clear="all">

right floating image

FIGURE 4.9 • The gallery images are floating at the left and right margins.

The CLEAR attribute value of **all** in the BR element causes following text or elements to clear any floating image. You also can set a CLEAR attribute value of **left** or **right**, which causes following text or elements to clear a left-aligned or right-aligned floating image, respectively.

practice Four more images are included in the online gallery. Use the first two images that you just set up as floating images as examples for setting up the remaining images in the gallery as floating images. Alternate the image floats from left to right, and use BR elements with a `clear="all"` attribute at the end of the caption text to stop following text or elements from also flowing around the images.

NOTE In line with the W3C's strategy of separating structure and meaning from presentation to enhance accessibility, the ALIGN, HSPACE, VSPACE, and CLEAR attributes are deprecated in HTML 4 and obsolete in HTML 5. The only exception is use of the ALIGN attribute inside tables in HTML 4 (but not in HTML 5, where all uses are obsolete). Following is an example of using CSS styles to substitute for these attributes:

```
<h2><img style="float: right; margin: 0 10px 0 10px;
src="flagonmoon2_th.jpg" width="200" height="169" alt="Astronaut
Edwin Aldrin posing next to U.S. flag on the moon.">U.S. Flag and
Edwin "Buzz" Aldrin on the Moon</h2>
<p>The Lunar Module "Eagle" is on the left. You can see the
footprints of the astronauts on the surface of the moon. The
picture was taken by Neil Armstrong on July 20, 1969.
<br style="clear: both;"></p>
```

The **float** property can be used with a **left** or **right** value to float an image (or other element) on the left or right margin of the containing block. The four values of the **margin** property correspond to the top, right, bottom, and left margins of the IMG element. The **clear** property can be used with the **left, right,** or **both** value to cause following text or elements to clear a left-floating or right-floating element, or to clear both.

A more detailed discussion and examples of CSS-based alternatives to using deprecated elements and attributes, see Chapter 7, *Designing Multi-Column Web Sites*.

Creating Image Links

An **image link** is an image that also functions as a hypertext link. To create an image link, you nest an inline image inside a hypertext link. An image link need not link to another image. It can link to any object that has an address on the Web.

A smaller-sized image that links to a larger-sized image is sometimes called a thumbnail image. For that reason, in the example file, the smaller-sized images have a "_th" at the end of their file names, while the larger-sized images do not have "_th" at the end of their file names.

Set up the first two floating images as image links:

1. Bracket the first two floating images with hypertext links that link to the corresponding fuller-sized images and add **border="1"** to the IMG elements (see Figure 4.10):

```
<hr>
<h2><a href="spacecapsules.jpg"><img align="left" border="1"
hspace="10" src="spacecapsules_th.jpg" width="200" height="166"
alt="Mercury, Gemini, and Apollo spacecraft."></a>Mercury,
Gemini, and Apollo Spacecraft</h2>
<p>The Mercury spacecraft carried one pilot, the Gemini
spacecraft carried two crew members, and the Apollo spacecraft
carried three crew members.<br clear="all"></p>


<hr>
<h2><a href="flagonmoon2.jpg"><img align="right" border="1"
hspace="10" src="flagonmoon2_th.jpg" width="200" height="169"
alt="Astronaut Edwin Aldrin posing next to U.S. flag on the
moon."></a>U.S. Flag and Edwin "Buzz" Aldrin on the Moon</h2>
```

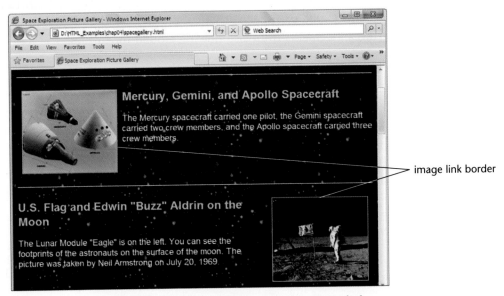

image link border

FIGURE 4.10 • The first two floating images are set as image links.

Internet Explorer and Mozilla Firefox automatically display a border around an image when it is nested inside of a hypertext link, but you cannot depend on that happening in other browsers. In the Opera and Safari browsers, for instance, **border="1"** must be added to the IMG element before a border will be displayed around an image link.

2. In your browser, click on the first image link to test it. The full-sized image should be displayed in the browser window (see Figure 4.11). Click your browser's Back button to return to the gallery page.

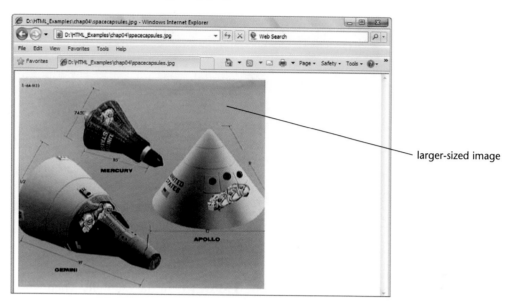

larger-sized image

FIGURE 4.11 • A full-sized image is displayed when a visitor clicks on a thumbnail image link.

practice Using the first two image links you created as a guide, set the four remaining floating images as image links. To do this, you will need to:

1. Create image links by adding A elements bracketing the images that link to larger-sized versions of the images. Remember that the thumbnail (smaller-sized) images have "_th" at the end of their file names, while the larger-sized images do not.
2. Insert **border="1"** to the IMG elements to ensure that Safari and Opera users will see borders around the image links.

After creating the image links, the results you see in your browser should match what is shown in Figure 4.12. Test the links to make sure they work properly.

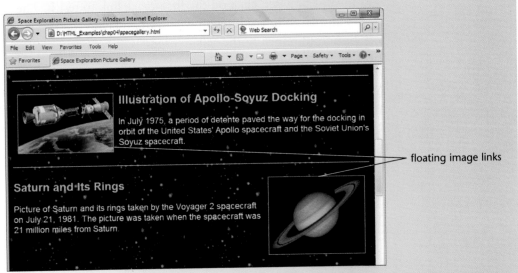

Illustration of Apollo-Soyuz Docking

In July 1975, a period of detente paved the way for the docking in orbit of the United States' Apollo spacecraft and the Soviet Union's Soyuz spacecraft.

floating image links

Saturn and Its Rings

Picture of Saturn and its rings taken by the Voyager 2 spacecraft on July 21, 1981. The picture was taken when the spacecraft was 21 million miles from Saturn.

FIGURE 4.12 • The remaining images have been floated, with following gallery sections set to "clear" the previous float.

CONTROLLING LINK TARGETS In the example, when you click on one of the image links, the object of the link is displayed in a browser window that replaces the current browser window. Some Web authors like to cause linked pages that are external to their own site to display in a second browser window, while the first browser window remains open in the background. They do this to keep visitors from simply taking an exit and never coming back. That way, when a visitor closes the second browser window, the first browser window should return to the foreground. The A element's TARGET attribute can be used to cause the object of a link to be displayed in a new browser window that does not replace the current browser window.

Cause the gallery's linked images to be displayed in a new browser window, rather than replacing the current browser window:

1. Insert a **target="_blank"** attribute in the first gallery image's link:

```
<h2><a href="spacecapsules.jpg" target="_blank"><img align="left"
hspace="10" src="spacecapsules_th.jpg" width="200" height="166"
alt="Mercury, Gemini, and Apollo spacecraft."></a>Mercury,
Gemini, and Apollo Spacecraft</h2>
```

2. Do the same for the other gallery images' links.
3. Save your document, and refresh the display of your page in your browser. Click on any of the image links (apollo-soyuz.jpg, for instance).
4. In the window that opens, notice that the Back button is not highlighted, which means that a new window has been opened (see Figure 4.13).

Back button
not active

Close button

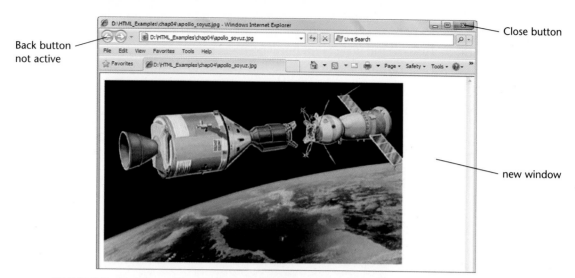

new window

FIGURE 4.13 • The apollo-soyuz.jpg image is opened in a new window.

5. Close the window to bring the window showing spacegallery.html back to the foreground. (In Windows, the Close button is a red button with a white "x" in the upper-right corner of a window; in Macintosh OS X, it is a round red button in the upper-left corner.)

Besides **_blank**, the other values of the TARGET attribute include: **_self**, **_parent**, and **_top**. They are used to target frames, opening the target in the same, parent, or top frame in a set of frames. You will learn about creating framed pages in Chapter 7, *Designing Multi-Column Web Sites*.

The TARGET attribute is deprecated in HTML 4 and obsolete in HTML 5. It is valid in HTML 4 only if the document has a DocType statement declaring it as conforming to the "transitional" or "frameset" definition of HTML 4 or 4.01 or XHTML 1.

To enable opening a link object in a new window in a document declared to conform to the "strict" definition of HTML 4 or 4.01, just replace `target="_blank"` with:

```
onclick="window.open(this.href); return false;"
```

Some argue that this violates the spirit, if not the letter, of the HTML 4 and 5 specifications, which discourage disabling the normal operation of the Back button in browsers. Commercial clients, on the other hand, not wanting to see potential customers follow external links never to return, taking their dollars with them, are likely to demand it. If so, this is a way to satisfy customer demand, while still complying with the HTML 4.01 "strict" and HTML 5 specifications.

TURNING OFF AN IMAGE LINK'S BORDER The introductory paragraph tells the visitor that the thumbnail images can be clicked on to view the full-size images. In this case, you can thus safely turn off the display of the image link border. You need to be careful, however, when turning off image link borders because visitors to your page might not be able to tell that an image link is a link if there is no border displayed around the image.

Turn off the image link borders:

1. Turn off the first image link border by changing the **border="1"** attribute you added previously to **border="0"**:

```
<h2><a href="spacecapsules.jpg" target="_blank"><img border="0"
align="left" hspace="10" src="spacecapsules_th.jpg" width="200"
height="166" alt="Mercury, Gemini, and Apollo spacecraft.">
</a>Mercury, Gemini, and Apollo Spacecraft</h2>
```

2. Do the same for the other image links (see Figure 4.14).

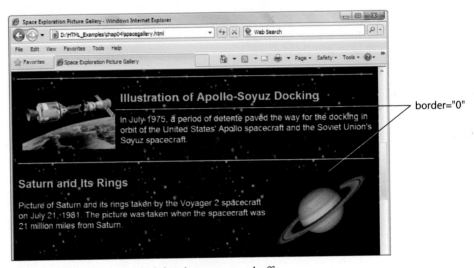

border="0"

FIGURE 4.14 • The image link borders are turned off.

Although the image link borders are turned off, when a visitor passes the mouse pointer over one of the image links, the image still behaves as a link, with a "hand" cursor displayed over the image and the URL of the link displayed on the browser's status bar when the mouse is passed over the image.

NOTE — The BORDER attribute, other than in the TABLE element, is deprecated in HTML 4; it is obsolete in HTML 5. CSS-based alternatives to using the BORDER element will be discussed in Chapter 7, *Designing Multi-Column Web Sites*.

USING RULES, BANNERS, AND BUTTONS

Using graphic rules and banners can add visual appeal to your page, as well as give it more of a 3-D look.

Using Graphic Rules

A **graphic rule** is an image of variable width (usually 400 to 500 pixels) that usually does not have a height of more than 5 to 10 pixels. Graphic rules are generally used as decorative separators and can be used in place of horizontal rules, giving your page a more colorful and 3-D look. An example graphic rule, **bluegreen_bar.jpg**, is included with this chapter's example files.

Replace the HR element with a graphic rule:

1. Replace the first HR element with the example graphic rule:

```
<hr>
<p align="center"><img src="bluegreen_bar.jpg" height="8"
width="100%" alt="Horizontal separator"></p>
<h2><a href="spacecapsules.jpg" target="_blank"><img border="0"
align="left" hspace="10" src="spacecapsules_th.jpg" width="200"
height="166" alt="Mercury, Gemini, and Apollo spacecraft.">
</a>Mercury, Gemini, and Apollo Spacecraft</h2>
```

2. Replace the remaining HR elements with the same example graphic rule (see Figure 4.15).

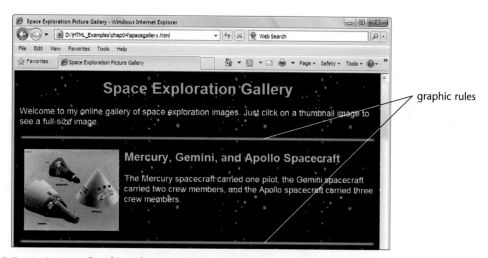

FIGURE 4.15 • Graphic rules can add visual impact to a page.

Notice that a percentage value (`width="100%"`) is used to set the width of the graphic rule. This is an exception to the general rule that you should specify the actual dimensions of an image and not a different size at which you want it to display. Varying the width of a graphic rule relative to the width of the browser window allows it to reduplicate the function of a horizontal rule (the width of which is also dynamically resized relative to the width of the browser window). This method also does not generally cause problems with image quality because a graphic rule's height is small (usually less than 10 pixels), so that increasing only its width is unlikely to magnify flaws within the image.

You can easily create your own graphic rules in your image editor. Most image editors allow you to add various effects to a graphic rule. The example graphic rule, for instance, was created in Corel Paint Shop Pro, using its Buttonize effect. A good width for a graphical rule is 450 pixels, which is short enough that it should not have its width reduced and is long enough that it should not undergo much distortion when being stretched to fill 100 percent of a browser's window.

Using a Transparent Banner Image

When displaying a background image, a **transparent GIF** image with one of its colors set to be transparent can make an effective visual impact. An example **banner image**, spacegallery.gif, with the color of its background set to be transparent, is included with this chapter's example files.

Add a transparent banner image and turn off the display of the H1 element:

1. Insert a banner image above the H1 element:

```
<div align="center">
<img src="spacegallery.gif" width="450" height="75" alt="Space
Gallery Banner Image">
<h1>Space Exploration Gallery</h1>
</div>
```

2. Edit the style sheet to turn off display of the H1 element (see Figure 4.16):

```
h1 {
    color: aqua;
    background: transparent;
    display: none;
    }
```

transparent GIF

FIGURE 4.16 • A transparent banner image can help give a page more of a 3-D look.

3. To close up the space below the banner image, insert a style that sets a negative bottom margin for the DIV element that contains the banner image (see Figure 4.17):

```
<div align="center" style="margin-bottom: -1em;">
<img src="spacegallery.gif" width"450" height="75" alt="Space
Gallery Banner Image">
<h1>Space Exploration Gallery</h1>
</div>
```

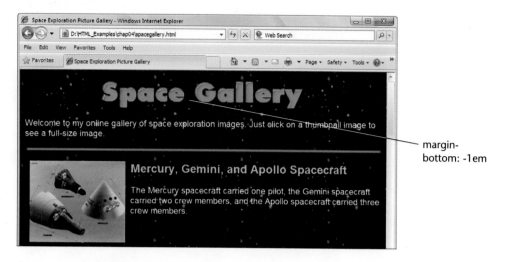

margin-bottom: -1em

FIGURE 4.17 • Setting a negative bottom margin on the containing DIV element reduces the vertical space below the banner image.

Notice in the example that the H1 element is left in the page but with its display turned off (by the **display: none** style property) instead of simply being replaced by the banner image. The reason for this is that some search engines place special weight on the content of your H1 element when indexing your page, so it pays to leave it in, even though turning off its display.

Using Navigation Icons and Button Links

A **navigation icon** is an image that portrays an action a visitor can take by clicking on the image. For instance, a graphic of a house functioning as an image link conveys the idea that it is a link to the home page of the site or author. A left-pointing arrow conveys the idea that the link goes to the previous page, while a right-pointing arrow conveys that the link goes to the next page in a series of pages.

A **button link** is similar to a navigational icon because its design (with 3-D borders) conveys its function (that it can be clicked on), while its label conveys the action or result that will occur when a visitor clicks on the button.

Because they graphically indicate their function and purpose, it is customary to turn off the border of navigation icons and button links. An example button image, gobutton.gif, with the word "Go" as its label, is included with the other example files for this chapter.

Add an image link to the bottom of the page, below the address block, that uses a button link to link to Shirley Johnson's home page (see Figure 4.18):

```
</address>
<p align="center"><a href="home.html" style="text-decoration:
none"><img src="gobutton.gif" width="100" height="50" alt="Go
button" border="0" hspace="8" align="middle">to my Home Page
</a></p>
```

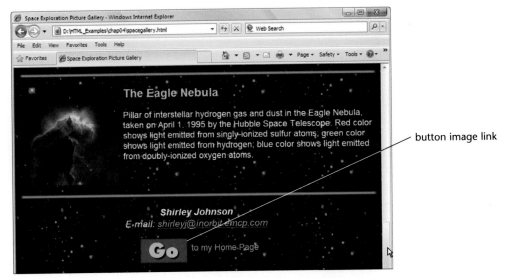

button image link

FIGURE 4.18 • A button image link graphically conveys that it can be clicked to go to an object or resource.

Notice that the ALIGN attribute is used here to vertically align the image relative to the text line on which it is inserted—in this case, the middle of the image is aligned with the image's text line. You also can specify `align="top"` to align the top of the image relative to its text line. Bottom-alignment is the default. If you set top-, middle-, or bottom-alignment, you cannot also set left- or right-alignment.

The inline style in the A element, `text-decoration: none;`, turns off the underline for the text following the button, which still functions as part of the link.

Visit the Internet Resource Center. To find online resources that provide clip art that you can use in your Web pages, visit the Chapter 4 section of this book's Internet Resource Center at **www.emcp.net/html2e.**

Finding Images on the Web

Many repositories of images are available on the Web. Always carefully read any terms of use that are posted relative to images you find on the Web (if you do not see a terms of use page, look for an FAQ page). Some images are true **public domain images** that you are free to use in any manner that you choose, due to either the lapsing of their copyright or a creator releasing them into the public domain. Many other images, however, are free to use only if you can satisfy the terms of use. Some images, for instance, are free for personal, non-commercial, or educational purposes, but not for commercial or for-profit purposes. Some providers also require a credit and a link back to their site if you use their images on your site.

A number of sites specifically provide clip art images that can be freely used by instructors and students in an educational environment. Many other Web art repositories allow free use of their art images for non-commercial or educational purposes.

CREATING YOUR OWN WEB IMAGES

You can create your own Web art images to give your page or site a unique or personalized appearance. To create your own Web art images, you need an **image editor** that can create and save GIF and JPEG images. A wide array of image editors can be used to create Web art images. If you do not already have an image editor you can use, here are some you can try out:

- **Adobe Photoshop CS4 (www.adobe.com/products/photoshop/).** The tool of choice preferred by many professional graphic designers (Windows and Macintosh OS X).
- **Adobe Photoshop Elements 7 (www.adobe.com/products/photoshopelwin/).** A less expensive version of Photoshop (Windows and Macintosh OS X).
- **Corel Paint Shop Pro Photo X2 (www.corel.com/servlet/Satellite/us/en/ Product/1184951547051).** Not just a photo editor, but a full-feature image editor that rivals Adobe Photoshop CS4 for features at 1/6th the price (Windows).
- **Ulead PhotoImpact X3 (www.ulead.com/pi/).** Not just a photo editor, but a full-feature image editor that rivals Adobe Photoshop CS4 for features at 1/10th the price (Windows).
- **GIMP (GNU Image Manipulation Program (www.gimp.org/).** Free image editor (cross-platform).
- **GIMPShop (www.gimpshop.com/).** A free image editor that replicates the feel of Adobe Photoshop (cross-platform).
- **Paint.NET (www.getpaint.net/).** A free image editor (Windows).
- **WebPainter by Totally Hip Software (www.totallyhip.com/webpainter.html).** A full-feature, inexpensive image editor (Windows and Macintosh Classic).

 **Visit the Internet Resource Center.** To find online resources that provide additional image editors and graphic utilities, visit the Chapter 4 section of this book's Internet Resource Center at **www.emcp.net/html2e** or the Tucows site at **www.tucows.com/**.

Choosing Image Formats

Beginning Web authors are often perplexed by which image format to use for displaying images on the Web. There are three different image formats that are supported by all recent browsers:

- GIF (Graphic Interchange Format)
- JPG (Joint Photographic Experts Group)
- PNG (Portable Network Graphics)

The **GIF image format** (*.gif) is an 8-bit image format (8-bits per pixel) that supports up to 256 colors. Because colors not included in a GIF image's color palette will be dithered, the GIF image format is best used for images that contain less than 256 colors. The exception to that rule is with images that contain text, since the compression algorithm used in JPEG images can cause text to appear blurry. For images with text, even if containing many more than 256 colors, a GIF image with an optimized color palette is often the better choice. (See "Working with GIF Images" later in this chapter for coverage of using optimized color palettes.) Because GIF images can have one color designated to be transparent, they are also frequently used whenever transparency is desired. GIF images also support **interlacing**, which in GIF images works by displaying the image in several passes, with progressively more lines displayed in each pass. This allows a visitor to see a representation of the image after the first pass, without having to wait for the whole image to download first. For more detailed guidance on using GIF images, see "Working with GIF Images" below.

The **JPEG image format** (*.jpg) is a 24-bit image format that supports up to 16.8 million colors (sometimes referred to as Truecolor). It is best used for images that contain many colors, such as photographs or images that contain continuous tones or blends. The exception is with images that contain text, as noted above. For more detailed guidance on using JPEG images, see "Working with JPEG Images" below.

The **PNG image format** (*.png) supports more colors than JPEG images and can specify ranges of colors to be transparent (**alpha-channel transparency**), rather than just one color as with GIF images. At first glance, the PNG image format would appear to combine the best of both the JPEG and GIF image formats. In reality, however, inconsistencies in how different browsers support the format have limited the degree to which PNG images have been used on the Web. Also, because PNG images use a **lossless compression scheme**, rather than a **lossy compression scheme**, as with JPEG images, an image saved as a PNG image can be larger (consume more bandwidth) than the same image saved as a JPEG image. For these reasons, most Web designers have chosen to stick with using GIF or JPEG images for displaying graphics on the Web. For more detailed guidance on using PNG images, see "Working with PNG Images" below.

Working with GIF Images

Although GIF images were not originally designed for display on the Web, a number of basic methods and techniques have been created by Web authors that make using GIF images over the Web effective. GIF images work best for images that include line art, flat colors, and fewer than 256 colors. When such an image is saved as a GIF, it produces a smaller image, measured in bytes, than if the image is saved as a JPEG or PNG image. GIF images are also often used to create images with a transparent background. The image spacegallery.gif, used earlier in this chapter, is a transparent GIF image. A GIF image can include multiple frames, which means it can be animated (a GIF animation).

GIF images can include three different kinds of color palettes: standard, Web-safe, and optimized. The **standard color palette** contains 256 colors, generally taken from the default 256-color palette of the system on which the image was created. The Web-safe color palette contains 216 colors that should be present on almost any system. (The Windows, Macintosh, and UNIX system palettes differ from each other.) An optimized color palette includes only colors that are present in the image (also called an adaptive color palette in Photoshop).

USING THE WEB-SAFE COLOR PALETTE The **Web-safe color palette** guarantees that an image will be displayed on any 256-color or higher system without dithering. **Dithering** is done by positioning pixels of different colors next to each other to simulate to the eye that a single color is present, which can result in colors with a speckled or mottled appearance that barely resembles the desired color. Without dithering, areas that use blends, gradients, or continuous tones might be displayed as a sequence of distinct color bands because only colors that are actually included in the palette can be displayed.

The problem with using the Web-safe palette, however, is that it works well only for images with relatively few colors or color gradations. Images that contain many colors that are not included in the Web-safe palette are likely to suffer considerably when saved using that palette. In other words, if you are concerned that some viewers of your image will see a lot of dithered colors, making sure that everyone sees dithered colors is hardly an optimum solution.

USING AN OPTIMIZED COLOR PALETTE Web designers today choose to focus their efforts on the vast majority of viewers who are using true-color graphics cards (capable of displaying colors selected from a palette of 16.7 million colors or more).

GIF images, however, can display only up to 256 colors. When you save an image that has many more than 256 colors as a GIF image using the Web-safe palette, the image quality can suffer tremendously. Instead, such images can be saved with an **optimized color palette** (also called an *adaptive* or *indexed palette* in Photoshop). An optimized palette, unlike the standard or Web-safe palettes, includes only colors that are present in the image.

When creating an optimized color palette, you can choose 256 or fewer as the number of colors. The fewer colors you can select and still retain acceptable image quality, the fewer bytes the resulting image will consume.

Many image editors also include wizards that help automate the creation of optimized GIF images. These editors often let you see the results of different settings as you are making them.

WORKING WITH IMAGES WITH TEXT Photographs or other images with continuous tones, blends, or gradients that require more than 256 colors should be saved as JPEG images. The exception to this rule is an image containing text, for which an optimized GIF image is usually the better choice. Due to the kind of compression it applies, the JPEG format tends to cause the edges of letterforms to appear fuzzy. To see this in action, open **image_compare.html** in your browser (see Figure 4.19).

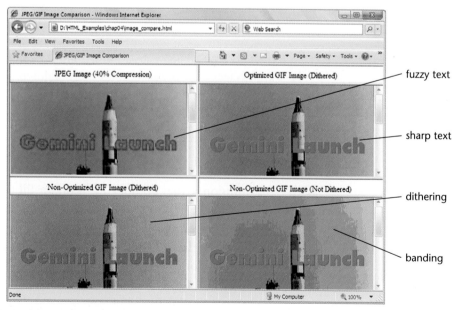

FIGURE 4.19 • An image containing text usually looks best when saved as an optimized GIF image.

USING TRANSPARENT GIF IMAGES GIF images allow you to specify one color as transparent. This can let you create text banners with a page's background color or image showing through the banner's negative (non-text) areas. You can also create a button with rounded corners, for instance, that will display transparently against a background color or image.

When creating transparent GIF images, some things to watch out for include:

- **Error diffusion.** This can cause an image's background to be diffused into a range of different colors, which can interfere with setting the background to be transparent, because only one color can be set to be transparent in a GIF image.
- **Anti-aliasing.** If creating a text banner where you want the text to be displayed transparently against a page's background, turning on anti-aliasing, which blends the letterforms with the image's background, can cause a visible "halo" effect along the edges of the letterforms, if the image background and the page background differ in tone or hue. See Figure 4.20.

FIGURE 4.20 • Anti-aliasing can cause text in a transparent GIF image to display a white halo effect if created against a white background, and displayed against a dark background.

NOTE If you are creating a GIF image with a transparent background color, using error diffusion can result in the color of your background being diffused into more than one color. Because only one color can be defined as transparent in a GIF image, this can interfere with setting the background of your image as entirely transparent. If you want to set a transparent background, your choices are to either turn off error diffusion or refill your image's background later with a solid color.

With error diffusion, either do not turn it on, or fill the diffused background with a single color (most image editors will let you fill a tonal range of colors, replacing them with a single color).

With anti-aliasing or drop shadows, either do not use the effect, or make sure your image's background color closely matches that of the Web page against which you want it to be displayed.

A Web page's background image can contain a number of colors. Most full-feature image editors contain an "eye-dropper" tool that lets you pick up a color from a background image and set it as the color of your foreground or background swatch. You can then use that color to fill the background of a **banner image**, for instance, and then assign that color as transparent. This method can be particularly effective when using a drop shadow effect (causing the drop shadows to appear to blend transparently with the page's background image or color).

Just open the background image in your image editor and "pick up" a color with the eye-dropper and assign it to the foreground or background swatch. Fill the image's background with the color, set it to be transparent, then assign the same color to the page background.

Picking the right color out of a background image to be used as a transparent background color in your image can take a little trial and error. Try to pick either the most prominent or one of the more common colors in the image.

USING INTERLACED GIF IMAGES

Interlacing refers to displaying an image in more than one pass, with only some of the lines in the image appearing in any one pass. Four passes are used to display an interlaced GIF image, with the last two passes filling in progressively more lines than the first two passes. The result is that a viewer can start seeing what a downloaded interlaced GIF image will look like much sooner than with a non-interlaced GIF image.

Many visitors just click the Back button if they think a site's images are taking too long to display. By saving your GIF images as interlaced, you can give visitors to your site a much earlier indication of what the images will look like. When you save a GIF image, most image editors let you choose an option to save your image as interlaced.

Working with JPEG Images

A photographic image or an image with a lot of colors or blends is usually best saved as a JPEG image. The exception to this rule, as noted earlier, is an image that includes text, which is often best saved as an optimized GIF image because a JPEG image's compression method tends to blur and fuzz the edges of letterforms.

When you save a JPEG image, most image editors let you set a **compression level** for the image. The higher the compression level, the smaller the resulting file size will be. The smaller the file size, the quicker the image will download and display. Some image editors have wizards that will automate finding the right compression level for an image, or you can just experiment by saving your image at different compression levels and then compare the results, to see which provides the best combination of preserving image quality and conserving bandwidth.

Realize, however, that some images can take much higher levels of compression than other images. The optimal level of compression can be different for each JPEG image you want to create. In general, however, you can usually compress JPEG images up to 20 to 30 percent without appreciable loss of image quality. Other images might take as much as a 50 or 60 percent compression.

JPEG images use a *lossy* compression scheme. A lossy compression scheme results in bits in the image being thrown away, which means that a JPEG image cannot be uncompressed after it has been compressed. A *lossless* compression scheme, on the other hand, does not throw away bits, which means that an image saved using such a scheme can later be uncompressed, with no bits being lost. You should not store original images you create as JPEG images but should save them in your image editor's proprietary format (PSD for Photoshop or PSP for Paint Shop Pro, for instance) or in an image format that uses a lossless compression scheme, such as PNG or TIFF.

Besides being able to save an image as a standard JPEG, many image editors also let you save an image as a progressive JPEG, which causes the image to display in a similar fashion to an interlaced GIF image. As with interlaced GIFs, viewers are able to see what the downloaded JPEG image will look like before it has completely downloaded. This increases the size of the image, however, which will increase the time it takes the entire image to display—a better idea is to take the time to find the optimal compression level for the image and speed up its download and display that way. Some earlier Web browsers can also have problems displaying progressive JPEG images.

Using the FONT element or styles, you are limited to displaying fonts that are available on a viewer's local computer. When creating your own Web images, however, you can use any font you have installed on your system, because you will be using them in a graphic instead of displaying them as part of your page's text. You can use a Dracula font, for instance, to create a banner graphic for your page if you have that font installed on your computer.

Visit the Internet Resource Center. To find online resources where you can download fonts, visit the Chapter 4 section of this book's Internet Resource Center at **www.emcp.net/html2e**. Before using a font, however, read the terms of use for copyright information and restrictions on use.

Using Other Image Formats

Many other image formats are available, including BMP, WMF, TIFF, PCX, PICT, and more. Although these image formats are fine for using in a desktop publishing program where you only need to display them on your local computer and print them on your printer, they should not be used for display in a Web page. Such files are uncompressed and result in images that are much larger in bytes than a GIF, JPEG, or PNG image. Only GIF, JPEG, and PNG digital images should be displayed in Web pages.

Because Internet Explorer displays BMP images, many beginning Web authors mistakenly think that it is okay to use BMP images in Web pages. Most other browsers do not display BMP images. The BMP image format also does not use any compression, so an image that has a size in the tens of kilobytes when saved as a JPEG image, for instance, can have a size of hundreds of kilobytes when saved as a BMP image. In other words, do not use BMP or WMF images in Web pages, even if you know everybody accessing your page will be using Internet Explorer.

Using Image Effects in Web Pages

There is a wide range of different effects you can create using an image editor such as Adobe Photoshop or Corel Paint Shop Pro.

- **Text effects.** While in HTML, you are limited to displaying fonts that are present on a user's system; when creating graphics, you can use any font that is on your system.
- **Drop shadows.** Adding a drop shadow effect to a transparent image can create much more of a 3D effect. However, if the backgrounds of the image and page differ significantly in tone or hue, a halo effect even more noticeable than with anti-aliasing will result.
- **Button effects.** Many image editors have wizards that automate creating three-dimensional buttons, which can serve as navigational icons and other Web objects.
- **Gradient effects.** A gradient blends two or more colors, from red to yellow, green to blue, and so on.

Figure 4.21 shows a three-dimensional button created in Corel Paint Shop Pro Photo X2 that also features text, drop shadow, and gradient fill effects.

FIGURE 4.21 • A three-dimensional button featuring text, drop shadow, and gradient fill effects.

USING ANIMATIONS

You can include media other than still graphics in a Web page. By adding animations to your pages, you can make them more dynamic and eye-catching than pages that include only still images (or no images at all).

Using GIF Animations

The GIF image format allows for the inclusion of multiple image frames within a single image, to create what is generally called a **GIF animation** (or animated GIF). When displayed in a Web browser, the image frames within an animated GIF are displayed at a frame rate that can be set when the image is created. An example GIF animation, go_anim.gif, is included with this chapter's example files.

If it is not already open, re-open **spacegallery.html** in your text editor and browser. Replace the previous navigation icon at the bottom of the page with a GIF animation, go_anim.gif, set the image's vertical spacing to 5 pixels, and insert a BR element to move the following text below the image (see Figure 4.22):

```
</address>
<p align="center"><a href="home.html" style="text-decoration:
none"><img src="go_anim.gif" vspace="5" width="100" height="50"
alt="Go button" border="0" hspace="8" align="middle"><br>to my
Home Page</a></p>
```

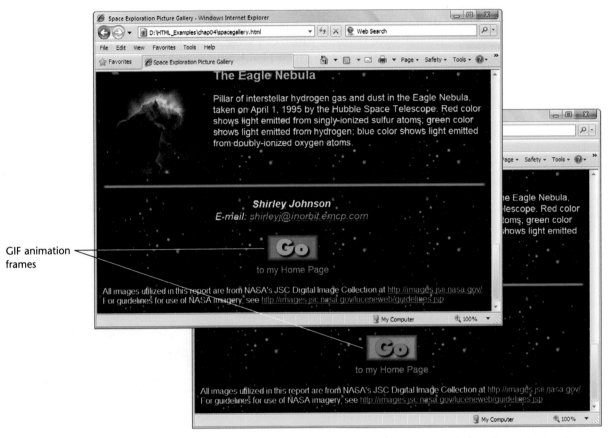

GIF animation frames

FIGURE 4.22 • A GIF animation also can function as an image link and a navigation icon.

Notice that a BR element is added that moves the following text below the GIF animation, and 5 pixels of vertical spacing is added to provide extra spacing between the animation and the following text. The `align="middle"` attribute is deleted because it has no effect with the following text moved below the image.

To create your own GIF animations, you need a GIF animation editor. Many GIF animation editors include animation wizards that make creating GIF animations as simple as selecting the images you want to use, the order in which you want them to appear, and the frame rate at which you want your animation to display. After you have created an animation, you can change the settings for individual frames, create transitions between frames, add and delete frames, preview the animation, and so on.

GIF animations, although they can include multiple image frames, are still GIF images. The color palette used to display all the frames within a GIF animation is still limited to no more than 256 colors. The result is that some GIF images included in a GIF animation can suffer visually, due to additional dithering, for instance, when a particular color is not present in the image's palette. Some GIF animators also let you import JPEG, PNG, or other true-color images that can suffer considerably from dithering when converted to GIF format within a GIF animation.

One way to try to fix this problem is to edit the individual images in your image editor and create optimized color palettes for each one that include only the minimal number of colors required to produce acceptable image quality. For instance, if you can reduce the total number of colors used by each image to 128 or 64 colors, you will reduce or eliminate the dithering that can result when the images are combined within a GIF animation.

File size is another issue to consider with GIF animations. For instance, in one GIF animation software program, saving 4-, 8-, and 16-frame animations resulted in file sizes of 8-, 14-, and 27 kilobytes, respectively. If you add any transition effects between frames, that can add many additional frames to your animation, depending on the effect being used. Also, the more image frames you include in your animation, the more likely that individual images in your animation will be dithered. For these reasons, it is usually best to limit the number of frames included in a GIF animation; you would not want to include a 200-KB GIF animation in a Web page, for instance (a more reasonable size would be 30-KB to 50-KB, or less).

Using Other Animations

GIF animations are not the only kinds of animations that can be included in a Web page. Flash or Java animations can include many more effects than GIF animations. These types of animations can also do much more than just provide dynamic movement; they can create multimedia effects (animation, video, and audio effects) that interact with user actions or respond to events.

 **Visit the Internet Resource Center.** To find online resources where you can download GIF animation and other animation software programs, visit the Chapter 4 section of this book's Internet Resource Center at **www.emcp.net/html2e** or the Tucows site at **www.tucows.com/**.

ADDING SOUND

You can add background sound that plays automatically when a Web page displays. An example WAV-format audio file, kennedy.wav, is included with this chapter's example files.

Embedding Audio Files

The EMBED element was originally introduced as an unofficial extension to HTML by Netscape and is supported by all current browsers. Despite wide support among browsers, the EMBED element was not included in HTML 3.2 or HTML 4, in favor of using the new OBJECT element instead.

NOTE
The EMBED element has, belatedly, been included in HTML 5, so concerns about forward-compatibility no longer counsel against using it. For your document to validate with an EMBED element in it, however, you will need to use an HTML 5 DocType statement (`<!DOCTYPE html>`) at the top of the document and exclude all elements and attributes that are obsolete in HTML 5.

PLAYING AN AUDIO FILE AUTOMATICALLY IN THE BACKGROUND You can embed an audio file that will play automatically in the background when the page is opened in a browser.

Add and test a WAV file that plays automatically in the background when the page is opened:

1. At the top of the page, use the EMBED element to insert an audio file that plays automatically in the background:

```
<div align="center" style="margin-bottom: -1em;">
<div><embed src="kennedy.wav" type="audio/wav" hidden="true"
autostart="true" loop="false"></div>
<img src="spacegallery.gif" width"450" height="75" alt="Space
Gallery Banner Image">
<h1>Space Exploration Gallery</h1>
```

2. Save your HTML file, switch to your browser, and click the Refresh (or Reload) button.

If your computer and browser are configured to play WAV audio files, an audio file of President John F. Kennedy announcing the program to land a man on the moon will start playing in the background.

If the WAV file does not play in your browser, you may need to download and install a plug-in for your browser or a player that will play WAV files. To download the latest version of the Windows Media Player, go to **www.microsoft.com/windows/windowsmedia/**.

Visit the Internet Resource Center. To find online resources that provide audio/video plug-ins and players you can download and use, visit the Chapter 4 section of this book's Internet Resource Center at **www.emcp.net/html2e**.

The SRC attribute specifies the media file being played. The `type="audio/wav"` attribute identifies the media file's MIME type. Although not required, this will speed up the time it takes for the file to start playing (otherwise, the file has to be downloaded once to identify its MIME type and then again to play). The `hidden="true"` attribute hides the **player console**, while the `autostart="true"` attribute causes the media to start playing automatically.

The `loop="false"` attribute causes the audio file to play only once, rather than being looped indefinitely. Especially when hiding the player console, indefinitely looping an audio file that plays automatically in the background is strongly discouraged because users have no way of turning it off, except by clicking the Back button or accessing their system's audio volume controls. Because some visitors find audio annoying, you could also set **autostart="false"**, especially if the embedded audio is on your front page.

A common error is to specify a numerical value for the EMBED element's LOOP attribute, to specify a set number of loops, such as **loop="2"**, for instance. This causes varying results in different players, with some defaulting to looping the media file only once, while others loop it indefinitely. Always set either **true** or **false** as the LOOP attribute's value.

PLAYING AN AUDIO FILE AUTOMATICALLY IN THE FOREGROUND If you want to automatically play an indefinitely looping audio file, you should set the dimensions of the player console to make it visible in the browser window, so users can turn off the audio if they wish.

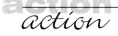

Edit the EMBED element to cause the player console to be visible:

1. Edit the EMBED element to unhide the player console, set its dimensions to 144 × 60 pixels, turn off autostart, and set the audio file to loop indefinitely:

```
<div><embed src="kennedy.wav" type="audio/wav" width="144"
height="60" hidden="true" autostart="false" loop="true"></div>
```

2. Save the document, switch over to your browser, and click the Refresh (or Reload) button (see Figure 4.23).

FIGURE 4.23 • The Windows Media Player 11 console is displayed on the page, letting a user turn off the playing of a looping or long audio file.

3. Click the player console's Play button to play the audio file.
4. Click the Stop button to stop the audio from looping.

The player console displayed in your browser will depend on which application, if any, is associated with WAV files on your system. The Apple QuickTime player is the most common audio player on Macintosh systems, although it might also be available on Windows systems. Different player consoles can have different dimensions, so you cannot depend on a player console being any particular size, or having a particular look. The Windows Media Player 11 console is shown in the figure, but a user might have an older or newer version of that player installed.

If WAV files are associated with the QuickTime player on a Windows system, to see the same player console as shown in Figure 4.23, you can download and install the Windows Media player from **www.microsoft.com/windows/windowsmedia/**.

Not automatically starting the audio lets users decide whether they want to listen to the audio. Some people are irritated by audio that plays automatically, or they might be working in an office environment, for instance, where audio might be inappropriate.

SPECIFYING A PLUG-IN PAGE One problem with including audio in Web pages is that a user needs to have an appropriate player or plug-in to play the audio. The EMBED element's PLUGINSPAGE attribute can be used to specify a URL for downloading an appropriate plug-in player for the audio format being played. The following code example shows a PLUGINSPAGE attribute that specifies the URL where the QuickTime player can be downloaded:

```
<div><embed src="kennedy.wav" type="audio/wav" width="144"
height="60" autostart="false" loop="true"
pluginspage="http://www.apple.com/quicktime/download/"></div>
```

If the browser does not have the appropriate plug-in player to play a particular media file, it will present the URL provided by the PLUGINSPAGE attribute, so that the user can download a plug-in player capable of playing the media file.

Using the OBJECT Element to Insert Audio Files

The OBJECT element is a standard element included in HTML 4 that is intended as a generic means to insert objects into Web pages. An object might be an image, a sound file, a video, a Java applet, and so on. You can even embed an HTML file inside another HTML file as an object. The PARAM (Parameter) element can be nested inside the OBJECT element to set display, behavior, and other parameters.

PLAYING AN AUDIO FILE AUTOMATICALLY IN THE FOREGROUND Previously, you used the EMBED element to insert a WAV audio file that plays automatically when the page is opened. The same thing can be accomplished using the OBJECT element.

Use HTML comments to comment out the EMBED element you added previously, and then use the OBJECT element to automatically play and loop a WAV audio file with the player console displayed (see Figure 4.24):

```
<!--<div><embed src="kennedy.wav" type="audio/wav" width="144"
height="60" autostart="false" loop="true"></div>-->
<img src="spacegallery.gif" width="450" height="75" alt="Space
Gallery Banner Image">
<div style="margin-top:-10px"><object data="kennedy.wav"
type="audio/wav" width="200" height="45">
<param name="src" value="kennedy.wav">
<param name="autoplay" value="true">
<param name="controller" value="true">
<param name="loop" value="true">
President Kennedy calling for landing a man on the moon.
</object></div>
```

player console
(OBJECT element)

FIGURE 4.24 • The OBJECT element, a standard HTML 4 element, can be used to embed an audio file in a Web page.

The current example starts playing the audio file automatically in the background. If you want the audio file to play only after the user clicks the play button, set a value of **false** for the **autostart** parameter.

The OBJECT element's TYPE attribute specifies the **MIME type** (or content type) of an object file. MIME stands for *Multipurpose Internet Mail Extensions* and was originally devised to identify different e-mail attachments but is now used more generally to identify files on the Internet. For instance, **audio/wav**, **image/gif**, and **text/css** are all MIME types for files that can be downloaded over the Web. MIME types have two parts, a type and a subtype, with **audio** specifying the type and **wav** specifying the subtype, for instance. Including the TYPE attribute in the OBJECT element is optional but recommended; if a browser does not recognize the MIME type, it can simply not download the object.

Various additional attributes can be used with the OBJECT element. For a listing, see Appendix A, *HTML Quick Reference*. For further explanation of how to use the OBJECT element, see the W3C's HTML 4.01 specification at **www.w3.org/TR/html401/**.

PLAYING AN AUDIO FILE AUTOMATICALLY IN THE BACKGROUND You also can use the OBJECT element to automatically play an audio file in the background when a Web page is opened.

Edit the example code to turn off display of the player console (controller) and not loop playing the audio file:

1. Edit the OBJECT element's WIDTH and HEIGHT attributes to have a value of **0** (zero); delete the third and fourth PARAM elements:

```
<div style="margin-top:-10px">
<object data="kennedy.wav" type="audio/wav" width="0" height="0">
<param name="src" value="kennedy.wav">
<param name="autoplay" value="true">
<param name="controller" value="true">
<param name="loop" value="true">
President Kennedy calling for landing a man on the moon.
</object>
</div>
```

2. Save your HTML file and then refresh its display in your browser. You should here the audio file play automatically in the background, without the player console visible on the page.

3. In your text editor, comment out the OBJECT element, so it will not play, but you can save the codes for later reference:

```
<!--
<div style="margin-top:-10px">
<object data="kennedy.wav" type="audio/wav" width="0" height="0">
<param name="src" value="kennedy.wav">
<param name="autoplay" value="true">
President Kennedy calling for landing a man on the moon.
</object>
</div>
-->
```

Setting the width and height of the OBJECT element to **0** hides it from view. The **controller** parameter is deleted because it is not needed to display the player console. The **loop** parameter is also deleted to not loop the audio file (**value="false"** is the default value).

Choosing Audio Formats

Many different audio formats can be used to play audio in a Web page. Some of the most commonly used audio formats are WAV, AIFF, MIDI, MP3, AU, and RealAudio. Table 4.1 shows many of the audio formats, along with their MIME types, that can be used in Web pages.

The WAV audio format is native to the Windows system, the AIFF format originated from the Macintosh, and the AU format originated from the Sun and Next computer platforms. The MIDI and MP3 formats are popular for playing music files.

TABLE 4.1 • Common Audio MIME Types

Media Object	Extensions	MIME Types
AU (Sun/Next Audio format)	AU, SND	audio/basic
AIFF (Audio Interchange File Format)	AIF, AIFF, AIFC	audio/x-aiff
OGG	OGG, OGA	audio/ogg
MIDI (Musical Instrument Digital Interface)	MID, MIDI, RMI	audio/mid
MPEG (Moving Picture Experts Group)	MPG, MPEG, MP2, MPE	audio/mpeg
MP3 audio	MP3	audio/mpeg3
RealAudio	RA	audio/x-realaudio
Windows (WAVE) audio	WAV	audio/wav
Windows Media Audio file	WMA	audio/x-ms-wma

ADDING VIDEO

You are not limited to including only still images or GIF animations in Web pages. Many video formats also can be inserted into a Web page using the EMBED or OBJECT elements. An example video file, biosphere.mpg, is included with this chapter's example files.

Using the EMBED Element to Insert a Video

You can use the EMBED element to insert a video file in a Web page.

Embed a video file at the bottom of the page:

1. Copy and paste the graphical rule at the bottom of your page, as shown here:

```
<p align="center"><img src="bluegreen_bar.jpg" height="8"
width="100%" alt="Horizontal separator"></p>
<p align="center"><img src="bluegreen_bar.jpg" height="8"
width="100%" alt="Horizontal separator"></p>
<address>
```

2. Use the EMBED element to insert a video file:

```
<p align="center"><img src="bluegreen_bar.jpg" height="8"
width="100%" alt="Horizontal separator"></p>
<div align="center">
<h2>Earth Biosphere Animation from NASA</h2>
<p><embed src="biosphere.mpg" autostart="false" loop="true"
width="320" height="255"></p>
</div>
<p align="center"><img src="bluegreen_bar.jpg" height="8"
width="100%" alt="Horizontal separator"></p>
<address>
```

3. Save your file, switch over to your browser, and click the Refresh (or Reload) button.
4. If the video and player console are displayed, click the Play button to start the video (see Figure 4.25).

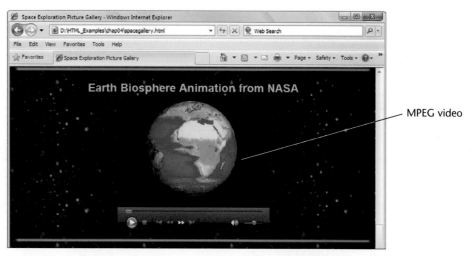

FIGURE 4.25 • The embedded MPEG video file, biosphere.mpg, starts to play when the Play button is clicked.

TROUBLE *spot*

Depending on the browser you are using, how it is configured, and which players or plug-ins are installed, what you see on your system might differ from what is shown in Figure 4.25. If you have trouble playing video files in your browser, download and install the latest video player for your platform: the Windows Media Player (**www.microsoft.com/windows/windowsmedia/**) for Windows and the Apple QuickTime Player (**www.apple.com/quicktime/**) for Macintosh OS X.

Using the OBJECT Element to Insert a Video

You also can use the OBJECT element to insert a video in a Web page.

Comment out the EMBED element, and use the OBJECT element to insert an AVI video:

```
<div align="center">
<h2>Earth Biosphere Animation from NASA</h2>
<!--
<p><embed src="biosphere.mpg" autostart="false" loop="true"
width="320" height="255"></p>
-->
<object data="biosphere.mpg" type="video/mpeg" width="320"
height="255">
<param name="src" value="biosphere.mpg">
<param name="autoplay" value="false">
<param name="controller" value="true">
<param name="loop" value="false">
</object>
</div>
```

If your browser supports the OBJECT element, the result you see in your browser should look the same as when using the EMBED element (refer to Figure 4.25) to embed the video file in your Web page. Table 4.2 shows some of the more common video formats, along with their MIME types, that are used on the Web.

TABLE 4.2 • Common Video MIME Types

Media Object	Extensions	MIME Types
ASF (Advanced Streaming Format)	ASF	video/x-ms-asf
MPEG video	MPEG, MPG, MPE	video/mpeg
MPEG-2 video	MPV2, MP2V	video/mpeg2
QuickTime video	MOV, QT	video/quicktime
OGG	OGV	video/ogg
RealMedia meta file	RM, RAM	application/vnd.rn-realmedia
RealVideo	RV	video/vnd.rn-realvideo
Video for Windows (Audio/Video Interleave)	AVI	video/avi
Windows Media Video file	WMV	video/x-ms-wmv
VDOLive streaming video	VDO	video/vdo
Vivo streaming video	VIV	video/vnd.vivo

UNDERSTANDING COPYRIGHT ISSUES

A lot of images, audio clips, and video files can be downloaded easily from the Web, but that does not mean you are free to use them. Always make sure you have the right to use an image or other media file before you use it.

When using images or other media files from online sources, be sure to save any pages or documents that provide permission for usage or guidelines for fair or allowed usage of images or other media files. Also, the use of an image of a recognizable living person might require separate permission from that person. In its guidelines, for instance, NASA advises that images of such persons in its collection can be used without permission if for communicative purposes, rather than for commercial exploitation.

Additional considerations apply to musical copyrights because a particular musical work's score (sheet music), arrangement, performance, recording, and sequencing might all be separately copyrighted. Both performance and distribution fees can be deemed due when offering copyrighted audio recordings for download over the Web.

Visit the Internet Resource Center. To find online resources that discuss copyright issues as they apply to the Web, visit the Chapter 4 section of this book's Internet Resource Center at **www.emcp.net/html2e.**

If you are creating a commercial Web site, many sites on the Web offer access to images, music, and video for a membership or subscription fee. These media files are usually referred to as royalty-free, to distinguish them from public domain media files. To locate vendors of royalty-free images, music, or video files, search at Google (**www.google.com/**) or Yahoo! (**www.yahoo.com/**) on the words "royalty free."

USING RELATIVE URLS

Until now, you have been working with examples that use files that are all located in the same folder. When working with a more complex Web site with many files, using a single folder can become cumbersome. To make working with a more complex Web site easier, you can organize the site's files into separate folders. Separating image files from HTML files, by organizing image files in their own folder, can make it easier to manage and work with both types of files.

You create links between two files located in different folders within your site by using a relative URL. As defined in Chapter 1, a **relative URL** states the location of a linked object relative to 1) the location of the linking file or 2) the root folder of a site. You should always use relative URLs when linking between files that are internal to your own site. The same relative URL will work equally well both when creating your site on your local machine and after you have published your site to the Web. You also can easily move a site that uses relative URLs from one domain to another, without having to fix a single internal link. However, if you had used absolute URLs to link to files internal to your own site, you would need to fix every single internal link in your site.

You have actually been using relative URLs all along in this book—using only the name of the file to link to it is the simplest form of a relative URL (because the linked and linking files are in the same folder, no other path information is required to create the link).

Some common types of relative URLs include:

- `href="banner.jpg"`—links to an object in the same folder as the linking file.
- `href="chapter1/"`—links to the index file (usually index.html) in a child folder (chapter1) of the linking file's folder.
- `href="part1/page1.html"`—links to page1.html in a child folder (part1) of the linking file's folder.
- `href="part1/chapter1/page1.html"`—links to page1.html in a grandchild folder (chapter1) of the linking file's folder.
- `href="../"`—links to the index file (usually index.html) in the parent folder of the linking file's folder.
- `href="./"`—links to the index file (usually index.html) in the same folder as the linking file.
- `src="../images/mypic.jpg"`—links to mypic.jpg in the child folder (images/) of the linking file's parent folder. The images folder, in this case, could be called a sibling folder of the linking file's folder.
- `href="../bio.html"`—links to bio.html in the parent folder of the linking file's folder.
- `href="../../"`—links to the index file (usually index.html) in the grandparent folder of the linking file's folder.
- `href="../../contact/"`—links to the index file (usually index.html) in a child folder (contact) of the grandparent folder of the linking file's folder. The contact folder, in this case, could be called an aunt (or uncle) folder.
- `href="/"`—links to the index file (usually index.html) in the site's root folder.
- `href="/contact/"`—links to the index file (usually index.html) in a child folder (contact) of the site's root folder.
- `href="/contact/jmiller/"`—links to the index file (usually index.html) in a child folder (contact) of the site's root folder.

NOTE The last three examples state the location of the linked object relative to the site's root folder, rather than relative to the linking file's location. For that reason, this kind of relative URL is sometimes called a *root URL*.

Figure 4.26 shows a diagram illustrating the different linking relationships. Table 4.3 shows some example URLs and their absolute URL equivalents (assuming a base URL of www.server.com/folder/project1/ for the linking file).

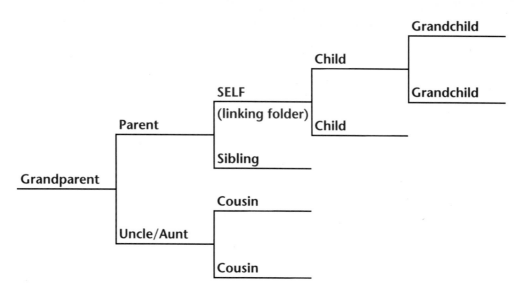

FIGURE 4.26 • This relative URL tree illustrates the linking relationships relative to the linking file's location.

TABLE 4.3 • Relative/Absolute URL Equivalents (assuming a base URL of server.emcp.com/folder/project1/)

Relative URLs	Absolute URL Equivalents
main.html	server.emcp.com/folder/project1/main.html
images/back.jpg	server.emcp.com/folder/project1/images/back.jpg
../project2/index.html	server.emcp.com/folder/project2/index.html
../../folder2/project-a/	server.emcp.com/folder2/project-a/
chap1/tbls/tbl1.html	server.emcp.com/folder/project1/chap1/tbls/tbl1.html
./index2.html	server.emcp.com/folder/project1/index2.html
./	server.emcp.com/folder/project1/
/support/	server.emcp.com/support/

CASE EXAMPLE: CONVERTING THE MERCURY PROJECT PAGE TO RELATIVE LINKS

“Shirley Johnson has decided she wants to reorganize her page on the Mercury Project by placing her HTML file in one folder and the images she is using in a separate images folder. She is then going to link from her HTML file to her images using relative URLs.”

In the previous examples in this book, all local links have been to images and files located in the same folder as the linking HTML file, stating the linked file's name as the value of the HREF or SRC attribute. As noted previously, this is actually a form of relative URL, in that it states that the linked file, relative to the linking file, is in the same folder.

In this example, you will be using relative links to link between an HTML file in one folder and images in another folder. In doing this, you will be using two folders, a project folder and an images folder, that are located in the chap04 folder. All of the images used in this example are located in the images folder.

action

Revise the Mercury Project page so that relative URLs are used in the image links (pointing to the images in the images folder):

1. In your text editor, open **mercury.html** from the chap04 folder in your working folder.

NOTE You created **mercury.html** at the start of this chapter. If you have not yet created this file, you will need to return and complete the case example, "Creating a Report with Floating Images," before proceeding with this example.

2. Save mercury.html as **mercury2.html** in the **project** folder that is located in the chap04 folder.
3. Edit the background image reference in the page's style sheet:

```
body {
    margin-bottom: 20em;
    color: #ffffcc;
    background: black url(../images/starcluster.jpg)
    }
```

4. Edit the atlas_mercury.jpg image reference in the "1915 to 1957" section:

```
<p><img src="../images/atlas_mercury.jpg" align="left"
hspace="10" alt="Atlas rocket with Mercury spacecraft"
width="175" height="238">
```

5. Find any other image references in mercury2.html, and convert them to relative URLs that point to the images folder. These include:

   astronauts.jpg
   chimp_ham.jpg
   glenn_grissom_shepard.jpg

6. In your browser, open **mercury2.html** from the **project** folder (see Figure 4.27).

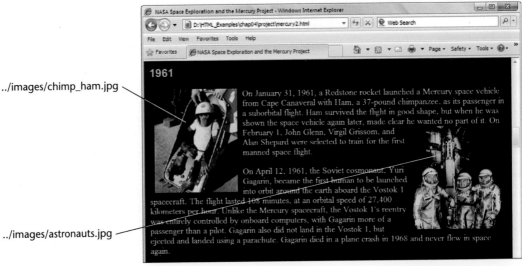

../images/chimp_ham.jpg

../images/astronauts.jpg

FIGURE 4.27 • The images in mercury2.html are now linked to using relative URLs.

practice

practice There are a number of additional images in the images folder that you can use to practice creating relative image links. Find appropriate places in mercury2.html where you can use relative URLs to display these images:

alan_shepard.jpg

earth_apollo17.jpg

flagonmoon.jpg

glenn_orbit.jpg

john_glenn.jpg

mercurylaunch.jpg

schirra_splash_down.jpg

white_eva.jpg

Float the images, with horizontal spacing separating the images from the text flowing around them.

CASE EXAMPLE: CREATING A GRAPHICAL FRONT END

Using an image map to create a graphical front end is a popular way to give a site a distinctive and attractive look. An image map is an image in which hotspots have been mapped; a hotspot is an area mapped to an image that is associated with a URL link. When visitors click on the hotspot, their browsers take them to the linked URL.

"Rhonda Andrews is an amateur chef and enjoys collecting recipes from family and friends. She wants to share her collection of recipes over the Web. She has decided to create a graphical front end for her site, which will allow visitors to access different kinds of recipes by clicking on an area in the image."

CREATING IMAGE MAPS

As stated previously, an **image map** is an image for which clickable hotspots have been mapped, and a **hotspot** is an area within an image that functions as a hypertext link. When a visitor clicks in a hotspot area, the browser opens the page or other object that is the target of the link.

Any image can be set up as an image map, but before you select or create an image you want to use, you should plan how you want your image map to appear and what you want it to do. It can be helpful, for instance, to first sketch out on a piece of paper the basic design you want to create.

"Rhonda has sketched out the basic design for her image map. She has decided to use the different recipe categories as design elements, presenting them in 3-D relief against the image's background. To give it a distinctive look, she has used two different wood-grain textures, as well as button, cutout, and drop shadow effects."

There are two example files that are used in this case example: recipes.gif and recipes_ex.html. Both are included with the example files in the chap04 folder in your working folder.

In this case example, you will:
1. Use an image map editor to draw hotspots on an image, recipes.gif, and export the image map codes as a text file.
2. Insert the image map codes into an HTML file, recipes.html, to enable displaying recipes.gif as a clickable image map.

Using an Image Map Editor

An **image map editor** is a program that allows you to draw (or map) areas in an image and then export HTML codes that turn the areas drawn in the image into clickable hotlink areas. Some image editors also include image mapping wizards or utilities. These all work in roughly the same way.

NOTE

The following example uses the GIMP image editor, which includes an image mapping wizard. GIMP was originally written for Linux but is now available for Windows and Macintosh OS X. It is free software, available under the GNU General Public License. Visit **www.gimp.org/** to download the version for your platform. Windows users can download GIMP at **www.gimp.org/windows/** and Macintosh users at **www.gimp.org/macintosh/**.

GIMP Version 2.66 for Windows is shown in the figures, but versions for other platforms and later versions should be quite similar. The name of the program is rendered differently on different platforms—GIMP in Windows, Gimp in Macintosh OS X, and gimp in Linux. In this chapter, it will be referred to as GIMP, regardless of the platform, unless referring to a specific menu option.

Using the GIMP image editor's image map wizard, draw clickable hotspots for recipes.gif and then save the image map codes to a text file:

Windows
1. Run GIMP from the Start menu.
2. Select File, Open, navigate to the **chap04** folder in your working folder, and double-click **recipes.gif** to open it in GIMP.

Macintosh
1. Run GIMP from the Dock. This will launch two applications, GIMP and X11.
2. With X11 in the foreground, go to the GNU Image Manipulation Program window, select File, and then Open. Navigate to the **chap04** folder in your working folder and double-click **recipes.gif** to open it in GIMP.

Both Platforms
3. Select Filters, Web, and Image Map. Select the rectangle icon in the left sidebar.
4. Click the mouse above and to the left of "Meats" in the image and move the mouse down and to the right, drawing a box around "Meats" (see Figure 4.28).

save icon

pointer tool icon

rectangle tool icon

rectangle hotspot

FIGURE 4.28 • A hotspot area is drawn in the image mapping wizard of GIMP.

5. Click the mouse button again to bring up the Area #1 Settings dialog box. In the *URL to activate when this area is clicked* text box, key **meat-recipes.html**. In the *ALT text* text box, key **Meat recipes - beef, chicken, pork, lamb**. Leave all other options as they are (see Figure 4.29).

6. Click Apply to add the area to the Selection list on the right and then click OK.

7. Repeat steps 3 through 5 to draw hotspots and assign URLs (file names) for the other words in the image (Seafood, Pasta, Soup, and so on). Two dummy files, meat-recipes.html and seafood-recipes.html, are included with the example files for this chapter. For the other hotspot areas, specify pasta-recipes.html, soup-recipes. html, barbecue-recipes.html, salad-recipes.html, bread-recipes.html, dessert-recipes. html, and drinks-recipes.html as the URLs (file names). Add what you think would be appropriate alternative text.

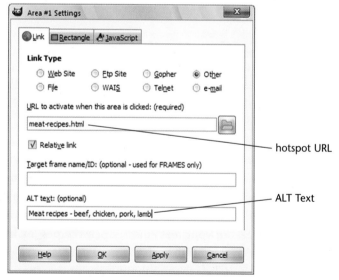

hotspot URL

ALT Text

FIGURE 4.29 • A URL (or file name) is specified for the hotspot area as well as alternative text.

tip

If you need to redraw an area, just select Edit and Undo Create.

8. After you have finished drawing the hotspot areas, select Mapping and Edit Map Info. Key **recipes** in the Title box, key **Rhonda Andrews** in the Author box, and key **recipes.html** in the Default URL box. Leave CSIM (Client-Side Image Map) selected as the Map File Format (see Figure 4.30). Click Apply and then click OK.

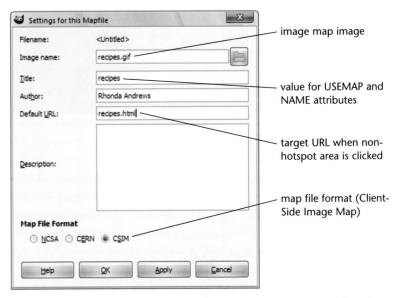

image map image

value for USEMAP and NAME attributes

target URL when non-hotspot area is clicked

map file format (Client-Side Image Map)

FIGURE 4.30 • A title (recipes), author, and default URL (recipes.html) are specified in the Settings for this Mapfile dialog box.

9. Save the image map codes: select File and Save As. Leave recipes.gif.map in the Name box. Click Browse for other folders and navigate to the **chap04** folder in your working folder. Click Save.

Setting Up the Image Map

GIMP's image map wizard exported the image map codes in a recipes.gif.map text file. Some other image map editors will insert the codes directly into your HTML file (recipes.html, in this case) but with GIMP you need to do that manually.

Set up the image map codes to work in recipes.html:

1. In your text editor, open **recipes.gif.map** from the **chap04** folder. Click and drag with the mouse to highlight everything in recipes.gif.map. Press Ctrl-C (in Windows) or Command-C (in Macintosh OS X) to copy the highlighted text.
2. In your text editor, open **recipes_ex.html** from the **chap04** folder. Save it as **recipes.html** in that same folder.
3. Click the mouse in front of the **<hr>** and press Ctrl-V (in Windows) or Command-V (in Macintosh OS X) to paste in the codes you copied in the previous step, as shown in the following code block:

NOTE — The coordinates and alternative text you see in your text editor will differ somewhat from what is shown in the following code block. The GIMP image map wizard saves image map codes in XHTML format, which is why "/" is inserted at the end of the AREA empty elements. The inserted symbol poses no problem in an HTML file.

```
<body bgcolor="#003300" text="white" link="yellow" vlink="yellow"
alink="yellow">
<img src="recipes.gif" width="575" height="375" border="0"
usemap="#recipes" />

<map name="recipes">
<!-- #$-:Image map file created by GIMP Image Map plug-in -->
<!-- #$-:GIMP Image Map plug-in by Maurits Rijk -->
<!-- #$-:Please do not edit lines starting with "#$" -->
<!-- #$VERSION:2.3 -->
<!-- #$AUTHOR:Rhonda Andrews -->
<area shape="rect" coords="33,111,180,167" alt="Meat recipes -
beef, chicken, pork, lamb" href="meat-recipes.html" />
<area shape="rect" coords="194,113,383,165" alt="Seafood recipes
- fish, crab, oysters, shrimp, clams"
href="seafood-recipes.html" />
<area shape="rect" coords="397,113,540,165" alt="Pasta recipes -
spaghetti, ravioli, lasagna, macaroni"
href="pasta-recipes.html" />
<area shape="rect" coords="33,190,155,252" alt="Soup recipes -
bisques, borsch, chowder, cream soups, gumbo"
href="soup-recipes.html" />
<area shape="rect" coords="170,193,390,249" alt="Barbecue recipes
- ribs, chops, chicken, marinade, sauce"
href="barbecue-recipes.html" />
<area shape="rect" coords="397,193,533,246" alt="Salad recipes -
lettuce, spinach, greens, caesar, waldorf, dressings"
href="salad-recipes.html" />
<area shape="rect" coords="30,274,173,326" alt="Bread recipes -
bread, rolls, biscuits, corn bread" href="bread-recipes.html" />
<area shape="rect" coords="187,274,369,329" alt="Dessert recipes
- cakes, pies, cookies, muffins, puddings"
href="dessert-recipes.html" />
<area shape="rect" coords="383,276,540,326" alt="Drink recipes -
coffee, espresso, tea, ades, punch" href="drinks-recipes.html" />
<area shape="default" href="recipes.html" />
</map>
<hr>
<address>
```

4. Edit the IMG element for the recipes.gif image: nest it inside a P element, center it using the DIV element, and and add some alternative text:

```
<body bgcolor="#003300" text="white" link="yellow" vlink="yellow"
alink="yellow">
<div align="center">
<p><img src="recipes.gif" width="575" height="375" border="0"
alt="Recipes image map: Meats, Seafood, Pasta, Soup, Barbecue,
Salad, Bread, Dessert, and Drinks" usemap="#recipes" /></p>
</div>
```

5. Save your file in your text editor. Switch to (or run) your browser and open **recipes.html** from the **chap04** folder.

6. When you pass the mouse over the hotspot areas, the cursor changes (to a "hand" in most browsers), and the URL for the hotspot is displayed in the status bar (see Figure 4.31).

mouse cursor

URL in status bar

FIGURE 4.31 • When the mouse passes over a hotspot, the cursor changes and its URL displays in the browser's status bar.

7. Click on the Meats hotspot area to open meat-recipes.html, which is included with the Chapter 4 example files (see Figure 4.32).

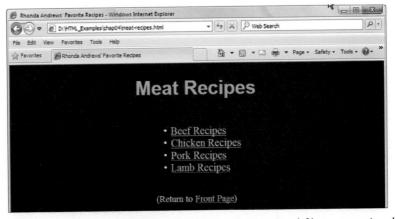

FIGURE 4.32 • After clicking the Meats hotspot, the associated file, meat-recipes.html, is opened in the browser viewport.

8. Click the Front Page link to return to recipes.html in your browser.

Following are some pointers to help you understand the code for this example:
- The MAP element identifies that nested AREA elements are used to define a client-side image map. (A different element, the ISMAP element, is used to specify a server-side image map.)
- The MAP element's NAME attribute names the image map, so it can be linked with the image that is being mapped.
- The nested AREA elements specify the coordinates and URL links for the hotspots.
- The SHAPE attribute (in the AREA element) specifies the type of hotspot area. Possible values of the SHAPE attribute are **rect**, **circle**, **poly**, and **default**. The

example uses the **rect** and **default** values but not the **circle** or **poly** values (which define circular and polygon-shaped hotspot areas).

- The COORDS attribute (in the AREA element) specifies the coordinates of the hotspot area, relative to the left and top edge of the image. For instance, in the coordinates for the Seafood hotspot area (200,110,379,167, for example), the first two numbers specify the distance in pixels that the upper-left corner of the hotspot is spaced in from the image's left and top edges, respectively, while the second two numbers specify the same thing for the hotspot's lower-right corner. (The other shape types, circle or poly, will have additional coordinate pairs to map out their positions.)

- In the last AREA element, the `shape="default"` attribute indicates that the entire image functions as a hotspot that is linked to the specified URL; when declaring a default shape for the image as a whole, no COORDS attribute is used (because the coordinates are the same as the image). Because this links to recipes.html, clicking outside of a hotspot area just refreshes the current page.

Other image map programs work similarly to GIMP's image mapping wizard. Some, like MapEdit and MapThis for Windows, will export the image map codes directly to the HTML file where the image is linked. (MapEdit will even insert the USEMAP attribute in the IMG element, `usemap="#recipes"`, for instance.)

 **Visit the Internet Resource Center.** To find online resources where you can download and try out other image map editors or graphics programs capable of creating image maps, visit the Chapter 4 section of this book's Internet Resource Center at **www.emcp.net/html2e**.

Creating Image Maps without an Image Map Editor

You do not need an image map editor to create image maps. Although it is more time-consuming, you can calculate hotspot area coordinates just using an image editor. For instance, in calculating the coordinates of a rectangular hotspot area:

- The first two coordinates specify the distance, in pixels, of the upper-left corner of the hotspot area from the left and top edges of the image.
- The second two coordinates specify the distance of the lower-right corner of the hotspot area from the left and top edges of the image.

A circular hotspot area, designated by `shape="circle"`, requires two coordinates, specifying the distance of the center of the circle from the left and top edges of the image, plus the radius of the circle. For instance, `coords="25,75,50"` defines a hotspot area with a radius of 50 pixels that is 25 pixels from the left edge and 50 pixels from the top edge of the image.

A polygon hotspot area, designated by `shape="poly"`, is more complicated, with a pair of coordinates required for each point in the shape.

To discover the coordinate position of any point within an image, in your image editor, just position the mouse cursor over any point in the image—the coordinate distances from the left and top edge of the image should be displayed in the image editor's status bar. For instance, in the example codes shown in this book, the upper-left corner of the Meats hotspot area is 33 pixels in from the image's left edge and 111 pixels down from the top edge, while the lower-right corner is 180 pixels in from the left edge and 167 pixels down from the top edge. (Your coordinates will differ somewhat from those shown in the example code.)

Planning for Accessibility and Backward Compatibility

When using an image map in your site, be aware that some visitors will not be able to see or use your image map for the following reasons:

- Users of text browsers and non-visual browsers will not be able to see an image map's image. This can leave someone with a visual handicap who is using a speech or Braille browser with literally nowhere to go when they come to your page, if all your page has on it is an image map.
- A significant number of users surf the Web with the display of graphics turned off in their browsers to speed up access to the textual content of Web pages. These users also will not be able to see your image map's image and thus might not be able to tell the function or purpose of your hotspot links.
- Some search engine robots might not be able to follow image map links to index the rest of your site. An image map page also might not have text content that a search engine can index.

For these reasons, it is important to provide alternative means, other than just an image map, that surfers and search engine robots can use to access the rest of your site.

The simplest way to do that is to include a **text-based link menu,** or separate links below your image map that link to the main pages in your site.

Add a one-line link menu below the image map (see Figure 4.33):

```
<div align="center">
<p><img src="recipes.gif" width="575" height="375" border="0"
alt="Recipes image map: Meats, Seafood, Pasta, Soup, Barbecue,
Salad, Bread, Dessert, and Drinks" usemap="#recipes" /></p>
<p><a href="meat-recipes.html">Meats</a> -
<a href="seafood-recipes.html">Seafood</a> -
<a href="pasta-recipes.html">Pasta</a> -
<a href="soup-recipes.html">Soup</a> -
<a href="barbecue-recipes.html">Barbecue</a> -
<a href="salad-recipes.html">Salad</a> -
<a href="bread-recipes.html">Bread</a> -
<a href="dessert-recipes.html">Dessert</a> -
<a href="drinks-recipes.html">Drinks</a></p>
</div>
```

FIGURE 4.33 • A link menu provides an alternative means for visitors or search engine robots to access the other pages in the site.

A neat trick that you can use here is to combine the alternative text menu with the CSS display property. By using CSS to turn off the display of the text menu, you can render it invisible to most browsers that support client-side image maps, while continuing to display it for early browsers that do not support client-side image maps.

action

Edit the text menu's paragraph so it will be invisible in all browsers that support the display property:

```
<p style="display: none"><a href="meat-recipes.html">Meats</a> -
<a href="seafood-recipes.html">Seafood</a> - <a href="pasta-
recipes.html">Pasta</a> - <a href="soup-recipes.html">Soup</a> -
<a href="barbecue-recipes.html">Barbecue</a> - <a href="salad-
recipes.html">Salad</a> - <a href="bread-recipes.html">Bread</a>
- <a href="dessert-recipes.html">Dessert</a> - <a href="drinks-
recipes.html">Drinks</a></p>
```

The result of this is that any archaic browsers that do not support client-side image maps will display the alternative text menu because they also do not support the display property (or any other CSS properties, for that matter). Older browsers that support client-side image maps but not the display property, such as Netscape Navigator 3 or Internet Explorer 3, will display both the image map and the text menu (which is exactly what the result would be in all browsers if no display property was present).

You should not use this trick, however, without also including informative ALT attributes in your image map's AREA elements in order to clue in visitors surfing with the display of graphics turned off.

GIMP's image map wizard allows you to specify alternative text for AREA elements while creating hotspots, but other image map programs might not (or you might choose not to include alternative text at that point). You should also be sure to include informative alternative text for the IMG element that specifies the image used for the image map, which you have already done.

The MAP and AREA elements are not included in XHTML 2, but they are included in HTML 5, so there should be no forward-compatibility issues involved in using them. Some designers, however, feel they are antiquated and can pose accessibility issues and prefer to use CSS to create clickable image maps.

Visit the Internet Resource Center. To find online resources that discuss creating image maps, as well as CSS image maps, visit the Chapter 4 section of this book's Internet Resource Center at **www.emcp.net/html2e**.

CHAPTER SUMMARY

You should now be familiar with using images and other media files in Web pages. When working with images, you should understand how to use floating images, image links, graphic rules, transparent banner images, navigation icons, button links, and GIF animations. You also should understand the differences between the GIF, JPEG, and PNG image formats, including which format to use to save which kinds of images, and when transparent and interlaced GIFs are used. You should also understand how to use color palettes with GIF images and how to set compression levels for JPEG images. You also should have experience using audio and video files in a Web page, including using both the EMBED element and the OBJECT element to play an audio file in the background, playing an audio file with the player console displayed at the top of the page, and inserting and playing a video in a Web page. You should also now be familiar with using relative URLs to link to files and images in other folders and creating and setting up an image map.

Code Review

`<img align="value"`	ALIGN attribute. In the IMG element, a **left** or **right** value floats an image to the left or right margin; a **top**, **middle**, or **bottom** value vertically aligns it relative to a line of text.
`<br clear="all">`	CLEAR attribute. In the BR element, causes following text to clear a floating image, rather than wrap around it. Values: **left** clears a left-aligned image, **right** clears a right-aligned image, and **all** clears both.
`<img hspace="n"`	HSPACE attribute. In the IMG or OBJECT element, adds horizontal spacing (in pixels) to the left and right of an image.
`<img vspace="n"`	VSPACE attribute. In the IMG or OBJECT element, adds vertical spacing (in pixels) above or below an image.
`<img border="1"`	BORDER attribute. In the IMG or OBJECT element, displays a border around the image.
`<img border="0"`	BORDER attribute. In the IMG or OBJECT element, eliminates any border displayed around an image. Internet Explorer and Firefox, for instance, automatically display a border around an image link.
`<img alt="text"`	ALT attribute. Provides an alternative description of an image for people who cannot see the image.
`<a target="_blank"`	In the A and AREA elements, opens a link target in a new window.
`<img src="imagename.gif"`	SRC attribute. Displays a GIF image.
`<img src="imagename.jpg"`	SRC attribute. Displays a JPEG image.
`<img src="imagename.png"`	SRC attribute. Displays a PNG image.
`<embed src="url"`	EMBED element. An element introduced by Netscape that allows audio and video to be embedded into a Web page. Not included in HTML 4, but included in HTML 5.

`<embed type="MIMEtype">`	TYPE attribute. In an EMBED element, specifies the MIME-type of a media file.
`<embed autostart="true|false">`	AUTOSTART attribute. In the EMBED element, causes an audio or video file to start playing automatically after the page where it is embedded is opened in a browser.
`<embed loop="true|false">`	LOOP attribute. In the EMBED element, causes an audio and video file to loop indefinitely, rather than play only once.
`<embed pluginspage="url">`	PLUGINSPAGE attribute. In the EMBED element, indicates a URL where an appropriate plug-in player for a media file can be downloaded, which a browser can convey to a user if no plug-in player for the media file is installed.
`<embed height="n" width="n">`	HEIGHT and WIDTH attributes. In the EMBED element, specify the dimensions of the player console but also can be used to hide the console [by assigning a 0 (zero) value].
`<object data="url">`	OBJECT element. An element introduced in HTML 4 used to include objects in HTML documents, including images, audio, video, Java animations, and more.
`<param name="src" value="url">`	PARAM element. In conjunction with the OBJECT element, an empty element that specifies display or behavior parameters for an object. Some other NAME attribute values include **autoplay**, **controller**, and **loop** (all paired up with `value="true|false"`).
`<img src="../">`	A relative URL that specifies the parent folder of the current folder.
`<img src="../../">`	A relative URL that specifies the grandparent folder of the current folder.
`<img src="./">`	A relative URL that specifies the current folder.
`<map name="mapname">`	MAP element. Defines a clickable client-side image map. The NAME attribute names the MAP element, so an image can be associated with it.
`<area href="url">`	AREA element. Specifies a hotspot area in an image map. The HREF attribute specifies the link target for the hotspot.
`<area shape="rect">`	SHAPE attribute. The **rect** value specifies the hotspot is a rectangle.
`<area shape="circle">`	SHAPE attribute. The **circle** value specifies the hotspot is a circle.
`<area shape="poly">`	SHAPE attribute. The **poly** value specifies the hotspot is a polygon.
`<area shape="default">`	SHAPE attribute. The **default** value specifies that any area in the image that has not been defined as a hotspot will function as a default hotspot.
`<area coords="coordinates">`	COORDS attribute. In the AREA element, specifies the coordinates of a hotspot area.
`<img usemap="#mapname">`	USEMAP attribute. Specifies a fragment identifier that associates an image with a MAP element's name. Case-sensitive.

KEY TERMS

For a review of the key terms bolded in this chapter, visit the Chapter 4 section of this book's Internet Resource Center at **www.emcp.net/html2e**. A complete glossary appears at the end of the book.

ONLINE QUIZ

An online self-check quiz that you can use to test your knowledge of the topics covered in this chapter can be found in the Chapter 4 section of this book's Internet Resource Center at **www.emcp.net/html2e**.

REVIEW EXERCISES

This section provides some hands-on review exercises to reinforce the information and material included within this chapter. Review using the elements, attributes, styles, and other features that were covered in this chapter, checking your results in your browser and troubleshooting any errors:

1. Open **mercury_ex.html** from the **chap04** and save it as **mercury-review.html** in that same folder. Using any of the example images in the chap04 folder, review using the IMG element's ALIGN attribute to float images:

    A. Insert at least two floating images, demonstrating floating images on the left and right margins. Add appropriate ALT, HEIGHT, and WIDTH attributes to the IMG elements.

    B. Insert two overlapping floating images, with text flowing between them. Add appropriate ALT, HEIGHT, and WIDTH attributes to the IMG elements.

    C. Use the IMG element's HSPACE attribute to add horizontal spacing to the left and right of the floating images.

2. Open **spacegallery_ex.html** from the **chap04** and save it as **spacegallery-review.html** in the same folder. Review using the IMG element's ALIGN attribute in combination with the BR element's CLEAR attribute to create a gallery layout using floating images:

    A. Float the first image to the right, the second image to the right, and so on (the opposite from the case example). Use the IMG element's HSPACE attribute to add horizontal spacing to the left and right of the floating images. Use the BR element's CLEAR attribute to cause a following gallery section to clear a preceding floating image.

    B. Bracket the gallery thumbnail images with A (Anchor) elements to turn them into image links, linking them with their full-sized versions (without "_th" in their file names). Use the IMG element's BORDER attribute to turn off the display of a border (in Internet Explorer and Firefox) around the image links. Use the A element's TARGET attribute to cause the linked full-sized images to be displayed in a new window.

    C. Using any image editor, create four more thumbnail images (with the largest dimension, height or width, set to no more than 200 pixels) from the other full-sized images in the chap04 folder, saving them as JPG images with "_th" appended to the file name. If you do not have an image editor, check out the online resources in the Chapter 4 section of this book's Internet Resource Center to find image editors for your platform you can download and try.

Use the new thumbnail images you have saved to add four more gallery sections to spacegallery-review.html, using the other gallery sections as a model. Write headings and descriptive text for the new sections (even if only dummy text).

3. Using **mercury-review.html**, review using the EMBED element to add an audio and a video file to the page:
   A. Find and download an audio file from the Web and use the EMBED element to cause it to play automatically in the background when the page is opened. Set the player to be hidden and to loop playing the audio file only once.
   B. Find and download a video file from the Web and use the EMBED element to cause it to play when the Play button on the player console is clicked. Set it to loop the video only once.

4. Using **spacegallery-review.html**, review using the OBJECT element to add an audio and a video file to the page:
   A. Using the audio file you downloaded in the previous review exercise, use the OBJECT element to cause it to play automatically in the background when the page is opened. Set the player to be hidden and to loop playing the audio file only once.
   B. Using the video file you downloaded in the previous review exercise, use the OBJECT element to cause it to play when the Play button on the player console is clicked. Set it to loop the video only once.

5. Open **recipes_ex.html** from the **chap04** and save it as **imagemap-review.html** in that same folder and use it to review creating an image map:
   A. Create an image using your image editor or download an image from the Web that you want to set up as an image map.
   B. Using an image map editor, such as GIMP's Image Map wizard, define rectangular, circular, or polygonal hotspots for the image and export the codes. In imagemap-review.html, using the exported codes, set up an image map using the IMG element and the MAP element. Note: GIMP's Image Map wizard exports both the IMG and MAP elements to a text file; other image map editors might export only the MAP element, but to a specified HTML file (already containing an IMG element linking to the image to be turned into an image link).

WEB-BASED LEARNING ACTIVITIES

The following Web-based learning activities can help you to further extend your learning and shore up your understanding of specific topic-areas:

- Visit the Chapter 4 section of this book's Internet Resource Center at **www.emcp.net/html2e** to find online resources that you can use to further investigate and explore the topics and subjects covered in this chapter. You can also find all Web sites cited in this chapter's notes listed there.
- Further research a specific topic introduced in this chapter using Google (**www.google.com/**), Yahoo! (**www.yahoo.com/**), Wikipedia (**www.wikipedia.org/**), Open Directory Project (**www.dmoz.org/**), or other online sources. Some topics covered in this chapter that you can further research include:
  - Available image editors for your platform that you can download and try.
  - Available image viewing software that can augment the built-in capabilities of your platform.

- Available GIF animation and other animation programs that can be used to create animations for display on the Web.
- Online sources for public domain clip art you can download and use in your Web pages.
- Copyright issues with using images from the Web in Web pages.
- Image creation issues with GIF, JPEG, and PNG images and how they impact their use on the Web.
- Available image map editors for your platform.
- Use the results of your online research into a particular topic to:
  - Write a review to be read in front of your classmates.
  - Write a report that can be read by your classmates.
  - Design a diagram, chart, or other graphic that illustrates a key topic or concept.
  - Create a presentation using PowerPoint (or other software) that can be shared with your classmates.
  - Give a stand-up presentation to your classmates.
  - Team up with one or more classmates to give a group presentation to your classmates.

PROJECTS

These projects can be done in class, in a computer lab, or at home. Use the skills you have developed in this and the previous chapters to create any of the following projects. In your project, demonstrate the correct use of the following HTML features covered in this chapter:

- At least two floating images, one floating at the left margin and the other at the right margin, with following text flowing around them.
- At least one instance of forcing following text or other elements to "clear" a floating image, using the method demonstrated in this chapter. (Do not simply insert multiple BR elements to do this.)
- At least one "thumbnail" image link, using a smaller image that links to a larger full-size image.
- At least two of the following features: 1) a transparent GIF image (displayed against a background color or image); 2) graphic navigation icons or buttons; 3) a graphic rule; 4) a GIF animation; 5) an audio or video file (using the EMBED or OBJECT element); or 6) an image map.
- All IMG elements should include properly used ALT, HEIGHT, and WIDTH attributes.

Project 1. Add images to a page you have already created.

Add floating images, graphical rules, a banner graphic, and a navigation icon to a page you have already created, such as a personal page, a page for a club or organization, a topical page, or any other page. Incorporate lessons you learned in previous chapters, including using a document menu, return links, and colors and backgrounds, for instance. Use images downloaded from the Web, or create your own images in an image editor. Optionally, incorporate audio or inline video.

If downloading images, use any of the links provided previously in the "Finding Images on the Web" section or in the Chapter 4 section of this book's Internet Resource Center at **www.emcp.net/html2e** to find images you can use in your page, or use Google (**www.google.com/**), AltaVista (**www.altavista.com/**), or Yahoo! (**www.yahoo.com/**) to find additional sources for images you can download and use. Use an image editor to resize, crop, and optimize the images.

If creating your own images, you can create your images from scratch in an image editor or use images that you have scanned in using a scanner or imported from a digital camera.

Visit the Chapter 4 section of this book's Internet Resource Center at **www.emcp.net/html2e** to find additional links to digital scanning and photography resources on the Web.

Project 2. Create your own online gallery.

Using this chapter's online gallery example as a guide, create your own online gallery from scratch. For instance, create a gallery of vacation photos or a gallery of other personal snapshots. If you are an artist, create a gallery of photos of your paintings, illustrations, drawings, or other artwork. If you are a photographer, create a gallery to display some of your photographic works. Use a scanner or digital camera to create the raw images you will use, or create your own images in an image editor. Crop, resize, sharpen, and apply other corrections or effects to prepare your images to be displayed on the Web. Save your images as either optimized JPEGs or optimized GIFs. Save smaller-sized thumbnail versions and larger-sized versions of each image.

Project 3. Create a Web site that utilizes a graphical front end using an image map.

Create a graphical front end using an image map. To do this, you will need to 1) create the image in an image editor that will be used for the image map, 2) create an HTML file to contain the image, 3) create at least one other HTML file that will be linked to from the image map, 4) draw and link hotspots for the image in Map This or other image mapping software, 5) export the image map codes to the image map HTML file, and 6) link the IMG element's USEMAP attribute with the MAP element's NAME attribute (if using Map This), add ALT attributes to the IMG and AREA elements, and create an alternative link menu. At least one of the hotspots should link to a real Web page (the others can link to dummy pages), where you can meet the other project requirements stated at the start of this section.

Project 4. Create a Web page using images.

Create any other kind of Web page from scratch that makes use of images (any kind of page you can imagine or conceive). Use images downloaded from the Web or images that you have scanned or imported from a digital camera. Optionally, incorporate audio and inline video. Apply skills learned in this chapter and any previous chapters.

CHAPTER 5

Working with Tables

PERFORMANCE OBJECTIVES

- Use the PRE element to format tabular data.
- Use the TABLE element to format tabular data in rows and columns.
- Span columns and rows within tables.
- Control the width and appearance of table columns.
- Control the appearance of row groups.
- Control the appearance of tables using styles.
- Create indented icon bullet lists.
- Format an online resume using a table.

Tables are one of the most commonly used features of HTML. They are used in Web pages for two different purposes, one being the purpose for which they were designed, to format tabular data, and the other being to create multi-column layouts that cannot be created using other HTML elements.

USING THE EXAMPLE FILES

If you have created a working folder for storing files you create, you will find the example files for this chapter located in the **chap05** folder within your working folder. You should save any HTML files you create in this chapter in that folder.

CASE EXAMPLE: FORMATTING A WORKSHEET

When creating published reports, it is common to include worksheet tables from spreadsheet programs. You also might want to include such data in tabular format within an HTML document.

> Chandra Nichols is an assistant to the president of the Parker-Ruff Corporation, a major firm with more than $80 million in quarterly sales. She is producing the company's quarterly sales report, which provides the sales results for all the company's sales representatives. Besides creating a printed sales report in Adobe InDesign, her boss also wants her to produce a version of the sales report for posting on the Web using data from Microsoft Excel.

To get started working with this example:

1. In your text editor, open **salesreport_ex.html** from the chap05 folder in your working folder.
2. Save salesreport_ex.html as **salesreport.html** in the chap05 folder.
3. In your browser, open **salesreport.html** from the chap05 folder.

FORMATTING TABULAR DATA AS PREFORMATTED TEXT

The easiest way to include tabular data in a Web page is as preformatted text. In HTML, the PRE element is used to insert preformatted text into a Web page. Before the introduction of the TABLE element, the PRE element was the only way to include **tabular data** in a Web page.

> Chandra has created the quarterly sales report as a worksheet in Microsoft Excel. She needs to export the worksheet data from Excel so that it can be formatted and displayed using HTML. She has opened Microsoft Excel and saved her worksheet file as a space-delimited PRN (.prn) file, which preserves all the spaces within the worksheet.

The **PRN text file format** is actually a "print" format file. It originated from Lotus 1-2-3, which provided a feature called "printing to a file." This allowed a user to save a copy of a **worksheet** (or range within a worksheet) as a text file with all relative spacing, as it appears in the worksheet, preserved. Originally the feature was primarily used to print a worksheet on a printer connected to another computer via "sneaker net," whereby you saved a PRN (*.prn) file to a floppy disk and walked it to another computer where it could be printed. This transportability now works just as well to import worksheet data into a Web page. In Microsoft Excel, for Windows or Macintosh OS X, to save your worksheet as a PRN file, select File, Save As, and then Formatted Text (Space delimited) (*.prn) as the file type. There is nothing official or standard about the PRN file format—this is just the file extension that Lotus 1-2-3 and Excel have used when saving this type of file. Other spreadsheet programs might use different file extensions for this type of file.

tip

For a quick and dirty way to transfer worksheet data to your text editor, in your spreadsheet program, click and drag to highlight the data cells you want to transfer, copy the highlighted data, and then paste it into your text editor. All the spacing will not be preserved, so you will have to insert or delete spaces to line up the columns.

An example PRN file, **sales.prn**, is included with the example files in the chap05 folder. This is just a regular text file that you can open directly in your text editor.

Open **sales.prn** in your text editor, and then paste it into salesreport.html as preformatted text:

1. In a new window of your text editor, open **sales.prn** from the chap05 folder in your working folder. (If you are using Windows Notepad, you will need to run a

second copy of that text editor to have both salesreport.html and sales.prn open in windows at the same time.)

2. If the data columns are out of alignment, it is because a proportional font is being used to display text in your text editor—you will need to change the font your text editor is using to a monospaced font.

   For instance, in Notepad for Windows, to specify that a monospaced font is to be used to display text, click and drag to highlight the contents of the file, and then select Format, Font, and choose a monospaced font (such as Lucida Console or Courier New). In some earlier versions of Notepad, you might have to select Edit, Set Font, and choose Fixedsys as the font. TextEdit for Macintosh OS X should default to using the Monaco monospaced font for plain text files, unless you have changed the default plain text font.

3. Click and drag with the mouse cursor to highlight the contents of sales.prn, and then copy it (Ctrl+C in Windows or Command+C on the Macintosh).

4. Switch to the text editor window that contains salesreport.html. Scroll down to and highlight **[Insert worksheet file here.]**, and then paste in the text that you copied in the previous step (Ctrl+V in Windows or Command+V on the Macintosh), as shown in the following example:

```
<p>Parker-Ruff is one of the top firms in our field in the
country and this sales report only reinforces that. We rank in
the top tier of firms in our field, with gross annual sales of
over $250 million. We trail only three other firms, all of which
have much larger sales forces and have been competing in the
field for longer periods of time. In the all-important category
of earnings as a percentage of gross sales, we are actually the
leader, which shows that we both try harder and can do more with
less. With current sales growth at over 20 percent per quarter,
we project that Parker-Ruff will be the leader in gross sales
inside of two years. The following table shows sales figures for
the quarter, broken down by individual sales representatives and
monthly sales figures:</p>

             Quarterly Sales Report
                ($1 = $1,000)


             Jan       Feb       Mar      Totals

Anderson   $ 1,954   $ 2,543   $ 1,844   $ 6,341
Bailey       5,693     2,999     6,235    14,927
Martini      3,594     4,635     2,689    10,918
Peters       8,655     5,869     9,254    23,778
Wang         4,678     3,694     5,458    13,830

Totals     $24,574   $19,740   $25,480   $69,794

<p>We are proud of what we have accomplished. We have a superior
product line, a top-notch sales program, and a great crew of
sales representatives. Congratulations on another outstanding
quarter! We look forward to seeing even higher results in the
remaining quarters!</p>
```

5. Nest the sales report data inside a PRE element, as shown in the following (see Figure 5.1):

```
<pre>
                    Quarterly Sales Report
                         ($1 = $1,000)


              Jan         Feb         Mar       Totals

Anderson    $ 1,954    $ 2,543    $ 1,844    $ 6,341
Bailey        5,693      2,999      6,235     14,927
Martini       3,594      4,635      2,689     10,918
Peters        8,655      5,869      9,254     23,778
Wang          4,678      3,694      5,458     13,830

Totals      $24,574    $19,740    $25,480    $69,794
</pre>
```

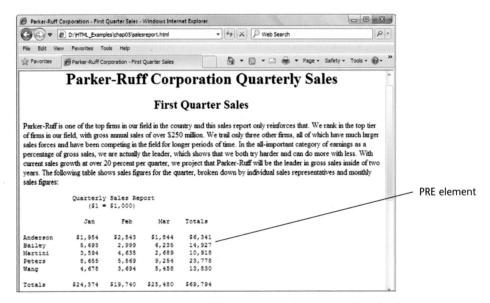

PRE element

FIGURE 5.1 • For text nested inside a PRE element, hard returns and multiple spaces are shown, rather than ignored.

Only inline elements can be nested inside the PRE element, such as the I, B, EM, STRONG, and FONT elements. You can even insert a hypertext link using the A element inside the PRE element. You cannot, however, insert IMG, OBJECT, BIG, SMALL, SUB, or SUP elements inside the PRE element. For instance, you could use the B element to bold the top two lines in the worksheet, and the FONT element to make the Totals row red.

Use inline elements to vary the display of the data worksheet:

1. Use the B element to bold the first two lines:

```
<b>Quarterly Sales Report</b>
     <b>($1 = $1,000)</b>
```

2. Use the FONT element to apply a red color to the bottom line (see Figure 5.2):

```
Wang          4,678      3,694      5,458     13,830
<font color="red">
Totals      $24,574    $19,740    $25,480    $69,794
</font>
</pre>
```

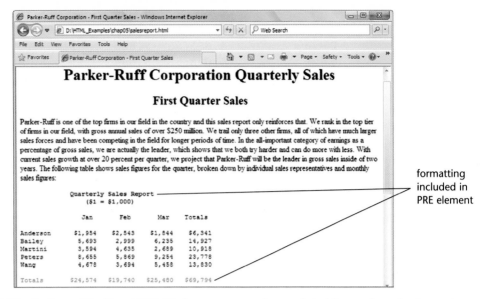

FIGURE 5.2 • The B and FONT elements are used to apply bolding and a red color to the preformatted text.

FORMATTING TABULAR DATA USING AN HTML TABLE

Another way to include tabular data in a Web page is to use the TABLE element. The TABLE element lets you format tabular data in cells that are arranged in rows and columns. The TABLE element gives you much more control over the appearance of tabular data than the PRE element.

Creating the Basic Table

The TABLE element is used in conjunction with the CAPTION, TR (Table Row), TH (Table Heading), and TD (Table Data) elements. The TABLE element brackets everything that is contained within the table, the CAPTION element brackets the table caption, and the TR element brackets each table row. The TH element defines table cells that function as column and row headings, whereas the TD element defines table cells that contain data.

Use the TABLE element to format the quarterly sales report:

1. Delete the PRE, B, and FONT elements you added in the previous example, and then nest the table text inside a TABLE element. Just leave any blank lines as they are, because they are only displayed when nested in a PRE element:

```
<table>
<pre>

          <b>Quarterly Sales Report</b>
            <b>($1 = $1,000)</b>


      Jan        Feb        Mar      Totals


Anderson     $ 1,954    $ 2,543    $ 1,844    $ 6,341
```

```
Bailey        5,693      2,999      6,235      14,927
Martini       3,594      4,635      2,689      10,918
Peters        8,655      5,869      9,254      23,778
Wang          4,678      3,694      5,458      13,830
<font color="red">
Totals       $24,574    $19,740    $25,480    $69,794
</font>
</pre>
</table>
```

2. Delete the spaces at the start of the first two lines, nest the first two lines inside a CAPTION element, and insert a BR element at the end of the first line:

```
<table>
<caption>Quarterly Sales Report<br>
($1 = $1,000)</caption>
```

3. Nest the lines inside of TR elements to define them as table rows:

```
<tr>               Jan      Feb      Mar      Totals</tr>

<tr>Anderson    $ 1,954  $ 2,543  $ 1,844  $ 6,341</tr>
<tr>Bailey        5,693    2,999    6,235    14,927</tr>
<tr>Martini       3,594    4,635    2,689    10,918</tr>
<tr>Peters        8,655    5,869    9,254    23,778</tr>
<tr>Wang          4,678    3,694    5,458    13,830</tr>

<tr>Totals     $24,574  $19,740  $25,480  $69,794</tr>
</table>
```

4. Use TH and TD elements to tag the remaining table items, defining them as either table heading cells or table data cells (delete any spaces not shown in the code example; see Figure 5.3):

```
<tr><th></th> <th>Jan</th> <th>Feb</th> <th>Mar</th> <th>Totals
</th></tr>

<tr><th>Anderson</th> <td>$ 1,954</td> <td>$ 2,543</td> <td>$
1,844</td> <td>$ 6,341</td></tr>
<tr><th>Bailey</th> <td>5,693</td> <td>2,999</td> <td>6,235</td>
<td>14,927</td></tr>
<tr><th>Martini</th> <td>3,594</td> <td>4,635</td> <td>2,689</td>
<td>10,918</td></tr>
<tr><th>Peters</th> <td>8,655</td> <td>5,869</td> <td>9,254</td>
<td>23,778</td></tr>
<tr><th>Wang</th> <td>4,678</td> <td>3,694</td> <td>5,458</td>
<td>13,830</td></tr>

<tr><th>Totals</th> <td>$24,574</td> <td>$19,740</td>
<td>$25,480</td> <td>$69,794</td></tr>
</table>
```

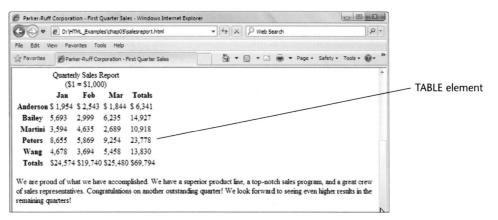

FIGURE 5.3 • The tabular data is formatted in rows and columns.

NOTE

In the previous example, an empty TH element is included at the start of the row because the first column in that row is empty, with the first month heading ("Jan") displaying in the second column.

Although the table is not very impressive at this point, you will make it look more presentable in the following sections.

Controlling the Table Border

The TABLE element's BORDER attribute draws a border around the table and its cells. Adding a border can help delineate the different parts of the table and make it easier for you to see them.

action

Add a one-pixel border around the table and its cells (see Figure 5.4):

```
<table border="1">
```

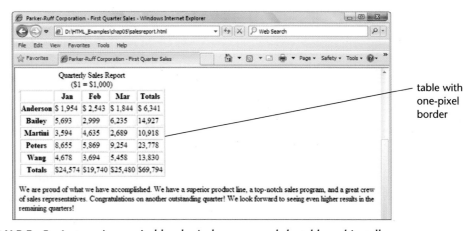

FIGURE 5.4 • A one-pixel border is drawn around the table and its cells.

Increasing the border size only increases the size of the border around the table, giving it a 3-D look, but the borders around the table cells remain unchanged.

Increase the size of the border to six pixels (see Figure 5.5):

```
<table border="6">
```

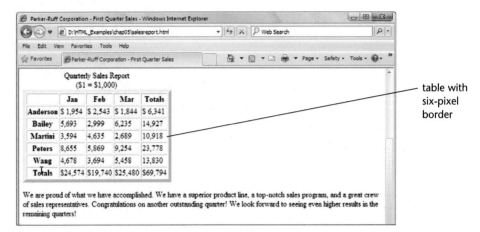

table with
six-pixel
border

FIGURE 5.5 • Increasing the border value only changes the style and increases the size of the outside border; the inner borders remain unchanged.

You should expect a good deal of variability in how different browsers display wider borders. Figure 5.6 shows how a table with a six-pixel table border is displayed in Mozilla Firefox 3.

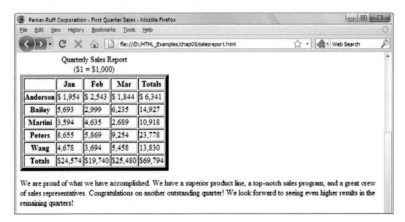

FIGURE 5.6 • How browsers display wider table borders can differ significantly, as shown here in Mozilla Firefox 3.

Controlling Spacing and Padding

The TABLE element's CELLPADDING and CELLSPACING attributes let you control the amount of cell padding displayed inside the cells and the amount of space displayed between the cells. **Cell padding** is space between a cell's content and its border, while **cell spacing** is space between the borders of different cells.

Add five pixels of padding and spacing to the table (see Figure 5.7):

```
<table border="6" cellpadding="5" cellspacing="5">
```

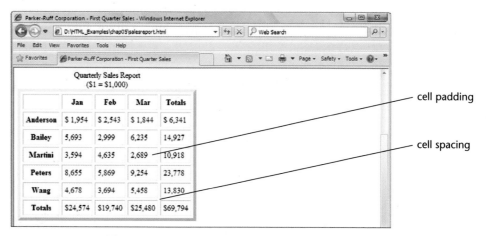

FIGURE 5.7 • Padding and spacing are added to the table's cells.

NOTE

Internet Explorer 8 and most other current browsers will draw a border around an empty table cell (TH or TD), but earlier versions of Internet Explorer as well as many other earlier browsers will not draw the border. If you want to ensure that a border is drawn around an empty table cell in all browsers, insert a **non-breaking space** character, ` ` or ` `, which will cause the cell to have content, although invisible.

Setting Table Width and Alignment

The TABLE element's WIDTH and ALIGN attributes let you control the table's width and horizontal alignment.

Center the table and set it to have a width of 85 percent (see Figure 5.8):

```
<table border="6" cellpadding="5" cellspacing="5" align="center"
width="85%">
```

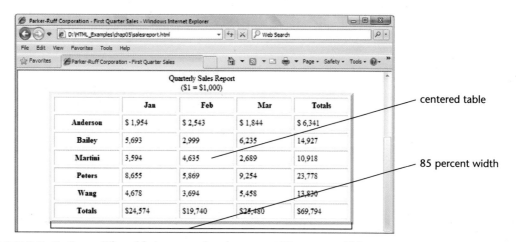

FIGURE 5.8 • The table is centered and set to an 85 percent width.

The WIDTH attribute can be set using a percentage or a numerical value. A percentage value sets the width of the table to a percentage of the browser window. For instance, if you set the browser width to 100 percent, the table will always be at least as wide as the browser window.

The ALIGN attribute sets the horizontal alignment of the table and can take a value of **center**, **left**, or **right**. Center-alignment works the same way as in the heading-level and paragraph elements. Left-alignment and right-alignment, on the other hand, work similarly to the IMG element, with the table floating to the left or right margin and following text or elements flowing around the table. As with the IMG element, the BR element's CLEAR attribute can be used to stop following text or elements from flowing around a table.

Setting Column Widths

The WIDTH attribute can be used in the TH or TD elements to set the width of a column. The attribute only needs to be inserted in one cell in a column to set the width of all cells within that column.

action

Set the width of the first cell in the second row to a width equal to 18 percent of the table width (see Figure 5.9):

```
<tr><th width="18%">Anderson</th> <td>$ 1,954</td> <td>$ 2,543
</td> <td>$ 1,844</td> <td>$ 6,341</td></tr>
```

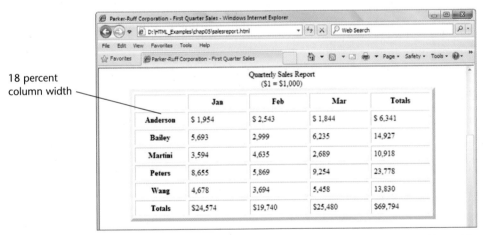

18 percent column width

FIGURE 5.9 • The first column is set to a width that is 18 percent of the table width.

You also could use the WIDTH attribute in the first cell in the first row to set the column width. It was set in the first cell in the second row, however, because you will be deleting the first cell in the first row in the next section, "Spanning Columns and Rows."

In a table without any WIDTH attributes set in the TABLE, TH, or TD elements, column widths are determined by the width of column content. If a WIDTH attribute is only set in the TABLE element, all current browsers apportion column widths equally so their sum is equal to the table width.

Because there are five columns in the example table, each column is equal to 20 percent of the table width as long as a different column width is not set in any of the columns. For current browsers, if one column is reduced or increased (to less or more than

20 percent in this case), the other column widths will be apportioned equally to fill the remaining width set for the table as a whole.

Although not included in this example, you also can use the HEIGHT attribute to set the height of cells within a row. For instance, to increase the first row to a height of 65 pixels, you just need to insert `height="65"` in any TH (or TD) element within that row.

Spanning Columns and Rows

The COLSPAN and ROWSPAN attributes can be used in TH and TD elements to create a **spanned cell**, which can span multiple columns or rows, or both.

Add a row to the example table that includes a cell that spans three columns (see Figure 5.10):

```
<tr><th></th> <th colspan="3">Monthly Sales Figures</th><th>
</th></tr>
<tr><th></th> <th>Jan</th> <th>Feb</th> <th>Mar</th> <th>Totals
</th></tr>
```

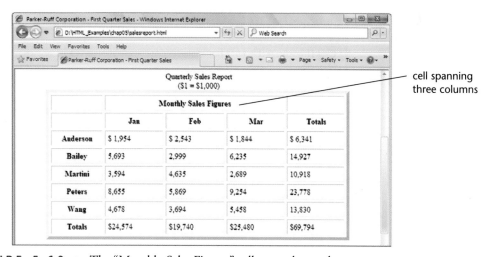

FIGURE 5.10 • The "Monthly Sales Figures" cell spans three columns.

Because the other rows of the table have five columns (five table cells in each row), the COLSPAN value (3) plus the non-spanned cells (2) should not exceed the total number of columns in the other rows (5).

Use the ROWSPAN element to create table cells in the upper-left and upper-right corners of the table that span two rows:

1. Because they are going to be spanned, delete the first and last TH elements in the second row:

```
<tr><th></th> <th colspan="3">Monthly Sales Figures</th><th>
</th></tr>
<tr><th></th> <th>Jan</th> <th>Feb</th> <th>Mar</th> <th>Totals
</th></tr>
```

2. Key **Sales Reps** as the content of the first cell and **Totals** as the content of the last cell in the first row. Use the ROWSPAN attribute in the first and last cells of that row to cause those cells to span two rows (see Figure 5.11):

```
<tr><th rowspan="2">Sales Reps</th> <th colspan="3">Monthly Sales
Figures</th><th rowspan="2">Totals</th></tr>
<tr><th>Jan</th> <th>Feb</th> <th>Mar</th></tr>
```

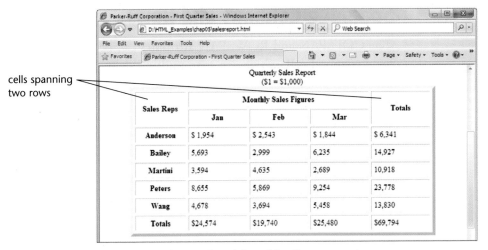

cells spanning two rows

FIGURE 5.11 • The "Sales Reps" and "Totals" cells are spanning two rows.

USING HTML TO CONTROL TABLE APPEARANCE

There are a number of ways to control the appearance of tables by using HTML alone. For instance, you can use the FONT element to set font characteristics (sizes, colors, and faces) inside table cells and use the BGCOLOR and BACKGROUND attributes in various elements to control background colors and background images within tables.

Save the current file so you can use it later as a base to further experiment with setting table display characteristics using HTML attributes:
1. In your text editor, save any changes you have made to **salesreport.html** (File, Save).
2. Resave salesreport.html as **salesreport2.html** in the chap05 folder.
3. Open **salesreport2.html** in your browser.

Vertically Aligning Cell Contents

By default, the contents of table cells are vertically aligned with the middle of the cell. The VALIGN attribute lets you vertically align the contents of table cells with the top, middle, or bottom of a cell, or along a common **baseline**.

Use the VALIGN attribute to vertically align the contents of the "Sales Reps" and "Totals" cells with the bottom of the cells (see Figure 5.12):

```
<tr><th rowspan="2" valign="bottom">Sales Reps</th>
<th colspan="3">Monthly Sales Figures</th><th rowspan="2"
valign="bottom">Totals</th></tr>
```

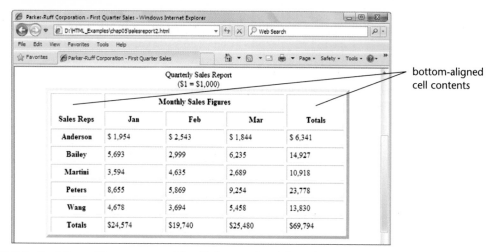

bottom-aligned cell contents

FIGURE 5.12 • The contents of the "Sales Reps" and "Totals" cells are bottom-aligned.

In addition to the **top**, **middle**, and **bottom** values, the VALIGN attribute also can take a **baseline** value, which causes text strings in different cells in a row to be aligned along their baselines.

Horizontally Aligning Cell Contents

TH elements are center-aligned by default, and TD elements are left-aligned by default. The ALIGN attribute can be used in the TR element to override the default horizontal alignment of the TH and TD elements.

Use the ALIGN attribute to right-align the table's data rows:

```
<tr align="right"><th>Anderson</th> <td>$ 1,954</td>
<td>$ 2,543</td> <td>$ 1,844</td> <td>$ 6,341</td></tr>
<tr align="right"><th>Bailey</th> <td>5,693</td> <td>2,999</td>
<td>6,235</td> <td>14,927</td></tr>
<tr align="right"><th>Martini</th> <td>3,594</td> <td>4,635</td>
<td>2,689</td> <td>10,918</td></tr>
<tr align="right"><th>Peters</th> <td>8,655</td> <td>5,869</td>
<td>9,254</td> <td>23,778</td></tr>
<tr align="right"><th>Wang</th> <td>4,678</td> <td>3,694</td>
<td>5,458</td> <td>13,830</td></tr>

<tr align="right"><th>Totals</th> <td>$24,574</td> <td>$19,740
</td> <td>$25,480</td> <td>$69,794</td></tr>
```

In its default standards mode, Internet Explorer 8 allows the overriding of the default horizontal alignment of TD cells, but not TH cells, when the alignment is set on the TR element. This is true whether an ALIGN attribute is used or a style is used (**text-align: right**). To make sure that Internet Explorer 8 treats this in the same way as other browsers, use the ALIGN attribute to directly right-align the row headings (TH elements) in the first column of the table (see Figure 5.13):

```
<tr align="right"><th align="right" width="18%">Anderson</th>
<td>$ 1,954</td> <td>$ 2,543</td> <td>$ 1,844</td> <td>$ 6,341
</td></tr>
<tr align="right"><th align="right">Bailey</th> <td>5,693</td>
```

```
<td>2,999</td> <td>6,235</td> <td>14,927</td></tr>
<tr align="right"><th align="right">Martini</th> <td>3,594</td>
<td>4,635</td> <td>2,689</td> <td>10,918</td></tr>
<tr align="right"><th align="right">Peters</th> <td>8,655</td>
<td>5,869</td> <td>9,254</td> <td>23,778</td></tr>
<tr align="right"><th align="right">Wang</th> <td>4,678</td>
<td>3,694</td> <td>5,458</td> <td>13,830</td></tr>

<tr align="right"><th align="right">Totals</th> <td>$24,574</td>
<td>$19,740</td> <td>$25,480</td> <td>$69,794</td></tr>
```

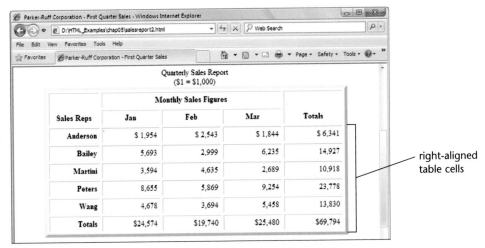

right-aligned
table cells

FIGURE 5.13 • The contents of the table data rows are right-aligned.

Future updates or versions of Internet Explorer might allow setting horizontal alignment on the TR element to override the TH element's default horizontal alignment, in which case, the previous code example will become unnecessary.

An alternative to inserting **align="right"** directly in the TH elements is to include a META-equiv statement in your page's HEAD section to trigger Internet Explorer 8's almost standards mode (or Internet Explorer 7 Standards Mode):

```
<meta http-equiv="Content-Type" content="text/html;
charset=utf-8">
<meta http-equiv="X-UA-Compatible" content="IE=7">
<title>Parker-Ruff Corporation - First Quarter Sales</title>
```

This, however, triggers an Internet Explorer 7 quirk, causing more horizontal spacing to be added below the table caption than in other browsers.

Substituting a style set on the TR element to set right-alignment also does not override the default horizontal alignment of TH elements in Internet Explorer 8. See "Using Styles to Control Table Appearance" later in this chapter for a more involved alternative that uses styles and the THEAD and TBODY elements to set horizontal alignment for both TD and TH elements.

Controlling Font Characteristics

You cannot bracket a table with a FONT element to change the font or color of text included in table cells. A FONT element must be inserted inside each cell in which a change in font or color is desired.

Use the FONT and B elements to change the appearance of text within the table:

1. Change the appearance of the caption and text in the first table row by using the FONT element:

```
<caption><font size="5">Quarterly Sales Report</font><br>
($1 = $1,000)</caption>

<tr><th rowspan="2" valign="bottom">Sales Reps</th>
<th colspan="3"><font color="blue" face="Arial, Helvetica">
Monthly Sales Figures</font></th><th rowspan="2" valign="bottom">
Totals</th></tr>
<tr><th>Jan</th> <th>Feb</th> <th>Mar</th></tr>
```

2. Change the appearance of the bottom row of totals by using the FONT and B elements (see Figure 5.14):

```
<tr align="right"><th align="right">Totals</th> <td>
<font color="red" face="Arial, Helvetica"><b>$24,574</b></font>
</td> <td><font color="red" face="Arial, Helvetica"><b>$19,740
</b></font></td> <td><font color="red" face="Arial, Helvetica">
<b>$25,480</b></font></td> <td><font color="red" face="Arial,
Helvetica"><b>$69,794</b></font></td></tr>
</table>
```

FIGURE 5.14 • The font characteristics of the caption, top row, and bottom row are changed.

NOTE

Inserting FONT elements within each and every TD or TH element to control the appearance of the content of table cells is not only deleterious to accessibility but also very inefficient for Web designers. Creating and maintaining complex table-based page designs that depend on the FONT element for formatting can be very laborious and time-consuming. It can also be harmful to usability, in that it can significantly increase the size of a page in bytes, increasing the time it takes to download and view a page and wasting bandwidth.

In the "Using Styles to Control Table Appearance" section later in this chapter, you will learn alternatives to using the FONT element to control the appearance of table cells that improve accessibility, usability, and efficiency.

Displaying a Background Color behind the Table

The BGCOLOR attribute lets you control the background color of the table, rows, or cells. It works exactly the same way as in the BODY element. You insert the BGCOLOR attribute in the TABLE element to display a background color behind the whole table.

Use the BGCOLOR attribute to assign a light blue color (one of the Web-safe colors) to the table background (see Figure 5.15):

```
<table border="6" cellpadding="5" cellspacing="5" align="center"
width="85%" bgcolor="#ccffff">
```

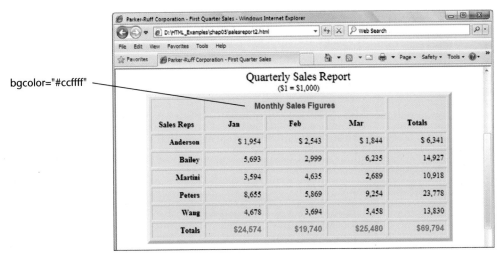

FIGURE 5.15 • The table background is now light blue.

Eliminating Spacing between Cells

The CELLSPACING attribute can be used to eliminate spacing between table cells, collapsing the double-line between cells to a single line.

Eliminate the spacing between the table's cells and increase the padding within the table's cells to eight pixels (see Figure 5.16):

```
<table border="6" cellpadding="8" cellspacing="0" align="center"
width="85%" bgcolor="#ccffff">
```

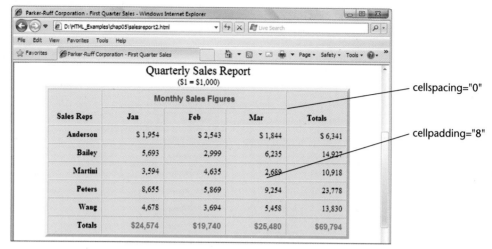

cellspacing="0"

cellpadding="8"

FIGURE 5.16 • The spacing between cells is eliminated and the padding within the cells in increased to eight pixels.

The eight-pixel padding amount roughly equals the previous padding and spacing amount, in that the spacing between cells was shared.

Displaying a Background Image Behind the Table

The BACKGROUND attribute can be used to display background images in tables.

You should be aware, however, that the BACKGROUND attribute is not part of the HTML 4 standard. It was originally a proprietary extension to HTML developed by Netscape that was never included in the HTML 3.2 or 4 standards, likely due to a lack in commonality in how earlier browsers (Netscape Navigator and Internet Explorer, in particular) interpreted it. All recent browsers consistently support the BACKGROUND attribute, but concerns with forward-compatibility counsel against its use in new Web pages, in that there is no guarantee that future browsers will continue to support this non-standard attribute. The example of using this attribute is presented solely so that you will understand how to handle this attribute in legacy Web pages.

In the "Using Styles to Control Table Appearance" section later in this chapter, you will learn how to use styles to display background images in tables.

Use the BACKGROUND attribute to set a background image for the table (see Figure 5.17):

```
<table border="6" cellpadding="8" cellspacing="0" align="center"
width="85%" bgcolor="#ccffff" background="back_clouds.jpg">
```

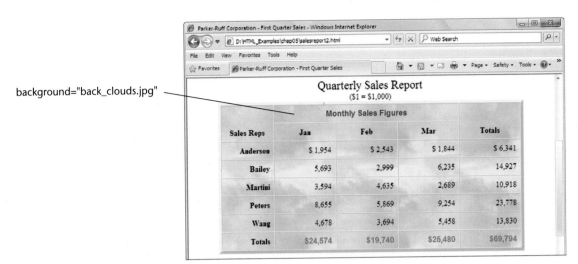

background="back_clouds.jpg"

Quarterly Sales Report ($1 = $1,000)				
Monthly Sales Figures				
Sales Reps	**Jan**	**Feb**	**Mar**	**Totals**
Anderson	$ 1,954	$ 2,543	$ 1,844	$ 6,341
Bailey	5,693	2,999	6,235	14,927
Martini	3,594	4,635	2,689	10,918
Peters	8,655	5,869	9,254	23,778
Wang	4,678	3,694	5,458	13,830
Totals	$24,574	$19,740	$26,480	$69,794

FIGURE 5.17 • A background image can give a table a dramatic look.

While all recent browsers consistently support using the BACKGROUND attribute to set a background image for the TABLE element, they are highly inconsistent in whether they support doing the same on the TH, TD, and TR elements. For that reason, if you should choose, against all better sense, to use this attribute, it should only be used in the TABLE element.

TROUBLE *spot*

Whenever displaying a background image, whether using the BACKGROUND attribute or styles, you also should specify a background color that resembles the color of your background image. That way, if users are surfing with the display of images turned off, they will still see your background color. This is especially important when displaying light text against a dark background image because with the display of images turned off, a visitor could end up seeing (or not seeing) white text against a white background, for instance.

Displaying Background Colors behind Rows and Cells

You can insert the BGCOLOR attribute in the TR, TH, or TD elements to display background colors behind table rows or table cells.

action

Use different background colors to highlight the different parts of the table:

1. Set a light green background color behind the first two rows:

```
<tr bgcolor="#ccffcc"><th rowspan="2" valign="bottom">Sales
Reps</th> <th colspan="3"><font color="blue" face="Arial,
Helvetica, sans-serif">Monthly Sales Figures</font></th>
<th rowspan="2" valign="bottom">Totals</th></tr>
<tr bgcolor="#ccffcc"><th>Jan</th> <th>Feb</th> <th>Mar</th></tr>
```

2. Set a light yellow color behind the row heading cells that contain the last names of the sales reps:

```
<tr align="right"><th bgcolor="#ffffcc" align="right" width="18%">
Anderson</th> <td width="20%">$ 1,954</td> <td width="20%">$ 2,543
</td> <td width="20%">$ 1,844</td> <td width="20%">$ 6,341</td>
</tr>
<tr align="right"><th bgcolor="#ffffcc" align="right">Bailey</th>
<td>5,693</td> <td>2,999</td> <td>6,235</td> <td>14,927</td></tr>
```

```
<tr align="right"><th bgcolor="#ffffcc" align="right">Martini
</th> <td>3,594</td> <td>4,635</td> <td>2,689</td> <td>10,918
</td></tr>
<tr align="right"><th bgcolor="#ffffcc" align="right">Peters</th>
<td>8,655</td> <td>5,869</td> <td>9,254</td> <td>23,778</td></tr>
<tr align="right"><th bgcolor="#ffffcc" align="right">Wang</th>
<td>4,678</td> <td>3,694</td> <td>5,458</td> <td>13,830</td></tr>
```

3. Set a light pink (or salmon) background color behind the bottom row in the table (see Figure 5.18):

```
<tr bgcolor="#ffcccc" align="right"><th align="right">Totals</th>
<td><font color="red" face="Arial, Helvetica"><b>$24,574</b>
</font></td> <td><font color="red" face="Arial, Helvetica"><b>
$19,740</b></font></td> <td><font color="red" face="Arial,
Helvetica"><b>$25,480</b></font></td> <td><font color="red"
face="Arial, Helvetica"><b>$69,794</b></font></td></tr>
</table>
```

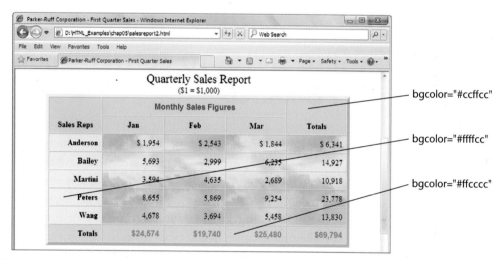

FIGURE 5.18 • Using different background colors helps highlight the different parts of the table.

As you will notice in Figure 5.18, background colors set for the TR, TH, and TD elements overlay any background (color or image) that is set for the TABLE element.

To see how the table will look with only a background color assigned to the TABLE element, remove the background image that you added to the table (see Figure 5.19):

```
<table border="6" cellpadding="8" cellspacing="0" align="center"
width="85%" bgcolor="#ccffff" background="back_clouds.jpg">
```

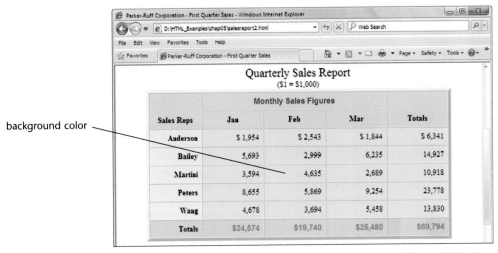

background color

	Quarterly Sales Report ($1 = $1,000)			
	Monthly Sales Figures			
Sales Reps	Jan	Feb	Mar	Totals
Anderson	$ 1,954	$ 2,543	$ 1,844	$ 6,341
Bailey	5,693	2,999	6,235	14,927
Martini	3,594	4,635	2,689	10,918
Peters	8,655	5,869	9,254	23,778
Wang	4,678	3,694	5,458	13,830
Totals	$24,574	$19,740	$25,480	$69,794

FIGURE 5.19 • The green, yellow, and pink background colors, set on TR and TH elements, overlay the blue background color, set on the TABLE element.

USING STYLES TO CONTROL TABLE APPEARANCE

The use of styles provides much more control over the appearance of tables than can be achieved through HTML alone. Styles are also much more efficient than using the FONT element to control table appearance. You have to insert the FONT element inside of each and every table cell where you want it to have effect, but a single entry in a style sheet can change the formatting of every table cell.

The use of styles to format tables also provides for better accessibility, in that styles separate the presentation of the table from its content and organization. A nonvisual browser, for instance, can easily ignore any presentation features defined by styles to concentrate on conveying the table's content and organization.

A number of table elements were introduced as part of HTML 4, which require the use of styles to provide visual formatting. By themselves, the TBODY, THEAD, TFOOT, COL, and COLGROUP elements have no visual formatting but can be used in conjunction with styles to format groups of rows and groups of columns in tables.

Using styles to format tables can also improve usability because complex table-based page designs created using styles can have significantly smaller file sizes in bytes than comparable pages formatted using the FONT element.

Visit the Internet Resource Center. The purpose of this section is to determine how certain HTML 4 features and elements, in conjunction with styles, can be used to provide more control over the appearance of tables. This section is not intended to provide an in-depth understanding of the use of styles in general. For links to resources that cover the use of styles in more depth, visit the Chapter 5 section of this book's Internet Resource Center at **www.emcp.net/html2e**.

Return to the copy of your example file that you saved earlier to do the following style examples:

1. Reopen **salesreport.html** in your text editor from the chap05 folder.

2. Save salesreport.html as **salesreport3.html** in the chap05 folder, and open it in your browser.

Changing Fonts and Colors

You can use styles to easily change fonts and colors.

Create a style sheet to transform the appearance of the table:

1. Create a style sheet that assigns fonts and colors to the table's contents (see Figure 5.20):

```
<title>Parker-Ruff Corporation - First Quarter Sales</title>
<style type="text/css">
table {
    color: #330066;
    background: #ffffcc;
    }
caption {
    font-family: Arial, Helvetica, sans-serif;
    color: #990000;
    background: transparent;
    font-size: 1.2em;
    }
th {
    font-family: Arial, Helvetica, sans-serif;
    color: #003399;
    background: transparent;
    }
</style>
</head>
```

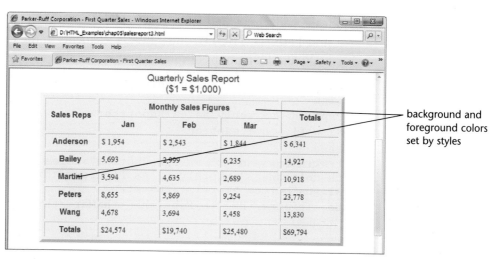

FIGURE 5.20 • Styles let you make global changes to the appearance of a table.

2. Use a style to add a background image to the table (see Figure 5.21):

```
<style type="text/css">
table {
    color: #330066;
    background: #ffffcc url("back_marblebeige.jpg");
    }
```

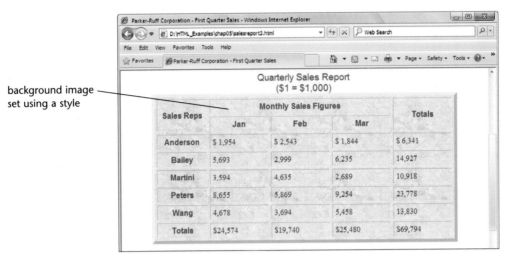

background image set using a style

FIGURE 5.21 • A background image gives a table a whole new look.

Controlling the Appearance of Row Groups

The TBODY, THEAD, and TFOOT elements are HTML 4 elements that let you set different display characteristics for a group of rows, or **row group**, within a table. By themselves, these elements have no visual formatting; you must use these elements in conjunction with styles to produce any visual result.

Use the TBODY, THEAD, and TFOOT elements to create separate display characteristics for the body, head, and foot of the table:

1. Add THEAD, TBODY, and TFOOT elements to the table to define table head, body, and foot groups of rows:

```
<table border="6" cellpadding="5" cellspacing="5" width="85%"
align="center">
<caption>Quarterly Sales Report<br>
($1 = $1,000)</caption>
<thead>
<tr><th rowspan="2" valign="bottom">Sales Reps</th>
<th colspan="3">Monthly Sales Figures</th><th rowspan="2"
valign="bottom">Totals</th></tr>
<tr><th>Jan</th> <th>Feb</th> <th>Mar</th></tr>
</thead>

<tbody>
<tr><th width="18%">Anderson</th> <td>$ 1,954</td> <td>$ 2,543
</td> <td>$ 1,844</td> <td>$ 6,341</td></tr>
<tr><th>Bailey</th> <td>5,693</td> <td>2,999</td> <td>6,235</td>
<td>14,927</td></tr>
<tr><th>Martini</th> <td>3,594</td> <td>4,635</td> <td>2,689</td>
<td>10,918</td></tr>
<tr><th>Peters</th> <td>8,655</td> <td>5,869</td> <td>9,254</td>
<td>23,778</td></tr>
```

```
<tr><th>Wang</th> <td>4,678</td> <td>3,694</td> <td>5,458</td>
<td>13,830</td></tr>

<tr><th>Totals</th> <td>$24,574</td> <td>$19,740</td>
<td>$25,480</td> <td>$69,794</td></tr>
</tbody>

<tfoot>
<tr><td colspan="5">All sales amounts are stated at $1 per
$1,000.</td></tr>
</tfoot>
</table>
```

2. Create styles to control the display of the table's head, body, and foot sections (see Figure 5.22):

```
th {
    font-family: Arial, Helvetica, sans-serif;
    color: #003399;
    background: transparent;
    }
thead {
    color: #330066;
    background: #ffff99 url("back_sandstone.jpg");
    }
tbody {
    color: #990000;
    background: transparent;
    }
tfoot {
    color: #330066;
    background: #ffff99 url("back_goldrock.jpg");
    font-weight: bold;
    text-align: center;
    }
</style>
```

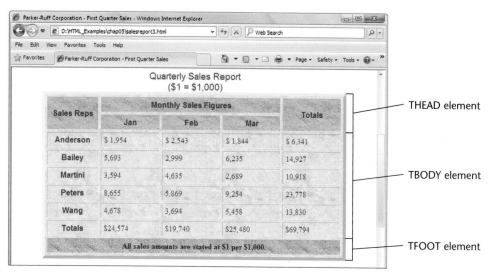

FIGURE 5.22 • Different display characteristics are applied to the table's head, body, and foot.

Including the TBODY element is optional. Any table rows not included in a THEAD or TFOOT element will be formatted using style properties assigned to the TBODY element in the style sheet, even if the TBODY element is not present.

Turning Off Spacing between Cells

Earlier, in the salesreport2.html example, you eliminated the spacing between table cells by setting a **cellspacing="0"** attribute in the TABLE element, while increasing the padding amount within the cells by setting a **cellpadding="8"** attribute. The same result can be achieved using styles and without using the CELLSPACING or CELLPADDING attributes.

Use styles to eliminate the spacing between the table cells, and set a black one-pixel border between the cells:

1. Remove the cell padding and cell spacing currently set in the TABLE element:

```
<table border="6" cellpadding="5" cellspacing="5" width="85%"
align="center" >
```

2. Collapse the spacing between the table cells:

```
table {
    color: #330066;
    background: #ffffcc url("back_marblebeige.jpg");
    border-collapse: collapse;
    border-spacing: 0;
    }
```

3. For the TH and TD elements, set eight pixels of padding, and set a one-pixel black border to be drawn around the table cells (see Figure 5.23):

```
th {
    font-family: Arial, Helvetica, sans-serif;
    color: #003399;
    background: transparent;
    }
th, td {
    padding: 8px;
    border: 1px solid black;
    }
```

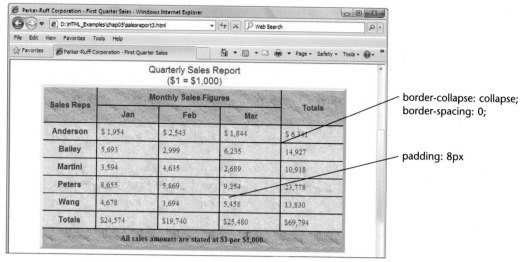

border-collapse: collapse;
border-spacing: 0;

padding: 8px

FIGURE 5.23 • Styles are used to remove the spacing between and increase the padding inside the table cells.

The style rule you just added (**th, td**) allows applying properties to a comma-separated list (or group) of elements, in this case, the TH and TD elements. In CSS this kind of selector is called a **group selector**. In Chapter 7, *Designing Multi-Column Web Sites*, you will learn more about using group and other CSS selectors.

The default setting for tables is **border-collapse: separate**. As long as that setting is active, each cell has its own separate border. To set a specific amount of spacing around the border of a cell, set the border-spacing property to the amount of spacing you want between cell borders (**border-spacing: 6px**, for instance).

Controlling Vertical Alignment

The Sales Reps and Totals cells in the THEAD section of the table still are middle-aligned, which is the default vertical alignment for table cells.

action

Set the TH elements in the THEAD section of the table so they are bottom-aligned (see Figure 5.24):

```
thead {
    color: #330066;
    background: #ffff99 url("back_sandstone.jpg");
    }
thead th {
    vertical-align: bottom;
    }
```

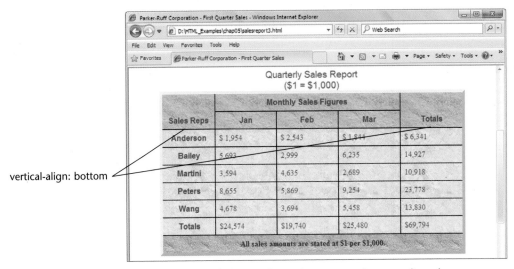

vertical-align: bottom

FIGURE 5.24 • The TH cells in the THEAD section are now bottom-aligned.

The style rule you just added (**thead th**) allows applying properties to an element that is the descendant (nested anywhere inside) of another element. In CSS this kind of selector is called a **descendant selector**. In this case, the property (**vertical-align: bottom;**) is applied to a TH element only if it is nested inside of the THEAD element, but not otherwise. In Chapter 7, *Designing Multi-Column Web Sites*, you will learn more about using descendant and other CSS selectors.

Other allowable values for the vertical-align property in tables include **top**, **middle**, and **baseline**. When **baseline** is used, cells will be vertically aligned based on the baseline of the first cell in a row.

Controlling Horizontal Alignment

The default horizontal alignment for TH and TD elements is center-alignment and left-alignment, respectively. In this kind of layout, they should both be right-aligned.

action

Right-align the TH and TD cells in the TBODY section (see Figure 5.25):

```
tbody {
    color: #990000;
    background: transparent;
    }
tbody th {
    text-align: right;
    }
tbody td {
    text-align: right;
    }
```

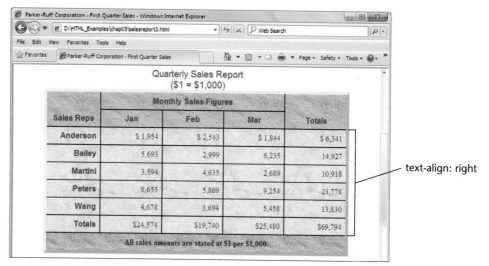

text-align: right

FIGURE 5.25 • The TH and TD cells in the TBODY section are now right-aligned.

These two styles can be combined in a single style that combines a group selector with two descendant selectors:

```
tbody th, tbody td {
    text-align: right;
    }
```

Controlling the Appearance of Columns

You also can control the appearance of columns using styles. You can do this by assigning table cells to a class, to which style properties can be applied, or by using a descendant selector.

Assign separate display characteristics to the "Sales Reps" column and the "Totals" column:

1. Assign the "Totals" column to a class so a style can be applied to it:

```
<tbody>
<tr><th width="18%">Anderson</th> <td>$ 1,954</td> <td>$ 2,543
</td> <td>$ 1,844</td> <td class="totalcol">$ 6,341</td></tr>
<tr><th>Bailey</th> <td>5,693</td> <td>2,999</td> <td>6,235</td>
<td class="totalcol">14,927</td></tr>
<tr><th>Martini</th> <td>3,594</td> <td>4,635</td> <td>2,689</td>
<td class="totalcol">10,918</td></tr>
<tr><th>Peters</th> <td>8,655</td> <td>5,869</td> <td>9,254</td>
<td class="totalcol">23,778</td></tr>
<tr><th>Wang</th> <td>4,678</td> <td>3,694</td> <td>5,458</td>
<td class="totalcol">13,830</td></tr>

<tr><th>Totals</th> <td>$24,574</td> <td>$19,740</td>
<td>$25,480</td> <td class="totalcol">$69,794</td></tr>
</tbody>
```

2. Define styles that apply formatting to the "Sales Reps" and "Totals" columns (see Figure 5.26):

```
tbody th {
    text-align: right;
    color: #ffffcc;
    background: #330066 url("back_blueslate.jpg");
    }
tbody td {
    text-align: right;
    }
.totalcol {
    font-weight: bold;
    color: navy;
    background: #990000 url("back_paper.jpg");
    }
```

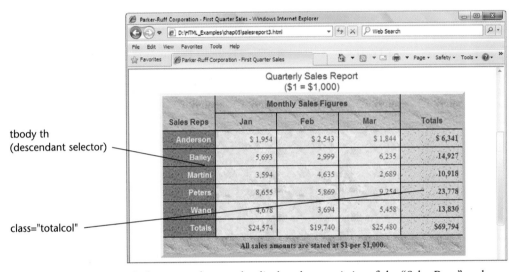

tbody th
(descendant selector)

class="totalcol"

FIGURE 5.26 • Styles are used to set the display characteristics of the "Sales Reps" and "Totals" columns.

In CSS, the "." in `.totalcol` signifies that it is a **class selector**. The style properties will be applied to any element included within the class (in this case, assigned by inserting `class="totalcol"` in the element's start tag). If you want the style applied only to TD elements assigned to the "totalcol" class, you can use a `td.totalcol` selector. If you want the style applied only to TD elements assigned to the "totalcol" class that are nested inside the TBODY element, you can use a `tbody td.totalcol` selector.

Two additional HTML elements, the COLGROUP and COL elements, can be used in conjunction with styles to control the appearance of column groups and individual columns. For guidance on implementing these elements, see the CSS 2.1 specification at **www.w3.org/TR/html401/**.

Setting Display Characteristics of Specific Rows and Cells

You also can apply display characteristics to specific rows and cells within the table.

Include specific cells or rows within classes, and then create styles that apply display characteristics to those classes:

    1. Assign the first row in the THEAD section to the "toprow" class, and then assign the last row in the TBODY section to the "totalrow" class:

```
<thead>
<tr class="toprow"><th rowspan="2">Sales Reps</th>
<th colspan="3">Monthly Sales Figures</th><th rowspan="2">
Totals</th></tr>
<tr><th>Jan</th> <th>Feb</th> <th>Mar</th></tr>
</thead>

[...]

<tr class="totalrow"><th>Totals</th> <td>$24,574</td>
<td>$19,740</td> <td>$25,480</td> <td class="totalcol">$69,794
</td></tr>
</tbody>
```

2. Delete the color and background properties from the th style, and then add two styles that set display characteristics for the two classes you just added (see Figure 5.27):

```
th {
    font-family: Arial, Helvetica, sans-serif;
    color: #003399;
    background: transparent;
    }
.toprow {
    color: #003399;
    background: transparent url("back_marblegreen.jpg");
    }
.totalrow td {
    font-weight: bold;
    color: #ffcc33;
    background: #990000 url("back_redstone.jpg");
    }
```

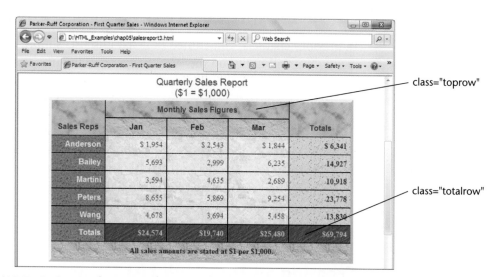

FIGURE 5.27 • Separate styles are applied to the "toprow" and "totalrow" classes.

3. Create an additional style that sets a separate format for the grand total cell (see Figure 5.28):

```
.totalrow .totalcol {
    font-family: Arial, Geneva, Helvetica, sans-serif;
    font-size: 1.1em;
    font-weight: bold;
    color: #ccff99;
    background: #990000 url("back_bluestone2.jpg");
    }
</style>
```

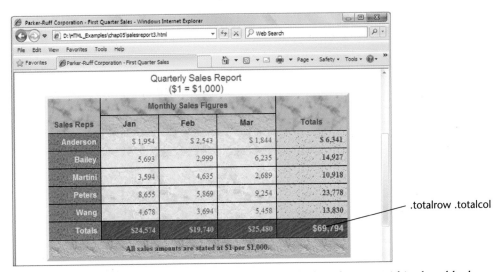

.totalrow .totalcol

FIGURE 5.28 • Different display characteristics are applied to elements within the table that are assigned to specific classes.

CASE EXAMPLE: CREATING INDENTED ICON LINK LISTS

In previous chapters, you created bulleted link lists simply by using the UL and LI elements. You will notice on the Web, however, many instances in which bulleted lists are created using graphical bullet icons.

> While surfing the Web, Johnny Watson has noticed that many sites make use of colorful graphical bullet icons when presenting lists. He decided that he wants to do the same in his personal page to add more color and visual appeal. Johnny removed the DIV (Division), UL (Unordered List), and LI (List Item) elements he used previously, nested his list of link items in a P element, added descriptions to the link list items in his page, and added BR elements where he wants line breaks.

Creating an Icon Link List Using a Table

A table can be used to create an **indented icon link list**.

Prepare to work with this example by following these steps:

1. In your text editor, open **watson4_ex.html** from the chap05 folder.
2. Save watson4_ex.html as **watson4.html** in the chap05 folder.
3. In your browser, open **watson4.html** from the chap05 folder.

You create an indented icon link list using a table by creating a two-column table, with the bullet icon inserted in the cells of the first column and the link text and descriptions inserted in the second column. An example icon bullet image, goldball.gif, is included with this chapter's example files.

action

Use a table to create an indented icon line list:

1. Add the following code before and after the first A element:

```
<table width="85%" align="center">
<tr valign="top"><td width="30">
<img src="goldball.gif" height="15" vspace="3" width="15" alt="*">
</td><td>
<a href="mybio.html">My biography</a> - Read about where I'm from, my family history, my interests and involvements, the accomplishments I'm most proud of, and my future plans.
</td></tr>
<tr valign="top"><td>
<img src="goldball.gif" height="15" vspace="3" width="15" alt="*">
</td><td>
<a href="myresume.html">My resume</a> - Look here for details about my studies, work experience, community involvements, and awards and honors.
```

2. Copy and paste the last section of code you added (starting with **</td></tr>** and ending with **</td><td>**) in front of each of the following A elements.

3. Add the following code after the last A element (see Figure 5.29):

```
<a href="http://www.wherever.emcp.com/jdoe/homepage.html">My friend Jane's site</a> - Jane is a very talented photographer. She's put up a gallery of photos from her recent trip to Olympic National Park in Washington state. Don't miss it!
</td></tr>
</table>
```

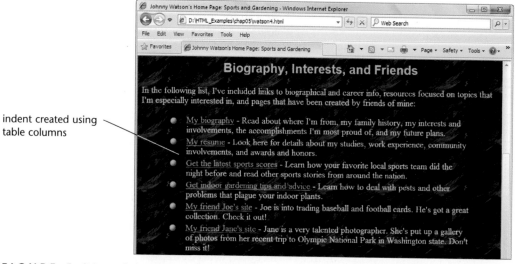

indent created using table columns

FIGURE 5.29 • It is easy to indent and center an icon link list created using a two-column table.

If you want to adjust the vertical position of the bullet icon image, just increase or decrease the VSPACE attribute values set on the IMG elements. You might need to decrease it if there is additional space included at the top of the bullet image, for instance.

The primary disadvantage of using tables to create indented icon link lists is that they tend to be somewhat labor-intensive to create and maintain, especially if you have a lot of list items. They also are less efficient and consume more bytes than using styles to create an indented icon link list.

Creating an Icon Link List Using Styles

Although using a table to format content other than tabular data is handy, it is discouraged by the W3C because it is counter to the semantic meaning of the TABLE element, which is the presentation of tabular data, and thus is considered to be harmful to accessibility on the Web. In this case, a screen reader might try to interpret the bullet icons as being data.

Prepare to work with this example by following these steps:

1. In your text editor, re-open **watson4_ex.html**.
2. Save watson4_ex.html as **watson5.html** in the chap05 folder.
3. In your browser, open **watson5.html** from the chap05 folder.

Instead of using a table to create an indented icon link list, you can use styles. This method of creating an indented icon link list involves positioning the bullet icon as a background image relative to the list item.

Create an indented icon link list using a background image and styles:

1. Use the UL and LI elements to set up the list of links and descriptions as an unordered list:

```
<ul>
<li><a href="mybio.html">My biography</a> - Read about where I'm
from, my family history, my interests and involvements, the
accomplishments I'm most proud of, and my future plans.
<li><a href="myresume.html">My resume</a> - Look here for details
about my studies, work experience, community involvements, and
awards and honors.
<li><a href="http://www.usatoday.com/sports/scores.htm">Get the
latest sports scores</a> - Learn how your favorite local sports
team did the night before and read other sports stories from
around the nation.
<li><a href="http://www.about-house-plants.com/">Get indoor
gardening tips and advice</a> - Learn how to deal with pests and
other problems that plague your indoor plants.
<li><a href="http://blank.emcp.com/jshmoe/">My friend Joe's
site</a> - Joe is into trading baseball and football cards. He's
got a great collection. Check it out!
<li><a href="http://wherever.emcp.com/jdoe/homepage.html">My
friend Jane's site</a> - Jane is a very talented photographer.
She's put up a gallery of photos from her recent trip to Olympic
National Park in Washington state. Don't miss it!
</ul>
```

2. Add styles to the style sheet that 1) turn off display of the default bullet for unordered lists and 2) position a bullet icon image as a non-tiled background image relative to the list's LI element (see Figure 5.30):

```
ul {
    list-style: none;
    }
li {
    background-image:url(redball.gif);
    background-repeat: no-repeat;
    background-position: 5px 5px;
    padding-left: 30px; padding-right:60px;
    }
</style>
```

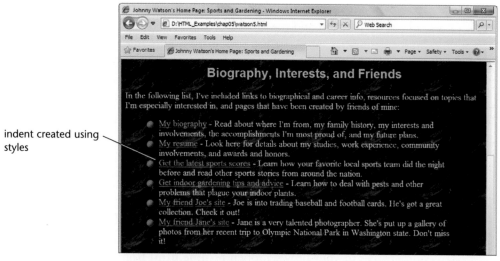

indent created using styles

FIGURE 5.30 • Styles provide a less labor-intensive method for creating indented icon link lists through positioning the bullet icon as a background image.

To adjust the vertical position of the bullet icon, increase or decrease the first background-position value. To adjust the separation between the bullet icon and the following text, increase or decrease the padding-left value.

Another method for creating indented bullet icon lists is to use the list-style-image style property in combination with an unordered list:

```
ul {
    list-style-image: url(redball.gif);
    }
ul li {
    padding-left: 15px;
    padding-right: 15px;
    margin-left: 15px;
    margin-right: 15px;
    }
```

The disadvantage of this method is that there is no way to adjust the vertical position of the bullet icon.

An advantage of using styles to create indented icon link lists is they are much easier to create and maintain and are much more efficient than using a table.

NOTE

The CSS examples in this section are presented to provide alternatives to using tables for formatting non-tabular data that can be implemented by the student without already having an in-depth knowledge of how styles work. Using styles will be covered in more detail in Chapter 7, *Designing Multi-Column Web Sites*.

CASE EXAMPLE: FORMATTING AN ONLINE RESUME

A common type of HTML document that many people want to create is an online resume. Having an attractive resume online can be a real asset in landing a job.

> Kristine Kochanski has been the controller of a medium-sized corporation for more than five years. She believes she is ready to step into a management position and has launched a job search because the opportunities for further advancement at her current firm are limited.
>
> Kristine has decided that creating an online resume will help in her job search. She has already written her resume and done the initial HTML formatting. She has been studying using HTML tables, however, and has decided to use them to finalize the formatting of her resume. For instance, one of the changes she wants to implement is to use tables to format the dates and following paragraphs as hanging indents.

Prepare to work with this example by following these steps:

1. In your text editor, open **resume_ex.html** from the chap05 folder.
2. Save resume_ex.html as **resume.html** in the chap05 folder.
3. In your browser, open **resume.html** from the chap05 folder (see Figure 5.31).

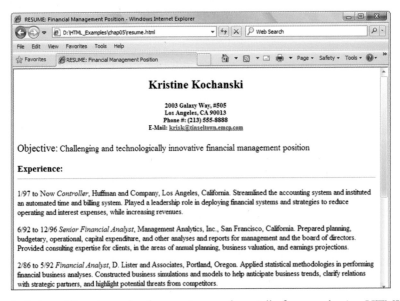

FIGURE 5.31 • The resume has been written and partially formatted using HTML but is far from optimal in its appearance.

Initially, the layout is not very efficient, and it does not look much like a resume. An HTML table can be used to create a more efficient layout that also looks much more like a resume.

Create an online resume using a table:

1. Use a two-column HTML table and COLSPAN attributes to create the resume layout:

```
<h2 align="center">Kristine Kochanski</h2>
<h5 align="center">2003 Galaxy Way, #505<br>
Los Angeles, CA 90013<br>
Phone #: (213) 555-8888<br>
E-Mail: <a href="mailto:krisk@tinseltown.emcp.com">
krisk@tinseltown.emcp.com</a></h5>


<table width="97%" cellpadding="3" cellspacing="3">
<tr valign="baseline">
<th width="112" align="right"><p><span style="font-size:1.3em">
Objective:</span></th>
<td><span style="font-size:1.1em">Challenging and technologically
innovative financial management position</span></td>
</tr>

<tr>
<th colspan="2"><h3>Experience:<hr></h3></th>
</tr>
<tr valign="top">
<th width="115" align="right"><p>1/97 to Now </th>
<td><i>Controller</i>, Huffman and Company, Los Angeles,
California. Streamlined the accounting system and instituted an
automated time and billing system. Played a leadership role in
deploying financial systems and strategies to reduce operating
and interest expenses, while increasing revenues.</td>
</tr>
<tr valign="top">
<th align="right"><p>6/92 to 12/96 </th>
<td><i>Senior Financial Analyst</i>, Management Analytics, Inc.,
San Francisco, California. Prepared planning, budgetary,
operational, capital expenditure, and other analyses and reports
for management and the board of directors. Provided consulting
expertise for clients, in the areas of annual planning, business
valuation, and earnings projections.</td>
</tr>
<tr valign="top">
<th align="right"><p>2/86 to 5/92 </th>
<td><i>Financial Analyst</i>, D. Lister and Associates, Portland,
Oregon. Applied statistical methodologies in performing financial
business analyses. Constructed business simulations and models to
help anticipate business trends, clarify relations with strategic
partners, and highlight potential threats from competitors.</td>
</tr>

<tr>
<th colspan="2"><h3>Education and Training:<hr></h3></th>
</tr>
<tr valign="top">
<th align="right"><p>9/84 to 6/86 </th>
<td><i>Master of Business Administration</i>, with concentrations
```

```
in Technology/Innovation Management and Finance, University of
Colorado at Boulder.</td>
</tr>
<tr valign="top">
<th align="right"><p>9/80 to 6/84 </th>
<td><i>Bachelor of Arts</i>, Business Administration, University
of Colorado at Boulder.</td></tr>

<tr>
<th colspan="2"><h3>Certifications and Memberships:<hr></h3></th>
</tr>
<tr valign="top">
<td colspan="2" align="center"><p><i>Certified Public Accountant
(CPA)</i>, San Francisco, California.<br>
<i>Personal Financial Planning (PFP)</i>, Portland, Oregon.<br>
<i>American Association of Financial Planners, senior member</i>,
Portland, Oregon.</td>
</tr>
</table>
<p align="center">References available upon request.</p>
```

2. Create a style sheet to control the spacing of the H2 and H4 elements, and set a different font for the H2, H4, and TH elements (see Figure 5.32):

```
<style type="text/css">
h2, h3, h4 {
    margin-top: 10px;
    margin-bottom: 0;
    padding: 0
    }
h2, h3, h4, th {
    font-family: Arial, Geneva, Helvetica, sans-serif;
    }
</style>
</head>
```

vertical spacing inserted above P element

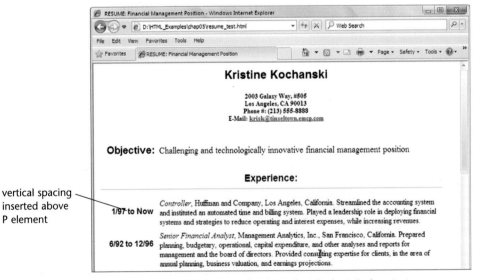

FIGURE 5.32 • The dates are not vertically aligned with the job descriptions.

TROUBLE *spot*

If you are using Internet Explorer 7, or earlier versions of that browser, you will not see the vertical spacing above the dates text because it incorrectly eliminates it for the first block element in a table cell. This can trick you into thinking that other browsers do the same, which they do not (including Internet Explorer 8).

3. As called out in Figure 5.32, the text strings for the dates, which are preceded by **<p>** start tags, are not vertically aligned with the following job position descriptions. To fix this, add a style that uses a **:first-child** selector to eliminate the top margin of any block element that is the first child of a TD or TH element (see Figure 5.33):

```
td :first-child, th :first-child {
   margin-top: 0;
   margin-bottom: 10px;
   }
</style>
```

th:first-child {
margin-top: 0; }

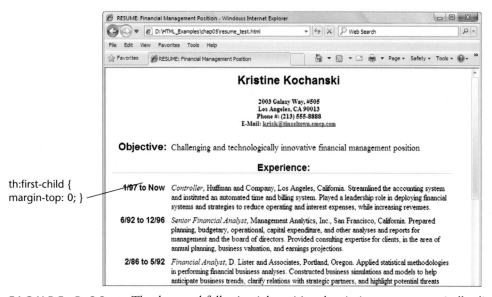

FIGURE 5.33 • The dates and following job position descriptions are now vertically aligned with each other.

A non-breaking space character (** **) is inserted following the dates to create more separation between the two table columns without having to globally increase the padding or spacing in the table.

The **:first-child** selector operates similarly to the **:link**, **:visited**, **:active**, and **:hover** selectors you used previously to control the appearance of links. They all assign display characteristics based on the specific state or position of an element. The W3C refers to the **:first-child** selector as a **pseudo-element**, since it functions similarly to a simple (or element) selector, except that properties are only applied to an element that is a **first child**. A **:link**, **:visited**, **:active**, or **:hover** selector is referred to as a **pseudo-class** because it operates on an element class without attaching a CLASS attribute to the element.

Most of the techniques applied in creating the online resume layout have been used in previous examples in this chapter. One feature that is new in this example is the use of the `valign="baseline"` attribute in the "Objective" table row. Because the text strings in the two table cells in the row are differently sized (in font sizes of 1.1 and 1.3 ems), this attribute causes the text strings to be vertically aligned along their baselines.

TROUBLE *spot*

Although not used in the previous example, inserting an image as the first or sole content of a table cell can lead to differences in how different browsers display the image. All current browsers add some spacing above the image, or above and below the image if it is the sole content of the table cell. Internet Explorer 7 and earlier versions of that browser, however, do not add in the vertical spacing in either case. Although adding in the spacing is correct according to the HTML 4 standard, there are situations where you might not want it, such as when using sliced images to create a graphical layout (arranging the sliced images next to each other like pieces in a jig-saw puzzle). To eliminate the vertical spacing above and below an image, in all recent browsers, when it is the first or sole content in a table cell, add the following to the page's style sheet:

```
td img, th img {
    display: block;
    margin: 0;
    }
```

CHAPTER SUMMARY

You should now be familiar with many of the HTML features and elements that are commonly used to create and format tables, including using the PRE element to format pre-formatted tabular data and the TABLE element for formatting raw data. You should know how to set table borders, width, and alignment on the page; control spacing and padding between table cells; horizontally and vertically align table contents; span columns and rows in tables; specify foreground and background colors for tables, rows, and cells; specify a background image for a table; and format tables using styles (using row groups, class selectors, group selectors, and descendant selectors). You should also be aware of accessibility, usability, and efficiency issues involved in using tables, especially if using tables in a counter-semantic fashion to present non-tabular data.

Code Review

`<pre>...</pre>`	PRE element. Used to display pre-formatted text, such as a worksheet saved as a .prn file, with all spaces and returns displayed.
`<table>...</table>`	TABLE element. Defines a table (data arranged in rows and columns) in HTML.
`<caption>...</caption>`	CAPTION element. Specifies a caption that can be displayed above or below a table.
`<tr>...</tr>`	TR element. Defines a row of cells in a table.
`<th>...</th>`	TH element. Defines a table heading cell, which can function as either a column heading or a row heading.
`<td>...</td>`	TD element. Defines a table data cell.
`<table border="1"`	BORDER attribute. In the TABLE element, draws a one-pixel border around the table and the table cells.
`<table border="6"`	BORDER attribute. In the TABLE element, draws a six-pixel border around a table, but leaves borders around table cells unchanged.
`<table cellpadding="5"`	CELLPADDING attribute. Specifies that five pixels of padding is displayed inside a table's cells (between a cell's content and its border).
`<table cellspacing="5"`	CELLSPACING attribute. Specifies that five pixels of spacing is displayed between a table's cells (between the borders around cells).
`<table width="85%"`	WIDTH attribute. In the TABLE element, specifies that the width of a table is 85 percent of the page (or containing block). Value can also be stated as an integer, designating pixels (`width="500"`, for instance).
`<table align="center"`	ALIGN attribute. In the TABLE element, centers the table in the page or containing block. A value of **left** or **right** floats the table to the left or right margin of the page (or containing block), with following text flowing around the table.
`<th width="18%"`	WIDTH attribute. In a TH or TD element, sets the width of a table column to 18 percent of the width of the table. Value can also be stated as an integer to set a specific column width in pixels (`width="50"`, for instance).

`<th colspan="3"`	COLSPAN attribute. In a TH or TD element, causes a table cell to span three columns. The span amount plus the unspanned cells must equal the total number of columns in the table.
`<th rowspan="2"`	ROWSPAN attribute. In a TH or TD element, causes a table cell to span two table rows. The span amount plus the unspanned cells in the column must equal the total number of rows in the table.
`<th valign="bottom"`	VALIGN attribute. In a TH or TD element, vertically aligns cell contents with the bottom of a cell. Other values include **middle** (the default) and **top**.
`<tr align="right"`	ALIGN attribute. In a table row, right-aligns the content of table cells. Other values include **left**, **center**, and **baseline** (see explanation of "baseline" below). In Internet Explorer 8, however, any horizontal alignment for TH cells that differs from the defaults (centered) must be individually set for each cell, rather than for the row as a whole.
`<th align="right"`	ALIGN attribute. In a TH or TD element, right-aligns the content of the cell. Other values include **left**, **center**, and **baseline** (see explanation of "baseline" below).
`<table bgcolor=` `"#ccffff"`	BGCOLOR attribute. In the TABLE, TR, TH, and TD elements, specifies a light blue background color (using the #ccffff hexadecimal RGB code). A color name can also be used (**bgcolor="silver"**, for instance).
`<table cellspacing=` `"0"`	CELLSPACING attribute. Eliminates the spacing displayed between table cells, collapsing double borders between cells to a single border.
`<table background=` `"url"`	BACKGROUND attribute. Non-standard attribute that specifies the URL (or file name) of a background image for the TABLE element. Supported by current browsers, but not included in HTML 4, XHTML 1, or HTML 5.
`<thead>...</thead>`	THEAD element. Specifies that nested table rows are part of the "table head" row group, so that styles can be separately applied to them.
`<tbody>...</tbody>`	TBODY element. Specifies that nested table rows are part of the "table body" row group, so that styles can be separately applied to them. Optional—in its absence, tbody styles are applied to any table rows not included in a THEAD or TFOOT element.
`<tfoot>...</tfoot>`	TFOOT element. Specifies that nested table rows are part of the "table foot" row group, so that styles can be separately applied to them.
`th, td {properties}`	Group selector. Allows applying style properties to a group of elements (specified as a comma-separated list). In this case, the group includes the TH and the TD elements.
`thead th` `{properties}`	Descendant selector. Allows applying style properties to an element (TH, in this instance) that is a descendant of (nested at any level within) another element (THEAD, in this instance).

`vertical-align: bottom`	When applied to the TH and/or TD elements, vertically aligns content with the bottom of a table cell. Other values include **middle** (the default for table cells), **top**, and **baseline**.
`text-align: right`	When applied to the TH and/or TD elements, horizontally aligns content with the right side of a table cell (exclusive of any padding that is set). Other values include **left** (the default for TD cells) and **center** (the default for TH cells). Can also be applied to the TR element, but Internet Explorer 8 in its default standards mode applies the horizontal alignment to only the TD cells in a row, not to the TH cells.
`class="totalcol"`	CLASS attribute. Allows assigning an element to the "totalcol" class. Used in the chapter example to specify that cells in a table column contain row totals.
`.totalcol {properties}`	Class selector. Allows applying styles to elements that have been assigned to the "totalcol" class. Used in the chapter example to format table cells (TD element) in a table column that contain row totals.
`border-collapse: collapse; border-spacing: 0;`	When applied to the TABLE element, style properties used together to collapse the borders around table cells to a single border between table cells. Substitute for the `cellspacing="0"`.
`padding: 8px`	When applied to a TH or TD element, specifies eight pixels of padding (spacing) to be displayed between a table cell's content and its border. Substitutes for the TABLE element's CELLPADDING attribute.
`border: 1px solid black`	When applied to a TH or TD element, draws a one-pixel border around a table cell.
`class="totalrow"`	CLASS attribute. Allows assigning an element to the "totalrow" class. Used in the chapter example to assign a table row (TR element) to the "totalrow" class.
`.totalrow td {properties}`	Combination class and descendant selector that applies properties to TD elements that are descendants of elements assigned to the "totalrow" class.
`list-style: none`	A style property value that turns off display of the bullets or numerals in a UL or OL list.
`background-image: url(url)`	Specifies the URL (or file name) of an image to be displayed in an element's background.
`background-repeat: no-repeat`	Turns off the tiling (repeating) of a background image.
`background-position: 5px 5px`	Positions a non-repeating background image relative to the left and top sides of an element. In the non-table example of creating an indented icon link list, the icon bullet is positioned five pixels in from the left and five pixels down from the top in the background of the LI element.
`padding-left: 30px; padding-right: 60px;`	Adds 30 pixels of padding to the left of an element's content and 60 pixels of padding to the right of an element's content, but inside its border.
`list-style-image: url(url)`	Specifies the URL (or file name) of an image to be used as the bullet icon in a bulleted list (UL element).

| `valign="baseline"` | Vertically aligns differently sized text strings contained in different cells in a table row along their baselines. Descenders, such as in the letters "g" and "y" extend below the baseline. |
| `:first-child` | A selector that applies a style to the first child of an element. |

KEY TERMS

For a review of key terms bolded in this chapter, visit the Chapter 5 section of this book's Internet Resource Center at **www.emcp.net/html2e**. A complete glossary appears at the end of the book.

ONLINE QUIZ

An online self-check quiz that you can use to test your knowledge of the topics covered in this chapter can be found in the Chapter 5 section of this book's Internet Resource Center at **www.emcp.net/html2e**.

REVIEW EXERCISES

This section provides some hands-on review exercises to reinforce the information and material included within this chapter. Review using the elements, attributes, styles, and other features that were covered in this chapter, checking your results in your browser and troubleshooting any errors:

1. Open **salesreport_ex.html** from the **chap05** folder and save it as **salesreport-review.html** in that same folder.
2. If you have access to Microsoft Excel or another spreadsheet program that can save a space-delimited text file (PRN file), practice saving a PRN file, opening it in your text editor, copying it, and then pasting it into an HTML file. You can create your own worksheet file to practice with, or you can use a worksheet file you have already created. Your spreadsheet program might also have sample worksheet files you can practice with.
3. Using a .prn file that you have created or the sales.prn file that is included with the example files in the chap05 folder, review using the PRE element to display tabular data as preformatted text.
4. Copy the tabular data from inside the PRE element and paste it in below the PRE element. Review using the TABLE, CAPTION, TR, TH, and TD elements. Review setting the width of a table and aligning it horizontally on the page.
5. Review setting table borders, cellspacing, cellpadding, column widths, column spans, and row spans.
6. Save **salesreport-review.html** as **salesreport-review2.html** and review using HTML elements and attributes to control table appearance:
   A. Horizontally and vertically align table cell contents.
   B. Use the FONT element's SIZE, COLOR, and FACE attributes to control the appearance of table cell contents.

C. Use the CELLSPACING attribute to eliminate the spacing between cells, so that a single border separates table cells. Review using the CELLPADDING attribute to increase or decrease padding within table cells.

D. Set background colors and background images in tables. Set a background color and a background image for a table. Set background colors for table rows and cells.

7. Re-open **salesreport-review.html** as **salesreport-review3.html** and review using styles to control table appearance.

A. Set foreground and background colors, font sizes, font families, and background images for a table as a whole.

B. Set display characteristics for table rows and cells.

C. Collapse borders between table cells to a single border.

D. Vertically and horizontally aligning table contents.

E. Set a background image for a table.

F. Set background colors for table rows and cells.

G. Use the CLASS attribute to assign table cells in a column to a class, and then use a class selector to apply styles to that class.

H. Use the CLASS attribute to assign a table row to a class, and then use a descendant selector to apply styles only to TD or TH elements in that row.

8. Open **watson4_ex.html** and save it as **watson4-review.html** and review creating indented icon link lists:

A. Use a table to create an indented icon link list.

B. In a separate list, use styles to display the icon bullet as a background image in creating an indented icon link list.

9. Open **resume_ex.html** and save it as **resume-review.html** and review using a table to format a resume.

WEB-BASED LEARNING ACTIVITIES

The following Web-based learning activities can help you to further extend your learning and shore up your understanding of specific topic-areas:

- Visit the Chapter 5 section of this book's Internet Resource Center at **www.emcp.net/html2e** to find online resources that you can use to further investigate and explore the topics and subjects covered in this chapter. You can also find all Web sites cited in this chapter's notes listed there.

- Further research a specific topic introduced in this chapter using Google (**www.google.com/**), Yahoo! (**www.yahoo.com/**), Wikipedia (**www.wikipedia.org/**), Open Directory Project (**www.dmoz.org/**), or other online sources. Some topics covered in this chapter that you can further research include:
  - Accessibility issues with using tables for page layout.
  - Problems with using nested tables and FONT elements to format table contents.
  - Advantages of using styles for page layout and to format table contents.

- Use the results of your online research into a particular topic to:
  - Write a review to be read in front of your classmates.
  - Write a report that can be read by your classmates.
  - Design a diagram, chart, or other graphic that illustrates a key topic or concept.
  - Create a presentation using PowerPoint (or other software) that can be shared with your classmates.

- Give a stand-up presentation to your classmates.
- Team up with one or more classmates to give a group presentation to your classmates.

PROJECTS

These projects can be done in class, in a computer lab, or at home. Use the skills you have developed in this and the previous chapters to create any of the following projects. In your project, demonstrate the correct use of the following HTML features covered in this chapter:

- Incorporation of tabular data using the TABLE element. Optionally, you can also include a spreadsheet worksheet formatted using the PRE element.
- Use of the TR, TH, TD, and CAPTION elements.
- Use of the BORDER, CELLSPACING, and CELLPADDING attributes.
- Use of the WIDTH and ALIGN attributes in the TABLE element.
- Use of the ALIGN, VALIGN, HEIGHT, and WIDTH attributes in the TD or TH elements.
- At least one instance each of using the ROWSPAN and COLSPAN attributes to join two or more cells in a row or column.
- Application of font size, color, and face changes to table content using the FONT element or styles.
- Application of background color changes to the table content using the BGCOLOR attribute. Optionally, you can also apply a background image to the table using the BACKGROUND attribute or styles.
- If applying a background image, always apply a background color, as well, that closely matches the most common color in the background image, in case a user has display of images turned off.
- If using styles to apply foreground and background color changes, always apply both for an element (even if only declaring the background to be transparent).

While creating your design, be sure to test your page in more than one browser—if working in Windows, test your page in Firefox, Opera, and Safari, in addition to Internet Explorer, for instance; if working in Macintosh OS X, test your page in Safari, Firefox, and Opera, for instance.

Project 1. Incorporate tabular data into a Web page.

Take the lessons learned in this chapter and apply them in incorporating an HTML table or tables for formatting tabular data into a Web page you have already created or that you create from scratch. This can be a personal page, a topical page, an online paper, or any other page you have created or can create that can profit from the inclusion of tabular data. Focus more on the organized and structured presentation of data than on the esthetic appearance of the tables.

Project 2. Coordinate the design of a table or tables with the overall design of a Web page using HTML attributes.

Take the lessons learned in this chapter and apply them to coordinating the design of an HTML table with the overall design of a Web page, using HTML attributes. Use a Web page you have already created or that you create from scratch. In this project, focus on using HTML attributes to create a consistent overall look for the page by making use of fonts, colors, and backgrounds.

Project 3. Coordinate the design of a table or tables with the overall design of a Web page using styles.

Take the lessons learned in this chapter and apply them to coordinating the design of an HTML table with the overall design of a Web page, using CSS styles. Use a Web page you have already created or that you create from scratch. In this project, focus on using styles to create a consistent overall look for the page by making use of fonts, colors, and backgrounds.

Project 4. Incorporate an icon link list into a Web page.

Take the lessons learned in this chapter and apply them in incorporating an icon link list into a Web page that you have already created or that you create from scratch. Use any of the three methods for creating indented icon link lists covered in this chapter. Select the bullet icon so that it is coordinated with the overall look and color scheme of your page. Use any of the bullet icons included with this chapter's example files or look in the Art folder that accompanies this book's example files for additional bullet icons you can use. You also can look online for sources of bullet icons that you can download and use.

Project 5. Format an online resume using a table.

Take the lessons learned in this chapter and apply them in formatting an online resume for yourself or a friend that uses a table to create a side-by-side format (with dates in one column and following text in a second column). Use the text for a resume you have already created or that you create from scratch. Research different ways in which a resume can be organized and laid out and choose one that is best suited to your skills and experience. Apply the techniques and methods you learned in this and prior chapters to achieve your desired layout and organization.

CHAPTER 6
Working with Forms

PERFORMANCE OBJECTIVES

- Create mailto and CGI forms.
- Create text boxes.
- Create radio buttons and check boxes.
- Create unfolding list menus.
- Create multi-line text area boxes.
- Handle form responses.
- Design form layouts.
- Validate form input using JavaScript.

Forms provide you with a means to gather information and data from visitors to a Web page. Forms can be as simple as a text area box that lets visitors send you a message or as complex as a survey or questionnaire that lets visitors fill out text boxes and select radio buttons, check boxes, and options from pull-down menus. You can gather information for your own use or you can format the data for presentation on the Web.

USING THE EXAMPLE FILES

If you have created a working folder for storing files you create, you will find the example files for this chapter located in the **chap06** folder within your working folder. Save any HTML files you create in this chapter in that folder.

MAILTO OR CGI FORMS?

Historically, there have been two basic kinds of forms that can be included in Web pages: mailto and CGI forms. A **mailto form**, originally introduced in the Netscape Navigator 2 browser, uses a mailto URL to send form responses to your e-mail address. A CGI form uses a CGI script to process form responses, either saving them to a folder on your server or forwarding them to your e-mail address. The first is a client-side action that relies on a user's local mail program to send form responses, while the second is a server-side action that relies on a CGI script located on a remote server to send form responses.

NOTE — CGI stands for *Common Gateway Interface* and is the means built into the architecture of the Web to allow access to and execution of server-side programs and scripts. Most CGI scripts are written in the Perl programming language, but other languages, including C/C++, Visual Basic, AppleScript, TCL, and UNIX Shell, for instance, can also be used.

Mailto forms are easier to set up and test, but not all users can use a mailto form. Among current major browsers, only Mozilla Firefox and Apple Safari support sending mailto form responses. Internet Explorer 8, however, brings up a blank mail composition window when a mailto form response is submitted, without any of the submitted form data attached, as does the Opera browser. Internet Explorer 6 and 7 also do not support sending mailto form responses.

Because mailto forms are not supported in the most widely used browser on the Web, they should not be published to the Web but should only be used to test sending and receiving form responses on your local computer.

The draft HTML 5 specification, however, does allow for mailto forms, as long as the user is alerted that an e-mail will be sent, which makes it more likely that Internet Explorer and other browsers that do not support them now will do so in the future. A user would still need to have an e-mail client installed and configured to send e-mail, however, so even if all browsers supported sending mailto form responses, there would still be users who would not be able to use them.

TROUBLE *spot* Publishing a mailto form to the Web, just like a mailto e-mail link, can expose your e-mail address to harvesting by spam robots (*spambots*). This is another reason why a server-side CGI script that allows hiding your e-mail address, and not a client-side mail program, should be used to submit form responses.

In the following section, you will be creating an example form that allows a user to submit data. This form will initially be set as a mailto form, which will allow you to test sending and receiving form responses without having to have access to a CGI script for processing form responses. To complete these action steps, you will need to have a browser and a mail program installed that support mailto forms.

Later you will learn how to create CGI forms and enable them in your Web pages.

NOTE — If you are accessing the Web through a local or wide area network (LAN or WAN) at school or work, you might not be able to use a mailto form, unless the system administrator provides you with a POP/IMAP mail address that includes use of an outgoing (SMTP) mail server. If you are receiving Internet access through Windows Live, you also might not be able to use a mailto form, because it does not normally provide POP/IMAP mail service.

Browsers that Support Mailto Forms

Internet Explorer 6, 7, and 8 do not support sending mailto form responses. They will open a mail message compose window addressed to the specified e-mail address, but they do not include the form data in the message's body or as an attachment.

Testing sending and receiving mailto form responses is optional. If using Internet Explorer to do the form example, you can test that the submit button works, but you will not be able to actually send and receive form responses.

If you want to test sending and receiving mailto form responses, you will need to download and install a browser that supports sending mailto form responses. You can download Firefox (for Windows, Macintosh OS X, or Linux) at **www.mozilla.org/firefox/** or Apple Safari (for Macintosh OS X or Windows) at **www.apple.com/safari/**.

Mail Programs that Support Mailto Forms

If your default mail program is Outlook Express, Thunderbird, or Eudora in Windows or Thunderbird or Entourage in Macintosh OS X, it should work fine for testing mailto form responses, as long as it is configured to send and receive e-mail.

However, if you are using AOL Mail in Windows or the Mail application in Macintosh OS X, for instance, as your mail program, you will not automatically be able to use a mailto form. If you are using Firefox as your browser, however, you can specify a mail program other than your default mail program to handle mailto form responses:

Windows: In Firefox, select Tools, Options, Applications, and scroll down and click the "mailto" item to highlight it. In the list box on the right, you can then select the mail program you want to associate with mailto actions. If the mail program you want to use is not listed, select Use Other and Browse to navigate to and select a mail program (from the Program Files folder).

Macintosh OS X: In Firefox, select Firefox, Preferences, Applications, and scroll down and click the "mailto" item to highlight it. In the list box on the right, you can then select the mail program you want to associate with mailto actions. If the mail program you want to use is not listed, select Use Other and navigate to and select a mail program (from the Applications folder).

If you are using Apple Safari as your browser, in Macintosh OS X or Windows, you have to change the default mail program (in the Mail application in Macintosh OS X or in the Control Panel's Internet Options in Windows, if you want to use a different mail program for mailto responses. If you do not wish to do that, you can either skip testing the sending and receiving of mailto form responses in this chapter or use Firefox instead.

Configuring Your Mail Program to Send Mail

If you can already send and receive mail in Outlook Express or Mozilla Thunderbird, you do not need to do anything to send and receive mailto form responses in Mozilla Firefox, other than having one or the other designated as your default mail client.

Providing detailed instructions for configuring a mail program so you can send and receive mail is beyond the scope of this book. You can choose to not test sending and receiving mailto form responses, if you wish. If you want to configure a mail program to send and receive mail, check with your ISP or system administrator for guidance.

The kinds of information you will need to configure a mail client include:

- **POP mail server** name (incoming mail)
- **SMTP mail server** name (outgoing mail)
- Your username and password (the same you use to log-in)
- Whether a secure connection or authentication is required to receive or send mail
- Whether any non-standard ports are used (other than Port 110 for incoming or Port 25 for outgoing mail)

You can use a form to gather data from visitors to your page or site and then republish it on the Web.

"Roger Yang is a computer science student who is taking a class in Web design. Through research, he found a bewildering array of Web hosting options. For a project to be completed for his class, he has decided to create a Web site that organizes different Web hosting options according to key features and characteristics. As part of that project, he has decided to create a user-input form that Web hosting companies can use to submit their Web hosting plans to be displayed on his site."

CREATING A FORM

In this section, you will create an HTML form containing a text area box, text boxes, radio buttons, check boxes, and pull-down lists. A starter page, hostsubmit_ex.html, also has been created for you that you will use to get started creating the example form for this chapter.

To start working with this example:

1. In your text editor open **hostsubmit_ex.html** from the chap06 folder.
2. Save hostsubmit_ex.html as **hostsubmit.html** in the chap06 folder in your working folder or disk.
3. In your Web browser open **hostsubmit.html**.

Using the FORM Element

The FORM element is used to create a user-input form in HTML. All other form elements are nested inside the FORM element.

Add a FORM element set to post the form response to a mailto e-mail address:

```
<h2 align="center">The Very Best Web Hosts</h2>

<h1 align="center">Hosting Plans Submission Form</h1>

<p>To submit a hosting plan to be published on my The Very Best
Web Hosting Plans page, fill out and submit the following form.
If you have any questions about this form, contact us at
<a href="mailto:hostplans@theverybesthosts.emcp.com">
hostplans@theverybesthosts.emcp.com</a>.</p>

<form action="mailto:hosts@theverybesthosts.emcp.com"
method="post">
</form>
</body>
```

The ACTION attribute specifies the URL to which the form response is to be sent. This particular attribute specifies that the form data should be sent to a mailto e-mail address. A CGI form would specify the URL of a CGI script as the value of the ACTION attribute.

The METHOD attribute specifies the method to be used to transfer the form data when it is submitted. The METHOD attribute has two possible values: **get** and **post**.

The basic difference between the get method and the post method is that in the **get method**, form data is encoded as appended to a URL (following a "?" character), while in the **post method**, form data is included in the message.

Generally, the get method is used for retrieving (getting) data from a server, such as in a database query, for instance, so it can be displayed in a browser or other user agent. On the other hand, the post method is used to send (or post) data to a server (if using a CGI form) or to an e-mail address (if using a mailto form). The get method is also limited in the number of characters it can send (from 256 to 2,000 characters, depending on the browser sending the request and the Web server processing the request), while the post method is not limited in the amount of data that can be sent. Because the get method exposes the form response as part of the URL, and might be saved in Web server logs or browser history lists, it is inherently less secure than the post method. Since in this chapter you will only be sending data, you will only be using the post method.

Creating Form Controls

A variety of different kinds of **form controls** can be added to a form, including text boxes, radio buttons, check boxes, list menus, text area boxes, submit buttons, reset buttons, password boxes, hidden controls, file select controls, and push buttons. These controls are created using a variety of different elements, including the INPUT, SELECT (with OPTION and/or OPTGROUP), TEXTAREA, and BUTTON elements.

Creating Text Boxes

The INPUT element's **type="text"** attribute specifies a **text box** to be added to the form.

Add text boxes to the form that gather information such as a provider's name, phone number, Web address, and so on (see Figure 6.1):

```
<form action="mailto:hosts@theverybesthosts.emcp.com"
method="post">

<p>Provider: <input type="text" name="Provider" size="40">
Phone #: <input type="text" name="Phone_Number" size="40"></p>

<p>Web Address: <input type="text" name="URL" size="40"> E-Mail:
<input type="text" name="EMail" size="40"></p>

<p>Plan Name: <input type="text" name="PlanName" size="30">
Setup Fee: <input type="text" name="Setup_Fee" size="15"
value="$">
Monthly Fee: <input type="text" name="Monthly_Fee" size="15"
value="$"></p>

</form>
```

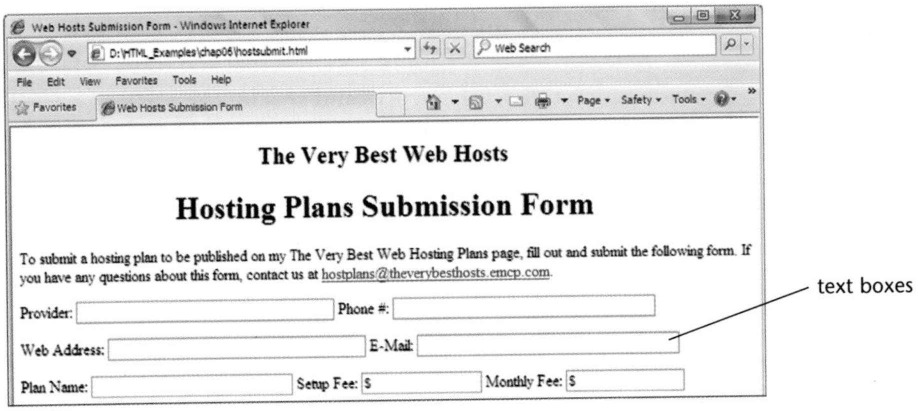

FIGURE 6.1 • Several text box form controls are added to the form.

The NAME attribute names the text field. NAME attribute values should not include spaces (use underscores instead). Each text box form control should have a unique name. When the form response data is submitted, the text keyed in the text box will be associated with the name of the text box field. If two text box form controls have the same name, the second box's data will overwrite the first text box's data when the form is submitted.

The SIZE attribute specifies the width of the text box in text characters (not pixels). This attribute, however, only sets the width of the text box; it does not delimit the amount of text that can be entered in a text box. To delimit the amount of text that can be entered in a text box, use a MAXLENGTH attribute, which limits the total number of characters that can be entered in a text box to the specified value. For instance, `maxlength="40"` would limit input to a total of 40 characters. You might want to do this, for instance, if you plan on importing the form responses into a database with length limits set on specific fields.

The VALUE attribute specifies an initial value to be displayed within a text box.

Creating Radio Buttons

The INPUT element's `type="radio"` attribute specifies a **radio button** option to be added to the form. Only one button from a group of radio buttons can be selected. The term *radio button* comes from older-style car radios, which as a safety feature used push buttons for selecting preset radio stations. Pushing any of the buttons would pop up any other button that had previously been pushed.

action

Add a group of radio buttons that allows a user to specify the type of host plan being submitted (see Figure 6.2):

```
<p>Plan Name: <input type="text" name="PlanName" size="30">
Setup Fee: <input type="text" name="Setup_Fee" size="15"
value="$">
Monthly Fee: <input type="text" name="Monthly_Fee" size="15"
value="$"></p>

<p>Plan Type:
<input type="radio" name="PlanType" value="Non-Virtual Host"
checked>Non-Virtual Host Plan  
```

```
<input type="radio" name="PlanType" value="Basic Virtual Host">
Basic Virtual Host Plan  
<input type="radio" name="PlanType" value="Advanced Virtual
Host">Advanced Virtual Host Plan  
<input type="radio" name="PlanType" value="Reseller">Reseller
Plan  
</p>

</form>
```

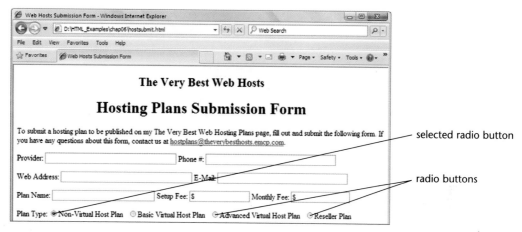

FIGURE 6.2 • A group of radio button options is added to the form.

Notice that a CHECKED attribute is included in the first radio button INPUT element. It specifies that the radio button should initially be selected. In the absence of a CHECKED attribute, none of the radio buttons will be selected initially. The same attribute can be used with check boxes (covered in the next section) to specify that a check box should initially be checked.

Unlike with text boxes, notice that the NAME attribute in each radio button form control specifies the same name. The NAME attribute, in this case, defines a group of radio button controls.

The VALUE attribute specifies the value to be submitted with the form response data if a radio button is selected (the data value will be associated with the name of the radio button control group).

Creating Check Boxes

The INPUT element's **type="checkbox"** attribute specifies a **check box** option to be added to the form. Unlike with radio buttons, multiple check boxes from a group of check boxes can be selected at the same time.

Add a group of check boxes to the form (see Figure 6.3):

```
<input type="radio" name="PlanType" value="Reseller">Reseller
Plan  
</p>

<p>Basic Features Included:</p>
<p><input type="checkbox" name="Basic_Features" value="stock CGI
scripts">stock CGI scripts  
```

```
<input type="checkbox" name="Basic_Features" value="FTP upload">
FTP upload  
<input type="checkbox" name="Basic_Features" value="extra e-mail
addresses">multiple e-mail addresses  
<input type="checkbox" name="Basic_Features" value="access
reports">access reports  
<input type="checkbox" name="Basic_Features" value="free domain
name registration">free domain name registration  </p>

    </form>
```

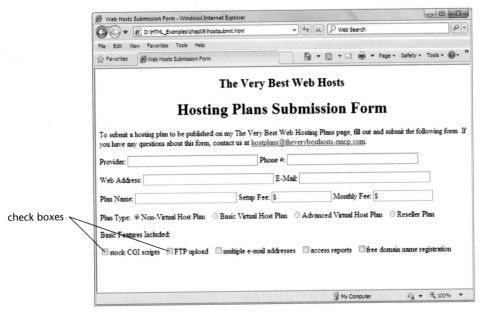

check boxes

FIGURE 6.3 • A group of check boxes is added to the form.

Unlike with text boxes, notice that the NAME attribute in each check box control specifies the same name. The NAME attribute, in this case, defines a group of check box controls.

The VALUE attribute specifies the value to be submitted with the form response data if a check box is selected (the data value will be associated with the name of the check box control group). If more than one check box is selected, a comma-separated list of selected values is returned.

Creating List Menus

The SELECT and OPTION elements are used to add a **list menu**, which presents a list of selectable options. Include a menu in the form that lets users select from a list of options.

Add a list menu to the form (see Figure 6.4):

```
<input type="checkbox" name="Basic_Features" value="free domain
name registration">free domain name registration  </p>

<p>Server Type:
<select name="ServerType">
  <option selected>Unix/Linux-Based Server
  <option>Windows-Based Server
```

```
    <option>Macintosh-Based Server
    <option>Other Server
  </select>
  </p>

  </form>
```

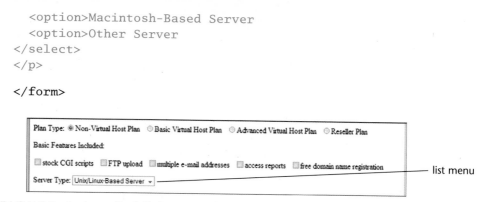

FIGURE 6.4 • By default, a menu list initially only shows the top option when it is included in a form.

When you click on the list menu (or the drop-down arrow), the remaining list options unfold, as shown in Figure 6.5.

FIGURE 6.5 • When the list menu is clicked, it unfolds to display the remaining options.

That there are no end tags included in the example for the OPTION element does not mean it is an empty (or standalone) element. Rather, in HTML 4, it is a container element with an implied ending. In XHTML 1 and 2, however, the end tag is required.

SETTING THE SIZE OF A LIST MENU By default, a list menu initially only displays the top option. You can use the SELECT element's SIZE attribute to specify the number of options that will be displayed initially in a list menu. For instance, to set all four options to be displayed, set a size of 4:

```
<select name="ServerType" size="4">
```

SPECIFYING OPTION VALUES By default, the text following the selected OPTION element in a list menu is sent with the form response data. You can use the OPTION element's VALUE attribute, however, to specify alternative data values that you want to have sent. This allows you to display more descriptive text as your options, for instance, while sending more abbreviated text as data in the form response:

```
<select name="ServerType">
  <option value="unix" selected>Unix/Linux-Based Server
  <option value="win">Windows-Based Server
  <option value="mac">Macintosh-Based Server
  <option value="other">Other Server
</select>
```

ENABLING MULTIPLE SELECTIONS IN A LIST MENU Normally, a user can select only one option from a list menu. The SELECT element's MULTIPLE attribute specifies that users can select multiple options from a list menu, either by holding down the Ctrl key (Windows) or the Command key (Macintosh OS X) to select separate options or by holding down the Shift key to select a range of options. For this to be practical, you need to preface the list menu with some kind of notice indicating that multiple options can be selected and instructing the user how to do it:

```
<p>Server Type (hold down CTRL or COMMAND to select multiple
options, or SHIFT to select a range of options):
<select name="ServerType" multiple>
  <option value="unix" selected>Unix/Linux-Based Server
  <option value="win">Windows-Based Server
  <option value="mac">Macintosh-Based Server
  <option value="other">Other Server
</select>
```

Creating Text Area Boxes

A text box created using the INPUT element limits a user to inputting text on a single line. The TEXTAREA element creates a **text area box**, which allows users to provide comments or expand on their previous selections with a multi-line text box.

Add a text area box that is 8 lines high and 75 characters wide (see Figure 6.6):

```
    <option>Other Server</select>
</p>

<p>Added Comments:</p>
<p><textarea name="Comments" rows="8" cols="75"></textarea></p>

</form>
```

FIGURE 6.6 • A text area box lets users include comments within a form.

The ROWS and COLS attributes determine the visible size of the text area box, with the first specifying the number of visible rows (or lines) in the box and the second the number of characters in a row. Text input by users, however, is not limited to the visible area of the box but can extend beyond it (in which case, scroll bars will be displayed).

Creating Control Buttons

Once you have added the elements for gathering data to your form, you need to add control buttons that allow the user to submit the form data or reset the form.

CREATING SUBMIT AND RESET BUTTONS Two additional controls can be created using the INPUT element, a **submit button** and a **reset button**, which users can click on to submit the form's data or reset the form.

Add submit and reset buttons to the form (see Figure 6.7):

```
<p><textarea name="Comments" rows="8" cols="75"></textarea></p>

<p><input type="submit" value="Submit"> <input type="reset"
value="Reset"></p>

</form>
```

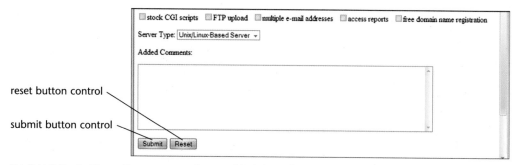

reset button control

submit button control

FIGURE 6.7 • Button controls are added that allow users to submit or reset the form.

The VALUE attribute specifies the label for the button. In this instance, the submit button label happens to be "Submit," but could just as easily be "Submit Form," "Send Form," or anything else that conveys the action of the button. When referring to a *submit button* or *reset button*, it is not the label that is being referred to, but the action. When a user clicks on a submit button, the form is submitted to the URL specified by the FORM element's ACTION attribute.

CREATING A GRAPHICAL SUBMIT BUTTON Alternatively, a **graphical submit button** can be created using an INPUT element that uses an image as the button. An example image, submit.gif, is used in this example and is included with this chapter's example files.

Add a graphical submit button to the form (see Figure 6.8):

```
<p><input type="submit" value="Submit"> <input type="reset"
value="Reset"></p>
<p><input type="image" src="submit.gif" alt="Submit Form Button"
border="0"></p>
```

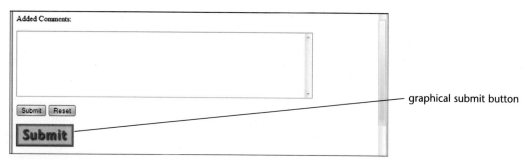

graphical submit button

FIGURE 6.8 • You also can use an image to create a graphical submit button.

USING THE **BUTTON** ELEMENT HTML 4 includes an additional element, the BUTTON element, which can also be used to create buttons for submitting or resetting a form. These buttons perform the exact same function as a submit or reset button created using the INPUT element, except that using the BUTTON element provides for richer rendering possibilities. The main problem with using the BUTTON element is that it degrades ungracefully for users of earlier browsers that do not support HTML 4, with such users being left without any way to submit or reset the form.

When using the Button element, the label text ("Submit" and "Reset" in this instance) is nested inside the BUTTON element, rather than being specified by the VALUE attribute, as with the INPUT element.

action

Using the Button element, create buttons to submit and reset the form (see Figure 6.9):

```
<p><input type="image" src="submit.gif" alt="Submit Form Button"
border="0"></p>
<p><button name="submit" value="submit" type="submit">
  <font size="4" color="green">Submit</font>
</button>  
<button name="reset" type="reset">
  <font size="4" color="maroon">Reset</font>
</button></p>
```

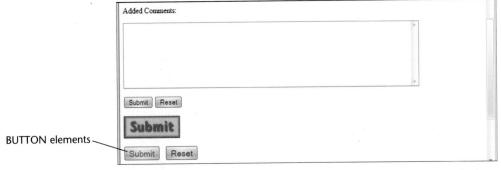

BUTTON elements

FIGURE 6.9 • Using the BUTTON element provides richer rendering possibilities for buttons to submit or reset forms, but it degrades ungracefully in some earlier browsers.

The NAME attribute names the control, whereas the VALUE attribute sets an initial value to be submitted with the form (and be associated with its name). The TYPE attribute value specifies the type of button being created, with the supported values being submit, reset, or button. If no TYPE attribute is specified, "submit" is the default value.

A **type="button"** attribute value can be used in conjunction with a script to create a push button to perform functions other than submitting or resetting a form.

You also can use a style to set the formatting of the BUTTON element, including specifying a background image for the button.

Because the BUTTON element degrades ungracefully in some earlier browsers that do not support it, you should not use it in a form that you want all visitors to be able to use. Use the INPUT element, instead, to create regular or graphical buttons to submit and reset forms.

For this example, a regular submit button, a graphical submit button, and a submit button created using the BUTTON element, as well as two types of reset buttons, are included in the same form for testing purposes; in normal practice, however, you would use only one submit or reset button in a form.

Creating Other Form Controls

There are a number of additional form controls that can be used that are not demonstrated in the current example, including the **hidden control**, **password control**, **file select control**, and **push button control**. Use of hidden controls is demonstrated in the "Creating CGI Forms" section later in this chapter. Some discussion of using passwords with secure forms is included in Appendix G, *Miscellaneous Technologies and Features*.

The file select control allows you to create a box where the name of a file to be uploaded can be specified. The button form control allows you to create a push button that can activate a JavaScript script, for instance. To learn more about these kinds of form controls and how they can be applied, see the HTML 4.01 specification's section on forms at **www.w3.org/TR/html401/interact/forms.html**.

Table 6.1 shows the different form controls that can be included in forms, along with example codes and the elements used to create them.

TABLE 6.1 • Form Controls

Control	Example	Element(s)
text box	`<input type="text"[...]`	INPUT
radio button	`<input type="radio"[...]`	INPUT
check box	`<input type="checkbox"[...]`	INPUT

list menu	`<select name="menuname">`
	`    <option selected>first option label`
	`    <option>second option label[...]`
		SELECT and OPTION

text area box	`<textarea name="controlname" rows="n"`
	`cols="n">`
	`</textarea>`
		TEXTAREA

(regular) submit button	`<input type="submit"[...]`	INPUT
(regular) reset button	`<input type="reset"[...]`	INPUT
graphical reset button	`<input type="image"[...]`	INPUT

submit button (w/BUTTON)	`<button name="controlname"`
	`type="submit">`
	`Submit</button>`
		BUTTON

reset button (w/BUTTON)	`<button name="controlname" type="reset">` `Reset</button>`	BUTTON
hidden control	`<input type="hidden"[...]`	INPUT
password control	`<input type="password"[...]`	INPUT
file select control	`<input type="file"[...]`	INPUT
push button	`<input type="button"[...]`	INPUT

Changing the Tabbing Order

Users can move from one form element to the next by pressing the Tab key. Normally, the **tabbing order** is the same as the order in which the form elements are inserted in the document. By using the TABINDEX attribute, however, you can set a different tabbing order. The following elements accept the TABINDEX attribute: A, AREA,

BUTTON, INPUT, OBJECT, SELECT, and TEXTAREA. Not all of these are form elements, but they would normally be included in the tabbing order.

The TABINDEX attribute takes a value from 0 to 32,767. The element with the lowest TABINDEX value is tabbed to first, the one with the second-lowest value is tabbed to second, and so on. The following example uses the TABINDEX value to reorder the tabbing order:

```
<p>Provider: <input type="text" name="Provider" size="40"
tabindex="1"> Phone #: <input type="text" name="Phone_Number"
size="40" tabindex="3"></p>
<p>Web Address: <input type="text" name="URL" size="40"
tabindex="2"> E-Mail: <input type="text" name="EMail" size="40"
tabindex="4"></p>
```

TESTING THE FORM

Now that you have created a form, you can test it. Depending on your browser/mail program combination and configuration, you might not be able to actually submit and retrieve a form response. You can, however, test all the elements of the form and make sure the buttons that submit and reset the form are working properly.

Filling in the Text Boxes

The top of the form contains a series of text boxes. You can use the mouse to locate the cursor in each text field, or you can press the Tab key to move from one text field to another.

Test the form you have just created:

1. With hostsubmit.html open in your browser, in the *Provider* text box, key **XYZ Hosting Company**.
2. In the *Phone #* text box, key **(212) 555-8743**.
3. In the *Web Address* text box, key **http://xyzhosting.emcp.com/**.
4. In the *E-Mail* text box, key **info@xyzhosting.emcp.com**.
5. In the *Plan Name* text box, key **ABC Host Plan**.
6. In the *Setup Fee* text box, key **$10.00**.
7. In the *Monthly Fee* text box, key **$12.95** (see Figure 6.10).

text boxes
filled in

FIGURE 6.10 • The form's text boxes are filled in.

Selecting a Radio Button

The next section of the form contains a group of radio buttons. You can select only one radio button out of a group.

action

Click on the *Basic Virtual Host Plan* radio button to select the plan type (see Figure 6.11). Notice that the *Non-Virtual Host Plan* radio button, which was selected previously, is no longer selected.

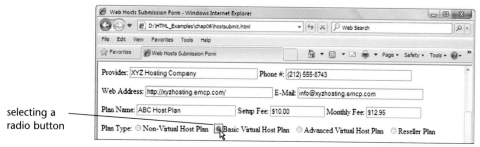

selecting a
radio button

FIGURE 6.11 • A radio button is selected to designate the plan type.

Selecting Check Boxes

The next section of the form contains a series of check boxes. Unlike radio buttons, you can select multiple check boxes within a check box group.

action

In the *Basic Features Included* group of check boxes, click on the first, second, and fourth check boxes (*stock CGI scripts*, *FTP upload*, and *access reports*) to select them, while leaving the other two check boxes unchecked (see Figure 6.12).

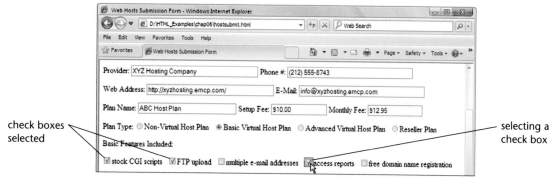

check boxes
selected

selecting a
check box

FIGURE 6.12 • You can select multiple check boxes in a group of check boxes.

Selecting an Option from a List Menu

The next line of the form contains a list menu that lets a user specify a server type.

Click on the list menu to unfold it, and then select the *Windows-Based Server* option (see Figure 6.13).

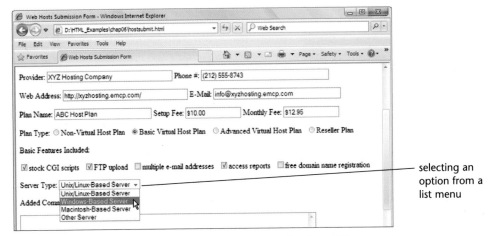

FIGURE 6.13 • The Windows-Based Server option is selected from the list menu.

Filling In the Text Area Box

You cannot key more than one line of text in a text box, but you can key multiple lines of text in a text area box.

In the *Added Comments* text area box, key **Same day e-mail support. 30-day money back guarantee. Redundant T3 connections to the Internet backbone.** (see Figure 6.14.)

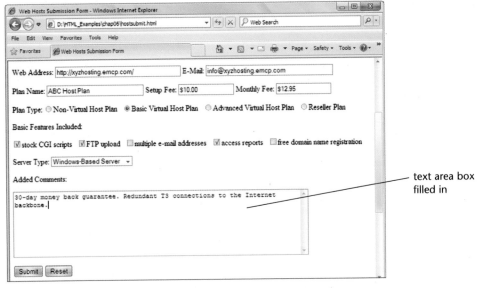

FIGURE 6.14 • You can key a multi-line comment in a text area box.

NOTE Note in Figure 6.14 that as text is being keyed in the text area box, Internet Explorer 8, unlike other browsers, highlights the button used to submit the form in a light blue color. Although you might think that means pressing the Enter key would submit the form, that is not true; doing so just starts a new line in the text area box.

SUBMITTING AND RESETTING THE FORM

The current form demonstrates three kinds of buttons that can be used to submit the form. In a normal form, you only have one button for submitting the form. You would also normally have only one reset button in a form, instead of two as in the current example.

Testing the Submit Button

You can test the different submit buttons you have added to the form.

Test the submit buttons:

1. Click the first Submit button, which was created using the INPUT element, with **type="submit"** set. If you are using a browser and a mail program that support sending mailto forms, a message composition window will open, with the form data included in the message body (see Figure 6.15). If you are using Internet Explorer 6 through 8, a pop-up box alerts you the form data is being sent via e-mail, asking if you want to continue. After clicking OK, a blank New Message window will open, but without any form data included in the message body.

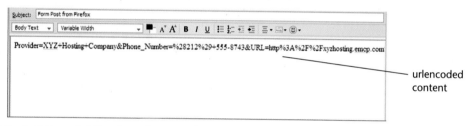
urlencoded content

FIGURE 6.15 • Mailto form data is included in the body of a message composition window when using Firefox.

2. Close the message composition window.
3. Click the second Submit button, which was created using the INPUT element, with **type="image"** set. The result should be the same as the previous step.
4. Click the third Submit button, which was created using the BUTTON element. The result should be the same as the previous steps.

Changing the Mailto Content Type

As you will notice in Figure 6.15, mailto form data is not sent in a human-friendly format. That is because the default content type (or encoding type) for mailto form responses is the **urlencoded content** type (application/x-www-form-urlencoded), which substitutes "+" characters for any spaces and control codes for hard returns, commas, ampersands, and other reserved characters. To send mailto form responses in a more human-friendly format, you must change the content type when the post method is used to plain text (text/plain) using the ENCTYPE (Encoding Type) attribute.

 Change the content type of the form data so that it is in a more user-friendly format:

1. In your text editor, edit the FORM element to change the content type to plain text, as shown here:

```
<form action="mailto:your e-mail address" method="post"
enctype="text/plain">
```

2. Save your HTML file, switch to your browser, and refresh the display of the page.

TROUBLE *spot*
In Safari, refreshing the display of the page brings up an alert that if you reload the page, your changes to the form will be lost. Click Reload. You will need to re-input your form data; just input some dummy data.
In Firefox, when you refresh the page, the changes to the form are not lost.

3. If using Firefox or Safari, click any of the Submit buttons. A mail composition window will open, showing the form data aligned in separate lines in the message body, making it much easier to read and interpret (see Figure 6.16). Close the window.

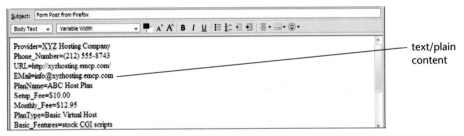

FIGURE 6.16 • By setting the content type to plain text, form data is presented in a much more human-friendly format.

Testing the Reset Buttons

The current form has two types of buttons that are used to reset the form, one created by using the INPUT element (with **type="reset"**) and the other by using the BUTTON element. Resetting the form returns it to its original state.

 Test resetting the form:

1. Click the first Reset button (in the first line of buttons). You will see that the form has reverted to its original state, with none of the fields filled out.
2. Key any text in the *Added Comments* text area box. Click the second Reset button (on the bottom line of buttons). You will see that the form has reverted to its original state, with none of the fields filled out (see Figure 6.17).

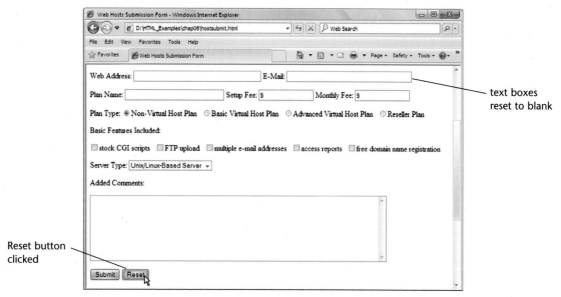

text boxes
reset to blank

Reset button
clicked

FIGURE 6.17 • When the Reset button is clicked, the form is reset to its original state.

SENDING AND RECEIVING MAILTO FORM RESPONSES

If you have not installed Mozilla Firefox or Apple Safari, or you are using a mail program that does not support sending mailto form responses, skip ahead to the next section, "Creating CGI Forms."

Sending a Mailto Form Response

In this section, you will edit the form so that it will send a mailto form response to your own e-mail address.

Edit the ACTION attribute so that it will send a mailto form response to your e-mail address and then send a form response to that address:

1. Revise the FORM element's ACTION attribute to refer to your e-mail address:

```
<form action="mailto:type your e-mail address here"
method="post">
```

3. Save your file, switch to your browser, and refresh its display.
4. Fill out text fields (using whatever text you like), select radio buttons, and select check boxes.
5. Click on any of the submit buttons.
6. When the message compose window opens, note your e-mail address on the To line and the form data you keyed in the body of the message. Click Send to send the message.

Receiving a Mailto Form Response

If you have successfully sent a mailto form response to yourself, you will find a message in your e-mail account's inbox containing the form response with a subject heading of "Form Post from Firefox." When opened, you will see the form data displayed in the message data (see Figure 6.18).

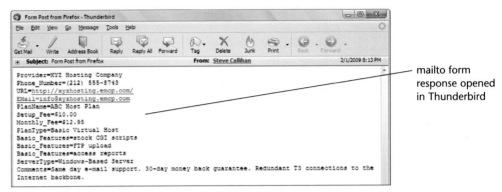

mailto form response opened in Thunderbird

FIGURE 6.18 • A mailto form response is opened in Mozilla Thunderbird.

Mailto form responses can sometimes be filtered out by spam filtering services, such as Postini, that might be provided by your ISP or Web site host. If your form response does not show up in your inbox, you might need to adjust your junk mail filter settings. With Postini, for instance, you can specify your own e-mail address as an exception or set a less aggressive level for filtering junk mail. Check with your ISP or Web host for guidance on how to change the settings of any spam filtering service they provide.

NOTE

Although mailto forms are not included in the HTML 4 specification, they are included in the HTML 5 draft specification, so other browsers in addition to Firefox and Safari will likely support mailto forms in the future.

Firefox and Safari insert mailto form data in the body of an e-mail message, but it is not guaranteed that other browsers will do the same. Previously, Internet Explorer 5 and 5.5, which supported mailto forms, included the form data as an attachment (POSTDATA.ATT), which had to be saved and reopened in a text editor to be viewed.

CREATING CGI FORMS

To create a form that everyone can use, you need to create a CGI form. A **CGI form** uses a program or script located on the Web server, generally referred to as a **CGI script**, to process and direct form responses. Many Web hosts provide a stock form-processing CGI script that you can use. If your Web host does not provide a stock form-processing CGI script and does not allow you to install your own CGI scripts, you will not be able to use a CGI form, at least not a form using a CGI script hosted by your Web host. There are, however, services that provide remotely hosted **form-processing CGI scripts** that you can use instead, usually in exchange for allowing them to display advertising along with the form submission confirmation.

In this section, you will learn how to set up a form to use the NMS FormMail.pl CGI script, which is used by many Web hosts. NMS FormMail is a drop-in alternative for the original FormMail.pl script that was written by Matt Wright. It has improved security to prevent the relaying of spam messages. It also allows you to set up an alias, so that you do not have to reveal your e-mail address. NMS FormMail is available at **nms-cgi.sourceforge.net/scripts.shtml**.

Setting Up a CGI Form

The following includes an example of setting up a CGI form using NMS MailForm as the form-processing CGI script. If you are using a different CGI script, check with your Web host for the specific configuration details.

Your form needs to be set up to send a CGI form response. This example includes your e-mail address in the form code. Later you will learn how to specify an *@alias* variable that will allow you to replace your e-mail address with an alias.

 Comment out the FORM start tag that you set up to send mailto form responses, and then replace it with one configured to send a CGI form response, replacing *yourname@yourdomain* with your e-mail address:

```
<!--<form action="mailto:yourname@yourdomain" method="post"
enctype="text/plain">-->

<form action="/cgi-bin/FormMail.pl" method="post">
<input type="hidden" name="recipient"
value="yourname@yourdomain">
```

For instance, if your site's domain is TheVeryBestWebHosts.emcp.com, then your e-mail address might be hostplans@theverybesthosts.emcp.com, just to cite a hypothetical case.

 For the form action to work, your Web host needs to have set up a cgi-bin folder for you, into which the FormMail.pl script has been uploaded (either by your Web host or yourself). If this has not been done, you will need to ask your Web host's technical support to set up a cgi-bin folder for you.

File names on a UNIX server are case-sensitive. If the actual file name of the CGI script is formmail.pl, then the ACTION attribute would need to read: **action="/cgi-bin/formmail.pl"**.

Setting Access Permissions

If your site is hosted on a UNIX or Linux server, before you can use a CGI script in your personal cgi-bin folder, **access permissions** must be set for it. If not, users might not be able to access the CGI script over the Web.

You may not need to set access permissions to allow visitors to your site to access your CGI script. If your Web host provides a stock CGI form processing script you can use, they may have already set the access permissions for you.

Most Web servers on the Web are running under UNIX. For that reason, the following instructions are for using FTP to set access permissions on a UNIX (or Linux) server. If your Web host's server is running under Windows or on a Macintosh, see their technical support notes for information on what you need to do to install and configure CGI scripts on those platforms.

Many **FTP programs** let you set CGI script permissions on a UNIX or Linux server. Some FTP programs that allow you to do this include:

- WS_FTP at **www.ipswitchft.com/solutions/personal.asp** (Windows)
- CuteFTP at **www.globalscape.com/products/** (Windows and Macintosh OS X)
- FTP Voyager at **www.ftpvoyager.com/** (Windows)
- FileZilla at **filezilla-project.org/** (Windows, Macintosh OS X, and Linux)

The first three are commercial programs that have free trial periods. Filezilla is an open source application and free to use. WS_FTP Home is available to educational institutions through a bulk license, so check with your school's technical support to see if it is available for you to use for free. You can also do a search for "WS_FTP LE," an older version that is free for educational uses. It is no longer available from ipswitchft.com but can still be found elsewhere on the Web.

For instance, if your site is hosted on a UNIX server, you can follow these steps to set CGI script permissions using any of the above FTP programs:

1. Run WS_FTP Home, CuteFTP, FTP Voyager, or FileZilla, and connect to your Web hosting account.
2. Change to your cgi-bin folder—if you have set your FTP program to automatically open your Web site's www folder, you will need to first change to the parent folder (your site's root folder) and then change to your cgi-bin folder.
3. Right-click on the CGI script (FormMail.pl). In WS_FTP Home or Voyager FTP, select Properties. In CuteFTP, select Properties/CHMOD. In FileZilla, select File attributes.
4. Key **755** in the *Numeric Value* text box (in WS_FTP Home, FTP Voyager, and FileZilla) or in the *Permissions* text box (in CuteFTP). (Confirm that the *Write* check boxes in the *Group* and *World* sections are unchecked.) See Figure 6.19. Click OK.

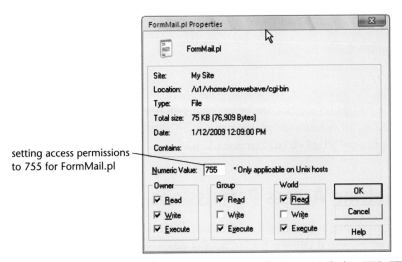

FIGURE 6.19 • Access permissions are set for FormMail.pl in WS_FTP Home.

NOTE If you are using WS_FTP LE, you should right-click on FormMail.pl, select *FTP Commands* and *SITE*, key **chmod 755 FormMail.pl**, and then press the Enter key.

Understanding the CHMOD Number

The CHMOD (Change Mode) command is used to set access permissions for the owner, the group, and all others in the form of a **CHMOD number**. The number, 755, used to set the permissions for the FormMail.pl script is not nearly as arcane as it might appear. Rather than a three-digit number, it actually represents three separate numbers: 7, 5, and 5. The first number sets permissions for the owner, the second for the group, and the third for everyone else.

You are the owner, of course, and the group is either everyone logged onto the server or a more restrictive listing of individuals who are assigned access privileges to access the file by the server administrator. Everyone else refers to the users who will visit your site and make use of the form. Table 6.2 shows how these access numbers are derived.

Thus, as shown in Table 6.2, if you want the owner to have read, write, and execute permissions for a file, you need to assign a value of 7 (or 4 + 2 + 1) in the first number. On the other hand, if you do want group members or others to have permission to read and execute a file, but not to write to that file, you need to assign a value of 5 (4 + 0 + 1) in the second two numbers, with the full resulting CHMOD value thus being 755.

TABLE 6.2 • How CHMOD Permission Numbers Are Derived

Access Permissions	Owner	Group	World
Read: (4=yes)	4	4	4
Write: (2=yes)	2	0	0
Execute: (1=yes)	1	1	1
CHMOD Number:	7	5	5

Configuring the NMS FormMail.pl Script

Your Web host might configure the NMS FormMail.pl script for you, in which case you should not need to edit the script to start using it in your Web pages. If you have uploaded the script to your cgi-bin folder or your Web host has not configured it for you, however, it needs to know the paths to where Perl and SendMail are located on your server. As long as the paths to Perl and SendMail are **/usr/bin/perl** and **/usr/lib/sendmail**, which they are in most cases, you will not need to edit the script. If either are different, however, you will need to edit the script and replace all instances of the above paths with the actual paths on your server. Check with your Web host's technical support if they have not provided this information to you.

Even if your Web host has configured the NMS FormMail.pl script for you, the script contains a User Configuration Section that allows you to configure script variables to specify:
- Domains from which form submissions are allowed.
- E-mail address that are allowed to receive form responses.
- Aliases that can be used in place of allowed e-mail addresses.

The main user-configurable variables in the script are presented in this manner:

```
@referers          = qw(yourdomain.com/ www.yourdomain.com);
@allow_mail_to     = qw(yourname@yourdomain.com, ruth@home.emcp.com);
@recipients        = ();
%recipient_alias = (
        'myself' => 'yourname@yourdomain.com',
        'ruth' => 'ruth@home.emcp.com');
```

In the code example, the *@referers* variable specifies which domains from which form submissions will be allowed, stopping someone from accessing the script from a remote form.

The *@allow_mail_to* variable specifies one or more e-mail addresses that are allowed to receive form responses.

The *@recipients* variable should be left blank, in that a mistake in the Perl expressions it requires could make the script available as a spam relay.

The *@recipient_alias* variable specifies one or more aliases. An alias can be used in place of an e-mail address to which you want the form data sent.

Setting Up Your Form to Use an E-Mail Alias

Using your e-mail address in your form's HTML code can expose it to spambots that rove the Web looking for e-mail addresses to harvest. If you have defined an **e-mail alias** in the NMS FormMail.pl script, you can use it instead.

To set up your form to use an alias for your e-mail address that you have specified in the FormMail.pl script, you would insert a VALUE attribute with the alias as its value in the first INPUT element:

```
<form action="/cgi-bin/FormMail.pl" method="post">
<input type="hidden" name="recipient" value="alias">
```

For instance, if you specified in the *@recipient_alias* variable that "myself" is an alias for your e-mail address, you would insert `value="myself"` in the hidden control.

Sending and Receiving CGI Form Responses

Unlike a mailto form, in most cases, you cannot test submitting CGI form responses on your local computer without publishing your page to a Web server and having access to a form-processing CGI script located on that Web server. The script might also need to be configured to allow sending form responses to your e-mail address.

The one exception is if you use a **remotely hosted CGI script**. See the following section for information on where to find remotely hosted CGI script providers.

When you submit a mailto form, if your browser/mail program combination and configuration supports using mailto forms, a pop-up window alerts you that you are sending a form via e-mail. When you submit a CGI form, the CGI script on the server generates an HTML page that confirms that the form response has been sent. Figure 6.20 shows a form response confirmation page generated by the NMS FormMail CGI script.

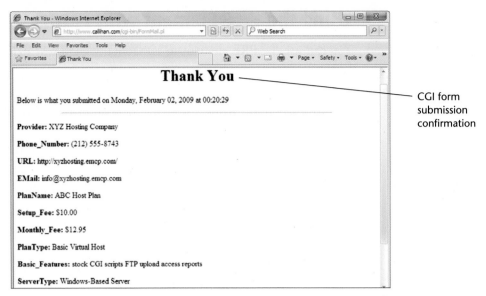

FIGURE 6.20 • When you submit a CGI form, the form-processing CGI script generates a page confirming that the form response has been sent to the recipient's e-mail address.

When you receive the form response in your inbox, the form response data is included in the body of the message. Figure 6.21 shows an example of a CGI form response.

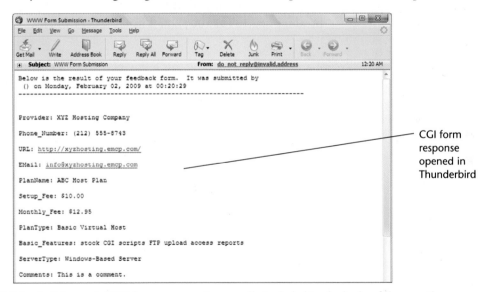

FIGURE 6.21 • A CGI form response is generally included in the body of the e-mail message.

Using a Remotely Hosted CGI Form Script

If your Web host does not allow CGI scripts or provide a CGI form script, you might choose to use a remotely hosted script. You can find a listing of remotely hosted form script providers at **cgi.resourceindex.com/Remotely_Hosted/Form_Processing/**.

DESIGNING FORMS

Until now in this chapter, you focused on using the different form elements and attributes, as well as understanding how to use, submit, and receive form responses. You also can design and format your forms further so they are more attractive and easier to read.

Using the PRE Element with Forms

You can use the PRE element to horizontally align text fields and other form elements.

Use the PRE element to horizontally align text fields and other form elements:

1. If **hostsubmit.html** is not already open in your text editor, re-open it from the chap06 folder.
2. Save hostsubmit.html as **hostsubmit2.html**. Open **hostsubmit2.html** in your browser.
3. Add a style sheet to the page that specifies a sans serif font for the FORM and INPUT elements:

```
<title>Web Hosts Submission Form</title>
<style type="text/css">
form, input {
    font-family: sans-serif;
    }
</style>
```

4. Delete any paragraph tags (**<p>** or **</p>**) that are nested inside the FORM element but leave any line breaks.
5. Insert any codes displayed in magenta. Delete any double spaces, including non-breaking spaces (** **), and insert spaces where · characters are displayed below:

TROUBLE spot Do not add additional hard returns inside of the PRE elements. When using the PRE element to align form controls in a form, you need to be aware that any hard returns nested inside of the PRE element will be displayed when the page is viewed in a browser.

```
<pre>Provider:·····<input type="text" name="Provider" size="40">
Phone #: <input type="text" name="Phone_Number" size="40"></pre>
```

```
<pre>Web Address:··<input type="text" name="URL" size="40">··
E-Mail: <input type="text" name="EMail" size="40"></pre>
```

```
<pre>Plan Name:·····<input type="text" name="PlanName"
size="30">··Setup Fee: <input type="text" name="Setup_Fee"
size="10" value="$">··Monthly Fee: <input type="text"
name="Monthly_Fee" size="10" value="$"></pre>
```

```
<pre>Plan Type:·····<input type="radio" name="PlanType"
value="Non-Virtual Host" checked>Non-Virtual Host
Plan·······<input type="radio" name="PlanType" value="Basic
Virtual Host">Basic Virtual Host Plan
·············<input type="radio" name="PlanType" value="Advanced
Virtual Host">Advanced Virtual Host Plan  <input type="radio"
name="PlanType" value="Reseller">Reseller Plan</pre>
```

```
<pre>Basic Features Included:
·············<input type="checkbox" name="Basic_Features"
value="stock CGI scripts">stock CGI scripts·<input
type="checkbox" name="Basic_Features" value="FTP upload">FTP
upload··<input type="checkbox" name="Basic_Features" value="extra
e-mail addresses">multiple e-mail addresses
```

```
· · · · · · · · · · · · · · ·<input type="checkbox" name="Basic_Features"
value="access reports">access reports· · · · ·<input type="checkbox"
name="Basic_Features" value="free domain name registration">free
domain name registration</pre>

<pre>Server Type:· · ·<select name="ServerType">
  <option selected>Unix/Linux-Based Server
  <option>Windows-Based Server
  <option>Macintosh-Based Server
  <option>Other Server
</select>
</pre>

<pre>Added Comments:
· · · · · · · · · · · · ·<textarea name="Comments" rows="8" cols="77">
</textarea>

· · · · · · · · · · · · ·<input type="submit" value="Submit">
<input type="reset" value="Reset"></pre>
```

TROUBLE *spot*

If you are using Safari to view the example, what you see will vary somewhat from what is shown in Figure 6.22, with the form aligning along the left side, but not the right side of the form. This is because Safari handles lengths set for form controls differently than Internet Explorer or Firefox.

6. Save your file (File, Save), and refresh the display of the form in your browser. Compare the horizontal spacing of your form with that shown in Figure 6.22.

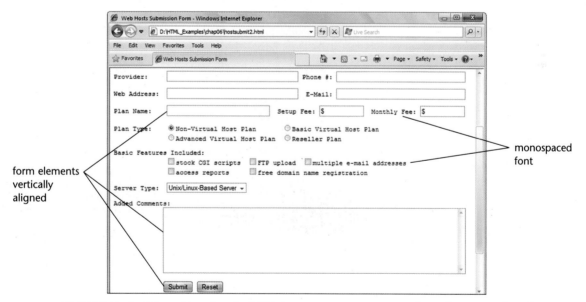

FIGURE 6.22 • By using the PRE element, you can space out form elements to line them up vertically.

7. Make any adjustments you need to make to your form, adding or removing spaces or returns, so that it matches what is shown in Figure 6.22. (If using Safari, just make sure the form elements are aligned along the left side of the form.)

Using Colors and Backgrounds with Forms

Using colors and backgrounds with forms can help make forms more attractive, as well as provide additional contrast between form element backgrounds (which stay white) and a background color or background image.

Specify text and background colors in the BODY element (see Figure 6.23):

```
<body bgcolor="#ccccff" text="#660000">
```

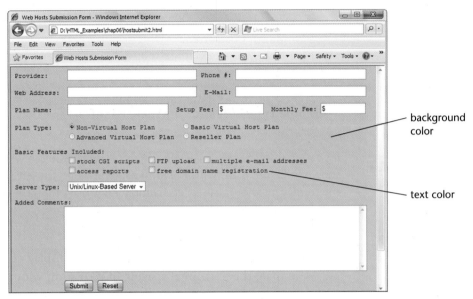

FIGURE 6.23 • Setting text and background colors can improve the visual appeal of a form, as well as provide increased contrast between form elements and the page's background.

Using Tables with Forms

The primary disadvantage of using the PRE element is that the form text has to be displayed in a monospaced font—otherwise, you cannot space out the input elements to line them up vertically. Alternatively, you can use a table to vertically line up elements within a form.

Format a form using tables:

1. Re-open **hostsubmit.html** in your text editor, and save it as **hostsubmit3.html**. Open **hostsubmit3.html** in your browser.

2. To create visual appeal and add contrast, set background, text, and link colors:

```
<body bgcolor="navy" text="white" link="aqua" vlink="silver"
alink="blue">
```

3. Delete any paragraph tags (**<p>** or **</p>**) that are nested inside the FORM element.

4. Delete any spaces, including nonbreaking spaces (** **) not shown below, and make any other adjustments needed to make your code match what is shown below (see Figure 6.24):

```
<table width="100%"><tr valign="bottom">
<td width="13%" height="20">Provider:</td> <td><input type="text"
name="Provider" size="40"></td>
<td>Phone #:</td> <td><input type="text" name="Phone_Number"
size="35"></td>
</tr><tr valign="bottom" height="35">
<td>Web Address:</td><td><input type="text" name="URL"
size="40"></td>
<td>E-Mail:</td><td><input type="text" name="EMail" size="35">
</td>
</tr></table>


<table width="100%"><tr valign="bottom" height="35">
<td width="13%">Plan Name:</td> <td><input type="text"
name="PlanName" size="30">
  Setup Fee: <input type="text" name="Setup_Fee"
size="15" value="$">
  Monthly Fee: <input type="text" name="Monthly_Fee"
size="15" value="$"></td></tr>
</table>


<table width="100%"><tr valign="bottom" height="35">
<td width="13%">Plan Type:</td> <td><input type="radio"
name="PlanType" value="Non-Virtual Host" checked>Non-Virtual Host
Plan  <input type="radio" name="PlanType" value="Basic
Virtual Host">Basic Virtual Host Plan  
<input type="radio" name="PlanType" value="Advanced Virtual
Host">Advanced Virtual Host Plan  
<input type="radio" name="PlanType" value="Reseller">Reseller
Plan  </td>
</tr></table>


<table width="100%"><tr valign="bottom" height="50">
<td width="13%">Basic Features Included:</td>
<td><input type="checkbox" name="Basic_Features" value="stock CGI
scripts">stock CGI scripts  
<input type="checkbox" name="Basic_Features" value="FTP
upload">FTP upload  
<input type="checkbox" name="Basic_Features" value="extra e-mail
addresses">multiple e-mail addresses  <input
type="checkbox" name="BasicFeatures" value="access
reports">access reports<br>
<input type="checkbox" name="Basic_Features" value="free domain
name registration">free domain name registration</td>
</tr></table>


<table width="100%"><tr valign="bottom" height="35">
<td width="13%">Server Type:</td>
<td><select name="ServerType">
  <option selected>Unix/Linux-Based Server
  <option>Windows-Based Server
  <option>Macintosh-Based Server
  <option>Other Server
</select></td>
</tr></table>


<table width="100%"><tr height="10">
<td></td></tr>
<tr valign="top">
```

```
<td width="13%">Added Comments:</td>
<td><textarea name="Comments" rows="8" cols="77"></textarea></td>
</tr></table>

<table width="100%"><tr valign="bottom" height="35">
<td width="13%"></td><td><input type="submit" value="Submit">
<input type="reset" value="Reset"></td>
</tr></table>
</form>
```

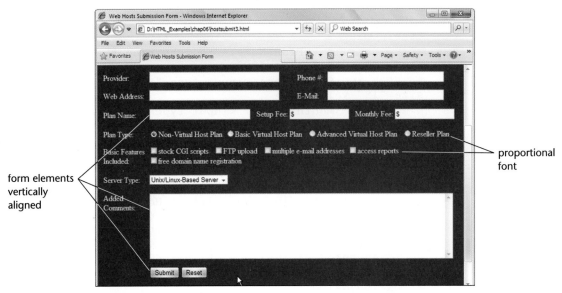

FIGURE 6.24 • You also can use tables to vertically align table elements.

NOTE

As was previously noted, you need to be aware when displaying light text against a dark background that users can have difficulty printing such a page, which in many browsers will print as light text against a white background (or, even worse, as white text against a white background). If you believe a user might want or need to print a completed form, to mail it to you, for instance, you should format it with dark text against a light or white background.

You can also use styles to control the appearance of forms, which will allow you to create forms that are more accessible than if using tables for formatting. Using styles to format HTML elements is covered in more depth in Chapter 7, *Designing Multi-Column Web Sites*.

VALIDATING FORM INPUT USING JAVASCRIPT

You can create a form using HTML, but you cannot check to make sure that a user has entered valid information. Using a JavaScript script, however, you can check user input to help ensure that it is valid. The following example uses **form input validation** to make sure that the Provider field has not been left blank and that an e-mail address (or at least a text string that includes the "@" and "." characters) has been input.

Add a JavaScript script that will validate the form input:

1. Re-open **hostsubmit.html** in your text editor and save it as **hostsubmit4.html**.

2. Add a JavaScript script to the file's HEAD section that creates a validForm() function that can be called when the form is submitted:

```
<title>Web Hosts Submission Form</title>
<script language="JavaScript" type="text/javascript">
<!-- start hiding script
function validForm(){
if (document.myform.Provider.value==document.myform.Provider.
defaultValue)
{
    alert('You have not filled in the Provider field.');
    document.myform.Provider.select();
    document.myform.Provider.focus();
    return false;
}
if (document.myform.EMail.value.indexOf('@',0)==-1 ||
document.myform.EMail.value.indexOf('.',0)==-1) {
    alert('Please provide a valid e-mail address.');
    document.myform.EMail.select();
    document.myform.EMail.focus();
    return false;
}
    else {
        {
        return true;
        }
}}
// end hiding script -->
</script>
</head>
```

3. Add a statement to the form's introductory paragraph that required fields are marked by an asterisk:

```
<p>To submit a hosting plan to be published on my The Very Best
Web Hosting Plans page, fill out and submit the following form.
If you have any questions about this form, contact us at
<a href="mailto:hostplans@theverybesthosts.emcp.com">
hostplans@theverybesthosts.emcp.com</a>. Required fields are
marked by an asterisk <span style="color:red; font-weight:bold;">
*</span>.</p>
```

4. If you previously set up the form as a CGI form, delete the comments around the mailto FORM element and delete the CGI FORM element along with the following hidden form control. (You are doing this so you will not get an error message when submitting the form.)

5. Add a NAME attribute to identify the form and an onSubmit event handler that will call the validForm() function when the form is submitted:

```
<form name="myform" onSubmit="return validForm()"
action="mailto:hosts@theverybesthosts.emcp.com" method="post">

<form name="myform" onSubmit="return validForm()"
action="/cgi-bin/FormMail.pl" method="post">
<input type="hidden" name="recipient" value="myself">
```

6. Use SPAN elements to insert bold red asterisks, to indicate that the Provider and E-Mail fields are required:

```
<p>Provider:<span style="color:red; font-weight:bold;">*</span>
<input type="text" name="Provider" size="40"> Phone #:
<input type="text" name="Phone_Number" size="40"></p>

<p>Web Address: <input type="text" name="URL" size="40">
E-Mail:<span style="color:red; font-weight:bold;">*</span>
<input type="text" name="EMail" size="40"></p>
```

7. Save your file in your text editor, switch to your browser, and open **hostsubmit4.html** in your browser from the **chap06** folder.

8. Leave the Provider field blank, and key **myemail** in the E-Mail field and click the Submit button. A pop-up message should be displayed, alerting you that you have not filled in the Provider field (see Figure 6.25). Click OK.

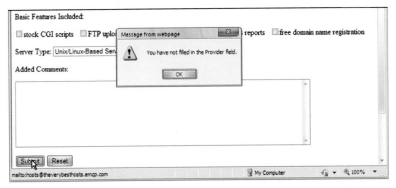

FIGURE 6.25 • The user is alerted that the Provider field has not been filled out.

9. Key **XYZ Hosts** in the Provider text box and click the Submit button again. This time, a pop-up message should be displayed, requesting that you provide a valid e-mail address (see Figure 6.26). Click OK.

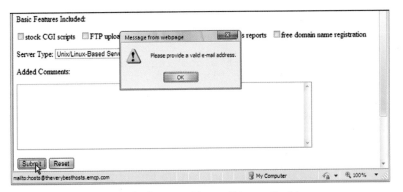

FIGURE 6.26 • The user is asked to provide a valid e-mail address.

The first IF routine checks to see if the value of the element with a name of "Provider" is equal to its default value (which is blank). If not, the alert message shown in Figure 6.26 is displayed. The second IF routine checks to see if both the "@" and "." characters are present in the "EMail" field. If not, the alert message shown in Figure 6.27 is displayed. Only when the Provider field is not empty and the E-Mail field contains both a "@" and a "." character will the form be submitted.

TROUBLE *spot*

For the JavaScript script to work, JavaScript must be enabled in your browser.

In Internet Explorer 8, select Tools, Internet Options, and click the Security tab. Select the Internet zone, if it is not already selected. Click the Custom Level button, and make sure Enable is selected for Active scripting, in the Scripting section.

To enable or disable JavaScript in other browsers: In Firefox 3 for Windows, select Tools and Options; in Firefox 3 for Macintosh OS X, select Firefox, Preferences, and Content; in Safari for Windows, select Edit, Preferences, and Security; in Safari for Macintosh OS X, select Safari, Preferences, and Security.

TROUBLE *spot*

If the example does not work as expected, carefully examine the code you keyed in to locate any errors. Make sure that what you have keyed in matches exactly what is shown in the code example, including any uppercase characters. Look to see if you have mistakenly substituted a "(" or ")" character for a "{" or "}" character. Make sure all script lines end with a ";" character. Check that you have not substituted a zero ("0") character for an uppercase letter "O" character, or the other way around. Look for any missing quotation marks.

MORE WAYS TO VALIDATE FORMS USING JAVASCRIPT

Following are some more ways in which JavaScript can be used with forms:

- Check that an integer value (rather than an alphanumeric text string) has been keyed in a field.
- Check that an integer value between a minimum and a maximum value (between 1 and 6, for instance) has been keyed in a field.
- Check that a valid phone number has been keyed in a field requesting a phone number.
- Check that a valid postal code has been keyed in a field requesting a ZIP or other postal code.
- Perform calculations on numerical values that have been keyed or selected in input fields. For instance, you might want to total the cost of items selected in an order form, calculate the sales tax, add shipping and handling, and then display the total amount.
- Check that text entered in a text area box does not exceed a set number of characters. Although you can use the MAXLENGTH attribute to limit the number of characters that can be keyed in a text box, it cannot be used to do the same thing in a text area box.
- Create a button element (using an INPUT element with a `type="button"` attribute) that performs an action when the button is clicked.
- Set other actions to be performed in response to user actions.
- Create a list menu that allows users to jump to different pages or other objects in your site. This is sometimes called a "jump menu," because it jumps to another location.

This is just a sampling of how you can use JavaScript to add versatility and functionality to forms.

Visit the Internet Resource Center. For links to online that discuss using JavaScript in forms, see the Chapter 6 section of this book's Internet Resource Center at **www.emcp.net/html2e**. See also Appendix F, *Working with JavaScript*, for additional guidance on using JavaScript in Web pages.

CHAPTER SUMMARY

You should now be familiar with how to create a wide array of different form elements and controls, including text boxes, radio button groups, check box groups, list menus, multi-line text area boxes, and various kinds of buttons to submit and reset forms. You gained practical experience using the PRE element and tables to create horizontally aligned form layouts, and you learned how to use colors and backgrounds with forms. You should be conversant in the differences between mailto and CGI forms and understand how to set up and use both types of forms. You should also understand how to set access permissions for a CGI form and how to configure a commonly used form-processing CGI script. You might have gained experience sending and receiving form responses. You should also have created a JavaScript script to validate form input and be aware of some of the other ways that JavaScript can extend the functionality of forms.

Code Review

`<form>...</form>`	FORM element. Defines a user-input form in an HTML file.
`<form action="url"`	ACTION attribute. In the FORM element, specifies the URL (mailto or CGI) to which form data is to be submitted.
`<form method="post|get"`	METHOD attribute. In the FORM element, specifies the method of submitting the form. Possible values are **post** and **get**, with the first being the more usual method for submitting online form data.
`<input>`	INPUT element. Defines a range of user form controls, including text boxes, radio buttons, check boxes, and more.
`<input type="text"`	TYPE element. In the INPUT element, specifies that an form control is a text box.
`<input type="text" size="n"`	SIZE attribute. In a text box form control, specifies the width of the text box in characters. Text entered in a text box can exceed the size of the box.
`<input type="text" maxlength="n"`	MAXLENGTH attribute. In a text box input element, specifies a maximum number of characters that can be keyed.
`<input type="text" value="text"`	VALUE attribute. For a text box control, specifies an initial value (text content) to be displayed in a text box.
`<input type="radio"`	TYPE attribute. In the INPUT element, specifies that an form control is a radio button.
`<input type="checkbox"`	TYPE attribute. In the INPUT element, specifies that an form control is a check box.
`<input name="name"`	NAME attribute. Assigns a name to a form control, in the INPUT, SELECT, TEXTAREA, and BUTTON elements. Names for text boxes are unique, while those for a group of radio buttons or check boxes are shared.
`<input value="text"`	VALUE attribute. For radio button or check box controls, specifies a value to be submitted with the form data if a radio button is selected or a check box is checked, as part of a name/value pair.

`<select>...</select>`	SELECT element. Defines a list menu (or dropdown menu).
`<select name="name"`	NAME attribute. Assigns a name to a menu list form control.
`<select multiple`	MULTIPLE attribute. In the SELECT element, a boolean attribute that specifies that multiple list options can be selected (otherwise, only one option can be selected).
`<select size="n"`	SIZE attribute. In the SELECT element, specifies the number of options to be initially displayed in a list menu (one option is the default).
`<option>`	OPTION element. Nested inside the SELECT element, defines an option in a menu list. In HTML 4 (but not in XHTML 1), the end tag is optional.
`<option selected`	SELECTED attribute. In the OPTION element, specifies that an option is selected by default.
`<option value="text"`	VALUE attribute. In the OPTION element, specifies alternative data values to be submitted with form data, in place of the nested content of the element.
`<textarea>...` `</textarea>`	TEXTAREA element. Defines a text area box, which allows users to key in multi-line comments.
`<textarea rows="n"` `cols="n"`	ROWS and COLS attributes. In the TEXTAREA element, defines the dimensions of a text area box. The ROWS attribute value specifies the number of text lines that are included in the box and the COLS attribute specifies the width of the box in text characters (not pixels).
`<input type="submit"`	TYPE attribute. In the INPUT element, specifies that a form control is a submit button.
`<input type="reset"`	`type="reset"`. In the INPUT element, specifies that a form control is a reset button.
`<input type="submit"` `value="label"`	VALUE attribute. In the INPUT element, specifies a label to be displayed on a submit button.
`<input type="reset"` `value="label"`	VALUE attribute. In the INPUT element, specifies a label to be displayed on a reset button.
`<input type="image"`	In the INPUT element, specifies that a form control is a graphical submit button. Graphical submit buttons function identically to regular submit button.
`<input type="image"` `src="url"`	SRC attribute. In the INPUT element, specifies the URL (or file name) of an image to be used for a graphical submit button.
`<input type="image"` `alt="text"`	ALT attribute. In the INPUT element, specifies alternative text for a graphical submit button, to be displayed in a non-visual user agent or if display of graphics is turned off.
`<button>...</button>`	BUTTON element. An HTML 4 element that can define a submit button or a reset button. BUTTON element submit and reset buttons function identically to regular submit and reset buttons (created using the INPUT element), except that they can be more richly rendered.

`<button type= "submit|reset |button"`	TYPE attribute. In the BUTTON element, specifies whether a submit button, reset button, or push button control is created. Submit and reset buttons created using the BUTTON element function identically to regular submit and reset buttons created using the INPUT element, but with richer rendering possibilities. A push button can trigger a script.
`<input type="hidden"`	TYPE attribute. In the INPUT element, specifies that a form control is hidden (not displayed in the browser). Commonly used in CGI forms.
`<input type="file"`	TYPE attribute. In the INPUT element, specifies that
`<input type= "password"`	TYPE attribute. In the INPUT element, allows the entry of a password. Text keyed in a password box is displayed as a series of asterisks.
`<input type="file"`	TYPE attribute. In the INPUT element, creates a file select element, which allows a user to select a file or files to be submitted (uploaded) with a form.
`<input tabindex="n"`	TABINDEX attribute. Resets the tabbing order for the INPUT and other elements (A, AREA, BUTTON, INPUT, OBJECT, SELECT, and TEXTAREA). A value of 1 places an element first in the tabbing order, a value of **2** second in the tabbing order, a value of **3** third in the tabbing order, and so on.
`<form action= "mailto:email- address"`	Specifies that a form is a mailto form, which uses a user's mail program to send the form response to an e-mail address.
`<form enctype= "text/plain"`	ENCTYPE (Encoding Type) attribute. In this case, in the FORM element, specifies **text/plain** as the content type (or MIME type). When post is the method, **application/x-www-form-urlencoded** is the default, which substitutes "+" characters for any spaces and control codes for hard returns, commas, ampersands, and other reserved characters.
`<form action= "/cgi-bin/script- name"`	Specifies that a form is a CGI form, which uses a CGI script on the page's server to transmit the send the form response.
`chmod 755 filename`	UNIX command used to set permissions for a CGI script file, so it can be accessed over the Web.
`<input value="alias"`	VALUE attribute. When creating a CGI form using the NMS FormMail.pl script, specifies an alias (set in the script) to be used in place of an e-mail address, to which form data will be sent.

KEY TERMS

For a review of the key terms bolded in this chapter, visit the Chapter 6 section of this book's Internet Resource Center at **www.emcp.net/html2e**. A complete glossary appears at the end of the book.

ONLINE QUIZ

Go to the Chapter 6 section of this book's Internet Resource Center at **www.emcp.net/html2e**, and take the online self-check quiz.

REVIEW EXERCISES

This section provides some hands-on practice exercises to reinforce the information and material included within this chapter. Review using the elements, attributes, styles, and other features that were covered in this chapter, checking your results in your browser and troubleshooting any errors:

1. Save **hostsubmit.html** as (**hostsubmit_review.html** in the **chap06** folder and review creating additional text boxes. For instance, under the line including the *Plan Name*, *Setup Fee*, and *Monthly Fee* text boxes, create two more lines containing the following text boxes:
   1st text box (1st line):
     lead-in text = Web Space:
     name = Space
     size = 40
   2nd text box (1st line)
     lead-in text = Extra Space:
     name = Extra_Space
     size = 35
   3rd text box (2nd line):
     lead-in text = Traffic:
     name = Traffic
     size = 40
   4th text box (2nd line):
     lead-in text = Extra Traffic:
     name = Extra_Traffic
     size = 35

2. Review creating a second radio button group following the *Plan Type* radio button group you already created:
   Lead-in text = Advanced Payment Discounts?
   1st radio button:
     name = Pay_Discount
     value = Y
     following text = Yes
   2nd radio button:
     name = Pay_Discount
     value = N
     following text = No

3. Still working with hostsubmit_practice.html, practice further creating a second drop-down list on the same line following the *Server Type* selection control list you have already created:
   Lead-in text = Connection Type:
   Name = ConnectType
   1st list menu option:
     text = Multiple DS-3 Connections

2nd list menu option:

    text = Single DS-3 Connection

3rd list menu option:

    text = Other

4. Review creating a second group of check boxes following the *Basic Features Included* check box group you have already created:

Lead-in text = Other Features Included:

1st check box:

    name = Other_Features

    value = custom CGI scripts

    following text = custom CGI scripts

2nd check box:

    name = Other_Features

    value = autoresponders

    following text = autoresponders

3rd check box:

    name = Other_Features

    value = shell account

    following text = shell account

4th check box:

    name = Other_Features

    value = access logs

    following text = access logs

5th check box:

    name = Other_Features

    value = RealMedia

    following text = RealMedia

6th check box:

    name = Other_Features

    value = FrontPage Extensions

    following text = FrontPage Extensions

7th check box:

    name = Other_Features

    value = password protected folders

    following text = password protected folders

8th check box:

    name = Other_Features

    value = database/MySQL

    following text = database/MySQL

9th check box:

    name = Other_Features

    value = Cold Fusion

    following text = Cold Fusion

10th check box:

    name = Other_Features

    value = PHP

    following text = PHP

11th check box:
    name = Other_Features
    value = ASP
    following text = ASP
12th check box:
    name = Other_Features
    value = multiple domain hosting
    following text = multiple domain hosting
13th check box:
    name = Other_Features
    value = shopping cart
    following text = shopping cart
14th check box:
    name = Other_Features
    value = 24/7 phone support
    following text = 24/7 phone support

5. If your browser and mail program support sending mailto form responses, review sending form responses directly to your e-mail address. Use your mail program to open and receive form responses. Experiment with sending form responses using both the "urlencoded" (the default) and "text/plain" content types.

6. If you have access to a Web space account on a UNIX or Linux server that provides a forms-processing CGI script, check the support area to find out the URL of the forms-processing CGI script and what you need to do to call it in your form. Confirm the locations of Perl and SendMail on the server. Confirm which form-processing script is used (NMS FormMail.pl or Matt Wright's FormMail.pl, for instance) and what version it is. Research on the Web to find out if there are any security issues with the form-processing script and if a later version is available that addresses those issues. Following instructions provided earlier in this chapter, use one of the FTP programs listed earlier to practice setting access permissions—set **755** as the access permissions for the CGI script.

7. Save hostsubmit-review.html as **hostsubmit-review2.html** in the chap06 folder. If you are using NMS FormMail.pl as your form-processing CGI script, follow the instructions provided previously to configure a form to send CGI form responses to your e-mail address. Review setting user-configuration variables in the script to specify domains from which submissions are allowed, e-mail addresses that are allowed to receive form responses, and aliases that can be used in place of allowed e-mail addresses. After editing your form, publish it to your Web site folder and test submitting CGI form responses in your browser and receiving them in your e-mail program.

8. If you have a Web space account, but it does not provide access to a forms-processing CGI script, go to **cgi.resourceindex.com/Remotely_Hosted/Form_Processing/** to find services that provide remotely hosted form-processing CGI scripts. Sign up for a service and follow its instructions to edit your form to use the service's forms-processing script to send form responses to your e-mail address. Publish the page with your form to your Web site, and test sending and receiving form responses using the remotely hosted forms-processing CGI script. (Note: If the remotely hosted form-processing script exposes your e-mail address, get a temporary Web-mail address and use it instead of your regular e-mail address.)

9. Save hostsubmit-review.html as **hostsubmit-review3.html** in the chap06 folder. Review setting different combinations of text, link, and background colors in your form. To refresh your memory about setting text, link, and background colors in Web pages, see Chapter 3, *Working with Fonts, Colors, and Backgrounds*. Try out several color schemes to find the color scheme you think works best with your form. When you find the color scheme you like, ask at least two classmates to critique your color choices.

10. Review organizing and laying of the form using the PRE element, using spaces to horizontally align form elements. Create an entirely different layout from the current layout. Adjust text box sizes (lengths) to fit your layout.

11. Save hostsubmit-review.html as **hostsubmit-review4.html** in the chap06 folder. Review using HTML tables to organize and layout your form.

12. Save hostsubmit-review.html as **hostsubmit-review5.html** in the chap06 folder. Review using a JavaScript script to validate form input. Using the script presented in this chapter as a reference, expand the number of required fields for which input is validated. Validate that at least two fields are not empty. Validate that a valid e-mail address is present. See if you can figure out how to validate that a phone number, in the format of (*nnn*) *nnn-nnnn*, is present (Hint: check for the presence of "(", ")," and "-"). Compose appropriate alert messages to be displayed if a required field does not validate.

WEB-BASED LEARNING ACTIVITIES

The following Web-based learning activities can help you to further extend your learning and shore up your understanding of specific topic-areas:

- Visit this chapter's section at the Internet Resource Center for this book at **www.emcp.net/html2e** to find online resources that you can use to further investigate and explore the topics and subjects covered in this chapter. You can also find all Web sites cited in this chapter's notes listed there.
- Further research a specific topic introduced in this chapter using Google (**www.google.com/**), Yahoo! (**www.yahoo.com/**), Wikipedia (**www.wikipedia.org/**), Open Directory Project (**www.dmoz.org/**), or other online sources. Some topics covered in this chapter that you can further research include:
    - The pros and cons of mailto and CGI forms.
    - Security issues involved with using poorly written form-processing CGI scripts and available alternative solutions.
    - Different ways in which JavaScript can be used with forms.
- Use the results of your online research into a particular topic to:
    - Write a review to be read in front of your classmates.
    - Write a report that can be read by your classmates.
    - Design a diagram, chart, or other graphic that illustrates a key topic or concept.
    - Create a presentation using PowerPoint (or other software) that can be shared with your classmates.
    - Give a stand-up presentation to your classmates.
    - Team up with one or more classmates to give a group presentation to your classmates.

PROJECTS

These projects can be done in class, in a computer lab, or at home. Use the skills you have developed in this and the previous chapters to create any of the following projects. In your project, demonstrate the correct use of the following HTML features covered in this chapter:

- Creation of a Web page incorporating at least one form (using the FORM element).
- Proper use of the METHOD and ACTION attributes to activate either a mailto or CGI form.
- Use of the INPUT element to create text, checkbox, and radio button controls.
- Use of the SELECT element and OPTION elements to create at least one list menu control.
- Use of the TEXTAREA element to create a multi-line comment box.
- Use of the INPUT element to create submit and reset form controls.

Project 1. Conceptualize and design a user feedback form.

For any page that you have created for yourself or for any of the fictional case example scenarios that you have worked with so far in this book, conceptualize and design a user feedback form from scratch that allows users to fill out a form to send you feedback. For instance, create a user feedback form for the page on NASA Space Exploration that you created in Chapter 4 that asks visitors their opinions about space exploration, whether money should be spent on space exploration, whether human beings should go to Mars, and so on. Include a text area box that lets a visitor provide a longer comment.
Create a user feedback form for any other page, whether as part of a fictional case example scenario or for a personal, topical, or other page that you have created for yourself.

Project 2. Create a survey form.

Create a form that surveys visitors' opinions about a particular topic, issue, or event. This can be on any topic or subject matter, so be creative and come up with something different that you think would elicit a relatively broad response. For instance, you might create a survey asking visitors what they ate (or drank) for breakfast. You can create a survey of opinions about global warming. You can create a survey of what visitors think about recent movies, asking them to rank them on a scale from 1 to 5 in different categories, for instance. Or, you can create a survey form on any other topic or subject you can conceive.

Project 3. Create an order form.

Look on the Web for examples of order forms that allow visitors to order products or services. Save examples you find as bookmarks or favorites, and use them as guides in conceptualizing and designing an order form of your own. For instance, you might create an order form that allows visitors to order a range of different size and color "widgets." You can have options for ordering 2-inch, 5-inch, and 10-inch widgets in orange, green, and purple colors.

Project 4. Create a product registration form.

When people buy a product, they are increasingly asked to register the product online. Use Yahoo! at **www.yahoo.com/** or Google at **www.google.com/** to search for examples of product registration forms. Save good examples you find as bookmarks or favorites, and then use them as guides in creating a fictional product registration form from scratch. This could be for a software product, a video camera, a car stereo, a foot massager, or just about anything. Try to make it realistic. Ask for the customer's first name, last name, title, company name, address, city, state, ZIP code, country, product name, model number, date purchased, use of the product (work, entertainment, education, or other, for instance), and any comments about the product.

Project 5. Create a dating service form.

Imagine that you are running a dating service. Create a form that allows people looking for dates to describe their interests, likes and dislikes, favorite things to do, favorite music, ambitions, what they are looking for in a date or partner, and so on. Make liberal use of radio buttons, check boxes, and selection lists to elicit responses to an array of different kinds of questions. Have fun with it. Be creative.

Project 6. Create a form for a site of your own.

Create a form for a site that you have already created for yourself, or design a site from scratch that includes a form. This can be any kind of form you care to design (totally open-ended). Decide whether you are going to use a mailto or a CGI form.

If using a mailto form, do not use your regular e-mail address, because doing so will expose it to being harvested by spambots; get a temporary e-mail address, through GMail, HotMail, or other Web mail provider, and use it instead.

If using a CGI form, you will need access to a forms-processing CGI script on your Web host's server or from a service that provides remotely hosted forms-processing CGI scripts. If you cannot or do not choose to set up an alias for your e-mail address, get a temporary e-mail address and use it instead.

CHAPTER 7
Designing Multi-Column Web Sites

PERFORMANCE OBJECTIVES

- Use frames to create multi-column and multi-row Web sites.
- Learn about CSS selectors, properties, and declarations.
- Use tables and styles to create a two-column Web page.
- Understand usability and accessibility issues involved in designing multi-column layouts using frames and tables.
- Use styles to create a fixed multi-column layout featuring a masthead, content area, sidebar, and footer.
- Review an example of using styles to create a fluid multi-column layout.
- Learn how to create and use external style sheets.

Until now, you have been working with single-column Web pages. Most commercial and many non-commercial Web sites, however, feature multi-column page layouts. These kinds of layouts allow a wider variety of content, including menus, advertising, and resource lists, to be brought **above the fold**, or above the bottom edge of a browser's viewport, when a page is first loaded.

N O T E Some of the layout techniques demonstrated in this chapter are not supported in some recent browsers. For that reason, it is recommended that you use a current browser to review this chapter's examples. Current browsers include Internet Explorer 8, Mozilla Firefox 3, Apple Safari 4, Opera 9, or higher versions of those browsers.

USING THE EXAMPLE FILES

The example files used in this chapter are located within the frames-layout, tables-layout, and styles-layout folders of the chap07 folder within your working folder. Save any HTML files you create in this chapter in the appropriate folder for the case example you are working on.

NOTE — This chapter provides an overview of and hands-on practical experience with creating multi-column Web page layouts using frames, using tables and styles, and using styles alone. The purpose of this chapter is not to teach you everything you might need to know about designing these kinds of layouts (that would take a book, not a chapter), but to familiarize you with the basic issues, features, capabilities, and methods involved in these approaches.

CASE EXAMPLE: CREATING A FRAMED WEB SITE

The FRAMESET, FRAME, and NOFRAME elements let you create a Web site composed of frames (or scrollable windows) that can be organized in columns and rows. A FRAMESET element and two or more nested FRAME elements are called a **frameset**. These elements are allowed, but are deprecated, in the "frameset" definition of HTML 4.01 and XHTML 1.0. For discussion of deprecation and what it means, see "What Is Deprecation?" in Chapter 3. These elements are also obsolete in HTML 5 because they are considered to be harmful to usability. For these reasons, use of frames in current Web pages is not recommended. This case example is presented so the student will know how to revise legacy pages that make use of frames. A client might also insist that frames be used in designing a Web site, because that was how his or her old site was designed, despite advice and reasons presented by the Web designer to do otherwise. For a more detailed discussion of why frames should not be used in current Web pages, see the "Why Not Use Frames?" sidebar later in this chapter.

"Arturo Rodriguez is a graphic designer and printer working for a full-service printing firm, A-Plus Printers. His boss has directed him to create a framed Web site for the company. His boss had argued for using alternatives to using frames to create multi-column page designs, but the client's old site had used frames and he insisted the same approach be used to add the capability of a scrollable main content window, while a sidebar menu remained fixed on the screen."

CREATING PAGE LAYOUTS USING FRAMES

Frames were originally introduced in the Netscape Navigator browser and have been included in HTML since HTML 4. All current graphical browsers support using frames. By using frames, you can create a wide variety of different multi-column, multi-row, and combination column-and-row layouts. Unlike tables, **frame layouts** can include separate windows (or frames) within which scrollable content can be displayed. A link in one frame, by using the TARGET attribute, can also control the content of another frame, allowing users to select pages from a **sidebar menu** to be displayed in a main content frame, for instance.

Creating a Two-Column Frame Page

You can arrange frames in columns or rows. In this case, you create a basic frames layout that uses two columns, with a sidebar menu in one column and the main content of the page in the other column.

CREATING THE FRAMESET PAGE A **frameset page** is a page that includes the instructions for laying out two or more frames in a Web page. You will be using a starter example page, **framestart_ex.html**, to start creating the different frame page examples in this chapter.

To start working with this example:
1. In your text editor, open **framestart_ex.html** from the frames-layout folder and save it as **twocol_frame.html** in that same folder.
2. In your Web browser, open **twocol_frame.html** from the frames-layout folder.

A frameset page is created using the FRAMESET and FRAME elements. A frameset page does not contain any displayable content but only pointers to the pages (or other files) to be displayed in the individual frames.

Create a frameset page that creates a two-column Web page, with a sidebar menu in the left column and the main content of the page in the right column:
1. Add a FRAMESET element that specifies a two-column layout with a 150-pixel wide column on the left and a column on the right that will expand to fill the page:

```
<!DOCTYPE HTML PUBLIC "-//W3C//DTD HTML 4.01 Frameset//EN"
 "http://www.w3.org/TR/html4/frameset.dtd">
<html>
<head>
<meta http-equiv="Content-Type" content="text/html;
charset=UTF-8">
<title>A-Plus Printers: Serving All Your Printing Needs Since
1975</title>
</head>
<frameset cols="150,*">
</frameset>
</html>
```

2. Use the FRAME element to define the frames that compose the columns and point to the documents to be displayed in them (see Figure 7.1):

```
<frameset cols="150,*">
  <frame src="sidebar.html">
  <frame src="main.html" name="main">
</frameset>
```

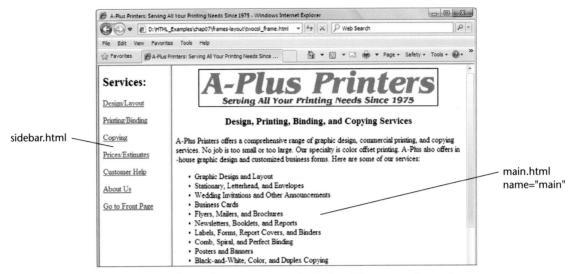

sidebar.html

main.html
name="main"

FIGURE 7.1 • The A-Plus Printers page is displayed in a two-column format.

3. Click on the Design/Layout link in the left sidebar (see Figure 7.2). Click on the Go to Front Page link in the left sidebar to return to the site's front page.

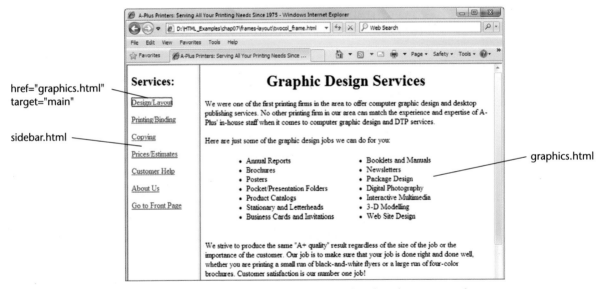

href="graphics.html"
target="main"

sidebar.html

graphics.html

FIGURE 7.2 • The graphics.html page is displayed in the main window.

There are several things to notice in this initial code:
- There is no BODY element. In a frameset page, the FRAMESET element replaces the BODY element.
- The COLS attribute (`cols="150,*"`) divides the frameset into two columns, one 150 pixels wide, and the other, by using the * wildcard, expandable to fill the available horizontal space.
- The SRC attributes specify the initial HTML files to be displayed in each frame (sidebar.html and main.html).
- The attribute `name="main"` names the main content frame so it can be a target for links. This allows links in the sidebar frame to control the content in the main frame.

TARGETING FRAME CONTENTS The TARGET attribute allows a link in one frame to control the content of another frame, as long as that frame has been named (**name="main"**, for instance). The file, sidebar.html, displayed in the sidebar frame, contains links (in the form of a sidebar menu) that use the TARGET attribute to control the content of the main frame:

```
<p><a href="graphics.html" target="main">Design/Layout</a></p>
<p><a href="printing.html" target="main">Printing/Binding</a></p>
<p><a href="copying.html" target="main">Copying</a></p>
<p><a href="prices.html" target="main">Prices/Estimates</a></p>
<p><a href="service.html" target="main">Customer Help</a></p>
<p><a href="about.html" target="main">About Us</a></p>
<p><a href="main.html" target="main">Go to Front Page</a>
```

The **target="main"** attribute tells a browser to display the specified file (graphics.html, printing.html, and so on) in a FRAME element with a **name="main"** attribute.

TARGET and NAME attribute values are case sensitive. If you have **target="main"** in your link, but **name="Main"** in your frameset page's FRAME element, the targeting will not work.

Creating a sidebar frame on the left side of the page is only one way to lay out a framed page. You could just as easily position the sidebar frame on the right side of the page, for instance, simply by switching the positions of the FRAME elements in the frameset page.

N O T E — Among the subpages, only graphics.html has been fully developed for this example. Dummy files have been created for the other subpages (printing.html, copying.html, service.html, and about.html).

Creating a Two-Row Frame Page

Another common way to lay out a framed page is by using two rows, with the top row containing a menu running along the top of the page.

CREATING THE FRAMESET PAGE As with creating a two-column frame page, you need to create a frameset page that specifies a two-row layout, using the ROWS attribute.

Create a two-row frame layout:
1. In your text editor, open **framestart_ex.html** from the frames-layout folder and save it as **tworow_frame.html** in that same folder.
2. In your browser, open **tworow_frame.html** from the frames-layout folder.
3. Define a top row with a height of 75 pixels and a bottom row that expands to vertically fill the page. Specify topbar.html as the first frame row's content and main.html as the second frame row's initial content (see Figure 7.3):

```
</head>
<frameset rows="25,*">
    <frame src="topbar.html" scrolling="no" marginheight="0">
    <frame src="main.html" name="main">
</frameset>
</html>
```

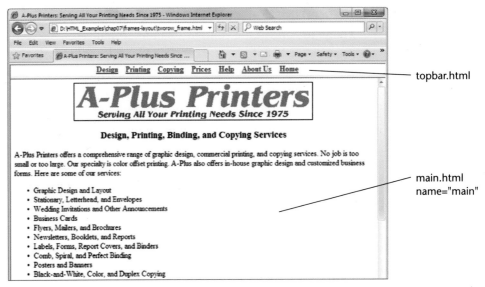

topbar.html

main.html
name="main"

FIGURE 7.3 • The A-Plus Printers page is displayed in a two-row format.

4. Click the Design link in the topbar frame (see Figure 7.4).

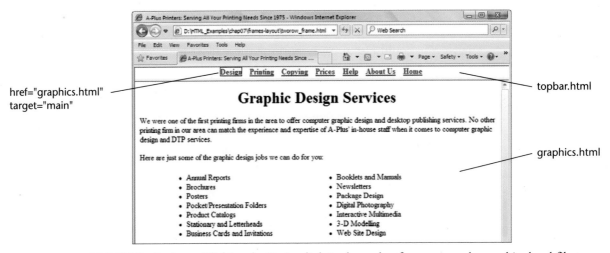

href="graphics.html"
target="main"

topbar.html

graphics.html

FIGURE 7.4 • Clicking the Design link in the topbar frame causes the graphics.html file to be displayed in the main frame.

This example differs from the previous example in the following ways:

- The ROWS attribute (`rows="75,*"`) divides the frameset into two rows, one 75 pixels high and the other expandable to fill the available vertical space in the viewport. Alternatively, a percentage value can be used.
- The `scrolling="no"` attribute in the first FRAME element turns off any scroll bars that might be displayed in the frame window.
- The `marginheight="0"` attribute in the first FRAME element sets the top and bottom margins of the frame to 0 (zero pixels), so that the content of the frame (topbar.html) will fit vertically within the frame. The MARGINWIDTH attribute can be used to set left and right margins for a frame.

UNDERSTANDING THE TOPBAR PAGE The topbar.html file is very similar to the sidebar.html file, except that the links are arranged horizontally across the topbar frame (with non-breaking spaces, ` `, providing extra space between the links), rather than vertically (in paragraph elements) down the sidebar frame, as in the previous example. The actual links are the same in both sidebar.html and topbar.html.

In topbar.html, an inline style (`style="margin-top: 0"`) is set on the P element to eliminate the top margin that most current browsers insert above the first block element in a frame. Without the inline style, the topbar menu would extend below the bottom of the topbar frame.

Creating a Frame Page with Columns and Rows

For a more complex frame layout, you can create a layout that contains both columns and rows by nesting one FRAMESET element within another.

For this example, you will start out using the two-column frame page layout you created previously. If you have not yet done that example, you should go back and do it first, before trying to do this example.

Create a combination frame layout that uses both rows and columns:

1. In your text editor, reopen **twocol_frame.html** from the frames-layout folder and save it as **combo_frame.html** in that same folder.
2. In your browser, open **combo_frame.html** from the frames-layout folder.
3. Create a frameset layout that nests one frameset element (using columns) inside another frameset element (using rows) (see Figure 7.5):

```
</head>
<frameset rows="85,*">
    <frame src="topbanner.html" scrolling="no" marginheight="0">
    <frameset cols="150,*">
        <frame src="sidebar2.html">
        <frame src="main2.html" name="main">
    </frameset>
</frameset>
</html>
```

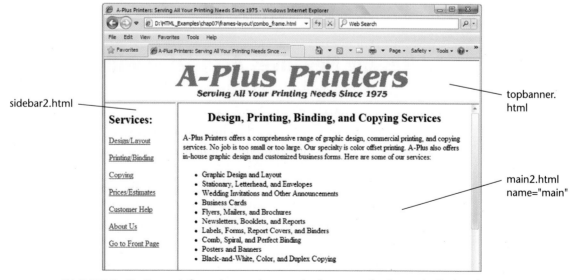

FIGURE 7.5 • A frame layout that uses both rows and columns is displayed.

4. Click on the Design/Layout link in the sidebar (see Figure 7.6).

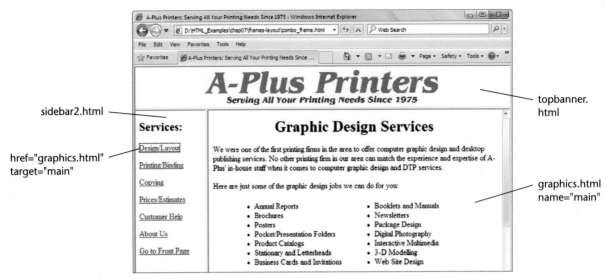

sidebar2.html

href="graphics.html"
target="main"

topbanner.
html

graphics.html
name="main"

FIGURE 7.6 • Clicking on the Design/Layout link causes the graphics.html file to be displayed in the "main" window.

The following are the main features of this example:
- The bracketing FRAMESET element defines an initial two-row layout, with a 85-pixel high top row and a bottom row set to expand vertically to fill the viewport.
- The first FRAME element defines the first row in the outside frameset. It links to a topbanner.html file that contains the A-Plus Printers' banner image. It also turns off scrolling and sets the top margin to 0.
- The nested FRAMESET element forms the second row in the outside frameset. It defines a two-column layout that is nested inside of the outside frameset's bottom row. It includes two frames that link to sidebar2.html and main2.html.

In the nested frameset the sidebar2.html file differs from the sidebar.html only in the "Go to Front Page" link, which links to main2.html, rather than main.html; the main2.html file differs from main.html only in that the banner image at the top of the page has been deleted, because it is now included in topbanner.html.

Addressing Negatives Associated with Frames

There are a number of things you can do to reduce, but not eliminate, some of the negatives associated with the use of frames.

The META element can be used to include a description and list of keywords in a frameset page's HEAD element, which search engines and directories can use in indexing and listing a framed site.

A NOFRAMES element can be used to include **noframes text**, which is content that will be displayed by older browsers that do not recognize framed pages. Noframes text can also provide content and links that search engine robots can index and follow. The NOFRAMES element should be inserted at the bottom the FRAMESET element (or the top-level frameset, if using a combination row and column frame layout):

```
<noframes>
<h3>A frames-compatible browser is required to view this page.
Please visit the <a href="main2.html">non-frames version</a> of
this site.</h3>
</noframes>
</frameset>
```

Make sure that pages linked to through a frameset can stand alone if accessed from outside the frameset. To do this, at minimum, include a link to the site's home page in the main and other framed pages. You can also include a menu at the bottom of pages linked to in the main content frame that links to the main pages of the site.

A link included inside of a frame will open inside that frame, if no TARGET attribute has been included. Linking this way, without permission from the site owner, is questionable, if not unethical. When linking to an external site from a framed page, you should always include either `target="_top"` or `target="_blank"`, so the link will be displayed outside of the frameset.

There have been a number of lawsuits over Web sites **deep linking** into another site's commercial content, from a single-column (or single-row) framed page (so that the frame is invisible). Linking this way, to commercial or non-commercial sites, is highly unethical and should never be done.

Visit the Internet Resource Center. To find online resources that discuss using frames for page layout, including usability and accessibility issues associated with their use, visit the Chapter 7 section of this book's Internet Resource Center at **www.emcp.net/html2e**.

Why Not Use Frames?

Frames present a number of drawbacks. These drawbacks might influence whether you choose to use frames or not:

- Frames can interfere with the bookmarking of specific pages within your site. What gets bookmarked is the top-level frameset page, which might be several levels away from the actual page a visitor wants to bookmark.
- Frames can interfere with visitors printing specific pages within a framed site. For instance, if you try to print twocol_frame.html in Internet Explorer 8, only sidebar2.html is printed. To print main2.html, a visitor needs to right-click inside the main frame and select Print.
- Although content within a framed Web page can remain fixed and always visible, this is at the expense of the space available for viewing the scrollable content of the page.

- A multi-page framed Web site can take longer to download and display than a single page because multiple pages must be downloaded.
- A complex framed site can be confusing to navigate and understand for someone using a screen reader or Braille browser.
- Visitors accessing the Web using mobile devices with constrained screen sizes can have trouble viewing and navigating framed Web sites.
- Because content pages are accessed through the frameset, search engines might see them as being deeper in the site and thus rank them lower in their listings.
- The FRAMESET, FRAME, and NOFRAMES elements, as well as the TARGET attribute, are obsolete in HTML 5, which means there is not assurance browsers will continue to support frames in the future.

UNDERSTANDING THE BASICS OF CSS

Prior to now, examples of using **Cascading Style Sheets** (CSS) have been presented that do not require any in-depth understanding of using **styles** for you to successfully implement them. Most of these examples were focused on providing one-for-one replacements for elements and attributes that are deprecated in HTML 4 or obsolete in HTML 5 due to usability and accessibility concerns.

The remaining examples in this chapter, however, make much more extensive use of style sheets, and not just to provide replacements for deprecated elements and attributes, but also to illustrate ways in which, using CSS, you can go beyond what HTML by itself can do. This section on the basics of CSS should help provide a foundation for understanding the more complex CSS examples provided in this chapter.

Why CSS?

CSS works with HTML on the premise of separating presentation from content, with HTML responsible for structuring and conveying the semantic meaning of document elements, while CSS is responsible for controlling presentation and appearance. Many of the deprecated elements and attributes in HTML 4 control how a Web page is presented, rather than designate the structural content of the page or the semantic meaning of its elements. This, however, can create barriers to access content on the Web for users with visual disabilities or impairments.

The FONT element, perhaps the most primary of the elements that has been deprecated for these reasons, is entirely involved in determining presentation, without having any import relative to the contextual structure or semantic meaning of a page. Some designers, however, abuse the FONT element, using it to give contextual and structural emphasis to nested text, such as substituting text enlarged with the FONT element for an H1 element. Others, conversely, use the H1 and other heading elements, without regard to their semantic meaning (as different levels of headings), simply to display text in different sizes.

Those learning HTML should be aware of and understand how to apply all of its aspects—including deprecated elements and attributes—because in the real world, Web designers might need to revise and edit legacy HTML documents that include those features. On the other hand, backward-compatibility issues involved in using CSS for page design have been greatly diminished, with all current major browsers now fully supporting CSS 2.1, while relatively simple workarounds are available to address most compatibility issues in recent browsers. (See Appendix C, *Cascading Style Sheet Sampler*, for details of the most common CSS workarounds.)

Many governmental agencies, educational institutions, and non-profit organizations are required under the terms of the Americans with Disabilities Act to ensure that their Web sites are accessible to people with disabilities, such as visual impairments. For more information on the importance of accessibility on the Web, see the Web Accessibility Initiative at **www.w3.org/WAI/**.

 **Visit the Internet Resource Center.** To find additional online resources that discuss accessibility and Web design, visit the Chapter 7 section of this book's Internet Resource Center at www.emcp.net/html2e/.

What Does "Cascading" Mean?

The term **cascading** in Cascading Style Sheets has to do with the fact that style information for presenting a document on the Web can have multiple sources. A browser, for instance, includes its own internal **style sheet** that determines how specific elements will be presented. A user also can set browser preferences or create a user-defined style sheet to assert control over how documents are to be displayed in the user's browser. Authors need to be aware, in other words, that other players are sitting at the table when it comes to how a Web page is displayed in a browser.

The mechanism that sorts all this out is called **the cascade**. In general, styles set by authors carry heavier weight than the same styles set by users, and styles set by users carry more weight than those set by browsers. However, if a user includes an **important declaration** (`body {font-size: 24px ! important;}`, for instance) in a user-defined style sheet, that carries more weight than an important declaration (for the same element or elements) by an author. The user, in other words, has the final say, if he or she chooses, and knows how, to have it. The reason for this is that a user might need to specify a larger font size, due to a visual impairment, for instance, and should not be barred from doing so. The cascade, in supporting browsers, falls like this:

1. `! important` declarations by users.
2. `! important` declarations by authors.
3. Normal declarations by authors.
4. Normal declarations by users.
5. User agent declarations.

NOTE

Browsers also apply a fairly complex system of assigning weights to style declarations, depending upon origin, importance, order, and specificity. For instance, an inline style applied to a specific instance of the H3 element has more weight than a different style applied to all H3 elements. A style property set for a group of elements (the H1, H2, and H3 elements, for instance) carries less weight than one set for the H1 element alone. To learn more about how the specific weight of a style declaration is calculated, see the W3C's section on Cascading Order at **www.w3.org/TR/CSS21/cascade.html#cascade**.

Anatomy of a Style

A **style rule** is composed of two parts, a **selector** and a **declaration**. A selector specifies (or selects) the object or objects to which the style's properties will be applied, while a declaration specifies (or declares) at least one **property** and its assigned value (or property:value pair) to be applied to the selected object. For instance:

```
selector { declaration }
```

A declaration is composed of one or more property:value pairs, separated by semi-colons:

```
selector { property1:value1; property2:value2; }
```

Style rules can also be arranged, using tabs or spaces, to make them more readable:

```
selector {
    property1: value1;
    property2: value2;
    }
```

Using Selectors

Selectors allow you to apply styles to documents in a variety of ways. You can apply styles to individual elements, a group of elements, or to elements only in certain contexts and situations. Table 7.1 lists selectors that are supported by current browsers.

These are some of the more commonly used CSS selectors. To find out about other kinds of selectors and ways to combine selectors, see the W3C's Selectors page at **www.w3.org/TR/CSS21/selector.html**.

TABLE 7.1 • CSS1 and CSS2 Selectors

Selector	Example/Description
CSS1 Selectors	
Type (or Simple)	`h1 { color: blue; background: transparent; }` Applied to all H1 elements.
Group	`h1, h2, h3 { font-family: Arial, sans-serif; }` Applied to all elements in the group.
Descendant (or Contextual)	`h1 em { color: red; background: transparent; }` Applied only to EM elements that are descendants of the H1 element (nested within it at any level).
Class	`.main	div.main` Applied to elements assigned to a class (`class="main"`). In the first example, the style is applied to all elements assigned to the class; in the second example, it is applied only to DIV elements assigned to the class.
ID	`#intro	p#intro` Applied to an element with an ID (`id="intro"`). Unlike CLASS attributes, an ID attribute value must be unique (cannot be assigned to more than one element). Including the element in the selector (`p#intro`) can increase the specificity, and thus the weight, of the selector.
Anchor Pseudo-Class	`a:link	a:visited	a:active	a:hover` Applied to links in specific states (unvisited, visited, active, or hovered over). a:hover is a CSS2 pseudo-class. In CSS1, pseudo-classes are only applied to the A element.
CSS2 Selectors	
Universal	`*	*p	*.main` Applied above to all elements, all P elements, and all elements assigned to the "main" class. p and *p, and .main and *.main, are functionally the same, except that browsers that support CSS1 but not CSS2 will recognize the first but not the second.
Child	`p > em	p>em` Applied to the child of an element but not to other descendants.
First-child	`td :first-child	div.main :first-child` Applied to the first child of an element but not to following children of that element. A child is nested directly inside of another element (compared to a descendant, which is nested at any level).

Note: **CSS1** refers to the Cascading Style Sheets, Level 1 specification, while **CSS2** refers to the Cascading Style Sheets, Level 2 specification. CSS1 selectors should be supported by all current and recent major browsers, but CSS2 selectors, while supported by current browsers, might not be supported by all recent browsers.

In the Example/Description column, the | character is not code, but is used to separate code alternatives.

Inheritance

Inheritance is a means by which a descendant element can inherit a property from a parent or other ancestor element. Many style properties, such as the color, font-family, and font-size properties can be inherited, while others cannot. An inheritable property applied to the BODY element, for instance, will be inherited by all elements nested in the BODY element (by all children and descendants of the BODY element). Other properties, such as the background, border, display, height, width, padding, and margin properties, cannot be inherited by child and descendant elements. At first glance, the background properties might seem to be inheritable, even though they are not, because the default background of elements is transparent. See Appendix C, *Cascading Style Sheets Sampler*, for descriptions of the most commonly used CSS properties, including whether they are inherited or not.

Horizontal and Vertical Margins

Horizontal (left and right) and vertical margins (top and bottom) are treated differently in CSS. Adjacent vertical margins are collapsed to the larger of the two margins, while adjacent horizontal margins are concatenated (or added to each other).

For instance, if a P element has a bottom margin of 15 pixels, and a following H2 element has a top margin of 20 pixels, the vertical spacing between the two elements will be collapsed to 20 pixels (the largest of the two adjacent vertical margins). However, if a P element with a left margin of 10 pixels is nested inside of a BODY element with a left margin of 15 pixels, the resulting horizontal spacing between the P element and the left side of the browser's viewport will be 25 pixels because adjacent horizontal margins are not collapsed but are concatenated, or added to each other.

Visit the Internet Resource Center. To find online resources that discuss using Cascading Style Sheets, visit the Chapter 7 section of this book's Internet Resource Center at **www.emcp.net/html2e.**

CASE EXAMPLE: CREATING A TWO-COLUMN LAYOUT USING TABLES AND STYLES

Prior to the introduction of styles, using tables was the primary way in which Web designers effected a multi-column layout in a Web page. Such layouts were created by using nested tables to vary cellpadding and cellspacing amounts and FONT elements to format table cell contents. Such layouts, however, are difficult to edit and maintain, present accessibility barriers to users who have to rely on a non-visual browser or screen reader to access a page's contents, and waste bandwidth.

Since the introduction of styles, Web designers have largely ceased using nested tables and the FONT element to create multi-column page designs because using styles to control padding, margins, font characteristics, and backgrounds is much more efficient and effective. Many Web designers, however, have continued to use tables to create multi-column page layouts, despite the accessibility issues using tables in that way can pose, because it can produce results that will display reliably in both current and recent browsers. For example, a designer may use a table to create equal-length, adjustable columns because they are much more difficult to create using styles.

"Shirley Johnson has decided that she wants to format her report on the Mercury space program in two columns, with a table of contents in a sidebar column. To reduce accessibility issues with using tables for layout, she has decided to rely as much as possible on styles to control the appearance of the layout, while avoiding using deprecated elements such as the FONT element. She has also decided not to use CELLPADDING, CELLSPACING, or nested tables."

The most basic layout you can do with tables is to create a two-column layout, with a sidebar column on the one side and a main content column on the other side. The method for doing this involves setting a width of 100 percent for the whole table, while setting the sidebar column within the table to a fixed pixel width. That way, the table as a whole, along with the main content column, can expand or contract along with the width of the viewport, while the sidebar column remains the same width.

action

Create a basic two-column layout:

1. In your text editor, open **mercury3_ex.html** from the tables-layout folder and save it as **mercury3.html** in that same folder.
2. In your browser, open **mercury3.html**.
3. Create a two-column table with the content of the page in the second column (see Figure 7.7):

```
<body>

<table width="100%" border="1">
<tr><td width="150" valign="top">

</td>
<td>

<h1 align="center"><a name="top"></a>NASA Space
Exploration<br>and the Mercury Project</h1>

[...]

</td></tr>
</table>
</body>
```

left column
(150 pixels wide)

right column
(expands horizontally
to fill viewport)

width="100%"

FIGURE 7.7 • A basic two-column layout is created, with the main content of the page in the right column.

Creating a Sidebar Menu

To create a sidebar menu, you just need to create a link list in the left column that jumps to the section headings in the right column.

Add a sidebar menu to the left column:

1. Click and drag to highlight the menu in the second column, and then cut it (Ctrl+X in Windows or Command+X on the Macintosh):

```
<a name="top"></a>
<h1 align="center">NASA Space Exploration<br>and the Mercury
Project</h1>
<h2 align="center">by Shirley Johnson</h2>

<p align="center" class="menu"><b>
[ <a href="#sect1">1915 - 1957</a>
]     
[ <a href="#sect2">1958 - 1960</a>
]     
[ <a href="#sect3">1961</a> ]     
[ <a href="#sect4">1962</a> ]     
[ <a href="#sect5">1963</a> ]     
[ <a href="#sect3">Gemini & Apollo</a> ]</b></p>
```

2. In the first column, paste in the menu codes and text (Ctrl+V in Windows or Command+V on the Macintosh), and then delete everything not shown in the following example:

```
<table width="100%" border="1">
<tr><td width="150" valign="top">
<p class="menu"><b>
<a href="#sect1">1915 - 1957</a>
<a href="#sect2">1958 - 1960</a>
```

```
<a href="#sect3">1961</a>
<a href="#sect4">1962</a>
<a href="#sect5">1963</a>
<a href="#sect3">Gemini & Apollo</a>
</b></p>
</td>
```

3. Add a heading, remove the center-alignment from the P element that you pasted in, and then set the links up so they are all in their own paragraphs (see Figure 7.8):

```
<table width="100%" border="1">
<tr><td width="150" valign="top">
<h4 class="menu">Menu:</h4>
<p class="menu"><b>
<a href="#sect1">1915 - 1957</a></b></p>
<p class="menu"><b>
<a href="#sect2">1958 - 1960</a></b></p>
<p class="menu"><b>
<a href="#sect3">1961</a></b></p>
<p class="menu"><b>
<a href="#sect4">1962</a></b></p>
<p class="menu"><b>
<a href="#sect5">1963</a></b></p>
<p class="menu"><b>
<a href="#sect3">Gemini & Apollo</a>
</b></p>
</td>
```

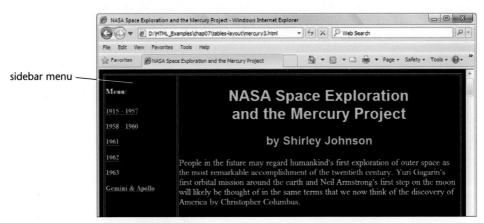

sidebar menu —

FIGURE 7.8 • A sidebar menu is inserted in the left column.

4. To eliminate margin spacing above the first block element in a table cell for all browsers, insert the following style in the page's style sheet (see Figure 7.9):

```
td :first-child, th :first-child {
    margin-top: 0;
    }
</style>
```

margin-top: 0;

FIGURE 7.9 • Margin spacing is eliminated above the first block element in a table cell.

TROUBLE *spot*

The code inserted in Step 4 is necessary in that current browsers, including Internet Explorer 8, display margin spacing above a block element that is the first child of a table cell or DIV element, while Internet Explorer 7 and earlier versions of that browser do not. To cause all current and recent browsers to treat this the same, in both table cells and DIV elements, you can include the following in a style sheet:

```
div :first-child, td :first-child, th :first-child {
    margin-top: 0;
    }
```

Varying the Padding Amounts

The CELLPADDING attribute allows you to specify the amount of cell padding (space between a cell's content and its border) but does not allow you to vary the amount of padding from one cell to another. When creating a two-column layout, however, the amount of padding set in the TABLE element can be too much for the sidebar column but too little for the main body column.

action

Add CLASS attributes to the table's cells so styles can be applied to them:

1. Add a **class="side"** attribute to the first table cell:

```
<table width="100%" border="1">
<tr><td class="side" width="150" valign="top">
<h4 class="menu">Menu:</h4>
```

2. Add a **class="main"** attribute to the second table cell:

```
<td class="main">
<h1 align="center"><a name="top"></a>NASA Space
Exploration<br>and the Mercury Project</h1>
```

TROUBLE *spot*

Note that the destination anchor, **<a name="top"></a>**, is inserted inside of the H1 element. Inserting it in front of the H1 element causes the margin spacing above that element to be displayed, rather than being turned off. It also is not standard to insert an inline element directly inside of a table cell.

3. Add .side and .main styles to the page's style sheet to apply variable left and right padding to the table columns (see Figure 7.10):

```
.side {
    padding-left: 5px;
```

```
        padding-right: 5px;
        }
.main {
        padding-left: 10px;
        padding-right: 10px;
        }
</style>
```

class="side" —

padding-left: 10px; —

padding-left: 5px; —

class="main"

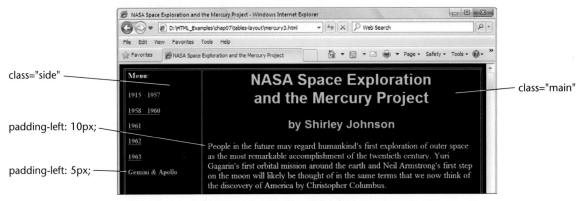

FIGURE 7.10 • Different left and right padding is added to the table columns.

Collapsing the Table Borders

You can use styles to collapse the cell borders, reducing the amount of cell spacing between cells to zero, so that only a single border is displayed between the cells.

Collapse the borders around the table's cells:

1. Add a **class="table-layout"** attribute to the TABLE element:

```
<table class="table-layout" width="100%" border="1">
<tr><td class="side" width="150" valign="top">
```

2. Add a style to the style sheet that will collapse the table borders (see Figure 7.11):

```
.table-layout {
        border-collapse: collapse;
        border-spacing: 0;
        }
</style>
```

border-collapse: collapse;
border-spacing: 0;

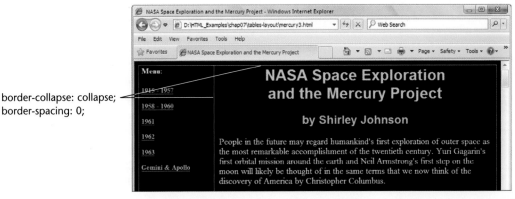

FIGURE 7.11 • The borders around the cells are collapsed to a single border between the cells.

Formatting the Heading Elements

You can improve the look of that layout by formatting the H4 element at the top of the sidebar.

Set display characteristics for the H4 and H1 headings, and increase the size of the sidebar menu's font (see Figure 7.12):

```css
h1, h2, h3, h4 {
    font-family: Arial, Geneva, Helvetica, sans-serif;
    }
h1 {
    color: #99ffff;
    background: transparent;
    padding-top: 15px;
    }
[...]

h4 {
    font-size: 1.25em;
    color: #ffcc00;
    background: transparent;
    padding-top: 15px;
    }
p.menu {
    color: yellow;
    background: transparent;
    font-size: 1.1em;
    }
```

padding-top: 15px;

font-size: 1.25em;
color: #ffcc00;

font-size: 1.1em;

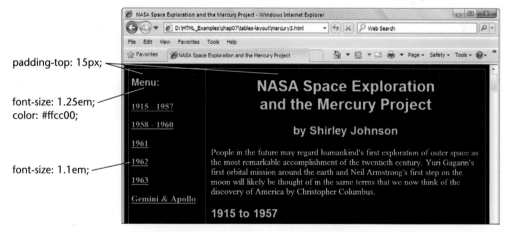

FIGURE 7.12 • The headings and sidebar text are reformatted.

Creating a Seamless Table Layout

In the current layout, the table is separated by margin space between it and the edge of the browser window. That space is actually the default page margin that the browser inserts.

Remove margins and add backgrounds to the side and main columns to give a "seamless" look to the Web page:

1. Set the page's top, right, bottom, and left margins, to 0, 0, 15em, and 0 respectively (the 15-em bottom margin leaves room to jump to the footnotes):

```
<style type="text/css">
body {
    color: #ffffcc;
    background: black;
    margin: 0 0 15em 0;
    }
```

2. Set a background color for the sidebar column:

```
.side {
    padding-left: 5px;
    padding-right: 5px;
    background: #660000;
    }
```

3. Turn off the table borders (see Figure 7.13):

```
<table class="table-layout" width="100%" border="1">
```

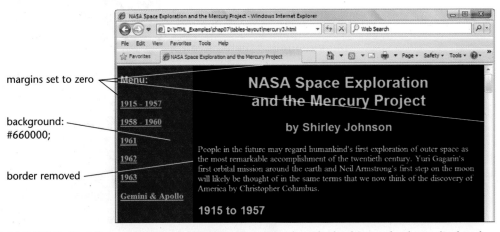

FIGURE 7.13 • Margins and borders are removed, and a background color is displayed behind the side column.

4. Set background images for the side and main columns (see Figure 7.14):

```
.side {
    padding-left: 5px;
    padding-right: 5px;
    background: #660000 url("images/back_nebula.jpg");
    }
.main {
    padding-left: 10px;
    padding-right: 10px;
    background: black url("images/starcluster.jpg");
    }
```

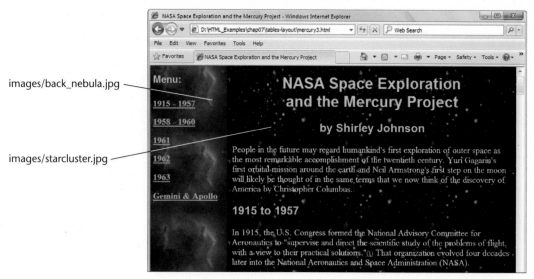

images/back_nebula.jpg

images/starcluster.jpg

FIGURE 7.14 • The table borders are turned, and background images are assigned to the side and main columns.

Adding a Floating Figure and Caption

Right now, the images are floated on the left or right margin using **align="left"** and **align="right"**. Using a SPAN element, you can turn the images into figures with captions.

action

Turn the first floating image, altas_mercury.jpg, into a floating figure and caption:

1. Nest the image in a SPAN element, remove the ALIGN and HSPACE attributes from the IMG element, and add a caption:

```
<p><span class="figure-left" style="width: 175px"><img
src="images/atlas_mercury.jpg" align="left" hspace="10"
alt="Atlas rocket with Mercury spacecraft" width="175"
height="238"><br style="clear: left"><i>Atlas rocket with Mercury
spacecraft</i></span>The Atlas rocket launch vehicle, which
lifted John Glenn into orbit, began being used following World
War II.
```

2. Add styles to the page's style sheet to float the SPAN element, set a right margin, and format the caption text (see Figure 7.15):

```
.figure-left {
    float: left;
    color: #ffcc00;
    font-size: .9em;
    margin-right: 10px;
    line-height: .9;
    }
.figure-left img {
    padding-bottom: 2px;
    }
</style>
```

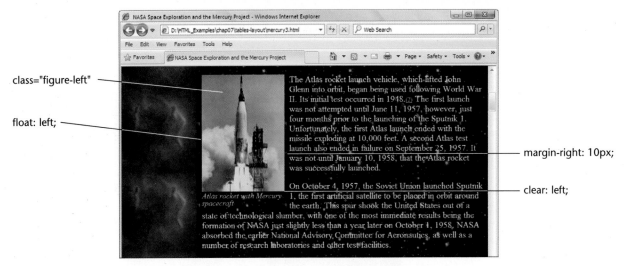

class="figure-left"

float: left;

margin-right: 10px;

clear: left;

FIGURE 7.15 • A left-aligned figure and caption are added.

3. Use the previous example as a model to turn the next floating image, astronauts.jpg, into a floating figure and caption, but floating on the right, instead of the left. Change the ALT, WIDTH, and HEIGHT attributes to fit the new image. You will need to create a second class, figure-right, and apply styles to it (see Figure 7.16).

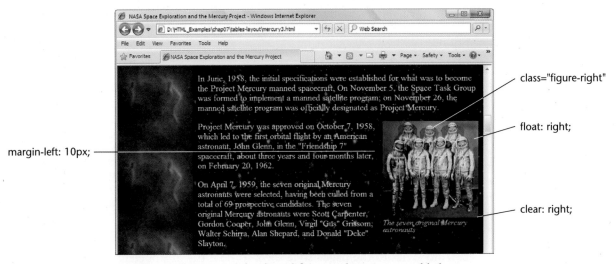

class="figure-right"

float: right;

margin-left: 10px;

clear: right;

FIGURE 7.16 • A right-aligned figure and caption are added.

Visit the Internet Resource Center. To find online resources that discuss using tables and Cascading Style Sheets for page layout, visit the Chapter 7 section of this book's Internet Resource Center at **www.emcp.net/html2e.**

CASE EXAMPLE: CREATING A FIXED TWO-COLUMN LAYOUT USING STYLES

The current standard for including styles in Web pages is CSS 2.1 (Cascading Style Sheets Level 2 Revision 1). CSS 2.1 is fully supported by all major current browsers.

With a minimal number of workarounds, CSS layouts can be designed to be backward-compatible with all major recent browsers.

A **fixed layout** created using CSS states all measurements in pixels, with the dimensions of the layout remaining fixed, regardless of the screen resolution or default font settings. This type of layout is sometimes called a **pixel-perfect layout**.

The primary drawback of a fixed layout, created using pixels instead of ems, is that it can interfere with users' controlling their own font settings (unless they set "! important" rules). All current browsers, however, allow users to zoom the size of their text, which alleviates some of the accessibility issues associated with this kind of layout.

A fixed page layout also does not let you easily create self-adjusting, equal-height columns, which is automatically done when creating a multi-column layout using tables. Instead, you need to manually adjust the height settings for the BODY element and other layout divisions to increase or decrease the length of the layout.

Following this case example, however, an example of creating a multicolumn **fluid layout** will be presented that does allow the automatic adjustment of column heights relative to content length. It is compatible, however, only with current browsers, while the fixed layout is compatible with both current and recent browsers.

NOTE

In this example, for convenience sake and to avoid repetitious verbiage, a DIV element with `id="page"` set will be referred to as *the "page" division*. A style using a #page ID selector will be referred to as *the #page style*.

" Amy Nguyen, a student at a technical college, has helped to organize a science club. Having just finished a course in Web design, she has volunteered to design a Web page for the club. She knows from research she did for her Web design class that more than 90 percent of users have systems with displays capable of at least 1024×768 pixels. She has decided to make that the target resolution for her design, while still accommodating users with displays of 800×600 pixels, by keeping the width of the main content area less than 800 pixels wide.

She has decided to further divide the main content area into two newspaper-style columns, primarily so that more than one article (or story) can be visible when the page is opened, but also to allow users with displays that are less than 800 pixels wide (such as cell phone users, for instance) to read the articles with a minimum of horizontal scrolling.

To ensure that the page will be accessible to all, she will not be using tables or any deprecated elements or attributes in designing the site, but will be laying out the page's design using the position property, which is part of CSS 2.1. Because others will be writing the stories to be included in the page, she will be using **lorum ipsum text**, which is commonly used in the publishing and graphic design fields to fill content areas until the actual content has been created. Lorum ipsum text looks like Latin but is actually nonsense text (gibberish) that is just made to look like it is Latin. "

NOTE

Previously in this book, screen captures have been done with a browser window sized at 800 × 600 pixels, primarily to facilitate readers easily being able to see the content of the examples in the figures. Technology moves on, however, and currently over 90 percent of users have systems with display resolutions of 1024 × 768 pixels or larger. Larger display resolutions enable organizing information more easily into columns (or vertical segments). Currently, most multi-column Web page layouts are designed to fit horizontally within a browser sized at 1024 × 768 pixels. For this case example, screen captures, unless otherwise noted, were done with a browser width of 1,024 pixels.

In the following sections, you will first create a basic multi-column layout, and then embellish its appearance.

Creating the Basic Layout

You will first create a basic layout, composed of a masthead, main content area, and sidebar. You will also set up **newspaper-style columns** in the main content area.

CENTERING THE PAGE Because some users will view the page with browsers sized larger than 1024 × 768 pixels, the page needs to be centered.

Center the page in the browser's viewport:
1. In your text editor, open **scienceclub_ex.html** and save it as **scienceclub.html** in that same folder.
2. Open **scienceclub.html** in your browser.
3. Nest the page's content inside of "center" and "page" divisions:

```
<body>
<div id="center">
<div id="page">

<h1>This is the masthead.</h1>

[...]

</div> <!-- end page -->
</div> <!-- end center -->
</body>
</html>
```

4. Add styles to the initial styles to the style sheet (see Figure 7.17):

```
<style type="text/css">
body {
    margin: 0;
    min-width: 990px;
    }
#center {
    width: 100%;
    text-align: center;
    background:#336699;
    }
```

```
#page {
    position: relative;
    top: 0;
    width: 970px;
    margin-left: auto;
    margin-right: auto;
    height: 1620px;
    background:#ccccff;
    text-align: left;
    }
div :first-child  {
    margin-top: 0;
    }
</style>
```

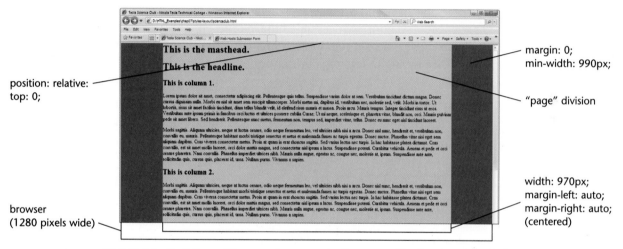

position: relative:
top: 0;

browser
(1280 pixels wide)

margin: 0;
min-width: 990px;

"page" division

width: 970px;
margin-left: auto;
margin-right: auto;
(centered)

FIGURE 7.17 • The page is automatically centered in the viewport of a browser set to 1280 pixels across.

Here are some pointers to help you understand the code inserted in Step 2:
- For the body style, the margins are set to zero to eliminate the default body margins. A minimum width of 990 pixels is set to keep the page from being collapsed inside that width if it should be viewed in a viewport with a width less than that.
- For the #center style, **width: 100%;** sets the width of the "center" division to be 100 percent of the width of the viewport. The **text-align: center;** declaration causes Internet Explorer 5.5 for Windows to center the nested "page" division (otherwise, the page would be displayed flush to the left margin in that browser).
- For the #page style, although **position: relative;** and **top: 0;** do not do anything visible, they give "position" to the "page" division, so that other divisions in the layout can be positioned in relation to the "page" division (rather than the body element).
- **width: 970px;** sets a width for the "page" division that is 20 pixels less than the minimum width set for the body, to preserve the left margin spacing when the page is viewed in a browser with a width of less than 1,024 pixels.
- **margin-left: auto;** and **margin-right: auto;** center the "page" division in the viewport (as shown in Figure 7.17).
- **text-align: center;** for the "center" division centers the "page" division in Internet Explorer 5.5 for Windows, which does not recognize the **auto** value for the margin properties.

- **height: 1620px;** sets the total height of the "page" division. The other parts of the layout (the masthead, main content area, sidebar, and footer) will all be sized to fit within that height.
- **text-align: left;** for the "page" division is necessary because center-alignment had to be set for the "center" division (to get Internet Explorer 5.5 for Windows to center the page).
- The **div :first-child** selector is used to eliminate top margin spacing for block elements that are the first child (the first element nested inside) of any DIV element.

This is the longest and most complex case example in the book. You can save copies of your work more frequently than called for in the chapter, if you wish. For instance, after adding the masthead to the layout in the next section, you can save scienceclub.html as scienceclub-a.html and continue working with that file, and then save it at any further point as scienceclub-b.html, scienceclub-c.html, and so on. That way, if you get stuck at any point in the example, you can step back to your last saved version and try again from that point, rather than having to retrace your steps or return to the beginning of the section.

ADDING A MASTHEAD TO THE LAYOUT A masthead extends across the width of the page, identifying the name or title of a publication, newspaper, newsletter, or Web site. In a Web site, it can also include other content, such as logos, search boxes, advertising, and menus.

action

Create and position a masthead at the top of the page:

1. Nest a "mast" division inside the "page" division:

```
<div id="center">
<div id="page">

<div id="mast">
<h1>This is the masthead.</h1>
</div> <!-- end Mast -->

<h1>This is the headline.</h1>
```

2. Add a #mast style to the style sheet (see Figure 7.18):

```
#mast {
    position: relative;
    top: 10px;
    width: 970px;
    height: 140px;
    background: #ffcccc;
    }
</style>
```

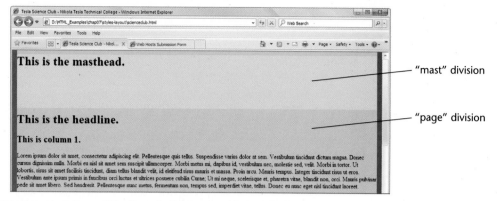

FIGURE 7.18 • The "mast" division is added to the layout.

The "mast" division, sized 970 × 140 pixels, is relatively positioned ten pixels down from its initial position. This has the affect of adding 10 pixels of margin spacing above the "mast" division. A background color is set so the dimensions of the division can be seen.

SETTING UP THE MAIN AND SIDEBAR COLUMNS The main content area will be the first of two side-by-side columns (the second column will be a sidebar).

Create and position the "main" and "side" divisions:

1. Nest a "main" division following the "mast" division:

```
<div id="mast">
<h1>This is the masthead.</h1>
</div> <!-- end mast -->

<div id="main">
<h1>This is the headline.</h1>

<h2>This is column 1.</h2>
[...]
<h2>This is column 2.</h2>
[...]
</div> <!-- end main -->

<h3>This is the sidebar.</h3>
```

2. Add a #main style to the style sheet:

```
#main {
    position: relative;
    top: 20px;
    width: 760px;
    height: 1340px;
    background: #ffffcc;
    }
</style>
```

3. Add a "side" division following the "main" division:

```
</div> <!-- end main -->

<div id="side">
<h3>This is the sidebar.</h3>
```

```
<h4>Recommended Sites:</h4>
<ul>
<li><a href="http://www.nsf.gov/">National Science Foundation</a>

[...]

<li><a href="../science/computer-science/">Computer Science</a>
</ul>
</div> <!-- end side -->

<h3>This is the footer.</h3>
```

4. Add a #side style to the style sheet:

```
#side {
    position: absolute;
    top: 160px;
    right: 0;
    width: 200px;
    height: 1340px;
    background: #ccffff;
    }
</style>
```

5. Remove the background color from the "page" division (see Figure 7.19):

```
#page {
    position: relative;
    top: 0;
    width: 970px;
    margin-left: auto;
    margin-right: auto;
    height: 1620px;
    background:#ccccff;
    text-align: left;
    }
```

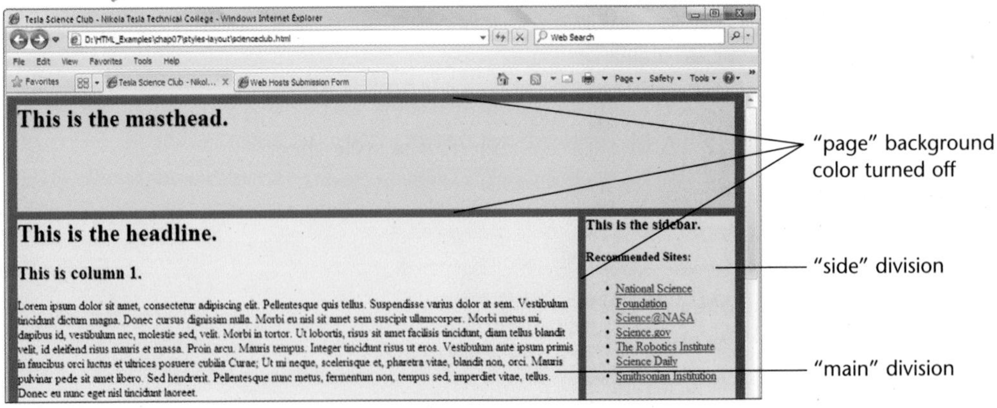

FIGURE 7.19 • The "main" and "side" divisions are added to the layout.

The "main" division is sized at 760 × 1340 pixels. Subtracting 760 pixels from 970 pixels (the width of the "page" and "mast" divisions) leaves 210 pixels available for positioning a 200 pixel wide "side" division to the right of the "main" division, with ten pixels of space remaining for a gutter between them.

The "main" division is relatively positioned 20 pixels down from its initial position. The 20 pixels include ten pixels to match the amount the "mast" division was repositioned, plus another ten pixels to create ten pixels of margin spacing between them.

Using **position: relative;** to reposition an element relative to its initial position does not affect the position of following elements, so when the "mast" division was moved down, the "main" division stayed where it was. A background color is set so the dimensions of the division can be seen.

For the "side" division, **position: absolute;**, instead of **position: relative;**, is used here, in conjunction with the top and right properties, to position the "side" division in relation to the top and right sides of the "page" division.

The "side" division is sized at 200 × 1340 pixels and absolutely positioned 160 pixels down from the top and 0 pixels in from the right side of the "page" division. The height of the "side" division is equal to the "main" division.

ADDING THE FOOTER TO THE LAYOUT The footer will be displayed below the "main" and "side" divisions.

Create and position the "footer" division:

1. Add a "footer" division following the "side" division:

```
<div id="footer">
<h3>This is the footer.</h3>

<p>Nikola Tesla Technical College - 2000 Crawford Lane, Valley
City, California 93700 - Phone: (559) 555-1920</p>
</div> <!-- end footer -->

</div> <!-- end page -->
</div> <!-- end center -->
</body>
```

2. Add a #footer style to the style sheet (see Figure 7.20):

```
#footer {
    position: absolute;
    bottom: 0;
    width: 970px;
    height: 100px;
    margin-bottom: 10px;
    background: #ccffcc;
    }
</style>
```

FIGURE 7.20 • The "footer" division is added to the layout.

The "footer" division is absolutely positioned, 0 pixels up from the bottom of the "page" division. This will not work if the "page" division has not been given "position"—otherwise, the "footer" division would be positioned from the bottom of the BODY element.

The "footer" division is sized at 970 × 100 pixels. The width is the same as the "page" and "mast" divisions: 140 pixels (the "mast" height) + 1340 pixels (the "main" height) + 100 pixels (the "footer" height) + 40 pixels (the amount of vertical spacing outside of those divisions) = 1620 pixels (the "page" height).

ADDING THE "HEADLINE" DIVISION AND NEWSPAPER COLUMNS Add a "headline" division, positioned at the top of the "main" division, followed by two newspaper-style columns.

Create and position the "headline" division:

1. Add a "headline" division inside the "main" division:

```
<div id="main">
<div id="headline">
<h1>This is the headline.</h1>
</div> <!-- end headline -->

<h2>This is column 1.</h2>
```

2. Add a #headline style to the style sheet:

```
#main {
    position: relative;
    top: 20px;
    width: 760px;
    height: 1340px;
    background: #ffffcc;
    }
#headline {
    width: 100%;
    height: 75px;
    background: #ccff99;
    }
```

3. To create the newspaper-style columns, add "main-col1" and "main-col2" divisions inside the "main" division:

```
<div id="main-col1">
<h2>This is column 1.</h2>
[...]
</div> <!-- end main-col1 -->

<div id="main-col2">
<h2>This is column 2.</h2>
[...]
</div> <!-- end main-col2 -->
</div> <!-- end main -->
```

4. Add #main-col1 and #main-col2 styles to the style sheet (see Figure 7.21):

```
#headline {
    width: 100%;
    height: 75px;
    background: #cff99;
    }
```

```
#main-col1 {
    float: left;
    width: 350px;
    height: 1230px;
    }
#main-col2 {
    float: right;
    width: 350px;
    height: 1230px;
    }
```

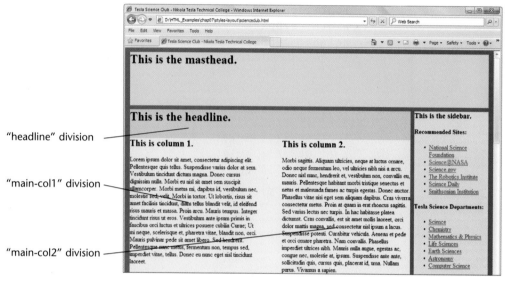

"headline" division

"main-col1" division

"main-col2" division

FIGURE 7.21 • A "header" division and two newspaper-style columns are added to the "main" division.

In this case, **float: left;** and **float: right;** are applied to the "main-col1" and "main-col2" divisions to align them side-by-side as columns.

This finalizes the two-column layout. The remainder of this case example illustrates ways in which you can embellish the layout and its content.

Embellishing the Layout

In this section, you will be embellishing the layout so it looks more attractive.

STYLING THE MASTHEAD AND ADDING A NAVIGATION BAR Because this is a school science club, the masthead should feature the school colors, which are navy and maize. A navigation menu (or bar) is often included in the masthead to provide links (or buttons) that allow visitors to navigate the site.

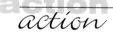

Style the masthead and its content:

1 In your text editor, save scienceclub.html as **scienceclub2.html** in the styles-layout folder.

2 In your browser, open **scienceclub2.html**.

3. Replace the dummy text in the "mast" division with some real content:

```
<div id="mast">
<h1>This is the masthead.</h1>
<h1>Nikola Tesla Science Club</h1>
</div>
```

4. Edit the #mast style, specifying maize yellow and navy blue as the foreground and background colors, and then use a descendant selector (**#mast h1**) to format the masthead's heading text:

```
#mast {
    position: relative;
    top: 10px;
    width: 970px;
    height: 140px;
    text-align: center;
    color: #ffcc00;
    background: #003399;
    }
#mast h1 {
    font-family: Arial, Helvetica, sans-serif;
    font-weight: bold;
    font-size: 54px;
    padding-top: 15px;
    width: 800px;
    margin-left: auto;
    margin-right: auto;
    border-bottom: 3px red ridge;
    }
```

5. Add a "navbar" division following the H1 element in the "mast" division:

```
<div id="mast">
<h1>Nikola Tesla Science Club</h1>
<div id="navbar">
    <span><a href="../../">Home</a></span>
    <span><a href="join.html/">Join!</a></span>
    <span><a href="calendar.html">Calendar</a></span>
    <span><a href="announcements.html">Announcements</a></span>
    <span><a href="advisors.html">Advisors</a></span>
    <span><a href="../">School Clubs</a></span>
</div>
</div> <!-- end mast -->
```

6. Add three styles to control the appearance of the navigation bar (see Figure 7.22):

```
#mast h1 {
    font-family: Arial, Helvetica, sans-serif;
    font-weight: bold;
    font-size: 54px;
    padding-top: 15px;
    width: 800px;
    margin-left: auto;
    margin-right: auto;
    border-bottom: 3px red ridge;
    }
#navbar {
    position: absolute;
```

```
        top: 95px;
        left: 0;
        padding-top: 5px;
        text-align: center;
        font-family: Arial, Helvetica, sans-serif;
        font-weight: bold;
        width: 100%;
        height: 30px;
        }
#navbar span {
        font-weight: bold;
        font-size: 18px;
        padding-left: 5px;
        padding-right: 5px;
        padding-top: 5px;
        }
#navbar a {
        color: #003399;
        background: #ffcc00;
        text-decoration: none;
        padding: 3px 20px 3px 20px;
        }
```

#mast h1
(descendant selector)

border-bottom: 3px red ridge;

"navbar" division

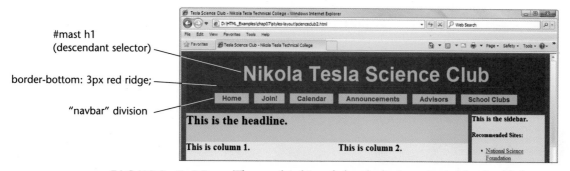

FIGURE 7.22 • The masthead is styled and a basic navigation bar is added.

The main thing to notice in the previous code is that the foreground and background colors are set for the "mast" division. That way, the foreground color is inherited by the H1 element, while the background color fills the background of the "mast" division.

A three-pixel, red, ridged border is drawn beneath the H1 element that is nested inside the "mast" division. Border styles that can be applied include solid, double, dotted, dashed, outset, inset, groove, and ridge. Open **borderstyles.html** from the styles-layout folder to see examples of these border styles. While browsers display the solid and double border styles consistently, there is a good deal of variety, however, in how the other border styles are displayed from browser to browser.

The navigation links are dummy links that do not link to any actual files. The "Home" and "School Clubs" links use relative URLs to link to fictional index files in the grand-parent and parent folders of the current folder, respectively. The other navigation links link to fictional files in the current folder. The URLs you would use in a navigation menu for an actual site you might create would depend on how the site was organized.

The links in the navigation bar are formatted by nesting them in SPAN elements and then using a **descendant selector** (**#navbar span**) to apply styles only to SPAN elements inside the "navbar" division but not to SPAN elements that might be located else-where in the page.

The `text-decoration: none;` declaration for the `#navbar a` descendant selector turns off the underlining that is normally displayed under links.

TROUBLE *spot*

Because both height and vertical padding values are assigned to the #navbar style, it is subject to the **box model bug** in Internet Explorer 5.5 for Windows, which misapplies the CSS box model by including padding and borders within an element's dimensions (width or height). The **box model hack** has been developed to address this bug, but since only about one percent of users currently use that browser, the choice has been made not to illustrate the box model hack in the case examples. It is exampled, along with other commonly used CSS workarounds, in Appendix C, *Cascading Style Sheet Sampler*.

TURNING THE NAVIGATION LINKS INTO HOVER BUTTONS Displaying the navigation links as buttons lets visitors know they are links that can be clicked (which is why the underlining was turned off in the previous section). By making use of the a:link, a:visited, a:active, and a:hover anchor pseudo-classes, you create **hover buttons**, which change appearance when the mouse cursor hovers over them.

action

Set up the hover buttons in the style sheet (see Figure 7.23):

```
#navbar a {
    color: #003399;
    background: #ffcc00;
    text-decoration: none;
    padding: 3px 20px 3px 20px;
    }
#navbar a:link, #navbar a:visited, #navbar a:active {
    border: 4px #ffcc00 outset;
    }
#navbar a:hover {
    color: #ffcc00;
    background: #cc0000;
    border: 4px #ff6699 outset;
    }
```

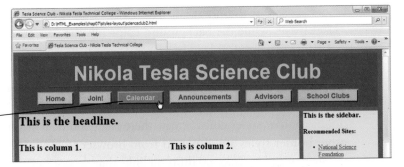

a:hover pseudo-class

FIGURE 7.23 • The navigation links are turned into hover buttons.

USING CSS COMMENTS **CSS comments** can be used to indicate the structure and organization of a style sheet to make returning to revise it later much easier. You cannot use HTML comments (`<!--` and `-->`) inside of a style sheet. CSS has its own form of comments, with `/*` starting a comment and `*/` ending a comment. Anything in between the two will be ignored by a browser's CSS parser.

Use CSS comments to show the structure and organization of the style sheet:

```css
/* Masthead Styles */
#mast {
    position: relative;
    top: 10px;
    width: 970px;
    height: 140px;
    text-align: center;
    color: #ffcc00;
    background: #003399;
    }
[...]
/* Main Content Area Styles */
#main {
    position: relative;
    top: 20px;
    width: 760px;
    height: 1340px;
    background: #ffffcc;
    }
[...]
/* Sidebar Styles */
#side {
    position: absolute;
    top: 160px;
    right: 0;
    width: 200px;
    height: 1340px;
    background: #ccffff;
    }

/* Footer Styles */
#footer {
    position: absolute;
    bottom: 0;
    width: 970px;
    height: 100px;
    margin-bottom: 10px;
    background: #ccffcc;
    }
```

CSS comments can also be used to troubleshoot a style sheet. By commenting out sections of the style sheet, you can isolate which codes are causing a result you do not like or expect. You can also preserve a style (or style rule), so you can experiment with other selectors, properties, and declarations, but still return to the original code if you desire.

CREATING THE HEADLINE The headline extends across the top of the main content area.

Replace the dummy headline with some real content, and then style it:

1. Edit the headline:

```
<div id="main">
<div id="headline">
<h1>This is the headline.</h1>
<h1>Tesla Science Team Earns Honors</h1>
</div> <!-- end headline -->
```

2. Edit the style sheet (see Figure 7.24):

```
#headline {
    width: 100%;
    height: 75px;
    background: transparent;
    font-family: Arial, Helvetica, sans-serif;
    text-align: center;
    margin-bottom: 10px;
    }
#headline h1 {
    position: relative;
    top: 20px;
    width: 700px;
    color: #990000;
    margin-left: auto;
    margin-right: auto;
    padding-bottom: 5px;
    border-bottom: 3px maroon ridge;
    }
#main-col1 {
    float: left;
    height: 1230px;
    width: 350px;
    }
```

#headline h1
(descendant selector) ——

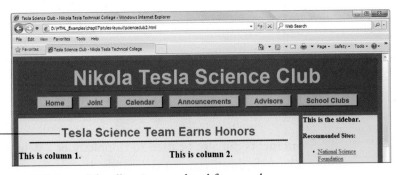

FIGURE 7.24 • A headline is created and formatted.

The colors you see in Figure 7.24 might not exactly match what you see on your monitor. That is because different monitors can have different settings, impacting how colors are displayed.

TROUBLE *spot*

Setting **width: 100%;** for the "headline" division causes the width of that element to equal the width of the containing "main" element. Changing the background of the "headline" division to transparent lets it share the background color set for the "main" division. A descendant selector is used to relatively position the H1 element, nested in the "headline" division, 20 pixels down from its initial position.

FORMATTING THE NEWSPAPER COLUMNS The newspaper-style columns currently extend to the left and right margins of the "main" element.

Replace the dummy column headings with some real content, and then style them:
1. Edit the column headings:

```
<div id="main-col1">
<h2>This is column 1.</h2>
<h2>Tesla Students Excel at Science Fair</h2>
[...]
<div id="main-col2">
<h2>This is column 2.</h2>
<h2>Celebrate Astronauts Week</h2>
```

2. Edit the style sheet to style the column headings and add padding to the left and right of the two columns (see Figure 7.25):

```
#main-col1 {
    float: left;
    width: 350px;
    height: 1230px;
    margin-left: 10px;
    }
#main-col2 {
    float: right;
    width: 350px;
    height: 1230px;
    margin-right: 10px;
    }
#main-col1 h2, #main-col2 h2 {
    font-family: Arial, Helvetica, sans-serif;
    font-style: italic;
    font-size: 18px;
    margin-top: 10px;
    margin-bottom: -10px;
    }
```

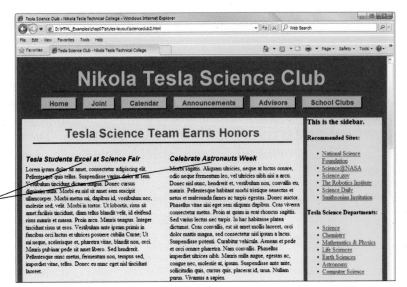

column headings

FIGURE 7.25 • The newspaper-style columns and column headings are formatted.

ADDING A COLUMN DIVIDER Adding a divider between text columns can make them look visually more appealing.

Add a divider between the two columns in the main content area:

1. Create an empty "divider" division:

```
</div> <!-- end main-col2 -->

<div id="divider">
</div>

</div> <!-- end main -->
```

2. Edit the style sheet to create a #divider style that defines and positions a 1-pixel wide vertical border (see Figure 7.26):

```
#divider {
    position: absolute;
    top: 85px;
    left: 375px;
    height: 1230px;
    width: 1px;
    border-right: 1px black solid;
    }
</style>
```

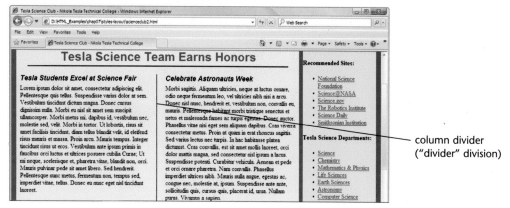

column divider
("divider" division)

FIGURE 7.26 • A divider line is positioned between the columns.

Either a border-right or border-left property can be used to specify the border that composes the divider, because the element is only 1-pixel wide.

FORMATTING THE SIDEBAR CONTENT Including a sidebar, either on the left or right side of the page, allows you to bring a wider variety of content "above the fold." That content might be a photograph of the author or owner of the site, a menu, a search box, recommended sites, advertising, or just about anything that will fit in that space.

Some sidebar content has been included with the original example file, in the form of two link lists, one to recommended sites and the other to Tesla Technical College science departments.

action

Format and add content to the sidebar:

1. Delete the dummy H3 heading, and then add a site search box and NASA and NSF logos to the sidebar:

```
<div id="side">
<h3>This is the sidebar.</h3>
<form id="search" method="post" action="/cgi-bin/searchsite.pl">
Search Tesla Tech:<br><input type="text" name="Search_String"
maxlength="75" size="18">
<input type="submit" value="Go">
</form>

[...]

<div class="logo">
<a href="http://www.nasa.org/"><img src="images/nasa.gif"
width="150" height="136" alt="NASA logo"></a>
</div>
<div class="logo">
<a href="http://www.nsf.org/"><img src="images/nsf.jpg"
width="150" height="150" alt="National Science Foundation
logo"></a>
</div>
</div> <!-- end side -->
```

2. Add styles to the stylesheet to format the search box, headings, link lists, and logo links (see Figure 7.27):

```
#side {
    position: absolute;
```

```
                top: 160px;
                right: 0;
                width: 200px;
                height: 1340px;
                background: #ccffff;
                }
        #search {
            font-family: Arial, Helvetica, sans-serif;
            font-weight: bold;
            color: #3366cc;
            background: transparent;
            margin: 5px;
            }
        #side h4 {
            font-family: Arial, Helvetica, sans-serif;
            color: #3366cc;
            background: transparent;
            margin-top: 15px;
            margin-bottom: 5px;
            padding-left: 5px;
            }
        #side ul {
            margin-top: 0;
            margin-left: 20px;
            padding-left: 5px;
            padding-right: 10px;
            }
        #side a:link, #side a:visited, #side a:active {
            color: #003399;
            background: transparent;
            }
        #side a:hover {
            color: #ffcc00;
            background: #003399;
            text-decoration: none;
            font-weight: bold;
            }
        .logo {
            text-align: center;
            margin-top: 20px;
            }
        .logo img {
            display: inline;
            border-style: none;
            }
```

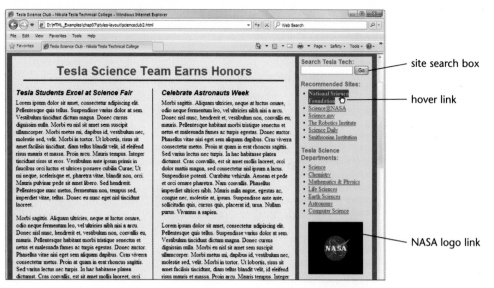

FIGURE 7.27 • The sidebar is formatted, and a search box and logos have been added.

The search box is a dummy box that does not actually search the Web page. For it to do a search, you would need to link to an actual CGI script for doing a site search. Google provides a site search box; the code for the site search box just needs to be pasted into a page's code. See Google Site Search at **www.google.com/sitesearch/**. For other site search CGI or remotely hosted scripts, see the CGI Resource Index at **cgi.resourceindex.com/**.

In the last style rule, `display: inline;` is used to specify that an IMG element, nested in a division assigned to the "logo" class, should be displayed as an inline element, which might seem strange at first glance, because the IMG element is an inline element by default. However, the display characteristic of the IMG element can be changed elsewhere in the style sheet—in this case, using `text-align: center;` on the containing division to center a contained image will work only if the image is displayed as an inline image. Reiterating that the image is indeed an inline image is done to make sure that it stays that way.

FORMATTING THE FOOTER CONTENT Including a footer at the bottom of the page allows inclusion of information you do not want to include in the other areas of the page. It can include information identifying the institution, agency, organization, or company to which the Web site belongs; where it is located; and how to contact it. The name of the designer or author responsible for creating the page, along with a link to his or her e-mail address, could also be included. Alternatively, the name of whoever is responding to requests or comments about the contents of the page could be used as the contact name. The footer can also include a copyright statement.

Format the contents of the footer:

1. Edit the footer:

```
<div id="footer">
<h3>This is the footer.</h3>
<p id="school"><a href="../">Nikola Tesla Technical College</a> -
2000 Crawford Lane, Valley City, California 93700 - Phone: (559)
555-1920</p>
<p id="designer">Designer: <a href="mailto:amynguyen@teslatech.
emcp.edu">Amy Nguyen</a>, Nikola Tesla Science Club</p>
```

```
<p id="copyright">&copy; Copyright 2010 by Nikola Tesla Technical
College - All Rights Reserved.</p>
</div> <!-- end footer -->
```

2. Edit the style sheet (see Figure 7.28):

```
/* Footer Styles */
#footer {
    position: absolute;
    bottom: 0;
    width: 970px;
    height: 100px;
    margin-bottom: 10px;
    background: #ccffcc;
    text-align: center;
    }
#footer p {
    font-family: Arial, Helvetica, sans-serif;
    color: #336699;
    background: transparent;
    margin-top: 8px;
    margin-bottom: 0;
    }
#school {
    font-size: 18px;
    font-weight: bold;
    }
#school a:link, #school a:visited, #school a:active {
    color: #cc0000;
    background: transparent;
    text-decoration: none;
    }
#designer a:link, #designer a:visited, #designer a:active {
    color: #cc0000;
    background: transparent;
    }
</style>
```

footer styles

Nikola Tesla Technical College - 2000 Crawford Lane, Valley City, California 93700 - Phone: (559) 555-1920
Designer: Amy Nugyen, Nikola Tesla Science Club
© Copyright 2010 by Nikola Tesla Technical College - All Rights Reserved.

My Computer   100%

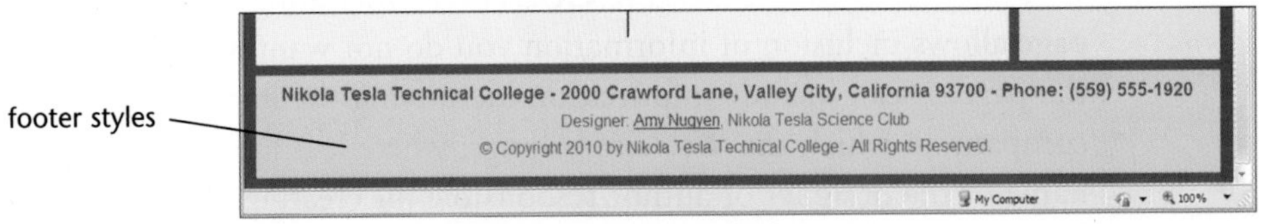

FIGURE 7.28 • The footer is formatted, and additional content has been added to it.

Changing the Page's Appearance

Some of the things you can do to give the page a different look and feel include adding borders, background images, and drop caps.

ADDING BORDERS AND BACKGROUND IMAGES Adding borders and background images can make your page's layout more dramatic. Adding borders to the layout divisions, however, requires that the heights and widths of their content areas be adjusted by an equal amount, if the layout is to be preserved. The positions or sizes of some of the other elements will also need to be adjusted, because their containing divisions will have less content area.

Add borders and background images to the "mast," "main," "side," and "footer" divisions:

1. In your text editor, save **scienceclub2.html** as **scienceclub3.html** in the styles-layout folder.
2. In your browser, open **scienceclub3.html**.
3. Add a 5-pixel border and a background image to the "mast" division, and reduce the width and height settings by 10 pixels to preserve the division's current dimensions:

```
#mast {
    position: relative;
    top: 10px;
    width: 970px;width: 960px;
    height: 140px;height: 130px;
    text-align: center;
    color: #ffcc00;
    background: #003399 url("images/back_bluewater.jpg");
    border: 5px #6699cc outset;
    }
```

4. Reduce the top padding of the H1 element and the "navbar" division by 5 pixels each to re-position them higher in the "mast" division (the content area that is now 10 pixels shorter):

```
#mast h1 {
    font-family: Arial, Helvetica, sans-serif;
    font-weight: bold;
    font-size: 54px;
    padding-top: 15px;padding-top: 10px;
    width: 800px;
    margin-left: auto;
    margin-right: auto;
    border-bottom: 3px red ridge;
    }
#navbar {
    position: absolute;
    top: 95px;
    padding-top: 5px; padding-top: 0;
    left: 0;
    width: 100%;
    text-align: center;
    font-family: Arial, Helvetica, sans-serif;
    font-weight: bold;
    height: 30px;
    }
```

5. Add borders and background images to the "main," "side," and "footer" divisions, and reduce the height and width of their content areas by 10 pixels:

```
#main {
    position: relative;
    top: 20px;
    width: 760px;width: 750px;
```

```
        height: 1340px;height: 1330px;
        background: #ffffcc url("images/back_parch.jpg");
        border: 5px #ffcc99 outset;
        }
[...]
#side {
        position: absolute;
        top: 160px;
        right: 0;
        width: 200px;width: 190px;
        height: 1340px;height: 1330px;
        background: #ccffff url("images/back_lightwater.jpg");
        border: 5px #99ccff outset;
        }
[...]
#footer {
        position: absolute;
        bottom: 0;
        width: 970px;width: 960px;
        height: 100px;width: 90px;
        margin-bottom: 10px;
        background: #ccffcc url("images/back_wall3.jpg");
        text-align: center;
        border: 5px #009999 outset;
        }
```

6. Adjust the left position of the "divider" line to move it 5 pixels to the left:

```
#divider {
        position: absolute;
        top: 85px;
        left: 375px;left: 370px;
        height: 1230px;
        width: 1px;
        border-right: 1px black solid;
        }
```

7. Shorten the size of the text input box for the search form, from 18 to 16, so it will fit inside the reduced width of the "side" division's content area (see Figure 7.29):

```
<div id="side">
<form id="search" method="post" action="/cgi-bin/searchsite.pl">
Search Tesla Tech:<br><input type="text" name="Search_String"
maxlength="75" size="18" size="16">
<input type="submit" value="Go">
</form>
```

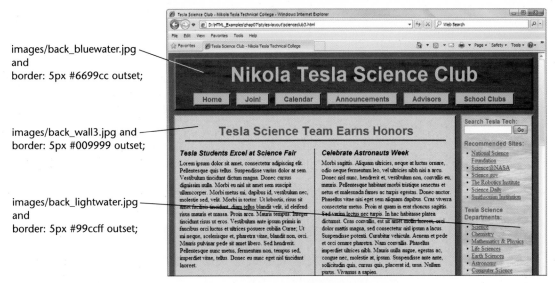

images/back_bluewater.jpg and border: 5px #6699cc outset;

images/back_wall3.jpg and border: 5px #009999 outset;

images/back_lightwater.jpg and border: 5px #99ccff outset;

FIGURE 7.29 • Borders and background images are added to the layout divisions.

TROUBLE *spot*

In the preceding code examples, 5-pixel borders are applied to the layout divisions (mast, main, side, and footer), which already have width and height attributes set for them. This will trigger the box model bug in Internet Explorer 5.5 for Windows. Because only about 1 percent of users still currently use that browser, no hacks or workarounds have been applied in this book's example code to address the box model bug. For guidance on using the box model hack and other workarounds, see "Compatibility Issues and Solutions" in Appendix C.

ADDING DROP CAPS Turning the first letter of an article into a **drop cap** can further highlight the start of the article.

Add drop caps to the "maincol1" and "maincol2" divisions:

1. Bracket the letters to be turned into drop caps with SPAN elements, assigned to the "drop" class:

```
<div id="main-col1">
<h2>Tesla Students Excel at Science Fair</h2>
<p><span class="drop">L</span>orem ipsum dolor sit amet,
consectetur adipiscing elit. [...]

<div id="main-col2">
<h2>Celebrate Astronauts Week</h2>
<p><span class="drop">M</span>orbi sagittis. Aliquam ultricies,
neque at luctus ornare, odio neque fermentum leo, vel ultricies
nibh nisi a arcu. [...]
```

2. Add a ".drop" style to the style sheet (see Figure 7.30):

```
#divider {
    position: absolute;
    top: 85px;
    left: 370px;
    height: 1230px;
    width: 1px;
    border-right: 1px black solid;
}
```

```
.drop {
    float: left;
    font-size: 230%;
    color: red;
    background: transparent;
    margin-bottom: -5px;
    margin-right: 5px;
}

/* Sidebar Styles */
```

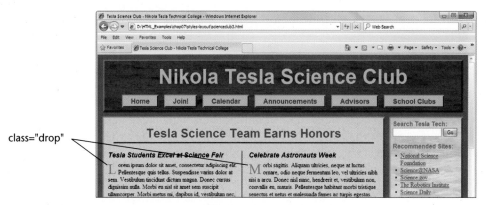

class="drop"

FIGURE 7.30 • Drop caps are added to the text columns.

A negative bottom margin (`margin-bottom: -7px;`) is used to cause the third line of text to wrap under the drop cap character. Otherwise, it is the fourth line that will wrap, leaving a blank space below the drop cap character.

CREATING FLUID MULTI-COLUMN LAYOUTS USING STYLES

The biggest criticism of using CSS for multi-column layouts has been that it is too difficult to create layouts featuring self-adjusting, equal-height columns, which are automatic when using tables for page layout.

Using Faux Columns

One technique using CSS to create self-adjusting, equal-height columns is commonly referred to as the **faux columns** technique. This technique involves using a background image on the BODY element, tiled only vertically, to simulate the look of self-adjusting, equal-height columns. The actual columns are then overlaid on top of the background-columns. Because the actual columns are transparent and without borders, you do not see that they have unequal heights. To learn more about using the faux columns technique, see the "Faux Columns" Wikipedia article at **en.wikipedia.org/wiki/Faux_columns**.

Using Display:Table Properties to Create Fluid Layouts

CSS has the ability to create layouts using self-adjusting, equal-height columns, without resorting to tricks like faux columns. Until recently, however, the ability has not been supported in the most widely used browser, Internet Explorer. The *display:table properties* (display:table, display:table-row, and display:table-cell) allow styling DIV elements so they emulate a table body, table row, or table cell and behave very much as though they were elements in an actual table.

NOTE

In the previous CSS code examples in this book, spaces have been inserted between a property and its value (`color: red`, for instance). This is optional in CSS, however. To facilitate readability, the display:table, display:table-row, and display:table-cell property:value pairs will be presented in this chapter without the inserted space. When referring to these as a group, the shorthand expression, "display:table properties," will be used.

Internet Explorer 7 and earlier versions of that browser, however, do not support the display:table properties, which means that Web pages coded using these property:value pairs degrade ungracefully in those browsers. Internet Explorer 8, however, does support them, bringing to that browser the capability of easily creating table-like layouts with self-adjusting, equal-height columns, without having to use tables. While the display:table properties still degrade ungracefully in earlier versions of Internet Explorer, those browsers now account for less than 35 percent of all browsers being used, and that percentage will rapidly shrink as Internet Explorer 8 is more widely adopted.

Included with the example files for this chapter is an example page layout, **fluid-layout. html**, which makes use of the display:table properties to create a multi-column layout featuring a masthead at the top; a footer at the bottom; and three equal-height, self-adjusting columns in between. The columns are composed of two fixed-width sidebar columns and a content column the width of which automatically adjusts relative to the width of the page. This allows for the easy creation of entirely fluid, multi-column page designs, using em measurements for text and self-adjusting widths and heights. To see how this works, open **fluid-layout.html** from the styles-layout folder in your browser and text editor (see Figures 7.31 and 7.32).

FIGURE 7.31 • A fluid multi-column layout is created using CSS.

FIGURE 7.32 • Using display:table, layouts with self-adjusting, equal-height columns are possible using CSS.

This example of creating a fluid page layout is organized just like a table, with a division with display:table set bracketing a division with display:table-row set, corresponding to the TABLE, TR, and TH/TD elements. This kind of layout is also called an **elastic layout**, since the layout can stretch vertically and/or horizontally to accommodate varying viewport widths, content lengths, and user-specified font sizes.

To alert users accessing the page using a version of Internet Explorer earlier than Version 8, a **conditional comment** is used to cause a message to be displayed to those users that they need to upgrade their browsers (see Figure 7.33).

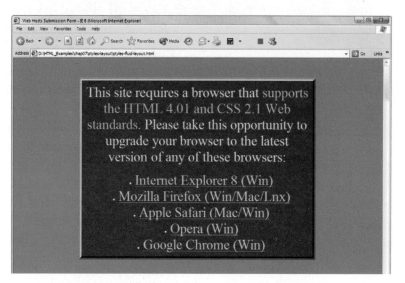

FIGURE 7.33 • A message is displayed alerting users of versions of Internet Explorer prior to Version 8 that they need to upgrade their browsers, as shown here in Internet Explorer 6.

Conditional comments are nested inside HTML comments and allow targeting content for specific versions of Internet Explorer. In the example file, the codes `<!--[if lt IE 8]>` and `<![endif]-->` cause nested elements and text to be displayed only in versions of Internet Explorer less than Version 8.

Visit the Internet Resource Center. To find examples or online resources that discuss using conditional comments to target content for specific versions of Internet Explorer, see Appendix C, *Cascading Style Sheets Sampler*, or visit this Chapter 7 section of this book's Internet Resource Center at **www.emcp.net/html2e**.

The current code demonstrates the use of the min-width property to ensure that columns do not collapse below a certain width. Some browsers such as Mozilla 1.7 or SeaMonkey, for instance, support the display:table property but do not recognize applying the min-width property to a table cell (whether created using tables or the display:table properties). The only way to get the layout to work in those browsers is to insert spacer images (spacer.gif) at the top of the left and right columns for which a width is set equal to that set by the min-width property. That is demonstrated in the example code, but is commented out, since only a very tiny percentage of users are using those browsers.

WORKING WITH EXTERNAL STYLE SHEETS

So far, all of the styles you have worked with have been set inline using the STYLE attribute or in an **internal style sheet** using the STYLE element. Alternatively, you can also use the LINK element or the **@import rule** to link to an **external style sheet**.

Advantages of Using External Style Sheets

External style sheets have a number of advantages:

- Styles in an external style sheet can be shared by more than one document.
- More than one style sheet can be linked, allowing modular external style sheets.
- Revising the layout and appearance of a Web site using an external style sheet can be done much faster than if every page had its own internal style sheet.
- An HTML file and external style sheet can be edited in different text editor windows, making scrolling between the content in the BODY element and an internal style sheet unnecessary.
- External style sheets can be linked that target specific media types, using the STYLE element's REL attribute or the @media rule, allowing the creation of special style sheets for printing, handheld devices, aural or Braille user agents, television sets, and more.

Using the LINK Element

The LINK element is an empty (or standalone) element that can be used in the HEAD element to link to external files, including external style sheet files. For instance, you could use the LINK element in scienceclub.html to link to an external style sheet, scienceclub.css, located in the same folder, in this manner:

```
<title>Tesla Science Club - Nikola Tesla Technical College
</title>
<link rel="stylesheet" type="text/css" href="scienceclub.css">
```

To change from using an internal to an external style sheet, copy all style rules between `<style type="text/css">` and `</style>`, paste them into a blank window in a text window, and then save it as an ASCII text file with a ,css extension.

Alternatively, you can use an @import rule to insert a link to an external style sheet inside an internal style sheet. You can also target specific media types, using the STYLE element's REL attribute or the @media rule, allowing the creation of special style sheets for printing, handheld devices, aural or Braille user agents, and more.

Visit the Internet Resource Center. There is much more to be understood about using styles to create multi-column page layouts than could be included in this chapter. To find online resources that discuss in more depth using fixed and fluid page layouts, faux columns, the display:table properties, external style sheets, and style sheets that target specific media types, see the Chapter 7 section of this book's Internet Resource Center at **www.emcp.net/html2e.**

CHAPTER SUMMARY

You should now be familiar with creating multi-column Web sites using frames, tables, and styles. You should also be cognizant of some of the pros and cons of using each of these solutions. You should be aware of steps that can be taken to reduce but not eliminate usability issues when using frames and accessibility issues when using tables for layout.

You should have created one CSS-only, multi-column layout using positioned divisions in this chapter, which is compatible with all recent browsers. You should also have reviewed another layout using display:table, display:table-row, and display:table-cell, that creates a table-like three-column layout with self-adjusting, equal-height columns, which is compatible with all current browsers.

You should understand how to use a variety of CSS selectors and properties to apply styles to HTML documents. You should also understand how to create and link to an external style sheet.

Code Review

`<frameset>...` `</frameset>`	FRAMESET element. Specifies a set of frames (or frameset), arrayed in columns and/or rows, and the files to be displayed in them. Replaces the BODY element.
`<frameset cols=` `"150,*">`	COLS attribute. Specifies frameset is composed of two columns, the first 150 pixels wide and the second expandable (through the use of the * wildcard) to fill available horizontal space in the viewport. Percentage values can also be used (`cols="25%,75%"`, for instance.
`<frameset rows=` `"25,*">`	ROWS attribute. Specifies frameset is composed of two rows, the first 25 pixels high and the second expandable (through the use of the * wildcard) to fill available vertical space in the viewport. Percentage values can also be used (`rows="15%,85%"`, for instance.
`<frame src="url"`	FRAME element. Defines a frame within a frameset, specifying the url of a file to be displayed in the frame.
`<frame name=` `"framename"`	NAME attribute. Assigns a name to a frame (`name="main"`, for instance), so it can used to target (or control) content in that frame from a link in another frame.
`<a target=` `"framename"`	TARGET attribute. Opens a linked file in a targeted frame with the same frame name as the TARGET attribute value. TARGET and NAME attribute values are case-sensitive and must match exactly.
`<frame scrolling=` `"no"`	SCROLLING attribute. In the FRAME element, turns off the display of scroll bars within a frame, even if content extends beyond the frame. A value of **yes** turns on the display of scroll bars, even if content does not extend beyond the frame. The default is **auto**, which turns on display of scroll bars only if content extends beyond the frame.
`<frame marginheight=` `"n"`	MARGINHEIGHT attribute. Sets the top and bottom margin heights in a frame in pixels. `marginheight="0"` sets the margin heights to zero.

`<frame marginwidth="n">`	MARGINWIDTH attribute. Sets the left and right margin widths in a frame in pixels. `marginwidth="0"` sets the margin widths to zero.
`<p style="margin-top: 0">`	Inline style that can be used in to turn off the default top margin that current and many recent browsers insert when a P element (or other block element) is the first block element in a frame.
`<noframes>...</noframes>`	NOFRAMES element. Allows presenting of information, and a link or links to access other pages in the site, to early browsers that do not support frames, as well as to search engine robots. Browsers that support frames ignore NOFRAMES content.
`font-size: 24px ! important`	`! important` declaration. Can be appended to a style declaration to give it priority over other style declarations without `! important` set. A user's declaration of importance, set in a user-created stylesheet, has priority over an author's.
`h1 {property declarations}`	Type (or simple) selector. Applies property declarations to a single type element (the H1 element, in this case).
`h1, h2, h3 {property declarations}`	Group selector. Applies property declarations to a group of elements (in a comma-separated list, listing the H1, H2, and H3 elements, in this case).
`h1 em {property declarations}.`	Descendant selector. Applies property declarations to an element that is the descendant (child, grandchild, and so on) of another element. In this case, property declarations are applied to any EM element that is a descendant (nested within) the H1 element.
`a:link	a:visited	a:active	a:hover`	Anchor pseudo-classes. Apply property declarations to links in specific states (unvisited, visited, active, and hovered).
`*	*p	*.main`	Universal selector. Universally applies property declarations, in this case, to all elements, all P elements, and all elements assigned to the "main" class.
`p > em`	Child selector. Applies property declarations to an element that is the child of another element (nested directly within it). In this case, property declarations are applied to any EM element that is a child of P element.
`td :first-child`	First child selector. Applies property declarations to an element that is the first child of another element (preceded by no other element).
`<table width="100%">`	WIDTH attribute. In the TABLE element, sets the width of a table at 100 percent of the width of the viewport.
`<table border="1">`	BORDER attribute. In the TABLE element, sets a one-pixel border around a table and its cells.
`<td width="150">`	WIDTH attribute. In any TD or TH element, sets the column in which the cell resides to 150 pixels. A percentage value (`width="20%"` can also be used.
`<td valign="top">`	VALIGN attribute. In a TD or TH element, aligns content vertically with the top of the cell. Other values are **middle** (the default), **bottom**, and **baseline**.

`<td class="classname"`	CLASS attribute. Assigns a TD element, in this case, to the a class (`class="side"`, for instance), so that a class selector can be used to apply styles to it (`.side {property declarations}`, for instance).
`.side {padding-left: 5px}`	The padding-left property. In this instance, applies five pixels of padding to the left side of any element assigned to the "side" class.
`.main {padding-right: 10px}`	The padding-right property. In this instance, applies five pixels of padding to the right side of any element assigned to the "main" class.
`border-collapse: collapse; border-spacing: 0;`	When applied to the TABLE element, collapses the borders around table cells to a single border between table cells.
`body {margin: 0 0 15em 0}`	Sets the top, right, bottom, and left margins of the body element to zero, zero, 15 ems, and zero.
`float: left`	Floats an element on the left margin of the containing element. Replaces `align="left"` in the IMG element. Other values are **none** (the default), **right**, and **inherit**.
`clear: left`	Causes an element to clear a left-floating element (wrapping to the left margin). Replaces `clear="left"` in the BR element. Other values are: **none** (the default), **right**, **both**, and **inherent**.
`<div>...</div>`	DIV element. Creates a division to which styles can be applied, including for layout.
`<div id="identity"`	ID attribute. Assigns a unique identity to an element, in this case, the DIV element, so that styles can be applied to just that element (`id="page"`, for instance).
`#identity {property declarations}`	ID selector. Applies property declarations to an element with a unique identity (`#page`, for instance).
`position: relative`	Position property. A **relative** value positions an element relative to the elements current position.
`margin-left: auto; margin-right: auto;`	Centers an element in the viewport, if a width has been set for it that is less than the viewport's width. Replaces `align="center"`
`position: absolute`	Position property. A **absolute** value positions an element in relation to the top, left, right, or bottom sides of a containing element that has already been positioned, or of the BODY element.
`top: 10px`	When used with `position: relative`, positions an element ten pixels down from its current position. When used with `position: absolute`, positions an element ten pixels down from the top side of a containing element that has already been positioned, or of the BODY element.
`right: 0`	When used with `position: absolute`, positions an element zero pixels from the right side of a containing element that has already been positioned, or of the BODY element.
`bottom: 0`	When used with `position: absolute`, positions an element zero pixels from the bottom side of a containing element that has already been positioned, or of the BODY element.

`text-decoration: none`	When applied to the A element, or any of the anchor pseudo-classes, turns off display of the underline under hypertext links.
`border: 4px #ffcc00 outset`	Draws a four-pixel border, with #ffcc00 as the color, in an "outset" border style. Other border styles include: **none** (the default), **solid, double, dashed, dotted, outset, inset, ridge, groove**, and **hidden**.
`/* comment */`	Format for including a comment in a style sheet that will be ignored by a browser.
`border-bottom: 3px maroon ridge`	Draws a three-pixel border, with maroon as the color, in a "ridge" border style.
`display:table`	Causes an element to be treated the same as a TABLE element.
`display:table-row`	Causes an element to be treated the same as a TR (Table Row) element.
`display:table-cell`	Causes an element to be treated the same as a table cell (TD or TH element).
`<link rel= "stylesheet" type="text/css" href="url.css"`	LINK element. In the HEAD element, an empty (or standalone) element that can be used to link to an external style sheet. The REL and TYPE attributes identify that it is a CSS style sheet that is being linked. The HREF attribute identifies the location and file name of the style sheet, which must have a .css file extension.

KEY TERMS

For a review of the key terms bolded in this chapter, visit the Chapter 7 section of this book's Internet Resource Center at **www.emcp.net/html2e**. A complete glossary appears at the end of the book.

ONLINE QUIZ

Go to the Chapter 7 section of this book's Internet Resource Center at **www.emcp.net/html2e/**, and take the online self-check quiz.

REVIEW EXERCISES

This section provides some hands-on review exercises to reinforce the information and material included within this chapter. Review using the elements, attributes, styles, and other features that were covered in this chapter, checking your results in your browser and troubleshooting any errors:

1. In the frames-layout folder, experiment further with creating different kinds of frameset layouts.
   A. Save **twocol_frame.html** as **twocol_frame-review.html**, and use that file to review revising a two-column frameset page. Change the left sidebar into a right sidebar. Revise the column settings. Create different content pages, and link to them through the FRAME element and sidebar.html.
   B. Save **tworow_frame.html** as **tworow_frame-review.html**, and use that file to practice revising a two-row frameset page. Change the top-bar frame into

a bottom-bar frame. Revise the row settings. Create different content pages, and link to them through the FRAME element and topbar.html.

C.   Save **combo_frame.html** as **combo_frame-review.html**, and use that file to practice revising a frameset page that contains both columns and rows. Change the top-banner row into a bottom-banner row. Change the left sidebar column into a right sidebar column. Create different banner and content pages, and link to them through the FRAME element and sidebar2.html.

D.   Save **framestart_ex.html** as **framestart-review.html**, and use that file to practice creating multi-column, multi-row, or combination row-column frameset pages from scratch. Use NAME attributes to name frames and TARGET attributes in links (in a sidebar or topbar menu) to open pages in the targeted frames.

2. In the tables-layout folder, experiment further with creating multi-column layouts using tables.

A.   Save **mercury3.html** as **mercury3-review.html**, and use that file to practice revising a two-column page created using tables. Change the width of the sidebar column. Change the sidebar column from a left sidebar to a right sidebar column. Change the left and right padding amounts for the sidebar and main content columns that are set in the style sheet. Add a third column to the layout.

B.   Save **mercury3_ex.html** as **mercury3-review2.html**, and use that file to practice using tables to create multi-column layouts from scratch. Create your own original content, including a main content column and a sidebar menu. Create links in the sidebar menu that jump to destination anchors in the main content column.

3. In the styles-layout folder, experiment further with creating multi-column layouts using styles.

A.   Save **scienceclub.html** as **scienceclub-review.html**, and use that file to practice revising a basic multi-column page layout using styles. Keeping the width of the page at 970 pixels (set in the #page style), practice changing the dimensions of the layout elements, changing the height or width dimensions of the masthead, main content, sidebar, and footer layout boxes. Adjust any properties that affect position, so the layout boxes are properly aligned with each other and are separated by the same amount of spacing. Adjust the height of the "page" division so changed heights for the other layout divisions fit within it.

B.   Save **scienceclub2.html** as **scienceclub2-review.html**, and use that file to practice formatting the content of a multi-column page layout created using styles. Change the formatting of the masthead (H1 element and "navbar" division), main content area (headline, newspaper columns, and divider), sidebar (headings and rollover links), and footer.

C.   Save **scienceclub3.html** as **scienceclub3-review.html**, and use that file to practice embellishing a multi-column layout using styles. Change the background images set for the masthead, main content area, sidebar, and footer. You can find additional background images in the art folder that is included with the example files (if you downloaded and extracted the art example files, art_examples_win.zip, for instance). You can also do a search for "background images" on the Web that you can use. Adjust foreground colors and background colors to match. Change the color and type of borders. Change the font and color of the drop caps. Look in the images folder in the styles-layout folder for images that you can use to practice floating images in the text columns.

D.   Save **scienceclub_ex.html** as **multicol-review.html**, and use that file to practice creating a multi-column layout using styles from scratch. Do not just replicate the layout example from this chapter, but create a different layout, such as one with the sidebar on the left and the main content area on the right. Draw your layout on paper, and then see if you can recreate it.

WEB-BASED LEARNING ACTIVITIES

The following Web-based learning activities can help you to further extend your learning and shore up your understanding of specific topic-areas:

*   Visit the Chapter 7 section of this book's Internet Resource Center at **www.emcp.net/html2e** to find online resources that you can use to further investigate and explore the topics and subjects covered in this chapter. You can also find all Web sites cited in this chapter's notes listed there.
*   Further research a specific topic introduced in this chapter using Google (**www.google.com/**), Yahoo! (**www.yahoo.com/**), Wikipedia (**www.wikipedia.org/**), Open Directory Project (**www.dmoz.org/**), or other online sources. Some topics covered in this chapter that you can further research include:
    *   Accessibility and usability issues with using frames for layout.
    *   Accessibility issues with using tables for layout.
    *   Pros and cons of using positioned divisions to create fixed (pixel-perfect) layouts using styles.
    *   Pros and cons of using the display:table properties to create fluid layouts using styles.
    *   Pros and cons of using external style sheets to control the appearance of a multi-page Web site.
*   Use the results of your online research into a particular topic to:
    *   Write a review to be read in front of your classmates.
    *   Write a report that can be read by your classmates.
    *   Design a diagram, chart, or other graphic that illustrates a key topic or concept.
    *   Create a presentation using PowerPoint (or other software) that can be shared with your classmates.
    *   Give a stand-up presentation to your classmates.
    *   Team up with one or more classmates to give a group presentation to your classmates.

FINAL PROJECTS

These projects can be done in class, in a computer lab, or at home. Use the skills you have developed in this and the previous chapters to create any of the following projects. In your project, demonstrate the correct use of the following HTML and CSS features covered in this chapter:

*   Creation of a Web site with a multi-column layout using tables and styles or using styles alone.

- If creating a Web site layout using tables, rely on styles as much as possible to control the appearance of the layout and its contents. Avoid using deprecated elements, such as the FONT element, but use styles to set font sizes, colors, and faces. Do not use the CELLPADDING or CELLSPACING attributes, but rely on styles to control padding within and spacing between cells, using the border-collapse and border-spacing properties to collapse borders between cells to a single border.
- If creating a Web site layout using styles alone, demonstrate an ability to create a page layout using either 1) positioned divisions or 2) the display:table, display:table-row, and display:table-cell property:value pairs.
- Do not just replicate a layout demonstrated in this chapter, but create an original layout of your own invention. Use the Web as a resource to find ideas for layouts that you can adapt or emulate. There are many different kinds of page layouts—you are limited only by your imagination.
- In the project, apply lessons learned in this and and the previous chapters of this book. Demonstrate skill in applying many of the features covered in this book, such as font sizes and faces, colors and backgrounds, menus and destination anchors, hover links and buttons, floating images, image links and thumbnail images, image maps, banner and logo images, graphic buttons and rules, unordered or ordered lists, icon link lists, and so on.
- Design at least three subpages with real content (not just dummy content or Lorum Ipsum text) that are linked from your site's front page, including an "About Me" page that introduces yourself and discusses your interest in Web design. Your front page and subpages should share a common design and visual theme.

Project 1. Create an informational or topical Web site.

Design a Web site using a multi-column layout that addresses a subject or topic that interests you and about which you have ideas, knowledge, or understanding you want to share.

Project 2. Create an advocacy Web site.

Design a Web site using a multi-column layout that addresses an issue or advocates a position on an issue about which you feel strongly.

Project 3. Create a social commentary Web site.

Design a Web site using a multi-column layout that discusses and illustrates a social phenomenon or trend that you believe is significant. This can be an analytical, humorous, or critical site but should not be an advocacy site.

Project 4. Create a commercial Web site.

Design a commercial Web site using a multi-column layout that promotes and markets a fictional product or service. Look at commercial Web sites on the Web to get ideas. Create a design and use a color scheme that is appropriate to the product or service being promoted.

Project 5. Create a technology Web site.

Design a Web site using a multi-column layout that discusses a technology that interests you or about which you have knowledge, or have done research, that you want to share.

Project 6. Create a family history Web site.

Design a Web site using a multi-column layout that presents information about your family history, including family tree, background, stories, trivia, photographs, and other information. Do not include information about living persons.

Project 7. Create some other kind of Web site.

Design some other kind of Web site that has not been described here using a multi-column layout. Make it interesting. Have fun.

APPENDIX A

HTML Quick Reference

This HTML quick reference consists of two parts. The first part includes a listing in alphabetical order of all of the standard elements of HTML 4.01 and their most commonly used attributes, as well as elements included in HTML 5. The second part covers generic and other attributes that are applied to many elements.

Elements and attributes first standardized in HTML 3.2 and 4, marked with "3.2" and "4.0," should be supported by all recent browsers. HTML 5 elements are marked with "5.0;" "Flow" content includes both block and inline elements. "Boolean" attributes are "true" if present, "false" if absent; expanded form (`selected="selected"`, instead of `selected`) is required in XHTML.

This reference can be used for both HTML (4 and 5) and XHTML 1 (1.0 and 1.1). All code examples are presented following HTML syntax and rules. See Appendix B, *HTML-to-XHTML Conversion Chart*, for a guide to creating documents compatible with both HTML and XHTML.

NOTE — HTML 4.01 is supported in all current browsers. HTML 5, however, is still a "draft" specification that is only partially supported by current browsers. Internet Explorer 8 does not support HTML 5, although it recognizes its DocType (<!DocType html>), which triggers IE 8's default standards mode. If you want to experiment with HTML 5, you should use the Opera browser, which currently provides the fullest support for HTML 5.

HTML ELEMENTS

A (Anchor)	**Type:** Inline/Container	**Content:** Inline
Attributes	name="*destination anchor name*"	See note
	href="*URL and/or fragment identifier*"	See note
	target="*frame name*"	Optional
Note: Either NAME or HREF is required.		
Example	`<a href="http://somesite.emcp.com/somedir/somepage.html">Go to my page.</a>`	

ABBR (Abbreviation) (4.0)   **Type:** Inline/Container   **Content:** Inline

Specifies the expanded form of an abbreviation. If the letters of a shortened expression are individually pronounced, such as ABC, FBI, BBC, NCAA, NAACP, WWW, CSS, and so on, it is an abbreviation.

Attributes   `title="expanded term"`

Example   `<p>J. Edgar Hoover was the first Director of the <abbr title="Federal Bureau of Investigation">FBI</abbr>.`

ACRONYM (4.0)   **Type:** Inline/Container   **Content:** Inline

Specifies the expanded form of an acronym. If the shortened expression is pronounced as a word, such as NATO, CERN, radar, laser, SOHO, SCUBA, and so on, it is an acronym. **(Obsolete in HTML 5.)**

Attributes   `title="expanded term"`

Example   `<p>The World Wide Web was invented by Tim Berners-Lee at <acronym title="Conseil European pour la Recherche Nucleaire/European Organization for Nuclear Research">CERN</acronym>.</p>`

ADDRESS   **Type:** Block/Container   **Content:** Inline

Identifies the author/owner of a Web page, along with a means to contact or provide feedback, such as a link to a contact page.

Note: The ALIGN attribute is not a legal attribute for the ADDRESS element, although many browsers recognize it. Block elements are not allowed within the ADDRESS element (although browsers do not care).

Example
```
<address>
Roger Dodger<br>
E-mail: <a href="mailto:rogdodg@blutto.emcp.com">rogdodg@blutto.emcp.com
</a>
</address>>
```

APPLET (3.2) (Deprecated)   **Type:** Inline/Container   **Content:** Block/Inline

Inserts a Java applet inline within an HTML document. **(Obsolete in HTML 5.)**

Attributes		
`code="applet class file"`	See Note
`object="applet class resource"` (4.0)	See Note
`alt="alternative text description"`	Recommended
`codebase="URL"`	Optional
`archive="comma-delimited list of URLs"` (4.0)	Optional
`width="n	n%"`	Optional
`height="n	n%"`	Optional
`name="applet name"`	Optional
`align="top|middle|bottom|left|right|center"`	Optional
`hspace="n"`	Optional
`vspace="n"`	Optional

Note: Either CODE or OBJECT is required. If both are present, they must reference the same applet class file name.

PARAM (3.2) (Deprecated in APPLET)   **Type:** Inline/Empty   **Content:** N/A

When nested inside an APPLET element, passes parameters to a Java applet. Also can be nested inside an OBJECT element; *see also* OBJECT.

| *Attributes* | name="*parameter name*" | Required |
| | value="*parameter value*" | Required |

Note: The NAME attribute value must start with a letter (A-Z or a-z), with the remainder of the value composed of letters, numbers, hyphens, or periods.

AREA (3.2)

See MAP.

ARTICLE (5.0)   **Type:** Section/Container   **Content:** Flow

A section in a document or page that stands independently on its own, such as a newsletter "article," for instance. Can also be used to mark up Web log (blog) entries, forum posts, user-submitted comments, or other independent content items.

ASIDE (5.0)   **Type:** Section/Container   **Content:** Flow

A section in a document or page that stands apart from surrounding content but is not independent of it, such as a sidebar.

AUDIO (5.0)   **Type:** Embedded/Container   **Content:** SOURCE/Transparent

A sound or audio stream. Content can be nested for display in non-supporting browsers that will be ignored by supporting browsers.

Attributes	src="*URL*"	Recommended
	autoplay	Boolean
	loop	Boolean
	controls	Boolean

See also: VIDEO (5.0).

SOURCE (5.0)   **Type:** None/Empty   **Content:** N/A

Specifies multiple media resources (audio files, for instance) for media elements (AUDIO or VIDEO).

| *Attributes* | src="*URL*" | Recommended |
| | type="*MIME type*" | Optional |

B (Bold)   **Type:** Inline/Container   **Content:** Inline

Specifies that nested text should be bolded. *See also* EM (Emphasis), STRONG (Strong Emphasis), and I (Italic).

Example   `<p>It is <b>important</b> that assignments be turned in on time.</p>`

BASE

See HEAD.

BASEFONT (3.2) (Deprecated)
Type: Inline/Empty   **Content:** N/A

Sets font characteristics for following text. BASEFONT is not implemented in many recent browsers and should be avoided. *See also* FONT. **(Obsolete in HTML 5.)**

Attributes	`size="1	2	3	4	5	6	7"`	Optional
	`color="color name	RGB color code"` (4.0)	Optional
	`face="font name	font name list"` (4.0)	Optional

BB (Browser Button) (5.0)
Type: Inline/Container   **Content:** FLOW, LI

A browser command that the user can invoke.

| *Attributes* | `type="makeapp"` | Recommended |

Example	`<ul>`
	`<li><a href="download-faq.html">Download Frequently Asked Questions</a>`
	`<li><bb type="makeapp">Standalone application download</bb>`
	`</ul>`

BDO (4.0)
Type: Inline/Container   **Content:** Inline

Changes the direction in which nested text is displayed.

| *Attributes* | `dir="ltr|rtl"` | Required |
| | `lang="language code"` | Optional |

BIG (3.2)
Type: Inline/Container   **Content:** Inline

Increases the size of nested text by one font size. The sizes correspond to the seven font sizes that can be set with the FONT and BASEFONT elements. *See also* SMALL. **(Obsolete in HTML 5.)**

| *Example* | `<p>In case of a fire alarm, walk, don't run, to the nearest <big>Exit` |
| | `</big> sign.</p>` |

BLOCKQUOTE
Type: Block/Container   **Content:** Block/SCRIPT

Displays a long quotation as an indented block.

| *Attributes* | `cite="URL"` | Optional |

Example	`<p>When starting a chess game, one should keep in mind the following`
	`basic principles, enumerated by the great American Grandmaster, Frank J.`
	`Marshall, in his book, <cite>Chess Step by Step</cite>:`
	`<blockquote>`
	`<p>In selecting a Sphere of Action, always move the pieces where they`
	`will command the greatest number of squares, have the greatest freedom`
	`of action, where they cannot be readily attacked or driven away, and`
	`where they will restrict or delay the opponent's development.</p>`
	`</blockquote>`

BODY
Type: Container   **Content:** Block

In a non-frameset page, one of two elements (along with HEAD) that is nested directly inside the HTML element. Both the start tag and end tag are optional in HTML 4.01. **(The following attributes are all obsolete in HTML 5.)**

Attributes	`text="color name|RGB color code"` (Deprecated)	Optional
	`link="color name|RGB color code"` (Deprecated)	Optional
	`vlink="color name|RGB color code"` (Deprecated)	Optional
	`alink="color name|RGB color code"` (Deprecated)	Optional
	`bgcolor="color name|RGB color code"` (Deprecated)	Optional
	`background="image URL"` (Deprecated)	Optional

Example
```
<body text="navy" link="red" vlink="#666600" alink="#666600"
bgcolor="#ffffcc" background="images/back_light.jpg">
```

BR (Break)   **Type:** Inline/Empty   **Content:** N/A

Causes a line break to be displayed.

Attributes	`clear="left|right|all|`**`none`**`"` (Deprecated)	Optional

Note: The CLEAR attribute causes text flowing around a floating image to move down until the left, right, or both margins are clear (not obstructed by the floating image).

Example
```
<h2>From "Auguries of Innocence" by William Blake:</h2>
<blockquote>
<p>To see a World in a Grain of Sand<br>
And a Heaven in a Wild Flower,<br>
Hold Infinity in the palm of your hand<br>
And Eternity in an hour.</p>
</blockquote>
```

BUTTON (4.0)

See FORM.

CANVAS (5.0)   **Type:** Embedded/Container   **Content:** Transparent

A resolution-independent bitmap canvas for rendering graphs or other graphics. Content can be nested for display in non-supporting browsers that will be ignored by supporting browsers. Used in conjunction with the SCRIPT element.

Attributes	`height="pixels"`	Optional
	`width="pixels"`	Optional

CAPTION (3.2)

See TABLE.

CENTER (3.2) (Deprecated)   **Type:** Block/Container   **Content:** Block/Inline

Centers nested text or elements horizontally on the page. In HTML 3.2 and HTML 4, the CENTER element is equivalent to a DIV element with an `align="center"` attribute set. **(Obsolete in HTML 5.)**

Example
```
<center>
<h2>Announcement:</h2>
<p>You can sign up for volunteer positions starting on Friday at 8:00
a.m.</p>
</center>
```

CITE   **Type:** Inline/Container   **Content:** Inline

Indicates that nested text is a citation of a source. Text nested in the CITE element is generally displayed in italics. EM or I can be used to achieve the same effect.

| *Example* | `<p>"There is no safe trusting to dictionaries and definitions," as Charles Lamb stressed, in "Popular Fallacies," <cite>Essays of Elia</cite>.` |

CODE (Computer Code)   Type: Inline/Container   Content: Inline

Indicates that nested text is a fragment of computer (or program) code. Text nested in the CODE element is generally displayed in a monospaced font.

| *Example* | `<p>Start by declaring a variable that sets a starting value for the count: <code>var count = 1;</code>.</p>` |

COL (Column) (4.0)

See Table.

COLGROUP (Column Group) (4.0)

See Table.

COMMAND (5.0)   Type: Phrasing/Empty   Content: N/A

A command that can be invoked by a user using an icon, radio button, or check box.

Attributes	`type="command/radio	checkbox"`	Optional
	`label="command name"`	Optional
	`icon="URL"`	Optional
	`disabled`	Boolean
	`checked`	Boolean
	`radiogroup="radiogroup name"`	w/type="radio"

DATAGRID (5.0)   Type: Interactive/Container   Content: Flow

Interactive tree, list, or tabular data. Can contain a TABLE, SELECT, or DATALIST element, and other flow elements.

Attributes	`multiple`	Boolean
	`disabled`	Boolean
	`class="pre-set values"`	Optional

Note: For a list of pre-set class values for this element and their effects, see the HTML 5 specification at **www.w3.org/html/wg/html5/**.

DATALIST (5.0)

See FORM.

DD (Definition Data)

See DL (Definition List).

DEL (Delete) (4.0)   Type: Inline/Container   Content: Inline

Marks nested text as a deletion. In browsers that support this element, nested text is generally displayed as strikeout text (with a line drawn through it). STRIKE and S also can be used to display strikeout text, with STRIKE being the most widely supported. *See also* INS (Insert).

| *Example* | `<h1><del>My </del>Frequently Asked Questions Page</h1>` |

DETAILS (5.0)   **Type:** Interactive/Container   **Content:** LEGEND/Flow

Additional details that the user can obtain.

Attributes   open   Boolean

Note: First child must be the LEGEND element, which can then be followed by flow content. If an OPEN attribute is present, the details are shown by default; if not present, they are hidden. A browser should provide a means for the user to open or close the display of details.

LEGEND (4.0)   **Type:** None/Container   **Content:** Inline (Phrasing)

If nested at the start of a DETAILS element, provides a summary. If not present, a browser should provide a default legend ("Details," for instance).

DFN (Definition) (3.2)   **Type:** Inline/Container   **Content:** Inline

Marks nested text as the defining instance of a term. Nested text is generally displayed in italics, but some earlier browsers might bold it.

Example
```
<p>JavaScript is an <dfn>object-oriented</dfn> scripting language, which
means that when you work with JavaScript, you are primarily involved in
defining and manipulating objects.</p>
```

DIALOG (5.0)   **Type:** Container   **Content:** DT/DD

Contains a dialog or conversation. Can be used in marking up a screenplay, for instance. DT elements indicate speakers, and DD elements indicate dialog.

Example
```
<dialog>
<dt>Estragon
<dd>Let's go.
<dt>Vladimir
<dd>We can't.
<dt>Estragon
<dd>Why not?
<dt>Vladimir
<dd>We're waiting for Godot.
</dialog>
```

DIR (Directory List) (Deprecated)   **Type:** Block/Container   **Content:** Block

The DIR element was originally intended for displaying multi-column directory lists, but this was never implemented in browsers. The UL element produces exactly the same result in all browsers and should be used instead. *See also* UL (Unordered List). **(Obsolete in HTML 5.)**

DIV (Division) (3.2)   **Type:** Block/Container   **Content:** Inline/Block

Marks a division within a document (a document division).

Note: The ALIGN attribute is the only HTML formatting that can be applied to a DIV element. All other formatting must be applied using an inline style (using the STYLE attribute), embedded style sheet (the STYLE element), or externally linked style sheet (using the LINK element). The **justify** value is not allowed in XHTML.

Example
```
<div align="center">
<h1>Causes of the American Revolution</h1>
<h2>by William Jefferson</h2>
</div>
```

DL (Definition List)
Type: Block/Container   **Content:** Block

Designates that nested text is a definition list (or glossary). Nested DT (Definition Term) and DD (Definition Data) elements designate the terms and definitions.

Attributes   compact (Deprecated)   Optional

Note: The COMPACT attribute is a hint to a browser that a definition list can be displayed in a more compact way. Browsers that support this, such as Internet Explorer 6, for instance, display the DT and DD elements on the same line, as long as the DT text does not include more than four characters. Most browsers, however, ignore the COMPACT element, so it is best avoided.

DT (Definition Term)
Type: Block/Container   **Content:** Inline

Designates nested text as a term in a definition list. The end tag is optional.

DD (Definition Data)
Type: Block/Container   **Content:** Inline/Block

Designates nested text as a definition in a definition list. The DD element is generally indented in from the left margin. The end tag is optional.

Example
```
<dl>
<dt>crippleware
<dd>A form of shareware software program in which one or more key
functions have been crippled.
<dt>demoware
<dd>A form of shareware software program that is distributed for
demonstration purposes only, usually with an evaluation period, after
which the software stops functioning.
</dl>
```

EM (Emphasis)
Type: Inline/Container   **Content:** Inline

Marks nested text as emphasized, which is displayed in italics in all browsers. Alternatively, the I (Italics) element can be used to achieve the same result. *See also* STRONG (Strong Emphasis), I (Italic), and B (Bold).

Example
```
<p>When moving, it is very <em>important</em> to submit a Change of
Address form at the post office.</p>
```

EMBED (5.0)
Type: Embedded/Empty   **Content:** N/A

Embeds plug-in content, including audio, video, animation, and interactive content (such as Adobe Flash).

Attributes

src="URL"	Required
type="mime-type"	Recommended
height="n"	Optional
width="n"	Optional
autostart="**true**|false"	Optional
loop="true|**false**"	Optional
hidden="true|**false**"	Optional
alt="alternative content"	Optional

Example
```
<p><embed src="anthem.wav" type="audio/wav" height="100" width="200">
</p>
```

EVENT-SOURCE (5.0) **Type:** Metadata/Phrasing/Empty **Content:** NA

Specifies a source for server-generated events.

Attributes   `src="URL"`   Required

Note: SRC must specify a URL that points to a resource using the text/event-stream format.

FIELDSET (4.0)

See FORM.

FIGURE (5.0) **Type:** Section/Container **Content:** LEGEND/Flow

Defines a figure that is apart from normal document flow. The LEGEND element can be nested before or after content to provide a caption.

Example
```
<p>For an example of an Impressionist work in pastel, see Figure 9.</p>
<figure id="9">
<img src="blue-dancers.png" alt="Blue Dancers, Impressionist work in
pastel, by Edgar Degas" width="100" height="135">
<legend>Figure 9. Blue Dancers by Edgar Degas</legend>
</figure>
```

FONT (3.2) (Deprecated) **Type:** Inline/Container **Content:** Inline

Designates font characteristics, including size, color, and face, that are to be applied to nested text.
(Obsolete in HTML 5, except for WYSIWYG editors.)

Attributes   `size="n[1|2|3|4|5|6|7] or +n|-n"`   See Note
                    `color="color name|RGB color code"`   Optional
                    `face="font name|font name list"`   Optional

Note: The default font size is equivalent to `size="3"`, unless it has been reset by a preceding BASEFONT element or a bracketing FONT element. A + or - sign preceding the size number designates a font size that is relative to the default font size.

Example   `<h1><font size="7" color="blue" face="Arial">Upcoming Schedule</font>`
                 `</h1>`

FOOTER (5.0) **Type:** Section/Container **Content:** Flow

Defines a footer providing information for a document or section, identifying the author, owner, and/or publisher, copyright data, related links, contact information, and so on. Contact information should be nested in an ADDRESS element.

Example
```
<footer>
<address>
<a href="./">The Eberhard Group</a><br>
Email: <a href="mailto:info@eberhard-group.com"> info@eberhard-group.
com</a>
</address>
<p>&copy; Copyright 2009 by The Eberhard Group.</p>
</footer>
```

Note: The FOOTER element cannot contain heading content (H1, H2, etc.), sectioning content (DIV, SECTION, ARTICLE, HEADER, ASIDE, etc.), or other FOOTER elements.

FORM
Type: Block/Container   **Content:** Block

Designates that nested elements are part of a form.

Attributes		
	`action="URL"`	Required
	`method="get|post"`	Optional
	`enctype="content type"`	Optional

Note: The ACTION attribute should specify an HTTP URL; behavior of user agents resulting from use of non-HTTP URLs (such as a mailto URL) is undefined. For user-input forms, use the **post** value with the METHOD attribute.

INPUT
Type: Inline/Empty   **Content:** N/A

Defines various input controls that can be included in forms, including text boxes, radio buttons, check boxes, and more.

Attributes		
	`type="text|password|checkbox|radio|submit` `|reset|file|hidden|image|button"`	See Note 1
	`name="control name"`	See Note 1
	`value="initial value"`	See Note 1
	`size="n"`	See Note 1
	`maxlength="n"`	See Note 1
	`checked`	See Note 1
	`src="URL"`	
	`alt="description"-`	See Note 1
	`disabled`	Optional
	`readonly`	Optional
	`autocomplete="on|off"` (5.0)	Optional
	`list="DATALIST ID value"` (5.0)	Optional
	`required` (5.0)	Optional
	`multiple` (5.0)	Optional
	`pattern="expression"` (5.0)	Optional
	`min="n"` (5.0)	Optional
	`max="n"` (5.0)	Optional
	`step="floating point number|any"` (5.0)	See Note 2
	`placeholder="hint"`	Optional

Note 1: The TYPE attribute is optional when creating text boxes, but required when creating other input controls. When submitted, values input by the user are associated with the NAME attribute value. The VALUE attribute is required for check boxes and radio buttons, but optional otherwise. The SIZE and MAXLENGTH attribute number specifies the width in character spaces for text box and password input controls, but in pixels for other input controls. The CHECKED attribute is recognized only for radio button and check box controls. The SRC attribute, specifying the location of an image, is required only when creating an image input control.

Note 2: For the STEP attribute (5.0), floating point mumber must parse to a number > 0.

A number of new input controls have been defined in HTML 5, implemented by the DATE, DATETIME, DATETIME-LOCAL, MONTH, WEEK, TIME, LIST, NUMBER, RANGE, EMAIL, and URL attributes. For details on using these attributes, see the HTML 5 specification at **www.w3.org/html/wg/html5/**.

Example	`<form action="http://www.mysite.com/cgi-bin/sendform.pl" method="post">`	

```
<form action="http://www.mysite.com/cgi-bin/sendform.pl" method="post">
<p><input type="hidden" name="recipient" value="bonzo@bedtime.com">
First Name/Initial: <input type="text" name="FirstName" size="30"><br>
Last Name: <input type="text" name="LastName" size="30"><br>
Gender: <input type="radio" name="Sex" value="Male"> <input type="radio"
name="Sex" value="Female">
Allergies: <input type="checkbox" name="Allergies" value="Food"> <input
type="checkbox" name="Allergies" value="Pets"> <input type="checkbox"
name="Allergies" value="Trees/Plants"> <input type="checkbox"
name="Allergies" value="Molds/Fungi"> <input type="checkbox"
name="Allergies" value="Chemicals"><p>
<p><input type="submit" value="Submit"> <input type="reset"
value="Reset"></p>
</form>
```

SELECT   **Type:** Inline/Container   **Content:** OPTGROUP/OPTION

Creates a list menu, in combination with the OPTION element and, optionally, the OPTGROUP element.

Attributes	`name="control name"`	Optional
	`size="n"`	Optional
	`multiple`	Boolean
	`disabled`	Boolean

Note: The SIZE attribute value specifies the number of visible rows (options) that will be displayed; the default value is **1**. MULTIPLE allows the selection of multiple options.

OPTION (Required in SELECT)   **Type:** Inline/Container   **Content:** Inline

Specifies an option in a list menu (required in the SELECT option). The end tag is optional.

Attributes	`selected`	Boolean
	`value="initial value"`	Optional
	`label="option label"` (4.0)	Optional

Note: The VALUE attribute specifies the initial value for an option; otherwise, the option value defaults to the OPTION element's content. The LABEL attribute is supposed to specify a label for an option, but this attribute is not widely supported; otherwise, the option label defaults to the OPTION element's content.

Example		

```
<select name="menu">
<option selected>Eenie</option>
<option>Meenie</option>
<option>Minie</option>
<option>Moe</option>
</select>
```

OPTGROUP (4.0) (Optional in SELECT)   **Type:** Inline/Container   **Content:** Inline

Specifies a group of options to be displayed in a list menu.

Attributes	`label="option group label"`	Required
	`disabled`	Boolean

```
<select name="Foods" size="13" multiple>
<optgroup label="Breakfast">
    <option value="cereal">Cold Cereal w/Milk</option>
    <option value="bacon">Bacon and Eggs</option>
    <option value="fruit">Fresh Fruit</option>
</optgroup>
<optgroup label="Lunch">
    <option value="bologna">Bologna/Cheese Sandwich</option>
    <option value="soup">Soup w/Salad</option>
    <option value="peanut">Peanut Butter Sandwich</option>
</optgroup>
<optgroup label="Dinner">
    <option value="steak">Steak w/Potatoes</option>
    <option value="fish">Broiled Fish w/Rice</option>
    <option value="chicken">Fried Chicken w/Fries</option>
    <option value="vegetable">Vegetable Tempura</option>
</optgroup>
</select>
```

TEXTAREA   **Type:** Inline/Container   **Content:** Text

Creates a multi-line text input box.

Attributes		
name="*control name*"		Optional
rows="*n*"		Required
cols="*n*"		Required
disabled		Boolean
readonly		Boolean

Note: Browsers should display text tested within the element, if there is any, as its initial value.

Example
```
<textarea name="comment" rows-"20" cols="80"
Type your comment here.
</textarea>
```

BUTTON (4.0)

An alternative to using the INPUT element to create submit and reset buttons, but with richer rendering possibilities. Also can be used to create push buttons that trigger scripts.

Attributes		
type="**submit**|reset|button"		Optional
name="*control-name*"		Optional
value="*initial value*"		Optional
tabindex="*n*"		Optional
accesskey="*character*"		Optional
disabled		Boolean

Note: The button label is provided by the text nested inside the BUTTON element; if an image is nested inside the BUTTON element, it is displayed as the button.

Example
```
<p><button type="submit" name="submit" value="submit">
    <font size="5" color="red">Submit</font></button>  
<button name="reset" type="reset">
    <font size="5" color="purple">Reset</font></button></p>
```

LABEL (4.0)   **Type:** Inline/Container   **Content:** Inline

Associates a label with a form control.

Attributes   `for="control ID"`   Optional

Note: Although visual browsers do nothing with the LABEL element, its use can help non-visual browsers and screen readers identify the purpose and function of a form control. This can be especially useful when using a table to lay out form controls in which the text identifying the control's purpose and function is located in a separate table cell. The FOR value references the ID value of the associated form control.

Example
```
<tr>
<th><label for="fname">First Name/Initial:</label></th>
<td><input name="first" id="fname"></td>
</tr>
```

FIELDSET (4.0)   **Type:** Block/Container   **Content:** Inline/Block

In conjunction with the LEGEND element, specifies a set of thematically related form controls and labels.

LEGEND (4.0)   **Type:** Container   **Content:** Inline

In conjunction with the FIELDSET element, provides a legend for a set of thematically related form controls.

Example
```
<fieldset>
<legend>Academic Interests</legend>
<input type="checkbox" name="Interest" value="arts"> Arts
<input type="checkbox" name="Interest" value="science"> Science
<input type="checkbox" name="Interest" value="business"> Business
</fieldset>
```

DATALIST (5.0)   **Type:** Container   **Content:** OPTION elements

Called by a LIST attribute (5.0) in a preceding INPUT element (with text, e-mail, URL, date-related, time-related, or numeric input types). Contains a set of OPTION elements, the VALUE attributes of which define a list of autocomplete hints that a user agent can offer, without foreclosing users from keying their own value.

Note: For more info on using this element, see the HTML 5 specification at **www.w3.org/html/wg/html5/**.

OPTION   **Type:** Inline/Container   **Content:** Phrasing

When contained as a series in a DATALIST element, provides a list of autocomplete hints.

OUTPUT (5.0)   **Type:** Container   **Content:** Phrasing

Specifies different types of output that are derived from other input values.

Example
```
<form>
<p>
<input name="a" type="number" step="any" value="0"> *
<input name="b" type="number" step="any" value="0"> =
<output name="total" onforminput="value = a.value * b.value">0</output>
</p>
</form>
```

Note: For more details on using this element, see the HTML 5 specification at **www.w3.org/html/wg/html5/**.

FRAME (4.0)

See FRAMESET.

FRAMESET (4.0)

Defines a set of framed windows to be displayed in a browser window. A page containing one or more FRAMESET elements is usually referred to as a frameset page and requires a DocType declaration declaring it to be compliant with the frameset definition of HTML 4.01 or XHTML 1.0. **(Obsolete in HTML 5.)**

Attributes	`rows="n,n,..."`	See Note
	`cols="n,n,..."`	See Note

Note: A FRAMESET element must contain either a ROWS or a COLS attribute, or it can contain both. The ROWS or COLS attribute value is a comma-separated list of two or more values specifying the vertical dimension of rows or the horizontal dimension of columns. The individual values can be of three types: pixel, percentage, or relative. A pixel value states a dimension in pixels; a percentage value states a dimension as a percentage of width or height of the browser window; a relative value expresses a dimension that is a ratio of the available vertical or horizontal space. For instance, `rows="25,1*,5%"` specifies a height of 25 pixels for the top row, a height of 5% of the browser window for the bottom row, and a height equivalent to 1 times the available space in the browser window for the middle row. The values 1* and * are equivalent. Likewise, `cols="50,5*,1*"` would set a width of 50 pixels for the first column, and then allot 5/6 and 1/6 of the remaining available browser space to the second and third columns.

FRAME (4.0)

Defines a single framed window within a frameset. **(Obsolete in HTML 5.)**

Attributes	`src="URL"`	See Note
	`name="frame name"`	See Note
	`frameborder="1|0"`	Optional
	`marginheight="n"`	Optional
	`marginwidth="n"`	Optional
	`scrolling="auto|yes|no"`	Optional
	`noresize`	Boolean
	`longdesc="URL"`	Optional

Note: SRC is required to display content within a frame; an empty frame is displayed if an SRC URL is not specified. NAME is required if you want to target a frame's name in a hypertext link using the TARGET attribute. NORESIZE stops the user from manually resizing frame dimensions using the mouse cursor. LONGDESC specifies the URL of a document that provides a long description of the contents of the frame, which can improve accessibility for individuals with visual impairments.

Example

```
<!DOCTYPE HTML PUBLIC "-//W3C//DTD HTML 4.01 Frameset//EN"
  "http://www.w3.org/TR/html4/frameset.dtd">
<html>
<head>
<meta http-equiv="Content-Type" content="text/html; charset=ISO-8859-1">
<title>NuShark Scuba Gear</title>
</head>
<frameset rows="85,*">
  <frame src="top.html" scrolling="no" marginheight="0">
  <frameset cols="150,*">
    <frame src="side.html">
    <frame src="front.html" name="main">
  </frameset>
</frameset>
</html>
```

NOFRAMES (4.0)   **Type:** Container   **Content:** BODY (optional), BLOCK

Provides content to be displayed in browsers that do not support frames (such as Internet Explorer 2.0, the default browser for Windows NT 4.0, for instance). The NOFRAMES element can be inserted inside the top-level FRAMESET element. The BODY element and any other elements normally nested inside the BODY element can be nested inside the NOFRAMES element. A hypertext link should be included in the NOFRAMES element that allows visitors using non-frames-capable browsers to access the rest of the site. **(Obsolete in HTML 5.)**

Example
```
<frameset rows="85,*">
  <frame src="top.html" scrolling="no" marginheight="0">
  <frameset cols="150,*">
    <frame src="side.html">
    <frame src="front.html" name="main">
  </frameset>
  <noframes>
  <p>A frames-capable browser is required to view this page. Please go
directly to my site's <a href="front.html">front page</a>.</p>
  </noframes>
</frameset>
```

H1, H2, H3, H4, H5, H6 (Heading Elements)   **Type:** Block/Container   **Content:** Inline

Allows the hierarchical organization of a document using six different heading levels. In practical terms, however, only the first four are likely to be used because the H5 and H6 elements are displayed by default in most browsers in a font that is smaller than the default text size. The H1 element is generally only inserted once, as the document's top-level heading (or title).

Attributes   `align="left|center|right|justify"`   Optional

Example
```
<<h1 align="center">My Life as an Emergency Room Attendant</h1>
<h2 align="center">by Ralph Green</h2>
```

HEAD (Header)   **Type:** Container   **Content:** HEAD elements

Along with the BODY element, one of two top-level elements that are nested directly inside the HTML element. The HEAD element is intended to contain elements that identify, describe, or direct the display of the page, whereas the BODY element contains all elements that are actually displayed within the page. Both the start tag and end tag are optional in HTML 4.01.

TITLE (Required)   **Type:** Container   **Content:** Inline

Specifies the title for a page, which is displayed on a browser's title bar.

Example
```
<html>
<head><title>Peter Locke's Political Science Site</title>
</head>
```

BASE   **Type:** Empty   **Content:** N/A

Specifies the absolute URL for the document that acts as a base for resolving relative URLs.

Attributes   `href="URL"`   Required

Example	`<head><title>John Peters' Political Science Site</title>`
	`<base href="http://www.somewhere.com/peters/polysci/index.html">`
	`</head>`
	`<body>`
	`<p align="center">Visit John Peter's <a href="../index.html">Home Page`
	`</a></p>`
	`<hr>`

Note: Because of the BASE URL, the relative URL in the BODY element correlates to an absolute URL of http://www.somewhere.com/peters/index.html.

ISINDEX (Deprecated)   Type: Empty   Content: N/A

Creates a one-line text-input control. The W3C recommends that Web authors use the INPUT element to create text-input controls. **(Obsolete in HTML 5.)**

Attributes	`prompt="prompt string"`	Optional

LINK   Type: Empty   Content: N/A

Defines a link in the HEAD element. A primary use for the LINK element is to link to external style sheets.

Attributes	`type="content-type"`	Optional
	`rel="link-type"`	Optional
	`rev="link-type"`	Optional
	`href="URL"`	Optional
	`media="media-descriptor"` (4.0)	Optional

Note: REL and REV can be used in combination with HREF to specify forward and reverse links. TYPE can be used in combination with HREF to specify a link to an external style sheet (**`type="text/css"`**). When linking to an external style sheet, MEDIA can be used to target a linked style sheet for a particular media. Because Netscape Navigator 4 ignores any LINK element with a MEDIA attribute other than **screen** set, the LINK element's MEDIA attribute can be used to block Netscape 4 users from accessing an external style sheet. Current allowable values for MEDIA include screen (the default), all, print, projection, handheld, tv, tty, aural, braille, and embossed.

Example	`<head><title>Peter Locke's Political Science Site</title>` `<link href="mystyles.css" rel="stylesheet" type="text/css" media="all">`

META   Type: Empty   Content: N/A

Specifies meta-information about the document.

Attributes	`name="meta-data identifier"`	See Note
	`http-equiv="refresh"`	See Note
	`content="meta-data data"`	Required

Note: Either NAME or HTTP-EQUIV is required.

Example	```<head><title>John Peters' Political Science Site</title>```
	```<meta name="description" content="Opinions and discussion of political```
	```science, including the theory of representative government, political```
	```constitutions, popular sovereignty, and other topics.">```
	```<meta name="keywords" content="political science, polysci, politics,```
	```constitution, civil rights, free speech, bill of rights, inalienable```
	```rights, liberty">```
	```</head>```
	or
	```<meta http-equiv="refresh"```
	```content="3;url="http://somewhere.emcp.com/peters/polysci/index.html">```

STYLE (3.2) **Type:** Container **Content:** Style Codes

Embeds a style sheet in the document's HEAD element. Multiple STYLE elements can be embedded.

Attributes	```type="content-type" (4.0)```	Required
	```media="media-descriptor" (4.0)```	Optional

Note: Only CSS style sheets can be used with HTML documents, so **`type="text/css"`** is always set for the STYLE element in HTML documents. In XHTML, however, other style sheet languages can be used, such as XSL, for instance. The MEDIA attribute allows the creation of style sheets that target specific media; current allowable values include **screen** (the default), **all**, **print**, **projection**, **handheld**, **tv**, **tty**, **aural**, **braille**, and **embossed**. This allows the embedding of a style sheet that will only be used when printing the document. Because only recent browsers support the MEDIA attribute, STYLE elements with a MEDIA attribute value other than **all** should precede any other STYLE elements in the HEAD element. Similar to the SCRIPT element, comment codes (`<!--` and `-->`) can be used to shield the content of the STYLE element from browsers that do not support it; style-aware browsers will ignore the comment codes.

Example	```<head><title>Peter Locke's Political Science Site</title>```
	```<style type="text/css">```
	```<!--```
	```h1, h2, h3 { color: blue; background: transparent; }```
	```p { font-family: Arial, Helvetica, sans-serif; }```
	```-->```
	```</style>```

HEADER (5.0) **Type:** Section/Container **Content:** Flow

Defines a header for a document or section, containing one or more heading elements (H1, H2,...). Can be used to group a title and subtitle. A HEADER element has the same heading rank as the H1 element.

Example	```<header>```
	```<h1>What I Did Last Summer</h2>```
	```<h2>A Cautionary Tale</h2>```
	```</header>```

HR (Horizontal Rule) **Type:** Block/Empty **Content:** N/A

Draws a horizontal rule across the page.

Attributes	```size="n" (Deprecated)```	Optional
	```width="n|n%" (Deprecated)```	Optional
	```align="left|center|right" (Deprecated)```	Optional
	```noshade```	Boolean

Note: SIZE specifies the height of the rule in pixels. ALIGN horizontally aligns the rule within the browser window, if WIDTH is set to a value of less than **100%** or a pixel-width is set that is less than the width of the browser window. NOSHADE turns off the 3-D shading for rules that is otherwise generally displayed by browsers.

Example   `<hr size="5" width="75%" align="center" noshade>`

HTML   Type: Container   Content: HEAD, BODY, FRAMESET

The top-level element in an HTML document. HTML 4.01 requires that a DocType declaration specifying the document's HTML conformance be inserted above the HTML element.

Example
```
<!DOCTYPE HTML PUBLIC "-//W3C//DTD HTML 4.01 Transitional//EN"
 "http://www.w3.org/TR/html4/loose.dtd">
<html>
All other elements in the document are nested here.
</html>
```

I (Italic)   Type: Inline/Container   Content: Inline

Causes nested text to be displayed in italics.

Example   `<p>One of my favorite books is <i>The Brothers Karamazov</i> by Fyodor Dostoevsky.</p>`

IFRAME (Inline Frame) (4.0)   Type: Inline/Container   Content: Inline

Creates an inline windowed frame within a Web page.

Attributes	
`src="URL"`	Required
`width="n"`	Optional
`height="n"`	Optional
`align="bottom|middle|top|left|right"`	Optional
`name="frame name"`	Optional
`marginheight="n"`	Optional
`marginwidth="n"`	Optional
`scrolling="auto|yes|no"`	Optional
`frameborder="1|0"`	Optional
`longdesc="URL"`	Optional

Note: Netscape 4 does not support inline frames. Content can be included in the IFRAME element to alert users of browsers that do not recognize the IFRAME element. NAME allows the targeting of an inline frame by a link using the TARGET attribute. The **left** and **right** values for the ALIGN attribute float the inline frame at the left or right margins, with following text flowing around the other side of the inline frame.

Example
```
<p><iframe src="insert.html" align="top" width="200" height="100">
[Note: This page uses inline frames, which is a feature not supported by
your browser. To find out how to upgrade to a browser that supports
current Web standards, see the <a href="http://www.webstandards.org/
upgrade/">Web Standard Project's Browser Upgrade Campaign</a>.]
</iframe></p>
```

IMG (Image)   Type: Inline/Empty   Content: N/A

Inserts an image inline within a Web page.

Attributes	src="*URL*"	Required
	alt="*alternate text*"	Required
	height="*n* | *n%*"	Recommended
	width="*n* | *n%*"	Recommended
	align="**bottom**|middle|top|left|right" (3.2)	Optional
	(Deprecated)	
	hspace="*n*" (3.2) (Deprecated)	Optional
	vspace="*n*" (3.2) (Deprecated)	Optional
	name="*image name*"	Optional
	usemap="*#mapname*|*URL*"	Optional
	border="1|0"	Optional

Note: ALIGN with **left** or **right** set floats the image on the left or right margin with following text or elements flowing around the other side of the image. VSPACE and HSPACE are used with floating images to add vertical and horizontal spacing outside the image. NAME allows the image to be targeted by a script. USEMAP links the image with the name of a client-side image map and is only used in conjunction with a fragment identifier that points to the NAME attribute of a MAP element or the URL of an external HTML file containing the associated MAP element. BORDER can turn the image border off (**border="0"**) when the image is an image link (nested inside the A element).

Example
```
<p align="center"><img src="mybanner.jpg" alt="Banner image"
height="125" width="175"></p>
```

INPUT

See FORM.

INS (Insert) (4.0) **Type:** Inline/Container **Content:** Inline

Marks nested text as an insertion. In browsers that support this element, nested text is generally displayed as underlined. INS can be used in combination with DEL (Delete) to display insertions and deletions in an HTML document. *See also* DEL (Delete).

| *Attributes* | cite="*URL*" | Optional |

Note: CITE can link to an HTML file providing details about why the document was revised, who revised it, when it was revised, and so on. No browser currently supports the CITE attribute.

Example
```
<h1><del>My </del><ins>Most </ins>Frequently Asked Questions Page</h1>
```

ISINDEX

See HEAD.

KBD (Keyboard) **Type:** Inline/Container **Content:** Inline

Can be used to indicate keyboard input. Text nested in the KBD element is generally displayed in a monospaced font. To distinguish KBD from the other monospaced text elements, it can be nested inside of (or bracket) a B (Bold) element.

Example
```
<p>At the prompt, key <b><kbd>newuser</kbd></b> and press the Enter
key.</p>
```

LABEL (4.0)

See FORM.

LEGEND (4.0)

Defines a caption, legend, or summary for the FIELDSET, DETAILS (5.0), or FIGURE (5.0) elements.

See FORM, DETAILS, *and* FIGURE.

LI (List Item)

See OL (Ordered List) *or* UL (Unordered List).

LINK

See HEAD.

MAP (Client-Side Image Map) (3.2) **Type:** Inline/Container **Content:** Block/AREA

In conjunction with the AREA element, defines a client-side image map.

Attributes	name="*mapname*"	Required

Note: In NAME, *mapname* must match (including uppercase and lowercase letters) the pointer included in the USEMAP attribute (**usemap="#*mapname*"**) of the IMG element being used for the image map.

AREA (3.2) **Type:** Inline/Empty **Content:** N/A

Defines an area within a client-side image map that functions as a hotspot link.

Attributes	shape="**rect**|circle|poly|default"	Optional
	coords="*coordinates*"	Optional
	href="*URL*"	Optional
	nohref	Boolean
	alt="*alternative text*"	Required

Example	

```
<p align="center"><img src="mymap.jpg" height="135" width="450"
alt="Image Map: Navigation Menu" usemap="#mymap" border=0></p>
<map name="mymap">
<area shape="rect" alt="Previous" coords="15,15,145,120" href="page1.
htm">
<area shape="rect" alt="Contents" coords="160,15,290,120" href="toc.
htm">
<area shape="rect" alt="Next" coords="305,15,435,120" href="page3.htm">
<area shape="default" nohref>
</map>
```

MARK (5.0) **Type:** Inline/Container **Content:** Phrasing

Marks or highlights a term or phrase for reference purposes.

Example	

```
<p>The SPAN element is an <mark>inline</mark> element, while the DIV
element is a <mark>block</mark> element.</p>
```

MENU (Deprecated) **Type:** Block/Container **Content:** Block

Originally intended for specifying a single-column menu, in contrast to the DIR element, originally intended for specifying a multi-column menu. Browsers treat MENU and DIR elements exactly like UL (Unordered List) elements, and the W3C recommends that Web authors use UL instead. **NOT obsolete in HTML 5.**

META (Meta Data)

See HEAD.

METER (5.0)
Type: Inline/Container   **Content:** Phrasing

Represents a scalar measurement for a known (non-arbitrary) range, such as a percentage, fraction, ratio, average, and so on.

Attributes	high="*n*"	Optional
	low="*n*"	Optional
	max="*n*"	Optional
	min="*n*"	Optional
	optimum="*n*"	Optional
	value="*n*"	Optional

Example   `<p>In a recent poll, Proposition 1 is supported by <meter>75 percent </meter> of likely voters.</p>`

NAV (5.0)
Type: Section/Container   **Content:** Flow

Contains navigation links and can function as a "navigation bar," similar to the ASIDE element functioning as a "sidebar."

Example
```
<nav>
Navigation: <a href="./">Home</a> <a href="articles/">Articles</a>
<a href="news/">News</a> <a href="forum/">Forum</a>
<a href="contact/">Contact</a>
</nav>
```

NOFRAMES (4.0)

See FRAMESET.

NOSCRIPT (4.0)

See SCRIPT.

OBJECT (4.0)
Type: Inline/Container   **Content:** Block/Inline

Generic mechanism for inserting inline objects into a Web page. Optionally used in conjunction with the PARAM (Parameter) element.

Attributes	classid="*URL*"	Optional
	codebase="*URL*"	Optional
	codetype="*content-type*"	Optional
	data="*URL*"	Optional
	type="*content-type*"	Optional
	standby="*standby message*"	Optional
	id="*objectname*"	Optional

PARAM (Parameter) (4.0)
Type: Empty   **Content:** N/A

Sets initial parameters for an object displayed by the OBJECT element.

Attributes	name="*parameter name*"	Required
	value="*parameter value*"	Optional
	valuetype="**data**|ref|object"	Optional
	type="*content-type*"	Optional

Note: NAME's value and case-sensitivity depends on the specific object implementation. VALUE is the value of the run-time parameter specified by NAME; the actual value is determined by the object implementation. VALUETYPE specifies the type of value being passed by the VALUE attribute; if **data**, the value is passed as a string; if **ref**, the value is passed as a URL; and if **object**, the value is passed as the ID value of the object.

Example
```
<object data="intro.wav" type="audio/wav" width="200" height="45"
vspace="5">
<param name="src" value="intro.wav">
<param name="autostart" value="true">
<param name="controller" value="true">
<param name="loop" value="false">
Audio introduction to site.
</object>
```

OL (Ordered List) **Type:** Block/Container **Content:** Block

Creates an ordered (or numbered) list.

Attributes		
	type="1|a|A|i|I"	Optional
	start="*n*"	Optional
	compact (Deprecated)	Optional

Note: TYPE specifies the numbering system, whether Arabic (**1**), lowercase alphabetic (**a**), uppercase alphabetic (**A**), lowercase Roman (**i**), or uppercase Roman (**I**). START can specify a starting number other than **1**.

LI (with OL) **Type:** Block/Container **Content:** Inline/Block

Specifies a list item, within an OL element in this case. The end tag for LI is optional. *See also* UL (Unordered List).

Attributes		
	type="1|a|A|i|I"	Optional
	value="*n*"	Optional

Note: VALUE specifies a value for the current list item. For instance, if **A** is the value of the TYPE attribute, **value="4"** corresponds to a value of D.

Example
```
<ol type="A">
<li>Breakfast
<li>Lunch
<li>Dinner
</ol>
```

OPTGROUP (Option Group) (4.0)

See FORM.

OPTION

See FORM.

OUTPUT (5.0)

See FORM.

P (Paragraph) **Type:** Block/Container **Content:** Inline

Indicates that nested text is a paragraph. The end tag is officially optional but should be included to avoid problems that can arise otherwise.

Attributes	align="**left**|center|right|justify" (3.2) (Deprecated)	Optional
Example	<p>Welcome to my home page!</p>	

PARAM (Parameter) (3.2/4.0)

See *APPLET* and *OBJECT*.

PRE (Preformatted Text)   **Type:** Block/Container   **Content:** Inline

Specifies that nested text be treated as preformatted text, with all included spaces and hard returns displayed by the browser. Inline elements that cannot be nested in a PRE element include IMG, OBJECT, BIG, SMALL, SUB, and SUP. Text in a PRE element is generally rendered in a monospaced font.

Attributes	width="*n*" (Deprecated)	Optional

Example

```
<pre>
                    QTR 1      QTR 2      QTR 3      QTR 4      Score
    Madison State     7          14         0          3         24
    Concord Tech      0          7          14         7         28
</pre>
```

PROGRESS (5.0)   **Type:** Inline/Container   **Content:** Phrasing

Indicates a progress bar, which can be updated by a script to show dynamic progress to completion of a task (loading a file, for instance).

Attributes	value="*n*"	Optional
	max="*n*"	Optional

Example   <p>Project completion: <progress value="75" max="100">75%</progress></p>

Q (Quote) (4.0)   **Type:** Inline/Container   **Content:** Inline

Marks nested text as an inline quotation. Browsers that support the Q element should automatically render quotation marks delimiting the quotation. Because few browsers support the Q element (Mozilla 1 does, but Internet Explorer 6, does not) and quotations marked by the Q element do not degrade gracefully in browsers that do not support the Q element (because no quotation marks at all are displayed), the Q element should probably be avoided.

Attributes	cite="*URL*"	Optional
	lang="*language-code*	Optional
	dir="ltr|rtl"	Optional

Note: CITE references the URL of the source of the quote. LANG specifies the language of the quotation (**lang="fr"**, if the language of the quotation is French, for instance).

S (Strike) (4.0) (Deprecated)   **Type:** Inline/Container   **Content:** Inline

Marks nested text as strikeout text, displayed with a line drawn through it. Previously proposed as part of the HTML 3.0 proposal, S (Strike) was included in HTML 4.0 but deprecated at the same time. STRIKE is more universally supported by earlier browsers and should probably be used instead. (**Obsolete in HTML 5.**)

SAMP (Sample Code)
Type: Inline/Container   **Content:** Inline

Marks nested text as sample code. All browsers display SAMP text in a monospaced font. The TT (Teletype Text) element can be used instead to achieve the same result.

SCRIPT (3.2)
Type: Container   **Content:** Script Code

Allows inclusion or linking of client-side scripts. The SCRIPT element can be inserted in either the HEAD or the BODY element.

Attributes		
	type="*content type*"	Required
	language="*script language*" (Deprecated)	Optional
	src="*URL*"	Optional

Note: TYPE identifies the MIME type of the scripting language (**text/javascript**, for instance). LANGUAGE is deprecated because it references non-standard script language identifiers. Some older browsers, however, recognize LANGUAGE, but not TYPE, in the SCRIPT element, so good practice dictates including both. Comment codes, `<!--` and `//-->`, can be used to shield browsers that are not script aware from displaying the content of the SCRIPT element. Script-aware browsers ignore the comment codes.

Example
```
<script type="text/JavaScript" src="mainscript.js"></script>
or
<script type="text/JavaScript" language="JavaScript">
<!-- hide script
function HiThere() {
    ident = window.prompt("Enter your name: ", "");
    alert ("Welcome to my page, "+ident+"!");
}
// end hiding script -->
</script>
```

NOSCRIPT (4.0)
Type: Container   **Content:** Block

Specifies content to be displayed in a browser that does not support the specified script language or is not script-aware. A script-aware browser ignores the content of the NOSCRIPT element, whereas a script-unaware browser displays the content of the NOSCRIPT element. **(Obsolete in HTML 5.)**

Example
```
<body>
<noscript>
<p>This page includes JavaScript scripts. Please go to the
<a href="no-js.html">non-JavaScript version</a> of this page.</p>
</noscript>
```

SECTION (5.0)
Type: Section/Container   **Content:** Flow

Indicates a section (or subsection) within a document or section.

Example
```
<section>
<h1>Part I: Mixing Colors</h1>
<p>Before you start painting, it is important that you understand the
basics of mixing colors on your palette.[...]
</section>
```

SELECT

See *FORM*.

SMALL (3.2)

Type: Inline/Container   **Content:** Inline

Marks text for display in a smaller font. Text is displayed in a font size that is one size smaller than the default font size, based on the seven font sizes specified by the FONT and BASEFONT elements' SIZE attribute. Nesting SMALL elements, although legal, is not recommended because it can result in an illegible font size in some Macintosh browsers, for instance. **(Redefined in HTML 5 as semantically referring to "small print," such as in a contract or disclaimer.)**

Example   `<p><small>&copy; Copyright 2010 by Alice Williams. All rights reserved.</small></p>`

SOURCE (5.0)

See AUDIO (5.0) *and* VIDEO (5.0).

SPAN (4.0)

Type: Inline/Container   **Content:** Inline

Marks a span of text, to which formatting using styles can be applied. By itself, the SPAN element has no formatting.

Example   `<p>Registration for <span style="font-family: Arial; color: maroon; background: transparent">Winter Quarter</span> classes will begin on January 5.</p>`

STRIKE (Strikeout) (3.2) (Deprecated)

Type: Inline/Container   **Content:** Inline

Marks nested text as strikeout text, displayed with a line drawn through it. STRIKE is more universally supported than either the S (Strike) or the DEL (Delete) element and should probably be used instead. **(Obsolete in HTML 5.)**

Example   `<p>Text to be deleted is marked as <strike>strikeout</strike>.</p>`

STRONG (Strong Emphasis)

Type: Inline/Container   **Content:** Inline

Marks nested text as strongly emphasized. Browsers display STRONG text identically to B (Bold) text. Either can be used.

Example   `<p><strong>Note:</strong> When creating Web sites, the unexpected is to be expected.</p>`

STYLE (3.2)

See HEAD.

SUB (Subscript) (3.2)

Type: Inline/Container   **Content:** Inline

Marks nested text as subscripted. To allow for earlier browsers that do not support SUB, subscripted text can be enclosed inside parentheses. *See also* SUP (Superscript).

SUP (Superscript) (3.2)

Type: Inline/Container   **Content:** Inline

Marks nested text as superscripted. To allow for earlier browsers that do not support SUP, superscripted text can be enclosed inside parentheses. *See also* SUB (Subscript).

Example   `<p>Eat Crumpies<sup>(tm)</sup>, the greatest thing since H<sub>(2) </sub>0!</p>`

TABLE (3.2)   **Type:** Block/Container   **Content:** Table Elements

Specifies that nested code is a table (arranged in columns and rows).

Attributes		
	`width="n|n%"`	Optional
	`border="n"`	Optional
	`cellpadding="n"`	Optional
	`cellspacing="n"`	Optional
	`align="left|center|right"`	Optional
	`bgcolor="color name|RGB color code"`	Optional
	`frame="void|above|below|hsides|`	
	`        lhs|rhs|vsides|box|border" (4.0)`	Optional
	`rules="none|groups|rows|cols|all" (4.0)`	Optional

Note: The ALIGN values of **left** and **right** have the effect of floating the table to the left or right margin and flowing following text or elements around the other side of the table. Current browsers also support the BACKGROUND attribute for specifying a background image for a table, but it is not a standard attribute, primarily due to differences in how it is implemented in browsers.

CAPTION (Table Caption)   **Type:** Block/Container   **Content:** Inline

Marks nested text as a table caption.

Attributes		
	`align="top|bottom|left|right" (Deprecated)`	Optional

Note: A **top** value centers the caption above the table. A **bottom** value for ALIGN causes the caption to be displayed below the table. Values of **left** and **right** left-aligns or right-aligns the caption (in the caption space) above the table.

TR (Table Row) (3.2)   **Type:** Container   **Content:** TH/TD

Delineates a row of cells in a table. The end tag is officially optional in HTML 4.01, but leaving it off might cause problems in earlier browsers.

Attributes		
	`align="left|center|right|justify"`	Optional
	`valign="top|middle|bottom|baseline"`	Optional

TH (Table Heading) and TD (Table Data) (3.2)   **Type:** Container   **Content:** Block/Inline

Designates a table heading (TH) or table data (TD) cell. TH content is centered and bolded, whereas TD content is left-aligned and displayed in a regular font. The end tag for TH and TD is officially optional in HTML 4.01, but leaving it off might cause problems in earlier browsers.

Attributes		
	`align="left|center|right|justify"`	Optional
	`valign="top|middle|bottom|baseline"`	Optional
	`colspan="n"`	Optional
	`rowspan="n"`	Optional
	`width="n|n%" (Deprecated)`	Optional
	`height="n|n%" (Deprecated)`	Optional
	`nowrap (Deprecated)`	Boolean

THEAD (Table Head), TBODY (Table Body), and TFOOT (Table Foot) (4.0)

Type: Container   **Content:** TR

Designates the head, body, and foot sections (or row groups) in a table. These elements have no formatting by themselves, but they can have styles applied to them to control their presentation. If not present, the whole table defaults to displaying styles set for TBODY (in HTML 4, but not XHTML 1). The end tags for THEAD, TBODY, and TFOOT are optional.

Attributes	`align="left|center|right|justify"`	Optional
	`valign="top|`**`middle`**`|bottom|baseline"`	Optional

Example
```
<style type="text/css">
<!--
thead tr.border th { border-bottom: 1px solid black; }
tbody tr.border th, tbody tr.border td { border-bottom: 3px double
black; }
tfoot th, tfoot td { color: red; background: transparent; }
-->
</style>
</head>
<body>
<table align="center" width="450" cellspacing="0">
<thead>
<tr><th></th><th colspan="3">Semi-Annual Sales Report</th></tr>
<tr class="border" align="right"><th>Salesperson</th><th>1st Qtr
</th><th>2nd Qtr</th><th>Totals</th></tr>
</thead>
<tbody>
<tr align="right"><th>Brady</th><td>$   525,000</td><td>$
   365,000</td><td>$   890,000</td></tr>
<tr align="right"><th>Crawford</th><td>400,000</td><td>500,000</td>
<td>900,000</td></tr>
<tr class="border" align="right"><th>Peters</th><td>250,000
</td><td>400,000</td><td>650,000</td></tr>
</tbody>
<tfoot>
<tr align="right"><th>Totals</th><td>$1,175,000</td><td>$1,265,000
</td><td>$2,440,000</td></tr>
</tfoot>
</table>
```

COLGROUP (Column Group) (4.0)

Type: Container   **Content:** COL

Designates a group of columns (specified by the COL element). The end tag is optional.

COL (Column) (4.0)　　　　　　　　　　　　Type: Empty　　Content: N/A

Example
```
<table width="75%" align="center" border="1">
<colgroup id="colg1">
  <col id="col1">
</colgroup>
<colgroup id="colg2">
  <col id="col2">
  <col id="col3">
  <col id="col4">
</colgroup>
<colgroup id="colg3">
  <col id="col5">
  <col id="col6">
  <col id="col7">
</colgroup>
```

TBODY (Table BODY) (4.0)

See TABLE.

TEXTAREA

See FORM.

TFOOT (Table Foot) (4.0)

See TABLE.

TH (Table Heading) and TD (Table Data)

See TABLE.

THEAD (Table Head) (4.0)

See TABLE.

TITLE

See HEAD.

TR (Table Row)

See TABLE.

TT (Teletype Text/Typewriter Text)　　　Type: Inline/Container　　Content: Inline

Marks nested text to be displayed in a monospaced font. **(Obsolete in HTML 5.)**

Example　　`<p>The message, <tt>Wait while downloading</tt>, is displayed.</p>`

U (Underline) (3.2)　　　　　　　　　　Type: Inline/Container　　Content: Inline

Marks nested text to be displayed as underlined. **(Obsolete in HTML 5.)**

Example　　`<p>The commissary will be <u>closed</u> on Friday.</p>`

UL (Unordered List)
Type: Block/Container   **Content:** Block

Creates an unordered (or bulleted) list.

Attributes	type="**disc**	circle	square"	Optional
	start="*n*"	Optional
	compact (Deprecated)	Boolean

Note: TYPE specifies the numbering system, whether Arabic (1), lowercase alphabetic (a), uppercase alphabetic (A), lowercase Roman (i), or uppercase Roman (I). START can specify a starting number other than 1.

LI (with OL)
Type: Block/Container   **Content:** Inline/Block

Specifies a list item, within an OL element in this case. The end tag for LI is optional. *See also* UL (Unordered List).

| *Attributes* | type="**1**|a|A|i|I" | Optional |
| | value="*n*" | Optional |

Note: VALUE specifies a value for the current list item. For instance, if **A** is the value of the TYPE attribute, **value="4"** corresponds to a value of D.

Example	<ol type="A">
	<li>Breakfast
	<li>Lunch
	<li>Dinner
	</ol>

VAR (Variable)
Type: Inline/Container   **Content:** Inline

Marks nested text as a variable. The VAR element is generally displayed in italics. Alternatively, the I (Italic) and EM (Emphasis) elements can be used to achieve the same effect.

| *Example* | <p>The <var>count</var> variable is incremented by one each time the loop is executed.</p> |

VIDEO (5.0)
Type: Embedded   **Content:** Transparent

A video stream. Content can be nested for display in non-supporting browsers that will be ignored by supporting browsers.

Attributes	src="*URL*"	Recommended
	autoplay	Boolean
	loop	Boolean
	controls	Boolean
	width="*n*"	Optional
	height="*n*"	Optional
	poster="*URL*"	Optional

POSTER specifies the location of an image file to be displayed in place of the video, if the video is still loading.

SOURCE (5.0)
Type: None   **Content:** Empty

Specifies multiple media resources (video files, for instance) for media elements (AUDIO or VIDEO).

| *Attributes* | src="*URL*" | Recommended |
| | type="*MIME type*" | Optional |

CORE AND OTHER ATTRIBUTES

class="*class name*" (All, except for BASE, BASEFONT, HEAD, HTML, META, PARAM, SCRIPT, STYLE, and TITLE)

id="*unique ID*" (All, except for BASE, HEAD, HTML, META, SCRIPT, STYLE, and TITLE)

style="*property1:value1; property2:value2;*" (All, except for BASE, BASEFONT, HEAD, HTML, META, PARAM, SCRIPT, STYLE, and TITLE)

title="*title*" (All, except for BASE, BASEFONT, HEAD, HTML, META, PARAM, SCRIPT, and TITLE; most useful in A, AREA, LINK, and IMG)

Other Common Attributes

accesskey="*character*" (A, AREA, BUTTON, INPUT, LABEL, LEGEND, and TEXTAREA)

align="**top**|bottom|left|right" (CAPTION) (Deprecated)

align="top|middle|bottom|left|right" (APPLET, FRAME, IMG, INPUT, and OBJECT) (Deprecated)

align="**left**|center|right|justify" (DIV, H1, H2, H3, H4, H5, H6, and P) (Deprecated)

align="left|center|right|justify|char" (COL, COLGROUP, TBODY, TH, THEAD, and TR) (Not Deprecated)

bgcolor="*color name*|*RGB color code*" (BODY, TABLE, TR, TD, and TH) (Deprecated)

border="*n*" (IMG, OBJECT, and TABLE)

charset="*character set*" (A, LINK, and SCRIPT)

disabled (BUTTON, INPUT, OPTGROUP, OPTION, SELECT, and TEXTAREA)

lang="*language code*" (All, except for APPLET, BASE, BASEFONT, BDO, BR, FRAME, FRAMESET, IFRAME, PARAM, and SCRIPT)

tabindex="*n*" (A, AREA, BUTTON, INPUT, OBJECT, SELECT, and TEXTAREA)

target="*frame name*" (A, AREA, BASE, FORM, and LINK)

valign="top|middle|bottom|baseline" (COL, COLGROUP, TBODY, TD, TFOOT, TH, THEAD, and TR)

Language Attributes (i18n)

lang="*language code*" ("fr" = French, "en" = English, etc.)

dir="ltr|rtl" (All, except for APPLET, BASE, BASEFONT, BDO, BR, FRAME, FRAMESET, IFRAME, PARAM, and SCRIPT)

Event Handler Attributes

onBlur="*script*" (See Note 1)

onChange="*script*" (INPUT, SELECT, and TEXTAREA)

onClick="*script*" (See Note 2)

onDblClick="*script*" (See Note 2)

onFocus="*script*" (See Note 1)

onLoad="*script*" (BODY, FRAMESET)

onKeyDown="*script*" (See Note 2)

onKeyPress="*script*" (See Note 2)

onKeyUp="*script*" (See Note 2)

onMouseDown="*script*" (See Note 2)

onMouseUp="*script*" (See Note 2)

onMouseMove="*script*" (See Note 2)

onMouseOut="*script*" (See Note 2)

onMouseOver="*script*" (See Note 2)

onReset="*script*" (FORM)

onSelect="*script*" (INPUT, TEXTAREA)

onSubmit="*script*" (FORM)

onUnload="*script*" (BODY, FRAMESET)

Note 1: A, AREA, BUTTON, INPUT, LABEL, SELECT, and TEXTAREA.

Note 2: All elements, except for APPLET, BASE, BASEFONT, BDO, BR, FONT, FRAME, FRAMESET, HEAD, HTML, IFRAME, ISINDEX, META, PARAM, SCRIPT, STYLE, and TITLE.

HTML 5 ELEMENTS AND ATTRIBUTES

HTML 5 New Elements

ASIDE, ARTICLE, AUDIO, CANVAS, COMMAND, DATAGRID, DATALIST, DETAILS, DIALOG, EMBED, EVENT-SOURCE, FIGURE, FOOTER, HEADER, MARK, METER, NAV, NEST, OUTPUT, PROGRESS, SECTION, SOURCE, and VIDEO

HTML 5 Obsolete Elements

ACRONYM, APPLET, BASEFONT, BIG, CENTER, DIR, FRAME, FRAMESET, ISINDEX, NOFRAMES, and TT

HTML 5 Attributes

HTML 5 Global Attributes

class, contenteditable, contextmenu, data-*, dir, draggable, id, hidden, lang, style, tabindex, and title

Other HTML 5 Attributes

New TYPE attribute values (on INPUT element): search, email, url, password, datetime, date, month, week, time, datetime-local, number, range, color, and file

class, contenteditable, contextmenu, data-*, dir, draggable, id, hidden, lang, style, tabindex, and title

All attributes deprecated in HTML 4.01, including background, bgcolor, alink, link, text, and vlink (on the BODY element)

Attributes not deprecated or deprecated only on some elements in HTML 4.01, but obsolete on all elements in HTML 5: align, border, cellpadding, cellspacing, frame, frameborder, marginheight, marginwidth, rules, scrolling, target, amd valign

The CELLPADDING and CELLSPACING attributes (on the TABLE element)

The HEIGHT attribute (except on IFRAME, IMG, and OBJECT)

The NAME attribute (on the A element), but allowed for transitional purposes (NAME and ID can be used on the same element, as long as both have the same value)

The SIZE attribute (on HR, INPUT, and SELECT, but allowed on FONT, which is included for WYSIWYG editors, but not for normal use)

The TYPE attribute (on LI, OL, and UL)

The WIDTH attribute (except on IFRAME, IMG, and OBJECT)

VALIDATING HTML (AND XHTML) MARKUP

The W3C HTML Validator, at **validator.w3.org/**, can check the validity of HTML (or XHTML) markup in Web pages against the latest standards. The W3C provides three ways in which you can validate your pages' markup, by clicking on the Validate by URI, Validate by File Upload, or Validate by Direct Input tabs.

Before validating an HTML (or XHTML) file, you should make sure that your file contains a valid HTML 4.01, XHTML 1.0, or HTML 5 DocType declaration, as well as a META element declaring the document's default character set (UTF-8, for instance). If validating an XHTML 1.0 file, a valid xmlns (XML name space) attribute should be present in the HTML element (see Appendix B, *HTML-to-XHTML Conversion Chart*, for an example of this, as well as other specific requirements for a valid XHTML document).

If validating your page against the "transitional" or "frameset" definitions of HTML 4.01 or XHTML 1.0, it should contain no obsolete elements or attributes; if against the "strict" definition of HTML 4.01 or XHTML 1.0, it should contain no obsolete or deprecated elements or attributes. You should also check for any obvious coding errors, such as overlapping elements, missing " or ">" characters, and so on.

Realize that one error can trigger the reporting of many other phantom errors that are not really errors in the code. Simply correct the topmost errors in your code and revalidate, and many following phantom errors should disappear. It is not uncommon to have to revalidate several times to eliminate all validation errors.

APPENDIX B

HTML-to-XHTML Conversion Chart

HTML 4.01 and XHTML 1.0 are closely related markup languages. XHTML 1.0 is based on and shares the same element and attribute definitions as HTML 4.01. Appendix A, *HTML Quick Reference*, along with this appendix, can be used as a reference to both HTML 4.01 and XHTML 1.0.

XHTML 1.0 was developed as a version of HTML based on XML (eXstensible Markup Language), while HTML was originally developed based on SGML (Standard Generalized Markup Language), which is widely used in the publishing and printing industries to mark up computer-generated documents.

There are a number of permutations of XHTML, including XHTML 1.0, XHTML Basic, XHTML 1.1, and XHTML 2.0. XHTML 1.0 is essentially HTML 4.01 but converted to adhere to the rules and syntax of XML. XHTML Basic is a subset of XHTML 1.0 that is optimized for the presentation of HTML documents on smaller-format wireless and mobile devices. XHTML 1.1 allows for extended XHTML modules (or families), such as MathML (Mathematical Markup Language) or SVG (Scalable Vector Graphics), for instance. XHTML 2.0, currently a draft recommendation, is an expansion of XHTML 1.1, which includes elements, attributes, and features that are not included in XHTML 1 or HTML 4. Some XHTML 2 elements have been included in HTML 5.

Most of the differences between the HTML 4.01 and XHTML 1.0 are syntactical, with XHTML 1.0 having stricter syntax than HTML 4.01. Students can use the following chart as a handy reference to:

- Convert any HTML 4.01 document into an XHTML 1.0 document.
- Create HTML documents that are compatible with both HTML 4.01 and XHTML 1.0.

This appendix presents a two-column chart that presents the differences between HTML 4.01 and XHTML 1.0 in a convenient side-by-side format. Students can follow this chart to convert any HTML 4.01-compliant document into an XHTML 1.0-compliant document. The resulting document can be declared to be an HTML 4.01 or XHTML 1.0 document. Other than the mostly syntactical differences detailed here, HTML 4.01 and XHTML 1.0 are the same.

N O T E ———— A utility, HTML Tidy, is available through SourceForge at **sourceforge.net/projects/tidy/**. This tool can be used to convert any HTML 4.01 document into an XHTML 1.0 document. The W3C's Amaya browser, available at **www.w3.org/Amaya/**, can also save HTML 4.01 documents as XHTML 1.0 documents.

In the following table, documents coded according to the first column comply with HTML 4.01 but not XHTML 1.0; documents coded according to the second column comply with XHTML 1.0 (if using an XHTML 1.0 DocType) or HTML 4.01 (if using an HTML 4.01 DocType). Where due to constrained margins it is necessary to wrap a code line other than at a space, the following line is indented to show that it and the preceding line should be keyed as one continuous line.

HTML-TO-XHTML CONVERSION CHART

HTML 4.01	XHTML 1.0
HTML Doctype required.	XHTML Doctype required. (Note 1)

```<!DOCTYPE HTML PUBLIC "-//W3C//DTD HTML 4.01//EN" "http://www.w3.org/TR/html4/strict.dtd">```
 	
or
 	
```<!DOCTYPE HTML PUBLIC "-//W3C//DTD HTML 4.01 Transitional//EN" "http://www.w3.org/TR/html4/loose.dtd">```
 	
or
 	
```<!DOCTYPE HTML PUBLIC "-//W3C//DTD HTML 4.01 Frameset//EN" "http://www.w3.org/TR/html4/frameset.dtd">```
	```<!DOCTYPE html PUBLIC "-//W3C//DTD XHTML 1.0//EN" "http://www.w3.org/TR/xhtml1/DTD /xhtml1-strict.dtd">```
	
	or
	
	```<!DOCTYPE html PUBLIC "-//W3C//DTD XHTML 1.0 Transitional//EN" "http://www.w3.org/TR/xhtml1/DTD /xhtml1-transitional.dtd">```
	
	or
	
	```<!DOCTYPE html PUBLIC "-//W3C//DTD XHTML 1.0 Frameset//EN" "http://www.w3.org/TR/xhtml1/DTD /xhtml1-frameset.dtd">```

No required attributes in `<html>` start tag.	xmnls (XML namespace) attribute in `<html>` start tag required. (Note 1)
`<html>`	```<html xmlns="http://www.w3.org/1999/ xhtml" xml:lang="en" lang="en">```
Optional elements allowed (HTML, HEAD, BODY, and TBODY).	Optional elements not allowed.

HTML	XHTML

`<!DOCTYPE HTML PUBLIC`
`"-//W3C//DTD HTML 4.01 Transitional//EN"`
`"http://www.w3.org/TR/html4/loose.dtd">`
`<meta http-equiv="Content-Type"`
`content="text/html; charset=UTF-8">`
`<title>John Allen's Home Page</title>`
`<h1>My Home Page</h1>`
	`<!DOCTYPE html PUBLIC`
	`-//W3C//DTD XHTML 1.0 Transitional//EN"`
	`"http://www.w3.org/TR/xhtml1/DTD/`
	`  xhtml1-transitional.dtd">`
	`<html xmlns="http://www.w3.org/1999/xhtml"`
	`xml:lang="en" lang="en">`
	`<head>`
	`<title>John Allen's Home Page</title>`
	`</head>`
	`<body>`
	`<h1>My Home Page</h1>`

Standalone elements allowed.	Standalone elements must end with / character. (Note 2)
`<img src="myimage.gif">` **or** `<hr>`	`<img src="myimage.gif" />` **or** `<hr />`
Element and attribute names are not case-sensitive.	Element and attribute names must be lowercase.
`<img src="myimage.gif">` **and** `<IMG SRC="myimage.gif">` **both allowed.**	`<img src="myimage.gif" />` **allowed, but not** `<IMG SRC="myimage.gif" />`.
Implied end tags are allowed.	Implied end tags are not allowed.

`<ul>`
`<li>List item 1.`
`<li>List item 2.`
`</ul>`
End tags for BODY, COLGROUP, DD, DT, HEAD, HTML, LI, OPTION, P, TBODY, TFOOT, TH, THEAD, and TR can optionally be omitted.
	`<ul>`
	`<li>List item 1.</li>`
	`<li>List item 2.</li>`
	`</ul>`

Quotes optional for attribute values without spaces.	Quotes required for all attribute values.
`rowspan="2"` **and** `rowspan=2` **both allowed.**	`rowspan="2"` **allowed, but not** `rowspan=2`.
Minimized (or Boolean) attributes allowed. (Note 3)	All attributes must be expanded.
`<input type="radio" name="sex"` `value="female" checked>` **or** `<td nowrap>`	`<input type="radio" name="sex"` `value="female" checked="checked" />` **or** `<td nowrap="nowrap">` **(nowrap not in "strict" definition)**
HTML justification of text allowed.	HTML justification of text not allowed; a style must be used instead.
`<p align="justify">`	`<p style="text-align:justify">`
Both NAME and ID attributes allowed.	ID attribute supercedes the NAME attribute. (Note 4)
`<a name="section1">`, `<a id="section1">`, **or** `<a name="section" id="section">`	`<a id="section">`

LANG attribute specifies language.	XML:LANG attribute takes precedence over LANG.

```
<span lang="fr">
```

```
<span xml:lang="fr" lang="fr">
```
(LANG attribute allowed for compatibility purposes in XHTML 1.0, but not XHTML 2.0.)

Standalone **&** and **<** allowed in body or embedded scripts, but not allowed in URLs or attribute values. (Browsers do not care, however.)	Standalone **&** and **<** not allowed anywhere. (Can lead to a browser, if using an XML parser, to fail to display the page.)

```
< Peter & John
```

```
&lt; Peter &amp; John
```

HTML (SGML) comment tags allowed inside STYLE or SCRIPT elements (to hide content from non-supporting browsers). CDATA wrapper allowed.	HTML (SGML) comment tags not allowed inside STYLE or SCRIPT elements. CDATA wrapper allowed. CDATA wrapper required around SCRIPT content that contains & or < characters.

```
<style type="text/css">
<!--
h1 { color:red; }
-->
</style>
```
or
```
<script type="text/javascript">
<!--
alert("This hides script contents from
older browsers.")
-->
</script>
```

```
<style type="text/css">
h1 { color:red; }
</style>
```
or
```
<script type="text/javascript">
/*<![CDATA[*//*---->*/
alert("This hides script comments from
XML parsers.")
/*--*//*]]>*/
</script>
```

Pre-defined attribute values are case-insensitive.	Pre-defined attribute values are case-sensitive.

```
<input type="radio" name="sex"
value="female"> or
<input type="RADIO" name="sex"
value="female">
```

```
<input type="radio" name="sex"
value="female" />, but not
<input type="RADIO" name="sex"
value="female" />
```

Hexadecimal values are case-insensitive.	Hexadecimal values are case-sensitive.

`&#ff6699;` **or** `&#FF6699;`

`&#ff6699;`, **but not** `&#FF6699;`

Sample document head:

```
<!DOCTYPE HTML PUBLIC
"-//W3C//DTD HTML 4.01 Transitional//EN"
"http://www.w3.org/TR/html4/loose.dtd">
<html>
<head>
<meta http-equiv="Content-Type"
content="text/html; charset=UTF-8">
<title>Transitional HTML Document with
UTF-8 Character Encoding</title>
</head>
```

Sample document heads:

Delivered as XHTML+XML:

```
<?xml version="1.0" encoding="UTF-8"?>
<!DOCTYPE html PUBLIC
"-//W3C//DTD XHTML 1.0 Transitional//EN"
"http://www.w3.org/TR/xhtml1/DTD/
    xhtml1-transitional.dtd">
<html xmlns="http://www.w3.org/1999/
    xhtml">
<head>
<title>Transitional Document with XML
Declaration</title>
</head>
```

Delivered as HTML or XHTML+XML (depending on browser):

```
<!DOCTYPE html PUBLIC
"-//W3C//DTD XHTML 1.0 Transitional//EN"
"http://www.w3.org/TR/xhtml1/DTD/
    xhtml1-transitional.dtd">
<html xmlns="http://www.w3.org/1999/
    xhtml">
<head>
<title>Transitional Document without XML
Declaration</title>
<meta http-equiv="Content-Type"
content="text/html;charset=UTF-8"/>
</head>
```

Note 1: XHTML DocType declarations can optionally be preceded by an XML declaration:

```
<?xml version="1.0" encoding="UTF-8"?>
<!DOCTYPE html PUBLIC "-//W3C//DTD XHTML 1.0 Transitional//EN"
"http://www.w3.org/TR/xhtml1/DTD/xhtml1-transitional.dtd">
```

If the declaration is absent, user agents will automatically use their XML parser, if they have one, to serve up the document as an XHTML document (`application/xhtml+xml` media type). Internet Explorer 8 and earlier versions of that browser do not have an XML parser and serve up XHTML documents as HTML documents (`text/html` media type).

Note 2: User agents parsing the document as an HTML document (or text/html media type) will simply ignore the trailing / character in the standalone element. The space preceding the / character (`<hr />` is not required by XHTML but is included to avoid confusing browsers parsing the document as HTML.

Note 3: A minimized (or Boolean) attribute turns on a feature by its presence, which is otherwise turned off by default. All HTML 4-compatible browsers recognize expanded Boolean attributes, but some earlier browsers might not.

Note 4: The NAME attribute is included in XHTML 1.0 for transitional purposes as a deprecated attribute, to allow for older browsers that do not recognize the ID attribute. The NAME attribute should not be used in a document declared to conform to the "strict" definition of XHTML 1.0. When both are included in an XHTML element, they must share the same unique value. The NAME attribute is obsolete in XHTML 2.0.

APPENDIX C
Cascading Style Sheets Sampler

Following is a sampler of the most commonly used and widely supported CSS1 (Cascading Style Sheets, level 1) and CSS2 (Cascading Style Sheets, level 2) properties. Current browsers support all of these properties, except where noted, but some recent browsers might not support all of the CSS2 properties. CSS1 properties are unmarked, while CSS2 properties are marked with "(2.0)." If it is important to maximize backward-compatibility with recent browsers, you should stick with using CSS1 properties and values unless also implementing hacks, filters, or browser redirections. See "Compatibility Issues and Solutions" for solutions to the most common compatibility issues.

N O T E ——— Initial values for properties (when they have them) are indicated by bold type. Anything other than a literal value is indicated by italics (for example *length* to indicate measurement values such as **10px** or **3em** or *n* to indicate a number).

SAMPLER OF CSS PROPERTIES

background	**Inherited:** no	**Application:** all elements

A shorthand property for controlling element backgrounds.

Property Values	*background-color\background-image\background-repeat\ background-attachment\background-position*
Example	`body { color: blue; background: black url(back_dark.jpg) fixed; }` `h1, h2, h3 { color: yellow; background: transparent; }` `p { color: #ffffcc; background: transparent; }`

See also: *background-color*, *background-image*, *background-repeat*, *background-attachment*, and *background-position*

background-attachment	**Inherited:** no	**Application:** all elements

Specifies whether a background image is fixed relative to the canvas or scrolls with the Web page.

Property Values	fixed|**scroll**
Example	`body { color: maroon; background: white; background-attachment: fixed; }`

This property is buggy in Internet Explorer prior to Version 7.

background-color   Inherited: no   Application: all elements

Specifies a background color for an element.

Property Values   *color*|**transparent**

color = a color name, a hexadecimal RGB color code, a decimal RGB color code, or a percentage RGB color code (see the color property listing for examples of using these).

Example
```
div.box { color: navy; background-color: #ccffcc; }
```

background-image   Inherited: no   Application: all elements

Specifies a background image for an element.

Property Values   url(*URL*)|**none**

Example
```
body { color: black; background-color: white; background-image:
url(back_light.jpg); }
```

background-repeat   Inherited: no   Application: all elements

Specifies whether and how a background image should be repeated in a Web page's background.

Property Values   repeat-x|repeat-y|**repeat**|no-repeat

Example
```
body { color: black; background-color: white; background-image:
url(back_twocol.jpg); background-repeat: repeat-y; }
```

repeat-x = horizontal, *repeat-y* = vertical, *repeat* = horizontal/vertical. The *no-repeat* value is usually used in conjunction with the background-position property (to position a watermark image, for instance).

background-position   Inherited: no   Application: block and replaced elements

Positions a background image in a Web page's background. Used in conjunction with a **no-repeat** value for the background-repeat property.

Property Values   *length length*|*n% n%*|*length*|*n%*|*length n%*|*n% length*|*keyword keyword*|
                            length|*n%*|*keyword*|0% 0%

length = px, em, ex, cm, in, mm, pt, and pc units (negative values allowed).
keyword (horizontal) = left, center, right.
keyword (vertical) = top, center, bottom.
n% = a percentage value. Negative percentages (*-n%*) are allowed.

Example
```
body { color: black; background-color: white; background-image:
url(watermark.gif); background-repeat: no-repeat; background-
position: 50% 150px; }
```

or

```
div { color: black; background-color: white; background-image:
url(logo.gif); background-repeat: no-repeat; background-position:
top center; }
```

The background image is positioned relative to the padding edge of the containing block.

length length|*n% n%*|*length n%*| *n% length* = horizontal (1st position) vertical (2nd position).
length|*n%* = horizontal (50% or center assumed for vertical).

Keyword values cannot be combined with length or percentage values.

border	**Inherited:** no	**Application:** all elements

A shorthand property for controlling border characteristics.

Property Values	*border-width, border-style, border-color*
Example	`div.frame { border: 4px solid red; }`

See also: *border-width*, *border-style*, and *border-color*.

border-collapse (CSS2)	**Inherited:** yes	**Application:** table elements

Specifies the formatting model for displaying adjacent borders in tables.

Property Values	collapse|**separate**|inherit

A **collapse** value collapses adjacent table borders to a single border, while a **separate** value retains separation between adjacent borders.

Example	`table { border-collapse: collapse; border-spacing: 0; border: 1px solid black; margin-left: auto; margin-right: auto; }`
	`th, td { padding: 4px; border: 1px solid black; }`

Netscape 6 does not recognize the border-collapse property but does recognize `border-spacing: 0` to achieve the same result. See *border-spacing* for more information on this property.

border-color	**Inherited:** no	**Application:** all elements

Specifies the border color to be drawn around an element.

Property Values	*color*|**transparent**|inherit

color = a color name, a hexadecimal RGB color code, a decimal RGB color code, or a percentage RGB color code (see the color property listing for examples of using these).

If a border-style property has been specified, but no border-color property, the element's color property value is inherited as the border color.

One to four values can be specified. One value = all four sides; two values = top/bottom and right/left; three values = top, right/left, and bottom; and four values = top, right, left, and bottom.

Example	`div.alert { border-color: green #0066ff blue #ff66cc; }`

border-spacing (CSS2)	**Inherited:** yes	**Application:** table elements

Specifies the amount of spacing to be displayed between adjacent table borders when `border-collapse: separate` is set.

Property Values	*length1* [*length2*]|inherit|**0**

One or two *length* values can be specified; if two, then the first specifies the horizontal spacing, and the second specifies the vertical spacing to be displayed between table borders.

Example	`table { border-collapse: separate; border-spacing: 3px; border: 1px solid black; margin-left: auto; margin-right: auto; }`
	`th, td { padding: 4px; border: 1px solid black; }`

Internet Explorer 6 for Windows and Internet Explorer 5 for the Macintosh do not support the border-spacing property. To control spacing between adjacent table borders in those browsers, you must use the CELLSPACING attribute in the TABLE element.

border-style
Inherited: no   **Application:** all elements

Specifies the style of border to be drawn around an element.

Property Values   dotted|dashed|solid|double| groove|ridge|inset|outset|**none**

One or two *length* values can be specified; if two, then the first specifies the horizontal spacing and the second specifies the vertical spacing to be displayed between table borders.

Example
```
div.announce { border-color: green; border-style: groove; }
table { border-collapse: separate; border-spacing: 3px; border: 1px
solid black; margin-left: auto; margin-right: auto; }
th, td { padding: 4px; border: 1px solid black; }
```

border-top, border-right, border-bottom, border-left
Inherited: no   **Application:** all elements

Shorthand properties for setting the border width, style, and color for the top, right, bottom, or left sides of an element.

Property Values   *border width, border style, border color*

Example
```
div.topbottom { border-top: groove green 5px; border-bottom: ridge
olive 3px; }
```

border-width
Inherited: no   **Application:** all elements

A shorthand property for setting the width of the borders around an element.

Property Values   *length*|thin|**medium**|thick

length = pixels (px), em units (em), ex units (ex), centimeters (cm), inches (in), millimeters (mm), points (pt), or picas (pc).

One value = all four sides; two values = top/bottom and right/left; three values = top, right/left, and bottom; and four values = top, right, left, and bottom.

Example
```
h2 { border-color: blue; border-top-style: solid; border-width: 6px
3px; }
```

clear
Inherited: no   **Application:** block elements

Clears a preceding floating element, moving down on the page until the left, right, or both margins are clear (not blocked by the floating element).

Property Values   left|right|both|**none**

See *float* for an example of using the clear property.

clip
Inherited: no   **Application:** block and replaced elements

Specifies an area within an element to be displayed (with the "clipped" areas rendered invisible).

Property Values   rect(*top right bottom left*)|**auto**|inherit

The rect values (*top*, *right*, *bottom*, and *left*) specify offsets (in pixels, ems, or percentages, for instance) from the respective sides of the element. Negative values can be used. An **auto** offset value also can be used to specify that an offset should be unchanged from what it would normally be.

Example
```
div.banner img { clip: rect(5px 20px 15px 30px); }
```

color	Inherited: yes	Application: all elements

Specifies the foreground color for an element.

Property Values   *color*

color = a color name, a hexadecimal RGB color code, a decimal RGB color code, or a percentage RGB color code (see the color property listing for examples of using these).

Example
```
h2 { color: navy; background: #ccffcc; }
span { color: rgb(128,255,0); background: transparent; }
```

display	Inherited: no	Application: all elements

Specifies how or whether an element will be displayed.

Property Values   block|**inline**|list-item|table|table-row|table-cell|none

Example
```
a.button { display: block; padding: 5px; border: ridge blue 3px;
color: red; background: yellow; }
.noshow { display: none; }
```

The **table**, **table-row**, and **table-cell** values are part of CSS 2 and might not be supported by all recent browsers (including Internet Explorer 7 and earlier versions).

It can sometimes be useful to turn inline elements into block elements, such as declaring A elements to be block elements, which avoids the need to use DIV, P, or BR elements to create a vertical menu or list of links.

display: none differs from **visibility: hidden** in that the element is not present and does not affect the page's layout, whereas with hiding an element using the visibility property, the element is still present, but just not visible, and thus affects the page's layout. The display property also is not inherited, whereas the visibility property is.

The table, table-row, and table-cell values for the display property allow the creation of table-like layouts using DIV elements, avoiding the counter-semantic use of the TABLE element for that purpose.

float	Inherited: no	Application: all elements

Floats an element to the left or right margin, with following text or other elements flowing around the other side of the element.

Property Values   left|right|**none**

Example
```
div.left { float: left; width: 200px; margin-right: 5px; }
h1, h2, h3 { clear: left; }
hr { clear: both: }
```

Unlike the **align="left"** and **align="right"** HTML attributes, which only be used to float the IMG, TABLE, OBJECT, and APPLET elements, the float property can float any displayable element.

The clear property is used in conjunction with the float property to cause following elements to clear a floating element.

font-family	Inherited: yes	Application: all elements

Specifies a font-family name or comma-separated list of font-family names.

Property Values   *font-family|generic font-family*

A specific font-family name should match the actual name of a font in use, such as Times New Roman, Trebuchet MS, Comic Sans MS, Palatino, New Century Schoolbook, and so on. Font-family names with spaces must be quoted.

Five generic font-family names can be used: **serif**, **sans-serif**, **monospace**, **cursive**, and **fantasy**, but only serif, sans-serif, and monospace are handled consistently by browsers.

Example   `h2 { font-family: 'Trebuchet MS', Arial, Helvetica, sans-serif; }`

A specific font-family has to be available on a local system to be displayed. In the example, if Trebuchet MS is not available, Arial will be displayed; if Arial is not available, Helvetica will be displayed; if Helvetica is not available, a system's default sans serif font will be displayed.

Although not required, it is good practice to list font-family names exactly, including any uppercase letters, because font names on some platforms are case-sensitive. It is also good practice to list PostScript fonts after TrueType fonts because some earlier Windows browsers display the embedded bitmap font if a PostScript font is listed first and Adobe Type Manager is not installed.

font-size   Inherited: yes   Application: all elements

Specifies the font size in which an element is to be displayed.

Property Values   *length*|*n%*|*relative-size*|
                      absolute-size (**medium**)

length = pixels (px), em units (em), ex units (ex), centimeters (cm), inches (in), millimeters (mm), points (pt), picas (pc).
relative-size = larger, smaller.
absolute-size = xxsmall, x-small, small, **medium**, large, x-large, xx-large.

Font sizes set in em units, ex units, and percentages are relative to the parent element's font size. Thus a font size of 1.5 ems set for an element would be one and a half times the font size set for that element's parent element.

When setting font sizes, other than on the BODY element, em units and percentages are equivalent (with 1.5 em and 150% both representing a font size that is one and a half times the font size of the parent element). An ex-unit should be relative to the x-height of the parent element's font, but many current browsers simply treat it as one-half of an em unit.

Example
```
h2 { font-size: 6.5em; }
p { font-size: 110%; }
address { font-size: smaller; }
```

Points (pt), picas (pc), centimeters (cm), inches (in), and millimeters (mm) should only be used where the dimensions of the output media are known, such as when creating a "print" media style sheet for printing to an 8.5 × 11.5-inch piece of paper.

Absolute-size keywords (xxsmall, x-small, small, medium, large, x-large, and xx-large) for setting font sizes are interpreted inconsistently in browsers and should probably be avoided.

font-style   Inherited: yes   Application: all elements

Specifies the style of an element's font.

Property Values   italic|oblique|**normal**

The **oblique** value is not normally used, since browsers do not generally distinguish between italic and oblique fonts. An italic font is individually crafted, while an oblique font is a normal font that has been slanted.

Example   `span.stress { font-style: italic; }`

font-weight	Inherited: yes	Application: all elements

Specifies the weight of an element's font.

Property Values   bold|bolder|lighter|**normal**|
100|200|300|400|500|600|700|800|900

A 400 font-weight should be equal to a normal font-weight, and a 700 font-weight should be equal to a bold font-weight. Most current browsers do not distinguish the other font-weights, displaying them in either a normal or a bold font-weight. Stick to specifying bold or normal font-weights, in other words, and do not bother with the rest.

Example   `blockquote { font-weight: bold; }`

height	Inherited: no	Application: block and replaced elements

Specifies the height of an element's font.

Property Values   *length*|*n%*|**auto**

Browsers are inconsistent in how they handle a percentage height (*n%*). To get consistent results, a height needs to be set for the containing block: `height: 100%;` for the BODY element or `height: 300px;` for other elements, for instance.

Example
```
div.insert {
        height: 400px;
        padding: 5px;
        border: 2px green solid;
```

In most browsers that support CSS, this will result in a division with a content area that is 400 pixels high, excluding any padding or borders that have been set. Internet Explorer 5.5 for Windows, however, incorrectly handles setting element heights and widths, which can result in a different heigth dimension displaying in that browser if padding or borders are are also set for the element. For a more detailed discussion of this issue and a solution, see "Compatibility Issues and Solutions" following this table.

letter-spacing	Inherited: yes	Application: all elements

Specifies additional spacing to be added between letters within an element.

Property Values   *length*|**normal**

A negative value (`letter-spacing: -2px`, for instance) can be set to reduce spacing between letters, but browsers can set implementation-specific limits (such as when also justifying text, for instance).

Example   `h2 { letter-spacing: 2px; }`

The letter-spacing property is not included in *CSS1 core*, which defines the core functionality required for a browser to be CSS1-compliant.

line-height	Inherited: yes	Application: all elements

Specifies the height of an element's line.

Property Values   *length*|*n*|*n%*|**normal**

n = an integer value that sets the line-height as a multiplication of the element's font size (with a value of 2, for instance, corresponding to double-spacing).

A percentage value (*n%*) differs from an integer value in that the computed value is inherited by a child element, while for an integer value, the specified value is inherited.

Example   `p { letter-height: 1.5; }`

list-style   Inherited: yes   Application: List item elements

A shorthand property for setting values for the list-style-type, list-style-position, and list-style-image properties.

Property Values	*list-style-type, list-style-position, list-style-image*
Example	`ul { list-style: circle url(bullet.gif) inside; }` `ol { list-style: A; }`

list-style-image   Inherited: yes   Application: list item elements

Specifies the URL of an image to be displayed in place of an unordered list's bullet character.

Property Values	url(*URL*)|**none**
Example	`ul { list-style-image: url(bullet.gif); }`

list-style-position   Inherited: yes   Application: list item elements

Specifies whether the list bullet or number is displayed inside or outside of a list item's element box.

Property Values	inside|**outside**
Example	`ol { list-style-position: inside; }` `ol ul { list-style-position: outside; }`

list-style-type   Inherited: yes   Application: list item elements

Specifies the type of unordered or ordered list to be displayed.

Property Values	**disc**|circle|square (for UL elements) **decimal**|lower-roman|upper-roman| lower-alpha|upper-alpha|none (for OL elements)

Example	`ol { list-style-type: square; }`
	`ol ol { list-style-type: disc; }`
	`ol ol ol { list-style-type: circle; }`
	`ul { list-style-type: upper-roman; }`
	`ul ul { list-style-type: upper-alpha; }`
	`ul ul ul { list-style-type: decimal; }`

margin   Inherited: no   Application: all elements

A shorthand property for setting the margin-top, margin-right, margin-bottom, and margin-left properties for an element.

Property Values	*length*|*n%*|auto|**0**

One to four values can be specified. One value applies to all four sides; two values apply to the top/bottom and right/left sides; three values apply to the top, right/left, and bottom sides; and four values apply to the top, right, left, and bottom sides.

For inline text elements, such as EM, STRONG, I, B, and so on, margin values are only applied to the left and right sides of the element. For the IMG element, however, which is also an inline element, margins are applied to all four sides.

Example	`body { margin: 2em; }` `div.inset { margin: 10px 20px; }`

Margin spacing is displayed outside of any borders or padding space that are set for an element.

margin-top, margin-right, margin-bottom, margin-left   **Inherited:** no   **Application:** all elements

These properties specify the amount of margin spacing to be displayed outside of the four sides of an element.

Property Values   *length*|*n%*|auto|**0**

Adjacent horizontal margins of nested elements are added together, while vertical margins between abutting elements collapse to the highest value of the two.

In CSS, an element with a width less than 100% of the browser window can be centered by setting the left and right margins to **auto**. Because of a bug, however, this does not work in Internet Explorer 5.5 for Windows. The workaround is to nest the element inside of a DIV element with a **text-align: center** property set, while setting **text-align: left** on the nested element. See the *text-align* listing for more information on using the text-align property.

Example

```
div.center { text-align: center; }
div.centered { width: 75%; margin-left: auto; margin-right: auto;
text-align: left; font-size: 110%; }
</style>
</head>
<body>
<div class="center">
<div class="centered">
<h2>Announcement:</h2>
<p>This semester's field trip is scheduled for next Friday. To be
excused, you must have a signed statement from a parent or
physician stating the reason you should be excused. Be sure to wear
proper walking shoes and bring protection against the rain, since
rain is not unheard of at this time of the year.</p>
</div>
</div>
```

Negative values can be set to reduce the margin spacing that would otherwise be displayed for an element. A problem can result, however, when trying to do this to reduce the default indenting of ordered or unordered lists because Internet Explorer and other browsers that follow its example indent a list by adding margin space to the left of the list, while Netscape and Mozilla indent a list by adding padding space to the left of the list. The workaround is to nest the list inside a DIV element and then set a negative left-margin on that element to reduce the default indenting of a list.

max-height, max-width (CSS2)   **Inherited:** no   **Application:** block and replaced elements

Set a maximum height or width for an element.

Property Values   *length*|*n%*|inherit|**none**

See *height* and *width* for descriptions of the *max-height* and *max-width* property values.

Example

```
div.container {
    max-height: 300px;
    max-width: 500px;
    }
```

min-height, min-width (CSS2)   **Inherited:** no   **Application:** block and replaced elements

Set a minimum height or width for an element.

Property Values   *length*|*n%*|inherit

The initial value is a length of 0. See *height* and *width* for descriptions of the *max-height* and *max-width* property values.

| *Example* | ```
div.container {
        min-height: 600px;
        min-width: 800px;
        }
``` |

overflow (CSS2) **Inherited:** no   **Application:** block and replaced elements

Specifies how content that overflows the dimensions of an element is to be treated.

Property Values **visible**|hidden|scroll|auto|inherit

A **visible** value indicates the element's content can overflow and be rendered outside of the element's boundaries. A **hidden** value hides content that overflows the element's boundaries. A **scroll** value causes scroll bars to be displayed, even if an element's content does not overflow its boundaries, while an **auto** value displays scroll bars only if the element's contents overflows its boundaries.

Example `div.wnd { height: 25em; overflow: auto; }`

padding **Inherited:** no   **Application:** all elements

A shorthand property for setting the padding-top, padding-right, padding-bottom, and padding-left properties for an element.

Property Values *length*|*n%*|auto|**0**

One to four values can be specified. One value applies to all four sides; two values apply to the top/bottom and right/left sides; three values apply to the top, right/left, and bottom sides; and four values apply to the top, right, left, and bottom sides.

Example `div.inset { margin: 10px 20px; border: 4px red groove; padding: 5px 10px 8px; }`

Padding is displayed outside of the element's content box but inside of any border.

padding-top, padding-right,
padding-bottom, padding-left **Inherited:** no   **Application:** all elements

These properties specify the amount of padding to be displayed around the four sides of an element.

Property Values *length*|*n%*|auto|**0**

Example ```
div.center { text-align: center; }
div.centered { width: 75%; padding-left: 10px; padding-right: 10px;
border: 4px ridge maroon; margin-left: auto; margin-right: auto;
text-align: left; font-size: 110%; }
```

position (CSS2) **Inherited:** no   **Application:** all elements (but not generated content)

Used in conjunction with the top, right, bottom, and left properties to position an element within the browser window.

Property Values **static**|relative|absolute|fixed|inherit

A **relative** value positions the element relative to its current position. An **absolute** value positions the element relative to the top, right, bottom, and left edges of the containing block's padding area. A **fixed** value works the same way as an **absolute** value, except the element remains fixed on the screen when the page is scrolled. See *top, right, bottom, and left* for an example.

Current and most recent browsers support the **fixed** value, but Internet Explorer 6 and earlier versions do not.

text-align   Inherited: yes   Application: block elements

Specifies how the content is horizontally aligned within an element.

Property Values   left|right|center|justify

Example   `p { text-align: justify; }`

The **justify** value is not included in *CSS1 core*, which defines the core functionality required for a browser to be CSS1-compliant; as a result, some earlier browsers ignore the **justify** value, enforcing the default text-alignment instead (left or right, depending on the default writing direction of the language in use).

text-decoration   Inherited: no   Application: all elements

Specifies how text is decorated (or highlighted) within an element.

Property Values   underline|overline|line-through|blink|**none**

A common use of the text-decoration property is to turn off display of the default underlining that most browsers display under hypertext links.

Browsers are not required to support the **blink** value. Generally, blinking text on the Web is considered to be irritating and rude and is best avoided.

Example   `h2 { text-decoration: overline; }`
                     `a { text-decoration: none; }`

text-indent   Inherited: yes   Application: block elements

Sets the amount of space the first line of an element is to be indented. Can be used to format tabbed paragraphs, for instance.

Property Values   *length*|*n%*|**0**

Example   `p { text-indent: 10px; margin-top: 0; margin-bottom: 0; }`

top, right, bottom, and left   Inherited: no   Application: positioned elements

Used in conjunction with the position property to position an element within the browser window.

Property Values   *length*|*n%*|**auto**|inherit

When absolutely positioning an element, the top, right, and left properties indicate the distance of the element's position from the top, right, and left edges of the containing block's padding area, while the bottom property positions it relative to the bottom of the browser window. When relatively positioning an element, the top, right, left, and bottom properties indicate the distance of the object from its current position. Negative values can be used.

Example   `div.pos1 { position: absolute; top: 24px; left: 100px; }`

vertical-align   Inherited: no   Application: inline and table-cell elements

Vertically aligns an element relative to its parent element.

Property Values   **baseline**|sub|super|top|text-top|middle|bottom|text-bottom|*n%*

The **baseline** value aligns the element with the parent element's baseline. The **sub** and **super** values subscript or superscript the element relative to the parent element. The **top**, **middle**, and **bottom** values align the element with the top, middle, or bottom of the parent element. The **text-top** and **text-bottom** values align the top or bottom of the element with the top or bottom of the parent element's text. A percentage value allows the incremental lowering or raising of the element relative to its parent element's box, with the percentage value being relative to the element's line-height. CSS2 also allows a length value (pixels or ems, for instance) to be specified.

| *Example* | `h3 { font-size: 2em; }` |
| | `h3 em { font-size: 2.5em; vertical-align: middle; }` |

| **visibility (CSS2)** | **Inherited:** no | **Application:** all elements |

Specifies whether an element's generated box is rendered.

| *Property Values* | **visible**|hidden|collapse|inherit |

The **visible** value renders the element's box visible, while the **hidden** value hides it. A `visibility: hidden` property value differs from a `display: none` property value, in that the first merely renders the element from being visible, which continues to occupy space within the document flow; while the second stops the element's box from being generated at all, without affecting the layout or positioning of surrounding elements. A **collapse** value applies only to table rows or columns; relative to other elements, a **collapse** value is equivalent to a **hidden** value.

| *Example* | `div.hide { visibility: hidden; }` |

| **white-space** | **Inherited:** yes | **Application:** block elements |

Specifies how *whitespace* within an element is to be treated. In CSS, whitespace is defined as being formed by spaces (Unicode 32), tabs (Unicode 9), line feeds (Unicode 10), carriage returns (Unicode 13), and form feeds (Unicode 12), but not by other characters forming spaces, such as em spaces (Unicode 8195), for instance.

| *Property Values* | nowrap|pre|**normal** |

The **nowrap** value causes the line to not wrap at whitespace characters, causing the line to extend past the right margin until a BR element is encountered. The **pre** value causes the element's content to be treated as though it were in a PRE element, with all spaces and hard returns preserved. The **normal** value causes whitespace characters to be treated as they normally are, with lines wrapping at the farthest whitespace character within a browser window and multiple whitespace characters, for instance, being collapsed to a single space.

In CSS, whitespace is defined as being formed by spaces (Unicode 32), tabs (Unicode 9), line feeds (Unicode 10), carriage returns (Unicode 13), and form feeds (Unicode 12), but not by other characters forming spaces, such as em spaces (Unicode 8195), for instance.

| *Example* | `code { display: block; white-space: pre; }` |

The white-space property is not included in *CSS1 core*, which defines the core functionality required for a browser to be CSS1-compliant. Some earlier browsers do not support it; Internet Explorer 5.5 for Windows supports the **nowrap** value, but not the **pre** value.

| **width** | **Inherited:** no | **Application:** block and replaced elements |

Specifies the width of the content area within an element.

| *Property Values* | *length*|*n%*|**auto** |

The width of an element is exclusive of any additional padding, borders, or margins that are defined for the element. When the width is undefined (or **auto** is set), the width is equal to the available space, minus any padding, borders, or margins. With a specific or percentage width, the right margin is adjusted to fill the available space (assuming the parent element is left-aligned), unless both the margin-left and margin-right properties are set to **auto**, in which case, both the left and right margins are adjusted to fill the available space (centering the element).

A percentage width is relative to the width of the containing block (the parent element).

Example

```
div.insert {
        width: 400px;
        padding: 5px;
        border: 2px green solid;
        margin-left: auto;
        margin-right: auto;
        }
```

In most browsers that support CSS, this will result in a center-aligned division, the content area of which is 400px wide, excluding any padding or borders that have been set. Internet Explorer 5.5 for Windows, however, incorrectly handles the width element, which can result in a different width dimension displaying in that browser if padding or borders are included in the object. For a more detailed discussion of this issue and a solution, see "Compatibility Issues and Solutions" following this table.

z-index (CSS2)	Inherited: no	Application: all elements

Specifies the stacking order of positioned elements.

Property Values   *n*|**auto**|inherit

Normally, a following positioned element is stacked on top of a preceding positioned element. A positioned element with a higher z-index value is stacked on top of one with a lower z-index value.

Example

```
height: 125px; width: 98.7%; background: aqua; }
div.left { z-index: 2; position: absolute; top: 135px; left: 10px;
height: 85em; width: 150px; background: lime; }
div.main { z-index: 1; position: absolute; top: 135px; left: 160px;
height: 85em; width: auto; background: yellow; }
```

NOTE

For additional resources and information on using CSS, see the Appendixes section at the IRC for this book at www.emcp.com/.

COMPATIBILITY ISSUES AND SOLUTIONS

CSS has only recently gained wide and consistent support in current browsers. Following are some of the main compatibility issues and some possible solutions.

Box Model Bug in Internet Explorer 5 and 5.5

Internet Explorer 5 and 5.5 for Windows incorrectly calculates the width of an element as including padding and border lengths, while all other recent CSS-supporting browsers, correctly following the CSS standards, calculate the width of an element as excluding padding and border lengths. Whenever using the width or height properties to set a specific or percentage length, this can cause the same box to appear shorter and/or thinner in Internet Explorer than in other browsers that correctly implement the W3C box model. Besides impacting Internet Explorer 5 and 5.5, the box model bug can also show up if quirks mode is triggered by a foreshortened or nonexistent DocType declaration.

SOLUTION #1: BOX IN A BOX This solution works simply by not assigning 1) a height or width and 2) padding or borders to the same element. Instead, you nest two DIV elements, setting a width on the outside DIV and padding and/or borders to the inside DIV:

```
<div style="width: 300px">
    <div style="padding: 4px; border: 2px green solid" >
    Some content...
    </div>
</div>
```

An inline style is used to illustrate this, but class selectors can just as easily be used (and allow styling more than one instance). This actually has the effect of forcing other browsers to follow the IE 5/5.5 box model, in that padding and borders are inserted inside the width-setting division. That means that once IE 5/5.5 completely disappears, the workaround cannot simply be removed without recalculating the width value. Another problem with this is that for more complex layouts, you end up with a lot of nested divisions.

SOLUTION #2: BOX MODEL HACK The box model hack was developed by Tantek Çelik, a leader of the Internet Explorer development team at Microsoft. The box model hack takes advantage of a parsing error in Internet Explorer 5/5.5 that causes it to ignore any style declarations following **voice-family: "\"}\""; voice-family: inherit;**. Here's an example:

```
div.side a {
    display: block;
    padding: 2px;
    border: 4px #f90 outset;
    width: 112px;
<!--Start Box Model Hack-->
    voice-family: "\"}\"";
    voice-family: inherit;
    width: 100px;
    }
html>body div.side a {
    width: 100px;
    }
<!--End Box Model Hack-->
```

The second part of the hack (**html>body div.side a**) is necessary for some earlier versions of the Opera browser, which have the same parsing error as Internet Explorer 5/5.5 but are not subject to the box model bug. It uses a CSS2 child selector that is recognized by Opera but is ignored by Internet Explorer 5/5.5.

In this example, Internet Explorer 5/5.5 applies the width of 112px but ignores the two width settings of 100px. Mozilla Firefox and other browsers not subject to the IE 5/5.5 parsing error apply the width of 112px, while Opera applies the second width of 112px. Because the element has 4 pixels in padding and 8 pixels in borders along either dimension, the difference in the two width settings needs to be 12 pixels (4 + 8 = 12).

If you are going to use the box model hack, you need to specify a full HTML 4.01 or XHTML 1.0 DocType declaration that does not trigger quirks mode in Internet Explorer 6 or 7. Those browsers are subject to the box model bug in quirks mode but not to the parsing error that makes the box model hack possible.

Internet Explorer 5/5.5 Centering Bug

With CSS, you can center an element with a specific or percentage width in the following manner:

```
<div style="width: 200px; margin-left: auto; margin-right: auto;">
Element content
</div>
```

Internet Explorer 5/5.5, or Internet Explorer 6/7 in quirks mode, however, sets the correct width for the element but left-aligns it because it does not recognize margins set to an **auto** value.

SOLUTION: TEXT-ALIGN WRAPPER A solution to this problem is to wrap the affected element in a DIV element with **text-align: center** set:

```
<div style="text-align: center">
    <div style="width: 200px; margin-left: auto;
    margin-right: auto; text-align: left">
    Element content
    </div>
</div>
```

Note that left-alignment is reset in the inner division, or both the division and its contents would be center-aligned. If you try to use this solution without resetting the text alignment for the nested division, any nested content will inherit the center-alignment from the wrapper division.

Advanced CSS Breaking Internet Explorer 7, 6, or Earlier Versions

Internet Explorer 8 supports the full panoply of CSS1 and CSS2, but if you try to apply **display:table**, **display:table-row**, and **display:table-cell** to lay out a three-column page design, or many other more advanced CSS features, your design will degrade ungracefully in earlier versions of Internet Explorer.

SOLUTION: MICROSOFT CONDITIONAL COMMENTS Microsoft has developed what it calls "conditional comments" that can be inserted in a Web page to target or filter content for a specific version or versions of Internet Explorer. This can be handy if you want to make full use of what CSS2 has to offer but do not want to resort to a lot of hacks to account for earlier versions of that browser.

For instance, if you design a site that uses the **display:table** attribute, which is not supported in versions of Internet Explorer prior to Version 8, you can use a conditional comment that will cause earlier versions of Internet Explorer (Version 7 and earlier) to display an advisory box on the screen, advising the user they need to upgrade their browser to one that supports the latest HTML and CSS standards:

```
<!--Start Conditional Comment that only versions of IE earlier
than IE8 will read and execute.-->
<!--[if lt IE 8]>
<div id="standards" align="center">This site requires a browser
that <span class="latest">supports the HTML 4.01 and CSS2.1 Web
standards</span>. Upgrade your browser now to the latest version
of any of these browsers:
```

```
<ul>
<li><a href="http://www.microsoft.com/windows/Internet-
explorer/">Internet Explorer 8 (Win)</a>
<li><a href="http://www.mozilla.org/firefox/">Mozilla Firefox
(Win/Mac/Lnx)</a>
<li><a href="">Apple Safari (Mac/Win)</a>
<li><a href="http://www.opera.com/">Opera (Win)</a>
<li><a href="http://www.google.com/chrome/">Google Chrome (Win)
</a>
</div>
<![endif]-->
<!--End Conditional Comment-->
```

This will cause Internet Explorer 5, 5.5, 6, and 7 to display the alert on the screen, while Internet Explorer 8 and all other browsers will ignore it.

However, sophisticated CSS-only multi-column layouts can be produced with minimal CSS hacks and workarounds, without the use of any conditional comments, which will display reliably in Internet Explorer 5 through 8 as well as in other current browsers. See the "Tesla Science Club" case example in Chapter 7, for an example.

The **class="standards"** attribute lets you position and format the alert. By applying a significant bottom margin to the "standards" class, for instance, you can push the rest of your page below the fold (the bottom edge of the browser's viewport), where it cannot be seen. For instance:

```
#standards {
    width:600px;
    margin-left:auto;
    margin-right:auto;
    margin-top:50px;
    margin-bottom:500px;
    padding:10px;
    font-size: 2.3em;
    color: #ffc;
    background: maroon;
    border: 8px #fcc outset;
    }
#standards :link, #standards :visited {
    color: #cfc;
    background: transparent;
    }
#standards .latest {
    color: #fc0;
    background: transparent;
    }
</style>
```

The background-attachment:fixed property value is buggy in versions of Internet Explorer prior to Version 7. You could use a conditional comment to make sure users of those earlier browsers get the default scrolled background image:

```
<style type="text/css">
body {
    background-attachment:fixed;
    }
</style>
```

```
<!--Start Conditional Comment that only versions of IE earlier
than IE7 will read and execute.-->
<!--[if lt IE 7]>
<style type="text/css">
body {
    background-attachment:scrolled;
    }
</style>
<![endif]-->
<!--End Conditional Comment-->
```

TABLE C.1 • Microsoft Conditional Comments

If Statement	Meaning
`<!--[if IE]>`	If any version of IE
`<!--[if IE 7]>`	If *equal to* IE 7
`<!--[if lte IE 7]>`	If *less than or equal* to IE 7
`<!--[if lt IE 7]>`	If *less than* IE 7
`<!--[if gt IE 5.5]>`	If *greater than* IE 5.5
`<!--[if gte IE 6]>`	If *greater than or equal* to IE
`<!--[if gt IE 5.5]>`	If *greater than* IE 5.5
`<!--[if (gt IE 5.5)&(lt IE 8)]>`	If *greater than* IE 5.5 and *less than* IE 8 (IE 6 or IE 7)

Shielding Other Noncompliant Browsers

Filtering content to alert users of Internet Explorer 7 and earlier versions of that browser so they see an alert notice instead of your page's content will keep most, but not all, users of noncompliant browsers from seeing your advanced CSS layout. Users of earlier browsers can still trip over your new page design. Combining one of the following methods with the Conditional Comments method shown earlier can shield almost all users still using browsers that do not fully support CSS1 and CSS2 from seeing a broken version of your CSS layout.

SOLUTION #1: THE INVISIBLE OBJECT METHOD The invisible object method is a method originally developed by the Web Standards Project (**www.webstandards.org/**). It works by adding an IFRAME element at the top of the page that is invisible to users of browsers that recognize the display:none style property. For instance:

```
<body>
<iframe style="display:none">
<p><big><big>This site is best viewed by a browser that supports
the latest Web standards. Please take this opportunity to upgrade
your browser to the latest version of any of these browsers:
</big></big></p>
<ul
<li><a href="http://www.microsoft.com/windows/Internet-
explorer/">Internet Explorer 8 (Win)</a>
<li><a href="http://www.mozilla.org/firefox/">Mozilla Firefox
(Win/Mac/Lnx)</a>
<li><a href="">Apple Safari (Mac/Win)</a>
<li><a href="http://www.opera.com/">Opera (Win)</a>
```

```
<li><a href="http://www.google.com/chrome/">Google Chrome (Win)
</a>
</ul>
<hr><br><br>
</iframe>
```

With this method, users of browsers that do not recognize **display:none** see the alert message, advising them that they need to upgrade their browser.

SOLUTION #2: THE DOM SNIFF METHOD The DOM sniff method is a method that was also originally developed by the Web Standards Project. It redirects any browser that does not support the W3C's Document Object Model (DOM). It works by inserting a short JavaScript script in the HEAD element that checks if a browser supports the W3C's DOM standard:

```
<script type="text/javascript" language="javascript">
<!-- //
if (!document.getElementById) {
    window.location = "upgrade.html"
}
// -->
</script>
</head>
```

If a user's browser does not support the W3C's DOM standard, it is redirected to an upgrade page (upgrade.html), where the user can be advised to upgrade the browser.

A Word of Caution

There is no shortage of hacks to address this or that CSS display quirk or bug in this or that browser. The problem with using hacks, however, is that they can have unintended consequences; that is, how future browsers will respond to them is an unknown. Wherever possible, workarounds should be used rather than hacks to support earlier browsers with less than full support for the CSS2.1 standard. In the solutions discussed earlier, there is only one hack presented, the box model hack—the other solutions are all workarounds. The box model hack has the virtue of being fairly bulletproof, because it relies on a parsing error that will not be reduplicated in future browsers. Once IE 5.5 passes from usage, or its users are numerically so small they can be safely left to their own desserts, the box model hack can be dispensed with entirely.

Validating CSS Code

The W3C's CSS Validator, at jigsaw.**w3.org/css-validator/**, can check the validity of CSS code in Web pages against the latest CSS standard (currently CSS 2.1). As with validating HTML using the W3C's HTML Validator, you can validate a CSS file (.css) or HTML file containing CSS by specifying a file address, uploading a file, or directly inputting (or pasting in) CSS code. It is recommended that you validate your page's HTML using the W3C's HTML Validator (see Appendix A) before using the CSS Validator to validate the page's CSS code.

APPENDIX D
Special Characters Chart

Because HTML documents are ASCII text documents, the number of characters that should be inserted directly from the keyboard is limited to the 128 ASCII characters. The ISO 8859-1 character set defines an additional 128 characters.

ASCII (KEYBOARD) CHARACTERS

The ASCII character set has 128 (0 through 127) positions. Positions 0 through 31 in the ASCII character set are control characters (Backspace, Tab, Cancel, and so on) that do not result in a displayable character. Positions 32 to 126 are characters that can be entered directly from the standard ASCII keyboard. Position 127 is a control character (Delete).

The displayable ASCII characters run from position 32 to 126. These constitute the only characters that should be directly entered from the keyboard into an HTML document.

NOTE

Keyboards for some Macintosh computers marketed in the United Kingdom substitute the British pound currency symbol (£) for the number sign (#). On those computers, press Option+3 (or Alt+3) to insert the number sign (#).

Character	Entity Number	Entity Name	Description
[ ]	#032;		space (brackets added)
!	#033;		exclamation mark
"	#034;	"	quotation mark
#	#035;		number sign
$	#036;		dollar sign
%	#037;		percent sign
&	#038;	&	ampersand
'	#039;	'	apostrophe
(	#040;		left parenthesis
)	#041;		right parenthesis

Character	Entity Number	Entity Name	Description
*	*		asterisk
+	+		plus sign
,	,		comma
-	-	−	hyphen, minus sign
.	.		period, decimal point
/	/		slash, solidus, virgule
0	0		numeral 0
1	1		numeral 1
2	2		numeral 2
3	3		numeral 3
4	4		numeral 4
5	5		numeral 5
6	6		numeral 6
7	7		numeral 7
8	8		numeral 8
9	9		numeral 9
:	:		colon
;	;		semicolon
<	<	<	less-than sign
=	=		equals sign
>	>	>	greater-than sign
?	?		question mark
@	@		at sign
A	A		capital A
B	B		capital B
C	C		capital C
D	D		capital D
E	E		capital E
F	F		capital F
G	G		capital G
H	H		capital H
I	I		capital I
J	J		capital J
K	K		capital K
L	L		capital L
M	M		capital M
N	N		capital N
O	O		capital O
P	P		capital P
Q	Q		capital Q
R	R		capital R
S	S		capital S
T	T		capital T

Character	Entity Number	Entity Name	Description
U	#085;		capital U
V	#086;		capital V
W	#087;		capital W
X	#088;		capital X
Y	#089;		capital Y
Z	#090;		capital Z
[	#091;		left square bracket
\	#092;		backslash, reverse solidus
]	#093;		right square bracket
^	#094;	&circ;	circumflex accent
_	#095;		underscore, low bar
`	#096;		gravé accent
a	#097;		small a
b	#098;		small b
c	#099;		small c
d	#100;		small d
e	#101;		small e
f	#102;		small f
g	#103;		small g
h	#104;		small h
i	#105;		small i
j	#106;		small j
k	#107;		small k
l	#108;		small l
m	#109;		small m
n	#110;		small n
o	#111;		small o
p	#112;		small p
q	#113;		small q
r	#114;		small r
s	#115;		small s
t	#116;		small t
u	#117;		small u
v	#118;		small v
w	#119;		small w
x	#120;		small x
y	#121;		small y
z	#122;		small z
{	#123;		left curly bracket
		#124;		vertical bar
}	#125;		right curly bracket
~	#126;		tilde

RESERVED CHARACTERS

A number of characters are used to indicate HTML codes and, depending on the circumstance, might need to be inserted into an HTML document using their entity number or entity name.

Character	Entity Number	Entity Name	Description
"	&#034;	&quot;	quotation mark
&	&#038;	&amp;	ampersand
<	&#060;	&lt;	less-than sign
>	&#062;	&gt;	greater-than sign

When displaying a < or > character in a Web page, always insert the character using either its entity number or entity name. Generally, standalone " and & characters do not need a substitute, unless they are part of an HTML code that you want to display, as is, in a Web page.

EXTENDED CHARACTERS (UNUSED)

Positions 128 through 159 reference extended characters that are in addition to the ASCII character set. Which characters in these positions are actually available depends upon the computer system and default character set being used. In the ISO 8859-1 character set, which is the standard character set for displaying Western European languages on the Web, the positions 128 through 159 are referenced as "unused" (or not to be used in Web pages). A number of browsers on the UNIX platform ignore entity numbers for all characters within this range. The following table shows the extended Latin-1 (ISO-8859-1) character set that is used in Microsoft Windows.

Character	Entity Number	Entity Name	Description
	&#128;		unused
	&#129;		unused
‚	&#130;		single quote (low)
ƒ	&#131;	&fnof;	function of, florin
„	&#132;		double quote (low)
…	&#133;	&hellip;	horizontal ellipsis
†	&#134;	&dagger;	dagger sign
‡	&#135;	&Dagger;	double dagger sign
ˆ	&#136;		small circumflex accent
‰	&#137;	&permil;	per thousand (mille) sign
Š	&#138;	&Scaron;	S-caron*
‹	&#139;	&lsaquo;	left single quillemet
Œ	&#140;	&OElig;	capital OE ligature
	&#141;		unused

* S-caron and s-caron characters are not available in the default character set of the "classic" Macintosh (OS 9 or earlier).

Character	Entity Number	Entity Name	Description
	&#142;		unused
	&#143;		unused
	&#144;		unused
'	&#145;	&lsquo;	left single quote
'	&#146;	&rsquo;	right single quote
"	&#147;	&ldquo;	left double quote
"	&#148;	&rdquo;	right double quote
•	&#149;	&bull;	round filled bullet
–	&#150;	&ndash;	en dash
—	&#151;	&mdash;	em dash
~	&#152;	&tilde;	small tilde
™	&#153;	&trade;	trademark
š	&#154;	&scaron;	s-caron*
›	&#155;	&rsaquo;	right single guillemet
œ	&#156;	&oelig;	small oe ligature
	&#157;		unused
	&#158;		unused
Ÿ	&#159;	&Yuml;	Y-umlaut

* S-caron and s-caron characters are not available in the default character set of the "classic" Macintosh (OS 9 or earlier).

SPECIAL CHARACTERS (ISO 8859-1)

The positions 160 through 255 include characters from the ISO 8859-1 (or Latin-1) character set that can be displayed in Web pages. Most of these characters are supported by most browsers.

TROUBLE *spot*   Current browsers support using ISO 8859-1 and Unicode entity names, but some earlier browsers only support using the entity names for the non-breakable space, copyright, registered trademark, and the accented characters (A-gravé, c-cedilla, and so on).

Character	Entity Number	Entity Name	Description
[ ]			non-breakable space (brackets added)
¡	&#161;	&iexcl;	inverted exclamation
¢	&#162;	&cent;	cent sign
£	&#163;	&pound;	British pound sign
¤	&#164;	&curren;	currency sign

* This character is missing from the native character set of the "classic" Macintosh. Internet Explorer 5 for the Macintosh substitutes the Latin-1 (ISO 8859-1) character set, so this character is displayed in that browser but might not be displayed in other browsers for the "classic" Macintosh.

Character	Entity Number	Entity Name	Description
¥	&#165;	&yen;	Japanese yen sign
¦	&#166;	&brvbar;	broken vertical bar*
§	&#167;	&sect;	section sign
¨	&#168;	&uml;	umlaut
©	&#169;	&copy;	copyright symbol
ª	&#170;	&ordf;	feminine ordinal
«	&#171;	&laquo;	left double guillemet
¬	&#172;	&not;	logical not sign
	&#173;	&shy;	soft hyphen
®	&#174;	&reg;	registered trademark
¯	&#175;	&macr;	macron accent
°	&#176;	&deg;	degree
±	&#177;	&plusmn;	plus/minus sign
²	&#178;	&sup2;	superscript 2*
³	&#179;	&sup3;	superscript 3*
´	&#180;	&acute;	acute accent
µ	&#181;	&micro;	micro sign
¶	&#182;	&para;	paragraph sign
·	&#183;	&middot;	middle dot
¸	&#184;	&cedil;	cedilla accent
¹	&#185;	&sup1;	superscript 1*
º	&#186;	&ordm;	masculine ordinal
»	&#187;	&raquo;	right double guillemet
¼	&#188;	&frac14;	1/4 fraction*
½	&#189;	&frac12;	1/4 fraction*
¾	&#190;	&frac34;	3/4 fraction*
¿	&#191;	&iquest;	inverted question mark
À	&#192;	&Agrave;	A-gravé
Á	&#193;	&Aacute;	A-acute
Â	&#194;	&Acirc;	A-circumflex
Ã	&#195;	&Atilde;	A-tilde
Ä	&#196;	&Auml;	A-umlaut
Å	&#197;	&Aring;	A-ring
Æ	&#198;	&AElig;	AE ligature
Ç	&#199;	&Ccedil;	C-cedilla
È	&#200;	&Egrave;	E-gravé
É	&#201;	&Eacute;	E-acute
Ê	&#202;	&Ecirc;	E-circumflex
Ë	&#203;	&Euml;	E-umlaut
Ì	&#204;	&Igrave;	I-gravé

* This character is missing from the native character set of the "classic" Macintosh. Internet Explorer 5 for the Macintosh substitutes the Latin-1 (ISO 8859-1) character set, so this character is displayed in that browser but might not be displayed in other browsers for the "classic" Macintosh.

Character	Entity Number	Entity Name	Description
Í	Í	Í	I-acute
Î	Î	Î	I-circumflex
Ï	Ï	Ï	I-umlaut
Ð	Ð	Ð	capital Eth*
Ñ	Ñ	Ñ	N-tilde
Ò	Ò	Ò	0-gravé
Ó	Ó	Ó	O-acute
Ô	Ô	Ô	O-circumflex
Õ	Õ	Õ	O-tilde
Ö	Ö	Ö	O-umlaut
×	×	×	multiplication sign*
Ø	Ø	Ø	O-slash
Ù	Ù	Ù	U-gravé
Ú	Ú	Ú	U-acute
Û	Û	Û	U-circumflex
Ü	Ü	Ü	U-umlaut
Ý	Ý	Ý	Y-acute*
Þ	Þ	Þ	capital Thorn*
ß	ß	ß	sharp s, sz ligature
à	à	à	a-gravé
á	á	á	a-acute
â	â	â	a-circumflex
ã	ã	ã	a-tilde
ä	ä	ä	a-umlaut
å	å	å	a-ring
æ	æ	æ	ae ligature
ç	ç	ç	c-cedilla
è	è	è	e-gravé
é	é	é	e-acute
ê	ê	ê	e-circumflex
ë	ë	ë	e-umlaut
ì	ì	ì	i-gravé
í	í	í	i-acute
î	î	î	i-circumflex
ï	ï	ï	i-umlaut
ð	ð	ð	small eth*
ñ	ñ	ñ	n-tilde
ò	ò	ò	o-gravé
ó	ó	ó	o-acute
ô	ô	ô	o-circumflex

* This character is missing from the native character set of the "classic" Macintosh. Internet Explorer 5 for the Macintosh substitutes the Latin-1 (ISO 8859-1) character set, so this character is displayed in that browser but might not be displayed in other browsers for the "classic" Macintosh.

Character	Entity Number	Entity Name	Description
õ	&#245;	&otilde;	o-tilde
ö	&#246;	&ouml;	o-umlaut
÷	&#247;	&divide;	division sign
ø	&#248;	&oslash;	o-slash
ù	&#249;	&ugrave;	u-gravé
ú	&#250;	&uacute;	u-acute
û	&#251;	&ucirc;	u-circumflex
ü	&#252;	&uuml;	u-umlaut
ý	&#253;	&yacute;	y-acute*
þ	&#254;	&thorn;	small thorn*
ÿ	&#255;	&yuml;	y-umlaut

* This character is missing from the native character set of the "classic" Macintosh. Internet Explorer 5 for the Macintosh substitutes the Latin-1 (ISO 8859-1) character set, so this character is displayed in that browser but might not be displayed in other browsers for the "classic" Macintosh.

Do not directly insert nonkeyboard characters into an HTML file by using the Windows Character Map utility, for instance, because what displays as one character on one platform might display as another character on another platform.

UNICODE CHARACTERS

ISO 8859-1 provides a total of 95 characters that can be inserted into HTML documents in addition to the ASCII "keyboard" characters that also can be used. This means, however, that many characters that desktop publishers, for instance, are accustomed to including in documents are not available in the ISO 8859-1 character set.

To overcome the limited number of characters that are available in ISO 8859-1, HTML 4 supports including characters in HTML documents from the Unicode character set. Unicode 3.0 supports the inclusion of more than 49,000 characters from a wide range of languages, including from the Americas, Europe, the Middle East, Africa, India, Asia, and the Pacific.

The Unicode characters shown in the following sections should be available on most recent Windows and Macintosh systems and display in most recent browsers. Other Unicode characters, however, might require additional Unicode-supporting fonts that include the characters to be installed on the system.

Some earlier browsers cannot display Unicode characters unless the document's character set is declared to be UTF-8:

```
<html>
<meta http-equiv="Content-Type" content="text/html;
charset=UTF-8">
```

Be aware that nonkeyboard characters that have been directly inserted into an HTML file, instead of being inserted using the characters' entity codes, might display entirely different characters or not display any characters at all. This is one more reason not to directly insert non-keyboard characters into an HTML file.

Latin Extended-A and Extended-B

Character	Entity Number	Entity Name	Description
Œ	&#338;	&OElig;	capital ligature OE
œ	&#339;	&oelig;	small ligature oe
Š	&#352;	&Scaron;	S-caron
š	&#353;	&scaron;	s-caron
Ÿ	&#376;	&Yuml;	Y-diaeresis
ƒ	&#402;	&fnof;	function, florin

Greek Capital Characters

Character	Entity Number	Entity Name	Description
Α	&#913;	&Alpha;	capital Alpha
Β	&#914;	&Beta;	capital Beta
Γ	&#915;	&Gamma;	capital Gamma
Δ	&#916;	&Delta;	capital Delta
Ε	&#917;	&Epsilon;	capital Epsilon
Ζ	&#918;	&Zeta;	capital Zeta
Η	&#919;	&Eta;	capital Eta
Θ	&#920;	&Theta;	capital Theta
Ι	&#921;	&Iota;	capital Iota
Κ	&#922;	&Kappa;	capital Kappa
Λ	&#923;	&Lambda;	capital Lambda
Μ	&#924;	&Mu;	capital Mu
Ν	&#925;	&Nu;	capital Nu
Ξ	&#926;	&Xi;	capital Xi
Ο	&#927;	&Omicron;	capital Omicron
Π	&#928;	&Pi;	capital Pi
Ρ	&#929;	&Rho;	capital Rho
(unused; there is no capital Sigma final character)			
Σ	&#931;	&Sigma;	capital Sigma
Τ	&#932;	&Tau;	capital Tau
Υ	&#933;	&Upsilon;	capital Upsilon
Φ	&#934;	&Phi;	capital Phi
Χ	&#935;	&Chi;	capital Chi
Ψ	&#936;	&Psi;	capital Psi
Ω	&#937;	&Omega;	capital Omega

Greek Small Characters

Character	Entity Number	Entity Name	Description
α	&#945;	&alpha;	small alpha
β	&#946;	&beta;	small beta
γ	&#947;	&gamma;	small gamma
δ	&#948;	&delta;	small delta
ε	&#949;	&epsilon;	small epsilon
ζ	&#950;	&zeta;	small zeta
η	&#951;	&eta;	small eta
θ	&#952;	&theta;	small theta
ι	&#953;	&iota;	small iota
κ	&#954;	&kappa;	small kappa
λ	&#955;	&lambda;	small lambda
μ	&#956;	&mu;	small mu
ν	&#956;	&nu;	small nu
ξ	&#958;	&xi;	small xi
ο	&#959;	&omicron;	small omicron
π	&#960;	&pi;	small pi
ρ	&#961;	&rho;	small rho
ς	&#962;	&sigmaf;	small sigma final
σ	&#963;	&sigma;	small sigma
τ	&#964;	&tau;	small tau
υ	&#965;	&upsilon;	small upsilon
φ	&#966;	&phi;	small phi
χ	&#967;	&chi;	small chi
ψ	&#968;	&psi;	small psi
ω	&#969;	&omega;	small omega

Miscellaneous Characters and Symbols

Character	Entity Number	Entity Name	Description
	&#8207;	&ndash;	en dash
—	&#8212;	&mdash;	em dash
'	&#8216;	&lsquo;	left single quotation mark
'	&#8217;	&rsquo;	right single quotation mark
‚	&#8218;	&sbquo;	single low-9 quotation mark
"	&#8220;	&ldquo;	left double quotation mark
"	&#8221;	&rdquo;	right double quotation mark
„	&#8222;	&bdquo;	double low-9 quotation mark
†	&#8224;	&dagger;	dagger
‡	&#8225;	&Dagger;	double dagger
•	&#8226;	&bull;	bullet
…	&#8230;	&hellip;	horizontal ellipsis

Character	Entity Number	Entity Name	Description
‰	&#8240;	&permil;	per mille sign
′	&#8242;	&prime;	prime, minutes, feet
″	&#8243;	&Prime;	double prime, seconds, inches
‹	&#8249;	&lsaquo;	single left angle quotation mark
›	&#8250;	&rsaquo;	single right angle quotation mark
⁄	&#8260;	&frasl;	fraction slash
€	&#8364;	&euro;	euro sign
™	&#8482;	&trade;	trademark
←	&#8592;	&larr;	left arrow
↑	&#8593;	&uarr;	up arrow
→	&#8594;	&rarr;	right arrow
↓	&#8595;	&darr;	down arrow
↔	&#8596;	&harr;	left-right arrow
⇒	&#8658;	&rArr;	right double arrow
⇔	&#8660;	&hArr;	left-right double arrow
∀	&#8704;	&forall;	for all
∂	&#8706;	&part;	part differential
∃	&#8707;	&exist;	there exists
∇	&#8711;	&nabla;	nabla/backward difference
∈	&#8712;	&isin;	element of (is in)
∋	&#8715;	&ni;	contains as member
∏	&#8719;	&prod;	product sign
∑	&#8721;	&sum;	n-ary summation
−	&#8722;	&minus;	minus sign
√	&#8730;	&radic;	square root/radical sign
∝	&#8733;	&prop;	proportional to
∞	&#8734;	&infin;	infinity
∠	&#8736;	&ang;	angle
∧	&#8743;	&and;	logical and
∨	&#8744;	&or;	logical or
∩	&#8745;	&cap;	intersection, cap
∪	&#8746;	&cup;	union, cup
∫	&#8747;	&int;	integral
∴	&#8756;	&there4;	therefore
∼	&#8764;	&sim;	similar to, tilde operator
≈	&#8776;	&asymp;	asymptomatic, almost equal
≠	&#8800;	&ne;	not equal
≡	&#8801;	&equiv;	equivalent
≤	&#8804;	&le;	less than or equal
≥	&#8805;	&ge;	greater than or equal
⊂	&#8834;	&sub;	subset of
⊃	&#8835;	&sup;	superset of

Character	Entity Number	Entity Name	Description
⊆	&#8838;	&sube;	subset of or equal to
⊇	&#9939;	&supe;	superset of or equal to
⊕	&#8853;	&oplus;	direct sum
⊥	&#8869;	&perp;	perpendicular
◊	&#9674;	&loz;	lozenge
♠	&#9824;	&spades;	spades suit
♣	&#9827;	&clubs;	clubs suit
♥	&#9829;	&hearts;	hearts suit
♦	&#9830;	&diams;	diamonds suit

Visit the Internet Resource Center. For additional resources and information on using character sets on the Web, see the Appendices section of this book's Internet Resource Center at **www.emcp.net/html2e.**

APPENDIX E

Web-Safe Color Chart

The Web-safe color palette contains 216 colors that display without being dithered on computer systems with display adapters that are limited to 256 colors. This color palette was originally called the "Netscape palette" because Netscape originated it. The 216 colors specified should all be present on the 256-color system palettes of most computers, whether running Windows, Macintosh OS, or UNIX. The Web-safe color palette also can help make it easier to select a color because you only have to choose between 216 colors, whereas the full True Color palette includes 16.3 million possible colors.

FFFFFF	FFFFCC	FFFF99	FFFF66	FFFF33	FFFF00
FFCCFF	FFCCCC	FFCC99	FFCC66	FFCC33	FFCC00
FF99FF	FF99CC	FF9999	FF9966	FF9933	FF9900
FF66FF	FF66CC	FF6699	FF6666	FF6633	FF6600
FF33FF	FF33CC	FF3399	FF3366	FF3333	FF3300
FF00FF	FF00CC	FF0099	FF0066	FF0033	FF0000

CCFFFF	CCFFCC	CCFF99	CCFF66	CCFF33	CCFF00
CCCCFF	CCCCCC	CCCC99	CCCC66	CCCC33	CCCC00
CC99FF	CC99CC	CC9999	CC9966	CC9933	CC9900
CC66FF	CC66CC	CC6699	CC6666	CC6633	CC6600
CC33FF	CC33CC	CC3399	CC3366	CC3333	CC3300
CC00FF	CC00CC	CC0099	CC0066	CC0033	CC0000

99FFFF	99FFCC	99FF99	99FF66	99FF33	99FF00
99CCFF	99CCCC	99CC99	99CC66	99CC33	99CC00
9999FF	9999CC	999999	999966	999933	999900
9966FF	9966CC	996699	996666	996633	996600
9933FF	9933CC	993399	993366	993333	993300
9900FF	9900CC	990099	990066	990033	990000

66FFFF	66FFCC	66FF99	66FF66	66FF33	66FF00
66CCFF	66CCCC	66CC99	66CC66	66CC33	66CC00
6699FF	6699CC	669999	669966	669933	669900
6666FF	6666CC	666699	666666	666633	666600
6633FF	6633CC	663399	663366	663333	663300
6600FF	6600CC	660099	660066	660033	660000

33FFFF	33FFCC	33FF99	33FF66	33FF33	33FF00
33CCFF	33CCCC	33CC99	33CC66	33CC33	33CC00
3399FF	3399CC	339999	339966	339933	339900
3366FF	3366CC	336699	336666	336633	336600
3333FF	3333CC	333399	333366	333333	333300
3300FF	3300CC	330099	330066	330033	330000

00FFFF	00FFCC	00FF99	00FF66	00FF33	00FF00
00CCFF	00CCCC	00CC99	00CC66	00CC33	00CC00
0099FF	0099CC	009999	009966	009933	009900
0066FF	0066CC	006699	006666	006633	006600
0033FF	0033CC	003399	003366	003333	003300
0000FF	0000CC	000099	000066	000033	000000

For additional resources and information on using color on the Web, see the Appendixes section of this book's Internet Resource Center at **www.emcp.net/html2e.**

APPENDIX F

Working with JavaScript

This appendix contains a basic introduction to using JavaScript in Web pages, including using functions, loops, variables, and arrays. Examples of some of the more commonly used types of scripts are included.

JavaScript is a client-side scripting language that was originally developed by Netscape for its Navigator 2 browser. The similarity in names has caused some to believe that JavaScript is a subset of Java, although other than in name, there is little similarity between the two. The only relation between the two is that they both borrow their basic syntax from the C programming language.

JavaScript is an *object-oriented* scripting language, which means that when you work with JavaScript, you are primarily involved in defining and manipulating objects. Although JavaScript contains some built-in objects, most objects that you control and manipulate are objects that are part of an HTML Web page, such as the document, windows, frames, and elements (forms, hypertext links, images, and so on). JavaScript scripts also can respond to and interact with mouse actions, link activation, form submissions, page loading or unloading, and other user actions or system events.

INTRODUCTION TO JAVASCRIPT

Following is a brief introduction to some of the key features of JavaScript, including comments, variables, conditional statements, functions, objects, arrays, and event handlers.

Writing a Simple JavaScript Script

The SCRIPT element is used to embed or insert JavaScript scripts in Web pages. The SCRIPT element can be used both in the HEAD and BODY elements—scripts that do not output directly to the page or contain functions are generally inserted in the HEAD section, so they will be loaded and parsed before the page body is loaded and displayed. The following is an example of a simple JavaScript script that displays an alert message (see Figure F.1):

```
<body>
<script type="text/JavaScript">
<!-- hide script
document.write("<h1 align='center'>Hi There!</h1>");
// end hide script -->
</script>
```

FIGURE F.1 • In this simple JavaScript script, "Hi There!", is displayed and centered at the top of the page.

The SCRIPT element is nested inside the BODY element. The script writes directly to the page and thus needs to be included in the body of the page. The TYPE attribute declares the script to be a JavaScript script.

The codes, `<!-- hide script` and `// end hide script -->`, hide the content of the script from browsers or other user agents that do not recognize JavaScript.

A JavaScript script is composed of one or more statements, such as `document.write("<h2 align='center'>Hi There!</h2>");`, for instance. Statements begin on a new line and end with a semi-colon. In this case, the statement instructs the browser to write the text string, `<h2 align='center'>Hi There!</h2>`, to the document where the script is located.

The ALIGN attribute value inside the text string is single-quoted because the text string within which it is nested is already double-quoted. To include double quotes inside a text string to be displayed as is, you need to escape them by preceding them with a "\" character (`\"Hi There!\"`, for instance).

Unlike HTML, JavaScript is case-sensitive. In the code line, `document.write` is correct, but `Document.Write` is not. A JavaScript interpreter ignores spaces, tabs, and non-breaking spaces (or). You should not insert hard returns inside JavaScript statements for formatting purposes.

USING JAVASCRIPT COMMENTS

There are two kinds of comments that can be used in a JavaScript script. The first, `//`, is inserted at the start of a line to comment out just that line; the second kind, `/*` and `*/`, is used to comment out multiple lines of code:

```
<body>
<script type="text/JavaScript">
<!-- hide script
// This is a single line comment
/* This starts a comment
document.write("<h1 align='center'>Hi There!</h1>");
This ends a comment */
// end hide script -->
</script>
```

UNDERSTANDING VARIABLES

Unlike many other programming languages, JavaScript is *untyped*, which means you do not have to declare the data type of a variable when it is declared. A variable name can start with an underscore or a letter but not with a number. For instance, the following are all variable declarations but for different data types:

```
<script type="text/JavaScript">
<!-- hide script
var course = "Web Design";        // string value
var credits = 5;                  // integer value
var tuition = 199.99;             // floating point value
var descript = document;          // object
var signup = true;                // boolean value (true or false)
var school                        // null value

descript.write("<h3>Course Description: " + course + "</h3>");
descript.write("<p>Credits: " + credits + "</p>");
descript.write("<p>Tuition: " + tuition + "</p>");
descript.write("<hr>");
// end hide script -->
</script>
```

Expressions and Operators

An *expression* assigns a value to a variable. For instance, the following expression assigns a value of 5 to a count variable:

```
var count = 5;
```

You also can omit the var keyword, although including it makes the variables you have assigned easier to track. Null values should always be assigned using the var keyword; if it is absent, such a variable will result in a runtime error when it is evaluated.

An *operator* performs an operation on a variable or value, such as adding, subtracting, multiplying, dividing, and so on, or compares one value with another. Table F.1 shows the most commonly used JavaScript operators.

TABLE F.1 • Basic JavaScript Operators

Operator	Action	Example
=	Assigns a variable value	var time = 60;

+	Addition (or string concatenation)	var cost = 50;
		var ship = 5;
		var total = cost + ship;
		document.write("Total: "+total);

–	Subtraction	var rev = 1000;
		var exp = 650;
		var profit = rev - exp;

*	Multiplication	var price = 1000;
		var tax = 0.08;
		var cost = price + (price*tax);

Operator	Action	Example

/	Division	var miles = 125;
		var hours = 3;
		var mph = miles/hours;

%	Modulo
	(remainder after division
	of one value by another)
		var a = 10;
		var b = 45;
		var c = a%b;

++	Increment (increase a value by 1)	var day = 1; var day2 = day++;
--	Decrement (decrease a value by 1)	var count = 100; var down = count--;
-[value/var]	Negative (changes value from positive to negative)	var start = -100; var flip = -start;

==	Returns true if equal	if (a == b)
		    document.write("same");
		else
		    document.write("different");

!=	Returns true if not equal	if (a != b)
		    document.write("different");
		else
		    document.write("same");

>	Greater than	if (a > b)
		    document.write("more");
		else
		    document.write("not more");

<	Less than	if (a < b)
		    document.write("less");
		else
		    document.write("not less");

>-	Greater than or equal to	if (a >- b)
		    document.write("same or more");
		else
		    document.write("less");

<-	Less than or equal to	if (a <- b)
		    document.write("same or less");
		else
		    document.write("more");

&&	Both true (Boolean AND)	if (x==0 && y==1)
||	Either true (Boolean OR)	if (x==0 || y==1)
!	Not true (Boolean NOT)	if (x==0 || !(y==1))

Reserved Keywords

JavaScript reserves certain keywords for its own use that cannot be used in naming variables or functions. Additional keywords are reserved for future use. Tables F.2 and F.3 show keywords that are currently reserved in JavaScript and keywords that are reserved for use in future versions of JavaScript.

TABLE F.2 • JavaScript Reserved Keywords

break	continue	delete
else	eval	false
for	function	if
in	new	null
return	this	true
var	while	with

TABLE F.3 • Keywords Reserved for Future Use

abstract	boolean	byte
byvalue	case	catch
class	const	default
do	double	extends
final	finally	float
goto	implements	import
instanceof	int	interface
long	native	package
short	static	super
switch	synchronized	threadsafe
throw	transient	try
void		

User-Defined Variables

You can include user-defined variables in your Web pages in a number of ways, including assigning variables using a prompt window, a form input field, or a designated user action. Variables also can be assigned based on polling various aspects of the user's system, such as the operating system and browser that are being used. For instance, to prompt the user for his or her name, you can use the following script (see Figure F.2):

```
<body>
<script type="text/JavaScript">
<!-- hide script
var visitor = window.prompt("Please enter your name: ", "");
document.write("<h1 align='center'>Hi " + visitor + "!</h1>");
// end hide script -->
</script>
```

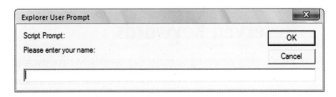

FIGURE F.2 • The user is prompted to enter his or her name.

The previous script example first prompts the user for a name and then assigns whatever the user has entered at the prompt as the value of the user variable. In this example, the second pair of double-quotes lets you specify a default content for the prompt box.

After the user enters his or her name at the prompt, the script writes an H1 element to the document that contains the content of the *visitor* variable to personalize it. For instance, if the user enters **Steve** at the prompt, an H1 element containing "Hi Steve!" will be written to the document (see Figure F.3).

FIGURE F.3 • A personalized H1 element is written to the document.

To write "Hi Steve!" to an alert box instead of to the document, substitute **alert** for **document.write** (see Figure F.4):

```
<body>
<script type="text/JavaScript">
<!-- hide script
var visitor = window.prompt("Please enter your name: ", "");
alert("Hi " + visitor + "!");
// end hide script -->
</script>
```

FIGURE F.4 • The user's name is displayed in an alert box.

USING CONDITIONAL STATEMENTS

A *conditional statement's* execution is dependent upon one or more conditions. You can create a variety of conditional statements using JavaScript.

Using IF/ELSE Statements

You can use IF/ELSE statements to create conditional statements that are executed (or not executed) based on a condition or set of conditions. For instance, the following example uses a combination of IF, ELSE IF, and ELSE statements to display a different alert message depending on the time of the day (see Figure F.5):

```
<body>
<script language="JavaScript" type="text/JavaScript">
<!-- hide script
var visitor = window.prompt("Please enter your name: ", "");
thismoment = new Date();
hour = thismoment.getHours();
if (hour >= 18) {
    alert("Good evening, "+ visitor +"!");
    }
else if (hour >= 12) {
    alert("Good afternoon, "+ visitor +"!");
```

```
    }
else {
    alert("Good morning, "+ visitor +"!");
    }
// end hide script -->
</script>
```

FIGURE F.5 • Depending on the time of day, the user is wished good morning, good afternoon, or good evening.

Using WHILE Loops

A while statement can be used to perform a conditional loop. The instruction is performed until a certain condition is no longer true. For instance, the following script assigns a value of 1 to the count variable and then increments that value by 1 for each loop, until the value reaches 5 (see Figure F.6):

```
<body>
<script type="text/JavaScript">
<!-- hide script
var count = 1;
while (count <= 5 ) {
    document.write("<p><big>The count is now " + count + ".
    </big></p>"); count++;
    }
// end hide script -->
</script>
```

FIGURE F.6 • A series of five numbered lines is written to the document.

As shown in Figure F.6, the result of the previous script is a series of numbered lines, running from 1 to 5. After the fifth line is reached, the WHILE loop is terminated.

Using FOR Loops

A FOR loop is similar to a WHILE loop, except that you get to set a start value, an end value, and a count value. The following is an example of a FOR loop (see Figure F.7):

```
<script type="text/JavaScript">
<!-- hide script
document.write("<p>")
for (a=1;a<=10;a=a+1) {
    document.write("Number " + a + ".<br>")
    }
document.write("</p>")
// end hide script -->
</script>
```

FIGURE F.7 • The FOR loop continues, incrementing the value of the a variable by 1, as long as its value is less than or equal to 10.

In this script, **a=1** sets the starting point (the value of 1 is assigned to the *a* variable), **a<=10** sets the stopping point (the loop continues as long as the value of *a* is less than or equal to 10), and **a=a+1** sets how much *a* is incremented in each loop (for each new loop, a is equal to a plus 1).

WORKING WITH FUNCTIONS

A *function* assigns a series of commands to be performed to a name. Later, the function's commands can be executed simply by calling its name. A function consists of the following parts:

```
function function_name(argument1, argument2,...n) {
    statement_1;
    statement_2;
    .
    .
    .
    statement_n;
    }
```

For example, the following function is nested in the HEAD element; it defines a variable (*ident*) and then specifies that variable as the content of an alert message:

```
<script type="text/JavaScript">
<!-- hide script
function HiThere() {
    ident = window.prompt("Please enter your name: ", "");
    alert("Welcome to my page, " + ident + "!");
    }
// end hide script -->
</script>
</head>
```

You can then cause this function to run automatically when the document is loaded, like this:

```
<body onLoad="HiThere()">
```

This example uses an onLoad event handler that calls the HiThere() function when the document is loaded. After the user enters his or her name at the prompt, an alert message appears welcoming him to the Web page (see Figure F.8).

FIGURE F.8 • The user is welcomed to the page, using the name provided by the user. afternoon, or good evening.

To call the function when a link is clicked, you might do the following:

```
<a href="javascript: HiThere()">This is the link text</a>
```

You also can create a function and then pass values to it. The value can be evaluated by the function and a response produced based on the value. Later in this appendix, you will create a jump menu that does just that.

WORKING WITH OBJECTS

Every element within an HTML document is an object, starting with the browser window (the window object), proceeding to the document (the document object), and then to every other object that is included in an HTML document. Objects also have properties (or attributes). For instance, an object might have a name, an ID, a size, a URL, a color, and so on.

For instance, you can refer to the VALUE property (or attribute) that belongs to an object; a BUTTON element named "mybutton", that is nested inside another object; and a FORM element named "myform", in the following manner:

```
window.document.myform.mybutton.value
```

The window object can be assumed and thus can be omitted. The reference also can be stated in this manner:

```
document.myform.mybutton.value
```

JavaScript also includes a number of built-in objects that are not part of the document. Table F.4 shows the built-in JavaScript objects that are not part of the document. JavaScript can also access objects through the HTML DOM (Document Object Model); some examples are shown in Table F.5.

TABLE F.4 • Built-In JavaScript Objects

Object	Description	Examples
window	The browser window	window.alert("Hi!")
document	The current document	window.document document.lastModified document.bgColor
navigator	Browser information	navigator.userAgent navigator.appVersion navigator.platform
frames	Frames in a window	window.frames[1] window.frames[2]
location	Document address	window.location
history	History list	window.history window.history.previous history.back()
Math	Math functions/constants	Math.PI Math.SQRT2 Math.log() Math.sin()
Date	Date and time	today = new Date()

TABLE F.5 • Selection of HTML DOM Objects

Object	Description	Examples
anchor	Anchors in a document	document.anchor[1] document.anchors.length
body	Body element	document.body document.body.p[3]
form	Form element	document.form document.*formname* document.forms.length
image	Image element	document.image[4] image.border image.complete
input	Input element	document.*formname.inputname*
input checkbox	Check box control	*formname.checkname*.checked
input hidden	Hidden control	*formname.hiddenname*.value=*value*
input radio	Radio button	*formname.radioname*[1].checked
input reset	Reset button	document.*formname*.reset
input submit	Submit button	document.*formname*.submit *submitname*.value *submitname*.name
option	Option element	*formname.selectname*.options[2]
select	Select element	*formname.selectname*.length
style	Style element	this.style.color getElementByID("*id*").style.color
table	Table element	*tablename*.insertRow(-1)
textarea	Textarea element	*formname.textareaname*.value

WORKING WITH ARRAYS

An array allows you to assign a series of values to a variable. For instance, you might assign the names of the 12 months to a *monthname* variable or the names of the days of the week to a *dayname* variable.

```
<script type="text/JavaScript">
<!--
thisdate = new Date();
day = thisdate.getDay();
month = thisdate.getMonth();
year = thisdate.getYear();
date = thisdate.getDate();

var dayname = new Array   ("Sunday","Monday","Tuesday",
"Wednesday","Thursday","Friday","Saturday");
var theday = dayname[day];
var monthname = new Array   ("January","February","March",
"April","May","June","July","August","September","October",
"November","December");
var themonth = monthname[month];
var theyear;
    if (year >= 100 && year <= 1999) theyear = 1900 + year;
        else theyear = year;
//-->
</script>
</head>
```

You can then write values to the document that correspond to specific values within the array. For instance, the following writes the day and date to the document (see Figure F.9):

```
<body>
<script type="text/JavaScript">
<!-- Hide script
document.write ("<h2>Today is "+ theday +", "+ themonth +"
"+ date +", "+ theyear +".</h2>");
// End hiding script -->
</script>
```

FIGURE F.9 • The day and date are written to the document.

Using Event Handlers

Event handlers allow JavaScript scripts to respond to user or system events, such as clicking on a link or passing the mouse cursor over or off an image. Event handlers can be expressed both as HTML attributes and as JavaScript code. For instance, the following is an example of using an event handler as an HTML attribute:

```
<img src="myimage.jpg" name="myimage" OnMouseOver="alert('That/'s
me!');"
```

Alternatively, this could also be expressed in JavaScript like this:

```
document.myimage.onmouseover = function() {
    alert('That/'s me!');
    }
```

Table F.6 shows the different JavaScript event handlers, along with their descriptions.

TABLE F.6 • JavaScript Event Handlers

Event Handler	Description
onAbort	When the loading of an image is aborted by the user.
onBlur	When an element loses focus, such as when a user tabs from one form input element to another. The flip-side of onFocus.
onFocus	When an element is given focus, such as when a user tabs to a form element or when a window is brought to the foreground.
onChange	When a list menu option or input control is selected or deselected, or when the content of a textarea box is changed.
onSelect	When a user selects text in a text input field.
onClick	When the user clicks once on an element.
onDblClick	When the user double-clicks on an element.
onError	When an error occurs while an image is loading.
onKeyDown	When a key is pressed and held down over an element.
onKeyPress	When a key is pressed and released over an element.
onKeyUp	When a key is released by a user.
onLoad	When a document is loaded into a browser window.
onUnload	When a document is unloaded.
onMouseDown	When a mouse button is pressed down over an element.
onMouseUp	When a mouse button is released over an element.
onMouseOut	When the mouse pointer passes off of an element.
onMouseOver	When the mouse pointer passes over an element.
OnMouseMove	When the mouse pointer is moved while positioned over an element.
onReset	When a form is reset.
onResize	When the window is resized.
onSubmit	When a form is submitted.

MISCELLANEOUS JAVASCRIPT EXAMPLES

Following are examples of kinds of JavaScript scripts that are often used in Web pages.

Displaying When a Page Was Last Updated

Displaying when a page was last updated can be helpful to visitors to your site. They can easily see if there have been any changes since their last visit, for instance. If you make frequent changes to a page, however, it can be a hassle, and you can easily forget to manually update the "last updated" line.

A better idea is to use a JavaScript to automatically insert the date when a page was last updated, as shown in the following example (see Figure F.10).

```
<hr>
<address>
Course: Web Design Fundamentals<br>
Instructor: Ruth Clearwater<br>
E-Mail: <a href="mailto:rclearwater@flat-iron.emcp.com">
rclearwater@flat-iron.emcp.com</a><br>
<script type="text/javascript">
<!-- Hide script
if (Date.parse(document.lastModified) > 0) {
    document.write("Page Last Modified: " +
    document.lastModified)
    }
// End hide script -->
</script>
</address>
```

Course: Web Design Fundamentals
Instructor: Ruth Clearwater
E-Mail: rclearwater@flat-iron.emcp.com
Page Last Modified: 07/06/2009 10:59:18

Done   My Computer   100%

FIGURE F.10 • The date and time when the page was last modified is displayed at the bottom of the ADDRESS element.

You could simply insert the **document.write("Page Last Modified: "** **+ document.lastModified)**, except that some systems will mistakenly report a date of 1970 (which is equal to year 0 in UNIX time). By using the IF statement, the last modified line is only inserted if the parse value for the lastModified date is greater than 0.

Creating Pop-Up Windows

Although you can open a page in a new browser window using just HTML (by using the **target="_blank"** attribute in the link's A element), you cannot control the size and position of the window, nor can you specify whether or not menu bars, status bars, scroll bars, or other window elements will be displayed. You can control all of these features, however, when using JavaScript to open a new window. When displaying an HTML file within a pop-up window, the main concern is that the content of the HTML file fits within the dimensions of the pop-up window you create.

First, create a script in the document's HEAD section that defines a function (PopWin) that will cause the pop-up window to open when it is called:

```
<script type="text/javascript">
<!-- hide script
function PopWin(url) {
    newwindow=window.open(url, "name", "height=250, width=250,
toolbar=no, status=no, menubar=no, location=no, resizable=yes,
scrollbars=auto, top=350, left=300");
    if (window.focus) {
        newwindow.focus()
        }
    }
// end hide script -->
</script>
</head>
```

Next, add a link to the page that calls the PopWin(url) function (see Figure F.11):

```
<p>Welcome to the <b><a href="javascript:PopWin('popup1.html')">
Web Design Fundamentals</a></b> course page.</p>
```

FIGURE F.11 • When the pop-up link is clicked, a 250- by 250-pixel pop-up window is displayed.

The parameters in the script set the dimensions of the window; turn off the tool bar, status bar, menu bar, and location (address) bar; set the window to be resizable and the scroll bars to automatically display; and position the window 300 pixels from the top and 300 pixels from the left side of the screen.

INCLUDING A CLOSE WINDOW LINK You can also include a link in the pop-up window's HTML file that a user can click to close the window (see Figure F-12).

```
<p align="center"><a href="javascript:window.close();">Close the
Window.</a></p>
</body>
```

FIGURE F.12 • A link is added to the pop-up window's page so the user can close the window.

AUTOMATICALLY CLOSING A POP-UP WINDOW You can also set the pop-up window to close automatically after a specified period of time. For instance, the following code will close the pop-up window after 5,000 milliseconds:

```
<body class="popup" onLoad="setTimeout(window.close, 5000)">
```

TROUBLE *spot*

If you insert an image as the sole content of a pop-up window, the page margins or padding will be displayed around the image. To eliminate them, just add the following to the pop-up page:

```
<body style="margin: 0; padding: 0;">
```

Creating a Jump Menu

A *jump menu* is a just a pull-down menu, created using the FORM, SELECT, and OPTION elements, that lets a user select an option and then go to the specified Web page that is associated with that option. There are two basic types of jump menus: a menu that automatically goes to a URL when a destination is selected and a menu that requires the user to click a "Go" button after selecting a destination.

CREATING AN AUTOMATIC JUMP MENU This kind of jump menu requires a user to execute a minimum of mouse clicks to select and go to a destination. The user only needs to click on the drop-down menu to unfold it and then click on the desired destination. Add a JavaScript script to the document's HEAD element that defines a function that will execute the jump:

```
<script type="text/JavaScript" >
<!-- hide script
function goDestination(a){
    if (document.mymenu.menuopts.value != "null") {
        document.location.href = a
        }
    }
// end hide script -->
</script>
</head>
```

Add a form to the page's body that uses an onChange event handler to pass a value, based on the destination selected by the user, to the goDestination function (see Figure F.13):

```
<body>
<p>Welcome to the <b><a href="javascript:PopWin('popup1.html')">
Web Design Fundamentals</a></b> course page. Select an option
from the following menu list:</p>
<form name="mymenu" style="margin-top: 0">
<select name="menuopts" onChange="goDestination
    (document.mymenu.menuopts.options
    [document.mymenu.menuopts.options.selectedIndex].value)">
<option>Jump to page--&gt;</option>
<option value="webdesign.html">Introduction</option>
<option value="descript.html">Description</option>
<option value="syllabus.html">Syllabus</option>
<option value="materials.html">Materials</option>
<option value="assignments.html">Assignments</option>
<option value="resources.html">Resources</option>
<option value="feedback.html">Feedback</option>
<option value="scores.html">Scores</option>
</select>
</form>
```

FIGURE F.13 • A jump menu is added to the page.

Click on the menu list (or on the menu's down arrow) to unfold the menu options. Pass the mouse over the unfolded menu to highlight any of the options (see Figure F.14).

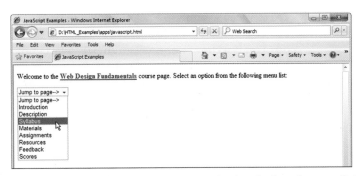

FIGURE F.14 • A series of destination options is displayed when the user clicks on the jump menu's box.

Clicking on any of the menu options will then jump to the page specified in the form.

This script works by passing an argument value from the onChange event handler in the form's SELECT element to the script in the document's HEAD element. The value that is passed is assigned to the "a" function argument. As long as the value of "a" is not equal to "null", the passed value is executed as the value of the `document.location.href` statement. That is, if the Description option is clicked on, "descript.html" is assigned as the value of `document.location.href`.

The FORM and SELECT elements are named "mymenu" and "menuopts", respectively. You can name these elements anything you wish, but the script in the document's head and the value of the onChange event handler in the SELECT element must match the names that you use.

A dummy option (an OPTION element without a VALUE attribute) is set as the default selected option. If this option is selected, a "null" value is passed to the script function in the document's HEAD element. This option is used to identify the purpose of the jump menu, which is to jump to a page within the site. Notice that an arrow is created by inserting two hyphens followed by the entity code (`&lt;`) for a right-arrow bracket. You can key in whatever you want as the content of this option, as long as it concisely and accurately conveys the purpose and function of the list menu.

TROUBLE *spot*

Using a jump menu that automatically jumps to a destination when it is selected poses a potential accessibility concern. Using keyboard input, rather than mouse actions, does not work for this kind of jump menu—a user can access the form and select an option using only keyboard input, but pressing the Enter key after selecting an option does not do anything. For this reason, especially in an educational situation, you should consider not using this kind of jump menu. The following section, "Creating a Jump Menu with a Go Button," covers a different way to create a jump menu, which is accessible using only keyboard input.

CREATING A JUMP MENU WITH A GO BUTTON With this type of jump menu, a user must unfold the list menu and select an option, and then click on a "Go" button to cause the browser to open the selected destination page. The advantage of this method is that users can access the menu and activate its options using only keyboard input, making it much more accessible. You also do not need to include a dummy option because the "Go" button label conveys the function and purpose of the jump menu (that it is a jump menu) to the user.

The following example of creating a jump menu that uses a "Go" button does not call a function, as in the previous example, but uses an onClick event handler to activate the jump (see Figure F.15):

```
<form name="mymenu" style="margin-top: 0">
<select name="menuopts">
<option value="webdesign.html">Introduction</option>
<option value="descript.html">Description</option>
<option value="syllabus.html">Syllabus</option>
<option value="materials.html">Materials</option>
<option value="assignments.html">Assignments</option>
<option value="resources.html">Resources</option>
<option value="feedback.html">Feedback</option>
<option value="scores.html">Scores</option>
<input type="button" onClick="location=document.mymenu.menuopts
.options[document.mymenu.menuopts.selectedIndex].value;"
value=" Go ">
</select>
</form>
```

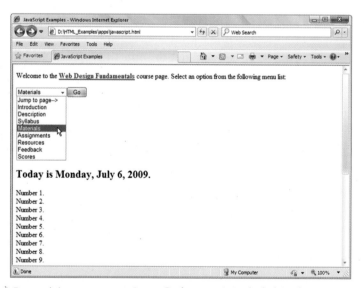

FIGURE F.15 • A jump menu, using a Go button, is included in the page.

Creating Rollover Buttons

A common use of JavaScript is to create rollover buttons, where rolling the mouse cursor over a button image causes the image to be swapped out for another image.

PRELOADING IMAGES When the rollover effect is initiated, there will be a delay while the rollover image downloads, unless the image is preloaded:

```
<script type="text/JavaScript">
<!-- hide script
img=new Image();
    img1.src="gobutton1.gif";
img=new Image();
    img2.src="gobutton2.gif";
// end hide script -->
</script>
</head>
```

CREATING THE ROLLOVER BUTTON A rollover button is added to the page's body:

```
<body>
<p><a href="home.html" class="off" onMouseOver="this.className =
'on'" onMouseOut="this.className = 'off'"></a></p>
```

CREATING THE ROLLOVER STYLES CSS styles are used to create the rollover effect (see Figure F.16):

```
<style type="text/css">
<!--
a.off {
    background-image: url(gobutton1.gif);
    display: block;
    width: 100px;
    height: 50px;
    margin-left: auto;
    margin-right: auto;
    }
a.on {
    background-image: url(gobutton2.gif);
    display: block;
    width: 100px;
    height: 50px;
    margin-left: auto;
    margin-right: auto;
    }
-->
</style>
```

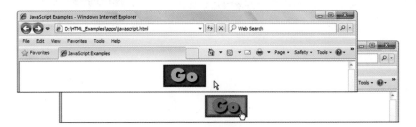

FIGURE F.16 • A rollover button is created using JavaScript.

Using a Push Button to Print the Page

You can also create a push button using the INPUT element's **type="button"** attribute, to activate a script action. The following example prints the document when the button is clicked (see Figure F.17):

```
<div align="center">
<form>
<input name="print" type="button" value="Print this Document!"
onClick="window.print()">
</form>
</div>
```

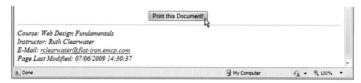

FIGURE F.17 • A push button is created that will print the page when it is clicked.

Visit the Internet Resource Center. This appendix barely scratches the surface of using JavaScript in Web pages. To find online resources that discuss using JavaScript in more depth, see the Appendices section of this book's Internet Resource Center at **www.emcp.net/html2e**.

APPENDIX G

Miscellaneous Technologies and Features

This appendix includes brief rundowns, including some examples, of various technologies and features not covered previously, but which students might find of interest or value in further pursuing the development of their Web design and authoring knowledge and skills. Features and technologies covered in this appendix include:

- FTP (File Transfer Protocol)
- Server-side includes (SSI)
- Cookies
- Password protection
- Client-side scripting and programming
- Server-side scripting and programming
- Online databases
- Secure forms and servers
- Dynamic HTML
- XML
- Flash and Silverlight
- Wireless and Mobile Web protocols and languages

USING FTP TO UPLOAD YOUR SITE TO YOUR SERVER

You need to use FTP (File Transfer Protocol) to upload your site to a server.

Finding a Web Host

Many options are available for finding a Web host for your Web pages:

- **Web space through your school.** Your school might provide you with free Web space on its Web server. The primary drawback of this is that you will lose the Web space when you graduate or leave.
- **Web space through your dial-up provider.** The dial-up provider you use to connect to the Internet also might provide you with free Web space. The amount of free space provided can vary considerably, from 5 MB to 20 MB.

- **Web space through a free Web space provider.** There are also many providers of free Web space. Generally, these sorts of Web space accounts require that you display a banner or pop-up window with advertising when your Web pages are opened.
- **Web space through a for-pay Web space provider.** To gain access to more features, additional e-mail addresses, domain name registration, and higher traffic and space allotments, you can sign up for an account with a for-pay Web space provider. Costs run anywhere from $10 to $30 a month, depending on the account and its features.
- **Web space through a reseller account.** A reseller account allows you to resell Web space accounts. This can be handy, for instance, if you want to both design and manage Web sites for clients; by using a reseller account, you also can sell Web space, domain registration, and other Web services to your design clients.

 For additional information on finding the right Web host for your Web pages, as well as links to resources for finding free and budget Web space providers, see the Appendices section at the Internet Resource Center of this book at **www.emcp.net/html2e**.

Uploading Options

You can use a dedicated FTP program to upload your site to your server, or you can use a Web publishing program, such as Adobe Dreamweaver, for instance. For guidance on using a Web publishing program, see its help documentation.

Choosing an FTP Program

Some FTP programs you can use to upload your site to a server include:
- Core FTP at **www.coreftp.com/** (Windows)
- FileZilla at **filezilla-project.org/** (Windows/Mac/Linux)
- WS FTP Home at **www.ipswitchft.com/solutions/personal.asp** (Windows)
- CuteFTP at **www.globalscape.com/products/** (Windows)
- FTP Voyager at **www.ftpvoyager.com/** (Windows)
- Transmit at **www.panic.com/transmit/** (Mac)

Core FTP and FileZilla are free programs. The other four are commercial programs that have free trial periods. WS_FTP Home is available to educational institutions through a bulk license, so check with your school's technical support to see if it is available for you to use free. You can also do a search for "WS_FTP LE," which is an older version that is free for educational uses. It is no longer available from ipswitchft.com, but can still be found elsewhere on the Web.

Understanding What You Need to Know

To transfer files from your local computer to your Web space folder on a remote Web server, you need or might need to know the following:
- **Host name (server name or Web address).** This is usually the name of the Web server on which your Web site folder is located (srv3.myhost.net, for instance). Some providers also let you use the Web address of your site, which might be

different from the server name (www.myhost.net/~myfolder/, for instance). If you have your own domain name, you can usually just specify it as the host name (*yoursite*.com).

- **Host type.** In most cases, you should not need to know this but can specify that the host type should be automatically detected (if asked for this information). If that does not work, your Web server might require that you identify the specific host type you are trying to connect to. Your Web space provider will need to provide that information, or you can just experiment with the different available options in your FTP program until you find the right one.

- **User name.** If you are using Web space provided by your dial-up provider, this will be the same user name you use to log on the Internet. If you are using Web space provided by a separate provider, you need to use the user name assigned to you by that provider. Your user name is case-sensitive.

- **Password.** If you are using Web space provided by your dial-up provider, this will be the same password you use to log on to the Internet. If you are using Web space provided by a separate provider, you need to use the password assigned to you by that provider. Your password is case-sensitive.

- **Initial remote folder.** This is not required to connect to your Web space folder but can specify that a particular folder, other than the root folder, be connected to. Web space folders are often organized into separate folders, one of which contains all the files and folders that are included in your Web site and into which you need to publish your Web page files. This folder is usually named **www** but can be named using any name your server administrator has decided to use. By specifying that folder as your initial remote folder, you will go directly to it when you connect to your site.

- **Firewall settings.** If your computer is located behind a firewall, you might need to specify additional information, such as the name or IP address of your firewall and your user name and password. To set these settings, in WS_FTP Home, for instance, click the Options button, and select Firewall from the Program Options menu. Generally, this should not affect you in uploading files to a remote server but might stop you from downloading files to your local computer. Check with your server administrator if you need to specify these additional settings.

- **Active or passive mode.** Files can be transferred to a server in either active or passive mode. In active mode, the server establishes the connection with the FTP client; in passive mode, the FTP client establishes the connection. Some servers require that passive mode be used. If you are behind a router-based firewall or a network gateway, you might also need to use passive mode. WS_FTP Home defaults to passive mode, but other FTP programs might default to active mode. If you have trouble getting your FTP program to connect to your server, try switching the transfer mode. In WS_FTP Home, click the Connect button, choose your site, click the Edit button, and select Advanced from the side menu. Check Use Passive mode for data connections to select passive mode; uncheck it to select active mode.

USING SERVER-SIDE INCLUDES

Many Web servers allow you to include files within other files by means of *server-side includes* (SSI). Your Web host, however, must configure your account to allow the use of server-side includes. Server-side includes enable you to easily include updateable content within any page.

Server-side includes date back to when virtually all Web servers were UNIX machines. Although server-side includes (or a close variant) are supported on some Windows-based and Macintosh-based servers, the commands and syntax that they require can differ significantly from what is required on a UNIX server. Although different UNIX-based servers can support slightly different implementations of server-side includes, the commands and syntax they use are generally the same. The code examples and information provided in this section applies only to UNIX-based servers.

There are some drawbacks to using server-side includes, however. A server must parse the file that contains the server-side include, rather than simply delivering it to the Web browser. Each include that is present within a file generates a separate server process. Because of the extra load that enabling server-side includes places on the server some Web hosts, especially the inexpensive or free ones, do not allow server-side includes.

Because files that include server-side includes must first be parsed by the server, before they are delivered to a browser (or other client-side agent), a special file extension, .shtml, is generally used to identify files that include server-side includes. Otherwise, a server would have no way of knowing which files contain server-side includes and which do not. By using a special extension, a server only needs to parse files with an .shtml extension before delivering them, while files with an .html extension can be delivered unparsed.

Server-side includes are inserted in HTML documents using HTML comment codes. The general format used is as follows:

```
<!--#command attribute=value attribute=value ...-->
```

Specifying the Date and Time

You can use a server-side include to specify the current date. For instance, the following server-side include causes a supporting server to display the current date:

```
<p><!--#echo var="DATE_LOCAL" --></p>
```

The previous example simply echoes the default date format, which might not be in the format that you prefer. You can use the CONFIG command to change the time format. For example:

```
<p><!--#config timefmt="%A, %B %d, %Y - %R %p" -->
Today is <!--#echo var="DATE_LOCAL" --></p>
```

Besides displaying the date in a different format, the previous example also displays the time. It is important to note, however, that the time reported through a server-side include corresponds to the time on the server and not to the time on a user's local computer, so it might not correspond to a user's own local time.

Displaying the Last Time a Document Was Modified

Another handy thing you can do using a server-side include is display the date when a document was last modified. The server-side include enables you to include that information in your document without manually updating it each time you make a change to the document. The following is an example of using a server-side include to display the last time the document was updated:

```
<!--#config timefmt="%A, %B %d, %Y" -->
This document was last modified on <!--#echo var="LAST_MODIFIED"
-->.
```

Including a File

Probably the most common use for server-side includes is to include a file inside a document. This can allow you, for instance, to create a document that contains a page's address block and then automatically include that file inside other pages within a site. This can be useful if sections or parts are duplicated across many pages (such as an address block, for instance). By using a server-side include, you only need to edit the file being included to update your entire site, in other words. The following is an example of using a server-side include to include a file within an HTML document:

```
<!--#include file="inclfile.html"-->
```

The previous example uses a relative URL to specify that the file to be included is located in the same folder as the document in which it is to be included. You cannot, however, use "../" to step back up the folder tree when using the file attribute. To specify the folder where a file to be included is located, use the virtual attribute, as shown here:

```
<!--#include virtual="/includes/inclfile.html"-->
```

In this case, if the file to be included is located at the address, **http://www.yourdomain.com/includes/inclfile.html**, just eliminate the first part of the URL. If you do not have your own domain name but have a folder within someone else's domain, you might use the following code (where *username* corresponds to your user name):

```
<!--#include virtual="/username/includes/inclfile.html"-->
```

USING COOKIES

A cookie is a file that is saved on a user's computer when a Web page is visited. Later, when a user visits the same page, the cookie can be read and updated. Cookies can keep track of when you last visited or how many times you have visited a page, as well as many other kinds of information. A shopping cart application, for instance, might save a cookie to your computer to remember what you have placed in your shopping cart. A cookie also can be used to remember a password or user name, for instance.

Cookies can be set either using a server-side program (a CGI script written in Perl, for instance) or a client-side script or program (a JavaScript script or a Java applet, for instance).

There is a great deal of misinformation and myth in regards to what cookies can and cannot do. Cookies are not programs but simple text files, so they cannot be executed to perform actions or look for information on a user's computer. One serious concern, however, is that a cookie can be used to track and monitor users' browsing history over many sites, rather than simply track their history and preferences relative to a single page or site. This is generally done through a third party that provides an advertising banner on another site; when the advertising banner is displayed, the third party sets a cookie tracking the banner being shown, if the person clicks on the banner, the page from which the banner originated is displayed, and so on. The information gathered is generally used to then tailor ads to the specific interests or preferences of that individual. Some are concerned that this type of gleaning of personal information could possibly be exploited in the future for less benign purposes. It is important to stress, however, that unless users volunteer their names or e-mail addresses, for instance, there is no way that cookies can discover that kind of information.

A number of proposals are in the works to change the protocol that enables the use of cookies to make it more difficult for third parties to track users' Web browsing habits. The most recent browsers also provide users with more capability to control how cookies are set and read on their computers. For instance, to change how cookies are handled in Internet Explorer 8 for Windows:

1. In Internet Explorer 8, select Tools, Internet Options, and click the Privacy tab.
2. To control how cookies are set and accessed on your computer, either use the slider to set a higher or lower level of privacy, or click on the Advanced button. You also can choose to override the cookie parameters you have set for individual sites by clicking the Edit button.
3. If you click on the Advanced button, you can select the check box to override automatic cookie handling. For instance, you might choose to accept cookies from first parties (set directly by sites that you visit and only readable by those sites) but choose to block cookies from third parties (set by third-party advertisers on a first-party site, for instance).

ADDING PASSWORD PROTECTION

There are many reasons why you might want or be called upon to password protect a Web page, a folder, or an entire site. For instance, you might be running a service that requires users to log in to use your service, so you can charge a subscription fee. You may also be running an administrative site that you do not want to be available to the general public. If running a subscription service, you may also want to implement automated sign-ups and authentication, so subscribers can sign up and receive a username and password, which they can then use to log into your site.

Setting up password protection that is relatively secure needs to be done on the server, but if you do not require strong security, JavaScript scripts for password protecting files can be used. Most JavaScript password-protection scripts work by requiring you to know the name of the file you are trying to access, which serves as the password. If you cannot provide the correct password, you get a "file not found" response.

If setting up password protection on the server, on a UNIX server, at minimum you will need to create or edit an .htaccess file for the folder or page you want to protect that points to another file, .htpasswd, which lists one or more usernames and passwords that can be used to access the folder or page. When users try to access the protected page, they will be prompted to enter a username and password.

To get more sophisticated, you will need to use an application that allows for automated sign-ups and updating of the password file. This can involve using a form and a CGI script (a Perl script, for instance) to process the data submitted with the form, which could then be automatically written to the password file to update it. If charging a fee or price for signing up, you may also need to have access to a secure server for gathering sensitive data, such as a credit card number. Larger sites with a large number of subscribers might need to access a MySQL database, for instance, for storing and updating user name and password data.

CLIENT SIDE SCRIPTING AND PROGRAMMING

JavaScript is the most commonly used client-side scripting language on the Web. VBScript is a client-side scripting language that is primarily used on Windows-based intranets, but much less commonly on the Internet, due to its not being supported by browsers other than Internet Explorer. Java is a client-side programming language, as is ActiveX (Java programs are called "applets," whereas ActiveX programs are called "controls"). Scripting languages create scripts, which are text-based lists of codes that can be embedded in Web pages or linked to externally. Java and ActiveX programs, on the other hand, are compiled, which means they are downloaded to your browser as binary data, instead of as text code.

SERVER-SIDE SCRIPTING AND PROGRAMMING

Server-side scripts and programs run on a server, with only their output downloaded to a browser to be displayed.

CGI

CGI (Common Gateway Interface) is not a programming language but a gateway protocol that allows a browser to access scripts and programs residing on a server. Such scripts and programs are server-side applications, in that they run on the server, rather than first being downloaded and run in the browser. One of the most common server-side scripting languages is Perl, which owes its popularity partly to its availability on most UNIX computers (and most servers on the Web still run some variant of UNIX). Other server-side scripting and programming languages can be used, however, including C, C++, Visual Basic, Python, TCL, UNIX Shell, ASP, PHP, ActiveX, Server-Side JavaScript, Enterprise Java (Java Servlets), Cold Fusion, and more (see the next two sections for descriptions of ASP and PHP).

ASP and ASP.NET

ASP (*Active Server Pages*) uses server-side scripting to dynamically generate Web pages. Most commonly, ASP is used with VBScript (*Visual Basic Script*) but also can be used with JScript (Microsoft's version of JavaScript) or other scripting languages. ASP Web pages have an extension of .asp, instead of .html or .htm. ASP requires server support to be used—ASP is supported by Windows-based Web servers, such as Microsoft Internet Information Server (IIS).

ASP pages can include HTML codes, client-side scripts (such as JavaScript scripts), and server-side scripts. When a user accesses an ASP page, the ASP server is called by the Web server, which then scans the page from top to bottom, parsing any server-side scripts. After executing the server-side scripts, it outputs the resulting HTML file and downloads it to the client (the browser).

ASP.NET is an expansion of the basic idea behind ASP into a server-side programming framework or platform that is designed to facilitate the building, deploying, and running of distributed Web applications that can run in any browser and on any platform. ASP.NET takes advantage of the .NET Common Language Runtime that is built into all newer versions of Windows and that provides access to lower-level services, such as user authentication, file management, network mapping, and so on. ASP.NET pages, unlike regular ASP pages, are compiled, which speeds up performance considerably. ASP. NET pages have an extension of .aspx.

PHP

PHP originally stood for *Personal Home Page*, but now stands for *PHP: Hypertext Preprocessor* (it is a recursive acronym, in that it refers to itself). PHP is a scripting language that runs on a server (a server-side scripting language). PHP is used to dynamically generate HTML pages on-the-fly. PHP code is embedded directly in HTML pages. Web servers that support PHP scan any files ending with .php, parsing any PHP codes they contain before downloading them to clients. A **<?php ... ?>** code alerts the server that a PHP command is enclosed. Some common uses of PHP include working with cookies and online databases (such as MySQL, SyBase, ODBC, Oracle, and more). PHP is an open-source scripting language that can be used on most platforms and server software. Here is a short example of PHP embedded in an HTML page:

```
<?php
    define("a','"Hello");
    echo a."<br>";
?>
```

Other Web Application Frameworks

A variety of other server-side Web application frameworks that work similarly to ASP and PHP have been developed, including Ajax (Asynchronous JavaScript and XML) and Ruby on Rails, both of which, like PHP, are open source rather than proprietary technologies. The Ajax programming language and Ruby on Rails can be used together, a combination that is sometimes referred to as Ajax on Rails.

ONLINE DATABASES

There are two basic approaches to publishing databases to the Web. The first is to export or convert database records to HTML documents before publishing them to the Web. The second is to actually publish a database to the Web that users can then query using SQL or MySQL. SQL stands for Structured Query Language and was originally developed by IBM. MySQL is the most popular relational database management system for use on the Web; it is often used in conjunction with PHP to create dynamic database-based Web sites.

The simplest way to publish information from databases to the Web is to format a report form that includes the necessary HTML codes. You then just need to generate a database report, which is then published to the Web. This is especially useful for formatting catalogs, for instance, as HTML documents. Additionally, various utilities can convert database data (such as in comma-delimited CSV files, for instance) to HTML documents. Many database software programs, such as FileMaker Pro or Microsoft Access, can export data in HTML format.

You can approximate the look-and-feel of an online database by generating HTML-formatted documents for various queries and then linking to them.

Actually publishing a database to the Web that can be queried by users can be either relatively simple or complex. Relatively simple options for publishing data to the Web include simple text-based and table-based datasets that can be queried using scripts, while more complex options include creating databases using MySQL with ASP and PHP. Some database programs, such as FileMaker Pro, for instance, also facilitate publishing flat-file or relational databases to the Web that can be queried by users.

SECURE FORMS AND SERVERS

If you want to add a form or a shopping cart application to your site that needs to collect and transmit credit card or other sensitive information, you should have access to a secure server running SSL (Secure Sockets Layer). Web pages located on a secure server are accessed using "https://" (HyperText Transfer Protocol over Secure Socket Layer), instead of "http://" (HyperText Transfer Protocol), as is the case with pages on a regular Web server. When you link to a page on an SSL server, any data transmitted between you and the server (or from the server to you) is encrypted and is next to impossible to intercept or decipher.

Digital Certificates

You will also need access to a digital certificate, either your own or one provided by the provider of your secure server space. A digital certificate authenticates the identity of a Web site to browsers. Generally, using a digital certificate provided by your secure server provider is less expensive but does not uniquely identify you when users view your digital certificate information (it identifies the provider of the secure server provider instead). In other words, if you want to instill the maximum degree of confidence in your customers when using a secure form or shopping cart application on your site, you should purchase your own digital certificate. For a smaller site that will not be handling a large number of orders, however, this is not necessary. Accounts that provide secure server access usually cost somewhat more per month (if using your provider's digital certificate) than a regular virtual hosting account.

Encryption

Different levels of encryption can be provided via SSL: 128-bit, 56-bit, and 40-bit encryption. 128-bit encryption is, by far, the more secure and, in fact, was considered so secure that the U.S. government until recently did not allow the export of software that included 128-bit encryption capability. All recent major Web browsers support 128-bit encryption.

One issue that is sometimes ignored is what happens to sensitive data after it has been submitted to a secure server. Many Web designers use a version of the formmail.pl form processing script to e-mail form responses to a designated e-mail address. This is inherently insecure, however, because normal e-mail is sent unencrypted over an insecure connection and is vulnerable to being intercepted. To ensure security for sensitive information (such as credit card numbers), any form responses should save form responses in an encrypted file or database on a secure server, rather than relay them to an e-mail address.

To retrieve the data, you would then log in to the server and provide the private key to gain access to the data. To keep it secure, the data should be left on the server and not downloaded to your desktop computer or laptop. If you need to download secure information, it should be transferred in an encrypted form using either FTPS (also called SSL/TLS) or SFTP. FTPS is FTP running over an SSL (Secure Sockets Layer) connection, while SFTP is FTP running on top of the SSH (Secure Shell) protocol. Most current FTP programs allow file transfers via FTPS or SFTP, or both. SFTP is supported by Linux or UNIX servers by default.

E-Commerce Programs

Many Web hosting companies offer e-commerce programs to handle secure transactions at rates even one-person or small companies can afford. There are also many secure e-commerce and shopping cart scripts available, at low cost or free, that you can install and use on your server.

You should be aware that if you fail to protect credit card information or other sensitive information that has been submitted to you and which you have promised to secure, you could be liable for any damages suffered as a result by a customer or customers (or by their credit card company).

DYNAMIC HTML (DHTML)

DHTML does not refer to a specific standard but to a combination of specifications that can be implemented in concert to create dynamic effects in Web pages. The four principal parts that comprise DHTML are a markup language (HTML, XHTML, or XML), a style sheet language (CSS or XSL), a scripting language (JavaScript, ECMAScript, JScript, or VBScript), and a Document Object Model (DOM). Initially, both Microsoft and Netscape supported differing DOMs, which in turn differed from the DOM promulgated by the W3C. That and a lack in uniformity in how CSS was implemented hampered widespread implementation of DHTML. Internet Explorer has supported the W3C DOM since Version 5. All current and recent major browsers now support the W3C DOM.

Following is a sample DHTML script that causes the position and other display characteristics of an H1 element to change when the mouse is passed over and off it:

```
<script type="text/javascript">
function change()
```

```
{
document.getElementById("heading1').style.position="relative";
document.getElementById("heading1').style.left="25px";
document.getElementById("heading1').style.top="-8px";
document.getElementById("heading1').style.color="blue";
document.getElementById("heading1').style.letterSpacing="0.2em";
document.getElementById("heading1').style.fontStyle="italic";
document.getElementById("heading1').style.fontSize="2.3em";
document.getElementById("heading1').style.width="85%";
document.getElementById("heading1').style.border="3px solid
green";
document.getElementById("heading1').style.background="yellow";
document.getElementById("heading1').style.textAlign="right";
}
function changeback()
{
document.getElementById("heading1').style.position="relative";
document.getElementById("heading1').style.left="0";
document.getElementById("heading1').style.top="0";
document.getElementById("heading1').style.color="red";
document.getElementById("heading1').style.letterSpacing="normal";
document.getElementById("heading1').style.fontStyle="normal";
document.getElementById("heading1').style.fontSize="2em";
document.getElementById("heading1').style.border="none";
document.getElementById("heading1').style.
background="transparent";
document.getElementById("heading1').style.textAlign="left";
}
</script>
</head>
<body>
<h1 id="heading1" style="color:red; font-size:2em;"
onmouseover="change()"
onmouseout="changeback()">
Move the mouse over this text.</h1>
```

To see how this works, open **dhmtl.html** from the **apps** folder in your working folder. Open it in your text editor, and then save it with a new name, to experiment changing the codes. You can use any CSS property—for instance, to specify the margin-top property, just change it to marginTop.

XML

XHTML 1.0 and 2.0 are versions of HTML formulated to be compatible with XML (Extensible Markup Language). In standalone XML documents, authors can freely create their own elements and then apply styles to them using either CSS (Cascading Style Sheets) or XSLT (Extensible Stylesheet Language Transformations). Following is an example of an XML file that formats a bibliography using CSS:

```
<?xml version="1.0" encoding="UTF-8" standalone="yes"?>
<?xml-stylesheet type="text/css" href="biblio.css"?>
<bibliography>
    <heading>A J.K. Rowling Bibliography</heading>
    <book>
        <title>Harry Potter and the Philosopher's Stone</title>
```

```
        <author>Rowling, J.K.</author>
        <publisher>Scholastic</publisher>
        <location>New York</location>
        <date>1997</date>
    </book>
    <book>
        <title>Harry Potter and the Chamber of Secrets</title>
        <author>Rowling, J.K.</author>
        <publisher>Scholastic</publisher>
        <location>New York</location>
        <date>1999</date>
    </book>
    <book>
        <title>Harry Potter and the Prisoner of Azbakan</title>
        <author>Rowling, J.K.</author>
        <publisher>Scholastic</publisher>
        <location>New York</location>
        <date>1999</date>
    </book>
    <book>
        <title>Harry Potter and the Goblet of Fire</title>
        <author>Rowling, J.K.</author>
        <publisher>Scholastic</publisher>
        <location>New York</location>
        <date>2000</date>
    </book>
    <book>
        <title>Harry Potter and the Order of the Phoenix</title>
        <author>Rowling, J.K.</author>
        <publisher>Scholastic</publisher>
        <location>New York</location>
        <date>2003</date>
    </book>
    <book>
        <title>Harry Potter and the Half-Blood Prince</title>
        <author>Rowling, J.K.</author>
        <publisher>Scholastic</publisher>
        <location>New York</location>
        <date>2005</date>
    </book>
    <book>
        <title>Harry Potter and the Deathly Hallows</title>
        <author>Rowling, J.K.</author>
        <publisher>Scholastic</publisher>
        <location>New York</location>
        <date>2007</date>
    </book>
</bibliography>
```

If you want to see what this looks like in your browser, just open **biblio.xml** from the apps folder in your working folder. To see it as created, open it and **biblio.css** in your text editor.

INTERACTIVE ANIMATION AND MULTIMEDIA

Increasing average bandwidth available to users has led to the development of sophisticated software for creating graphically rich and interactive Web applications featuring interactive animation and multimedia.

Adobe Flash

Flash is a software program that allows the creation of interactive vector-based animations for the Web. It was originally created as FutureSplash Animator by FutureWave Software, but was acquired by Macromedia in 1996 and renamed as Flash (a contraction of Future and Splash). Adobe acquired Flash in 2006, releasing it as part of their CS3 suite of applications in 2007.

Flash works in conjunction with ActionScript, which uses the same syntax as JavaScript, but has a different programming framework and class libraries. ActionScript 3.0 added object-oriented programming capability.

A Flash animation uses the .swf file extension and can be embedded in an HTML file in the following manner:

```
<object data="animation-name.swf"
type="application/x-shockwave-flash" width="300" height="300">
    <param name="movie" value="animation-name.swf" />
</object>
```

There are a number of lower-cost or free substitutes for Flash that are available over the Web, including Swish (Windows) and OpenLazlo (Windows, Mac OS X, and Linux).

Microsoft Silverlight

Silverlight is a programmable browser plug-in that enables rich Internet applications featuring interactive animation, vector graphics, and audio/video playback. Version 2.0 supports the .NET languages and development tools. It is viewed as a direct competitor with Adobe Flash.

WIRELESS AND MOBILE ACCESS TO THE WEB

Not everyone connects to and surfs the Web using a computer. More and more people are connecting to the Web using other devices, such as mobile phones, PDAs, TV set-top boxes (such as MSN TV, for instance), car navigation systems, mobile game machines, digital book readers, and other devices that do not feature the screen or resolution size necessary to present a Web page as it might normally be displayed on a computer screen. These devices also do not use mouse interfaces, which requires the specification of different means for accessing menus, links, scrolling, and so on. Users of mobile devices face constrained screens, input facilities, processing power, memory, and bandwidth, compared to those accessing the Web through desktop or laptop computers with broadband connections.

WAP and WML

WAP (Wireless Application Protocol) and WML (Wireless Markup Language) were developed to enable the publishing and transmission of content on the Web that is tailored to presentation on wireless and other small-format devices. Handheld Device Markup Language (HDML) and CompactHTML (CHTML) are markup languages similar to WML. WAP 2.0 uses XHTML Mobile Profile as its markup language.

XHTML Basic 1.0 and XHTML-MP

More recently, however, support for enabling wireless and mobile access to the Web has migrated to the use of XHTML (XHTML Basic) and CSS (CSS Mobile Profile), developed by the W3C, to enable presenting text, images, forms, basic tables, and other objects on wireless/mobile devices. XHTML Basic is a simplified version of XHTML 1.0, which can be extended with custom modules to provide for richer markup capabilities for specific environments.

XHTML-MP (XHTML Mobile Profile) is based on XHTML Basic 1.0 and was developed by the Open Mobile Alliance (OMA) and its predecessor, the WAP Forum. It provides more extensive form controls and scripting support than XHTML Basic 1.0.

XHTML Basic 1.1

XHTML Basic 1.1 was developed through collaboration between OMA and the W3C, superceding both XHTML Basic 1.0 and XHTML-MP 1.2. It became a W3C recommendation in July 2008. If a browser supports XHTML-MP, it should support most features of XHTML Basic 1.1. It is the most widely supported markup language for wireless and mobile devices.

To declare a document as conforming to XHTML Basic 1.1, you would include the following DocType declaration above the HTML element:

```
<!DOCTYPE html
    PUBLIC "-//W3C//DTD XHTML Basic 1.1//EN"
    "http://www.w3.org/TR/xhtml-basic/xhtml-basic11.dtd">
```

Otherwise, you create an XHTML Basic 1.1 document just as you would an XHTML document, except only a subset of the XHTML elements and attributes are available for use. There are no I, B, CENTER, or FONT elements, for instance. Nested tables are not allowed. Features added to XHTML Basic 1.1 include XHTML Forms, Intrinsic Events, styles, XHTML Presentation, and the inputmode attribute.

An XHTML Basic document should be delivered as an application/xhtml+xml media-type, according to the W3C, but in practice, delivering it as text/html works just as well.

To learn more about XHTML Basic 1.1, see **www.w3.org/TR/xhtml-basic/**.

CSS Mobile Profile 2.0 is a subset of CSS 2.1, focused on those features of most value to users of constrained devices. To learn more about CSS Mobile Profile 2.0, see **www.w3.org/TR/css-mobile/**.

For links to many resources that further discuss the topics covered in this appendix, see the Appendices section at the Internet Resource Center of this book at **www.emcp.net/html2e**.

GLOSSARY

@import rule A rule that can be inserted in a style sheet (internal or external) that will import styles from an external style sheet.

A

above the fold A term originating from the newspaper business, where advertising above a paper's fold commanded higher prices than advertising below the fold. In Web design, it refers to information that is immediately visible above the bottom edge of a browser's viewport, without having to scroll down to see it.

absolute font sizes Using the FONT element, absolute font sizes are indicated by any of seven different font sizes, numbered from 1 to 7. The default font size is usually size 3. Size 7 is one size bigger than the default size of an H1 element.

absolute URL A URL that points to a location on the Web.

access permissions Need to be set on a UNIX or Linux server to enable access to a form-processing or other CGI script.

address block A block of text created using the ADDRESS element that can include the identity of the author or owner of a Web page, contact information, and a means to provide feedback.

alias A prefix to a domain name that stands for a resource located within that domain. A common alias used on the Web is "www."

almost standards mode A mode in which a browser implements almost all of the most recent HTML or CSS standards. Many recent browsers default to almost standards mode (including Internet Explorer 6 and 7).

alpha-channel transparency Involves assigning an 8-bit channel (or alpha-channel) to an RGB image, allowing multiple-color transparency effects.

alternative text Text included in an IMG element using the ALT attribute that describes the content and/or function of the image for users of non-visual browsers or who are surfing with display of graphics turned off.

anchor pseudo-class CSS1 selector that applies property values to specific link states (unvisited, visited, active, or hover).

anti-aliasing Blends (or "blurs") the edges of letterforms with an image's or display's background. It is generally used to smooth jagged (or pixelated) edges, but can cause problems when displaying text in an image against a transparent background (because there is no longer a discreet edge between letterforms and their background).

ARPAnet A computer network, commissioned in 1969, that was a progenitor of the Internet, established by the Defense Department's Advanced Research Projects Agency (ARPA) to link four universities involved in defense research (UCLA, Stanford, UCSB, and Utah).

ASCII American Standard Code for Information Interchange, which defines a standard set of characters and control codes that are recognized by almost all computer systems. Sometimes referred to as US-ASCII, since it includes the "$" symbol for U.S. currency.

ASCII text file A text file that includes only codes and characters that are included in the American Standard Code for Information Interchange encoding scheme.

attribute A property or characteristic that can be included in an element's start (or empty) tag. An attribute is composed of a name and a value: *name="value"*.

attribute name The name of an attribute: width, height, href, align, and src are some examples.

attribute value A value that can be assigned to an attribute: *center* in **align="center"** is an example.

B

background color A color set to be displayed in the background of a Web page. Can be set using color names or hexadecimal RGB codes.

backward-compatibility A concern with how Web pages are displayed in older browsers that do not support or poorly support the latest HTML or CSS features.

background image Generally, a small image that can be seamlessly "tiled" to display a continuous graphical background for a page. A background image will overlay any background color set for a page.

bandwidth The capacity of a network or network connection to carry data.

banner image An image, wider than it is tall, that is often displayed across the top of a page.

baseline The line upon which a text font sits, not including descenders, such as in the "y" or "g" letters, which descend below the baseline.

block element An element, the content of which is displayed as a separate block, with vertical spacing inserted above and below the element.

box model bug A misapplication of the CSS box model in Internet Explorer 5.x for Windows, which includes padding and border lengths in the element width (in the CSS box model, the element width is exclusive of any padding or border lengths).

box model hack A hack (or workaround) that takes advantage of a parsing error in Internet Explorer 5.x to deliver one set of style rules to that browser and a different set to other browsers.

bulleted list A list where the items are preceded by a bullet. Also called an *unordered list* because it is created using the UL (Unordered List) element.

button link A hypertext link that contains a graphical "button" as its content. Button links generally have the image borders turned off, since the content of the link (a button) indicates the image is linked.

C

cascading The order of precedence given to styling information originating from different sources (author, user, and browser).

Cascading Style Sheets (CSS) The standard for creating style sheets for the Web.

case examples The case examples are real-world example Web designs that the student creates in order to learn different features of HTML, CSS, and Web design. Each chapter features one or more case examples.

cell padding Spacing within a table cell, separating the cell content from the cell border.

cell spacing Spacing between the borders of different table cells.

CGI Common Gateway Interface, a specification by which a Web server (running HTTP) can interface with its host computer, allowing clients to run server-side programs or scripts.

CGI form A type of form that accesses a CGI script to send form responses. Requires access to and configuration of a server-side form processing script.

CGI script A server-side script, usually residing in a cgi-bin folder, most often written in the Perl language, but written in other languages as well.

check box A form control created using the INPUT element that allows the selection of one or more check boxes out of a check box group.

child selector CSS2 selector that applies property values to any child of a specified element, but not to other descendants.

CHMOD number A number issued using UNIX's CHMOD (Change Mode) command to set access permissions for CGI scripts. The CHMOD number most commonly used to set

access permissions for CGI form-processing scripts is 755, which provides read, write, and execute permissions to the owner (7), but only read and execute permissions to the group (5) or the world (5).

class selector CSS1 selector that applies property values to any element belonging to a specified class (set with the CLASS attribute).

client A computer that requests and receives services from a server on a network.

client-server model A model by which one computer (a client) requests a service from another computer (a server).

client-side application A program or script that is downloaded to be executed by a client.

color name A standard color name that is included in the HTML standard. There are 16 color names: blue, red, yellow, green, purple, aqua, maroon, olive, navy, fuchsia, lime, teal, silver, gray, black, and white. Note that "orange" is not one of the standard color names in HTML, but has been included in CSS 2.1.

color-vision deficiency An issue that can impact accessibility for pages that use foreground and background colors. Ten percent of males have a form of this type of vision deficiency. Common forms of color blindness are the inability to distinguish between red and green or blue and yellow colors with the same tonal value.

comment Text that can be added to an HTML document that will not be displayed when opened in a browser.

compression level In JPEG images, varying degrees of compression can be applied. The higher the compression, the smaller the image will be in bytes, but image quality can suffer. Optimizing JPEG images involves finding the optimal compression level, which saves the most bytes without overly compromising image quality.

conditional comment A conditional expression, enclosed in HTML comment codes, that is recognized only by the Internet Explorer browser (Version 5.x and later). Allows targeting content for specific versions of that browser.

conformance level HTML 4 (and XHTML 1.0) defines three conformance levels that can be declared for an HTML document: *transitional* allows deprecated elements/attributes, *frameset* allows frameset and deprecated elements/attributes, and *strict* does not allow deprecated or frameset elements/attributes.

container element Composed of a start tag, an end tag, and the contained content in between.

counter-semantic use The use of an element in a way that runs counter to its semantic meaning, such as using the BLOCKQUOTE element simply as a formatting device (to indent margins) rather than to display a quoted block of text.

CSS comments Any text or code inserted between /* and */ codes, which a browser's parser will ignore.

CSS styles Cascading Style Sheets. Styles (presentational changes) can be applied to HTML elements using either inline styles or style sheets.

CSS1 The Cascading Style Sheets, Level 1 specification.

CSS2 The Cascading Style Sheets, Level 2 specification.

D

declaration Declares which property values will be applied to the subject or subjects of a selector.

deep linking Linking to pages buried deep within another's site. Can be unethical if done from within a frame, without `target="_blank"` or `target="_top"`.

degrades ungracefully What happens when a later HTML feature being displayed in an earlier non-supporting browser makes access to the document's content more difficult or impossible. The Q element, for instance, degrades ungracefully in earlier browsers that do not recognize that element, since the generated quote marks are not displayed.

deprecated The word *deprecate* means "to disapprove." In HTML, Web authors are discouraged from using deprecated elements and attributes that are deemed harmful to accessibility or usability. Web authors are encouraged to use alternatives that achieve similar or superior results and are not harmful to accessibility or usability, such as Cascading Style Sheets (CSS).

deprecated elements HTML elements that have been outdated by newer constructs, primarily for accessibility and usability issues. Web authors are discouraged from using them, although they are still allowed.

deprecated attributes Attributes that Web authors are discouraged from using in Web documents, in many cases because they are considered harmful to accessibility or usability. Web authors are encouraged to use alternatives that achieve similar or superior results and are not harmful to accessibility or usability, such as Cascading Style Sheets (CSS). The philosophy of HTML 4 and XHTML 1 is to use HTML to determine structure and CSS to determine appearance.

descendant selector Indicates style properties are applied to an element that is the descendant of another element. Also called a contextual selector.

destination anchor An A element, with a NAME attribute, that marks a landing spot (or destination) of a hypertext link in the current or another document.

destination element In HTML 4 and XHTML 1.0, any element with an ID attribute can serve as the destination for a jump link. Not supported by all browsers. While current browsers should support this, not all older browsers do.

display:table properties The display:table, display:table-row, and display:table-cell property:value pairs, which can be applied to divisions (DIV elements) to create fluid table-like layouts with self-adjusting, equal-height columns.

dithering The adjustment of the colors of adjacent pixels so that they appear to the eye to be a single color, allowing the display of a color that is not included in a system's or image's color palette.

DocType declaration Short for *document type declaration.* Specifies the version of HTML and conformance level to which a document conforms.

DocType switching A means of triggering different modes using different DocType declarations or no DocType declaration including standards, almost standards, and quirks modes. A foreshortened DocType statement, without a DTD file reference, will trigger quirks mode in most recent and current browsers.

document menu A menu of links at the top of a document that jump to subsections within that document.

docuverse A term coined by Ted Nelson to denote the universe of hypertext-linked documents.

domain name A domain name is a unique name that identifies a domain (or IP address) on the Internet and the Web—yahoo.com, for instance.

dot pitch A measurement applied to computer monitors that describes the distance between same-color dots (or sub-pixels) in a monitor's display screen. Roughly corresponds to the dots-per-inch (dpi) a display is capable of displaying.

drop cap A larger initial letter that drops below the first line in a paragraph.

DTD Document Type Definition. The formal definition of any specification that is based on SGML, including HTML 4.01 and earlier versions of HTML. HTML 5, however, is no longer linked to SGML and no longer uses a DTD.

E

elastic layout A page layout that can stretch vertically and/or horizontally to accommodate varying viewport widths, content lengths, and user-specified font sizes.

element The basic building block of an HTML document—every HTML document is composed of elements.

element content The content of a container element, between a start tag and an end tag.

em A printer's measurement that traditionally was equal to the width of the letter M in a particular typeface. In CSS, it is a relative measurement that sets an element's font size relative to its parent element's font size. Thus `font-size: 1.5em` would set an element's font size to 1.5 times its parent-element's font size.

e-mail alias A means provided in some form-processing CGI scripts to specify an alias to be used in place of an e-mail address when submitting a form.

empty element A single-tag element that is empty of content. Also called a *stand alone element* or a *void element.*

end tag The finishing code component that ends an HTML element.

entity code A code that inserts an entity (or non-keyboard character) in an HTML document.

error diffusion When converting a JPEG image (which can include any of 16.8 million colors) to a GIF image (which can include only 256 colors), for instance, error diffusion is used to diffuse any quantization errors across neighboring pixels, so they are less visually evident in the resulting image. It can cause problems, however, when displaying text in an image against a transparent background (since it is no longer a single color).

example files The case examples for each chapter make use of author-created example files to help reduce the amount of redundant code the student needs to key in or that the book needs to present. Example graphic files that are used in the case examples are also included in the example files. The example files are available for download from the book's Internet Resource Center at www.emcp.net/html2e.

external style sheet A style sheet file (with a .css file extension) containing style rules that can be linked to using the LINK element or the @import rule. Allows applying one or several style sheets to multiple HTML documents.

F

faux columns A technique, using a vertically tiled background image, that gives a page the appearance that it contains equal-height columns, even if it does not. Because the actual columns are transparent and without borders, you do not see that they have unequal heights.

file select control A control that allows the uploading of a file along with the form response.

first child An element that is the first child (initial nested element) of another element.

first-child selector CSS2 selector that applies property values to the first child of a specified element, but not to other children.

fixed layout A layout in which all dimensions are set in pixels.

float The action of aligning an image or object with the left or right margins from the point of insertion, with following text flowing, or wrapping, around the right or left side of the image.

fluid design A page design that uses ems or percentages, rather than pixels, so that element and font sizes can adjust fluidly to user font-size preferences. Fluid designs are more accessible, but can vary in layout and look, depending on a user's font preferences and screen resolution.

fluid layout A layout in which dimensions are set in ems or percentages. Sometimes called a "liquid" layout.

font Traditionally, a "font" is a set of characters in a particular size and style (16-point Arial Bold, for instance), while a "typeface" is a family of fonts (Arial, Arial Bold, and Arial Italic, for instance). On the Web, however, "font" or "font face" has come to designate a particular typeface (Arial, Times New Roman, or Helvetica, for instance). Most browsers default to displaying body text using Times New Roman or some variant of it.

font face A term derived from the FONT element and its FACE attribute, which corresponds roughly to "typeface" in typography. The terms "font" and "font face" are generally used interchangeably on the Web.

font list A list that can be used to display text if available on a user's system: **<font face="Arial, Geneva, Helvetica, sans-serif">**, for instance.

foreground color Generally, any color set for text or link fonts in an HTML document. Web pages can have more than one foreground color. Can be set using color names or hexadecimal RGB codes.

form controls Controls, such as a text box, radio button, and check box controls, that can be used to input different types of data or perform actions through an HTML form, through the INPUT, SELECT, TEXTAREA, and BUTTON elements.

form input validation The ability, often provided through a JavaScript script, to validate that data has been input in required fields or that it has been input in an expected format (containing a "@" and a "." character if an e-mail address is expected, for instance).

form-processing CGI script A CGI script that processes form responses. One of the most commonly used form-processing scripts on UNIX or Linux servers is NMS FormMail.pl.

forward-compatibility A concern with how Web pages will be displayed in future browsers. Workarounds used with one generation of browsers to ensure backward-compatibility and cross-browser compabitibility can fail to work in a following generation of browsers. Current browsers support deprecated elements and attributes, but might not do so if they are declared obsolete in a future version of HTML (as many have been in the draft specification for HTML 5).

fragment identifier An HREF value, starting with a # character followed by the name or ID of a destination anchor, that enables a link to jump to another location in the current or another document.

frame layout A multi-column, multi-row, or combination column/row layout created using the FRAMESET and FRAME elements.

frames Scrollable windows created using the FRAMESET and FRAME elements, arranged in rows and/or columns.

frameset conformance Allows the usage of frameset and deprecated elements and attributes in HTML 4 and XHTML 1 documents.

frameset page A page that contains the code for laying out a framed page and designating the URLs for the content of the frames. Derived from the FRAMESET element.

FTP programs Programs that use File Transfer Protocol to download files from or upload files to a Web server. They can also be used to set access permissions for CGI scripts.

G

generic font-family names Names for generic types of fonts, including **serif**, **sans-serif**, **monospace**, **cursive**, and **fantasy**. They can be used with the FONT element's FACE attribute or CSS's **font-family** property to direct a browser to use its default font for the type of font specified. Only the first three are widely supported in browsers.

get method A method that appends form data to the form response URL. Limited in the number of characters that can be sent and not secure. Primarily used to interact with a CGI script, make database queries, and so on.

GIF animation A GIF image that takes advantage of the ability of that image format to contain multiple image frames. Also called an animated GIF.

GIF image format Graphic Interchange Format, an 8-bit image format that supports up to 256 colors, interlacing, and transparency (one color). Originated by Compuserve to facilitate exchanging images on its network. File extension: *.gif.

graphic rule A graphical image that can be displayed in place of a horizontal rule.

graphical submit button A form control for submitting form data, with an image designated as the button, created using the INPUT element.

group selector CSS1 selector that applies property values to a group of elements or pseudo-elements.

H

heading-level elements The H1, H2, through H6 elements that are used to define hierarchical headings and subheadings in a document.

hexadecimal numbering system A base-16 numbering system (0, 1, 2, 3, 4, 5, 6, 7, 8, 9, A, B, C, D, E, F) that programmers often prefer to use since any of 256 number values can be expressed using just two numbers.

hexadecimal RGB codes A code that states the RGB (red-green-blue) values for a particular color using hexadecimal numbers. Stated in the form: *#rrggbb*.

hidden control A control the content of which is not displayed by a browser, but is included when a form response is sent. Can be used by an author to identify a form or required by a form processing script to specify parameters.

horizontal spacing Spacing to the left or right of an image or object. Set for the IMG element using the HSPACE attribute.

host name A name, which is a combination of an alias and a domain name, that can be substituted for an IP address.

hotspot An area mapped to an image that is associated with a URL link.

hover buttons Buttons that change their appearance when the mouse cursor hovers over them.

HTML Hypertext Markup Language, the common language that facilitates the universal exchange of information over the Web. HTML allows the "marking up" of documents to facilitate the presentation of structured information and data.

HTTP Hypertext Transfer Protocol, which formalizes the interchange of data between computers (clients and servers) on the Web.

hypermedia A term coined by Ted Nelson to denote the non-sequential linking of different media.

hypertext A term invented by Ted Nelson to denote the dynamic and non-linear interlinking of textual documents, which he described as "nonsequential writing."

hypertext link A link that allows a user (or reader) to jump from an anchor in one position in a text document to the object or target of the link, which can be another document or a position in the same or another document, as well as a non-text object, such as an image, audio file, video clip, animation, and so on. In HTML, the A element is used to create hypertext links.

I

ID selector CSS1 selector that applies property values to an element with a specified ID (set with the ID attribute).

image editor A software program that enables the creation and editing of graphic images.

image link An image that is nested inside a hypertext link (the A element).

image map An image with areas set as hypertext hotspots.

image map editor A program, utility, or wizard that allows users to draw hotspot areas on an image and export HTML codes to enable displaying the image as a clickable image map.

important declaration A means by which a user or author can declare that a declaration is important and not to be trumped by other declarations for the same element or elements. A user's important declaration, in a user-defined style sheet, however, trumps an author's important declaration.

indented icon link list A list of links that uses an icon image as the bullet, with following text indented from the margin.

index page The name of an HTML file, most often index.html, that is loaded automatically when no object file is included in a URL.

inheritance The means by which a descendant element can inherit properties from a parent or other ancestor element. Some properties are inheritable, such as the color, font-family, or font-size elements, while other properties are not, such as the border, height, width, padding, margin, and background properties.

inline element An element that is displayed inline (or "in a line") and not as a separate block.

inline image An image displayed "inline" in a Web page, inserted using the IMG (Image) element, which is an inline, not a block, element.

inline style A style that is inserted *inline*, using the STYLE attribute, which allows applying styles to any displayable element.

interlacing Displaying an image using several passes, allowing a user to see an image's content before it has completely downloaded. With GIF images, the first pass displays every eighth line, the second pass every fourth line, and so on.

internal style sheet A style sheet that is inserted in an HTML file using the STYLE element.

internet A "network of networks." What started as a networking of networks involved in defense research, an *internet*, eventually evolved into the *Internet*.

Internet Society An international organization responsible for establishing Internet infrastructure standards.

IP address A set of numbers that uniquely identifies a device on the Internet (221.96.64.21, for instance).

J

JPEG image format Joint Photographic Experts Group format, a 24-bit image format that supports up to 1,677,216 colors. Three versions, standard, progressive, and lossless. File extension: *.jpg.

jump link A link that jumps to a location (marked by a destination anchor) in the same or another document.

K

keywords Words included in a Web page's content that might be used by a search engine to index its content.

L

link list A list composed of hypertext links (and optional descriptive text).

link text Text displayed as a link, inserted between the start and end tags of the A element.

list menu A form control created using the SELECT and OPTION elements (and optionally the OPTGROUP element) that allows selection from a list of options (or menu). Sometimes called a dropdown or pulldown menu, because only the initial option is displayed, with the other options unfolding when the menu box is clicked on.

literal elements How the I (Italic) and B (Bold) elements are sometimes described, because their names literally describe their appearance.

logical elements How the EM (Emphasis) and STRONG (Strong Emphasis) elements are sometimes described, because their names logically indicate their function, rather than describe their appearance.

lorum ipsum text Dummy text that has traditionally been used by the publishing and design industries to include text in layouts when the actual text has yet to be created. Often mistaken for Latin, but it is actually gibberish that is made to look like Latin.

lossless compression scheme A compression scheme used in PNG images that allows lost bits to be recovered after compression.

lossy compression scheme A compression scheme used in JPEG images that does not allow lost bits to be recovered after compression.

M

mailto address A form of Web address that allows visitors to send a message to an e-mail address using a user's default mail program.

mailto form A type of form that uses a mailto link to send form responses to an e-mail address, using a user's default e-mail program. Supported by Mozilla Firefox and Apple Safari, among current browsers, but not by Internet Explorer 8.

markup language A language that enables the marking up of documents or manuscripts so they can be printed, published, or displayed.

memex A proposal by Vannevar Bush in an article, "As We May Think," in the July 1945 issue of *Atlantic Monthly* magazine, which he described as being an "intricate web of trails," and which many consider to be a foreshadowing and precursor of what eventually became the World Wide Web.

metadata Data that is about or describes a document, rather than being part of its content. Described by the W3C as "machine understandable information," it is inserted in an HTML document's HEAD section using the META element. HTML metadata can include the character set, description, and keywords that are associated with a document.

Microsoft extensions Unofficial extensions to HTML that were introduced in Microsoft's Internet Explorer browser. Of these, only the FACE attribute for the FONT element has been included in later versions of HTML, but as deprecated. The most notable Microsoft extension that has not been included in standard HTML is the MARQUEE element.

MIME type Multipurpose Internet Mail Extension, originally used to identify attachments to e-mail messages, but now used more generally to identify file types on the Internet.

monospaced font A font in which all characters, including letters, numbers, punctuation marks, and even spaces are the same width. Examples of monospaced fonts include Lucida Console and Courier New in Windows and Monaco and Courier in Macintosh OS X. Also called a *fixed-pitch font*.

Mosaic The first widely distributed Web browser.

N

named entity code References the name of an entity. The named entity code for the copyright symbol is **©**, for instance.

namespace An abstract container holding a grouping of names (identifiers, terms, etc.). When creating an XHTML document, you declare it as belonging to the XHTML namespace within XML, which defines all the names (for elements and attributes) that belong to that language.

navigation icon An image that iconically depicts a navigational object or action, such as going to the home page (icon of a "house"), the previous page (icon of a "left-arrow"), and the next page (icon of a "right-arrow").

nesting The insertion of an element within another element, so the first is the content, or part of the content, of the second. The second element is the bracketing (or containing) element. Elements are not always nestable (a block element cannot be nested inside an inline element, for instance). Elements should never overlap each other.

Netscape extensions Unofficial extensions to HTML that were introduced in the Netscape's Navigator browser. The FONT, BASEFONT, CENTER, SCRIPT, APPLET, FRAMESET, FRAME, NOFRAME, and MAP elements, as well as the BODY element's TEXT, LINK, VLINK, ALINK, BGCOLOR, and BACKGROUND attributes, were later incorporated into HTML 3.2 or HTML 4, but as deprecated elements. The EMBED element (but not NOEMBED) is included in HTML 5. The most notable Netscape extension that has never been included in a later version of HTML is the BLINK element (causing the display of tagged text to blink on and off).

newspaper-style columns Also called snaking columns, in that the bottom of a preceding column continues at the top of a following column.

noframes text Text inserted in a NOFRAMES element in a frameset page, for the benefit of users using browsers that do not support frames. Also a way of including text in a frameset page that can be indexed by search engines.

non-breaking space A space that will not break when a line of text wraps. Can be inserted in an empty table cell to cause a border to be drawn around it (empty table cells do not have borders).

NSFNet A network established in 1986 by the National Science Foundation linking five supercomputing centers (at Princeton, UCSD, Illinois, Cornell, and Pittsburgh) along a high-speed backbone (initially at a speed of 56 KBps, but later at 1.544 KBps, or T1).

numbered list A list where the items are preceded by an ordered sequence of numbers (1, 2, 3, etc.) or letters (A, B, C, etc.). Also called an *ordered list* because it is created using the OL (Ordered List) element.

numeric entity code References the numerical position of an entity in a document's default character set. The numerical entity code for the copyright symbol in the ISO 8859-1 character set is `&#169;`, for instance.

O

object of a URL The file or other resource being linked to in a URL.

obsolete attributes Attributes that should not be used in HTML documents. Current browsers are not required to support obsolete attributes.

obsolete elements Elements that should not be used, because current Web browsers need not support them. Current browsers are not required to support obsolete elements.

optimized color palette A color palette of 256 or fewer colors that includes only colors that are present in a GIF image, in contrast with the standard color palette, which can contain many colors that are not present in the image. Also called an adaptive color palette (in Adobe Photoshop).

P

packet switching A method of communication on a network or between networks whereby messages are broken down into *packets* that can be transmitted (or switched) through separate channels (or paths) toward their destination, leading to a more efficient utilization of network transmission resources.

packets The pieces into which a message is broken by TCP.

password control Similar to a text box, but with the content hidden (as a series of asterisks).

personal Web page A Web page created by a person that has that person's interests, experiences, and other personal information as its primary content.

pixel The smallest piece of information in a digital image; short for "picture element." Screen resolutions are stated in pixels: 1024 × 768 pixels, for instance.

pixel-perfect design A page design that uses pixels, rather than ems or percentages, so that element and font sizes are fixed relative to a specific resolution. Also called a *fixed design*. Commercial clients and designers often prefer pixel-perfect designs, because they can exactly duplicate a specific look or layout.

pixel-perfect layout Another name for a fixed layout.

player console An object displayed in a browser window that allows the playing and pausing of an audio or video file.

PNG image format Portable Network Graphics format, which can select colors from a 32-bit or 48-bit palette. Supports setting transparency for an alpha-channel, allowing multiple partial transparency levels to be set for images.

POP mail server Post Office Protocol mail server. Receives and stores incoming e-mail.

post method A method that includes form data in the body of the HTTP request. Not limited in the number of characters that can be sent and inherently more secure than the get method. In almost all cases, the post method, and not the get method, should be used to send form responses.

PostScript font A type of font introduced by Adobe for use in the Apple Laserwriter and other PostScript-enabled printers. Common examples include Times, Helvetica, Courier, Palatino, Bookman, New Century Schoolbook, Avant Garde, and Zapf Chancery. These are the fonts most often used in the desktop publishing and graphic design fields.

preformatted text Text contained within a PRE element, which is displayed in a monospace font and in which all tabs, returns, and multiple spaces are displayed rather than ignored (as in all other HTML elements).

PRN text file format A file format resulting from "printing to a file" a worksheet or range within a worksheet, preserving all spaces so the columns continue to be aligned, so it could be printed later. Originated with Lotus 1-2-3 and was later incorporated into Microsoft Excel.

property An element characteristic that can be changed using styles, such as margins, padding, color, height, width, font-size, and so on.

protocols Sets of agreed upon rules that control how systems connect, communicate, and exchange data.

pseudo-class An abstract class to which properties can be applied. The `:visited` pseudo-class, for instance, applies style properties only to links (A elements) that have been previously visited.

pseudo-element An abstract element to which properties can be applied. The `:first-child` pseudo-element, for instance, applies style properties to the first child of an element.

public domain images Images for which their copyrights have expired or that have been released into the public domain by their authors or owners.

push button control A button that can be created, using the INPUT element, not to submit or reset a form, but to activate a script.

Q

quirks mode A mode in which a browser reverts to displaying a page according to the quirks (or bugs) of a previous version or versions of that browser.

R

radio button A form control created using the INPUT element that allows the selection of one radio button out of a radio button group.

Refresh button Refreshes (or reloads) the display of a Web page in Internet Explorer.

relative font sizes Using the FONT element, relative font sizes are indicated by a "+" or "-" in front of a SIZE attribute:

`<font size="+1">`, for instance. They increase or decrease the font size a specified number of steps, relative to the base font size (normally, size 3). The BIG and SMALL elements, on the other hand, increase or decrease the font size by one step relative to the current element's font size. There are a total of seven font sizes.

relative URL A URL that states the position of a linked object relative to the linking file.

Reload button Reloads (or refreshes) the display of a Web page in Mozilla Firefox.

remotely hosted CGI script A CGI script hosted by a third-party remote server, rather than on a Web author's own server.

reset button A form control for resetting a form to its initial state, created using the INPUT or BUTTON element.

resource path Specifies the folder path to the location of a resource in a Web site.

return link A link following a destination anchor that allows a user to return to that anchor's targeting link, or a link that allows a user to return to the top of the page.

rich text format The RTF document format was developed by Microsoft for cross-platform document exchange. It has a file extension of ".rtf" and can include additional formatting commands that are not included in a plain (or ASCII) text file.

router A device on a network that forwards, or routes, a message to its destination.

row group A group of table rows to which style properties can be applied, designated by the THEAD, TBODY, and TFOOT elements.

S

sans serif font A sans serif font, as its name implies, lacks the serifs (or strokes) that a serif font has. Sans serif fonts are more generally used in headings and display text. Magazine articles and advertising copy often use a sans serif font as body text because it has a more modern look.

scheme Identifies the service (and protocol) being used ("http://," for instance).

selector Selects where a style will be applied (to an element, a group of elements, descendants of an element, etc.).

serif font A serif font has strokes (serifs) that accentuate the ends of letterforms, making them easier to read when reading a larger volume of text. Newspapers and books generally print body text in a serif font for that reason.

server A computer that responds to requests for services from and delivers services to client computers on a network.

server-side application A program or script that is run on a server.

SGML Standard Generalized Markup Language, upon which HTML was originally based.

sidebar menu A list of links displayed in a sidebar column that provides access to sections within a page or to pages within a site.

SMTP mail server Simple Mail Transfer Protocol mail server. Typically used by client-side mail programs to send e-mail messages.

spam Unsolicited and unwanted e-mail messages.

spanned cell A table cell that spans two or more rows and/or columns.

special characters Non-keyboard characters that must be inserted into an HTML document using entity codes, such as the copyright and registered symbols. Characters included in the ISO 8859-1 or Unicode character sets can be inserted.

standard color palette The default color palette for a GIF image, which includes 256 colors, generally taken from the default 256-color palette of the system on which the image was created.

standards mode A mode in which a browser displays a page according to the most recent HTML or CSS standards. All current major browsers default to standards mode (including Internet Explorer 8).

start tag The initial code component that starts an HTML element.

strict conformance Disallows the usage of deprecated or frameset elements and attributes in HTML 4 and XHTML 1 documents.

style rule The basic constituency of a style sheet, composed of a selector and a declaration. Also called a style.

style sheet A list (or sheet) of styles that can be included in or linked to from Web pages.

styles Codes included in a style sheet that specify how document elements will be formatted.

submit button A form control for submitting form data, created using the INPUT or BUTTON element.

T

tabbing order The order in which form elements can be accessed using the Tab key. The default tabbing order is the order in which they are inserted in the document. By using the TABINDEX attribute, Web authors can specify a different tabbing order than the default.

tabular data Data arranged in rows and columns.

tags Code components that delimit the start and end of an element.

TCP/IP Transmission Control Protocol/Internet Protocol, the key suite of protocols that enables the exchange of data over the Internet. TCP breaks messages into smaller packets and reassembles them at their destination. IP routes packets to their intended destinations.

text area box A form control created using the TEXTAREA element that allows inputting a multi-line comment or message.

text box A form control created using the INPUT element that provides a one-line box of specified length into which text can be input.

text editor A program that enables the editing of ASCII, or plain, text files. Some editors only edit ASCII files, such as Windows Notepad, while others can also function as RTF or HTML editors. TextEdit on Macintosh OS X defaults to editing RTF files, but also can edit ASCII and HTML files.

text-based link menu Separate links below an image map that link to pages in a site. A technique for planning for accessibility of a Web page.

thumbnails Smaller versions of images that are often used to link to full-sized versions of the images. Displaying thumbnail images, instead of full-sized images, on a Web page can save bandwidth.

top-level elements Those elements that define the overall structure of an HTML document: html, head, and body.

transitional conformance Allows the usage of deprecated elements and attributes in HTML 4 and XHTML 1 documents.

transparent GIF image In a GIF image, one color, usually the background, can be set to be transparent, allowing underlying colors or images to show through the transparent areas of the image.

TrueType font A type of font introduced by Microsoft in Windows as a replacement for Adobe's PostScript fonts, with Times New Roman, Arial, and Courier New replacing Times, Helvetica, and Courier. TrueType fonts are the most widely used fonts on the Web.

type (or simple) selector CSS1 selector that applies property values to all instances of a specific element.

U

universal selector CSS2 selector that applies property values to all elements (*), all instances (*p) of a particular element, all instances of a particular class (*.main), and so on.

URI Uniform Resource Identifier, which is how the W3C now refers to a URL.

URL Uniform Resource Locator. Also called a *Web address*. A URL is minimally composed of a scheme (http://, for instance), host (alias and domain name: www.yahoo.com, for instance), resource path (users/jwatson, for instance), and an object file (mypage.html, for instance). Also called a *URI* (Uniform Resource Indicator).

urlencoded content A content type (or encoding type) that replaces spaces with "+" characters and hard returns, commas, ampersands, and other reserved characters with control codes.

user agent Software that operates as a user's agent in making requests of a server. A Web browser and an FTP program, for instance, are user agents.

V

vertical spacing Spacing above or below an image or object. Set for the IMG element using the VSPACE attribute.

W

Web browser Client software (or user agent) that requests services from a Web server.

Web page A document on the Web, which might more accurately described as a "Web scroll."

Web server Software on a computer that enables it to respond to requests from and deliver services to a Web client (such as a Web browser).

Web-safe color palette A color palette for GIF images originally developed by Netscape that includes 216 colors that are present in the native palettes of almost all computer systems.

Web-safe colors Colors guaranteed not to be dithered on systems that can display only 256 colors.

Web-safe palette Another way of referring to the Web-safe color palette.

working folder The folder in which the student creates the case examples for each chapter. To create their working folders, students (or the instructor) download a ZIP archive file and extract its contents, which will create an HTML_Examples folder, in which all the example files used in the book can be found. The example files ZIP file is available for download in two versions: one version for Windows and the other version for Macintosh OS X and Linux/UNIX.

worksheet Data arranged in rows and columns in a spreadsheet program, such as Microsoft Excel.

World Wide Web Now more commonly referred to as simply "the Web," an invention of Tim Berners-Lee while working at CERN in Switzerland, facilitating the sharing of information and ideas over the Internet, which he initially described as "a wide area hypermedia information retrieval initiative aiming to give universal access to a large universe of documents."

World Wide Web Consortium Formed in 1994 at MIT to foster and develop specifications and standards for the Web. Broadly known colloquially as the "W3C."

X

x-height The height of lowercase letters (or the height of a lowercase "x"), stated as a ratio of the height of uppercase letters in a font. Different fonts of the same font size can have differing x-heights. Verdana has a larger x-height than Arial, for instance.

XHTML Extensible Hypertext Markup Language. Versions of HTML written to conform with XML, not SGML, including XHTML 1.0, XHTML 1.1, XHTML 2.0, and XHTML Basic.

XML Extensible Markup Language, which facilitates (and lays down the ground rules for) the presentation of structured data.

Z

ZIP archive file A file within which other files can be archived and compressed, reducing the amount of bandwidth that is used while downloading. After downloading, the files can be extracted (uncompressed). Both Windows and Mac OS X support creating ZIP archive files (Windows calls them *compressed* folders). Numerous other third-party programs facilitate working with ZIP archive files.

INDEX